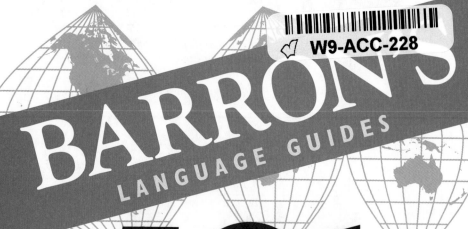

BARRON'S LANGUAGE GUIDES

501 ENGLISH VERBS

SECOND EDITION

Fully conjugated in all the tenses
in a new, easy-to-learn format,
alphabetically arranged

by

Thomas R. Beyer, Jr., Ph.D.

Professor
Middlebury College
Middlebury, Vermont

Chicago
Public
Library

Dedicated to the hundreds of millions
who have learned English
to communicate with the other
hundreds of millions of native speakers.

For my understanding wife, Dorothea,
my most faithful supporters,
Carina, Stefanie, and Alexandra,
and Rich who loves action words.

All inquiries should be addressed to:
Barron's Educational Series, Inc.
250 Wireless Boulevard
Hauppauge, NY 11788
www.barronseduc.com

ISBN-13: 978-0-7641-3548-4 (book only)
ISBN-10: 0-7641-3548-1 (book only)
ISBN-13: 978-0-7641-7985-3 (book & CD-ROM package)
ISBN-10: 0-7641-7985-3 (book & CD-ROM package)

Library of Congress Catalog Card No. 2006040682

Library of Congress Cataloging-in-Publication Data

Beyer, Thomas R.
    501 English verbs : fully conjugated in all the tenses in a new easy-to-learn format,
  alphabetically arranged / by Thomas R. Beyer, Jr.—2nd ed.
        p. cm.
    Includes index.
    ISBN-13: 978-0-7641-3548-4 (alk. paper)
    ISBN-10: 0-7641-3548-1 (alk. paper)
    1. English language—Verb—Tables. I. Title. Five hundred one English verbs. II. Title:
  Five hundred and one English verbs. III. Title.

PE1273.B49   2007
428.2—dc22   2006040682

PRINTED IN CANADA
9 8 7 6 5 4 3 2 1

Contents

The English Verb

Introduction

For everything you do, or want to be or how you feel, you need a verb. A verb can indicate an action (I write, she buys, they talk) or a state of being (we feel, you care). The verb is an essential element of English—only the nouns occur more frequently in the spoken and written language. Structurally the verb is one of the easiest parts of speech, since there really are only four or five different forms. Native speakers of English rarely think about verbs. In actual practice, however, verbs are misused and abused by native speakers and learners of English alike. The English verb has confounded generations worrying whether to use "lie" or "lay," "gone" or "went," "shall" or "will." For those learning English the verb can be one of the most complex word forms, with over 300 irregular verbs and 200 possible combinations for all the possible verbal usages. It is the disparity between this paucity of verbal endings and the numerous and flexible uses of English verbs that has given birth to this book.

The English verb in comparison to many other Indo-European languages has lost most of the endings that indicate the categories of voice, mood, tense, aspect, person, and number. English has about a dozen auxiliary or helping verbs (more about them later), but most English verbs are full verbs that may be either regular or irregular. Regular verbs form the past tense by adding "d" or "ed" to the simple form: accepted, pulled, moved. Irregular verbs (some languages call them "strong" verbs) have different ways of forming that past tense: bring–brought, drive–drove, sing–sang, spend–spent. There are about 300 hundred irregular verbs in English and all but those rarely used are found in *501 English Verbs*.

501 English Verbs gives the conjugations or conjugated forms of the irregular and regular verbs most frequently used in speech and writing. Conjugation means to "join with": we attach endings to the basic form of the verb to distinguish voice, mood, tense, aspect, person, and number. These categories may be more familiar to the learner of English than to the native speaker. Discussions and analyses of grammatical categories in English have disappeared from many American schools. The traditional categories are better suited to a highly inflected language—one with many changes such as Classical Greek and Latin, or modern Russian and German. At one time English was more heavily inflected—it had many more endings than at present.

Since the original publication of *501 English Verbs* the language and its use have witnessed dramatic changes. The ever-growing use of technology and the role of English in electronic communication have expanded not only the vocabulary, but the number of those who come into contact with the language every day. This Second Edition has tried to be mindful of those changes and incorporate some of the most popular and most recent additions to English.

How to Use This Book

What follows is an example of the verb accept accompanied by an overview and explanation of the categories of verbs and the formation of those forms as they are presented in our book.

Conjugation of the Full Verb "accept"

accept (active voice)	PRINCIPAL PARTS: accepts, accepting, accepted, accepted	be accepted (passive voice)

INDICATIVE MOOD

Pres.	I, we, you, they **accept**	I **am accepted**
		we, you, they **are accepted**
	he, she, it **accepts**	he, she, it **is accepted**
Pres.	I **am accepting**	I **am being accepted**
Prog.	we, you, they **are accepting**	we, you, they **are being accepted**
	he, she, it **is accepting**	he, she, it **is being accepted**
Pres.	I, we, you, they **do accept**	I, we, you, they **do get accepted**
Int.	he, she, it **does accept**	he, she, it **does get accepted**
Fut.	I, he, she, it,	I, he, she, it,
	we, you, they **will accept**	we, you, they **will be accepted**
Past	I, he, she, it,	I, he, she, it **was accepted**
	we, you, they **accepted**	we, you, they **were accepted**
Past	I, he, she, it **was accepting**	I, he, she, it **was being accepted**
Prog.	we, you, they **were accepting**	we, you, they **were being accepted**
Past	I, he, she, it,	I, he, she, it,
Int.	we, you, they **did accept**	we, you, they **did get accepted**
Pres.	I, we, you, they **have accepted**	I, we, you, they **have been accepted**
Perf.	he, she, it **has accepted**	he, she, it **has been accepted**
Past	I, he, she, it,	I, he, she, it,
Perf.	we, you, they **had accepted**	we, you, they **had been accepted**
Fut.	I, he, she, it, we, you, they	I, he, she, it, we, you, they
Perf.	**will have accepted**	**will have been accepted**

IMPERATIVE MOOD

accept	**be accepted**

SUBJUNCTIVE MOOD

Pres.	if I, he, she, it,	if I, he, she, it,
	we, you, they **accept**	we, you, they **be accepted**
Past	if I, he, she, it,	if I, he, she, it,
	we, you, they **accepted**	we, you, they **were accepted**
Fut.	if I, he, she, it,	if I, he, she, it,
	we, you, they **should accept**	we, you, they **should be accepted**

Transitive and intransitive.

The boss accepted his resignation.
Your apology is accepted.

Basic Form

Verbs are normally listed in English language dictionaries according to the basic or simple form. In this book, the basic form of each verb appears on the top line in bold face, followed by the notation "active voice" in parentheses for verbs that can be transitive. This form is used for the present tense and infinitive.

Principal Parts

In addition to their basic forms, English verbs have four other forms. These other principal parts may be listed in English language dictionaries according to their "irregularity." In the middle of the top line, we provide the other four principal parts for all verbs in this order:

- accepts   the third person singular present tense or "-s" form
- accepting   the present participle or "-ing" form
- accepted   the past tense or "-ed" form
- accepted   the past participle

The third person singular present (the "he," "she," or "it") form is made by adding "s" or "es" to the simple form: she accepts. Since this change is not difficult for the native speaker the form is included in dictionaries only when the correct spelling is not obvious.

The present participle or "-ing" form also poses little problem for the native speaker and it too rarely occurs in dictionaries.

The simple past is usually formed by adding to the basic form "ed" after a consonant and "d" after a vowel. Verbs that form their past tense in this way are considered regular verbs.

The past participle for regular verbs is the same as the past tense. Some English verbs have alternate forms for the past tense and/or the past participle. These are normally listed in the order in which they appear in the *American Heritage Dictionary of the English Language* (Third Edition).

After the principal parts the top line contains the passive voice form if the verb is transitive, followed by the notation "passive voice."

The convention of listing the active voice on the left side of the page and the passive voice on the right side is maintained throughout *501 English Verbs*.

Voice

A verb is in the active voice when some subject (the doer) performs some action or activity on someone or something:

Mary accepts the invitation.

When there is a complement—a direct or indirect object—for these verbs, they are transitive verbs and permit a passive construction. When a verb is in the passive voice, the object of the action becomes the grammatical subject of the verb:

The invitation was accepted by Mary.

In both cases "Mary" was the doer and the "invitation" was the object of "accepted."

Beneath the line following the principal parts of the verb, there are normally eight forms, four active and four passive: infinitive, perfect infinitive, present participle, and past participle.

Infinitives (nonfinite verb form).

Infinitives are forms of the verb not limited by time. They have no tense or mood. Often (but not always) the infinitive is preceded by to:

I like to take showers.

The Present Infinitive refers to the present or future.
The Present Active Infinitive is identical to the basic form of the verb.
The Present Passive Infinitive is a compound form composed of be and the past participle.

The Perfect Infinitive relates to an activity or state existing prior to the main verb.
The Past Active Infinitive is a compound form composed of have and the past participle.
The Past Passive Infinitive is a compound form composed of have been and the past participle.

Participles

Participles also have no tense or mood, but they are used together with auxiliaries to form the progressive and perfect tenses and the passive voice.

The Present Participle refers to an action in the present or future.
The Present Active Participle is formed by adding "ing" to the basic form: accepting. When a verb ends in a silent "e," that letter is dropped before adding the "ing": come–coming.
The Present Passive Participle is a compound form composed of being and the past participle.

The Past Participle refers to an action in the past. Since it is used in combination with auxiliary verbs to form the passive voice, the past participle is sometimes called the "passive participle."
The Past Active Participle is normally the same as the past tense form of the verb. For regular verbs this is the "-ed" form: accepted.
The Past Passive Participle is a compound form combining been and the past participle.

Mood

English has three moods or modes of speech: indicative, imperative, and subjunctive.

The Indicative Mood is used to make a statement or an exclamation, or to ask a question:

I like strawberries.
Mary was accepted to Harvard!
Are you going to the movies?

Tense

Tense is used to express the time when an action takes place. Traditionally there are three primary categories of tense: present, past, and future. (Recent English grammars consider only the present and the past true tenses, because only they have distinct grammatical forms.)

The Present (*Pres.*) is used for an action or state that exists at the present moment (or the moment of speech or writing). This may also include something that began in the past and continues now in the present, and might include something that continues into the future.
The Present Active for most full verbs has two forms to distinguish between person and number.

Person and Number

In English we have three persons (first, second, third) and two numbers (singular and plural).

> First person singular, the I form, refers to the speaker.
> First person plural, the we form, refers to the speaker and one or more other persons.
> Second person singular and plural, the you form, refers to the person or persons spoken to.
> Third person singular, the he, she, it form, refers to someone or something other than the speaker or the person spoken to.
> Third person plural, the they form, refers to more than one person or thing other than the speaker or the person spoken to.

The Present Active for the first person singular and plural, the second person singular and plural, and the third person plural is the basic form:

I accept your invitation.
We accept.
Do you accept?*
They accept!

The Present Active for the third person singular (he, she, it) is normally formed by adding "s" after most consonants and all silent vowels:

She runs, he plays, it snows, she moves, he hides, it drives.

After the combinations of "ss," "zz," "ch," "sh," "x," or after a vowel that is pronounced, we add "es."

She passes, it buzzes, he catches, she pushes, he boxes, he goes, she does.

When a verb ends in "y" after a consonant, the "y" changes to an "i" and is followed by "es."

He cries, she tries, it fries.

In a few instances when the basic form ends in a single "s," you add "ses":

The district busses, she focusses.

The Present Passive is a compound form combining the conjugated form of be with the past participle.

I am accepted.
We, you, they are registered.
He, she, it is required.

Aspect

In addition to the simple present, past, and future, English has a progressive and a perfect aspect relaying how an action or mood is experienced or viewed by the speaker.

The Progressive Aspect, sometimes called the continuous aspect, describes something in progress at the time of the verb's action.

---

* Note that English today uses you to refer to one or more than one person. Sometimes you may find the archaic second person singular form thou instead of you. The thou form is then followed by the old form of the verb.

The Present Progressive (*Pres. Prog.*) is an action still going on in the present.

The Present Progressive Active is formed by combining the present tense form of the verb be with the present participle.

I am reading.
We, you, they are thinking.
He is riding, she is driving, it is snowing.

The Present Progressive Passive combines am being, are being, or is being with the passive participle.

I am being driven.
We, you, they are being sent.
She is being tested.

The Intensive

This form is used for emphasis and is also a key to negation in English and for asking questions.[*]

The Present Intensive (*Pres. Int.*) emphasizes that an action can or does take place.

The Present Intensive Active is formed by combining the auxiliary form do or does with the basic form.

I, we, you, they do accept your conditions.
He does want to come, but she does not want to come.

The Present Intensive Passive combines do get or does get with the past participle.

I, we, you, they do get appreciated.
He or she does get presented a variety of views.

The Future (*Fut.*) of a verb indicates an action or state that does not yet exist. Strictly speaking, it is not a separate tense in modern English.

The Future Active is a compound formed with the help of the auxiliary verb will (or shall)[**] and sometimes contracted as 'll followed by the basic form of the verb. (In the spoken language future time is often indicated by am, are, is going to and the basic form of the verb).

I, she, he, it, we, you, they will survive.

The Future Passive is formed by combining will be and the past participle.

I, he, she, it, we, you, they will be discovered.

---

[*] In the latest English grammar texts there is no mention of the intensive or emphatic as a separate category. The auxiliary verb do is called a "dummy operator" when used to form negations and questions. Because these do forms are so essential I have followed the convention of Hopper, *English Verb Conjugations*, and provided the present and the past intensive for each verb.

[**] I have consistently used will as the auxiliary verb for the future. Traditionally school children were taught to use shall for the first person singular and plurals to indicate simple future: "I shall come, we shall overcome." "I will" and "we will" were to be used for special emphasis. Similarly we were taught to write "he, she, it, you, they will" unless we wished to emphasize the statement with "she, he, it, you, they shall." The distinction was then and probably for the entire twentieth century very artificial. Recent research has indicated that this rule was rarely ever observed in actual practice and in modern standard American English shall is rarely used except in legal documents and in some specific phrases: "We shall overcome." "Shall we dance?" One should, however, be aware of the historical distinction and recognize shall for the first person singular and plural and in questions and some formulaic statements.

The Past *(Past)* tense describes some action or mood that occurred or existed prior to or before the moment of speech or writing.

The Past Active form of regular verbs is formed for all three persons, singular and plural, by adding "d," "ed," or "d." First we provide the most common forms.

After a vowel the letter "d" is added:

> He closed, continued, decided.

After a consonant the letters "ed" are added:

> She worked, opened, passed, packed.

When a "y" comes after a consonant it changes to "i" before the ending "ed":

> He cried, tried, carried, married.

There are cases where the general rule requires some modification.

Verbs that end with a "c" sometimes have an added "k" before the "ed" ending:

> She panicked, because he trafficked in drugs.

Sometimes a word's final consonant is doubled—when it is spelled with a single letter and the vowel before it is stressed—before adding "ed." (In words of a single syllable this is always the case.)

> He begged, gunned, stopped.

American English differs from British English in verbs ending in a single "l" or "p." American English permits a single final consonant.

> She traveled (travelled), he worshiped (worshipped).

American English also accepts a single "m" for the past tense of verbs ending in "m":

> She programed (programmed).

After some final vowels the letters "ed" are added:

> She echoed, radioed, taxied.

After some final vowel sounds an "d" is added:

> She FTP'd, IM'd.

The Past Passive form combines was or were and the past participle.

> I, he, she, it was added at the last moment.
> We, you, they were all added later.

The Past Progressive *(Past Prog.)* indicates an action that was proceeding in the past.

The Past Progressive Active combines was or were with the present participle.

> I, he, she, it was riding in a car.
> We, you, they were keeping tabs.

The Past Progressive Passive combines was being or were being with the past participle.

> I, she, he, it was being improved.
> We, you, they were being preserved.

The Past Intensive (*Past Int.*) emphasizes that an action did take place in the past. It is also used for negation and questions in the past.

The Past Intensive Active combines did (the past tense of do) with the basic form of the verb.

I did complete the assignment.
She did not stop to smell the roses.
Did we hear you correctly?
You and they did do the exercises.

The Past Intensive Passive combines did get and the past participle.

I did get recognized.
It did not get removed.
Did we get called last evening?
You and they did not get summoned.

The Perfect Aspect

The three perfect tenses refer to an action or state that precedes some other action or state.

The Present Perfect (*Pres. Perf.*) describes an action or state begun in the past and leading up to the present.

The Present Perfect Active combines the auxiliary present tense form of have or has with the past participle.

I, we, you, they have arrived.
He has worried, she has heard, it has rained.

The Present Perfect Passive uses have been or has been plus the past participle. (This is the same as adding have/had to the past passive participle.)

I, we, you, they have been wondering.
Neither she nor he has been supported by their friends.

The Past Perfect (*Past Perf.*) (sometimes called the Pluperfect) describes an action or state begun sometime prior to another past reference point.

The Past Perfect Active form uses had (the past tense of have) with the past participle.

I, he, she, it, we, you, they had all taken the ferry.

The Past Perfect Passive uses had been with the past participle (which is the same as adding had to the past passive participle).

I, she, he, it, we, you, they had been convinced.

The Future Perfect (*Fut. Perf.*) refers to a future action or state that will have begun prior to some other future time event.

The Future Perfect Active combines will have (shall have) with the past participle.

I, he, she, it, we, you, they will have written the letter before tomorrow.

The Future Perfect Passive combines will have been with the past participle (or will have with the past passive participle).

I, he, she, we, you, they will have been married twenty-five years next fall.

The Progressive Perfect*

One can combine the perfect and progressive aspects for the compound forms Present Perfect Progressive and Past Perfect Progressive.

The Present Perfect Progressive describes an action begun in the past and continuing into the present.

The Present Perfect Progressive Active combines have or has plus been and the present participle form of the verb.

> I, we, you, they have been training since January.
> He has been swimming since he was three years old.

The Present Perfect Progressive Passive combines have or has plus been being and the past participle form of the verb.

> I, he, she, it, we, you, they have been being observed since our plane arrived.

The Past Perfect Progressive describes an action ongoing in the past that no longer exists.

The Past Perfect Progressive Active combines had and been with the present participle form of the verb.

> I, he, she, it, we, you, they had been training regularly before the accident.

The Past Perfect Progressive Passive combines had plus been being with the past participle form of the verb.

> I, he, she, it, we, you, they had been being examined when the storm began.

The Future Perfect Progressive describes an ongoing action in the future prior to another future action.

The Future Perfect Progressive Active combines will have and been with the present participle form of the verb.

> I, he, she, it, we, you, they will have been playing
> chess for ten hours before the match ends.

The Future Perfect Progressive Passive combines will have plus been being with the past participle form of the verb.

> I, he, she, it, we, you, they will have been being examined
> for over three months before the report will be issued.

The Imperative Mood

The Imperative Mood is used to give an order, command, demand, or request. Sometimes it is used in giving directions.

The Active Imperative form is the same as the basic form of the verb.

> Go. Stop. Write. Listen. Sing. Eat and drink.
> Bring me your homework.
> Please pass the butter.
> Drive straight ahead and turn right at the light.

---

* Since these forms represent a combination of two forms already presented, they are not listed for each individual verb.

The Passive Imperative* combines be with the past participle.

Be frightened.
Don't be found.

The Subjunctive Mood

The Subjunctive Mood is used for expressing a wish, reporting something that was said, or describing something hypothetical.

The Present Subjunctive is used with a "that" clause after verbs, adjectives or nouns; for a condition; in some set expressions of desire.

The Present Subjunctive Active uses the verb's basic form (except for the verb be). Note the third person singular form has no "s."

We suggested that she travel to London this summer.
I demanded that he refund my money.

The Present Subjunctive Passive is made by combining be and the past participle.

I insist that you be heard.
He requested that she be invited.

The Past Subjunctive describes something hypothetical or unreal. It often occurs after words like "if," "as if," "though," "wish," "suppose."

The Past Subjunctive Active** (sometimes called the were form) is identical to the forms of the past except for the verb be, in which case the form were is used for all persons.

If she tried, she could do it.
If we slept, we could do better.
If he were rich, he would buy me a diamond ring.
I wish that I were in Oklahoma.

The Past Subjunctive Passive combines were with the past participle.

I wish that we were warned.
We would be delighted, if our invitation were accepted.

The Future Subjunctive*** (should) refers to an action or state that may come into being.

The Future Subjunctive Active is formed by combining the auxiliary verb should with the basic form of the verb form.

If ever you should leave me, I would die.
If I should be in town next week, I will call you.

---

* Another way to form a passive imperative is with the word get and the past participle: "Get hired." "Get dressed." "Don't get lost." "Don't get caught."

** In modern American English the indicative past tense is often substituted: "I wish I was there." A Past Perfect Subjunctive is also possible using had or had been plus the past particple: "If we had written, they would have come." "If we had been driven, we would not have arrived too late for the show."

*** As with other recent references to future time, the future subjunctive is not listed in the two most recent English grammar texts. The use of should is considered a special use as "putative" in conditional sentences. Nonetheless, should is regularly used to describe a future condition: "How should I know?" "If I should see him, I'll tell him." I have followed the example of Hopper in including the future form here for the sake of consistency.

The Future Subjunctive Passive combines should be and the past participle.

If he should be harmed, you will all be punished.
Should she be awoken, please inform me immediately.

Transitive and Intransitive Verbs

Most regular verbs are either transitive or intransitive. When a single verb can be both transitive and intransitive, it has been noted at the bottom of the page.

A Transitive verb is one that has a complement, either a direct or indirect object.

Mary gave me the book.

An Intransitive verb is one that has no complement.

He tires easily.
My head aches.

Auxiliary Verbs

English has a dozen auxiliary verbs, normally divided into three categories: primary, modal, and marginal. Auxiliary verbs are often referred to as "helpers" or "operators." They help in the construction of English sentences.

They can come before the negative particle not.

I am not coming.
She did not buy the dress.
He has not set the time.

They can be inverted in questions.

Are you coming?
Must I go?
Will they be there?

They can form contractions.

I'll be ready.
We can't decide.
They couldn't accept our offer.
John won't use a computer.

They can be used as emphatics.

You should do it.
He must come.

The Primary Auxiliaries: be, have, do.

The three verbs be, have, and do, can stand alone, but they also serve as auxiliaries to form other tenses.

The verb be combines with the present participle to form the progressive tenses and with the past participle to form the passive.

I am working.
He was notified.

The verb have combines with the past participle to form the perfect tenses.

You have made great progress.
He had listened.
She will have arrived by evening.

The verb do forms the intensive and is used in negations and questions.

We do like to read often.
They did not come any more.
Do you prefer an aisle or window seat?

The Modal Auxiliaries: can/could, may/might, must, shall/should, will/would

They have no distinctive "s" form for the third person singular in the present.

I will go, and she will come.

They combine with the basic or infinitive form without the word "to."

He can leave.
I might stay.
We must stop for lunch.

The Marginal Auxiliaries: dare, need, ought to, used to.

These verbs may all be used as main verbs in addition to their auxiliary function. When used as auxiliaries, the third person singular form has no "s."

She dare not go.
He need not try.

Phrasal Verbs

Phrasal verbs are combinations of a verb and an adverb or preposition in which the meaning cannot always be understood as the sum of its parts. One can "run up a hill," but this is not the same as the phrasal verb run up as in "run up a bill."

Some phrasal verbs are intransitive, that is, they take no complement: act up, burn out. Others are transitive and take an object: call off, cut down.

We have included a special section of the most common phrasal verbs for the 501 English verbs in this book.

Catenatives

Catenatives are verbs that are not auxiliary verbs but can be followed by another verb.
They can occur with the simple form:

He helped clean the car.

Some have the basic form with to.

I always wanted to write.

Others are followed by the "-ing" form.

I like buying jewelry.
I hate watching television.
She kept calling.

Questions

English has two main types of questions: yes-no, and wh- (who, what, where, when, why, etc.). A question (the interrogative sentence) can be formed in English by using an auxiliary verb before the subject. Many questions in English rely on inversion—changing the position of the order of the subject and the auxiliary.

Are you coming?
Had she listened?
What can I do for you?
Where can I find that telephone number?

When the subject of the question is who, there is no inversion.

Who is coming to the party?

Even when the declarative sentence has no auxiliary, one is used for questions.

The baby drinks milk.	Does she drink juice?
We work every morning.	Do they work?

Negations

Negation in English is also dependent upon auxiliaries placed after the subject and before not plus the required form of the verb.

I am not going.
She has not been seen.
We do not feel like leaving.
You were not watching.
They will not want dinner.

Negative sentences can also be formed using another negation word, such as never, nothing, nobody, and so forth.

I never went to class unprepared.
Nothing can stop us now.
Nobody likes to pay taxes.

Which 501 English Verbs?

Where did these 501 English verbs come from? One cannot write a book like this without expressing a debt to those who have come before. A pioneer in attempting to list all the forms of English irregular verbs was Vincent F. Hopper, whose list of 123 irregular verbs in *English Verb Conjugations* (Barron's, 1975) was both an inspiration and a starting point for the 501 verbs here. I have attempted to determine all of the irregular verbs in English. Most sources refer to over 200. Dictionaries, grammars, and handbooks provided a list of almost 300—although that included several compounds, such as "reread," "underwrite," and so forth. I consulted the word frequency lists for the spoken language *Word Frequencies of Spoken American English* (1979), by Hartvig Dahl, who notes that "only 848 words account for 90% of spoken usage" (p. vii). I have included all verbs found in the first 1,000 words of the spoken sample.

Similarly I have included verbs in the first 2,000 words of written speech as determined by the Brown corpus in W. Nelson Francis and Henry Kucera's *Frequency Analysis of English Usage* (Boston: Houghton Mifflin, 1982). At the final stage I carefully compared my list to the entire body of the *American Heritage Dictionary of the English Language* (Third Edition, 1992) to seek out forms that might cause difficulty for learners and native speakers alike. For all of the entries, I have compared the *American Heritage* entries to those of the *Oxford Modern English Dictionary* (Second Edition, 1996), *Merriam Webster's Collegiate Dictionary* (Tenth Edition, 1993), and *Webster's New World Dictionary* (Third Edition, 1990).

In the course of my work it became clear that there are several accepted forms and some disagreements. This is as it should be. English has resisted most efforts to prescribe "correct" usage. A living language spoken natively by hundreds of millions living in the United States, Great Britain, Australia, New Zealand, and Canada, it is also spoken by hundreds of millions who learn English in addition to their native languages. I have relied on two of the most recent grammars in English for guidance: Randolf Quirk, Sidney Greenbaum, et al., *A Comprehensive Grammar of the English Language* (1985) and Sidney Greenbaum, *The Oxford English Grammar* (1996). I have also consulted Kenneth G. Wilson, *The Columbia Guide to Standard American English* (1993).

My purpose has been to describe what can and may occur. I make no claim that each and every form of the verbs presented here has or will actually occur in speech or writing. They are all potential forms, and even when one must imagine possible situations or figurative usages for some of them, the forms are here for your information.

I have also become convinced of how complex the entire verbal system is, and how much work is required by native speakers and learners alike to master all the forms. *501 English Verbs* is itself a pioneering attempt and I look forward to your comments and suggestions for the next edition.

Thomas R. Beyer, Jr.
Middlebury College
Middlebury, Vermont

P.S. In responding to comments from readers to the first edition, I have tried to answer their concerns and include their suggestions. I have inserted fifty new verbs in the body of the book. I have relied on the latest resources, the *New Oxford American Dictionary* (Second Edition, 2005) and the *Random House Webster's Unabridged Dictionary* (Second Edition, 2001). I have also consulted electronic sources, *Merriam-Webster Online Dictionary* (www.m-w.com), and *Word Frequencies in Written and Spoken English: Based on the British National Corpus* (http://www.comp.lancs.ac.uk/ucrel/bncfreq/flists.html). I have included words new to the language, or words used in a new sense. Many of these reflect our changing world and the new technological age.

In the first edition I tried to include in the body for the text almost all the irregular verbs in English. Many of these are rarely used. To make way for fifty new verbs, I have moved fifty of the original verbs to the section entitled Another 550 Problem Verbs. Thus no verb forms have been lost.

A new feature in this edition are the Essential 55 Verbs. Beginning students should pay attention to the 55 verbs highlighted as "essential" throughout the book. They were chosen because they are useful for learning essential conjugations, tricky spelling changes, and common usage.

One other comment concerned providing forms for verbs that might likely never be encountered. In some cases I, too, have stretched my imagination to include a form such as "I am cried." But in literary language it is not impossible to conceive of an inanimate object, a river or a tear, that gives voice to that form. *I have italicized my original statement above, but have decided to retain those "potential forms."*

This revised edition has been made richer by the comments of the original book's readers and reviewers. As the language continues to change, I hope that some of the more than one billion native speakers and learners of English will continue to offer me their comments and suggestions.

Essential 55 Verb List

Beginning students should pay careful attention to the verbs in this list. We have chosen them because they represent important spelling changes and popular usage. If you study these essential verbs you will be able to conjugate just about any verb you come across and express yourself in correct idiomatic English.

Allow	**Look**
Ask	**Make**
Be	**Mean**
Become	**Meet**
Begin	**Move**
Believe	**Need**
Bring	**Pay**
Call	**Play**
Come	**Provide**
Do	**Put**
Feel	**Run**
Find	**Say**
Follow	**See**
Get	**Seem**
Give	**Set**
Go	**Show**
Happen	**Stand**
Have	**Start**
Hear	**Take**
Heave	**Tell**
Hold	**Think**
Include	**Try**
Keep	**Turn**
Know	**Use**
Lead	**Want**
Leave	**Work**
Like	**Write**
Live	

Abbreviations

Pres.	Present
Pres. Prog.	Present Progressive
Pres. Int.	Present Intensive
Fut.	Future
Past Prog.	Past Progressive
Past Int.	Past Intensive
Pres. Perf.	Present Perfective
Past Perf.	Past Perfective
Fut. Perf.	Future Perfective

501 English Verbs
Fully Conjugated,
Arranged Alphabetically

abide
(active voice)

PRINCIPAL PARTS: **abides, abiding, abode/abided, abided/abode**

be abided/abode
(passive voice)

INDICATIVE MOOD

Pres.	I, we, you, they **abide**	I **am abided**
		we, you, they **are abided**
	he, she, it **abides**	he, she, it **is abided**
Pres.	I **am abiding**	I **am being abided**
Prog.	we, you, they **are abiding**	we, you, they **are being abided**
	he, she, it **is abiding**	he, she, it **is being abided**
Pres.	I, we, you, they **do abide**	I, we, you, they **do get abided**
Int.	he, she, it **does abide**	he, she, it **does get abided**
Fut.	I, he, she, it,	I, he, she, it,
	we, you, they **will abide**	we, you, they **will be abided**
Past	I, he, she, it,	I, he, she, it **was abided**
	we, you, they **abode**	we, you, they **were abided**
Past	I, he, she, it **was abiding**	I, he, she, it **was being abided**
Prog.	we, you, they **were abiding**	we, you, they **were being abided**
Past	I, he, she, it,	I, he, she, it,
Int.	we, you, they **did abide**	we, you, they **did get abided**
Pres.	I, we, you, they **have abided**	I, we, you, they **have been abided**
Perf.	he, she, it **has abided**	he, she, it **has been abided**
Past	I, he, she, it,	I, he, she, it,
Perf.	we, you, they **had abided**	we, you, they **had been abided**
Fut.	I, he, she, it, we, you, they	I, he, she, it, we, you, they
Perf.	**will have abided**	**will have been abided**

IMPERATIVE MOOD

abide   **be abided**

SUBJUNCTIVE MOOD

Pres.	if I, he, she, it,	if I, he, she, it,
	we, you, they **abide**	we, you, they **be abided**
Past	if I, he, she, it,	if I, he, she, it,
	we, you, they **abode**	we, you, they **were abided**
Fut.	if I, he, she, it,	if I, he, she, it,
	we, you, they **should abide**	we, you, they **should be abided**

Transitive and intransitive. In the past tense ABODE and ABIDED are acceptable. For the past participle, ABIDED is now more frequently used. ABODE has a "literary" ring. As an intransitive verb ABODE means "to dwell or live somewhere." *The Oxford Modern English Dictionary* prefers **"abided** or rarely **abode."**

They are abiding in temporary housing.
They abided by the judge's decisions.
The pressures of the job could be abided by the new employee.

accept
(active voice)

be accepted
(passive voice)

INDICATIVE MOOD

Pres.	I, we, you, they **accept**	I **am accepted**
		we, you, they **are accepted**
	he, she, it **accepts**	he, she, it **is accepted**
Pres.	I **am accepting**	I **am being accepted**
Prog.	we, you, they **are accepting**	we, you, they **are being accepted**
	he, she, it **is accepting**	he, she, it **is being accepted**
Pres.	I, we, you, they **do accept**	I, we, you, they **do get accepted**
Int.	he, she, it **does accept**	he, she, it **does get accepted**
Fut.	I, he, she, it,	I, he, she, it,
	we, you, they **will accept**	we, you, they **will be accepted**
Past	I, he, she, it,	I, he, she, it **was accepted**
	we, you, they **accepted**	we, you, they **were accepted**
Past	I, he, she, it **was accepting**	I, he, she, it **was being accepted**
Prog.	we, you, they **were accepting**	we, you, they **were being accepted**
Past	I, he, she, it,	I, he, she, it,
Int.	we, you, they **did accept**	we, you, they **did get accepted**
Pres.	I, we, you, they **have accepted**	I, we, you, they **have been accepted**
Perf.	he, she, it **has accepted**	he, she, it **has been accepted**
Past	I, he, she, it,	I, he, she, it,
Perf.	we, you, they **had accepted**	we, you, they **had been accepted**
Fut.	I, he, she, it, we, you, they	I, he, she, it, we, you, they
Perf.	**will have accepted**	**will have been accepted**

IMPERATIVE MOOD

accept   **be accepted**

SUBJUNCTIVE MOOD

Pres.	if I, he, she, it,	if I, he, she, it,
	we, you, they **accept**	we, you, they **be accepted**
Past	if I, he, she, it,	if I, he, she, it,
	we, you, they **accepted**	we, you, they **were accepted**
Fut.	if I, he, she, it,	if I, he, she, it,
	we, you, they **should accept**	we, you, they **should be accepted**

Transitive and intransitive.

The boss accepted his resignation.
Your apology is accepted.

achieve
(active voice)

be achieved
(passive voice)

INDICATIVE MOOD

Pres.	I, we, you, they **achieve**	I **am achieved**
		we, you, they **are achieved**
	he, she, it **achieves**	he, she, it **is achieved**
Pres.	I **am achieving**	I **am being achieved**
Prog.	we, you, they **are achieving**	we, you, they **are being achieved**
	he, she, it **is achieving**	he, she, it **is being achieved**
Pres.	I, we, you, they **do achieve**	I, we, you, they **do get achieved**
Int.	he, she, it **does achieve**	he, she, it **does get achieved**
Fut.	I, he, she, it,	I, he, she, it,
	we, you, they **will achieve**	we, you, they **will be achieved**
Past	I, he, she, it,	I, he, she, it **was achieved**
	we, you, they **achieved**	we, you, they **were achieved**
Past	I, he, she, it **was achieving**	I, he, she, it **was being achieved**
Prog.	we, you, they **were achieving**	we, you, they **were being achieved**
Past	I, he, she, it,	I, he, she, it,
Int.	we, you, they **did achieve**	we, you, they **did get achieved**
Pres.	I, we, you, they **have achieved**	I, we, you, they **have been achieved**
Perf.	he, she, it **has achieved**	he, she, it **has been achieved**
Past	I, he, she, it,	I, he, she, it,
Perf.	we, you, they **had achieved**	we, you, they **had been achieved**
Fut.	I, he, she, it, we, you, they	I, he, she, it, we, you, they
Perf.	**will have achieved**	**will have been achieved**

IMPERATIVE MOOD

achieve   **be achieved**

SUBJUNCTIVE MOOD

Pres.	if I, he, she, it,	if I, he, she, it
	we, you, they **achieve**	we, you, they **be achieved**
Past	if I, he, she, it,	if I, he, she, it,
	we, you, they **achieved**	we, you, they **were achieved**
Fut.	if I, he, she, it,	if I, he, she, it,
	we, you, they **should achieve**	we, you, they **should be achieved**

Transitive and intransitive.

All children are achieving high grades in this course.
All believed that much had been achieved during the meeting.

| act
(active voice) | PRINCIPAL PARTS: **acts, acting, acted,**
acted | be acted
(passive voice) |

INDICATIVE MOOD

Pres.	I, we, you, they **act**	I **am acted** we, you, they **are acted**
	he, she, it **acts**	he, she, it **is acted**
Pres. *Prog.*	I **am acting** we, you, they **are acting** he, she, it **is acting**	I **am being acted** we, you, they **are being acted** he, she, it **is being acted**
Pres. *Int.*	I, we, you, they **do act** he, she, it **does act**	I, we, you, they **do get acted** he, she, it **does get acted**
Fut.	I, he, she, it, we, you, they **will act**	I, he, she, it, we, you, they **will be acted**
Past	I, he, she, it, we, you, they **acted**	I, he, she, it **was acted** we, you, they **were acted**
Past *Prog.*	I, he, she, it **was acting** we, you, they **were acting**	I, he, she, it **was being acted** we, you, they **were being acted**
Past *Int.*	I, he, she, it, we, you, they **did act**	I, he, she, it, we, you, they **did get acted**
Pres. *Perf.*	I, we, you, they **have acted** he, she, it **has acted**	I, we, you, they **have been acted** he, she, it **has been acted**
Past *Perf.*	I, he, she, it, we, you, they **had acted**	I, he, she, it, we, you, they **had been acted**
Fut. *Perf.*	I, he, she, it, we, you, they **will have acted**	I, he, she, it, we, you, they **will have been acted**

IMPERATIVE MOOD

act	**be acted**

SUBJUNCTIVE MOOD

Pres.	if I, he, she, it, we, you, they **act**	if I, he, she, it, we, you, they **be acted**
Past	if I, he, she, it, we, you, they **acted**	if I, he, she, it, we, you, they **were acted**
Fut.	if I, he, she, it, we, you, they **should act**	if I, he, she, it, we, you, they **should be acted**

Transitive and intransitive.

It is time to cease talking and act.
The bills were acted upon by the legislature.

add
(active voice)

be added
(passive voice)

A

INDICATIVE MOOD

Pres.	I, we, you, they **add**	I **am added**
		we, you, they **are added**
	he, she, it **adds**	he, she, it **is added**
Pres.	I **am adding**	I **am being added**
Prog.	we, you, they **are adding**	we, you, they **are being added**
	he, she, it **is adding**	he, she, it **is being added**
Pres.	I, we, you, they **do add**	I, we, you, they **do get added**
Int.	he, she, it **does add**	he, she, it **does get added**
Fut.	I, he, she, it,	I, he, she, it,
	we, you, they **will add**	we, you, they **will be added**
Past	I, he, she, it,	I, he, she, it **was added**
	we, you, they **added**	we, you, they **were added**
Past	I, he, she, it **was adding**	I, he, she, it **was being added**
Prog.	we, you, they **were adding**	we, you, they **were being added**
Past	I, he, she, it,	I, he, she, it,
Int.	we, you, they **did add**	we, you, they **did get added**
Pres.	I, we, you, they **have added**	I, we, you, they **have been added**
Perf.	he, she, it **has added**	he, she, it **has been added**
Past	I, he, she, it,	I, he, she, it,
Perf.	we, you, they **had added**	we, you, they **had been added**
Fut.	I, he, she, it, we, you, they	I, he, she, it, we, you, they
Perf.	**will have added**	**will have been added**

IMPERATIVE MOOD

add   **be added**

SUBJUNCTIVE MOOD

Pres.	if I, he, she, it,	if I, he, she, it,
	we, you, they **add**	we, you, they **be added**
Past	if I, he, she, it,	if I, he, she, it,
	we, you, they **added**	we, you, they **were added**
Fut.	if I, he, she, it,	if I, he, she, it,
	we, you, they **should add**	we, you, they **should be added**

Transitive and intransitive.

You simply add two plus two to get four.
The new letter of recommendation was added to his file.

PRINCIPAL PARTS: **admits, admitting, admitted, admitted**

be admitted
(passive voice)

INDICATIVE MOOD

Pres.	I, we, you, they **admit**	I **am admitted**
		we, you, they **are admitted**
	he, she, it **admits**	he, she, it **is admitted**
Pres.	I **am admitting**	I **am being admitted**
Prog.	we, you, they **are admitting**	we, you, they **are being admitted**
	he, she, it **is admitting**	he, she, it **is being admitted**
Pres.	I, we, you, they **do admit**	I, we, you, they **do get admitted**
Int.	he, she, it **does admit**	he, she, it **does get admitted**
Fut.	I, he, she, it,	I, he, she, it,
	we, you, they **will admit**	we, you, they **will be admitted**
Past	I, he, she, it,	I, he, she, it **was admitted**
	we, you, they **admitted**	we, you, they **were admitted**
Past	I, he, she, it **was admitting**	I, he, she, it **was being admitted**
Prog.	we, you, they **were admitting**	we, you, they **were being admitted**
Past	I, he, she, it,	I, he, she, it,
Int.	we, you, they **did admit**	we, you, they **did get admitted**
Pres.	I, we, you, they **have admitted**	I, we, you, they **have been admitted**
Perf.	he, she, it **has admitted**	he, she, it **has been admitted**
Past	I, he, she, it,	I, he, she, it,
Perf.	we, you, they **had admitted**	we, you, they **had been admitted**
Fut.	I, he, she, it, we, you, they	I, he, she, it, we, you, they
Perf.	**will have admitted**	**will have been admitted**

IMPERATIVE MOOD

admit   **be admitted**

SUBJUNCTIVE MOOD

Pres.	if I, he, she, it,	if I, he, she, it,
	we, you, they **admit**	we, you, they **be admitted**
Past	if I, he, she, it,	if I, he, she, it,
	we, you, they **admitted**	we, you, they **were admitted**
Fut.	if I, he, she, it,	if I, he, she, it,
	we, you, they **should admit**	we, you, they **should be admitted**

Transitive and intransitive.

We are not admitting any more students this year.
The criminal admitted his guilt.
Theatergoers are not admitted inside after the third bell.

| agree
(active voice) | PRINCIPAL PARTS: **agrees, agreeing,
agreed, agreed** | be agreed
(passive voice) |

INDICATIVE MOOD

Pres.	I, we, you, they **agree**	I **am agreed** we, you, they **are agreed**
	he, she, it **agrees**	he, she, it **is agreed**
Pres. *Prog.*	I **am agreeing** we, you, they **are agreeing** he, she, it **is agreeing**	I **am being agreed** we, you, they **are being agreed** he, she, it **is being agreed**
Pres. *Int.*	I, we, you, they **do agree** he, she, it **does agree**	I, we, you, they **do get agreed** he, she, it **does get agreed**
Fut.	I, he, she, it, we, you, they **will agree**	I, he, she, it, we, you, they **will be agreed**
Past	I, he, she, it, we, you, they **agreed**	I, he, she, it **was agreed** we, you, they **were agreed**
Past *Prog.*	I, he, she, it **was agreeing** we, you, they **were agreeing**	I, he, she, it **was being agreed** we, you, they **were being agreed**
Past *Int.*	I, he, she, it, we, you, they **did agree**	I, he, she, it, we, you, they **did get agreed**
Pres. *Perf.*	I, we, you, they **have agreed** he, she, it **has agreed**	I, we, you, they **have been agreed** he, she, it **has been agreed**
Past *Perf.*	I, he, she, it, we, you, they **had agreed**	I, he, she, it, we, you, they **had been agreed**
Fut. *Perf.*	I, he, she, it, we, you, they **will have agreed**	I, he, she, it, we, you, they **will have been agreed**

IMPERATIVE MOOD

agree	**be agreed**

SUBJUNCTIVE MOOD

Pres.	if I, he, she, it, we, you, they **agree**	if I, he, she, it, we, you, they **be agreed**
Past	if I, he, she, it, we, you, they **agreed**	if I, he, she, it, we, you, they **were agreed**
Fut.	if I, he, she, it, we, you, they **should agree**	if I, he, she, it, we, you, they **should be agreed**

Intransitive and transitive.

We are all agreeing to the time and place of our next meeting.
The rules were agreed upon in advance.

| allow
(active voice) | PRINCIPAL PARTS: **allows, allowing,
allowed, allowed** | be allowed
(passive voice) |

INDICATIVE MOOD

Pres.	I, we, you, they **allow**	I **am allowed** we, you, they **are allowed**
	he, she, it **allows**	he, she, it **is allowed**
Pres. *Prog.*	I **am allowing** we, you, they **are allowing** he, she, it **is allowing**	I **am being allowed** we, you, they **are being allowed** he, she, it **is being allowed**
Pres. *Int.*	I, we, you, they **do allow** he, she, it **does allow**	I, we, you, they **do get allowed** he, she, it **does get allowed**
Fut.	I, he, she, it, we, you, they **will allow**	I, he, she, it, we, you, they **will be allowed**
Past	I, he, she, it, we, you, they **allowed**	I, he, she, it **was allowed** we, you, they **were allowed**
Past *Prog.*	I, he, she, it **was allowing** we, you, they **were allowing**	I, he, she, it **was being allowed** we, you, they **were being allowed**
Past *Int.*	I, he, she, it, we, you, they **did allow**	I, he, she, it, we, you, they **did get allowed**
Pres. *Perf.*	I, we, you, they **have allowed** he, she, it **has allowed**	I, we, you, they **have been allowed** he, she, it **has been allowed**
Past *Perf.*	I, he, she, it, we, you, they **had allowed**	I, he, she, it, we, you, they **had been allowed**
Fut. *Perf.*	I, he, she, it, we, you, they **will have allowed**	I, he, she, it, we, you, they **will have been allowed**

IMPERATIVE MOOD

allow	**be allowed**

SUBJUNCTIVE MOOD

Pres.	if I, he, she, it, we, you, they **allow**	if I, he, she, it, we, you, they **be allowed**
Past	if I, he, she, it, we, you, they **allowed**	if I, he, she, it, we, you, they **were allowed**
Fut.	if I, he, she, it, we, you, they **should allow**	if I, he, she, it, we, you, they **should be allowed**

Transitive and intransitive.

I will not allow you to stay out late during the week.
Loud talking is not allowed.

AN ESSENTIAL
55 VERB

AN ESSENTIAL 55 VERB

allow

Examples

Smoking is not allowed in most buildings.

I will not allow it.

She allows for questions during her lectures.

They had never allowed rude conduct.

Am I allowed to leave?

The new students were not allowed into the meeting.

In their house everything was allowed.

The dog was not allowed outside without a leash.

We will allow one more comment.

Allow me to express my concerns.

Words and expressions related to this verb

Allow for some damage in transport.

She is allowed an hour for lunch.

Their plan does not allow for the unexpected.

Allow children to be happy in their own way.

Recording devices are not allowed.

You are not allowed to bring your cell phone into the room.

Have you allowed for all contingencies?

I allowed myself a piece of chocolate cake.

Who is allowed to vote?

What items are not allowed in my luggage?

announce
(active voice)

PRINCIPAL PARTS: **announces,
announcing, announced, announced**

be announced
(passive voice)

INDICATIVE MOOD

Pres.	I, we, you, they **announce**	I **am announced**
		we, you, they **are announced**
	he, she, it **announces**	he, she, it **is announced**
Pres.	I **am announcing**	I **am being announced**
Prog.	we, you, they **are announcing**	we, you, they **are being announced**
	he, she, it **is announcing**	he, she, it **is being announced**
Pres.	I, we, you, they **do announce**	I, we, you, they **do get announced**
Int.	he, she, it **does announce**	he, she, it **does get announced**
Fut.	I, he, she, it,	I, he, she, it,
	we, you, they **will announce**	we, you, they **will be announced**
Past	I, he, she, it,	I, he, she, it **was announced**
	we, you, they **announced**	we, you, they **were announced**
Past	I, he, she, it **was announcing**	I, he, she, it **was being announced**
Prog.	we, you, they **were announcing**	we, you, they **were being announced**
Past	I, he, she, it,	I, he, she, it,
Int.	we, you, they **did announce**	we, you, they **did get announced**
Pres.	I, we, you, they **have announced**	I, we, you, they **have been announced**
Perf.	he, she, it **has announced**	he, she, it **has been announced**
Past	I, he, she, it,	I, he, she, it,
Perf.	we, you, they **had announced**	we, you, they **had been announced**
Fut.	I, he, she, it, we, you, they	I, he, she, it, we, you, they
Perf.	**will have announced**	**will have been announced**

IMPERATIVE MOOD

announce   **be announced**

SUBJUNCTIVE MOOD

Pres.	if I, he, she, it,	if I, he, she, it,
	we, you, they **announce**	we, you, they **be announced**
Past	if I, he, she, it,	if I, he, she, it,
	we, you, they **announced**	we, you, they **were announced**
Fut.	if I, he, she, it,	if I, he, she, it,
	we, you, they **should announce**	we, you, they **should be announced**

Transitive and intransitive.

They are announcing the winners.
Their engagement was officially announced by their parents.

annoy (active voice)	PRINCIPAL PARTS: **annoys, annoying,** **annoyed, annoyed**	**be annoyed** (passive voice)

INDICATIVE MOOD

Pres.	I, we, you, they **annoy**	I **am annoyed** we, you, they **are annoyed**
	he, she, it **annoys**	he, she, it **is annoyed**
Pres. *Prog.*	I **am annoying** we, you, they **are annoying** he, she, it **is annoying**	I **am being annoyed** we, you, they **are being annoyed** he, she, it **is being annoyed**
Pres. *Int.*	I, we, you, they **do annoy** he, she, it **does annoy**	I, we, you, they **do get annoyed** he, she, it **does get annoyed**
Fut.	I, he, she, it, we, you, they **will annoy**	I, he, she, it, we, you, they **will be annoyed**
Past	I, he, she, it, we, you, they **annoyed**	I, he, she, it **was annoyed** we, you, they **were annoyed**
Past *Prog.*	I, he, she, it **was annoying** we, you, they **were annoying**	I, he, she, it **was being annoyed** we, you, they **were being annoyed**
Past *Int.*	I, he, she, it, we, you, they **did annoy**	I, he, she, it, we, you, they **did get annoyed**
Pres. *Perf.*	I, we, you, they **have annoyed** he, she, it **has annoyed**	I, we, you, they **have been annoyed** he, she, it **has been annoyed**
Past *Perf.*	I, he, she, it, we, you, they **had annoyed**	I, he, she, it, we, you, they **had been annoyed**
Fut. *Perf.*	I, he, she, it, we, you, they **will have annoyed**	I, he, she, it, we, you, they **will have been annoyed**

IMPERATIVE MOOD

annoy	**be annoyed**

SUBJUNCTIVE MOOD

Pres.	if I, he, she, it, we, you, they **annoy**	if I, he, she, it, we, you, they **be annoyed**
Past	if I, he, she, it, we, you, they **annoyed**	if I, he, she, it, we, you, they **were annoyed**
Fut.	if I, he, she, it, we, you, they **should annoy**	if I, he, she, it, we, you, they **should be annoyed**

Transitive and intransitive.

The children annoy their babysitters until the lights are turned off.
I was annoyed by your behavior.

INDICATIVE MOOD

Pres. I, we, you, they **appear**

    he, she, it **appears**

Pres. I **am appearing**
Prog. we, you, they **are appearing**
    he, she, it **is appearing**

Pres. I, we, you, they **do appear**
Int.   he, she, it **does appear**

Fut.   I, he, she, it,
    we, you, they **will appear**

Past I, he, she, it,
    we, you, they **appeared**

Past I, he, she, it **was appearing**
Prog. we, you, they **were appearing**

Past I, he, she, it,
Int.   we, you, they **did appear**

Pres. I, we, you, they **have appeared**
Perf. he, she, it **has appeared**

Past I, he, she, it,
Perf. we, you, they **had appeared**

Fut.   I, he, she, it, we, you, they
Perf. **will have appeared**

IMPERATIVE MOOD

    appear

SUBJUNCTIVE MOOD

Pres. if I, he, she, it,
    we, you, they **appear**

Past if I, he, she, it,
    we, you, they **appeared**

Fut.   if I, he, she, it,
    we, you, they **should appear**

They are appearing on the quiz show today.
He has appeared once before for just a brief time.

apply
(active voice)

PRINCIPAL PARTS: **applies, applying, applied, applied**

be applied
(passive voice)

INDICATIVE MOOD

Pres.	I, we, you, they **apply**	I **am applied**
		we, you, they **are applied**
	he, she, it **applies**	he, she, it **is applied**
Pres.	I **am applying**	I **am being applied**
Prog.	we, you, they **are applying**	we, you, they **are being applied**
	he, she, it **is applying**	he, she, it **is being applied**
Pres.	I, we, you, they **do apply**	I, we, you, they **do get applied**
Int.	he, she, it **does apply**	he, she, it **does get applied**
Fut.	I, he, she, it,	I, he, she, it,
	we, you, they **will apply**	we, you, they **will be applied**
Past	I, he, she, it,	I, he, she, it **was applied**
	we, you, they **applied**	we, you, they **were applied**
Past	I, he, she, it **was applying**	I, he, she, it **was being applied**
Prog.	we, you, they **were applying**	we, you, they **were being applied**
Past	I, he, she, it,	I, he, she, it,
Int.	we, you, they **did apply**	we, you, they **did get applied**
Pres.	I, we, you, they **have applied**	I, we, you, they **have been applied**
Perf.	he, she, it **has applied**	he, she, it **has been applied**
Past	I, he, she, it,	I, he, she, it,
Perf.	we, you, they **had applied**	we, you, they **had been applied**
Fut.	I, he, she, it, we, you, they	I, he, she, it, we, you, they
Perf.	**will have applied**	**will have been applied**

IMPERATIVE MOOD

apply　　　　　　　　**be applied**

SUBJUNCTIVE MOOD

Pres.	if I, he, she, it,	if I, he, she, it,
	we, you, they **apply**	we, you, they **be applied**
Past	if I, he, she, it,	if I, he, she, it,
	we, you, they **applied**	we, you, they **were applied**
Fut.	if I, he, she, it,	if I, he, she, it,
	we, you, they **should apply**	we, you, they **should be applied**

Transitive and intransitive.

I am constantly applying for a new job.
The makeup was applied just before she went on stage.

argue
(active voice)

be argued
(passive voice)

INDICATIVE MOOD

Pres.	I, we, you, they **argue**	I **am argued**
		we, you, they **are argued**
	he, she, it **argues**	he, she, it **is argued**
Pres.	I **am arguing**	I **am being argued**
Prog.	we, you, they **are arguing**	we, you, they **are being argued**
	he, she, it **is arguing**	he, she, it **is being argued**
Pres.	I, we, you, they **do argue**	I, we, you, they **do get argued**
Int.	he, she, it **does argue**	he, she, it **does get argued**
Fut.	I, he, she, it,	I, he, she, it,
	we, you, they **will argue**	we, you, they **will be argued**
Past	I, he, she, it,	I, he, she, it **was argued**
	we, you, they **argued**	we, you, they **were argued**
Past	I, he, she, it **was arguing**	I, he, she, it **was being argued**
Prog.	we, you, they **were arguing**	we, you, they **were being argued**
Past	I, he, she, it,	I, he, she, it,
Int.	we, you, they **did argue**	we, you, they **did get argued**
Pres.	I, we, you, they **have argued**	I, we, you, they **have been argued**
Perf.	he, she, it **has argued**	he, she, it **has been argued**
Past	I, he, she, it,	I, he, she, it,
Perf.	we, you, they **had argued**	we, you, they **had been argued**
Fut.	I, he, she, it, we, you, they	I, he, she, it, we, you, they
Perf.	**will have argued**	**will have been argued**

IMPERATIVE MOOD

argue   **be argued**

SUBJUNCTIVE MOOD

Pres.	if I, he, she, it,	if I, he, she, it,
	we, you, they **argue**	we, you, they **be argued**
Past	if I, he, she, it,	if I, he, she, it,
	we, you, they **argued**	we, you, they **were argued**
Fut.	if I, he, she, it,	if I, he, she, it,
	we, you, they **should argue**	we, you, they **should be argued**

Transitive and intransitive.

The newlyweds are arguing for the first time.
That case was argued in Superior Court.

arise　　　　　　　　PRINCIPAL PARTS: **arises, arising,**
　　　　　　　　　　　　　　arose, arisen

INDICATIVE MOOD

Pres.　　I, we, you, they **arise**

　　　　　he, she, it **arises**

Pres.　　I **am arising**
Prog.　　we, you, they **are arising**
　　　　　he, she, it **is arising**

Pres.　　I, we, you, they **do arise**
Int.　　 he, she, it **does arise**

Fut.　　 I, he, she, it,
　　　　　we, you, they **will arise**

Past　　 I, he, she, it,
　　　　　we, you, they **arose**

Past　　 I, he, she, it **was arising**
Prog.　　we, you, they **were arising**

Past　　 I, he, she, it,
Int.　　 we, you, they **did arise**

Pres.　　I, we, you, they **have arisen**
Perf.　　 he, she, it **has arisen**

Past　　 I, he, she, it,
Perf.　　 we, you, they **had arisen**

Fut.　　 I, he, she, it, we, you, they
Perf.　　 **will have arisen**

IMPERATIVE MOOD

　　　　　arise

SUBJUNCTIVE MOOD

Pres.　　if I, he, she, it,
　　　　　we, you, they **arise**

Past　　 if I, he, she, it,
　　　　　we, you, they **arose**

Fut.　　 if I, he, she, it,
　　　　　we, you, they **should arise**

A new day is arising.
The problem arose when they discovered the leak.
Those concerns had arisen at the beginning of their relationship.

ask (active voice)	PRINCIPAL PARTS: **asks, asking, asked, asked**	be asked (passive voice)

INDICATIVE MOOD

Pres.	I, we, you, they **ask**	I **am asked** we, you, they **are asked**
	he, she, it **asks**	he, she, it **is asked**
Pres. *Prog.*	I **am asking** we, you, they **are asking**	I **am being asked** we, you, they **are being asked**
	he, she, it **is asking**	he, she, it **is being asked**
Pres. *Int.*	I, we, you, they **do ask**	I, we, you, they **do get asked**
	he, she, it **does ask**	he, she, it **does get asked**
Fut.	I, he, she, it, we, you, they **will ask**	I, he, she, it, we, you, they **will be asked**
Past	I, he, she, it, we, you, they **asked**	I, he, she, it **was asked** we, you, they **were asked**
Past *Prog.*	I, he, she, it **was asking** we, you, they **were asking**	I, he, she, it **was being asked** we, you, they **were being asked**
Past *Int.*	I, he, she, it, we, you, they **did ask**	I, he, she, it, we, you, they **did get asked**
Pres. *Perf.*	I, we, you, they **have asked**	I, we, you, they **have been asked**
	he, she, it **has asked**	he, she, it **has been asked**
Past *Perf.*	I, he, she, it, we, you, they **had asked**	I, he, she, it, we, you, they **had been asked**
Fut. *Perf.*	I, he, she, it, we, you, they **will have asked**	I, he, she, it, we, you, they **will have been asked**

IMPERATIVE MOOD

ask	**be asked**

SUBJUNCTIVE MOOD

Pres.	if I, he, she, it, we, you, they **ask**	if I, he, she, it, we, you, they **be asked**
Past	if I, he, she, it, we, you, they **asked**	if I, he, she, it, we, you, they **were asked**
Fut.	if I, he, she, it, we, you, they **should ask**	if I, he, she, it, we, you, they **should be asked**

Transitive and intransitive.

Please do not be afraid to ask me about anything.
That question has been asked and answered.

AN ESSENTIAL
55 VERB

AN ESSENTIAL 55 VERB

ask

Examples

You can ask him anything.

She is asking for your help.

He asks for trouble.

The prisoner was asked the same question ten times.

You were not asked to come.

Ask me anything.

Who will ask her?

Ask for the menu.

I had asked her once before.

Have they been asked to make a donation?

Words and expressions related to this verb

Don't ask, don't tell.

May I ask you a question?

May I ask you to leave?

Were you really asked to leave?

He asked for her hand in matrimony.

You asked for it.

We were asked for a contribution.

You cannot be asked to testify against yourself.

He was just asking about.

Could I ask you out for Friday evening?

She asked him over for coffee.

assume
(active voice)

be assumed
(passive voice)

INDICATIVE MOOD

Pres. I, we, you, they **assume**

he, she, it **assumes**

I **am assumed**
we, you, they **are assumed**
he, she, it **is assumed**

Pres. I **am assuming**
Prog. we, you, they **are assuming**
he, she, it **is assuming**

I **am being assumed**
we, you, they **are being assumed**
he, she, it **is being assumed**

Pres. I, we, you, they **do assume**
Int. he, she, it **does assume**

I, we, you, they **do get assumed**
he, she, it **does get assumed**

Fut. I, he, she, it,
we, you, they **will assume**

I, he, she, it,
we, you, they **will be assumed**

Past I, he, she, it,
we, you, they **assumed**

I, he, she, it **was assumed**
we, you, they **were assumed**

Past I, he, she, it **was assuming**
Prog. we, you, they **were assuming**

I, he, she, it **was being assumed**
we, you, they **were being assumed**

Past I, he, she, it,
Int. we, you, they **did assume**

I, he, she, it,
we, you, they **did get assumed**

Pres. I, we, you, they **have assumed**
Perf. he, she, it **has assumed**

I, we, you, they **have been assumed**
he, she, it **has been assumed**

Past I, he, she, it,
Perf. we, you, they **had assumed**

I, he, she, it,
we, you, they **had been assumed**

Fut. I, he, she, it, we, you, they
Perf. **will have assumed**

I, he, she, it, we, you, they
will have been assumed

IMPERATIVE MOOD

assume

be assumed

SUBJUNCTIVE MOOD

Pres. if I, he, she, it,
we, you, they **assume**

if I, he, she, it,
we, you, they **be assumed**

Past if I, he, she, it,
we, you, they **assumed**

if I, he, she, it,
we, you, they **were assumed**

Fut. if I, he, she, it,
we, you, they **should assume**

if I, he, she, it,
we, you, they **should be assumed**

We are not assuming that you are unsympathetic to our needs.
It was assumed by all that he would attend the meeting.

attack
(active voice)

PRINCIPAL PARTS: **attacks, attacking, attacked, attacked**

be attacked
(passive voice)

INDICATIVE MOOD

Pres.	I, we, you, they **attack**	I **am attacked**
		we, you, they **are attacked**
	he, she, it **attacks**	he, she, it **is attacked**
Pres.	I **am attacking**	I **am being attacked**
Prog.	we, you, they **are attacking**	we, you, they **are being attacked**
	he, she, it **is attacking**	he, she, it **is being attacked**
Pres.	I, we, you, they **do attack**	I, we, you, they **do get attacked**
Int.	he, she, it **does attack**	he, she, it **does get attacked**
Fut.	I, he, she, it,	I, he, she, it,
	we, you, they **will attack**	we, you, they **will be attacked**
Past	I, he, she, it,	I, he, she, it **was attacked**
	we, you, they **attacked**	we, you, they **were attacked**
Past	I, he, she, it **was attacking**	I, he, she, it **was being attacked**
Prog.	we, you, they **were attacking**	we, you, they **were being attacked**
Past	I, he, she, it,	I, he, she, it,
Int.	we, you, they **did attack**	we, you, they **did get attacked**
Pres.	I, we, you, they **have attacked**	I, we, you, they **have been attacked**
Perf.	he, she, it **has attacked**	he, she, it **has been attacked**
Past	I, he, she, it,	I, he, she, it,
Perf.	we, you, they **had attacked**	we, you, they **had been attacked**
Fut.	I, he, she, it, we, you, they	I, he, she, it, we, you, they
Perf.	**will have attacked**	**will have been attacked**

IMPERATIVE MOOD

attack   **be attacked**

SUBJUNCTIVE MOOD

Pres.	if I, he, she, it,	if I, he, she, it,
	we, you, they **attack**	we, you, they **be attacked**
Past	if I, he, she, it,	if I, he, she, it,
	we, you, they **attacked**	we, you, they **were attacked**
Fut.	if I, he, she, it,	if I, he, she, it,
	we, you, they **should attack**	we, you, they **should be attacked**

Transitive and intransitive.

The students are attacking the problem with great enthusiasm.
If we are attacked, we will naturally defend ourselves.

attend
(active voice)

be attended
(passive voice)

INDICATIVE MOOD

Pres.	I, we, you, they **attend**	I **am attended**
		we, you, they **are attended**
	he, she, it **attends**	he, she, it **is attended**
Pres.	I **am attending**	I **am being attended**
Prog.	we, you, they **are attending**	we, you, they **are being attended**
	he, she, it **is attending**	he, she, it **is being attended**
Pres.	I, we, you, they **do attend**	I, we, you, they **do get attended**
Int.	he, she, it **does attend**	he, she, it **does get attended**
Fut.	I, he, she, it,	I, he, she, it,
	we, you, they **will attend**	we, you, they **will be attended**
Past	I, he, she, it,	I, he, she, it **was attended**
	we, you, they **attended**	we, you, they **were attended**
Past	I, he, she, it **was attending**	I, he, she, it **was being attended**
Prog.	we, you, they **were attending**	we, you, they **were being attended**
Past	I, he, she, it,	I, he, she, it,
Int.	we, you, they **did attend**	we, you, they **did get attended**
Pres.	I, we, you, they **have attended**	I, we, you, they **have been attended**
Perf.	he, she, it **has attended**	he, she, it **has been attended**
Past	I, he, she, it,	I, he, she, it,
Perf.	we, you, they **had attended**	we, you, they **had been attended**
Fut.	I, he, she, it, we, you, they	I, he, she, it, we, you, they
Perf.	**will have attended**	**will have been attended**

IMPERATIVE MOOD

attend   **be attended**

SUBJUNCTIVE MOOD

Pres.	if I, he, she, it,	if I, he, she, it,
	we, you, they **attend**	we, you, they **be attended**
Past	if I, he, she, it,	if I, he, she, it,
	we, you, they **attended**	we, you, they **were attended**
Fut.	if I, he, she, it,	if I, he, she, it,
	we, you, they **should attend**	we, you, they **should be attended**

Transitive and intransitive.

Are you going to attend your daughter's graduation?
I am so glad that the concert was well attended.

avoid
(active voice)

be avoided
(passive voice)

INDICATIVE MOOD

Pres.	I, we, you, they **avoid**	I **am avoided**
		we, you, they **are avoided**
	he, she, it **avoids**	he, she, it **is avoided**
Pres.	I **am avoiding**	I **am being avoided**
Prog.	we, you, they **are avoiding**	we, you, they **are being avoided**
	he, she, it **is avoiding**	he, she, it **is being avoided**
Pres.	I, we, you, they **do avoid**	I, we, you, they **do get avoided**
Int.	he, she, it **does avoid**	he, she, it **does get avoided**
Fut.	I, he, she, it,	I, he, she, it,
	we, you, they **will avoid**	we, you, they **will be avoided**
Past	I, he, she, it,	I, he, she, it **was avoided**
	we, you, they **avoided**	we, you, they **were avoided**
Past	I, he, she, it **was avoiding**	I, he, she, it **was being avoided**
Prog.	we, you, they **were avoiding**	we, you, they **were being avoided**
Past	I, he, she, it,	I, he, she, it,
Int.	we, you, they **did avoid**	we, you, they **did get avoided**
Pres.	I, we, you, they **have avoided**	I, we, you, they **have been avoided**
Perf.	he, she, it **has avoided**	he, she, it **has been avoided**
Past	I, he, she, it,	I, he, she, it,
Perf.	we, you, they **had avoided**	we, you, they **had been avoided**
Fut.	I, he, she, it, we, you, they	I, he, she, it, we, you, they
Perf.	**will have avoided**	**will have been avoided**

IMPERATIVE MOOD

avoid   **be avoided**

SUBJUNCTIVE MOOD

Pres.	if I, he, she, it,	if I, he, she, it,
	we, you, they **avoid**	we, you, they **be avoided**
Past	if I, he, she, it,	if I, he, she, it,
	we, you, they **avoided**	we, you, they **were avoided**
Fut.	if I, he, she, it,	if I, he, she, it,
	we, you, they **should avoid**	we, you, they **should be avoided**

The important thing is to avoid making mistakes.
Were the obstacles successfully avoided?

awake (active voice)	PRINCIPAL PARTS: **awakes, awaking,** **awoke/awaked, awaked/awoken**	be awaked (passive voice)

INDICATIVE MOOD

Pres.	I, we, you, they **awake**	I **am awaked**
		we, you, they **are awaked**
	he, she, it **awakes**	he, she, it **is awaked**
Pres.	I **am awaking**	I **am being awaked**
Prog.	we, you, they **are awaking**	we, you, they **are being awaked**
	he, she, it **is awaking**	he, she, it **is being awaked**
Pres.	I, we, you, they **do awake**	I, we, you, they **do get awaked**
Int.	he, she, it **does awake**	he, she, it **does get awaked**
Fut.	I, he, she, it,	I, he, she, it,
	we, you, they **will awake**	we, you, they **will be awaked**
Past	I, he, she, it,	I, he, she, it **was awaked**
	we, you, they **awoke**	we, you, they **were awaked**
Past	I, he, she, it **was awaking**	I, he, she, it **was being awaked**
Prog.	we, you, they **were awaking**	we, you, they **were being awaked**
Past	I, he, she, it,	I, he, she, it,
Int.	we, you, they **did awake**	we, you, they **did get awaked**
Pres.	I, we, you, they **have awaked**	I, we, you, they **have been awaked**
Perf.	he, she, it **has awaked**	he, she, it **has been awaked**
Past	I, he, she, it,	I, he, she, it,
Perf.	we, you, they **had awaked**	we, you, they **had been awaked**
Fut.	I, he, she, it, we, you, they	I, he, she, it, we, you, they
Perf.	**will have awaked**	**will have been awaked**

IMPERATIVE MOOD

awake	**be awaked**

SUBJUNCTIVE MOOD

Pres.	if I, he, she, it,	if I, he, she, it,
	we, you, they **awake**	we, you, they **be awaked**
Past	if I, he, she, it,	if I, he, she, it,
	we, you, they **awoke**	we, you, they **were awaked**
Fut.	if I, he, she, it,	if I, he, she, it,
	we, you, they **should awake**	we, you, they **should be awaked**

Transitive and intransitive. Both forms of the past, AWOKE and AWAKED, are standard as are the past participles AWAKED and AWOKEN. The verb AWAKE and the related AWAKEN are synonymous with WAKE and WAKEN, but the former are more often used figuratively. The *Oxford Modern English Dictionary* lists only AWOKE for the past tense and AWOKEN for the past participle. *Merriam-Webster's Collegiate Dictionary* accepts AWOKE as a past participle.

This challenge is awaking their competitive spirit.
We awoke at dawn.
The child was awoken by the thunder.

awaken
(active voice)

be awakened
(passive voice)

A

INDICATIVE MOOD

Pres.	I, we, you, they **awaken**	I **am awakened**
		we, you, they **are awakened**
	he, she, it **awakens**	he, she, it **is awakened**
Pres.	I **am awakening**	I **am being awakened**
Prog.	we, you, they **are awakening**	we, you, they **are being awakened**
	he, she, it **is awakening**	he, she, it **is being awakened**
Pres.	I, we, you, they **do awaken**	I, we, you, they **do get awakened**
Int.	he, she, it **does awaken**	he, she, it **does get awakened**
Fut.	I, he, she, it,	I, he, she, it,
	we, you, they **will awaken**	we, you, they **will be awakened**
Past	I, he, she, it,	I, he, she, it **was awakened**
	we, you, they **awakened**	we, you, they **were awakened**
Past	I, he, she, it **was awakening**	I, he, she, it **was being awakened**
Prog.	we, you, they **were awakening**	we, you, they **were being awakened**
Past	I, he, she, it,	I, he, she, it,
Int.	we, you, they **did awaken**	we, you, they **did get awakened**
Pres.	I, we, you, they **have awakened**	I, we, you, they **have been awakened**
Perf.	he, she, it **has awakened**	he, she, it **has been awakened**
Past	I, he, she, it,	I, he, she, it,
Perf.	we, you, they **had awakened**	we, you, they **had been awakened**
Fut.	I, he, she, it, we, you, they	I, he, she, it, we, you, they
Perf.	**will have awakened**	**will have been awakened**

IMPERATIVE MOOD

awaken **be awakened**

SUBJUNCTIVE MOOD

Pres.	if I, he, she, it,	if I, he, she, it,
	we, you, they **awaken**	we, you, they **be awakened**
Past	if I, he, she, it,	if I, he, she, it,
	we, you, they **awakened**	we, you, they **were awakened**
Fut.	if I, he, she, it,	if I, he, she, it,
	we, you, they **should awaken**	we, you, they **should be awakened**

Transitive and intransitive.

We awakened to all of the implications of the tragedy.
I would like to be awakened at 7 A.M.

bar
(active voice)

be barred
(passive voice)

INDICATIVE MOOD

Pres.	I, we, you, they **bar**	I **am barred**
		we, you, they **are barred**
	he, she, it **bars**	he, she, it **is barred**
Pres.	I **am barring**	I **am being barred**
Prog.	we, you, they **are barring**	we, you, they **are being barred**
	he, she, it **is barring**	he, she, it **is being barred**
Pres.	I, we, you, they **do bar**	I, we, you, they **do get barred**
Int.	he, she, it **does bar**	he, she, it **does get barred**
Fut.	I, he, she, it,	I, he, she, it,
	we, you, they **will bar**	we, you, they **will be barred**
Past	I, he, she, it,	I, he, she, it **was barred**
	we, you, they **barred**	we, you, they **were barred**
Past	I, he, she, it **was barring**	I, he, she, it **was being barred**
Prog.	we, you, they **were barring**	we, you, they **were being barred**
Past	I, he, she, it,	I, he, she, it,
Int.	we, you, they **did bar**	we, you, they **did get barred**
Pres.	I, we, you, they **have barred**	I, we, you, they **have been barred**
Perf.	he, she, it **has barred**	he, she, it **has been barred**
Past	I, he, she, it,	I, he, she, it,
Perf.	we, you, they **had barred**	we, you, they **had been barred**
Fut.	I, he, she, it, we, you, they	I, he, she, it, we, you, they
Perf.	**will have barred**	**will have been barred**

IMPERATIVE MOOD

bar

be barred

SUBJUNCTIVE MOOD

Pres.	if I, he, she, it,	if I, he, she, it,
	we, you, they **bar**	we, you, they **be barred**
Past	if I, he, she, it,	if I, he, she, it,
	we, you, they **barred**	we, you, they **were barred**
Fut.	if I, he, she, it,	if I, he, she, it,
	we, you, they **should bar**	we, you, they **should be barred**

We are barring the door and letting no one enter.
His way was barred by the bouncer.

24

bare
(active voice)

be bared
(passive voice)

INDICATIVE MOOD

Pres.	I, we, you, they **bare**	I **am bared**
		we, you, they **are bared**
	he, she, it **bares**	he, she, it **is bared**
Pres.	I **am baring**	I **am being bared**
Prog.	we, you, they **are baring**	we, you, they **are being bared**
	he, she, it **is baring**	he, she, it **is being bared**
Pres.	I, we, you, they **do bare**	I, we, you, they **do get bared**
Int.	he, she, it **does bare**	he, she, it **does get bared**
Fut.	I, he, she, it,	I, he, she, it,
	we, you, they **will bare**	we, you, they **will be bared**
Past	I, he, she, it,	I, he, she, it **was bared**
	we, you, they **bared**	we, you, they **were bared**
Past	I, he, she, it **was baring**	I, he, she, it **was being bared**
Prog.	we, you, they **were baring**	we, you, they **were being bared**
Past	I, he, she, it,	I, he, she, it,
Int.	we, you, they **did bare**	we, you, they **did get bared**
Pres.	I, we, you, they **have bared**	I, we, you, they **have been bared**
Perf.	he, she, it **has bared**	he, she, it **has been bared**
Past	I, he, she, it,	I, he, she, it,
Perf.	we, you, they **had bared**	we, you, they **had been bared**
Fut.	I, he, she, it, we, you, they	I, he, she, it, we, you, they
Perf.	**will have bared**	**will have been bared**

IMPERATIVE MOOD

bare   **be bared**

SUBJUNCTIVE MOOD

Pres.	if I, he, she, it,	if I, he, she, it,
	we, you, they **bare**	we, you, they **be bared**
Past	if I, he, she, it,	if I, he, she, it,
	we, you, they **bared**	we, you, they **were bared**
Fut.	if I, he, she, it,	if I, he, she, it,
	we, you, they **should bare**	we, you, they **should be bared**

BARE meaning "uncover" is pronounced like the verb BEAR meaning "carry."

They are baring their most precious secrets.
He bared his head as he entered the school.
Their innermost thoughts were bared in the course of the discussion.

base
(active voice)

PRINCIPAL PARTS: bases, basing,
based, based

be based
(passive voice)

INDICATIVE MOOD

Pres.	I, we, you, they **base** he, she, it **bases**	I **am based** we, you, they **are based** he, she, it **is based**
Pres. *Prog.*	I **am basing** we, you, they **are basing** he, she, it **is basing**	I **am being based** we, you, they **are being based** he, she, it **is being based**
Pres. *Int.*	I, we, you, they **do base** he, she, it **does base**	I, we, you, they **do get based** he, she, it **does get based**
Fut.	I, he, she, it, we, you, they **will base**	I, he, she, it, we, you, they **will be based**
Past	I, he, she, it, we, you, they **based**	I, he, she, it **was based** we, you, they **were based**
Past *Prog.*	I, he, she, it **was basing** we, you, they **were basing**	I, he, she, it **was being based** we, you, they **were being based**
Past *Int.*	I, he, she, it, we, you, they **did base**	I, he, she, it, we, you, they **did get based**
Pres. *Perf.*	I, we, you, they **have based** he, she, it **has based**	I, we, you, they **have been based** he, she, it **has been based**
Past *Perf.*	I, he, she, it, we, you, they **had based**	I, he, she, it, we, you, they **had been based**
Fut. *Perf.*	I, he, she, it, we, you, they **will have based**	I, he, she, it, we, you, they **will have been based**

IMPERATIVE MOOD

base   **be based**

SUBJUNCTIVE MOOD

Pres.	if I, he, she, it, we, you, they **base**	if I, he, she, it, we, you, they **be based**
Past	if I, he, she, it, we, you, they **based**	if I, he, she, it, we, you, they **were based**
Fut.	if I, he, she, it, we, you, they **should base**	if I, he, she, it, we, you, they **should be based**

We are basing our conclusions on the evidence.
My actions are based on my beliefs.

be   PRINCIPAL PARTS: **is, being, was/were, been**

INDICATIVE MOOD

B

Pres.   I **am**
          we, you, they **are**
          he, she, it **is**

Pres.   I **am being**
Prog.   we, you, they **are being**
          he, she, it **is being**

Fut.   I, he, she, it,
          we, you, they **will be**

Past   I, he, she, it, **was**
          we, you, they **were**

Past   I, he, she, it **was being**
Prog.   we, you, they **were being**

Pres.   I, we, you, they **have been**
Perf.   he, she, it **has been**

Past   I, he, she, it,
Perf.   we, you, they **had been**

Fut.   I, he, she, it, we, you, they
Perf.   **will have been**

IMPERATIVE MOOD

          be

SUBJUNCTIVE MOOD

Pres.   if I, he, she, it,
          we, you, they **be**

Past   if I, he, she, it,
          we, you, they **were**

Fut.   if I, he, she, it,
          we, you, they **should be**

BE is the only English verb with a distinct form for the first person singular present, I AM, and two forms for the past, WAS and WERE. BE is often contracted: I am = I'm, he is = he's, you are = you're. It is also contracted in the negative forms: they aren't, he isn't. There is no correct contraction for "I am not" or "Am I not." The colloquial and substandard **ain't** is often heard for "I am not," "he is not," "we are not," etc. "Aren't I" is more often heard in British English. BE is also used as an auxiliary verb for the progressive tenses and the passive voice. The forms THOU ART and THOU WERT are archaic.

I am yours and you are mine. You are what you are.
We are being quiet about the accident.
This is the way we were.
This is the way it always has been.

AN ESSENTIAL 55 VERB

AN ESSENTIAL 55 VERB

Examples

To be or not to be, that is the question.

I think, therefore I am.

See me, be me, touch me, feel me.

Will you be my girl?

Been there, done that.

Be on time.

Be my Valentine.

I am what I am.

You are so beautiful to me.

What is to be done?

Where were you last night?

You are the sunshine of my life.

If I were a rich man!

Words and expressions related to this verb

I'm so lonely.

You're late.

He's in the money.

She's in the running.

We're in Florida next week.

They'll be home on Monday.

I'll be there.

You'll be sorry.

He'll be in the lobby.

She'll be on time.

We'll be missing you in all the old familiar places.

They'll be O.K.

bear
(active voice)

PRINCIPAL PARTS: bears, bearing, bore, borne/born

be borne/born
(passive voice)

INDICATIVE MOOD

Pres.	I, we, you, they **bear**	I **am borne**
		we, you, they **are borne**
	he, she, it **bears**	he, she, it **is borne**
Pres. *Prog.*	I **am bearing** we, you, they **are bearing** he, she, it **is bearing**	I **am being borne** we, you, they **are being borne** he, she, it **is being borne**
Pres. *Int.*	I, we, you, they **do bear** he, she, it **does bear**	I, we, you, they **do get borne** he, she, it **does get borne**
Fut.	I, he, she, it, we, you, they **will bear**	I, he, she, it, we, you, they **will be borne**
Past	I, he, she, it, we, you, they **bore**	I, he, she, it **was borne** we, you, they **were borne**
Past *Prog.*	I, he, she, it **was bearing** we, you, they **were bearing**	I, he, she, it **was being borne** we, you, they **were being borne**
Past *Int.*	I, he, she, it, we, you, they **did bear**	I, he, she, it, we, you, they **did get borne**
Pres. *Perf.*	I, we, you, they **have borne** he, she, it **has borne**	I, we, you, they **have been borne** he, she, it **has been borne**
Past *Perf.*	I, he, she, it, we, you, they **had borne**	I, he, she, it, we, you, they **had been borne**
Fut. *Perf.*	I, he, she, it, we, you, they **will have borne**	I, he, she, it, we, you, they **will have been borne**

IMPERATIVE MOOD

bear   **be borne**

SUBJUNCTIVE MOOD

Pres.	if I, he, she, it, we, you, they **bear**	if I, he, she, it, we, you, they **be borne**
Past	if I, he, she, it, we, you, they **bore**	if I, he, she, it, we, you, they **were borne**
Fut.	if I, he, she, it, we, you, they **should bear**	if I, he, she, it, we, you, they **should be borne**

Transitive and intransitive. The participle has two acceptable forms: BORNE relates to being "carried," while BORN relates to "birth."
"The little girl was being borne on her father's shoulders. She was born just a year ago."

All men over eighteen must bear arms.
They bore gifts to the newlyweds.
The little girl was born just six days ago and was now being borne in her daddy's arms.

beat
(active voice)

be beaten/beat
(passive voice)

INDICATIVE MOOD

Pres.	I, we, you, they **beat**	I **am beaten**
		we, you, they **are beaten**
	he, she, it **beats**	he, she, it **is beaten**
Pres.	I **am beating**	I **am being beaten**
Prog.	we, you, they **are beating**	we, you, they **are being beaten**
	he, she, it **is beating**	he, she, it **is being beaten**
Pres.	I, we, you, they **do beat**	I, we, you, they **do get beaten**
Int.	he, she, it **does beat**	he, she, it **does get beaten**
Fut.	I, he, she, it, we, you, they **will beat**	I, he, she, it, we, you, they **will be beaten**
Past	I, he, she, it, we, you, they **beat**	I, he, she, it **was beaten** we, you, they **were beaten**
Past	I, he, she, it **was beating**	I, he, she, it **was being beaten**
Prog.	we, you, they **were beating**	we, you, they **were being beaten**
Past	I, he, she, it, we, you, they **did beat**	I, he, she, it, we, you, they **did get beaten**
Int.		
Pres.	I, we, you, they **have beaten**	I, we, you, they **have been beaten**
Perf.	he, she, it **has beaten**	he, she, it **has been beaten**
Past	I, he, she, it, we, you, they **had beaten**	I, he, she, it, we, you, they **had been beaten**
Perf.		
Fut.	I, he, she, it, we, you, they **will have beaten**	I, he, she, it, we, you, they **will have been beaten**
Perf.		

IMPERATIVE MOOD

beat   **be beaten**

SUBJUNCTIVE MOOD

Pres.	if I, he, she, it, we, you, they **beat**	if I, he, she, it, we, you, they **be beaten**
Past	if I, he, she, it, we, you, they **beat**	if I, he, she, it, we, you, they **were beaten**
Fut.	if I, he, she, it, we, you, they **should beat**	if I, he, she, it, we, you, they **should be beaten**

Transitive and intransitive.

The little boy beats on his drums every chance he gets.
We beat a better team this evening.
The eggs must be beaten before you add them to the cake mix.

become (active voice)	Principal Parts: **becomes, becoming, became, become**	**be become** (passive voice)

INDICATIVE MOOD

Pres.	I, we, you, they **become**	I **am become**
		we, you, they **are become**
	he, she, it **becomes**	he, she, it **is become**
Pres. *Prog.*	I **am becoming** we, you, they **are becoming** he, she, it **is becoming**	I am being **become** we, you, they **are being become** he, she, it **is being become**
Pres. *Int.*	I, we, you, they **do become** he, she, it **does become**	I, we, you, they **do get become** he, she, it **does get become**
Fut.	I, he, she, it, we, you, they **will become**	I, he, she, it, we, you, they **will be become**
Past	I, he, she, it, we, you, they **became**	I, he, she, it **was become** we, you, they **were become**
Past *Prog.*	I, he, she, it **was becoming** we, you, they **were becoming**	I, he, she, it **was being become** we, you, they **were being become**
Past *Int.*	I, he, she, it, we, you, they **did become**	I, he, she, it, we, you, they **did get become**
Pres. *Perf.*	I, we, you, they **have become** he, she, it **has become**	I, we, you, they **have been become** he, she, it **has been become**
Past *Perf.*	I, he, she, it, we, you, they **had become**	I, he, she, it, we, you, they **had been become**
Fut. *Perf.*	I, he, she, it, we, you, they **will have become**	I, he, she, it, we, you, they **will have been become**

IMPERATIVE MOOD

become	**be become**

SUBJUNCTIVE MOOD

Pres.	if I, he, she, it, we, you, they **become**	if I, he, she, it, we, you, they **be become**
Past	if I, he, she, it, we, you, they **became**	if I, he, she, it, we, you, they **were become**
Fut.	if I, he, she, it, we, you, they **should become**	if I, he, she, it, we, you, they **should be become**

Intransitive and transitive.

That blouse becomes you.
I am becoming an accomplished musician.
She became famous.
It has become the main issue.

AN ESSENTIAL 55 VERB

become

Examples

She wants to become a physicist.

He became a soccer coach.

What will become of us?

Who will become the next president?

It has become a habit.

That hairdo becomes you.

It is becoming more popular every year.

In ten years computers will have become old fashioned.

Become a teacher.

Don't become a burden to your friends.

Words and expressions related to this verb

You can become anything you want to be.

What became of her?

What will become of us?

What becomes of the brokenhearted?

Are we becoming more or less healthy?

Don't become a grouchy old man.

You should become an actor.

What becomes of old cars?

That has already become outdated.

He was concerned about what might become of his fortune.

beg
(active voice)

be begged
(passive voice)

B

INDICATIVE MOOD

Pres.	I, we, you, they **beg**	**I am begged**
		we, you, they **are begged**
	he, she, it **begs**	he, she, it **is begged**
Pres.	**I am begging**	I am being begged
Prog.	we, you, they **are begging**	we, you, they **are being begged**
	he, she, it **is begging**	he, she, it **is being begged**
Pres.	I, we, you, they **do beg**	I, we, you, they **do get begged**
Int.	he, she, it **does beg**	he, she, it **does get begged**
Fut.	I, he, she, it,	I, he, she, it,
	we, you, they **will beg**	we, you, they **will be begged**
Past	I, he, she, it,	I, he, she, it **was begged**
	we, you, they **begged**	we, you, they **were begged**
Past	I, he, she, it **was begging**	I, he, she, it **was being begged**
Prog.	we, you, they **were begging**	we, you, they **were being begged**
Past	I, he, she, it,	I, he, she, it,
Int.	we, you, they **did beg**	we, you, they **did get begged**
Pres.	I, we, you, they **have begged**	I, we, you, they **have been begged**
Perf.	he, she, it **has begged**	he, she, it **has been begged**
Past	I, he, she, it,	I, he, she, it,
Perf.	we, you, they **had begged**	we, you, they **had been begged**
Fut.	I, he, she, it, we, you, they	I, he, she, it, we, you, they
Perf.	**will have begged**	**will have been begged**

IMPERATIVE MOOD

beg　　　　　　　　　　**be begged**

SUBJUNCTIVE MOOD

Pres.	if I, he, she, it,	if I, he, she, it,
	we, you, they **beg**	we, you, they **be begged**
Past	if I, he, she, it,	if I, he, she, it,
	we, you, they **begged**	we, you, they **were begged**
Fut.	if I, he, she, it,	if I, he, she, it,
	we, you, they **should beg**	we, you, they **should be begged**

Transitive and intransitive.

We are begging for mercy for our son.
He begged her to stay.
They were begged to go before the hurricane.

begin
(active voice)

be begun
(passive voice)

INDICATIVE MOOD

Pres. I, we, you, they **begin**

he, she, it **begins**

I **am begun**
we, you, they **are begun**
he, she, it **is begun**

Pres. I **am beginning**
Prog. we, you, they **are beginning**
he, she, it **is beginning**

I **am being begun**
we, you, they **are being begun**
he, she, it **is being begun**

Pres. I, we, you, they **do begin**
Int. he, she, it **does begin**

I, we, you, they **do get begun**
he, she, it **does get begun**

Fut. I, he, she, it,
we, you, they **will begin**

I, he, she, it,
we, you, they **will be begun**

Past I, he, she, it,
we, you, they **began**

I, he, she, it **was begun**
we, you, they **were begun**

Past I, he, she, it **was beginning**
Prog. we, you, they **were beginning**

I, he, she, it **was being begun**
we, you, they **were being begun**

Past I, he, she, it,
Int. we, you, they **did begin**

I, he, she, it,
we, you, they **did get begun**

Pres. I, we, you, they **have begun**
Perf. he, she, it **has begun**

I, we, you, they **have been begun**
he, she, it **has been begun**

Past I, he, she, it,
Perf. we, you, they **had begun**

I, he, she, it,
we, you, they **had been begun**

Fut. I, he, she, it, we, you, they
Perf. **will have begun**

I, he, she, it, we, you, they
will have been begun

IMPERATIVE MOOD

begin

be begun

SUBJUNCTIVE MOOD

Pres. if I, he, she, it,
we, you, they **begin**

if I, he, she, it,
we, you, they **be begun**

Past if I, he, she, it,
we, you, they **began**

if I, he, she, it,
we, you, they **were begun**

Fut. if I, he, she, it,
we, you, they **should begin**

if I, he, she, it,
we, you, they **should be begun**

Intransitive and transitive.

I am beginning to understand.
The concert began ten minutes late.
The operation was begun on schedule.

AN ESSENTIAL
55 VERB

Examples

You may begin.

He begins his day with a prayer.

She began early in the morning.

When does the class begin?

It begins at 8:00 A.M.

The concert had already begun.

Begin with a summary of your argument.

We will begin promptly.

Has he begun his assignment?

Begin on my signal.

Words and expressions related to this verb

Begin at the beginning.

Think before you begin.

He who begins too much accomplishes little.

Where do I begin?

I began to think about it seriously.

They failed to prepare adequately before they began.

He has begun to doubt himself.

Who began the universe?

He arrived just as they were beginning the ceremony.

Begin and end on time.

PRINCIPAL PARTS: believes, believing,
believed, believed

be believed
(passive voice)

INDICATIVE MOOD

Pres.	I, we, you, they **believe**	I **am believed**
		we, you, they **are believed**
	he, she, it **believes**	he, she, it **is believed**
Pres.	I **am believing**	I **am being believed**
Prog.	we, you, they **are believing**	we, you, they **are being believed**
	he, she, it **is believing**	he, she, it **is being believed**
Pres.	I, we, you, they **do believe**	I, we, you, they **do get believed**
Int.	he, she, it **does believe**	he, she, it **does get believed**
Fut.	I, he, she, it,	I, he, she, it,
	we, you, they **will believe**	we, you, they **will be believed**
Past	I, he, she, it,	I, he, she, it **was believed**
	we, you, they **believed**	we, you, they **were believed**
Past	I, he, she, it **was believing**	I, he, she, it **was being believed**
Prog.	we, you, they **were believing**	we, you, they **were being believed**
Past	I, he, she, it,	I, he, she, it,
Int.	we, you, they **did believe**	we, you, they **did get believed**
Pres.	I, we, you, they **have believed**	I, we, you, they **have been believed**
Perf.	he, she, it **has believed**	he, she, it **has been believed**
Past	I, he, she, it,	I, he, she, it,
Perf.	we, you, they **had believed**	we, you, they **had been believed**
Fut.	I, he, she, it, we, you, they	I, he, she, it, we, you, they
Perf.	**will have believed**	**will have been believed**

IMPERATIVE MOOD

believe **be believed**

SUBJUNCTIVE MOOD

Pres.	if I, he, she, it,	if I, he, she, it,
	we, you, they **believe**	we, you, they **be believed**
Past	if I, he, she, it,	if I, he, she, it,
	we, you, they **believed**	we, you, they **were believed**
Fut.	if I, he, she, it,	if I, he, she, it,
	we, you, they **should believe**	we, you, they **should be believed**

Transitive and intransitive.

Honestly, I am not believing anything he says.
She was believed by a majority of the audience.

AN ESSENTIAL
55 VERB

AN ESSENTIAL 55 VERB

Examples

She believed his story.

He believes almost anything.

The witness was not believed.

Have you ever believed in yourself?

I will believe.

They could not believe their good fortune.

I used to believe that my father could do everything.

I do not believe it can be repaired.

We had never believed that version.

I could not believe that it was you.

Words and expressions related to this verb

Please believe me.

He doesn't believe you.

Believe in yourself.

Do you believe in magic?

She doesn't believe in miracles.

Do you believe in immortality?

Believe in luck.

Don't believe everything they tell you.

I believe in karma.

I can't believe that you did that.

bend
(active voice)

PRINCIPAL PARTS: **bends, bending, bent, bent**

be bent
(passive voice)

INDICATIVE MOOD

Pres.	I, we, you, they **bend**	I **am bent**
		we, you, they **are bent**
	he, she, it **bends**	he, she, it **is bent**
Pres. Prog.	I **am bending**	I **am being bent**
	we, you, they **are bending**	we, you, they **are being bent**
	he, she, it **is bending**	he, she, it **is being bent**
Pres. Int.	I, we, you, they **do bend**	I, we, you, they **do get bent**
	he, she, it **does bend**	he, she, it **does get bent**
Fut.	I, he, she, it,	I, he, she, it,
	we, you, they **will bend**	we, you, they **will be bent**
Past	I, he, she, it,	I, he, she, it **was bent**
	we, you, they **bent**	we, you, they **were bent**
Past Prog.	I, he, she, it **was bending**	I, he, she, it **was being bent**
	we, you, they **were bending**	we, you, they **were being bent**
Past Int.	I, he, she, it,	I, he, she, it,
	we, you, they **did bend**	we, you, they **did get bent**
Pres. Perf.	I, we, you, they **have bent**	I, we, you, they **have been bent**
	he, she, it **has bent**	he, she, it **has been bent**
Past Perf.	I, he, she, it,	I, he, she, it,
	we, you, they **had bent**	we, you, they **had been bent**
Fut. Perf.	I, he, she, it, we, you, they **will have bent**	I, he, she, it, we, you, they **will have been bent**

IMPERATIVE MOOD

bend   **be bent**

SUBJUNCTIVE MOOD

Pres.	if I, he, she, it,	if I, he, she, it,
	we, you, they **bend**	we, you, they **be bent**
Past	if I, he, she, it,	if I, he, she, it,
	we, you, they **bent**	we, you, they **were bent**
Fut.	if I, he, she, it,	if I, he, she, it,
	we, you, they **should bend**	we, you, they **should be bent**

Transitive and intransitive.

Try not to bend the rules.
The handle bars of the bicycle had clearly been bent.

bet
(active voice)

be bet/betted
(passive voice)

INDICATIVE MOOD

Pres.	I, we, you, they **bet**	I **am bet**
		we, you, they **are bet**
	he, she, it **bets**	he, she, it **is bet**
Pres.	I **am betting**	I **am being bet**
Prog.	we, you, they **are betting**	we, you, they **are being bet**
	he, she, it **is betting**	he, she, it **is being bet**
Pres.	I, we, you, they **do bet**	I, we, you, they **do get bet**
Int.	he, she, it **does bet**	he, she, it **does get bet**
Fut.	I, he, she, it,	I, he, she, it,
	we, you, they **will bet**	we, you, they **will be bet**
Past	I, he, she, it,	I, he, she, it **was bet**
	we, you, they **bet**	we, you, they **were bet**
Past	I, he, she, it **was betting**	I, he, she, it **was being bet**
Prog.	we, you, they **were betting**	we, you, they **were being bet**
Past	I, he, she, it,	I, he, she, it,
Int.	we, you, they **did bet**	we, you, they **did get bet**
Pres.	I, we, you, they **have bet**	I, we, you, they **have been bet**
Perf.	he, she, it **has bet**	he, she, it **has been bet**
Past	I, he, she, it,	I, he, she, it,
Perf.	we, you, they **had bet**	we, you, they **had been bet**
Fut.	I, he, she, it, we, you, they	I, he, she, it, we, you, they
Perf.	**will have bet**	**will have been bet**

IMPERATIVE MOOD

bet **be bet**

SUBJUNCTIVE MOOD

Pres.	if I, he, she, it,	if I, he, she, it,
	we, you, they **bet**	we, you, they **be bet**
Past	if I, he, she, it,	if I, he, she, it,
	we, you, they **bet**	we, you, they **were bet**
Fut.	if I, he, she, it,	if I, he, she, it,
	we, you, they **should bet**	we, you, they **should be bet**

Transitive and intransitive. BETTED is becoming rare. Use BET for the past tense and past participle.

He is betting on the wrong party.
She bet on the cutest horse.
The less likely outcome had been bet on by several experts.

INDICATIVE MOOD

Pres.	I, we, you, they **bid**	I **am bid** we, you, they **are bid**
	he, she, it **bids**	he, she, it **is bid**
Pres. *Prog.*	I **am bidding** we, you, they **are bidding** he, she, it **is bidding**	I **am being bid** we, you, they **are being bid** he, she, it **is being bid**
Pres. *Int.*	I, we, you, they **do bid** he, she, it **does bid**	I, we, you, they **do get bid** he, she, it **does get bid**
Fut.	I, he, she, it, we, you, they **will bid**	I, he, she, it, we, you, they **will be bid**
Past	I, he, she, it, we, you, they **bid**	I, he, she, it **was bid** we, you, they **were bid**
Past *Prog.*	I, he, she, it **was bidding** we, you, they **were bidding**	I, he, she, it **was being bid** we, you, they **were being bid**
Past *Int.*	I, he, she, it, we, you, they **did bid**	I, he, she, it, we, you, they **did get bid**
Pres. *Perf.*	I, we, you, they **have bid** he, she, it **has bid**	I, we, you, they **have been bid** he, she, it **has been bid**
Past *Perf.*	I, he, she, it, we, you, they **had bid**	I, he, she, it, we, you, they **had been bid**
Fut. *Perf.*	I, he, she, it, we, you, they **will have bid**	I, he, she, it, we, you, they **will have been bid**

IMPERATIVE MOOD

bid   **be bid**

SUBJUNCTIVE MOOD

Pres.	if I, he, she, it, we, you, they **bid**	if I, he, she, it, we, you, they **be bid**
Past	if I, he, she, it, we, you, they **bid**	if I, he, she, it, we, you, they **were bid**
Fut.	if I, he, she, it, we, you, they **should bid**	if I, he, she, it, we, you, they **should be bid**

Transitive and intransitive. BID has the past tense and participle form BID when it means "offering." BID when it means "directing" or "inviting" has an alternate past tense BADE and participle form BIDDEN, both of which are considered archaic.

We are bidding on the exercise equipment.
Have you ever bid on an item at an auction?
That chair has been bid on by several individuals.

bide
(active voice)

PRINCIPAL PARTS: **bides, biding, bided/bode, bided**

be bided
(passive voice)

INDICATIVE MOOD

Pres.	I, we, you, they **bide**	I **am bided**
		we, you, they **are bided**
	he, she, it **bides**	he, she, it **is bided**
Pres.	I **am biding**	I **am being bided**
Prog.	we, you, they **are biding**	we, you, they **are being bided**
	he, she, it **is biding**	he, she, it **is being bided**
Pres.	I, we, you, they **do bide**	I, we, you, they **do get bided**
Int.	he, she, it **does bide**	he, she, it **does get bided**
Fut.	I, he, she, it,	I, he, she, it,
	we, you, they **will bide**	we, you, they **will be bided**
Past	I, he, she, it,	I, he, she, it **was bided**
	we, you, they **bided**	we, you, they **were bided**
Past	I, he, she, it **was biding**	I, he, she, it **was being bided**
Prog.	we, you, they **were biding**	we, you, they **were being bided**
Past	I, he, she, it,	I, he, she, it,
Int.	we, you, they **did bide**	we, you, they **did get bided**
Pres.	I, we, you, they **have bided**	I, we, you, they **have been bided**
Perf.	he, she, it **has bided**	he, she, it **has been bided**
Past	I, he, she, it,	I, he, she, it,
Perf.	we, you, they **had bided**	we, you, they **had been bided**
Fut.	I, he, she, it, we, you, they	I, he, she, it, we, you, they
Perf.	**will have bided**	**will have been bided**

IMPERATIVE MOOD

bide

be bided

SUBJUNCTIVE MOOD

Pres.	if I, he, she, it,	if I, he, she, it,
	we, you, they **bide**	we, you, they **be bided**
Past	if I, he, she, it,	if I, he, she, it,
	we, you, they **bided**	we, you, they **were bided**
Fut.	if I, he, she, it,	if I, he, she, it,
	we, you, they **should bide**	we, you, they **should be bided**

Intransitive and transitive. In the past tense, BIDED and BODE are acceptable. For the past participle, only BIDED is now used.

We are biding our time.
Their demand had been bided for too long.

bind
(active voice)

be bound
(passive voice)

INDICATIVE MOOD

Pres.	I, we, you, they **bind**	**I am bound**
		we, you, they **are bound**
	he, she, it **binds**	he, she, it **is bound**
Pres.	**I am binding**	**I am being bound**
Prog.	we, you, they **are binding**	we, you, they **are being bound**
	he, she, it **is binding**	he, she, it **is being bound**
Pres.	I, we, you, they **do bind**	I, we, you, they **do get bound**
Int.	he, she, it **does bind**	he, she, it **does get bound**
Fut.	I, he, she, it,	I, he, she, it,
	we, you, they **will bind**	we, you, they **will be bound**
Past	I, he, she, it,	I, he, she, it **was bound**
	we, you, they **bound**	we, you, they **were bound**
Past	I, he, she, it **was binding**	I, he, she, it **was being bound**
Prog.	we, you, they **were binding**	we, you, they **were being bound**
Past	I, he, she, it,	I, he, she, it,
Int.	we, you, they **did bind**	we, you, they **did get bound**
Pres.	I, we, you, they **have bound**	I, we, you, they **have been bound**
Perf.	he, she, it **has bound**	he, she, it **has been bound**
Past	I, he, she, it,	I, he, she, it,
Perf.	we, you, they **had bound**	we, you, they **had been bound**
Fut.	I, he, she, it, we, you, they	I, he, she, it, we, you, they
Perf.	**will have bound**	**will have been bound**

IMPERATIVE MOOD

bind   **be bound**

SUBJUNCTIVE MOOD

Pres.	if I, he, she, it,	if I, he, she, it,
	we, you, they **bind**	we, you, they **be bound**
Past	if I, he, she, it,	if I, he, she, it,
	we, you, they **bound**	we, you, they **were bound**
Fut.	if I, he, she, it,	if I, he, she, it,
	we, you, they **should bind**	we, you, they **should be bound**

Transitive and intransitive.

The nurse is here to bind up your wound.
We felt bound by the terms of the agreement.

bite
(active voice)

PRINCIPAL PARTS: **bites, biting, bit, bitten/bit**

be bitten/bit
(passive voice)

INDICATIVE MOOD

Pres.	I, we, you, they **bite**	I **am bitten**
		we, you, they **are bitten**
	he, she, it **bites**	he, she, it **is bitten**
Pres.	I **am biting**	I **am being bitten**
Prog.	we, you, they **are biting**	we, you, they **are being bitten**
	he, she, it **is biting**	he, she, it **is being bitten**
Pres.	I, we, you, they **do bite**	I, we, you, they **do get bitten**
Int.	he, she, it **does bite**	he, she, it **does get bitten**
Fut.	I, he, she, it, we, you, they **will bite**	I, he, she, it, we, you, they **will be bitten**
Past	I, he, she, it, we, you, they **bit**	I, he, she, it **was bitten** we, you, they **were bitten**
Past	I, he, she, it **was biting**	I, he, she, it **was being bitten**
Prog.	we, you, they **were biting**	we, you, they **were being bitten**
Past	I, he, she, it, we, you, they **did bite**	I, he, she, it, we, you, they **did get bitten**
Int.		
Pres.	I, we, you, they **have bitten**	I, we, you, they **have been bitten**
Perf.	he, she, it **has bitten**	he, she, it **has been bitten**
Past	I, he, she, it, we, you, they **had bitten**	I, he, she, it, we, you, they **had been bitten**
Perf.		
Fut.	I, he, she, it, we, you, they **will have bitten**	I, he, she, it, we, you, they **will have been bitten**
Perf.		

IMPERATIVE MOOD

bite be bitten

SUBJUNCTIVE MOOD

Pres.	if I, he, she, it, we, you, they **bite**	if I, he, she, it, we, you, they **be bitten**
Past	if I, he, she, it, we, you, they **bit**	if I, he, she, it, we, you, they **were bitten**
Fut.	if I, he, she, it, we, you, they **should bite**	if I, he, she, it, we, you, they **should be bitten**

The past participle may be either BITTEN or BIT.

They say you should not be biting the hand that feeds you.
The snake bit him in the leg.
The little boy was bitten several times by the puppy.

bleed
(active voice)

be bled
(passive voice)

INDICATIVE MOOD

Pres.	I, we, you, they **bleed**	**I am bled**
		we, you, they **are bled**
	he, she, it **bleeds**	he, she, it **is bled**
Pres.	**I am bleeding**	**I am being bled**
Prog.	we, you, they **are bleeding**	we, you, they **are being bled**
	he, she, it **is bleeding**	he, she, it **is being bled**
Pres.	I, we, you, they **do bleed**	I, we, you, they **do get bled**
Int.	he, she, it **does bleed**	he, she, it **does get bled**
Fut.	I, he, she, it,	I, he, she, it,
	we, you, they **will bleed**	we, you, they **will be bled**
Past	I, he, she, it,	I, he, she, it **was bled**
	we, you, they **bled**	we, you, they **were bled**
Past	I, he, she, it **was bleeding**	I, he, she, it **was being bled**
Prog.	we, you, they **were bleeding**	we, you, they **were being bled**
Past	I, he, she, it,	I, he, she, it,
Int.	we, you, they **did bleed**	we, you, they **did get bled**
Pres.	I, we, you, they **have bled**	I, we, you, they **have been bled**
Perf.	he, she, it **has bled**	he, she, it **has been bled**
Past	I, he, she, it,	I, he, she, it,
Perf.	we, you, they **had bled**	we, you, they **had been bled**
Fut.	I, he, she, it, we, you, they	I, he, she, it, we, you, they
Perf.	**will have bled**	**will have been bled**

IMPERATIVE MOOD

bleed　　　　　　**be bled**

SUBJUNCTIVE MOOD

Pres.	if I, he, she, it,	if I, he, she, it,
	we, you, they **bleed**	we, you, they **be bled**
Past	if I, he, she, it,	if I, he, she, it,
	we, you, they **bled**	we, you, they **were bled**
Fut.	if I, he, she, it,	if I, he, she, it,
	we, you, they **should bleed**	we, you, they **should be bled**

Intransitive and transitive.

Lately I have noticed that I bleed easily when I am shaving.
The victim bled for hours.
The airline's profit was slowly being bled away by high fuel costs.

blend
(active voice)

be blended/blent
(passive voice)

B

INDICATIVE MOOD

Pres.	I, we, you, they **blend**	I **am blended** we, you, they **are blended**
	he, she, it **blends**	he, she, it **is blended**
Pres. *Prog.*	I **am blending** we, you, they **are blending** he, she, it **is blending**	I **am being blended** we, you, they **are being blended** he, she, it **is being blended**
Pres. *Int.*	I, we, you, they **do blend** he, she, it **does blend**	I, we, you, they **do get blended** he, she, it **does get blended**
Fut.	I, he, she, it, we, you, they **will blend**	I, he, she, it, we, you, they **will be blended**
Past	I, he, she, it, we, you, they **blended**	I, he, she, it **was blended** we, you, they **were blended**
Past *Prog.*	I, he, she, it **was blending** we, you, they **were blending**	I, he, she, it **was being blended** we, you, they **were being blended**
Past *Int.*	I, he, she, it, we, you, they **did blend**	I, he, she, it, we, you, they **did get blended**
Pres. *Perf.*	I, we, you, they **have blended** he, she, it **has blended**	I, we, you, they **have been blended** he, she, it **has been blended**
Past *Perf.*	I, he, she, it, we, you, they **had blended**	I, he, she, it, we, you, they **had been blended**
Fut. *Perf.*	I, he, she, it, we, you, they **will have blended**	I, he, she, it, we, you, they **will have been blended**

IMPERATIVE MOOD

blend   **be blended**

SUBJUNCTIVE MOOD

Pres.	if I, he, she, it, we, you, they **blend**	if I, he, she, it, we, you, they **be blended**
Past	if I, he, she, it, we, you, they **blended**	if I, he, she, it, we, you, they **were blended**
Fut.	if I, he, she, it, we, you, they **should blend**	if I, he, she, it, we, you, they **should be blended**

Transitive and intransitive. The past tense and participle forms BLENDED and BLENT are both acceptable. The *Oxford Dictionary* lists BLENT as poetic for the past tense and past participle.

She blended the music after the recording.
The ingredients were blended into a delicious new ice-cream flavor.

PRINCIPAL PARTS: **blesses, blessing,
blessed/blest, blessed/blest**

INDICATIVE MOOD

Pres.	I, we, you, they **bless**	**I am blessed**
		we, you, they **are blessed**
	he, she, it **blesses**	he, she, it **is blessed**
Pres.	**I am blessing**	**I am being blessed**
Prog.	we, you, they **are blessing**	we, you, they **are being blessed**
	he, she, it **is blessing**	he, she, it **is being blessed**
Pres.	I, we, you, they **do bless**	I, we, you, they **do get blessed**
Int.	he, she, it **does bless**	he, she, it **does get blessed**
Fut.	I, he, she, it,	I, he, she, it,
	we, you, they **will bless**	we, you, they **will be blessed**
Past	I, he, she, it,	I, he, she, it **was blessed**
	we, you, they **blessed**	we, you, they **were blessed**
Past	I, he, she, it **was blessing**	I, he, she, it **was being blessed**
Prog.	we, you, they **were blessing**	we, you, they **were being blessed**
Past	I, he, she, it,	I, he, she, it,
Int.	we, you, they **did bless**	we, you, they **did get blessed**
Pres.	I, we, you, they **have blessed**	I, we, you, they **have been blessed**
Perf.	he, she, it **has blessed**	he, she, it **has been blessed**
Past	I, he, she, it,	I, he, she, it,
Perf.	we, you, they **had blessed**	we, you, they **had been blessed**
Fut.	I, he, she, it, we, you, they	I, he, she, it, we, you, they
Perf.	**will have blessed**	**will have been blessed**

IMPERATIVE MOOD

bless   **be blessed**

SUBJUNCTIVE MOOD

Pres.	if I, he, she, it,	if I, he, she, it,
	we, you, they **bless**	we, you, they **be blessed**
Past	if I, he, she, it,	if I, he, she, it,
	we, you, they **blessed**	we, you, they **were blessed**
Fut.	if I, he, she, it,	if I, he, she, it,
	we, you, they **should bless**	we, you, they **should be blessed**

According to the *Oxford Dictionary*, BLEST is the poetic form of the past tense and past participle.

The chaplain blessed the soldiers before their first parachute jump.
We have been truly blessed in our thirty years of marriage.

PRINCIPAL PARTS: **blogs, blogging, blogged, blogged**

INDICATIVE MOOD

Pres.   I, we, you, they **blog**

he, she, it **blogs**

Pres.   I **am blogging**
Prog.   we, you, they **are blogging**
he, she, it **is blogging**

Pres.   I, we, you, they **do blog**
Int.   he, she, it **does blog**

Fut.   I, he, she, it,
we, you, they **will blog**

Past   I, he, she, it,
we, you, they **blogged**

Past   I, he, she, it **was blogging**
Prog.   we, you, they **were blogging**

Past   I, he, she, it,
Int.   we, you, they **did blog**

Pres.   I, we, you, they **have blogged**
Perf.   he, she, it **has blogged**

Past.   I, he, she, it,
Perf.   we, you, they **had blogged**

Fut.   I, he, she, it, we, you, they
Perf.   will **have blogged**

IMPERATIVE MOOD

blog

SUBJUNCTIVE MOOD

Pres.   if I, he, she, it,
we, you, they **blog**

Past   if I, he, she, it,
we, you, they **blogged**

Fut.   if I, he, she, it,
we, you, they **should blog**

I keep an electronic journal as I am blogging.
He has blogged for two years.

blow
(active voice)

be blown
(passive voice)

INDICATIVE MOOD

Pres.	I, we, you, they **blow**	I **am blown**
		we, you, they **are blown**
	he, she, it **blows**	he, she, it **is blown**
Pres.	I **am blowing**	I **am being blown**
Prog.	we, you, they **are blowing**	we, you, they **are being blown**
	he, she, it **is blowing**	he, she, it **is being blown**
Pres.	I, we, you, they **do blow**	I, we, you, they **do get blown**
Int.	he, she, it **does blow**	he, she, it **does get blown**
Fut.	I, he, she, it,	I, he, she, it,
	we, you, they **will blow**	we, you, they **will be blown**
Past	I, he, she, it,	I, he, she, it **was blown**
	we, you, they **blew**	we, you, they **were blown**
Past	I, he, she, it **was blowing**	I, he, she, it **was being blown**
Prog.	we, you, they **were blowing**	we, you, they **were being blown**
Past	I, he, she, it,	I, he, she, it,
Int.	we, you, they **did blow**	we, you, they **did get blown**
Pres.	I, we, you, they **have blown**	I, we, you, they **have been blown**
Perf.	he, she, it **has blown**	he, she, it **has been blown**
Past	I, he, she, it,	I, he, she, it,
Perf.	we, you, they **had blown**	we, you, they **had been blown**
Fut.	I, he, she, it, we, you, they	I, he, she, it, we, you, they
Perf.	**will have blown**	**will have been blown**

IMPERATIVE MOOD

blow **be blown**

SUBJUNCTIVE MOOD

Pres.	if I, he, she, it,	if I, he, she, it,
	we, you, they **blow**	we, you, they **be blown**
Past	if I, he, she, it,	if I, he, she, it,
	we, you, they **blew**	we, you, they **were blown**
Fut.	if I, he, she, it,	if I, he, she, it,
	we, you, they **should blow**	we, you, they **should be blown**

Intransitive and transitive.

Dad blew up several balloons because he always blows too hard.
All of the balloons for the party have been blown up.

boot
(active voice)

be booted
(passive voice)

B

INDICATIVE MOOD

Pres.	I, we, you, they **boot**	I **am booted**
		we, you, they **are booted**
	he, she, it **boots**	he, she, it **is booted**
Pres.	I **am booting**	I **am being booted**
Prog.	we, you, they **are booting**	we, you, they **are being booted**
	he, she, it **is booting**	he, she, it **is being booted**
Pres.	I, we, you, they **do boot**	I, we, you, they **do get booted**
Int.	he, she, it **does boot**	he, she, it **does get booted**
Fut.	I, he, she, it,	I, he, she, it,
	we, you, they **will boot**	we, you, they **will be booted**
Past	I, he, she, it,	I, he, she, it **was booted**
	we, you, they **booted**	we, you, they **were booted**
Past	I, he, she, it **was booting**	I, he, she, it **was being booted**
Prog.	we, you, they **were booting**	we, you, they **were being booted**
Past	I, he, she, it,	I, he, she, it,
Int.	we, you, they **did boot**	we, you, they **did get booted**
Pres.	I, we, you, they **have booted**	I, we, you, they **have been booted**
Perf.	he, she, it **has booted**	he, she, it **has been booted**
Past	I, he, she, it,	I, he, she, it,
Perf.	we, you, they **had booted**	we, you, they **had been booted**
Fut.	I, he, she, it, we, you, they	I, he, she, it, we, you, they
Perf.	**will have booted**	**will have been booted**

IMPERATIVE MOOD

boot

be booted

SUBJUNCTIVE MOOD

Pres.	if I, he, she, it,	if I, he, she, it,
	we, you, they **boot**	we, you, they **be booted**
Past	if I, he, she, it,	if I, he, she, it,
	we, you, they **booted**	we, you, they **were booted**
Fut.	if I, he, she, it,	if I, he, she, it,
	we, you, they **should boot**	we, you, they **should be booted**

Transitive and intransitive.

Does anyone here know how to boot this computer?
The computer crashed as soon as it was booted.
He was booted out of the club for his bad behavior.

bother
(active voice)

PRINCIPAL PARTS: **bothers, bothering, bothered, bothered**

be bothered
(passive voice)

INDICATIVE MOOD

Pres.	I, we, you, they **bother** he, she, it **bothers**	I **am bothered** we, you, they **are bothered** he, she, it **is bothered**
Pres. *Prog.*	I **am bothering** we, you, they **are bothering** he, she, it **is bothering**	I **am being bothered** we, you, they **are being bothered** he, she, it **is being bothered**
Pres. *Int.*	I, we, you, they **do bother** he, she, it **does bother**	I, we, you, they **do get bothered** he, she, it **does get bothered**
Fut.	I, he, she, it, we, you, they **will bother**	I, he, she, it, we, you, they **will be bothered**
Past	I, he, she, it, we, you, they **bothered**	I, he, she, it **was bothered** we, you, they **were bothered**
Past *Prog.*	I, he, she, it **was bothering** we, you, they **were bothering**	I, he, she, it **was being bothered** we, you, they **were being bothered**
Past *Int.*	I, he, she, it, we, you, they **did bother**	I, he, she, it, we, you, they **did get bothered**
Pres. *Perf.*	I, we, you, they **have bothered** he, she, it **has bothered**	I, we, you, they **have been bothered** he, she, it **has been bothered**
Past *Perf.*	I, he, she, it, we, you, they **had bothered**	I, he, she, it, we, you, they **had been bothered**
Fut. *Perf.*	I, he, she, it, we, you, they **will have bothered**	I, he, she, it, we, you, they **will have been bothered**

IMPERATIVE MOOD

bother

be bothered

SUBJUNCTIVE MOOD

Pres.	if I, he, she, it, we, you, they **bother**	if I, he, she, it, we, you, they **be bothered**
Past	if I, he, she, it, we, you, they **bothered**	if I, he, she, it, we, you, they **were bothered**
Fut.	if I, he, she, it, we, you, they **should bother**	if I, he, she, it, we, you, they **should be bothered**

Transitive and intransitive.

Please do not bother him while he studying.
We are often bothered by the loud music coming from our neighbors' apartment.

break
(active voice)

PRINCIPAL PARTS: breaks, breaking, broke, broken

be broken
(passive voice)

INDICATIVE MOOD

Pres.	I, we, you, they **break**	I **am broken**
		we, you, they **are broken**
	he, she, it **breaks**	he, she, it **is broken**
Pres.	I **am breaking**	I **am being broken**
Prog.	we, you, they **are breaking**	we, you, they **are being broken**
	he, she, it **is breaking**	he, she, it **is being broken**
Pres.	I, we, you, they **do break**	I, we, you, they **do get broken**
Int.	he, she, it **does break**	he, she, it **does get broken**
Fut.	I, he, she, it,	I, he, she, it,
	we, you, they **will break**	we, you, they **will be broken**
Past	I, he, she, it,	I, he, she, it **was broken**
	we, you, they **broke**	we, you, they **were broken**
Past	I, he, she, it **was breaking**	I, he, she, it **was being broken**
Prog.	we, you, they **were breaking**	we, you, they **were being broken**
Past	I, he, she, it,	I, he, she, it,
Int.	we, you, they **did break**	we, you, they **did get broken**
Pres.	I, we, you, they **have broken**	I, we, you, they **have been broken**
Perf.	he, she, it **has broken**	he, she, it **has been broken**
Past	I, he, she, it,	I, he, she, it,
Perf.	we, you, they **had broken**	we, you, they **had been broken**
Fut.	I, he, she, it, we, you, they	I, he, she, it, we, you, they
Perf.	**will have broken**	**will have been broken**

IMPERATIVE MOOD

break   **be broken**

SUBJUNCTIVE MOOD

Pres.	if I, he, she, it,	if I, he, she, it,
	we, you, they **break**	we, you, they **be broken**
Past	if I, he, she, it,	if I, he, she, it,
	we, you, they **broke**	we, you, they **were broken**
Fut.	if I, he, she, it,	if I, he, she, it,
	we, you, they **should break**	we, you, they **should be broken**

Transitive and intransitive. The past tense BRAKE and past participle BROKE are archaic.

They went into overtime to break the tie.
I am sorry that I broke my promise not to tell.
By the end of the evening several bottles had been broken.

breed
(active voice)

be bred
(passive voice)

INDICATIVE MOOD

Pres.	I, we, you, they **breed**	I **am bred**
		we, you, they **are bred**
	he, she, it **breeds**	he, she, it **is bred**
Pres.	I **am breeding**	I **am being bred**
Prog.	we, you, they **are breeding**	we, you, they **are being bred**
	he, she, it **is breeding**	he, she, it **is being bred**
Pres.	I, we, you, they **do breed**	I, we, you, they **do get bred**
Int.	he, she, it **does breed**	he, she, it **does get bred**
Fut.	I, he, she, it,	I, he, she, it,
	we, you, they **will breed**	we, you, they **will be bred**
Past	I, he, she, it,	I, he, she, it **was bred**
	we, you, they **bred**	we, you, they **were bred**
Past	I, he, she, it **was breeding**	I, he, she, it **was being bred**
Prog.	we, you, they **were breeding**	we, you, they **were being bred**
Past	I, he, she, it,	I, he, she, it,
Int.	we, you, they **did breed**	we, you, they **did get bred**
Pres.	I, we, you, they **have bred**	I, we, you, they **have been bred**
Perf.	he, she, it **has bred**	he, she, it **has been bred**
Past	I, he, she, it,	I, he, she, it,
Perf.	we, you, they **had bred**	we, you, they **had been bred**
Fut.	I, he, she, it, we, you, they	I, he, she, it, we, you, they
Perf.	**will have bred**	**will have been bred**

IMPERATIVE MOOD

breed

be bred

SUBJUNCTIVE MOOD

Pres.	if I, he, she, it,	if I, he, she, it,
	we, you, they **breed**	we, you, they **be bred**
Past	if I, he, she, it,	if I, he, she, it,
	we, you, they **bred**	we, you, they **were bred**
Fut.	if I, he, she, it,	if I, he, she, it,
	we, you, they **should breed**	we, you, they **should be bred**

Transitive and intransitive.

Our friends bred horses before they retired.
They are certainly well-bred.

bring
(active voice)

be brought
(passive voice)

B

INDICATIVE MOOD

Pres.	I, we, you, they **bring**	I am **brought**
		we, you, they **are brought**
	he, she, it **brings**	he, she, it **is brought**
Pres.	I **am bringing**	I **am being brought**
Prog.	we, you, they **are bringing**	we, you, they **are being brought**
	he, she, it **is bringing**	he, she, it **is being brought**
Pres.	I, we, you, they **do bring**	I, we, you, they **do get brought**
Int.	he, she, it **does bring**	he, she, it **does get brought**
Fut.	I, he, she, it,	I, he, she, it,
	we, you, they **will bring**	we, you, they **will be brought**
Past	I, he, she, it,	I, he, she, it **was brought**
	we, you, they **brought**	we, you, they **were brought**
Past	I, he, she, it **was bringing**	I, he, she, it **was being brought**
Prog.	we, you, they **were bringing**	we, you, they **were being brought**
Past	I, he, she, it,	I, he, she, it,
Int.	we, you, they **did bring**	we, you, they **did get brought**
Pres.	I, we, you, they **have brought**	I, we, you, they **have been brought**
Perf.	he, she, it **has brought**	he, she, it **has been brought**
Past	I, he, she, it,	I, he, she, it,
Perf.	we, you, they **had brought**	we, you, they **had been brought**
Fut.	I, he, she, it, we, you, they	I, he, she, it, we, you, they
Perf.	**will have brought**	**will have been brought**

IMPERATIVE MOOD

bring   **be brought**

SUBJUNCTIVE MOOD

Pres.	if I, he, she, it,	if I, he, she, it,
	we, you, they **bring**	we, you, they **be brought**
Past	if I, he, she, it,	if I, he, she, it,
	we, you, they **brought**	we, you, they **were brought**
Fut.	if I, he, she, it,	if I, he, she, it,
	we, you, they **should bring**	we, you, they **should be brought**

Transitive and intransitive.

Is there anything we can bring to the party?
What have your other guests already brought?
They were brought to the courtroom under tight security.

AN ESSENTIAL
55 VERB

bring

Examples

I am bringing the wine.

She brings her dog everywhere.

Who brought the delicious pie?

The hurricane brought heavy rain.

The package was brought by the postman.

Bring two sharpened pencils to the exam.

I will bring the reports.

Juries usually bring forth verdicts in a few hours.

She brought out the very best in him.

He was brought to after a few seconds.

Words and expressions related to this verb

Bring it on.

Can you bring them around?

The chairperson brought forth an innovative plan.

Don't bring that up until the end of the meeting.

You bring me great joy.

They are bringing up three children.

He brings a lot to our group.

They were finally brought to justice.

Our fathers brought forth a new nation.

Bring it home.

broadcast
(active voice)

PRINCIPAL PARTS: **broadcasts, broad-
casting, broadcast/broadcasted,
broadcast/broadcasted**

**be broadcast/
broadcasted**
(passive voice)

INDICATIVE MOOD

Pres.	I, we, you, they **broadcast**	I **am broadcast**
		we, you, they **are broadcast**
	he, she, it **broadcasts**	he, she, it **is broadcast**
Pres.	I **am broadcasting**	I **am being broadcast**
Prog.	we, you, they **are broadcasting**	we, you, they **are being broadcast**
	he, she, it **is broadcasting**	he, she, it is **being broadcast**
Pres.	I, we, you, they **do broadcast**	I, we, you, they **do get broadcast**
Int.	he, she, it **does broadcast**	he, she, it **does get broadcast**
Fut.	I, he, she, it,	I, he, she, it,
	we, you, they **will broadcast**	we, you, they **will be broadcast**
Past	I, he, she, it,	I, he, she, it **was broadcast**
	we, you, they **broadcast**	we, you, they **were broadcast**
Past	I, he, she, it **was broadcasting**	I, he, she, it **was being broadcast**
Prog.	we, you, they **were broadcasting**	we, you, they **were being broadcast**
Past	I, he, she, it,	I, he, she, it,
Int.	we, you, they **did broadcast**	we, you, they **did get broadcast**
Pres.	I, we, you, they **have broadcast**	I, we, you, they **have been broadcast**
Perf.	he, she, it **has broadcast**	he, she, it **has been broadcast**
Past	I, he, she, it,	I, he, she, it,
Perf.	we, you, they **had broadcast**	we, you, they **had been broadcast**
Fut.	I, he, she, it, we, you, they	I, he, she, it, we, you, they
Perf.	**will have broadcast**	**will have been broadcast**

IMPERATIVE MOOD

broadcast	**be broadcast**

SUBJUNCTIVE MOOD

Pres.	if I, he, she, it,	if I, he, she, it,
	we, you, they **broadcast**	we, you, they **be broadcast**
Past	if I, he, she, it,	if I, he, she, it,
	we, you, they **broadcast**	we, you, they **were broadcast**
Fut.	if I, he, she, it,	if I, he, she, it,
	we, you, they **should broadcast**	we, you, they **should be broadcast**

Transitive and intransitive. The past tense and past participle may be BROADCAST or BROAD-CASTED. The *Oxford Dictionary* recognizes BROADCASTED only as a past participle.

He broadcast live from Times Square in New York City on New Year's Eve.
The World Cup of Soccer is broadcast all around the world.

browse
(active voice)

be browsed
(passive voice)

INDICATIVE MOOD

Pres.	I, we, you, they **browse**	**I am browsed** we, you, they **are browsed**
	he, she, it **browses**	he, she, it **is browsed**
Pres. *Prog.*	I **am browsing** we, you, they **are browsing** he, she, it **is browsing**	I **am being browsed** we, you, they **are being browsed** he, she, it **is being browsed**
Pres. *Int.*	I, we, you, they **do browse** he, she, it **does browse**	I, we, you, they **do get browsed** he, she, it **does get browsed**
Fut.	I, he, she, it, we, you, they **will browse**	I, he, she, it, we, you, they **will be browsed**
Past	I, he, she, it, we, you, they **browsed**	I, he, she, it **was browsed** we, you, they **were browsed**
Past *Prog.*	I, he, she, it **was browsing** we, you, they **were browsing**	I, he, she, it **was being browsed** we, you, they **were being browsed**
Past *Int.*	I, he, she, it, we, you, they **did browse**	I, he, she, it, we, you, they **did get browsed**
Pres. *Perf.*	I, we, you, they **have browsed** he, she, it **has browsed**	I, we, you, they **have been browsed** he, she, it **has been browsed**
Past *Perf.*	I, he, she, it, we, you, they **had browsed**	I, he, she, it, we, you, they **had been browsed**
Fut. *Perf.*	I, he, she, it, we, you, they **will have browsed**	I, he, she, it, we, you, they **will have been browsed**

IMPERATIVE MOOD

browse   **be browsed**

SUBJUNCTIVE MOOD

Pres.	if I, he, she, it, we, you, they **browse**	if I, he, she, it, we, you, they **be browsed**
Past	if I, he, she, it, we, you, they **browsed**	if I, he, she, it, we, you, they **were browsed**
Fut.	if I, he, she, it, we, you, they **should browse**	if I, he, she, it, we, you, they **should be browsed**

Intransitive and transitive.

She is browsing the Internet daily.
The most popular web sites are browsed several million times each day.

build
(active voice)

be built
(passive voice)

B

INDICATIVE MOOD

Pres.	I, we, you, they **build**	I **am built**
		we, you, they **are built**
	he, she, it **builds**	he, she, it **is built**
Pres.	I **am building**	I **am being built**
Prog.	we, you, they **are building**	we, you, they **are being built**
	he, she, it **is building**	he, she, it **is being built**
Pres.	I, we, you, they **do build**	I, we, you, they **do get built**
Int.	he, she, it **does build**	he, she, it **does get built**
Fut.	I, he, she, it,	I, he, she, it,
	we, you, they **will build**	we, you, they **will be built**
Past	I, he, she, it,	I, he, she, it **was built**
	we, you, they **built**	we, you, they **were built**
Past	I, he, she, it **was building**	I, he, she, it **was being built**
Prog.	we, you, they **were building**	we, you, they **were being built**
Past	I, he, she, it,	I, he, she, it,
Int.	we, you, they **did build**	we, you, they **did get built**
Pres.	I, we, you, they **have built**	I, we, you, they **have been built**
Perf.	he, she, it **has built**	he, she, it **has been built**
Past	I, he, she, it,	I, he, she, it,
Perf.	we, you, they **had built**	we, you, they **had been built**
Fut.	I, he, she, it, we, you, they	I, he, she, it, we, you, they
Perf.	**will have built**	**will have been built**

IMPERATIVE MOOD

build   **be built**

SUBJUNCTIVE MOOD

Pres.	if I, he, she, it,	if I, he, she, it,
	we, you, they **build**	we, you, they **be built**
Past	if I, he, she, it,	if I, he, she, it,
	we, you, they **built**	we, you, they **were built**
Fut.	if I, he, she, it,	if I, he, she, it,
	we, you, they **should build**	we, you, they **should be built**

Transitive and intransitive. *Webster's New World Dictionary* lists BUILDED as an archaic form of the past tense and past participle.

We built a shed for our garden tools.
Rome wasn't built in a day.

burn
(active voice)

be burned/burnt
(passive voice)

INDICATIVE MOOD

Pres.	I, we, you, they **burn**	I **am burned**
		we, you, they **are burned**
	he, she, it **burns**	he, she, it **is burned**
Pres.	I **am burning**	I **am being burned**
Prog.	we, you, they **are burning**	we, you, they **are being burned**
	he, she, it **is burning**	he, she, it **is being burned**
Pres.	I, we, you, they **do burn**	I, we, you, they **do get burned**
Int.	he, she, it **does burn**	he, she, it **does get burned**
Fut.	I, he, she, it,	I, he, she, it,
	we, you, they **will burn**	we, you, they **will be burned**
Past	I, he, she, it,	I, he, she, it **was burned**
	we, you, they **burned**	we, you, they **were burned**
Past	I, he, she, it **was burning**	I, he, she, it **was being burned**
Prog.	we, you, they **were burning**	we, you, they **were being burned**
Past	I, he, she, it,	I, he, she, it,
Int.	we, you, they **did burn**	we, you, they **did get burned**
Pres.	I, we, you, they **have burned**	I, we, you, they **have been burned**
Perf.	he, she, it **has burned**	he, she, it **has been burned**
Past	I, he, she, it,	I, he, she, it,
Perf.	we, you, they **had burned**	we, you, they **had been burned**
Fut.	I, he, she, it, we, you, they	I, he, she, it, we, you, they
Perf.	**will have burned**	**will have been burned**

IMPERATIVE MOOD

burn **be burned**

SUBJUNCTIVE MOOD

Pres.	if I, he, she, it,	if I, he, she, it,
	we, you, they **burn**	we, you, they **be burned**
Past	if I, he, she, it,	if I, he, she, it,
	we, you, they **burned**	we, you, they **were burned**
Fut.	if I, he, she, it,	if I, he, she, it,
	we, you, they **should burn**	we, you, they **should be burned**

Transitive and intransitive. The past tense and past participle are BURNED and BURNT. The *Oxford Dictionary* lists BURNT before BURNED.

They were severely burned by the sun on their vacation.
All of their firewood was burned for heat this winter.

58

PRINCIPAL PARTS: **bursts, bursting, burst, burst**

be burst
(passive voice)

INDICATIVE MOOD

Pres.	I, we, you, they **burst**	I **am burst**
		we, you, they **are burst**
	he, she, it **bursts**	he, she, it **is burst**
Pres.	I **am bursting**	I **am being burst**
Prog.	we, you, they **are bursting**	we, you, they **are being burst**
	he, she, it **is bursting**	he, she, it **is being burst**
Pres.	I, we, you, they **do burst**	I, we, you, they **do get burst**
Int.	he, she, it **does burst**	he, she, it **does get burst**
Fut.	I, he, she, it,	I, he, she, it,
	we, you, they **will burst**	we, you, they **will be burst**
Past	I, he, she, it,	I, he, she, it **was burst**
	we, you, they **burst**	we, you, they **were burst**
Past	I, he, she, it **was bursting**	I, he, she, it **was being burst**
Prog.	we, you, they **were bursting**	we, you, they **were being burst**
Past	I, he, she, it,	I, he, she, it,
Int.	we, you, they **did burst**	we, you, they **did get burst**
Pres.	I, we, you, they **have burst**	I, we, you, they **have been burst**
Perf.	he, she, it **has burst**	he, she, it **has been burst**
Past	I, he, she, it,	I, he, she, it,
Perf.	we, you, they **had burst**	we, you, they **had been burst**
Fut.	I, he, she, it, we, you, they	I, he, she, it, we, you, they
Perf.	**will have burst**	**will have been burst**

IMPERATIVE MOOD

burst

be burst

SUBJUNCTIVE MOOD

Pres.	if I, he, she, it,	if I, he, she, it,
	we, you, they **burst**	we, you, they **be burst**
Past	if I, he, she, it,	if I, he, she, it,
	we, you, they **burst**	we, you, they **were burst**
Fut.	if I, he, she, it,	if I, he, she, it,
	we, you, they **should burst**	we, you, they **should be burst**

Intransitive and transitive. *Merriam Webster's* lists BURSTED as an alternative past tense and past participle.

His artery burst during the surgery.
The balloons were burst by children seeking the prizes inside.

| **bust**
(active voice) | PRINCIPAL PARTS: **busts, busting,**
busted, busted | **be busted**
(passive voice) |

INDICATIVE MOOD

Pres.	I, we, you, they **bust** he, she, it **busts**	I **am busted** we, you, they **are busted** he, she, it **is busted**
Pres. *Prog.*	I **am busting** we, you, they **are busting** he, she, it **is busting**	I **am being busted** we, you, they **are being busted** he, she, it **is being busted**
Pres. *Int.*	I, we, you, they **do bust** he, she, it **does bust**	I, we, you, they **do get busted** he, she, it **does get busted**
Fut.	I, he, she, it, we, you, they **will bust**	I, he, she, it, we, you, they **will be busted**
Past	I, he, she, it, we, you, they **busted**	I, he, she, it **was busted** we, you, they **were busted**
Past *Prog.*	I, he, she, it **was busting** we, you, they **were busting**	I, he, she, it **was being busted** we, you, they **were being busted**
Past *Int.*	I, he, she, it, we, you, they **did bust**	I, he, she, it, we, you, they **did get busted**
Pres. *Perf.*	I, we, you, they **have busted** he, she, it **has busted**	I, we, you, they **have been busted** he, she, it **has been busted**
Past *Perf.*	I, he, she, it, we, you, they **had busted**	I, he, she, it, we, you, they **had been busted**
Fut. *Perf.*	I, he, she, it, we, you, they **will have busted**	I, he, she, it, we, you, they **will have been busted**

IMPERATIVE MOOD

| **bust** | **be busted** |

SUBJUNCTIVE MOOD

Pres.	if I, he, she, it, we, you, they **bust**	if I, he, she, it, we, you, they **be busted**
Past	if I, he, she, it, we, you, they **busted**	if I, he, she, it, we, you, they **were busted**
Fut.	if I, he, she, it, we, you, they **should bust**	if I, he, she, it, we, you, they **should be busted**

Considered slang in many instances, BUST can often be found in standard speech "bust the budget" or "bust a union." *Merriam Webster's* and the *Oxford Dictionary* recognize BUST as an alternate past tense and past participle form.

Without a tax increase the new expenses busted the budget.
The crooked union was busted by the government.

buy
(active voice)

be bought
(passive voice)

INDICATIVE MOOD

Pres.	I, we, you, they **buy**	I am **bought**
		we, you, they **are bought**
	he, she, it **buys**	he, she, it **is bought**
Pres.	I **am buying**	I **am being bought**
Prog.	we, you, they **are buying**	we, you, they **are being bought**
	he, she, it **is buying**	he, she, it **is being bought**
Pres.	I, we, you, they **do buy**	I, we, you, they **do get bought**
Int.	he, she, it **does buy**	he, she, it **does get bought**
Fut.	I, he, she, it,	I, he, she, it,
	we, you, they **will buy**	we, you, they **will be bought**
Past	I, he, she, it,	I, he, she, it **was bought**
	we, you, they **bought**	we, you, they **were bought**
Past	I, he, she, it **was buying**	I, he, she, it **was being bought**
Prog.	we, you, they **were buying**	we, you, they **were being bought**
Past	I, he, she, it,	I, he, she, it,
Int.	we, you, they **did buy**	we, you, they **did get bought**
Pres.	I, we, you, they **have bought**	I, we, you, they **have been bought**
Perf.	he, she, it **has bought**	he, she, it **has been bought**
Past	I, he, she, it,	I, he, she, it,
Perf.	we, you, they **had bought**	we, you, they **had been bought**
Fut.	I, he, she, it, we, you, they	I, he, she, it, we, you, they
Perf.	**will have bought**	**will have been bought**

IMPERATIVE MOOD

buy   **be bought**

SUBJUNCTIVE MOOD

Pres.	if I, he, she, it,	if I, he, she, it,
	we, you, they **buy**	we, you, they **be bought**
Past	if I, he, she, it,	if I, he, she, it,
	we, you, they **bought**	we, you, they **were bought**
Fut.	if I, he, she, it,	if I, he, she, it,
	we, you, they **should buy**	we, you, they **should be bought**

Transitive and intransitive.

Where do you buy your clothes?
I bought this dress at a secondhand shop.
Have any of these purchases been bought on your trip out of the country?

61

call
(active voice)

be called
(passive voice)

INDICATIVE MOOD

Pres.	I, we, you, they **call**	I **am called**
		we, you, they **are called**
	he, she, it **calls**	he, she, it **is called**
Pres.	I **am calling**	I **am being called**
Prog.	we, you, they **are calling**	we, you, they **are being called**
	he, she, it **is calling**	he, she, it **is being called**
Pres.	I, we, you, they **do call**	I, we, you, they **do get called**
Int.	he, she, it **does call**	he, she, it **does get called**
Fut.	I, he, she, it,	I, he, she, it,
	we, you, they **will call**	we, you, they **will be called**
Past	I, he, she, it,	I, he, she, it **was called**
	we, you, they **called**	we, you, they **were called**
Past	I, he, she, it **was calling**	I, he, she, it **was being called**
Prog.	we, you, they **were calling**	we, you, they **were being called**
Past	I, he, she, it,	I, he, she, it,
Int.	we, you, they **did call**	we, you, they **did get called**
Pres.	I, we, you, they **have called**	I, we, you, they **have been called**
Perf.	he, she, it **has called**	he, she, it **has been called**
Past	I, he, she, it,	I, he, she, it,
Perf.	we, you, they **had called**	we, you, they **had been called**
Fut.	I, he, she, it, we, you, they	I, he, she, it, we, you, they
Perf.	**will have called**	**will have been called**

IMPERATIVE MOOD

call   **be called**

SUBJUNCTIVE MOOD

Pres.	if I, he, she, it,	if I, he, she, it,
	we, you, they **call**	we, you, they **be called**
Past	if I, he, she, it,	if I, he, she, it,
	we, you, they **called**	we, you, they **were called**
Fut.	if I, he, she, it,	if I, he, she, it,
	we, you, they **should call**	we, you, they **should be called**

Transitive and intransitive.

She called this morning.
I was called very late last evening.

AN ESSENTIAL
55 VERB

Examples

She calls her mother once a week.

He called yesterday.

Were all the parents called?

I am calling to tell you the results.

Will you call?

May I ask who's calling?

You should have called before coming.

Call me later.

I need to know if anyone called.

I have never been called by her.

Words and expressions related to this verb

Call on me and I'll be there.

Don't call me, I'll call you.

He was called away on business.

Please call over to the school.

He was called up to active duty.

Let's call on them.

This calls for a prompt response.

I am calling about your offer in the newspaper.

I just called to say I love you.

Don't forget to call me.

The experiment was unexpectedly called off.

can*
(active voice)

be canned
(passive voice)

INDICATIVE MOOD

Pres.	I, we, you, they **can**	I am **canned**
		we, you, they **are canned**
	he, she, it **cans**	he, she, it **is canned**
Pres.	I am **canning**	I **am being canned**
Prog.	we, you, they **are canning**	we, you, they **are being canned**
	he, she, it **is canning**	he, she, it **is being canned**
Pres.	I, we, you, they **do can**	I, we, you, they **do get canned**
Int.	he, she, it **does can**	he, she, it **does get canned**
Fut.	I, he, she, it,	I, he, she, it,
	we, you, they **will can**	we, you, they **will be canned**
Past	I, he, she, it,	I, he, she, it **was canned**
	we, you, they **canned**	we, you, they **were canned**
Past	I, he, she, it **was canning**	I, he, she, it **was being canned**
Prog.	we, you, they **were canning**	we, you, they **were being canned**
Past	I, he, she, it,	I, he, she, it,
Int.	we, you, they **did can**	we, you, they **did get canned**
Pres.	I, we, you, they **have canned**	I, we, you, they **have been canned**
Perf.	he, she, it **has canned**	he, she, it **has been canned**
Past	I, he, she, it,	I, he, she, it,
Perf.	we, you, they **had canned**	we, you, they **had been canned**
Fut.	I, he, she, it, we, you, they	I, he, she, it, we, you, they
Perf.	**will have canned**	**will have been canned**

IMPERATIVE MOOD

can **be canned**

SUBJUNCTIVE MOOD

Pres.	if I, he, she, it,	if I, he, she, it,
	we, you, they **can**	we, you, they **be canned**
Past	if I, he, she, it,	if I, he, she, it,
	we, you, they **canned**	we, you, they **were canned**
Fut.	if I, he, she, it,	if I, he, she, it,
	we, you, they **should can**	we, you, they **should be canned**

---

*Meaning to place in a container for preservation.

Are you canning the extra tomatoes?
These pineapples were canned in Hawaii.

care (active voice)	PRINCIPAL PARTS: **cares, caring, cared, cared**	be cared (passive voice)

INDICATIVE MOOD

Pres.	I, we, you, they **care**	I **am cared** we, you, they **are cared**
	he, she, it **cares**	he, she, it **is cared**
Pres. *Prog.*	I **am caring** we, you, they **are caring** he, she, it **is caring**	I **am being cared** we, you, they **are being cared** he, she, it **is being cared**
Pres. *Int.*	I, we, you, they **do care** he, she, it **does care**	I, we, you, they **do get cared** he, she, it **does get cared**
Fut.	I, he, she, it, we, you, they **will care**	I, he, she, it, we, you, they **will be cared**
Past	I, he, she, it, we, you, they **cared**	I, he, she, it **was cared** we, you, they **were cared**
Past *Prog.*	I, he, she, it **was caring** we, you, they **were caring**	I, he, she, it **was being cared** we, you, they **were being cared**
Past *Int.*	I, he, she, it, we, you, they **did care**	I, he, she, it, we, you, they **did get cared**
Pres. *Perf.*	I, we, you, they **have cared** he, she, it **has cared**	I, we, you, they **have been cared** he, she, it **has been cared**
Past *Perf.*	I, he, she, it, we, you, they **had cared**	I, he, she, it, we, you, they **had been cared**
Fut. *Perf.*	I, he, she, it, we, you, they **will have cared**	I, he, she, it, we, you, they **will have been cared**

IMPERATIVE MOOD

care	**be cared**

SUBJUNCTIVE MOOD

Pres.	if I, he, she, it, we, you, they **care**	if I, he, she, it, we, you, they **be cared**
Past	if I, he, she, it, we, you, they **cared**	if I, he, she, it, we, you, they **were cared**
Fut.	if I, he, she, it, we, you, they **should care**	if I, he, she, it, we, you, they **should be cared**

Transitive and intransitive.

It is unjust to say that he is not caring for his animals.
But they say their needs were not adequately cared for.

carry
(active voice)

PRINCIPAL PARTS: **carries, carrying, carried, carried**

be carried
(passive voice)

INDICATIVE MOOD

Pres.	I, we, you, they **carry**	**I am carried**
	he, she, it **carries**	we, you, they **are carried**
		he, she, it **is carried**
Pres.	**I am carrying**	**I am being carried**
Prog.	we, you, they **are carrying**	we, you, they **are being carried**
	he, she, it **is carrying**	he, she, it **is being carried**
Pres.	I, we, you, they **do carry**	I, we, you, they **do get carried**
Int.	he, she, it **does carry**	he, she, it **does get carried**
Fut.	I, he, she, it,	I, he, she, it,
	we, you, they **will carry**	we, you, they **will be carried**
Past	I, he, she, it,	I, he, she, it **was carried**
	we, you, they **carried**	we, you, they **were carried**
Past	I, he, she, it **was carrying**	I, he, she, it **was being carried**
Prog.	we, you, they **were carrying**	we, you, they **were being carried**
Past	I, he, she, it,	I, he, she, it,
Int.	we, you, they **did carry**	we, you, they **did get carried**
Pres.	I, we, you, they **have carried**	I, we, you, they **have been carried**
Perf.	he, she, it **has carried**	he, she, it **has been carried**
Past	I, he, she, it,	I, he, she, it,
Perf.	we, you, they **had carried**	we, you, they **had been carried**
Fut.	I, he, she, it, we, you, they	I, he, she, it, we, you, they
Perf.	**will have carried**	**will have been carried**

IMPERATIVE MOOD

carry   **be carried**

SUBJUNCTIVE MOOD

Pres.	if I, he, she, it,	if I, he, she, it,
	we, you, they **carry**	we, you, they **be carried**
Past	if I, he, she, it,	if I, he, she, it,
	we, you, they **carried**	we, you, they **were carried**
Fut.	if I, he, she, it,	if I, he, she, it,
	we, you, they **should carry**	we, you, they **should be carried**

Transitive and intransitive.

Why is Mom carrying the heaviest suitcase?
The child was carried in her mother's arms.

cast (active voice)	PRINCIPAL PARTS: casts, casting, cast, cast	be cast (passive voice)

INDICATIVE MOOD

Pres.	I, we, you, they **cast**	I **am cast** we, you, they **are cast**
	he, she, it **casts**	he, she, it **is cast**
Pres. *Prog.*	I **am casting** we, you, they **are casting** he, she, it **is casting**	I **am being cast** we, you, they **are being cast** he, she, it **is being cast**
Pres. *Int.*	I, we, you, they **do cast** he, she, it **does cast**	I, we, you, they **do get cast** he, she, it **does get cast**
Fut.	I, he, she, it, we, you, they **will cast**	I, he, she, it, we, you, they **will be cast**
Past	I, he, she, it, we, you, they **cast**	I, he, she, it **was cast** we, you, they **were cast**
Past *Prog.*	I, he, she, it **was casting** we, you, they **were casting**	I, he, she, it **was being cast** we, you, they **were being cast**
Past *Int.*	I, he, she, it, we, you, they **did cast**	I, he, she, it, we, you, they **did get cast**
Pres. *Perf.*	I, we, you, they **have cast** he, she, it **has cast**	I, we, you, they **have been cast** he, she, it **has been cast**
Past *Perf.*	I, he, she, it, we, you, they **had cast**	I, he, she, it, we, you, they **had been cast**
Fut. *Perf.*	I, he, she, it, we, you, they **will have cast**	I, he, she, it, we, you, they **will have been cast**

IMPERATIVE MOOD

cast	**be cast**

SUBJUNCTIVE MOOD

Pres.	if I, he, she, it, we, you, they **cast**	if I, he, she, it, we, you, they **be cast**
Past	if I, he, she, it, we, you, they **cast**	if I, he, she, it, we, you, they **were cast**
Fut.	if I, he, she, it, we, you, they **should cast**	if I, he, she, it, we, you, they **should be cast**

Transitive and intransitive.

Years ago they simply cast trash overboard at sea.
Did you hear that she was cast for the leading role in the school play?

catch
(active voice)

be caught
(passive voice)

INDICATIVE MOOD

Pres.	I, we, you, they **catch**	I **am caught**
		we, you, they **are caught**
	he, she, it **catches**	he, she, it **is caught**
Pres.	I **am catching**	I **am being caught**
Prog.	we, you, they **are catching**	we, you, they **are being caught**
	he, she, it **is catching**	he, she, it **is being caught**
Pres.	I, we, you, they **do catch**	I, we, you, they **do get caught**
Int.	he, she, it **does catch**	he, she, it **does get caught**
Fut.	I, he, she, it,	I, he, she, it,
	we, you, they **will catch**	we, you, they **will be caught**
Past	I, he, she, it,	I, he, she, it **was caught**
	we, you, they **caught**	we, you, they **were caught**
Past	I, he, she, it **was catching**	I, he, she, it **was being caught**
Prog.	we, you, they **were catching**	we, you, they **were being caught**
Past	I, he, she, it,	I, he, she, it,
Int.	we, you, they **did catch**	we, you, they **did get caught**
Pres.	I, we, you, they **have caught**	I, we, you, they **have been caught**
Perf.	he, she, it **has caught**	he, she, it **has been caught**
Past	I, he, she, it,	I, he, she, it,
Perf.	we, you, they **had caught**	we, you, they **had been caught**
Fut.	I, he, she, it, we, you, they	I, he, she, it, we, you, they
Perf.	**will have caught**	**will have been caught**

IMPERATIVE MOOD

catch   **be caught**

SUBJUNCTIVE MOOD

Pres.	if I, he, she, it,	if I, he, she, it,
	we, you, they **catch**	we, you, they **be caught**
Past	if I, he, she, it,	if I, he, she, it,
	we, you, they **caught**	we, you, they **were caught**
Fut.	if I, he, she, it,	if I, he, she, it,
	we, you, they **should catch**	we, you, they **should be caught**

Transitive and intransitive.

Catch a falling star and put it your pocket.
I caught a nasty cold.
Has the student who was smoking been caught?

cause
(active voice)

be caused
(passive voice)

C

INDICATIVE MOOD

Pres.	I, we, you, they **cause**	I **am caused**
		we, you, they **are caused**
	he, she, it **causes**	he, she, it **is caused**
Pres.	I **am causing**	I **am being caused**
Prog.	we, you, they **are causing**	we, you, they **are being caused**
	he, she, it **is causing**	he, she, it **is being caused**
Pres.	I, we, you, they **do cause**	I, we, you, they **do get caused**
Int.	he, she, it **does cause**	he, she, it **does get caused**
Fut.	I, he, she, it,	I, he, she, it,
	we, you, they **will cause**	we, you, they **will be caused**
Past	I, he, she, it,	I, he, she, it **was caused**
	we, you, they **caused**	we, you, they **were caused**
Past	I, he, she, it **was causing**	I, he, she, it **was being caused**
Prog.	we, you, they **were causing**	we, you, they **were being caused**
Past	I, he, she, it,	I, he, she, it,
Int.	we, you, they **did cause**	we, you, they **did get caused**
Pres.	I, we, you, they **have caused**	I, we, you, they **have been caused**
Perf.	he, she, it **has caused**	he, she, it **has been caused**
Past	I, he, she, it,	I, he, she, it,
Perf.	we, you, they **had caused**	we, you, they **had been caused**
Fut.	I, he, she, it, we, you, they	I, he, she, it, we, you, they
Perf.	**will have caused**	**will have been caused**

IMPERATIVE MOOD

cause   **be caused**

SUBJUNCTIVE MOOD

Pres.	if I, he, she, it,	if I, he, she, it,
	we, you, they **cause**	we, you, they **be caused**
Past	if I, he, she, it,	if I, he, she, it,
	we, you, they **caused**	we, you, they **were caused**
Fut.	if I, he, she, it,	if I, he, she, it,
	we, you, they **should cause**	we, you, they **should be caused**

The broken traffic signal is causing a major traffic jam.
The flood caused the closing of the road.
My mistake was caused by a lack of attention.

PRINCIPAL PARTS: changes, changing, changed, changed

be changed
(passive voice)

INDICATIVE MOOD

Pres.	I, we, you, they **change**	I **am changed**
		we, you, they **are changed**
	he, she, it **changes**	he, she, it **is changed**
Pres.	I **am changing**	I **am being changed**
Prog.	we, you, they **are changing**	we, you, they **are being changed**
	he, she, it **is changing**	he, she, it **is being changed**
Pres.	I, we, you, they **do change**	I, we, you, they **do get changed**
Int.	he, she, it **does change**	he, she, it **does get changed**
Fut.	I, he, she, it,	I, he, she, it,
	we, you, they **will change**	we, you, they **will be changed**
Past	I, he, she, it,	I, he, she, it **was changed**
	we, you, they **changed**	we, you, they **were changed**
Past	I, he, she, it **was changing**	I, he, she, it **was being changed**
Prog.	we, you, they **were changing**	we, you, they **were being changed**
Past	I, he, she, it,	I, he, she, it,
Int.	we, you, they **did change**	we, you, they **did get changed**
Pres.	I, we, you, they **have changed**	I, we, you, they **have been changed**
Perf.	he, she, it **has changed**	he, she, it **has been changed**
Past	I, he, she, it,	I, he, she, it,
Perf.	we, you, they **had changed**	we, you, they **had been changed**
Fut.	I, he, she, it, we, you, they	I, he, she, it, we, you, they
Perf.	**will have changed**	**will have been changed**

IMPERATIVE MOOD

change

be changed

SUBJUNCTIVE MOOD

Pres.	if I, he, she, it,	if I, he, she, it,
	we, you, they **change**	we, you, they **be changed**
Past	if I, he, she, it,	if I, he, she, it,
	we, you, they **changed**	we, you, they **were changed**
Fut.	if I, he, she, it,	if I, he, she, it,
	we, you, they **should change**	we, you, they **should be changed**

Transitive and intransitive.

If he is changing just one thing in his life, what should it be?
The ballerina changed costumes three times in the performance.
The engine oil was changed just three months ago.

chat

PRINCIPAL PARTS: chats, chatting, chatted, chatted

INDICATIVE MOOD

Pres. I, we, you, they **chat**

he, she, it **chats**

Pres. I **am chatting**
Prog. we, you, they **are chatting**
he, she, it **is chatting**

Pres. I, we, you, they **do chat**
Int. he, she, it **does chat**

Fut. I, he, she, it,
we, you, they **will chat**

Past I, he, she, it,
we, you, they **chatted**

Past I, he, she, it **was chatting**
Prog. we, you, they **were chatting**

Past I, he, she, it,
Int. we, you, they **did chat**

Pres. I, we, you, they **have chatted**
Perf. he, she, it **has chatted**

Past. I, he, she, it,
Perf. we, you, they **had chatted**

Fut. I, he, she, it, we, you, they
Perf. will **have chatted**

IMPERATIVE MOOD

chat

SUBJUNCTIVE MOOD

Pres. if I, he, she, it,
we, you, they **chat**

Past if I, he, she, it,
we, you, they **chatted**

Fut. if I, he, she, it,
we, you, they **should chat**

They are chatting online again.
We chatted for over an hour.

choose
(active voice)

be chosen
(passive voice)

INDICATIVE MOOD

Pres.	I, we, you, they **choose**	I **am chosen**
		we, you, they **are chosen**
	he, she, it **chooses**	he, she, it **is chosen**
Pres.	I **am choosing**	I **am being chosen**
Prog.	we, you, they **are choosing**	we, you, they **are being chosen**
	he, she, it **is choosing**	he, she, it **is being chosen**
Pres.	I, we, you, they **do choose**	I, we, you, they **do get chosen**
Int.	he, she, it **does choose**	he, she, it **does get chosen**
Fut.	I, he, she, it,	I, he, she, it,
	we, you, they **will choose**	we, you, they **will be chosen**
Past	I, he, she, it,	I, he, she, it **was chosen**
	we, you, they **chose**	we, you, they **were chosen**
Past	I, he, she, it **was choosing**	I, he, she, it **was being chosen**
Prog.	we, you, they **were choosing**	we, you, they **were being chosen**
Past	I, he, she, it,	I, he, she, it,
Int.	we, you, they **did choose**	we, you, they **did get chosen**
Pres.	I, we, you, they **have chosen**	I, we, you, they **have been chosen**
Perf.	he, she, it **has chosen**	he, she, it **has been chosen**
Past	I, he, she, it,	I, he, she, it,
Perf.	we, you, they **had chosen**	we, you, they **had been chosen**
Fut.	I, he, she, it, we, you, they	I, he, she, it, we, you, they
Perf.	**will have chosen**	**will have been chosen**

IMPERATIVE MOOD

choose   **be chosen**

SUBJUNCTIVE MOOD

Pres.	if I, he, she, it,	if I, he, she, it,
	we, you, they **choose**	we, you, they **be chosen**
Past	if I, he, she, it,	if I, he, she, it,
	we, you, they **chose**	we, you, they **were chosen**
Fut.	if I, he, she, it,	if I, he, she, it,
	we, you, they **should choose**	we, you, they **should be chosen**

Transitive and intransitive.

Which color are you choosing?
We chose the chocolate ice cream instead of the vanilla.
Which of the students were chosen to represent the class?

click	PRINCIPAL PARTS: clicks, clicking,	be clicked
(active voice)	clicked, clicked	(passive voice)

INDICATIVE MOOD

Pres.	I, we, you, they **click**	I **am clicked** we, you, they **are clicked**
	he, she, it **clicks**	he, she, it **is clicked**
Pres. *Prog.*	I **am clicking** we, you, they **are clicking** he, she, it **is clicking**	I **am being clicked** we, you, they **are being clicked** he, she, it **is being clicked**
Pres. *Int.*	I, we, you, they **do click** he, she, it **does click**	I, we, you, they **do get clicked** he, she, it **does get clicked**
Fut.	I, he, she, it, we, you, they **will click**	I, he, she, it, we, you, they **will be clicked**
Past	I, he, she, it, we, you, they **clicked**	I, he, she, it **was clicked** we, you, they **were clicked**
Past *Prog.*	I, he, she, it **was clicking** we, you, they **were clicking**	I, he, she, it **was being clicked** we, you, they **were being clicked**
Past *Int.*	I, he, she, it, we, you, they **did click**	I, he, she, it, we, you, they **did get clicked**
Pres. *Perf.*	I, we, you, they **have clicked** he, she, it **has clicked**	I, we, you, they **have been clicked** he, she, it **has been clicked**
Past *Perf.*	I, he, she, it, we, you, they **had clicked**	I, he, she, it, we, you, they **had been clicked**
Fut. *Perf.*	I, he, she, it, we, you, they **will have clicked**	I, he, she, it, we, you, they **will have been clicked**

IMPERATIVE MOOD

click   **be clicked**

SUBJUNCTIVE MOOD

Pres.	if I, he, she, it, we, you, they **click**	if I, he, she, it, we, you, they **be clicked**
Past	if I, he, she, it, we, you, they **clicked**	if I, he, she, it, we, you, they **were clicked**
Fut.	if I, he, she, it, we, you, they **should click**	if I, he, she, it, we, you, they **should be clicked**

Intransitive and transitive.

Have you learned how to point and click with your computer mouse?
That button has been clicked once too often.

PRINCIPAL PARTS: **clings, clinging, clung, clung**

INDICATIVE MOOD

Pres. I, we, you, they **cling**

he, she, it **clings**

Pres.
Prog. I **am clinging**
we, you, they **are clinging**
he, she, it **is clinging**

Pres.
Int. I, we, you, they **do cling**
he, she, it **does cling**

Fut. I, he, she, it,
we, you, they **will cling**

Past I, he, she, it,
we, you, they **clung**

Past
Prog. I, he, she, it **was clinging**
we, you, they **were clinging**

Past
Int. I, he, she, it,
we, you, they **did cling**

Pres.
Perf. I, we, you, they **have clung**
he, she, it **has clung**

Past
Perf. I, he, she, it,
we, you, they **had clung**

Fut.
Perf. I, he, she, it, we, you, they
will have clung

IMPERATIVE MOOD

cling

SUBJUNCTIVE MOOD

Pres. if I, he, she, it,
we, you, they **cling**

Past if I, he, she, it,
we, you, they **clung**

Fut. if I, he, she, it,
we, you, they **should cling**

Some people often cling to hope, long after others have abandoned it.
We, too, clung to our mother's apron.

close
(active voice)

be closed
(passive voice)

C

INDICATIVE MOOD

Pres.	I, we, you, they **close**	I **am closed**
		we, you, they **are closed**
	he, she, it **closes**	he, she, it **is closed**
Pres.	I **am closing**	I **am being closed**
Prog.	we, you, they **are closing**	we, you, they **are being closed**
	he, she, it **is closing**	he, she, it **is being closed**
Pres.	I, we, you, they **do close**	I, we, you, they **do get closed**
Int.	he, she, it **does close**	he, she, it **does get closed**
Fut.	I, he, she, it,	I, he, she, it,
	we, you, they **will close**	we, you, they **will be closed**
Past	I, he, she, it,	I, he, she, it **was closed**
	we, you, they **closed**	we, you, they **were closed**
Past	I, he, she, it **was closing**	I, he, she, it **was being closed**
Prog.	we, you, they **were closing**	we, you, they **were being closed**
Past	I, he, she, it,	I, he, she, it,
Int.	we, you, they **did close**	we, you, they **did get closed**
Pres.	I, we, you, they **have closed**	I, we, you, they **have been closed**
Perf.	he, she, it **has closed**	he, she, it **has been closed**
Past	I, he, she, it,	I, he, she, it,
Perf.	we, you, they **had closed**	we, you, they **had been closed**
Fut.	I, he, she, it, we, you, they	I, he, she, it, we, you, they
Perf.	**will have closed**	**will have been closed**

IMPERATIVE MOOD

close   **be closed**

SUBJUNCTIVE MOOD

Pres.	if I, he, she, it,	if I, he, she, it,
	we, you, they **close**	we, you, they **be closed**
Past	if I, he, she, it,	if I, he, she, it,
	we, you, they **closed**	we, you, they **were closed**
Fut.	if I, he, she, it,	if I, he, she, it,
	we, you, they **should close**	we, you, they **should be closed**

Transitive and intransitive.

Is someone closing the door?
The store was already closed for the day when we arrived.

clothe
(active voice)

PRINCIPAL PARTS: **clothes, clothing, clothed/clad, clothed/clad**

be clothed/clad
(passive voice)

INDICATIVE MOOD

Pres.	I, we, you, they **clothe**	I **am clothed**
		we, you, they **are clothed**
	he, she, it **clothes**	he, she, it **is clothed**
Pres.	I **am clothing**	I **am being clothed**
Prog.	we, you, they **are clothing**	we, you, they **are being clothed**
	he, she, it **is clothing**	he, she, it **is being clothed**
Pres.	I, we, you, they **do clothe**	I, we, you, they **do get clothed**
Int.	he, she, it **does clothe**	he, she, it **does get clothed**
Fut.	I, he, she, it,	I, he, she, it,
	we, you, they **will clothe**	we, you, they **will be clothed**
Past	I, he, she, it,	I, he, she, it **was clothed**
	we, you, they **clothed**	we, you, they **were clothed**
Past	I, he, she, it **was clothing**	I, he, she, it **was being clothed**
Prog.	we, you, they **were clothing**	we, you, they **were being clothed**
Past	I, he, she, it,	I, he, she, it,
Int.	we, you, they **did clothe**	we, you, they **did get clothed**
Pres.	I, we, you, they **have clothed**	I, we, you, they **have been clothed**
Perf.	he, she, it **has clothed**	he, she, it **has been clothed**
Past	I, he, she, it,	I, he, she, it,
Perf.	we, you, they **had clothed**	we, you, they **had been clothed**
Fut.	I, he, she, it, we, you, they	I, he, she, it, we, you, they
Perf.	**will have clothed**	**will have been clothed**

IMPERATIVE MOOD

clothe

be clothed

SUBJUNCTIVE MOOD

Pres.	if I, he, she, it,	if I, he, she, it,
	we, you, they **clothe**	we, you, they **be clothed**
Past	if I, he, she, it,	if I, he, she, it,
	we, you, they **clothed**	we, you, they **were clothed**
Fut.	if I, he, she, it,	if I, he, she, it,
	we, you, they **should clothe**	we, you, they **should be clothed**

The *Oxford Dictionary* lists CLAD as the poetic or archaic past and past participle.

We are clothing the poor in our community.
They clothed their children in designer jeans.
In spite of the cold, he was clothed only in a thin sweater.

76

club
(active voice)

be clubbed
(passive voice)

C

INDICATIVE MOOD

Pres.	I, we, you, they **club**	I **am clubbed**
		we, you, they **are clubbed**
	he, she, it **clubs**	he, she, it **is clubbed**
Pres.	I **am clubbing**	I **am being clubbed**
Prog.	we, you, they **are clubbing**	we, you, they **are being clubbed**
	he, she, it **is clubbing**	he, she, it **is being clubbed**
Pres.	I, we, you, they **do club**	I, we, you, they **do get clubbed**
Int.	he, she, it **does club**	he, she, it **does get clubbed**
Fut.	I, he, she, it,	I, he, she, it,
	we, you, they **will club**	we, you, they **will be clubbed**
Past	I, he, she, it,	I, he, she, it **was clubbed**
	we, you, they **clubbed**	we, you, they **were clubbed**
Past	I, he, she, it **was clubbing**	I, he, she, it **was being clubbed**
Prog.	we, you, they **were clubbing**	we, you, they **were being clubbed**
Past	I, he, she, it,	I, he, she, it,
Int.	we, you, they **did club**	we, you, they **did get clubbed**
Pres.	I, we, you, they **have clubbed**	I, we, you, they **have been clubbed**
Perf.	he, she, it **has clubbed**	he, she, it **has been clubbed**
Past	I, he, she, it,	I, he, she, it,
Perf.	we, you, they **had clubbed**	we, you, they **had been clubbed**
Fut.	I, he, she, it, we, you, they	I, he, she, it, we, you, they
Perf.	**will have clubbed**	**will have been clubbed**

IMPERATIVE MOOD

club   **be clubbed**

SUBJUNCTIVE MOOD

Pres.	if I, he, she, it,	if I, he, she, it,
	we, you, they **club**	we, you, they **be clubbed**
Past	if I, he, she, it,	if I, he, she, it,
	we, you, they **clubbed**	we, you, they **were clubbed**
Fut.	if I, he, she, it,	if I, he, she, it,
	we, you, they **should club**	we, you, they **should be clubbed**

As a transitive verb, this means to "hit or strike with a club." As an intransitive verb, it means to "go out to a club."

The young people are clubbing every Friday night.
Several of the customers were clubbed in the fight.

INDICATIVE MOOD

Pres.	I, we, you, they **come** he, she, it **comes**
Pres. *Prog.*	I **am coming** we, you, they **are coming** he, she, it **is coming**
Pres. *Int.*	I, we, you, they **do come** he, she, it **does come**
Fut.	I, he, she, it, we, you, they **will come**
Past	I, he, she, it, we, you, they **came**
Past *Prog.*	I, he, she, it **was coming** we, you, they **were coming**
Past *Int.*	I, he, she, it, we, you, they **did come**
Pres. *Perf.*	I, we, you, they **have come** he, she, it **has come**
Past *Perf.*	I, he, she, it, we, you, they **had come**
Fut. *Perf.*	I, he, she, it, we, you, they **will have come**

IMPERATIVE MOOD

come

SUBJUNCTIVE MOOD

Pres.	if I, he, she, it, we, you, they **come**
Past	if I, he, she, it, we, you, they **came**
Fut.	if I, he, she, it we, you, they **should come**

Are you coming to my birthday party?
Last year they came without a gift.
They had come totally unprepared.

AN ESSENTIAL
55 VERB

Examples

Are you coming?

Come in.

The bluebird comes early in the morning.

I should have come sooner.

He came late again.

I will come again.

He has come for the package.

The letter has finally come.

The notice came too late for any response.

Is it too early to come over?

Words and expressions related to this verb

Come on, you can do it.

Come here.

Then came the rain.

The bus always comes on time.

You could have come with us.

I'm coming home.

When does the mail come?

Your time has come.

Summer has come and gone.

The sun comes up in the east.

He came clean about the crime.

compare
(active voice)

Principal Parts: **compares, comparing,**
compared, compared

be compared
(passive voice)

INDICATIVE MOOD

Pres.	I, we, you, they **compare**	I **am compared**
		we, you, they **are compared**
	he, she, it **compares**	he, she, it **is compared**
Pres.	I **am comparing**	I **am being compared**
Prog.	we, you, they **are comparing**	we, you, they **are being compared**
	he, she, it **is comparing**	he, she, it **is being compared**
Pres.	I, we, you, they **do compare**	I, we, you, they **do get compared**
Int.	he, she, it **does compare**	he, she, it **does get compared**
Fut.	I, he, she, it,	I, he, she, it,
	we, you, they **will compare**	we, you, they **will be compared**
Past	I, he, she, it,	I, he, she, it **was compared**
	we, you, they **compared**	we, you, they **were compared**
Past	I, he, she, it **was comparing**	I, he, she, it **was being compared**
Prog.	we, you, they **were comparing**	we, you, they **were being compared**
Past	I, he, she, it,	I, he, she, it,
Int.	we, you, they **did compare**	we, you, they **did get compared**
Pres.	I, we, you, they **have compared**	I, we, you, they **have been compared**
Perf.	he, she, it **has compared**	he, she, it **has been compared**
Past	I, he, she, it,	I, he, she, it,
Perf.	we, you, they **had compared**	we, you, they **had been compared**
Fut.	I, he, she, it, we, you, they	I, he, she, it, we, you, they
Perf.	**will have compared**	**will have been compared**

IMPERATIVE MOOD

compare   **be compared**

SUBJUNCTIVE MOOD

Pres.	if I, he, she, it,	if I, he, she, it,
	we, you, they **compare**	we, you, they **be compared**
Past	if I, he, she, it,	if I, he, she, it,
	we, you, they **compared**	we, you, they **were compared**
Fut.	if I, he, she, it,	if I, he, she, it,
	we, you, they **should compare**	we, you, they **should be compared**

Transitive and intransitive.

Are you comparing the quality of the two items?
They compared apples and oranges.
They have unjustly been compared to more accomplished athletes.

concern
(active voice)

be concerned
(passive voice)

C

INDICATIVE MOOD

Pres.	I, we, you, they **concern**	I **am concerned**
		we, you, they **are concerned**
	he, she, it **concerns**	he, she, it **is concerned**
Pres.	I **am concerning**	I **am being concerned**
Prog.	we, you, they **are concerning**	we, you, they **are being concerned**
	he, she, it **is concerning**	he, she, it **is being concerned**
Pres.	I, we, you, they **do concern**	I, we, you, they **do get concerned**
Int.	he, she, it **does concern**	he, she, it **does get concerned**
Fut.	I, he, she, it,	I, he, she, it,
	we, you, they **will concern**	we, you, they **will be concerned**
Past	I, he, she, it,	I, he, she, it **was concerned**
	we, you, they **concerned**	we, you, they **were concerned**
Past	I, he, she, it **was concerning**	I, he, she, it **was being concerned**
Prog.	we, you, they **were concerning**	we, you, they **were being concerned**
Past	I, he, she, it,	I, he, she, it,
Int.	we, you, they **did concern**	we, you, they **did get concerned**
Pres.	I, we, you, they **have concerned**	I, we, you, they **have been concerned**
Perf.	he, she, it **has concerned**	he, she, it **has been concerned**
Past	I, he, she, it,	I, he, she, it,
Perf.	we, you, they **had concerned**	we, you, they **had been concerned**
Fut.	I, he, she, it, we, you, they	I, he, she, it, we, you, they
Perf.	**will have concerned**	**will have been concerned**

IMPERATIVE MOOD

concern **be concerned**

SUBJUNCTIVE MOOD

Pres.	if I, he, she, it,	if I, he, she, it,
	we, you, they **concern**	we, you, they **be concerned**
Past	if I, he, she, it,	if I, he, she, it,
	we, you, they **concerned**	we, you, they **were concerned**
Fut.	if I, he, she, it,	if I, he, she, it,
	we, you, they **should concern**	we, you, they **should be concerned**

We all concerned ourselves with this matter.
Where children are concerned, we must act with great sensitivity.

INDICATIVE MOOD

Pres.   I, we, you, they **conference**

       he, she, it **conferences**

Pres.   **I am conferencing**
Prog.   we, you, they **are conferencing**
       he, she, it **is conferencing**

Pres.   I, we, you, they **do conference**
Int.   he, she, it **does conference**

Fut.   I, he, she, it,
       we, you, they **will conference**

Past   I, he, she, it,
       we, you, they **conferenced**

Past   I, he, she, it **was conferencing**
Prog.   we, you, they **were conferencing**

Past   I, he, she, it,
Int.   we, you, they **did conference**

Pres.   I, we, you, they **have conferenced**
Perf.   he, she, it **has conferenced**

Past   I, he, she, it,
Perf.   we, you, they **had conferenced**

Fut.   I, he, she, it, we, you, they
Perf.   **will have conferenced**

IMPERATIVE MOOD

conference

SUBJUNCTIVE MOOD

Pres.   if I, he, she, it,
       we, you, they **conference**

Past   if I, he, she, it,
       we, you, they **conferenced**

Fut.   if I, he, she, it,
       we, you, they **should conference**

They are conferencing long distance using videophones.
The trustees could be conferenced via cell phone.

confuse
(active voice)

PRINCIPAL PARTS: **confuses, confusing, confused, confused**

be confused
(passive voice)

INDICATIVE MOOD

Pres.	I, we, you, they **confuse**	I **am confused**
		we, you, they **are confused**
	he, she, it **confuses**	he, she, it **is confused**
Pres.	I **am confusing**	I **am being confused**
Prog.	we, you, they **are confusing**	we, you, they **are being confused**
	he, she, it **is confusing**	he, she, it **is being confused**
Pres.	I, we, you, they **do confuse**	I, we, you, they **do get confused**
Int.	he, she, it **does confuse**	he, she, it **does get confused**
Fut.	I, he, she, it,	I, he, she, it,
	we, you, they **will confuse**	we, you, they **will be confused**
Past	I, he, she, it,	I, he, she, it **was confused**
	we, you, they **confused**	we, you, they **were confused**
Past	I, he, she, it **was confusing**	I, he, she, it **was being confused**
Prog.	we, you, they **were confusing**	we, you, they **were being confused**
Past	I, he, she, it,	I, he, she, it,
Int.	we, you, they **did confuse**	we, you, they **did get confused**
Pres.	I, we, you, they **have confused**	I, we, you, they **have been confused**
Perf.	he, she, it **has confused**	he, she, it **has been confused**
Past	I, he, she, it,	I, he, she, it,
Perf.	we, you, they **had confused**	we, you, they **had been confused**
Fut.	I, he, she, it, we, you, they	I, he, she, it, we, you, they
Perf.	**will have confused**	**will have been confused**

IMPERATIVE MOOD

confuse   **be confused**

SUBJUNCTIVE MOOD

Pres.	if I, he, she, it,	if I, he, she, it,
	we, you, they **confuse**	we, you, they **be confused**
Past	if I, he, she, it,	if I, he, she, it,
	we, you, they **confused**	we, you, they **were confused**
Fut.	if I, he, she, it,	if I, he, she, it,
	we, you, they **should confuse**	we, you, they **should be confused**

I am not confusing coincidence with causality.
The twins are often confused for one another.

connect
(active voice)

be connected
(passive voice)

INDICATIVE MOOD

Pres.	I, we, you, they **connect**	I am **connected**
		we, you, they **are connected**
	he, she, it **connects**	he, she, it **is connected**
Pres.	I am **connecting**	I am **being connected**
Prog.	we, you, they **are connecting**	we, you, they **are being connected**
	he, she, it **is connecting**	he, she, it **is being connected**
Pres.	I, we, you, they **do connect**	I, we, you, they **do get connected**
Int.	he, she, it **does connect**	he, she, it **does get connected**
Fut.	I, he, she, it,	I, he, she, it,
	we, you, they **will connect**	we, you, they **will be connected**
Past	I, he, she, it,	I, he, she, it **was connected**
	we, you, they **connected**	we, you, they **were connected**
Past	I, he, she, it **was connecting**	I, he, she, it **was being connected**
Prog.	we, you, they **were connecting**	we, you, they **were being connected**
Past	I, he, she, it,	I, he, she, it,
Int.	we, you, they **did connect**	we, you, they **did get connected**
Pres.	I, we, you, they **have connected**	I, we, you, they **have been connected**
Perf.	he, she, it **has connected**	he, she, it **has been connected**
Past	I, he, she, it,	I, he, she, it,
Perf.	we, you, they **had connected**	we, you, they **had been connected**
Fut.	I, he, she, it, we, you, they	I, he, she, it, we, you, they
Perf.	**will have connected**	**will have been connected**

IMPERATIVE MOOD

connect

be connected

SUBJUNCTIVE MOOD

Pres.	if I, he, she, it,	if I, he, she, it,
	we, you, they **connect**	we, you, they **be connected**
Past	if I, he, she, it,	if I, he, she, it,
	we, you, they **connected**	we, you, they **were connected**
Fut.	if I, he, she, it,	if I, he, she, it,
	we, you, they **should connect**	we, you, they **should be connected**

Transitive and intransitive.

We connected electronically with our suppliers.
They were connected by blood and conviction.

consider
(active voice)

PRINCIPAL PARTS: **considers, considering, considered, considered**

be considered
(passive voice)

INDICATIVE MOOD

Pres.	I, we, you, they **consider**	I **am considered**
		we, you, they **are considered**
	he, she, it **considers**	he, she, it **is considered**
Pres.	I **am considering**	I **am being considered**
Prog.	we, you, they **are considering**	we, you, they **are being considered**
	he, she, it **is considering**	he, she, it **is being considered**
Pres.	I, we, you, they **do consider**	I, we, you, they **do get considered**
Int.	he, she, it **does consider**	he, she, it **does get considered**
Fut.	I, he, she, it,	I, he, she, it,
	we, you, they **will consider**	we, you, they **will be considered**
Past	I, he, she, it,	I, he, she, it **was considered**
	we, you, they **considered**	we, you, they **were considered**
Past	I, he, she, it **was considering**	I, he, she, it **was being considered**
Prog.	we, you, they **were considering**	we, you, they **were being considered**
Past	I, he, she, it,	I, he, she, it,
Int.	we, you, they **did consider**	we, you, they **did get considered**
Pres.	I, we, you, they **have considered**	I, we, you, they **have been considered**
Perf.	he, she, it **has considered**	he, she, it **has been considered**
Past	I, he, she, it,	I, he, she, it,
Perf.	we, you, they **had considered**	we, you, they **had been considered**
Fut.	I, he, she, it, we, you, they	I, he, she, it, we, you, they
Perf.	**will have considered**	**will have been considered**

IMPERATIVE MOOD

consider   **be considered**

SUBJUNCTIVE MOOD

Pres.	if I, he, she, it,	if I, he, she, it,
	we, you, they **consider**	we, you, they **be considered**
Past	if I, he, she, it,	if I, he, she, it,
	we, you, they **considered**	we, you, they **were considered**
Fut.	if I, he, she, it,	if I, he, she, it,
	we, you, they **should consider**	we, you, they **should be considered**

Transitive and intransitive.

Which of the items should we consider next?
All sides of the issue were carefully considered.

consult
(active voice)

be consulted
(passive voice)

INDICATIVE MOOD

Pres.	I, we, you, they **consult**	I **am consulted**
		we, you, they **are consulted**
	he, she, it **consults**	he, she, it **is consulted**
Pres.	I **am consulting**	I **am being consulted**
Prog.	we, you, they **are consulting**	we, you, they **are being consulted**
	he, she, it **is consulting**	he, she, it **is being consulted**
Pres.	I, we, you, they **do consult**	I, we, you, they **do get consulted**
Int.	he, she, it **does consult**	he, she, it **does get consulted**
Fut.	I, he, she, it,	I, he, she, it,
	we, you, they **will consult**	we, you, they **will be consulted**
Past	I, he, she, it,	I, he, she, it **was consulted**
	we, you, they **consulted**	we, you, they **were consulted**
Past	I, he, she, it **was consulting**	I, he, she, it **was being consulted**
Prog.	we, you, they **were consulting**	we, you, they **were being consulted**
Past	I, he, she, it,	I, he, she, it,
Int.	we, you, they **did consult**	we, you, they **did get consulted**
Pres.	I, we, you, they **have consulted**	I, we, you, they **have been consulted**
Perf.	he, she, it **has consulted**	he, she, it **has been consulted**
Past	I, he, she, it,	I, he, she, it,
Perf.	we, you, they **had consulted**	we, you, they **had been consulted**
Fut.	I, he, she, it, we, you, they	I, he, she, it, we, you, they
Perf.	**will have consulted**	**will have been consulted**

IMPERATIVE MOOD

consult   **be consulted**

SUBJUNCTIVE MOOD

Pres.	if I, he, she, it,	if I, he, she, it,
	we, you, they **consult**	we, you, they **be consulted**
Past	if I, he, she, it,	if I, he, she, it,
	we, you, they **consulted**	we, you, they **were consulted**
Fut.	if I, he, she, it,	if I, he, she, it,
	we, you, they **should consult**	we, you, they **should be consulted**

Transitive and intransitive.

Nowadays you have to consult with technical experts.
No one was consulted before he made the decision.

contain
(active voice)

PRINCIPAL PARTS: **contains, containing, contained, contained**

be contained
(passive voice)

INDICATIVE MOOD

Pres.	I, we, you, they **contain**	I am **contained**
		we, you, they **are contained**
	he, she, it **contains**	he, she, it **is contained**
Pres. *Prog.*	I am **containing**	I am **being contained**
	we, you, they **are containing**	we, you, they **are being contained**
	he, she, it **is containing**	he, she, it **is being contained**
Pres. *Int.*	I, we, you, they **do contain**	I, we, you, they **do get contained**
	he, she, it **does contain**	he, she, it **does get contained**
Fut.	I, he, she, it,	I, he, she, it,
	we, you, they **will contain**	we, you, they **will be contained**
Past	I, he, she, it,	I, he, she, it **was contained**
	we, you, they **contained**	we, you, they **were contained**
Past *Prog.*	I, he, she, it **was containing**	I, he, she, it **was being contained**
	we, you, they **were containing**	we, you, they **were being contained**
Past *Int.*	I, he, she, it,	I, he, she, it,
	we, you, they **did contain**	we, you, they **did get contained**
Pres. *Perf.*	I, we, you, they **have contained**	I, we, you, they **have been contained**
	he, she, it **has contained**	he, she, it **has been contained**
Past *Perf.*	I, he, she, it,	I, he, she, it,
	we, you, they **had contained**	we, you, they **had been contained**
Fut. *Perf.*	I, he, she, it, we, you, they	I, he, she, it, we, you, they
	will have contained	**will have been contained**

IMPERATIVE MOOD

contain   **be contained**

SUBJUNCTIVE MOOD

Pres.	if I, he, she, it,	if I, he, she, it,
	we, you, they **contain**	we, you, they **be contained**
Past	if I, he, she, it,	if I, he, she, it,
	we, you, they **contained**	we, you, they **were contained**
Fut.	if I, he, she, it,	if I, he, she, it,
	we, you, they **should contain**	we, you, they **should be contained**

Transitive and intransitive.

The book contains many interesting passages.
The outbreak of the flu was confined to one small town.

continue
(active voice)

be continued
(passive voice)

INDICATIVE MOOD

Pres.	I, we, you, they **continue**	I **am continued**
		we, you, they **are continued**
	he, she, it **continues**	he, she, it **is continued**
Pres.	I **am continuing**	I **am being continued**
Prog.	we, you, they **are continuing**	we, you, they **are being continued**
	he, she, it **is continuing**	he, she, it **is being continued**
Pres.	I, we, you, they **do continue**	I, we, you, they **do get continued**
Int.	he, she, it **does continue**	he, she, it **does get continued**
Fut.	I, he, she, it,	I, he, she, it,
	we, you, they **will continue**	we, you, they **will be continued**
Past	I, he, she, it,	I, he, she, it **was continued**
	we, you, they **continued**	we, you, they **were continued**
Past	I, he, she, it **was continuing**	I, he, she, it **was being continued**
Prog.	we, you, they **were continuing**	we, you, they **were being continued**
Past	I, he, she, it,	I, he, she, it,
Int.	we, you, they **did continue**	we, you, they **did get continued**
Pres.	I, we, you, they **have continued**	I, we, you, they **have been continued**
Perf.	he, she, it **has continued**	he, she, it **has been continued**
Past	I, he, she, it,	I, he, she, it,
Perf.	we, you, they **had continued**	we, you, they **had been continued**
Fut.	I, he, she, it, we, you, they	I, he, she, it, we, you, they
Perf.	**will have continued**	**will have been continued**

IMPERATIVE MOOD

continue be continued

SUBJUNCTIVE MOOD

Pres.	if I, he, she, it,	if I, he, she, it,
	we, you, they **continue**	we, you, they **be continued**
Past	if I, he, she, it,	if I, he, she, it,
	we, you, they **continued**	we, you, they **were continued**
Fut.	if I, he, she, it,	if I, he, she, it,
	we, you, they **should continue**	we, you, they **should be continued**

Intransitive and transitive.

She continues to insist on coming.
I regret to inform you that the skater is not continuing.
The case had been continued until both attorneys could be present.

cost	PRINCIPAL PARTS: **costs, costing,**	be cost
(active voice)	**cost, cost**	(passive voice)

INDICATIVE MOOD

Pres.	I, we, you, they **cost**	I **am cost**
		we, you, they **are cost**
	he, she, it **costs**	he, she, it **is cost**
Pres.	I **am costing**	I **am being cost**
Prog.	we, you, they **are costing**	we, you, they **are being cost**
	he, she, it **is costing**	he, she, it **is being cost**
Pres.	I, we, you, they **do cost**	I, we, you, they **do get cost**
Int.	he, she, it **does cost**	he, she, it **does get cost**
Fut.	I, he, she, it,	I, he, she, it,
	we, you, they **will cost**	we, you, they **will be cost**
Past	I, he, she, it,	I, he, she, it **was cost**
	we, you, they **cost**	we, you, they **were cost**
Past	I, he, she, it **was costing**	I, he, she, it **was being cost**
Prog.	we, you, they **were costing**	we, you, they **were being cost**
Past	I, he, she, it,	I, he, she, it,
Int.	we, you, they **did cost**	we, you, they **did get cost**
Pres.	I, we, you, they **have cost**	I, we, you, they **have been cost**
Perf.	he, she, it **has cost**	he, she, it **has been cost**
Past	I, he, she, it,	I, he, she, it,
Perf.	we, you, they **had cost**	we, you, they **had been cost**
Fut.	I, he, she, it, we, you, they	I, he, she, it, we, you, they
Perf.	**will have cost**	**will have been cost**

IMPERATIVE MOOD

cost	**be cost**

SUBJUNCTIVE MOOD

Pres.	if I, he, she, it,	if I, he, she, it,
	we, you, they **cost**	we, you, they **be cost**
Past	if I, he, she, it,	if I, he, she, it,
	we, you, they **cost**	we, you, they **were cost**
Fut.	if I, he, she, it,	if I, he, she, it,
	we, you, they **should cost**	we, you, they **should be cost**

Intransitive and transitive. The forms COSTED, especially with the preposition OUT for the past tense and past participle, are used when referring to "estimating or determining the price of something."

Gasoline costs far more than it cost just a year ago.
It had cost more than he was willing to pay.
The alternatives were costed out by our accountant.

cover (active voice)	Principal Parts: **covers, covering,** **covered, covered**	be covered (passive voice)

INDICATIVE MOOD

Pres.	I, we, you, they **cover**	I **am covered**
		we, you, they **are covered**
	he, she, it **covers**	he, she, it **is covered**
Pres. *Prog.*	I **am covering** we, you, they **are covering** he, she, it **is covering**	I **am being covered** we, you, they **are being covered** he, she, it **is being covered**
Pres. *Int.*	I, we, you, they **do cover** he, she, it **does cover**	I, we, you, they **do get covered** he, she, it **does get covered**
Fut.	I, he, she, it, we, you, they **will cover**	I, he, she, it, we, you, they **will be covered**
Past	I, he, she, it, we, you, they **covered**	I, he, she, it **was covered** we, you, they **were covered**
Past *Prog.*	I, he, she, it **was covering** we, you, they **were covering**	I, he, she, it **was being covered** we, you, they **were being covered**
Past *Int.*	I, he, she, it, we, you, they **did cover**	I, he, she, it, we, you, they **did get covered**
Pres. *Perf.*	I, we, you, they **have covered** he, she, it **has covered**	I, we, you, they **have been covered** he, she, it **has been covered**
Past *Perf.*	I, he, she, it, we, you, they **had covered**	I, he, she, it, we, you, they **had been covered**
Fut. *Perf.*	I, he, she, it, we, you, they **will have covered**	I, he, she, it, we, you, they **will have been covered**

IMPERATIVE MOOD

cover	**be covered**

SUBJUNCTIVE MOOD

Pres.	if I, he, she, it, we, you, they **cover**	if I, he, she, it, we, you, they **be covered**
Past	if I, he, she, it, we, you, they **covered**	if I, he, she, it, we, you, they **were covered**
Fut.	if I, he, she, it, we, you, they **should cover**	if I, he, she, it, we, you, they **should be covered**

Transitive and intransitive.

You should cover your head before you sit out in the sun.
The statue was covered by a cloth until its dedication.

90

crash
(active voice)

be crashed
(passive voice)

C

INDICATIVE MOOD

Pres.	I, we, you, they **crash**	I **am crashed**
		we, you, they **are crashed**
	he, she, it **crashes**	he, she, it **is crashed**
Pres.	I **am crashing**	I **am being crashed**
Prog.	we, you, they **are crashing**	we, you, they **are being crashed**
	he, she, it **is crashing**	he, she, it **is being crashed**
Pres.	I, we, you, they **do crash**	I, we, you, they **do get crashed**
Int.	he, she, it **does crash**	he, she, it **does get crashed**
Fut.	I, he, she, it,	I, he, she, it,
	we, you, they **will crash**	we, you, they **will be crashed**
Past	I, he, she, it,	I, he, she, it **was crashed**
	we, you, they **crashed**	we, you, they **were crashed**
Past	I, he, she, it **was crashing**	I, he, she, it **was being crashed**
Prog.	we, you, they **were crashing**	we, you, they **were being crashed**
Past	I, he, she, it,	I, he, she, it,
Int.	we, you, they **did crash**	we, you, they **did get crashed**
Pres.	I, we, you, they **have crashed**	I, we, you, they **have been crashed**
Perf.	he, she, it **has crashed**	he, she, it **has been crashed**
Past	I, he, she, it,	I, he, she, it,
Perf.	we, you, they **had crashed**	we, you, they **had been crashed**
Fut.	I, he, she, it, we, you, they	I, he, she, it, we, you, they
Perf.	**will have crashed**	**will have been crashed**

IMPERATIVE MOOD

crash   **be crashed**

SUBJUNCTIVE MOOD

Pres.	if I, he, she, it,	if I, he, she, it,
	we, you, they **crash**	we, you, they **be crashed**
Past	if I, he, she, it,	if I, he, she, it,
	we, you, they **crashed**	we, you, they **were crashed**
Fut.	if I, he, she, it,	if I, he, she, it,
	we, you, they **should crash**	we, you, they **should be crashed**

Transitive and intransitive.

Do you know why my computer just crashed?
The car was crashed to study the effect of such a collision on passengers.

create
(active voice)

be created
(passive voice)

INDICATIVE MOOD

Pres.	I, we, you, they **create**	I **am created**
		we, you, they **are created**
	he, she, it **creates**	he, she, it **is created**
Pres.	I **am creating**	I **am being created**
Prog.	we, you, they **are creating**	we, you, they **are being created**
	he, she, it **is creating**	he, she, it **is being created**
Pres.	I, we, you, they **do create**	I, we, you, they **do get created**
Int.	he, she, it **does create**	he, she, it **does get created**
Fut.	I, he, she, it,	I, he, she, it,
	we, you, they **will create**	we, you, they **will be created**
Past	I, he, she, it,	I, he, she, it **was created**
	we, you, they **created**	we, you, they **were created**
Past	I, he, she, it **was creating**	I, he, she, it **was being created**
Prog.	we, you, they **were creating**	we, you, they **were being created**
Past	I, he, she, it,	I, he, she, it,
Int.	we, you, they **did create**	we, you, they **did get created**
Pres.	I, we, you, they **have created**	I, we, you, they **have been created**
Perf.	he, she, it **has created**	he, she, it **has been created**
Past	I, he, she, it,	I, he, she, it,
Perf.	we, you, they **had created**	we, you, they **had been created**
Fut.	I, he, she, it, we, you, they	I, he, she, it, we, you, they
Perf.	**will have created**	**will have been created**

IMPERATIVE MOOD

create **be created**

SUBJUNCTIVE MOOD

Pres.	if I, he, she, it,	if I, he, she, it,
	we, you, they **create**	we, you, they **be created**
Past	if I, he, she, it,	if I, he, she, it,
	we, you, they **created**	we, you, they **were created**
Fut.	if I, he, she, it,	if I, he, she, it,
	we, you, they **should create**	we, you, they **should be created**

Transitive and intransitive.

I envy those who are creating good music today.
There is real controversy over how and when humans were created.

INDICATIVE MOOD

Pres.   I, we, you, they **creep**
          he, she, it **creeps**

Pres.   I **am creeping**
Prog.   we, you, they **are creeping**
          he, she, it **is creeping**

Pres.   I, we, you, they **do creep**
Int.   he, she, it **does creep**

Fut.   I, he, she, it,
          we, you, they **will creep**

Past   I, he, she, it,
          we, you, they **crept**

Past   I, he, she, it **was creeping**
Prog.   we, you, they **were creeping**

Past   I, he, she, it,
Int.   we, you, they **did creep**

Pres.   I, we, you, they **have crept**
Perf.   he, she, it **has crept**

Past   I, he, she, it,
Perf.   we, you, they **had crept**

Fut.   I, he, she, it, we, you, they
Perf.   **will have crept**

IMPERATIVE MOOD

creep

SUBJUNCTIVE MOOD

Pres.   if I, he, she, it,
          we, you, they **creep**

Past   if I, he, she, it,
          we, you, they **crept**

Fut.   if I, he, she, it,
          we, you, they **should creep**

My new plant already crept halfway up the wall.
The deadline has crept up on us unexpectedly.

| cry
(active voice) | PRINCIPAL PARTS: **cries, crying,
cried, cried** | be cried
(passive voice) |

INDICATIVE MOOD

Pres.	I, we, you, they **cry** he, she, it **cries**	I **am cried** we, you, they **are cried** he, she, it **is cried**
Pres. *Prog.*	I am **crying** we, you, they **are crying** he, she, it **is crying**	I **am being cried** we, you, they **are being cried** he, she, it **is being cried**
Pres. *Int.*	I, we, you, they **do cry** he, she, it **does cry**	I, we, you, they **do get cried** he, she, it **does get cried**
Fut.	I, he, she, it, we, you, they **will cry**	I, he, she, it, we, you, they **will be cried**
Past	I, he, she, it, we, you, they **cried**	I, he, she, it **was cried** we, you, they **were cried**
Past *Prog.*	I, he, she, it **was crying** we, you, they **were crying**	I, he, she, it **was being cried** we, you, they **were being cried**
Past *Int.*	I, he, she, it, we, you, they **did cry**	I, he, she, it, we, you, they **did get cried**
Pres. *Perf.*	I, we, you, they **have cried** he, she, it **has cried**	I, we, you, they **have been cried** he, she, it **has been cried**
Past *Perf.*	I, he, she, it, we, you, they **had cried**	I, he, she, it, we, you, they **had been cried**
Fut. *Perf.*	I, he, she, it, we, you, they **will have cried**	I, he, she, it, we, you, they **will have been cried**

IMPERATIVE MOOD

| **cry** | **be cried** |

SUBJUNCTIVE MOOD

Pres.	if I, he, she, it, we, you, they **cry**	if I, he, she, it, we, you, they **be cried**
Past	if I, he, she, it, we, you, they **cried**	if I, he, she, it, we, you, they **were cried**
Fut.	if I, he, she, it, we, you, they **should cry**	if I, he, she, it, we, you, they **should be cried**

Intransitive and transitive.

Sometimes I wish that she was crying.
We have cried enough.
His tears were cried in vain.

cut
(active voice)

be cut
(passive voice)

C

INDICATIVE MOOD

Pres.	I, we, you, they **cut**		I **am cut**
			we, you, they **are cut**
	he, she, it **cuts**		he, she, it **is cut**
Pres.	I **am cutting**		I **am being cut**
Prog.	we, you, they **are cutting**		we, you, they **are being cut**
	he, she, it **is cutting**		he, she, it **is being cut**
Pres.	I, we, you, they **do cut**		I, we, you, they **do get cut**
Int.	he, she, it **does cut**		he, she, it **does get cut**
Fut.	I, he, she, it,		I, he, she, it,
	we, you, they **will cut**		we, you, they **will be cut**
Past	I, he, she, it,		I, he, she, it **was cut**
	we, you, they **cut**		we, you, they **were cut**
Past	I, he, she, it **was cutting**		I, he, she, it **was being cut**
Prog.	we, you, they **were cutting**		we, you, they **were being cut**
Past	I, he, she, it,		I, he, she, it,
Int.	we, you, they **did cut**		we, you, they **did get cut**
Pres.	I, we, you, they **have cut**		I, we, you, they **have been cut**
Perf.	he, she, it **has cut**		he, she, it **has been cut**
Past	I, he, she, it,		I, he, she, it,
Perf.	we, you, they **had cut**		we, you, they **had been cut**
Fut.	I, he, she, it, we, you, they		I, he, she, it, we, you, they
Perf.	**will have cut**		**will have been cut**

IMPERATIVE MOOD

cut   **be cut**

SUBJUNCTIVE MOOD

Pres.	if I, he, she, it,		if I, he, she, it,
	we, you, they **cut**		we, you, they **be cut**
Past	if I, he, she, it,		if I, he, she, it,
	we, you, they **cut**		we, you, they **were cut**
Fut.	if I, he, she, it,		if I, he, she, it,
	we, you, they **should cut**		we, you, they **should be cut**

Transitive and intransitive.

Some are cutting their grass each week.
They cut themselves on the bushes.
That tree will have to be cut down in the spring.

95

dance
(active voice)

be danced
(passive voice)

INDICATIVE MOOD

Pres. I, we, you, they **dance**

he, she, it **dances**

I **am danced**
we, you, they **are danced**
he, she, it **is danced**

Pres. I am **dancing**
Prog. we, you, they **are dancing**
he, she, it **is dancing**

I **am being danced**
we, you, they **are being danced**
he, she, it **is being danced**

Pres. I, we, you, they **do dance**
Int. he, she, it **does dance**

I, we, you, they **do get danced**
he, she, it **does get danced**

Fut. I, he, she, it,
we, you, they **will dance**

I, he, she, it,
we, you, they **will be danced**

Past I, he, she, it,
we, you, they **danced**

I, he, she, it **was danced**
we, you, they **were danced**

Past I, he, she, it **was dancing**
Prog. we, you, they **were dancing**

I, he, she, it **was being danced**
we, you, they **were being danced**

Past I, he, she, it,
Int. we, you, they **did dance**

I, he, she, it,
we, you, they **did get danced**

Pres. I, we, you, they **have danced**
Perf. he, she, it **has danced**

I, we, you, they **have been danced**
he, she, it **has been danced**

Past I, he, she, it,
Perf. we, you, they **had danced**

I, he, she, it,
we, you, they **had been danced**

Fut. I, he, she, it, we, you, they
Perf. **will have danced**

I, he, she, it, we, you, they
will have been danced

IMPERATIVE MOOD

dance

be danced

SUBJUNCTIVE MOOD

Pres. if I, he, she, it,
we, you, they **dance**

if I, he, she, it,
we, you, they **be danced**

Past if I, he, she, it,
we, you, they **danced**

if I, he, she, it,
we, you, they **were danced**

Fut. if I, he, she, it,
we, you, they **should dance**

if I, he, she, it,
we, you, they **should be danced**

Intransitive and transitive.

The team is dancing every afternoon.
She could have danced all night.
The main role was danced by the youngest ballerina.

dare
(active voice)

PRINCIPAL PARTS: **dares/dare, daring, dared, dared**

be dared
(passive voice)

D

INDICATIVE MOOD

Pres.	I, we, you, they **dare**	**I am dared**
		we, you, they **are dared**
	he, she, it **dares/dare**	he, she, it **is dared**
Pres.	**I am daring**	I **am being dared**
Prog.	we, you, they **are daring**	we, you, they **are being dared**
	he, she, it **is daring**	he, she, it **is being dared**
Pres.	I, we, you, they **do dare**	I, we, you, they **do get dared**
Int.	he, she, it **does dare**	he, she, it **does get dared**
Fut.	I, he, she, it,	I, he, she, it,
	we, you, they **will dare**	we, you, they **will be dared**
Past	I, he, she, it,	I, he, she, it **was dared**
	we, you, they **dared**	we, you, they **were dared**
Past	I, he, she, it **was daring**	I, he, she, it **was being dared**
Prog.	we, you, they **were daring**	we, you, they **were being dared**
Past	I, he, she, it,	I, he, she, it,
Int.	we, you, they **did dare**	we, you, they **did get dared**
Pres.	I, we, you, they **have dared**	I, we, you, they **have been dared**
Perf.	he, she, it **has dared**	he, she, it **has been dared**
Past	I, he, she, it,	I, he, she, it,
Perf.	we, you, they **had dared**	we, you, they **had been dared**
Fut.	I, he, she, it, we, you, they	I, he, she, it, we, you, they
Perf.	**will have dared**	**will have been dared**

IMPERATIVE MOOD

dare   **be dared**

SUBJUNCTIVE MOOD

Pres.	if I, he, she, it,	if I, he, she, it,
	we, you, they **dare**	we, you, they **be dared**
Past	if I, he, she, it,	if I, he, she, it,
	we, you, they **dared**	we, you, they **were dared**
Fut.	if I, he, she, it,	if I, he, she, it,
	we, you, they **should dare**	we, you, they **should be dared**

Intransitive and transitive. DARE can behave like an auxiliary verb (may, can) and then has the third person singular form DARE: "How dare he?" In this usage it does not need "do" in questions. There is also no "to" after this verb and before another: "Don't you dare break your promise."

Is he daring to enter without knocking?
He had been dared by his fellow workers to ask for a raise.

deal
(active voice)

be dealt
(passive voice)

INDICATIVE MOOD

Pres.	I, we, you, they **deal**	I **am dealt**
		we, you, they **are dealt**
	he, she, it **deals**	he, she, it **is dealt**
Pres.	I **am dealing**	I **am being dealt**
Prog.	we, you, they **are dealing**	we, you, they **are being dealt**
	he, she, it **is dealing**	he, she, it **is being dealt**
Pres.	I, we, you, they **do deal**	I, we, you, they **do get dealt**
Int.	he, she, it **does deal**	he, she, it **does get dealt**
Fut.	I, he, she, it,	I, he, she, it,
	we, you, they **will deal**	we, you, they **will be dealt**
Past	I, he, she, it,	I, he, she, it **was dealt**
	we, you, they **dealt**	we, you, they **were dealt**
Past	I, he, she, it **was dealing**	I, he, she, it **was being dealt**
Prog.	we, you, they **were dealing**	we, you, they **were being dealt**
Past	I, he, she, it,	I, he, she, it,
Int.	we, you, they **did deal**	we, you, they **did get dealt**
Pres.	I, we, you, they **have dealt**	I, we, you, they **have been dealt**
Perf.	he, she, it **has dealt**	he, she, it **has been dealt**
Past	I, he, she, it,	I, he, she, it,
Perf.	we, you, they **had dealt**	we, you, they **had been dealt**
Fut.	I, he, she, it, we, you, they	I, he, she, it, we, you, they
Perf.	**will have dealt**	**will have been dealt**

IMPERATIVE MOOD

deal

be dealt

SUBJUNCTIVE MOOD

Pres.	if I, he, she, it,	if I, he, she, it,
	we, you, they **deal**	we, you, they **be dealt**
Past	if I, he, she, it,	if I, he, she, it,
	we, you, they **dealt**	we, you, they **were dealt**
Fut.	if I, he, she, it,	if I, he, she, it,
	we, you, they **should deal**	we, you, they **should be dealt**

Transitive and intransitive.

Who deals the cards first in this game?
Were you dealt with fairly at the service desk?

decide
(active voice)

PRINCIPAL PARTS: decides, deciding, decided, decided

be decided
(passive voice)

INDICATIVE MOOD

Pres.	I, we, you, they **decide**	I **am decided**
		we, you, they **are decided**
	he, she, it **decides**	he, she, it **is decided**
Pres.	I **am deciding**	I **am being decided**
Prog.	we, you, they **are deciding**	we, you, they **are being decided**
	he, she, it **is deciding**	he, she, it **is being decided**
Pres.	I, we, you, they **do decide**	I, we, you, they **do get decided**
Int.	he, she, it **does decide**	he, she, it **does get decided**
Fut.	I, he, she, it,	I, he, she, it,
	we, you, they **will decide**	we, you, they **will be decided**
Past	I, he, she, it,	I, he, she, it **was decided**
	we, you, they **decided**	we, you, they **were decided**
Past	I, he, she, it **was deciding**	I, he, she, it **was being decided**
Prog.	we, you, they **were deciding**	we, you, they **were being decided**
Past	I, he, she, it,	I, he, she, it,
Int.	we, you, they **did decide**	we, you, they **did get decided**
Pres.	I, we, you, they **have decided**	I, we, you, they **have been decided**
Perf.	he, she, it **has decided**	he, she, it **has been decided**
Past	I, he, she, it,	I, he, she, it,
Perf.	we, you, they **had decided**	we, you, they **had been decided**
Fut.	I, he, she, it, we, you, they	I, he, she, it, we, you, they
Perf.	**will have decided**	**will have been decided**

IMPERATIVE MOOD

decide   **be decided**

SUBJUNCTIVE MOOD

Pres.	if I, he, she, it,	if I, he, she, it,
	we, you, they **decide**	we, you, they **be decided**
Past	if I, he, she, it,	if I, he, she, it,
	we, you, they **decided**	we, you, they **were decided**
Fut.	if I, he, she, it,	if I, he, she, it,
	we, you, they **should decide**	we, you, they **should be decided**

Transitive and intransitive.

We are deciding on our choice of cars today.
I decided not to go on vacation with them this year.
Has the question been decided?

describe
(active voice)

PRINCIPAL PARTS: **describes, describing, described, described**

be described
(passive voice)

INDICATIVE MOOD

Pres.   I, we, you, they **describe**

he, she, it **describes**

I **am described**
we, you, they **are described**
he, she, it **is described**

Pres.
Prog.   I **am describing**
we, you, they **are describing**
he, she, it **is describing**

I **am being described**
we, you, they **are being described**
he, she, it **is being described**

Pres.
Int.   I, we, you, they **do describe**
he, she, it **does describe**

I, we, you, they **do get described**
he, she, it **does get described**

Fut.   I, he, she, it,
we, you, they **will describe**

I, he, she, it,
we, you, they **will be described**

Past   I, he, she, it,
we, you, they **described**

I, he, she, it **was described**
we, you, they **were described**

Past
Prog.   I, he, she, it **was describing**
we, you, they **were describing**

I, he, she, it **was being described**
we, you, they **were being described**

Past
Int.   I, he, she, it,
we, you, they **did describe**

I, he, she, it,
we, you, they **did get described**

Pres.
Perf.   I, we, you, they **have described**
he, she, it **has described**

I, we, you, they **have been described**
he, she, it **has been described**

Past
Perf.   I, he, she, it,
we, you, they **had described**

I, he, she, it,
we, you, they **had been described**

Fut.
Perf.   I, he, she, it, we, you, they
will have described

I, he, she, it, we, you, they
will have been described

IMPERATIVE MOOD

describe

be described

SUBJUNCTIVE MOOD

Pres.   if I, he, she, it,
we, you, they **describe**

if I, he, she, it,
we, you, they **be described**

Past   if I, he, she, it,
we, you, they **described**

if I, he, she, it,
we, you, they **were described**

Fut.   if I, he, she, it,
we, you, they **should describe**

if I, he, she, it,
we, you, they **should be described**

Are they describing the other vehicle?
He has been described as thoughtful and considerate.

design
(active voice)

PRINCIPAL PARTS: **designs, designing, designed, designed**

be designed
(passive voice)

INDICATIVE MOOD

Pres.	I, we, you, they **design**	I **am designed**
		we, you, they **are designed**
	he, she, it **designs**	he, she, it **is designed**
Pres.	I **am designing**	I **am being designed**
Prog.	we, you, they **are designing**	we, you, they **are being designed**
	he, she, it **is designing**	he, she, it **is being designed**
Pres.	I, we, you, they **do design**	I, we, you, they **do get designed**
Int.	he, she, it **does design**	he, she, it **does get designed**
Fut.	I, he, she, it,	I, he, she, it,
	we, you, they **will design**	we, you, they **will be designed**
Past	I, he, she, it,	I, he, she, it **was designed**
	we, you, they **designed**	we, you, they **were designed**
Past	I, he, she, it **was designing**	I, he, she, it **was being designed**
Prog.	we, you, they **were designing**	we, you, they **were being designed**
Past	I, he, she, it,	I, he, she, it,
Int.	we, you, they **did design**	we, you, they **did get designed**
Pres.	I, we, you, they **have designed**	I, we, you, they **have been designed**
Perf.	he, she, it **has designed**	he, she, it **has been designed**
Past	I, he, she, it,	I, he, she, it,
Perf.	we, you, they **had designed**	we, you, they **had been designed**
Fut.	I, he, she, it, we, you, they	I, he, she, it, we, you, they
Perf.	**will have designed**	**will have been designed**

IMPERATIVE MOOD

design　　　　　　　　　　　**be designed**

SUBJUNCTIVE MOOD

Pres.	if I, he, she, it,	if I, he, she, it,
	we, you, they **design**	we, you, they **be designed**
Past	if I, he, she, it,	if I, he, she, it,
	we, you, they **designed**	we, you, they **were designed**
Fut.	if I, he, she, it,	if I, he, she, it,
	we, you, they **should design**	we, you, they **should be designed**

Transitive and intransitive.

My daughter designs cars.
This building was designed by a famous architect.

determine
(active voice)

be determined
(passive voice)

INDICATIVE MOOD

Pres.	I, we, you, they **determine**	I **am determined**
		we, you, they **are determined**
	he, she, it **determines**	he, she, it **is determined**
Pres. *Prog.*	I **am determining**	I **am being determined**
	we, you, they **are determining**	we, you, they **are being determined**
	he, she, it **is determining**	he, she, it **is being determined**
Pres. *Int.*	I, we, you, they **do determine**	I, we, you, they **do get determined**
	he, she, it **does determine**	he, she, it **does get determined**
Fut.	I, he, she, it,	I, he, she, it,
	we, you, they **will determine**	we, you, they **will be determined**
Past	I, he, she, it,	I, he, she, it **was determined**
	we, you, they **determined**	we, you, they **were determined**
Past *Prog.*	I, he, she, it **was determining**	I, he, she, it **was being determined**
	we, you, they **were determining**	we, you, they **were being determined**
Past *Int.*	I, he, she, it,	I, he, she, it,
	we, you, they **did determine**	we, you, they **did get determined**
Pres. *Perf.*	I, we, you, they **have determined**	I, we, you, they **have been determined**
	he, she, it **has determined**	he, she, it **has been determined**
Past *Perf.*	I, he, she, it,	I, he, she, it,
	we, you, they **had determined**	we, you, they **had been determined**
Fut. *Perf.*	I, he, she, it, we, you, they	I, he, she, it, we, you, they
	will have determined	**will have been determined**

IMPERATIVE MOOD

determine

be determined

SUBJUNCTIVE MOOD

Pres.	if I, he, she, it,	if I, he, she, it,
	we, you, they **determine**	we, you, they **be determined**
Past	if I, he, she, it,	if I, he, she, it,
	we, you, they **determined**	we, you, they **were determined**
Fut.	if I, he, she, it,	if I, he, she, it,
	we, you, they **should determine**	we, you, they **should be determined**

Transitive and intransitive.

Who is determining the winner of the competition?
The order of the march was determined in advance.

develop
(active voice)

be developed
(passive voice)

INDICATIVE MOOD

Pres.	I, we, you, they **develop**	I **am developed**
		we, you, they **are developed**
	he, she, it **develops**	he, she, it **is developed**
Pres.	I **am developing**	I **am being developed**
Prog.	we, you, they **are developing**	we, you, they **are being developed**
	he, she, it **is developing**	he, she, it **is being developed**
Pres.	I, we, you, they **do develop**	I, we, you, they **do get developed**
Int.	he, she, it **does develop**	he, she, it **does get developed**
Fut.	I, he, she, it,	I, he, she, it,
	we, you, they **will develop**	we, you, they **will be developed**
Past	I, he, she, it,	I, he, she, it **was developed**
	we, you, they **developed**	we, you, they **were developed**
Past	I, he, she, it **was developing**	I, he, she, it **was being developed**
Prog.	we, you, they **were developing**	we, you, they **were being developed**
Past	I, he, she, it,	I, he, she, it,
Int.	we, you, they **did develop**	we, you, they **did get developed**
Pres.	I, we, you, they **have developed**	I, we, you, they **have been developed**
Perf.	he, she, it **has developed**	he, she, it **has been developed**
Past	I, he, she, it,	I, he, she, it,
Perf.	we, you, they **had developed**	we, you, they **had been developed**
Fut.	I, he, she, it, we, you, they	I, he, she, it, we, you, they
Perf.	**will have developed**	**will have been developed**

IMPERATIVE MOOD

develop   **be developed**

SUBJUNCTIVE MOOD

Pres.	if I, he, she, it,	if I, he, she, it,
	we, you, they **develop**	we, you, they **be developed**
Past	if I, he, she, it,	if I, he, she, it,
	we, you, they **developed**	we, you, they **were developed**
Fut.	if I, he, she, it,	if I, he, she, it,
	we, you, they **should develop**	we, you, they **should be developed**

Transitive and intransitive. The *Oxford Dictionary* lists DEVELOP with no final *e*. While the spellings DEVELOPE and DEVELOPES can be found, the *Columbia Guide to Standard American English* declares that there is no *e* after the *p*.

We will need to develop a plan of action.
Where do you have your photos developed?

dial
(active voice)

PRINCIPAL PARTS: **dials, dialing, dialling,** | **be dialed/dialled**
dialed/dialled, dialed/dialled | (passive voice)

INDICATIVE MOOD

Pres.	I, we, you, they **dial**	I **am dialed**
		we, you, they **are dialed**
	he, she, it **dials**	he, she, it **is dialed**
Pres.	I **am dialing**	I **am being dialed**
Prog.	we, you, they **are dialing**	we, you, they **are being dialed**
	he, she, it **is dialing**	he, she, it **is being dialed**
Pres.	I, we, you, they **do dial**	I, we, you, they **do get dialed**
Int.	he, she, it **does dial**	he, she, it **does get dialed**
Fut.	I, he, she, it,	I, he, she, it,
	we, you, they **will dial**	we, you, they **will be dialed**
Past	I, he, she, it,	I, he, she, it **was dialed**
	we, you, they **dialed**	we, you, they **were dialed**
Past	I, he, she, it **was dialing**	I, he, she, it **was being dialed**
Prog.	we, you, they **were dialing**	we, you, they **were being dialed**
Past	I, he, she, it,	I, he, she, it,
Int.	we, you, they **did dial**	we, you, they **did get dialed**
Pres.	I, we, you, they **have dialed**	I, we, you, they **have been dialed**
Perf.	he, she, it **has dialed**	he, she, it **has been dialed**
Past	I, he, she, it,	I, he, she, it,
Perf.	we, you, they **had dialed**	we, you, they **had been dialed**
Fut.	I, he, she, it, we, you, they	I, he, she, it, we, you, they
Perf.	**will have dialed**	**will have been dialed**

IMPERATIVE MOOD

dial | **be dialed**

SUBJUNCTIVE MOOD

Pres.	if I, he, she, it,	if I, he, she, it,
	we, you, they **dial**	we, you, they **be dialed**
Past	if I, he, she, it,	if I, he, she, it,
	we, you, they **dialed**	we, you, they **were dialed**
Fut.	if I, he, she, it,	if I, he, she, it,
	we, you, they **should dial**	we, you, they **should be dialed**

Transitive and intransitive. In the present participle DIALING and DIALLING are acceptable, just as in the past tense and past participle are DIALED and DIALLED. The *Oxford Dictionary* prefers the DIALLED as British, noting DIALING-DIALED as American.

Are you dialing the phone company?
Excuse me. I must have dialed the wrong number.
The numbers are dialed randomly by a computer.

INDICATIVE MOOD

Pres.	I, we, you, they **die**
	he, she, it **dies**
Pres. *Prog.*	I **am dying** we, you, they **are dying** he, she, it **is dying**
Pres. *Int.*	I, we, you, they **do die** he, she, it **does die**
Fut.	I, he, she, it, we, you, they **will die**
Past	I, he, she, it, we, you, they **died**
Past *Prog.*	I, he, she, it **was dying** we, you, they **were dying**
Past *Int.*	I, he, she, it, we, you, they **did die**
Pres. *Perf.*	I, we, you, they **have died** he, she, it **has died**
Past *Perf.*	I, he, she, it, we, you, they **had died**
Fut. *Perf.*	I, he, she, it, we, you, they **will have died**

D

IMPERATIVE MOOD

die

SUBJUNCTIVE MOOD

Pres.	if I, he, she, it, we, you, they **die**
Past	if I, he, she, it, we, you, they **died**
Fut.	if I, he, she, it, we, you, they **should die**

DIE/DYING means to lose one's life. Another verb, DIE, DIEING, DIED, DIED, means to stamp out or mold.

I am dying for a piece of chocolate.
The poet died at a very young age.
Many had died of neglect.

| die
(active voice) | PRINCIPAL PARTS: **dies, dieing,
died, died** | be died
(passive voice) |

INDICATIVE MOOD

Pres.	I, we, you, they **die**	I **am died** we, you, they **are died**
	he, she, it **dies**	he, she, it **is died**
Pres. *Prog.*	I **am dieing** we, you, they **are dieing** he, she, it **is dieing**	I **am being died** we, you, they **are being died** he, she, it **is being died**
Pres. *Int.*	I, we, you, they **do die** he, she, it **does die**	I, we, you, they **do get died** he, she, it **does get died**
Fut.	I, he, she, it, we, you, they **will die**	I, he, she, it, we, you, they **will be died**
Past	I, he, she, it, we, you, they **died**	I, he, she, it **was died** we, you, they **were died**
Past *Prog.*	I, he, she, it **was dieing** we, you, they **were dieing**	I, he, she, it **was being died** we, you, they **were being died**
Past *Int.*	I, he, she, it, we, you, they **did die**	I, he, she, it, we, you, they **did get died**
Pres. *Perf.*	I, we, you, they **have died** he, she, it **has died**	I, we, you, they **have been died** he, she, it **has been died**
Past *Perf.*	I, he, she, it, we, you, they **had died**	I, he, she, it, we, you, they **had been died**
Fut. *Perf.*	I, he, she, it, we, you, they **will have died**	I, he, she, it, we, you, they **will have been died**

IMPERATIVE MOOD

| **die** | **be died** |

SUBJUNCTIVE MOOD

Pres.	if I, he, she, it, we, you, they **die**	if I, he, she, it, we, you, they **be died**
Past	if I, he, she, it, we, you, they **died**	if I, he, she, it, we, you, they **were died**
Fut.	if I, he, she, it, we, you, they **should die**	if I, he, she, it, we, you, they **should be died**

This verb means to "cut or form as with a die."

This machine is dieing twenty pieces of metal per minute.
These bolts were died at our own plant.

D

INDICATIVE MOOD

Pres. I, we, you, they **diet**

   he, she, it **diets**

Pres. I **am dieting**
Prog. we, you, they **are dieting**
   he, she, it **is dieting**

Pres. I, we, you, they **do diet**
Int. he, she, it **does diet**

Fut. I, he, she, it,
   we, you, they **will diet**

Past I, he, she, it,
   we, you, they **dieted**

Past I, he, she, it **was dieting**
Prog. we, you, they **were dieting**

Past I, he, she, it,
Int. we, you, they **did diet**

Pres. I, we, you, they **have dieted**
Perf. he, she, it **has dieted**

Past I, he, she, it,
Perf. we, you, they **had dieted**

Fut. I, he, she, it, we, you, they
Perf. **will have dieted**

IMPERATIVE MOOD

diet

SUBJUNCTIVE MOOD

Pres. if I, he, she, it,
   we, you, they **diet**

Past if I, he, she, it,
   we, you, they **dieted**

Fut. if I, he, she, it,
   we, you, they **should diet**

We know that in order to maintain your weight you will have to diet.
His meals were strictly dieted by his physician.

dig
(active voice)

be dug
(passive voice)

INDICATIVE MOOD

Pres.	I, we, you, they **dig**	I **am dug**
		we, you, they **are dug**
	he, she, it **digs**	he, she, it **is dug**
Pres.	I **am digging**	I **am being dug**
Prog.	we, you, they **are digging**	we, you, they **are being dug**
	he, she, it **is digging**	he, she, it **is being dug**
Pres.	I, we, you, they **do dig**	I, we, you, they **do get dug**
Int.	he, she, it **does dig**	he, she, it **does get dug**
Fut.	I, he, she, it,	I, he, she, it,
	we, you, they **will dig**	we, you, they **will be dug**
Past	I, he, she, it,	I, he, she, it **was dug**
	we, you, they **dug**	we, you, they **were dug**
Past	I, he, she, it **was digging**	I, he, she, it **was being dug**
Prog.	we, you, they **were digging**	we, you, they **were being dug**
Past	I, he, she, it,	I, he, she, it,
Int.	we, you, they **did dig**	we, you, they **did get dug**
Pres.	I, we, you, they **have dug**	I, we, you, they **have been dug**
Perf.	he, she, it **has dug**	he, she, it **has been dug**
Past	I, he, she, it,	I, he, she, it,
Perf.	we, you, they **had dug**	we, you, they **had been dug**
Fut.	I, he, she, it, we, you, they	I, he, she, it, we, you, they
Perf.	**will have dug**	**will have been dug**

IMPERATIVE MOOD

dig

be dug

SUBJUNCTIVE MOOD

Pres.	if I, he, she, it,	if I, he, she, it,
	we, you, they **dig**	we, you, they **be dug**
Past	if I, he, she, it,	if I, he, she, it,
	we, you, they **dug**	we, you, they **were dug**
Fut.	if I, he, she, it,	if I, he, she, it,
	we, you, they **should dig**	we, you, they **should be dug**

Transitive and intransitive.

The children are digging for buried treasures.
They dug deep in their search for gold.
The ditch was dug using a new piece of machinery.

digitize
(active voice)

PRINCIPAL PARTS: **digitizes, digitizing,**
digitized, digitized

be digitized
(passive voice)

INDICATIVE MOOD

Pres.	I, we, you, they **digitize**	I **am digitized**
		we, you, they **are digitized**
	he, she, it **digitizes**	he, she, it **is digitized**
Pres.	I **am digitizing**	I **am being digitized**
Prog.	we, you, they **are digitizing**	we, you, they **are being digitized**
	he, she, it **is digitizing**	he, she, it **is being digitized**
Pres.	I, we, you, they **do digitize**	I, we, you, they **do get digitized**
Int.	he, she, it **does digitize**	he, she, it **does get digitized**
Fut.	I, he, she, it,	I, he, she, it,
	we, you, they **will digitize**	we, you, they **will be digitized**
Past	I, he, she, it,	I, he, she, it **was digitized**
	we, you, they **digitized**	we, you, they **were digitized**
Past	I, he, she, it **was digitizing**	I, he, she, it **was being digitized**
Prog.	we, you, they **were digitizing**	we, you, they **were being digitized**
Past	I, he, she, it,	I, he, she, it,
Int.	we, you, they **did digitize**	we, you, they **did get digitized**
Pres.	I, we, you, they **have digitized**	I, we, you, they **have been digitized**
Perf.	he, she, it **has digitized**	he, she, it **has been digitized**
Past	I, he, she, it,	I, he, she, it,
Perf.	we, you, they **had digitized**	we, you, they **had been digitized**
Fut.	I, he, she, it, we, you, they	I, he, she, it, we, you, they
Perf.	**will have digitized**	**will have been digitized**

IMPERATIVE MOOD

digitize   **be digitized**

SUBJUNCTIVE MOOD

Pres.	if I, he, she, it,	if I, he, she, it,
	we, you, they **digitize**	we, you, they **be digitized**
Past	if I, he, she, it,	if I, he, she, it,
	we, you, they **digitized**	we, you, they **were digitized**
Fut.	if I, he, she, it,	if I, he, she, it,
	we, you, they **should digitize**	we, you, they **should be digitized**

Are you digitizing your music files for the first time?
All of your old photos have now been digitized.

109

PRINCIPAL PARTS: **dines, dining,**
dined, dined

INDICATIVE MOOD

Pres.	I, we, you, they **dine**	I **am dined**
		we, you, they **are dined**
	he, she, it **dines**	he, she, it **is dined**
Pres.	I **am dining**	I **am being dined**
Prog.	we, you, they **are dining**	we, you, they **are being dined**
	he, she, it **is dining**	he, she, it **is being dined**
Pres.	I, we, you, they **do dine**	I, we, you, they **do get dined**
Int.	he, she, it **does dine**	he, she, it **does get dined**
Fut.	I, he, she, it,	I, he, she, it,
	we, you, they **will dine**	we, you, they **will be dined**
Past	I, he, she, it,	I, he, she, it **was dined**
	we, you, they **dined**	we, you, they **were dined**
Past	I, he, she, it **was dining**	I, he, she, it **was being dined**
Prog.	we, you, they **were dining**	we, you, they **were being dined**
Past	I, he, she, it,	I, he, she, it,
Int.	we, you, they **did dine**	we, you, they **did get dined**
Pres.	I, we, you, they **have dined**	I, we, you, they **have been dined**
Perf.	he, she, it **has dined**	he, she, it **has been dined**
Past	I, he, she, it,	I, he, she, it,
Perf.	we, you, they **had dined**	we, you, they **had been dined**
Fut.	I, he, she, it, we, you, they	I, he, she, it, we, you, they
Perf.	**will have dined**	**will have been dined**

IMPERATIVE MOOD

dine   **be dined**

SUBJUNCTIVE MOOD

Pres.	if I, he, she, it,	if I, he, she, it,
	we, you, they **dine**	we, you, they **be dined**
Past	if I, he, she, it,	if I, he, she, it,
	we, you, they **dined**	we, you, they **were dined**
Fut.	if I, he, she, it,	if I, he, she, it,
	we, you, they **should dine**	we, you, they **should be dined**

Intransitive and transitive.

Are you dining with me this evening?
The prospective employee was wined and dined by the office manager.

discover
(active voice)

PRINCIPAL PARTS: discovers, discovering, discovered, discovered

be discovered
(passive voice)

INDICATIVE MOOD

Pres.	I, we, you, they **discover**	I **am discovered**
		we, you, they **are discovered**
	he, she, it **discovers**	he, she, it **is discovered**
Pres.	I **am discovering**	I **am being discovered**
Prog.	we, you, they **are discovering**	we, you, they **are being discovered**
	he, she, it **is discovering**	he, she, it **is being discovered**
Pres.	I, we, you, they **do discover**	I, we, you, they **do get discovered**
Int.	he, she, it **does discover**	he, she, it **does get discovered**
Fut.	I, he, she, it,	I, he, she, it,
	we, you, they **will discover**	we, you, they **will be discovered**
Past	I, he, she, it,	I, he, she, it **was discovered**
	we, you, they **discovered**	we, you, they **were discovered**
Past	I, he, she, it **was discovering**	I, he, she, it **was being discovered**
Prog.	we, you, they **were discovering**	we, you, they **were being discovered**
Past	I, he, she, it,	I, he, she, it,
Int.	we, you, they **did discover**	we, you, they **did get discovered**
Pres.	I, we, you, they **have discovered**	I, we, you, they **have been discovered**
Perf.	he, she, it **has discovered**	he, she, it **has been discovered**
Past	I, he, she, it,	I, he, she, it,
Perf.	we, you, they **had discovered**	we, you, they **had been discovered**
Fut.	I, he, she, it, we, you, they	I, he, she, it, we, you, they
Perf.	**will have discovered**	**will have been discovered**

IMPERATIVE MOOD

discover   **be discovered**

SUBJUNCTIVE MOOD

Pres.	if I, he, she, it,	if I, he, she, it,
	we, you, they **discover**	we, you, they **be discovered**
Past	if I, he, she, it,	if I, he, she, it,
	we, you, they **discovered**	we, you, they **were discovered**
Fut.	if I, he, she, it,	if I, he, she, it,
	we, you, they **should discover**	we, you, they **should be discovered**

Transitive and intransitive.

I remembered when I first discovered classical music.
So many memories of our past are still to be discovered.

discuss
(active voice)

be discussed
(passive voice)

INDICATIVE MOOD

Pres.	I, we, you, they **discuss**	I **am discussed**
		we, you, they **are discussed**
	he, she, it **discusses**	he, she, it **is discussed**
Pres.	I **am discussing**	I **am being discussed**
Prog.	we, you, they **are discussing**	we, you, they **are being discussed**
	he, she, it **is discussing**	he, she, it **is being discussed**
Pres.	I, we, you, they **do discuss**	I, we, you, they **do get discussed**
Int.	he, she, it **does discuss**	he, she, it **does get discussed**
Fut.	I, he, she, it,	I, he, she, it,
	we, you, they **will discuss**	we, you, they **will be discussed**
Past	I, he, she, it,	I, he, she, it **was discussed**
	we, you, they **discussed**	we, you, they **were discussed**
Past	I, he, she, it **was discussing**	I, he, she, it **was being discussed**
Prog.	we, you, they **were discussing**	we, you, they **were being discussed**
Past	I, he, she, it,	I, he, she, it,
Int.	we, you, they **did discuss**	we, you, they **did get discussed**
Pres.	I, we, you, they **have discussed**	I, we, you, they **have been discussed**
Perf.	he, she, it **has discussed**	he, she, it **has been discussed**
Past	I, he, she, it,	I, he, she, it,
Perf.	we, you, they **had discussed**	we, you, they **had been discussed**
Fut.	I, he, she, it, we, you, they	I, he, she, it, we, you, they
Perf.	**will have discussed**	**will have been discussed**

IMPERATIVE MOOD

discuss   **be discussed**

SUBJUNCTIVE MOOD

Pres.	if I, he, she, it,	if I, he, she, it,
	we, you, they **discuss**	we, you, they **be discussed**
Past	if I, he, she, it,	if I, he, she, it,
	we, you, they **discussed**	we, you, they **were discussed**
Fut.	if I, he, she, it,	if I, he, she, it,
	we, you, they **should discuss**	we, you, they **should be discussed**

The director was eager to discuss the proposal.
The alterations were discussed at some length.

dive (active voice)	PRINCIPAL PARTS: **dives, diving,** **dived/dove, dived**	be dived (passive voice)

INDICATIVE MOOD

Pres.	I, we, you, they **dive**	I **am dived**
		we, you, they **are dived**
	he, she, it **dives**	he, she, it **is dived**
Pres. *Prog.*	I **am diving** we, you, they **are diving** he, she, it **is diving**	I **am being dived** we, you, they **are being dived** he, she, it **is being dived**
Pres. *Int.*	I, we, you, they **do dive** he, she, it **does dive**	I, we, you, they **do get dived** he, she, it **does get dived**
Fut.	I, he, she, it, we, you, they **will dive**	I, he, she, it, we, you, they **will be dived**
Past	I, he, she, it, we, you, they **dived/dove**	I, he, she, it **was dived** we, you, they **were dived**
Past *Prog.*	I, he, she, it **was diving** we, you, they **were diving**	I, he, she, it **was being dived** we, you, they **were being dived**
Past *Int.*	I, he, she, it, we, you, they **did dive**	I, he, she, it, we, you, they **did get dived**
Pres. *Perf.*	I, we, you, they **have dived** he, she, it **has dived**	I, we, you, they **have been dived** he, she, it **has been dived**
Past *Perf.*	I, he, she, it, we, you, they **had dived**	I, he, she, it, we, you, they **had been dived**
Fut. *Perf.*	I, he, she, it, we, you, they **will have dived**	I, he, she, it, we, you, they **will have been dived**

D

IMPERATIVE MOOD

dive	**be dived**

SUBJUNCTIVE MOOD

Pres.	if I, he, she, it, we, you, they **dive**	if I, he, she, it, we, you, they **be dived**
Past	if I, he, she, it, we, you, they **dived/dove**	if I, he, she, it, we, you, they **were dived**
Fut.	if I, he, she, it, we, you, they **should dive**	if I, he, she, it, we, you, they **should be dived**

This is normally an intransitive verb, but it can be transitive and thus have a passive voice when it means someone forcing something down, such as, "The pilot dived the plane." The past tense forms DIVED and DOVE are both accepted in American English.

At what age are your kids diving from the high board?
He dived into the lake after her.
The submarine was dived by the captain to avoid a collision.

| do
(active voice) | PRINCIPAL PARTS: **does, doing,**
did, done | be done
(passive voice) |

INDICATIVE MOOD

Pres.	I, we, you, they **do**	I **am done**
		we, you, they **are done**
	he, she, it **does**	he, she, it **is done**
Pres.	I **am doing**	I am being **done**
Prog.	we, you, they **are doing**	we, you, they **are being done**
	he, she, it **is doing**	he, she, it **is being done**
Pres.	I, we, you, they **do do**	I, we, you, they **do get done**
Int.	he, she, it **does do**	he, she, it **does get done**
Fut.	I, he, she, it,	I, he, she, it,
	we, you, they **will do**	we, you, they **will be done**
Past	I, he, she, it,	I, he, she, it **was done**
	we, you, they **did**	we, you, they **were done**
Past	I, he, she, it **was doing**	I, he, she, it **was being done**
Prog.	we, you, they **were doing**	we, you, they **were being done**
Past	I, he, she, it,	I, he, she, it,
Int.	we, you, they **did do**	we, you, they **did get done**
Pres.	I, we, you, they **have done**	I, we, you, they **have been done**
Perf.	he, she, it **has done**	he, she, it **has been done**
Past	I, he, she, it,	I, he, she, it,
Perf.	we, you, they **had done**	we, you, they **had been done**
Fut.	I, he, she, it, we, you, they	I, he, she, it, we, you, they
Perf.	**will have done**	**will have been done**

IMPERATIVE MOOD

do	**be done**

SUBJUNCTIVE MOOD

Pres.	if I, he, she, it,	if I, he, she, it,
	we, you, they **do**	we, you, they **be done**
Past	if I, he, she, it,	if I, he, she, it,
	we, you, they **did**	we, you, they **were done**
Fut.	if I, he, she, it,	if I, he, she, it,
	we, you, they **should do**	we, you, they **should be done**

As a transitive verb, DO means "performing, fulfilling." As an intransitive verb, it means "behaving." DO is also an auxiliary verb used to form the intensive tenses. It can be contracted in the negative forms: do not = don't, does not = doesn't, did not = didn't.

Can you do it? We are doing it.
I already did it.
It was actually done over an hour ago.

AN ESSENTIAL
55 VERB

AN ESSENTIAL
55 VERB

do

Examples

I do the dishes.

She does her homework every evening.

He did the work reluctantly.

Who will do your taxes?

The building was done in less than a year.

The hurricane did great damage.

You could have done better.

I will do better next time.

What are we to do?

Do it now.

Words and expressions related to this verb

I don't do math. I just don't.

He doesn't do wrong. He doesn't.

They didn't do it.

Don't do it.

Can you do me a favor?

Do you know what you are doing?

It was no sooner said than done.

I was done in by the false claims.

Do it right the first time.

He was done up as a pirate.

download
(active voice)

PRINCIPAL PARTS: **downloads, downloading, downloaded, downloaded**

be downloaded
(passive voice)

INDICATIVE MOOD

Pres.	I, we, you, they **download** he, she, it **downloads**	I **am downloaded** we, you, they **are downloaded** he, she, it **is downloaded**
Pres. *Prog.*	I **am downloading** we, you, they **are downloading** he, she, it **is downloading**	I **am being downloaded** we, you, they **are being downloaded** he, she, it **is being downloaded**
Pres. *Int.*	I, we, you, they **do download** he, she, it **does download**	I, we, you, they **do get downloaded** he, she, it **does get downloaded**
Fut.	I, he, she, it, we, you, they **will download**	I, he, she, it, we, you, they **will be downloaded**
Past	I, he, she, it, we, you, they **downloaded**	I, he, she, it **was downloaded** we, you, they **were downloaded**
Past *Prog.*	I, he, she, it **was downloading** we, you, they **were downloading**	I, he, she, it **was being downloaded** we, you, they **were being downloaded**
Past *Int.*	I, he, she, it, we, you, they **did download**	I, he, she, it, we, you, they **did get downloaded**
Pres. *Perf.*	I, we, you, they **have downloaded** he, she, it **has downloaded**	I, we, you, they **have been downloaded** he, she, it **has been downloaded**
Past *Perf.*	I, he, she, it, we, you, they **had downloaded**	I, he, she, it, we, you, they **had been downloaded**
Fut. *Perf.*	I, he, she, it, we, you, they **will have downloaded**	I, he, she, it, we, you, they **will have been downloaded**

IMPERATIVE MOOD

download   **be downloaded**

SUBJUNCTIVE MOOD

Pres.	if I, he, she, it, we, you, they **download**	if I, he, she, it, we, you, they **be downloaded**
Past	if I, he, she, it, we, you, they **downloaded**	if I, he, she, it, we, you, they **were downloaded**
Fut.	if I, he, she, it, we, you, they **should download**	if I, he, she, it, we, you, they **should be downloaded**

Before you can utilize that material you must download it to your own computer.
Do you know how many songs were downloaded just yesterday?

drag
(active voice)

be dragged
(passive voice)

D

INDICATIVE MOOD

Pres.	I, we, you, they **drag**	I **am dragged** we, you, they **are dragged**
	he, she, it **drags**	he, she, it **is dragged**
Pres. *Prog.*	I **am dragging** we, you, they **are dragging** he, she, it **is dragging**	I **am being dragged** we, you, they **are being dragged** he, she, it **is being dragged**
Pres. *Int.*	I, we, you, they **do drag** he, she, it **does drag**	I, we, you, they **do get dragged** he, she, it **does get dragged**
Fut.	I, he, she, it, we, you, they **will drag**	I, he, she, it, we, you, they **will be dragged**
Past	I, he, she, it, we, you, they **dragged**	I, he, she, it **was dragged** we, you, they **were dragged**
Past *Prog.*	I, he, she, it **was dragging** we, you, they **were dragging**	I, he, she, it **was being dragged** we, you, they **were being dragged**
Past *Int.*	I, he, she, it, we, you, they **did drag**	I, he, she, it, we, you, they **did get dragged**
Pres. *Perf.*	I, we, you, they **have dragged** he, she, it **has dragged**	I, we, you, they **have been dragged** he, she, it **has been dragged**
Past *Perf.*	I, he, she, it, we, you, they **had dragged**	I, he, she, it, we, you, they **had been dragged**
Fut. *Perf.*	I, he, she, it, we, you, they **will have dragged**	I, he, she, it, we, you, they **will have been dragged**

IMPERATIVE MOOD

drag

be dragged

SUBJUNCTIVE MOOD

Pres.	if I, he, she, it, we, you, they **drag**	if I, he, she, it, we, you, they **be dragged**
Past	if I, he, she, it, we, you, they **dragged**	if I, he, she, it, we, you, they **were dragged**
Fut.	if I, he, she, it, we, you, they **should drag**	if I, he, she, it, we, you, they **should be dragged**

Transitive and intransitive.

He is clicking and dragging in order to reposition that text in the document.
She was dragged to shore by the lifeguards.

draw (active voice)	PRINCIPAL PARTS: **draws, drawing, drew, drawn**	be drawn (passive voice)

INDICATIVE MOOD

Pres.	I, we, you, they **draw** he, she, it **draws**	I **am drawn** we, you, they **are drawn** he, she, it **is drawn**
Pres. *Prog.*	I **am drawing** we, you, they **are drawing** he, she, it **is drawing**	I **am being drawn** we, you, they **are being drawn** he, she, it **is being drawn**
Pres. *Int.*	I, we, you, they **do draw** he, she, it **does draw**	I, we, you, they **do get drawn** he, she, it **does get drawn**
Fut.	I, he, she, it, we, you, they **will draw**	I, he, she, it, we, you, they **will be drawn**
Past	I, he, she, it, we, you, they **drew**	I, he, she, it **was drawn** we, you, they **were drawn**
Past *Prog.*	I, he, she, it **was drawing** we, you, they **were drawing**	I, he, she, it **was being drawn** we, you, they **were being drawn**
Past *Int.*	I, he, she, it, we, you, they **did draw**	I, he, she, it, we, you, they **did get drawn**
Pres. *Perf.*	I, we, you, they **have drawn** he, she, it **has drawn**	I, we, you, they **have been drawn** he, she, it **has been drawn**
Past *Perf.*	I, he, she, it, we, you, they **had drawn**	I, he, she, it, we, you, they **had been drawn**
Fut. *Perf.*	I, he, she, it, we, you, they **will have drawn**	I, he, she, it, we, you, they **will have been drawn**

IMPERATIVE MOOD

draw	**be drawn**

SUBJUNCTIVE MOOD

Pres.	if I, he, she, it, we, you, they **draw**	if I, he, she, it, we, you, they **be drawn**
Past	if I, he, she, it, we, you, they **drew**	if I, he, she, it, we, you, they **were drawn**
Fut.	if I, he, she, it, we, you, they **should draw**	if I, he, she, it, we, you, they **should be drawn**

Transitive and intransitive.

Who drew that picture of the teacher on the board?
The moth was naturally drawn to the light.

dream
(active voice)

be dreamed/dreamt
(passive voice)

D

INDICATIVE MOOD

Pres.	I, we, you, they **dream**	I **am dreamed**
		we, you, they **are dreamed**
	he, she, it **dreams**	he, she, it **is dreamed**
Pres.	I **am dreaming**	I **am being dreamed**
Prog.	we, you, they **are dreaming**	we, you, they **are being dreamed**
	he, she, it **is dreaming**	he, she, it **is being dreamed**
Pres.	I, we, you, they **do dream**	I, we, you, they **do get dreamed**
Int.	he, she, it **does dream**	he, she, it **does get dreamed**
Fut.	I, he, she, it,	I, he, she, it,
	we, you, they **will dream**	we, you, they **will be dreamed**
Past	I, he, she, it,	I, he, she, it **was dreamed**
	we, you, they **dreamed**	we, you, they **were dreamed**
Past	I, he, she, it **was dreaming**	I, he, she, it **was being dreamed**
Prog.	we, you, they **were dreaming**	we, you, they **were being dreamed**
Past	I, he, she, it,	I, he, she, it,
Int.	we, you, they **did dream**	we, you, they **did get dreamed**
Pres.	I, we, you, they **have dreamed**	I, we, you, they **have been dreamed**
Perf.	he, she, it **has dreamed**	he, she, it **has been dreamed**
Past	I, he, she, it,	I, he, she, it,
Perf.	we, you, they **had dreamed**	we, you, they **had been dreamed**
Fut.	I, he, she, it, we, you, they	I, he, she, it, we, you, they
Perf.	**will have dreamed**	**will have been dreamed**

IMPERATIVE MOOD

dream   **be dreamed**

SUBJUNCTIVE MOOD

Pres.	if I, he, she, it,	if I, he, she, it,
	we, you, they **dream**	we, you, they **be dreamed**
Past	if I, he, she, it,	if I, he, she, it,
	we, you, they **dreamed**	we, you, they **were dreamed**
Fut.	if I, he, she, it,	if I, he, she, it,
	we, you, they **should dream**	we, you, they **should be dreamed**

Intransitive and transitive. Both DREAMED and DREAMT are acceptable past and past participle forms. DREAMED is more popular in American English.

I dreamed a dream of days gone by.
That plan was dreamed up in his free time.

drink
(active voice)

PRINCIPAL PARTS: **drinks, drinking, drank, drunk**

be drunk
(passive voice)

INDICATIVE MOOD

Pres.	I, we, you, they **drink**	I **am drunk**
		we, you, they **are drunk**
	he, she, it **drinks**	he, she, it **is drunk**
Pres.	I **am drinking**	I **am being drunk**
Prog.	we, you, they **are drinking**	we, you, they **are being drunk**
	he, she, it **is drinking**	he, she, it **is being drunk**
Pres.	I, we, you, they **do drink**	I, we, you, they **do get drunk**
Int.	he, she, it **does drink**	he, she, it **does get drunk**
Fut.	I, he, she, it,	I, he, she, it,
	we, you, they **will drink**	we, you, they **will be drunk**
Past	I, he, she, it,	I, he, she, it **was drunk**
	we, you, they **drank**	we, you, they **were drunk**
Past	I, he, she, it **was drinking**	I, he, she, it **was being drunk**
Prog.	we, you, they **were drinking**	we, you, they **were being drunk**
Past	I, he, she, it,	I, he, she, it,
Int.	we, you, they **did drink**	we, you, they **did get drunk**
Pres.	I, we, you, they **have drunk**	I, we, you, they **have been drunk**
Perf.	he, she, it **has drunk**	he, she, it **has been drunk**
Past	I, he, she, it,	I, he, she, it,
Perf.	we, you, they **had drunk**	we, you, they **had been drunk**
Fut.	I, he, she, it, we, you, they	I, he, she, it, we, you, they
Perf.	**will have drunk**	**will have been drunk**

IMPERATIVE MOOD

drink   **be drunk**

SUBJUNCTIVE MOOD

Pres.	if I, he, she, it,	if I, he, she, it,
	we, you, they **drink**	we, you, they **be drunk**
Past	if I, he, she, it,	if I, he, she, it,
	we, you, they **drank**	we, you, they **were drunk**
Fut.	if I, he, she, it,	if I, he, she, it,
	we, you, they **should drink**	we, you, they **should be drunk**

Transitive and intransitive. *Merriam Webster's* lists DRANK as an alternate past participle. *Webster's* characterizes that form as colloquial.

Who drank all the orange juice?
All of the diet soft drinks had been drunk before I got to choose.

drive
(active voice)

PRINCIPAL PARTS: **drives, driving, drove, driven**

be driven
(passive voice)

D

INDICATIVE MOOD

Pres.	I, we, you, they **drive**	I **am driven**
		we, you, they **are driven**
	he, she, it **drives**	he, she, it **is driven**
Pres.	I **am driving**	I **am being driven**
Prog.	we, you, they **are driving**	we, you, they **are being driven**
	he, she, it **is driving**	he, she, it **is being driven**
Pres.	I, we, you, they **do drive**	I, we, you, they **do get driven**
Int.	he, she, it **does drive**	he, she, it **does get driven**
Fut.	I, he, she, it,	I, he, she, it,
	we, you, they **will drive**	we, you, they **will be driven**
Past	I, he, she, it,	I, he, she, it **was driven**
	we, you, they **drove**	we, you, they **were driven**
Past	I, he, she, it **was driving**	I, he, she, it **was being driven**
Prog.	we, you, they **were driving**	we, you, they **were being driven**
Past	I, he, she, it,	I, he, she, it,
Int.	we, you, they **did drive**	we, you, they **did get driven**
Pres.	I, we, you, they **have driven**	I, we, you, they **have been driven**
Perf.	he, she, it **has driven**	he, she, it **has been driven**
Past	I, he, she, it,	I, he, she, it,
Perf.	we, you, they **had driven**	we, you, they **had been driven**
Fut.	I, he, she, it, we, you, they	I, he, she, it, we, you, they
Perf.	**will have driven**	**will have been driven**

IMPERATIVE MOOD

drive **be driven**

SUBJUNCTIVE MOOD

Pres.	if I, he, she, it,	if I, he, she, it,
	we, you, they **drive**	we, you, they **be driven**
Past	if I, he, she, it,	if I, he, she, it,
	we, you, they **drove**	we, you, they **were driven**
Fut.	if I, he, she, it,	if I, he, she, it,
	we, you, they **should drive**	we, you, they **should be driven**

Transitive and intransitive.

At the age of eighteen he is already driving in New York City.
Who drove you home?
The children were driven to their dance lessons by one of the fathers.

121

drop	PRINCIPAL PARTS: **drops, dropping,**	**be dropped**
(active voice)	**dropped, dropped**	(passive voice)

INDICATIVE MOOD

Pres.   I, we, you, they **drop**

he, she, it **drops**

I am dropped
we, you, they **are dropped**
he, she, it **is dropped**

Pres.   I **am dropping**
Prog.   we, you, they **are dropping**
he, she, it **is dropping**

I am being dropped
we, you, they **are being dropped**
he, she, it **is being dropped**

Pres.   I, we, you, they **do drop**
Int.   he, she, it **does drop**

I, we, you, they **do get dropped**
he, she, it **does get dropped**

Fut.   I, he, she, it,
we, you, they **will drop**

I, he, she, it,
we, you, they **will be dropped**

Past   I, he, she, it,
we, you, they **dropped**

I, he, she, it **was dropped**
we, you, they **were dropped**

Past   I, he, she, it **was dropping**
Prog.   we, you, they **were dropping**

I, he, she, it **was being dropped**
we, you, they **were being dropped**

Past   I, he, she, it,
Int.   we, you, they **did drop**

I, he, she, it,
we, you, they **did get dropped**

Pres.   I, we, you, they **have dropped**
Perf.   he, she, it **has dropped**

I, we, you, they **have been dropped**
he, she, it **has been dropped**

Past   I, he, she, it,
Perf.   we, you, they **had dropped**

I, he, she, it,
we, you, they **had been dropped**

Fut.   I, he, she, it, we, you, they
Perf.   **will have dropped**

I, he, she, it, we, you, they
will have been dropped

IMPERATIVE MOOD

drop   **be dropped**

SUBJUNCTIVE MOOD

Pres.   if I, he, she, it,
we, you, they **drop**

if I, he, she, it,
we, you, they **be dropped**

Past   if I, he, she, it,
we, you, they **dropped**

if I, he, she, it,
we, you, they **were dropped**

Fut.   if I, he, she, it,
we, you, they **should drop**

if I, he, she, it,
we, you, they **should be dropped**

Intransitive and transitive.

We are dropping that client from our list.
The boys were dropped off at the airport.

PRINCIPAL PARTS: **dwells, dwelling, dwelt/dwelled, dwelt/dwelled**

D

INDICATIVE MOOD

Pres.   I, we, you, they **dwell**

he, she, it **dwells**

Pres.   I **am dwelling**
Prog.   we, you, they **are dwelling**
he, she, it **is dwelling**

Pres.   I, we, you, they **do dwell**
Int.   he, she, it **does dwell**

Fut.   I, he, she, it,
we, you, they **will dwell**

Past   I, he, she, it,
we, you, they **dwelt**

Past   I, he, she, it **was dwelling**
Prog.   we, you, they **were dwelling**

Past   I, he, she, it,
Int.   we, you, they **did dwell**

Pres.   I, we, you, they **have dwelt**
Perf.   he, she, it **has dwelt**

Past   I, he, she, it,
Perf.   we, you, they **had dwelt**

Fut.   I, he, she, it, we, you, they
Perf.   **will have dwelt**

IMPERATIVE MOOD

dwell

SUBJUNCTIVE MOOD

Pres.   if I, he, she, it,
we, you, they **dwell**

Past   if I, he, she, it,
we, you, they **dwelt**

Fut.   if I, he, she, it,
we, you, they **should dwell**

The past tense and past participle may be DWELT or DWELLED.

Who could possibly dwell in these shacks?
The problem was dwelt on in great detail.

dye
(active voice)

be dyed
(passive voice)

INDICATIVE MOOD

Pres.	I, we, you, they **dye**	I **am dyed** we, you, they **are dyed**
	he, she, it **dyes**	he, she, it **is dyed**
Pres. *Prog.*	I **am dyeing** we, you, they **are dyeing** he, she, it **is dyeing**	I **am being dyed** we, you, they **are being dyed** he, she, it **is being dyed**
Pres. *Int.*	I, we, you, they **do dye** he, she, it **does dye**	I, we, you, they **do get dyed** he, she, it **does get dyed**
Fut.	I, he, she, it, we, you, they **will dye**	I, he, she, it, we, you, they **will be dyed**
Past	I, he, she, it, we, you, they **dyed**	I, he, she, it **was dyed** we, you, they **were dyed**
Past *Prog.*	I, he, she, it **was dyeing** we, you, they **were dyeing**	I, he, she, it **was being dyed** we, you, they **were being dyed**
Past *Int.*	I, he, she, it, we, you, they **did dye**	I, he, she, it, we, you, they **did get dyed**
Pres. *Perf.*	I, we, you, they **have dyed** he, she, it **has dyed**	I, we, you, they **have been dyed** he, she, it **has been dyed**
Past *Perf.*	I, he, she, it, we, you, they **had dyed**	I, he, she, it, we, you, they **had been dyed**
Fut. *Perf.*	I, he, she, it, we, you, they **will have dyed**	I, he, she, it, we, you, they **will have been dyed**

IMPERATIVE MOOD

dye **be dyed**

SUBJUNCTIVE MOOD

Pres.	if I, he, she, it, we, you, they **dye**	if I, he, she, it, we, you, they **be dyed**
Past	if I, he, she, it, we, you, they **dyed**	if I, he, she, it, we, you, they **were dyed**
Fut.	if I, he, she, it, we, you, they **should dye**	if I, he, she, it, we, you, they **should be dyed**

Transitive and intransitive.

You are not dyeing those jeans another color.
Were those T-shirts dyed professionally?

earn
(active voice)

PRINCIPAL PARTS: **earns, earning, earned, earned**

be earned
(passive voice)

INDICATIVE MOOD

Pres.	I, we, you, they **earn** he, she, it **earns**	I **am earned** we, you, they **are earned** he, she, it **is earned**
Pres. *Prog.*	I **am earning** we, you, they **are earning** he, she, it **is earning**	I **am being earned** we, you, they **are being earned** he, she, it **is being earned**
Pres. *Int.*	I, we, you, they **do earn** he, she, it **does earn**	I, we, you, they **do get earned** he, she, it **does get earned**
Fut.	I, he, she, it, we, you, they **will earn**	I, he, she, it, we, you, they **will be earned**
Past	I, he, she, it, we, you, they **earned**	I, he, she, it **was earned** we, you, they **were earned**
Past *Prog.*	I, he, she, it **was earning** we, you, they **were earning**	I, he, she, it **was being earned** we, you, they **were being earned**
Past *Int.*	I, he, she, it, we, you, they **did earn**	I, he, she, it, we, you, they **did get earned**
Pres. *Perf.*	I, we, you, they **have earned** he, she, it **has earned**	I, we, you, they **have been earned** he, she, it **has been earned**
Past *Perf.*	I, he, she, it, we, you, they **had earned**	I, he, she, it, we, you, they **had been earned**
Fut. *Perf.*	I, he, she, it, we, you, they **will have earned**	I, he, she, it, we, you, they **will have been earned**

IMPERATIVE MOOD

earn   **be earned**

SUBJUNCTIVE MOOD

Pres.	if I, he, she, it, we, you, they **earn**	if I, he, she, it, we, you, they **be earned**
Past	if I, he, she, it, we, you, they **earned**	if I, he, she, it, we, you, they **were earned**
Fut.	if I, he, she, it, we, you, they **should earn**	if I, he, she, it, we, you, they **should be earned**

You can earn bonus points if you complete the work ahead of time.
Everything I have was earned by sweat and tears.

eat (active voice)	PRINCIPAL PARTS: eats, eating, ate, eaten	be eaten (passive voice)

INDICATIVE MOOD

Pres.	I, we, you, they **eat** he, she, it **eats**	I **am eaten** we, you, they **are eaten** he, she, it **is eaten**
Pres. *Prog.*	I **am eating** we, you, they **are eating** he, she, it **is eating**	I **am being eaten** we, you, they **are being eaten** he, she, it **is being eaten**
Pres. *Int.*	I, we, you, they **do eat** he, she, it **does eat**	I, we, you, they **do get eaten** he, she, it **does get eaten**
Fut.	I, he, she, it, we, you, they **will eat**	I, he, she, it, we, you, they **will be eaten**
Past	I, he, she, it, we, you, they **ate**	I, he, she, it **was eaten** we, you, they **were eaten**
Past *Prog.*	I, he, she, it **was eating** we, you, they **were eating**	I, he, she, it **was being eaten** we, you, they **were being eaten**
Past *Int.*	I, he, she, it, we, you, they **did eat**	I, he, she, it, we, you, they **did get eaten**
Pres. *Perf.*	I, we, you, they **have eaten** he, she, it **has eaten**	I, we, you, they **have been eaten** he, she, it **has been eaten**
Past *Perf.*	I, he, she, it, we, you, they **had eaten**	I, he, she, it, we, you, they **had been eaten**
Fut. *Perf.*	I, he, she, it, we, you, they **will have eaten**	I, he, she, it, we, you, they **will have been eaten**

IMPERATIVE MOOD

eat　　　　　　　　　　　　　**be eaten**

SUBJUNCTIVE MOOD

Pres.	if I, he, she, it, we, you, they **eat**	if I, he, she, it, we, you, they **be eaten**
Past	if I, he, she, it, we, you, they **ate**	if I, he, she, it, we, you, they **were eaten**
Fut.	if I, he, she, it, we, you, they **should eat**	if I, he, she, it, we, you, they **should be eaten**

Transitive and intransitive.

When do you plan to eat?
I'm sorry, but we already ate dinner.
Have all the cookies been eaten?

echo
(active voice)

be echoed
(passive voice)

E

INDICATIVE MOOD

Pres.	I, we, you, they **echo**	I **am echoed**
		we, you, they **are echoed**
	he, she, it **echoes**	he, she, it **is echoed**
Pres.	I **am echoing**	I **am being echoed**
Prog.	we, you, they **are echoing**	we, you, they **are being echoed**
	he, she, it **is echoing**	he, she, it **is being echoed**
Pres.	I, we, you, they **do echo**	I, we, you, they **do get echoed**
Int.	he, she, it **does echo**	he, she, it **does get echoed**
Fut.	I, he, she, it,	I, he, she, it,
	we, you, they **will echo**	we, you, they **will be echoed**
Past	I, he, she, it,	I, he, she, it **was echoed**
	we, you, they **echoed**	we, you, they **were echoed**
Past	I, he, she, it **was echoing**	I, he, she, it **was being echoed**
Prog.	we, you, they **were echoing**	we, you, they **were being echoed**
Past	I, he, she, it,	I, he, she, it,
Int.	we, you, they **did echo**	we, you, they **did get echoed**
Pres.	I, we, you, they **have echoed**	I, we, you, they **have been echoed**
Perf.	he, she, it **has echoed**	he, she, it **has been echoed**
Past	I, he, she, it,	I, he, she, it,
Perf.	we, you, they **had echoed**	we, you, they **had been echoed**
Fut.	I, he, she, it, we, you, they	I, he, she, it, we, you, they
Perf.	**will have echoed**	**will have been echoed**

IMPERATIVE MOOD

echo

be echoed

SUBJUNCTIVE MOOD

Pres.	if I, he, she, it,	if I, he, she, it,
	we, you, they **echo**	we, you, they **be echoed**
Past	if I, he, she, it,	if I, he, she, it,
	we, you, they **echoed**	we, you, they **were echoed**
Fut.	if I, he, she, it,	if I, he, she, it,
	we, you, they **should echo**	we, you, they **should be echoed**

Transitive and intransitive.

The speaker is echoing our sentiments completely.
We echoed the opinion of our professor.
My thoughts were echoed by others at the conference.

e-mail
(active voice)

be e-mailed
(passive voice)

INDICATIVE MOOD

Pres.	I, we, you, they **e-mail**	I **am e-mailed** we, you, they **are e-mailed**
	he, she, it **e-mails**	he, she, it **is e-mailed**
Pres. *Prog.*	I **am e-mailing** we, you, they **are e-mailing** he, she, it **is e-mailing**	I **am being e-mailed** we, you, they **are being e-mailed** he, she, it **is being e-mailed**
Pres. *Int.*	I, we, you, they **do e-mail** he, she, it **does e-mail**	I, we, you, they **do get e-mailed** he, she, it **does get e-mailed**
Fut.	I, he, she, it, we, you, they **will e-mail**	I, he, she, it, we, you, they **will be e-mailed**
Past	I, he, she, it, we, you, they **e-mailed**	I, he, she, it **was e-mailed** we, you, they **were e-mailed**
Past *Prog.*	I, he, she, it **was e-mailing** we, you, they **were e-mailing**	I, he, she, it **was being e-mailed** we, you, they **were being e-mailed**
Past *Int.*	I, he, she, it, we, you, they **did e-mail**	I, he, she, it, we, you, they **did get e-mailed**
Pres. *Perf.*	I, we, you, they **have e-mailed** he, she, it **has e-mailed**	I, we, you, they **have been e-mailed** he, she, it **has been e-mailed**
Past *Perf.*	I, he, she, it, we, you, they **had e-mailed**	I, he, she, it, we, you, they **had been e-mailed**
Fut. *Perf.*	I, he, she, it, we, you, they **will have e-mailed**	I, he, she, it, we, you, they **will have been e-mailed**

IMPERATIVE MOOD

e-mail   **be e-mailed**

SUBJUNCTIVE MOOD

Pres.	if I, he, she, it, we, you, they **e-mail**	if I, he, she, it, we, you, they **be e-mailed**
Past	if I, he, she, it, we, you, they **e-mailed**	if I, he, she, it, we, you, they **were e-mailed**
Fut.	if I, he, she, it, we, you, they **should e-mail**	if I, he, she, it, we, you, they **should be e-mailed**

We can e-mail each other to confirm our arrivals.
The proposal was e-mailed to you yesterday.

embarrass
(active voice)

PRINCIPAL PARTS: embarrasses, embarrassing, embarrassed, embarrassed

be embarrassed
(passive voice)

INDICATIVE MOOD

Pres.	I, we, you, they **embarrass**	I **am embarrassed**
		we, you, they **are embarrassed**
	he, she, it **embarrasses**	he, she, it **is embarrassed**
Pres.	I **am embarrassing**	I **am being embarrassed**
Prog.	we, you, they **are embarrassing**	we, you, they **are being embarrassed**
	he, she, it **is embarrassing**	he, she, it **is being embarrassed**
Pres.	I, we, you, they **do embarrass**	I, we, you, they **do get embarrassed**
Int.	he, she, it **does embarrass**	he, she, it **does get embarrassed**
Fut.	I, he, she, it,	I, he, she, it,
	we, you, they **will embarrass**	we, you, they **will be embarrassed**
Past	I, he, she, it,	I, he, she, it **was embarrassed**
	we, you, they **embarrassed**	we, you, they **were embarrassed**
Past	I, he, she, it **was embarrassing**	I, he, she, it **was being embarrassed**
Prog.	we, you, they **were embarrassing**	we, you, they **were being embarrassed**
Past	I, he, she, it,	I, he, she, it,
Int.	we, you, they **did embarrass**	we, you, they **did get embarrassed**
Pres.	I, we, you, they **have embarrassed**	I, we, you, they **have been embarrassed**
Perf.	he, she, it **has embarrassed**	he, she, it **has been embarrassed**
Past	I, he, she, it,	I, he, she, it, we, you, they
Perf.	we, you, they **had embarrassed**	**had been embarrassed**
Fut.	I, he, she, it, we, you, they	I, he, she, it, we, you, they
Perf.	**will have embarrassed**	**will have been embarrassed**

IMPERATIVE MOOD

embarrass　　　　　　　　　　**be embarrassed**

SUBJUNCTIVE MOOD

Pres.	if I, he, she, it,	if I, he, she, it,
	we, you, they **embarrass**	we, you, they **be embarrassed**
Past	if I, he, she, it,	if I, he, she, it,
	we, you, they **embarrassed**	we, you, they **were embarrassed**
Fut.	if I, he, she, it,	if I, he, she, it,
	we, you, they **should embarrass**	we, you, they **should be embarrassed**

That performance embarrassed me and my family.
Have you ever been embarrassed by your actions?

end
(active voice)

be ended
(passive voice)

INDICATIVE MOOD

Pres.	I, we, you, they **end**	I **am ended**
		we, you, they **are ended**
	he, she, it **ends**	he, she, it **is ended**
Pres.	I **am ending**	I **am being ended**
Prog.	we, you, they **are ending**	we, you, they **are being ended**
	he, she, it **is ending**	he, she, it **is being ended**
Pres.	I, we, you, they **do end**	I, we, you, they **do get ended**
Int.	he, she, it **does end**	he, she, it **does get ended**
Fut.	I, he, she, it, we, you, they **will end**	I, he, she, it, we, you, they **will be ended**
Past	I, he, she, it, we, you, they **ended**	I, he, she, it **was ended** we, you, they **were ended**
Past	I, he, she, it **was ending**	I, he, she, it **was being ended**
Prog.	we, you, they **were ending**	we, you, they **were being ended**
Past	I, he, she, it, we, you, they **did end**	I, he, she, it, we, you, they **did get ended**
Int.		
Pres.	I, we, you, they **have ended**	I, we, you, they **have been ended**
Perf.	he, she, it **has ended**	he, she, it **has been ended**
Past	I, he, she, it, we, you, they **had ended**	I, he, she, it, we, you, they **had been ended**
Perf.		
Fut.	I, he, she, it, we, you, they **will have ended**	I, he, she, it, we, you, they **will have been ended**
Perf.		

IMPERATIVE MOOD

end **be ended**

SUBJUNCTIVE MOOD

Pres.	if I, he, she, it, we, you, they **end**	if I, he, she, it, we, you, they **be ended**
Past	if I, he, she, it, we, you, they **ended**	if I, he, she, it, we, you, they **were ended**
Fut.	if I, he, she, it, we, you, they **should end**	if I, he, she, it, we, you, they **should be ended**

Transitive and intransitive.

You should always end your speech with an anecdote.
The class was ended by the bell.

enjoy
(active voice)

be enjoyed
(passive voice)

INDICATIVE MOOD

Pres.	I, we, you, they **enjoy**	I **am enjoyed**
		we, you, they **are enjoyed**
	he, she, it **enjoys**	he, she, it **is enjoyed**
Pres.	I **am enjoying**	I **am being enjoyed**
Prog.	we, you, they **are enjoying**	we, you, they **are being enjoyed**
	he, she, it **is enjoying**	he, she, it **is being enjoyed**
Pres.	I, we, you, they **do enjoy**	I, we, you, they **do get enjoyed**
Int.	he, she, it **does enjoy**	he, she, it **does get enjoyed**
Fut.	I, he, she, it,	I, he, she, it,
	we, you, they **will enjoy**	we, you, they **will be enjoyed**
Past	I, he, she, it,	I, he, she, it **was enjoyed**
	we, you, they **enjoyed**	we, you, they **were enjoyed**
Past	I, he, she, it **was enjoying**	I, he, she, it **was being enjoyed**
Prog.	we, you, they **were enjoying**	we, you, they **were being enjoyed**
Past	I, he, she, it,	I, he, she, it,
Int.	we, you, they **did enjoy**	we, you, they **did get enjoyed**
Pres.	I, we, you, they **have enjoyed**	I, we, you, they **have been enjoyed**
Perf.	he, she, it **has enjoyed**	he, she, it **has been enjoyed**
Past	I, he, she, it,	I, he, she, it,
Perf.	we, you, they **had enjoyed**	we, you, they **had been enjoyed**
Fut.	I, he, she, it, we, you, they	I, he, she, it, we, you, they
Perf.	**will have enjoyed**	**will have been enjoyed**

IMPERATIVE MOOD

enjoy　　　　　　　　　　**be enjoyed**

SUBJUNCTIVE MOOD

Pres.	if I, he, she, it,	if I, he, she, it,
	we, you, they **enjoy**	we, you, they **be enjoyed**
Past	if I, he, she, it,	if I, he, she, it,
	we, you, they **enjoyed**	we, you, they **were enjoyed**
Fut.	if I, he, she, it,	if I, he, she, it,
	we, you, they **should enjoy**	we, you, they **should be enjoyed**

Transitive and intransitive.

We all enjoyed your performance.
A good wine is to be enjoyed.

enter (active voice)	PRINCIPAL PARTS: **enters, entering, entered, entered**	be entered (passive voice)

INDICATIVE MOOD

Pres.	I, we, you, they **enter**	I **am entered** we, you, they **are entered**
	he, she, it **enters**	he, she, it **is entered**
Pres. *Prog.*	I **am entering** we, you, they **are entering** he, she, it **is entering**	I **am being entered** we, you, they **are being entered** he, she, it **is being entered**
Pres. *Int.*	I, we, you, they **do enter** he, she, it **does enter**	I, we, you, they **do get entered** he, she, it **does get entered**
Fut.	I, he, she, it, we, you, they **will enter**	I, he, she, it, we, you, they **will be entered**
Past	I, he, she, it, we, you, they **entered**	I, he, she, it **was entered** we, you, they **were entered**
Past *Prog.*	I, he, she, it **was entering** we, you, they **were entering**	I, he, she, it **was being entered** we, you, they **were being entered**
Past *Int.*	I, he, she, it, we, you, they **did enter**	I, he, she, it, we, you, they **did get entered**
Pres. *Perf.*	I, we, you, they **have entered** he, she, it **has entered**	I, we, you, they **have been entered** he, she, it **has been entered**
Past *Perf.*	I, he, she, it, we, you, they **had entered**	I, he, she, it, we, you, they **had been entered**
Fut. *Perf.*	I, he, she, it, we, you, they **will have entered**	I, he, she, it, we, you, they **will have been entered**

IMPERATIVE MOOD

enter	**be entered**

SUBJUNCTIVE MOOD

Pres.	if I, he, she, it, we, you, they **enter**	if I, he, she, it, we, you, they **be entered**
Past	if I, he, she, it, we, you, they **entered**	if I, he, she, it, we, you, they **were entered**
Fut.	if I, he, she, it, we, you, they **should enter**	if I, he, she, it, we, you, they **should be entered**

Transitive and intransitive.

When they entered they removed their boots.
The building was entered by the firemen in search of the gas leak.

132

envelop
(active voice)

be enveloped
(passive voice)

INDICATIVE MOOD

Pres.	I, we, you, they **envelop**	I **am enveloped**
		we, you, they **are enveloped**
	he, she, it **envelops**	he, she, it **is enveloped**
Pres.	I **am enveloping**	I **am being enveloped**
Prog.	we, you, they **are enveloping**	we, you, they **are being enveloped**
	he, she, it **is enveloping**	he, she, it **is being enveloped**
Pres.	I, we, you, they **do envelop**	I, we, you, they **do get enveloped**
Int.	he, she, it **does envelop**	he, she, it **does get enveloped**
Fut.	I, he, she, it,	I, he, she, it,
	we, you, they **will envelop**	we, you, they **will be enveloped**
Past	I, he, she, it,	I, he, she, it **was enveloped**
	we, you, they **enveloped**	we, you, they **were enveloped**
Past	I, he, she, it **was enveloping**	I, he, she, it **was being enveloped**
Prog.	we, you, they **were enveloping**	we, you, they **were being enveloped**
Past	I, he, she, it,	I, he, she, it,
Int.	we, you, they **did envelop**	we, you, they **did get enveloped**
Pres.	I, we, you, they **have enveloped**	I, we, you, they **have been enveloped**
Perf.	he, she, it **has enveloped**	he, she, it **has been enveloped**
Past	I, he, she, it,	I, he, she, it,
Perf.	we, you, they **had enveloped**	we, you, they **had been enveloped**
Fut.	I, he, she, it, we, you, they	I, he, she, it, we, you, they
Perf.	**will have enveloped**	**will have been enveloped**

IMPERATIVE MOOD

envelop | **be enveloped**

SUBJUNCTIVE MOOD

Pres.	if I, he, she, it,	if I, he, she, it,
	we, you, they **envelop**	we, you, they **be enveloped**
Past	if I, he, she, it,	if I, he, she, it,
	we, you, they **enveloped**	we, you, they **were enveloped**
Fut.	if I, he, she, it,	if I, he, she, it,
	we, you, they **should envelop**	we, you, they **should be enveloped**

You will want to envelop your property with bushes.
They were enveloped by cheering admirers.

establish
(active voice)

be established
(passive voice)

INDICATIVE MOOD

Pres.	I, we, you, they **establish**	**I am established** we, you, they **are established**
	he, she, it **establishes**	he, she, it **is established**
Pres. *Prog.*	**I am establishing** we, you, they **are establishing** he, she, it **is establishing**	**I am being established** we, you, they **are being established** he, she, it **is being established**
Pres. *Int.*	I, we, you, they **do establish** he, she, it **does establish**	I, we, you, they **do get established** he, she, it **does get established**
Fut.	I, he, she, it, we, you, they **will establish**	I, he, she, it, we, you, they **will be established**
Past	I, he, she, it, we, you, they **established**	I, he, she, it **was established** we, you, they **were established**
Past *Prog.*	I, he, she, it **was establishing** we, you, they **were establishing**	I, he, she, it **was being established** we, you, they **were being established**
Past *Int.*	I, he, she, it, we, you, they **did establish**	I, he, she, it, we, you, they **did get established**
Pres. *Perf.*	I, we, you, they **have established** he, she, it **has established**	I, we, you, they **have been established** he, she, it **has been established**
Past *Perf.*	I, he, she, it, we, you, they **had established**	I, he, she, it, we, you, they **had been established**
Fut. *Perf.*	I, he, she, it, we, you, they **will have established**	I, he, she, it, we, you, they **will have been established**

IMPERATIVE MOOD

establish   **be established**

SUBJUNCTIVE MOOD

Pres.	if I, he, she, it, we, you, they **establish**	if I, he, she, it, we, you, they **be established**
Past	if I, he, she, it, we, you, they **established**	if I, he, she, it, we, you, they **were established**
Fut.	if I, he, she, it, we, you, they **should establish**	if I, he, she, it, we, you, they **should be established**

We established our claims based on the contract.
When was this institution first established?

excuse
(active voice)

be excused
(passive voice)

INDICATIVE MOOD

Pres.	I, we, you, they **excuse**	I **am excused**
		we, you, they **are excused**
	he, she, it **excuses**	he, she, it **is excused**
Pres. *Prog.*	I **am excusing**	I **am being excused**
	we, you, they **are excusing**	we, you, they **are being excused**
	he, she, it **is excusing**	he, she, it **is being excused**
Pres. *Int.*	I, we, you, they **do excuse**	I, we, you, they **do get excused**
	he, she, it **does excuse**	he, she, it **does get excused**
Fut.	I, he, she, it,	I, he, she, it,
	we, you, they **will excuse**	we, you, they **will be excused**
Past	I, he, she, it,	I, he, she, it **was excused**
	we, you, they **excused**	we, you, they **were excused**
Past *Prog.*	I, he, she, it **was excusing**	I, he, she, it **was being excused**
	we, you, they **were excusing**	we, you, they **were being excused**
Past *Int.*	I, he, she, it,	I, he, she, it,
	we, you, they **did excuse**	we, you, they **did get excused**
Pres. *Perf.*	I, we, you, they **have excused**	I, we, you, they **have been excused**
	he, she, it **has excused**	he, she, it **has been excused**
Past *Perf.*	I, he, she, it,	I, he, she, it,
	we, you, they **had excused**	we, you, they **had been excused**
Fut. *Perf.*	I, he, she, it, we, you, they	I, he, she, it, we, you, they
	will have excused	**will have been excused**

IMPERATIVE MOOD

excuse   **be excused**

SUBJUNCTIVE MOOD

Pres.	if I, he, she, it,	if I, he, she, it,
	we, you, they **excuse**	we, you, they **be excused**
Past	if I, he, she, it,	if I, he, she, it,
	we, you, they **excused**	we, you, they **were excused**
Fut.	if I, he, she, it,	if I, he, she, it,
	we, you, they **should excuse**	we, you, they **should be excused**

We are excusing his mistakes because of his inexperience.
May I please be excused from the table?

INDICATIVE MOOD

Pres.   I, we, you, they **exist**

            he, she, it **exists**

Pres.   **I am existing**
Prog.   we, you, they **are existing**
            he, she, it **is existing**

Pres.   I, we, you, they **do exist**
Int.   he, she, it **does exist**

Fut.   I, he, she, it,
            we, you, they **will exist**

Past   I, he, she, it,
            we, you, they **existed**

Past   I, he, she, it **was existing**
Prog.   we, you, they **were existing**

Past   I, he, she, it,
Int.   we, you, they **did exist**

Pres.   I, we, you, they **have existed**
Perf.   he, she, it **has existed**

Past   I, he, she, it,
Perf.   we, you, they **had existed**

Fut.   I, he, she, it, we, you, they
Perf.   **will have existed**

IMPERATIVE MOOD

exist

SUBJUNCTIVE MOOD

Pres.   if I, he, she, it,
            we, you, they **exist**

Past   if I, he, she, it,
            we, you, they **existed**

Fut.   if I, he, she, it,
            we, you, they **should exist**

Our business exists to make loans to future homeowners.
These difficulties have existed for several years.

PRINCIPAL PARTS: **expects, expecting, expected, expected**

INDICATIVE MOOD

Pres.	I, we, you, they **expect**	**I am expected** we, you, they **are expected**
	he, she, it **expects**	he, she, it **is expected**
Pres. *Prog.*	**I am expecting** we, you, they **are expecting** he, she, it **is expecting**	**I am being expected** we, you, they **are being expected** he, she, it **is being expected**
Pres. *Int.*	I, we, you, they **do expect** he, she, it **does expect**	I, we, you, they **do get expected** he, she, it **does get expected**
Fut.	I, he, she, it, we, you, they **will expect**	I, he, she, it, we, you, they **will be expected**
Past	I, he, she, it, we, you, they **expected**	I, he, she, it **was expected** we, you, they **were expected**
Past *Prog.*	I, he, she, it **was expecting** we, you, they **were expecting**	I, he, she, it **was being expected** we, you, they **were being expected**
Past *Int.*	I, he, she, it, we, you, they **did expect**	I, he, she, it, we, you, they **did get expected**
Pres. *Perf.*	I, we, you, they **have expected** he, she, it **has expected**	I, we, you, they **have been expected** he, she, it **has been expected**
Past *Perf.*	I, he, she, it, we, you, they **had expected**	I, he, she, it, we, you, they **had been expected**
Fut. *Perf.*	I, he, she, it, we, you, they **will have expected**	I, he, she, it, we, you, they **will have been expected**

IMPERATIVE MOOD

expect	**be expected**

SUBJUNCTIVE MOOD

Pres.	if I, he, she, it, we, you, they **expect**	if I, he, she, it, we, you, they **be expected**
Past	if I, he, she, it, we, you, they **expected**	if I, he, she, it, we, you, they **were expected**
Fut.	if I, he, she, it, we, you, they **should expect**	if I, he, she, it, we, you, they **should be expected**

Transitive and intransitive. As an intransitive verb used with the progressive tenses, this verb means to "be pregnant" or "looking forward to the birth of a child."

I expected you to be on time.
When is the baby expected?

explain
(active voice)

PRINCIPAL PARTS: explains, explaining, explained, explained

be explained
(passive voice)

INDICATIVE MOOD

Pres.	I, we, you, they **explain**	I **am explained**
		we, you, they **are explained**
	he, she, it **explains**	he, she, it **is explained**
Pres.	I **am explaining**	I **am being explained**
Prog.	we, you, they **are explaining**	we, you, they **are being explained**
	he, she, it **is explaining**	he, she, it **is being explained**
Pres.	I, we, you, they **do explain**	I, we, you, they **do get explained**
Int.	he, she, it **does explain**	he, she, it **does get explained**
Fut.	I, he, she, it,	I, he, she, it,
	we, you, they **will explain**	we, you, they **will be explained**
Past	I, he, she, it,	I, he, she, it **was explained**
	we, you, they **explained**	we, you, they **were explained**
Past	I, he, she, it **was explaining**	I, he, she, it **was being explained**
Prog.	we, you, they **were explaining**	we, you, they **were being explained**
Past	I, he, she, it,	I, he, she, it,
Int.	we, you, they **did explain**	we, you, they **did get explained**
Pres.	I, we, you, they **have explained**	I, we, you, they **have been explained**
Perf.	he, she, it **has explained**	he, she, it **has been explained**
Past	I, he, she, it,	I, he, she, it,
Perf.	we, you, they **had explained**	we, you, they **had been explained**
Fut.	I, he, she, it, we, you, they	I, he, she, it, we, you, they
Perf.	**will have explained**	**will have been explained**

IMPERATIVE MOOD

explain	**be explained**

SUBJUNCTIVE MOOD

Pres.	if I, he, she, it,	if I, he, she, it,
	we, you, they **explain**	we, you, they **be explained**
Past	if I, he, she, it,	if I, he, she, it,
	we, you, they **explained**	we, you, they **were explained**
Fut.	if I, he, she, it,	if I, he, she, it,
	we, you, they **should explain**	we, you, they **should be explained**

Transitive and intransitive.

You must explain yourself clearly and concisely.
All of this was explained when you first came onboard the ship.

express
(active voice)

be expressed
(passive voice)

INDICATIVE MOOD

Pres.   I, we, you, they **express**

      he, she, it **expresses**

I **am expressed**
we, you, they **are expressed**
he, she, it **is expressed**

Pres.   I **am expressing**
Prog.   we, you, they **are expressing**
      he, she, it **is expressing**

I **am being expressed**
we, you, they **are being expressed**
he, she, it **is being expressed**

Pres.   I, we, you, they **do express**
Int.   he, she, it **does express**

I, we, you, they **do get expressed**
he, she, it **does get expressed**

Fut.   I, he, she, it,
      we, you, they **will express**

I, he, she, it,
we, you, they **will be expressed**

Past   I, he, she, it,
      we, you, they **expressed**

I, he, she, it **was expressed**
we, you, they **were expressed**

Past   I, he, she, it **was expressing**
Prog.   we, you, they **were expressing**

I, he, she, it **was being expressed**
we, you, they **were being expressed**

Past   I, he, she, it,
Int.   we, you, they **did express**

I, he, she, it,
we, you, they **did get expressed**

Pres.   I, we, you, they **have expressed**
Perf.   he, she, it **has expressed**

I, we, you, they **have been expressed**
he, she, it **has been expressed**

Past   I, he, she, it,
Perf.   we, you, they **had expressed**

I, he, she, it,
we, you, they **had been expressed**

Fut.   I, he, she, it, we, you, they
Perf.   **will have expressed**

I, he, she, it, we, you, they
will have been expressed

IMPERATIVE MOOD

      express

be expressed

SUBJUNCTIVE MOOD

Pres.   if I, he, she, it,
      we, you, they **express**

if I, he, she, it,
we, you, they **be expressed**

Past   if I, he, she, it,
      we, you, they **expressed**

if I, he, she, it,
we, you, they **were expressed**

Fut.   if I, he, she, it,
      we, you, they **should express**

if I, he, she, it,
we, you, they **should be expressed**

We would like to express our gratitude for your hospitality.
All of our concerns were expressed to the landowner in a letter.

extend
(active voice)

be extended
(passive voice)

INDICATIVE MOOD

Pres.	I, we, you, they **extend**	I **am extended** we, you, they **are extended**
	he, she, it **extends**	he, she, it **is extended**
Pres. *Prog.*	I **am extending** we, you, they **are extending** he, she, it **is extending**	I **am being extended** we, you, they **are being extended** he, she, it **is being extended**
Pres. *Int.*	I, we, you, they **do extend** he, she, it **does extend**	I, we, you, they **do get extended** he, she, it **does get extended**
Fut.	I, he, she, it, we, you, they **will extend**	I, he, she, it, we, you, they **will be extended**
Past	I, he, she, it, we, you, they **extended**	I, he, she, it **was extended** we, you, they **were extended**
Past *Prog.*	I, he, she, it **was extending** we, you, they **were extending**	I, he, she, it **was being extended** we, you, they **were being extended**
Past *Int.*	I, he, she, it, we, you, they **did extend**	I, he, she, it, we, you, they **did get extended**
Pres. *Perf.*	I, we, you, they **have extended** he, she, it **has extended**	I, we, you, they **have been extended** he, she, it **has been extended**
Past *Perf.*	I, he, she, it, we, you, they **had extended**	I, he, she, it, we, you, they **had been extended**
Fut. *Perf.*	I, he, she, it, we, you, they **will have extended**	I, he, she, it, we, you, they **will have been extended**

IMPERATIVE MOOD

extend **be extended**

SUBJUNCTIVE MOOD

Pres.	if I, he, she, it, we, you, they **extend**	if I, he, she, it, we, you, they **be extended**
Past	if I, he, she, it, we, you, they **extended**	if I, he, she, it, we, you, they **were extended**
Fut.	if I, he, she, it, we, you, they **should extend**	if I, he, she, it, we, you, they **should be extended**

Transitive and intransitive.

You should extend an official invitation to all the parents.
The wings of the bird were extended to their full length.

140

face
(active voice)

be faced
(passive voice)

F

INDICATIVE MOOD

Pres.	I, we, you, they **face**	I **am faced**
		we, you, they **are faced**
	he, she, it **faces**	he, she, it **is faced**
Pres.	I **am facing**	I **am being faced**
Prog.	we, you, they **are facing**	we, you, they **are being faced**
	he, she, it **is facing**	he, she, it **is being faced**
Pres.	I, we, you, they **do face**	I, we, you, they **do get faced**
Int.	he, she, it **does face**	he, she, it **does get faced**
Fut.	I, he, she, it,	I, he, she, it,
	we, you, they **will face**	we, you, they **will be faced**
Past	I, he, she, it,	I, he, she, it **was faced**
	we, you, they **faced**	we, you, they **were faced**
Past	I, he, she, it **was facing**	I, he, she, it **was being faced**
Prog.	we, you, they **were facing**	we, you, they **were being faced**
Past	I, he, she, it,	I, he, she, it,
Int.	we, you, they **did face**	we, you, they **did get faced**
Pres.	I, we, you, they **have faced**	I, we, you, they **have been faced**
Perf.	he, she, it **has faced**	he, she, it **has been faced**
Past	I, he, she, it,	I, he, she, it,
Perf.	we, you, they **had faced**	we, you, they **had been faced**
Fut.	I, he, she, it, we, you, they	I, he, she, it, we, you, they
Perf.	**will have faced**	**will have been faced**

IMPERATIVE MOOD

face   **be faced**

SUBJUNCTIVE MOOD

Pres.	if I, he, she, it,	if I, he, she, it,
	we, you, they **face**	we, you, they **be faced**
Past	if I, he, she, it,	if I, he, she, it,
	we, you, they **faced**	we, you, they **were faced**
Fut.	if I, he, she, it,	if I, he, she, it,
	we, you, they **should face**	we, you, they **should be faced**

Transitive and intransitive.

You will be facing your opponent this afternoon.
The misbehaving children were faced to the wall.

141

fail
(active voice)

be failed
(passive voice)

INDICATIVE MOOD

Pres.	I, we, you, they **fail**	I **am failed**
		we, you, they **are failed**
	he, she, it **fails**	he, she, it **is failed**
Pres.	I **am failing**	I **am being failed**
Prog.	we, you, they **are failing**	we, you, they **are being failed**
	he, she, it **is failing**	he, she, it **is being failed**
Pres.	I, we, you, they **do fail**	I, we, you, they **do get failed**
Int.	he, she, it **does fail**	he, she, it **does get failed**
Fut.	I, he, she, it,	I, he, she, it,
	we, you, they **will fail**	we, you, they **will be failed**
Past	I, he, she, it,	I, he, she, it **was failed**
	we, you, they **failed**	we, you, they **were failed**
Past	I, he, she, it **was failing**	I, he, she, it **was being failed**
Prog.	we, you, they **were failing**	we, you, they **were being failed**
Past	I, he, she, it,	I, he, she, it,
Int.	we, you, they **did fail**	we, you, they **did get failed**
Pres.	I, we, you, they **have failed**	I, we, you, they **have been failed**
Perf.	he, she, it **has failed**	he, she, it **has been failed**
Past	I, he, she, it,	I, he, she, it,
Perf.	we, you, they **had failed**	we, you, they **had been failed**
Fut.	I, he, she, it, we, you, they	I, he, she, it, we, you, they
Perf.	**will have failed**	**will have been failed**

IMPERATIVE MOOD

fail | **be failed**

SUBJUNCTIVE MOOD

Pres.	if I, he, she, it,	if I, he, she, it,
	we, you, they **fail**	we, you, they **be failed**
Past	if I, he, she, it,	if I, he, she, it,
	we, you, they **failed**	we, you, they **were failed**
Fut.	if I, he, she, it,	if I, he, she, it,
	we, you, they **should fail**	we, you, they **should be failed**

Intransitive and transitive.

We must not fail in our primary mission.
The test was failed by over half the class.

PRINCIPAL PARTS: **falls, falling, fell, fallen**

INDICATIVE MOOD

Pres. I, we, you, they **fall**

he, she, it **falls**

Pres. I **am falling**
Prog. we, you, they **are falling**
he, she, it **is falling**

Pres. I, we, you, they **do fall**
Int. he, she, it **does fall**

Fut. I, he, she, it,
we, you, they **will fall**

Past I, he, she, it,
we, you, they **fell**

Past I, he, she, it **was falling**
Prog. we, you, they **were falling**

Past I, he, she, it,
Int. we, you, they **did fall**

Pres. I, we, you, they **have fallen**
Perf. he, she, it **has fallen**

Past I, he, she, it,
Perf. we, you, they **had fallen**

Fut. I, he, she, it, we, you, they
Perf. **will have fallen**

IMPERATIVE MOOD

fall

SUBJUNCTIVE MOOD

Pres. if I, he, she, it,
we, you, they **fall**

Past if I, he, she, it,
we, you, they **fell**

Fut. if I, he, she, it,
we, you, they **should fall**

Intransitive. In the meaning of to "fell a tree," this verb can be transitive.

It is very easy to fall into a trap.
The rider fell from his bicycle on the steep mountain.
Rain had fallen all day and all night.

PRINCIPAL PARTS: **faxes, faxing, faxed, faxed**

INDICATIVE MOOD

Pres.	I, we, you, they **fax**	I **am faxed**
		we, you, they **are faxed**
	he, she, it **faxes**	he, she, it **is faxed**
Pres.	I **am faxing**	I **am being faxed**
Prog.	we, you, they **are faxing**	we, you, they **are being faxed**
	he, she, it **is faxing**	he, she, it **is being faxed**
Pres.	I, we, you, they **do fax**	I, we, you, they **do get faxed**
Int.	he, she, it **does fax**	he, she, it **does get faxed**
Fut.	I, he, she, it,	I, he, she, it,
	we, you, they **will fax**	we, you, they **will be faxed**
Past	I, he, she, it,	I, he, she, it **was faxed**
	we, you, they **faxed**	we, you, they **were faxed**
Past	I, he, she, it **was faxing**	I, he, she, it **was being faxed**
Prog.	we, you, they **were faxing**	we, you, they **were being faxed**
Past	I, he, she, it,	I, he, she, it,
Int.	we, you, they **did fax**	we, you, they **did get faxed**
Pres.	I, we, you, they **have faxed**	I, we, you, they **have been faxed**
Perf.	he, she, it **has faxed**	he, she, it **has been faxed**
Past	I, he, she, it,	I, he, she, it,
Perf.	we, you, they **had faxed**	we, you, they **had been faxed**
Fut.	I, he, she, it, we, you, they	I, he, she, it, we, you, they
Perf.	**will have faxed**	**will have been faxed**

IMPERATIVE MOOD

fax   **be faxed**

SUBJUNCTIVE MOOD

Pres.	if I, he, she, it,	if I, he, she, it,
	we, you, they **fax**	we, you, they **be faxed**
Past	if I, he, she, it,	if I, he, she, it,
	we, you, they **faxed**	we, you, they **were faxed**
Fut.	if I, he, she, it,	if I, he, she, it,
	we, you, they **should fax**	we, you, they **should be faxed**

Transitive and intransitive.

Is it possible to fax those documents to me today?
The contracts were faxed this morning.

feed
(active voice)

be fed
(passive voice)

INDICATIVE MOOD

Pres.	I, we, you, they **feed**	I **am fed**
		we, you, they **are fed**
	he, she, it **feeds**	he, she, it **is fed**
Pres.	I **am feeding**	I **am being fed**
Prog.	we, you, they **are feeding**	we, you, they **are being fed**
	he, she, it **is feeding**	he, she, it **is being fed**
Pres.	I, we, you, they **do feed**	I, we, you, they **do get fed**
Int.	he, she, it **does feed**	he, she, it **does get fed**
Fut.	I, he, she, it,	I, he, she, it,
	we, you, they **will feed**	we, you, they **will be fed**
Past	I, he, she, it,	I, he, she, it **was fed**
	we, you, they **fed**	we, you, they **were fed**
Past	I, he, she, it **was feeding**	I, he, she, it **was being fed**
Prog.	we, you, they **were feeding**	we, you, they **were being fed**
Past	I, he, she, it,	I, he, she, it,
Int.	we, you, they **did feed**	we, you, they **did get fed**
Pres.	I, we, you, they **have fed**	I, we, you, they **have been fed**
Perf.	he, she, it **has fed**	he, she, it **has been fed**
Past	I, he, she, it,	I, he, she, it,
Perf.	we, you, they **had fed**	we, you, they **had been fed**
Fut.	I, he, she, it, we, you, they	I, he, she, it, we, you, they
Perf.	**will have fed**	**will have been fed**

F

IMPERATIVE MOOD

feed   **be fed**

SUBJUNCTIVE MOOD

Pres.	if I, he, she, it,	if I, he, she, it,
	we, you, they **feed**	we, you, they **be fed**
Past	if I, he, she, it,	if I, he, she, it,
	we, you, they **fed**	we, you, they **were fed**
Fut.	if I, he, she, it,	if I, he, she, it,
	we, you, they **should feed**	we, you, they **should be fed**

Transitive and intransitive.

We will be feeding ten hungry teenagers tonight at our house.
The mission fed hundreds of poor each day.
They all appeared well dressed and well fed.

INDICATIVE MOOD

Pres.	I, we, you, they **feel**	I **am felt**
		we, you, they **are felt**
	he, she, it **feels**	he, she, it **is felt**
Pres.	I **am feeling**	I **am being felt**
Prog.	we, you, they **are feeling**	we, you, they **are being felt**
	he, she, it **is feeling**	he, she, it **is being felt**
Pres.	I, we, you, they **do feel**	I, we, you, they **do get felt**
Int.	he, she, it **does feel**	he, she, it **does get felt**
Fut.	I, he, she, it,	I, he, she, it,
	we, you, they **will feel**	we, you, they **will be felt**
Past	I, he, she, it,	I, he, she, it **was felt**
	we, you, they **felt**	we, you, they **were felt**
Past	I, he, she, it **was feeling**	I, he, she, it **was being felt**
Prog.	we, you, they **were feeling**	we, you, they **were being felt**
Past	I, he, she, it,	I, he, she, it,
Int.	we, you, they **did feel**	we, you, they **did get felt**
Pres.	I, we, you, they **have felt**	I, we, you, they **have been felt**
Perf.	he, she, it **has felt**	he, she, it **has been felt**
Past	I, he, she, it,	I, he, she, it,
Perf.	we, you, they **had felt**	we, you, they **had been felt**
Fut.	I, he, she, it, we, you, they	I, he, she, it, we, you, they
Perf.	**will have felt**	**will have been felt**

IMPERATIVE MOOD

feel	**be felt**

SUBJUNCTIVE MOOD

Pres.	if I, he, she, it,	if I, he, she, it,
	we, you, they **feel**	we, you, they **be felt**
Past	if I, he, she, it,	if I, he, she, it,
	we, you, they **felt**	we, you, they **were felt**
Fut.	if I, he, she, it,	if I, he, she, it,
	we, you, they **should feel**	we, you, they **should be felt**

Transitive and intransitive.

Can you feel the tips of your toes in those boots?
We felt that our concerns had not been properly discussed.
The argument was felt to be rather weak.

AN ESSENTIAL 55 VERB

feel

Examples

How are you feeling today?

He felt her pulse.

She felt cold to the touch.

I will feel better in the morning.

She has not felt this well in years.

Feel this mattress.

I've felt worse.

The shock in the audience could be felt by all.

He was not felt to be qualified.

Feel the music.

Words and expressions related to this verb

I feel good.

Can you feel the love tonight?

That felt good.

I don't feel like it.

She does not feel up to visitors yet.

Have you ever felt something so soft?

She rarely tells us how she feels.

What do you feel about that?

Why does she feel so offended?

My new shoes feel so good.

Can you feel them out about a deal?

fight
(active voice)

be fought
(passive voice)

INDICATIVE MOOD

Pres.	I, we, you, they **fight**	I am **fought**
		we, you, they **are fought**
	he, she, it **fights**	he, she, it **is fought**
Pres.	I **am fighting**	I **am being fought**
Prog.	we, you, they **are fighting**	we, you, they **are being fought**
	he, she, it **is fighting**	he, she, it **is being fought**
Pres.	I, we, you, they **do fight**	I, we, you, they **do get fought**
Int.	he, she, it **does fight**	he, she, it **does get fought**
Fut.	I, he, she, it,	I, he, she, it,
	we, you, they **will fight**	we, you, they **will be fought**
Past	I, he, she, it,	I, he, she, it **was fought**
	we, you, they **fought**	we, you, they **were fought**
Past	I, he, she, it **was fighting**	I, he, she, it **was being fought**
Prog.	we, you, they **were fighting**	we, you, they **were being fought**
Past	I, he, she, it,	I, he, she, it,
Int.	we, you, they **did fight**	we, you, they **did get fought**
Pres.	I, we, you, they **have fought**	I, we, you, they **have been fought**
Perf.	he, she, it **has fought**	he, she, it **has been fought**
Past	I, he, she, it,	I, he, she, it,
Perf.	we, you, they **had fought**	we, you, they **had been fought**
Fut.	I, he, she, it, we, you, they	I, he, she, it, we, you, they
Perf.	**will have fought**	**will have been fought**

IMPERATIVE MOOD

fight

be fought

SUBJUNCTIVE MOOD

Pres.	if I, he, she, it,	if I, he, she, it,
	we, you, they **fight**	we, you, they **be fought**
Past	if I, he, she, it,	if I, he, she, it,
	we, you, they **fought**	we, you, they **were fought**
Fut.	if I, he, she, it,	if I, he, she, it,
	we, you, they **should fight**	we, you, they **should be fought**

Intransitive and transitive.

Must the two of you always fight?
My father fought in the last great war.
The battles of World War I were fought in the trenches.

figure
(active voice)

be figured
(passive voice)

INDICATIVE MOOD

Pres.	I, we, you, they **figure**	I **am figured**
		we, you, they **are figured**
	he, she, it **figures**	he, she, it **is figured**
Pres.	I **am figuring**	I **am being figured**
Prog.	we, you, they **are figuring**	we, you, they **are being figured**
	he, she, it **is figuring**	he, she, it **is being figured**
Pres.	I, we, you, they **do figure**	I, we, you, they **do get figured**
Int.	he, she, it **does figure**	he, she, it **does get figured**
Fut.	I, he, she, it,	I, he, she, it,
	we, you, they **will figure**	we, you, they **will be figured**
Past	I, he, she, it,	I, he, she, it **was figured**
	we, you, they **figured**	we, you, they **were figured**
Past	I, he, she, it **was figuring**	I, he, she, it **was being figured**
Prog.	we, you, they **were figuring**	we, you, they **were being figured**
Past	I, he, she, it,	I, he, she, it,
Int.	we, you, they **did figure**	we, you, they **did get figured**
Pres.	I, we, you, they **have figured**	I, we, you, they **have been figured**
Perf.	he, she, it **has figured**	he, she, it **has been figured**
Past	I, he, she, it,	I, he, she, it,
Perf.	we, you, they **had figured**	we, you, they **had been figured**
Fut.	I, he, she, it, we, you, they	I, he, she, it, we, you, they
Perf.	**will have figured**	**will have been figured**

IMPERATIVE MOOD

figure   **be figured**

SUBJUNCTIVE MOOD

Pres.	if I, he, she, it,	if I, he, she, it,
	we, you, they **figure**	we, you, they **be figured**
Past	if I, he, she, it,	if I, he, she, it,
	we, you, they **figured**	we, you, they **were figured**
Fut.	if I, he, she, it,	if I, he, she, it,
	we, you, they **should figure**	we, you, they **should be figured**

Transitive and intransitive.

I am already figuring our taxes for last year.
Ancient symbols were figured on the door of the cathedral.

file
(active voice)

be filed
(passive voice)

INDICATIVE MOOD

Pres.	I, we, you, they **file**	I **am filed**
		we, you, they **are filed**
	he, she, it **files**	he, she, it **is filed**
Pres.	I **am filing**	I **am being filed**
Prog.	we, you, they **are filing**	we, you, they **are being filed**
	he, she, it **is filing**	he, she, it **is being filed**
Pres.	I, we, you, they **do file**	I, we, you, they **do get filed**
Int.	he, she, it **does file**	he, she, it **does get filed**
Fut.	I, he, she, it,	I, he, she, it,
	we, you, they **will file**	we, you, they **will be filed**
Past	I, he, she, it,	I, he, she, it **was filed**
	we, you, they **filed**	we, you, they **were filed**
Past	I, he, she, it **was filing**	I, he, she, it **was being filed**
Prog.	we, you, they **were filing**	we, you, they **were being filed**
Past	I, he, she, it,	I, he, she, it,
Int.	we, you, they **did file**	we, you, they **did get filed**
Pres.	I, we, you, they **have filed**	I, we, you, they **have been filed**
Perf.	he, she, it **has filed**	he, she, it **has been filed**
Past	I, he, she, it,	I, he, she, it,
Perf.	we, you, they **had filed**	we, you, they **had been filed**
Fut.	I, he, she, it, we, you, they	I, he, she, it, we, you, they
Perf.	**will have filed**	**will have been filed**

IMPERATIVE MOOD

file   **be filed**

SUBJUNCTIVE MOOD

Pres.	if I, he, she, it,	if I, he, she, it,
	we, you, they **file**	we, you, they **be filed**
Past	if I, he, she, it,	if I, he, she, it,
	we, you, they **filed**	we, you, they **were filed**
Fut.	if I, he, she, it,	if I, he, she, it,
	we, you, they **should file**	we, you, they **should be filed**

Transitive and intransitive.

You are filing a claim to receive compensation.
They filed yesterday for divorce.
All our papers were filed over a month ago.

150

fill
(active voice)

be filled
(passive voice)

F

INDICATIVE MOOD

Pres.	I, we, you, they **fill**	I **am filled**
		we, you, they **are filled**
	he, she, it **fills**	he, she, it **is filled**
Pres.	I **am filling**	I **am being filled**
Prog.	we, you, they **are filling**	we, you, they **are being filled**
	he, she, it **is filling**	he, she, it **is being filled**
Pres.	I, we, you, they **do fill**	I, we, you, they **do get filled**
Int.	he, she, it **does fill**	he, she, it **does get filled**
Fut.	I, he, she, it,	I, he, she, it,
	we, you, they **will fill**	we, you, they **will be filled**
Past	I, he, she, it,	I, he, she, it **was filled**
	we, you, they **filled**	we, you, they **were filled**
Past	I, he, she, it **was filling**	I, he, she, it **was being filled**
Prog.	we, you, they **were filling**	we, you, they **were being filled**
Past	I, he, she, it,	I, he, she, it,
Int.	we, you, they **did fill**	we, you, they **did get filled**
Pres.	I, we, you, they **have filled**	I, we, you, they **have been filled**
Perf.	he, she, it **has filled**	he, she, it **has been filled**
Past	I, he, she, it,	I, he, she, it,
Perf.	we, you, they **had filled**	we, you, they **had been filled**
Fut.	I, he, she, it, we, you, they	I, he, she, it, we, you, they
Perf.	**will have filled**	**will have been filled**

IMPERATIVE MOOD

fill

be filled

SUBJUNCTIVE MOOD

Pres.	if I, he, she, it,	if I, he, she, it,
	we, you, they **fill**	we, you, they **be filled**
Past	if I, he, she, it,	if I, he, she, it,
	we, you, they **filled**	we, you, they **were filled**
Fut.	if I, he, she, it,	if I, he, she, it,
	we, you, they **should fill**	we, you, they **should be filled**

Transitive and intransitive.

We are filling our prescription this week.
He filled the new position promptly.
The lake was filled with trout.

151

fillet
(active voice)

be filletted
(passive voice)

INDICATIVE MOOD

Pres.	I, we, you, they **fillet**	I **am filletted**
		we, you, they **are filletted**
	he, she, it **fillets**	he, she, it **is filletted**
Pres.	I **am filletting**	I **am being filletted**
Prog.	we, you, they **are filletting**	we, you, they **are being filletted**
	he, she, it **is filletting**	he, she, it **is being filletted**
Pres.	I, we, you, they **do fillet**	I, we, you, they **do get filletted**
Int.	he, she, it **does fillet**	he, she, it **does get filletted**
Fut.	I, he, she, it,	I, he, she, it,
	we, you, they **will fillet**	we, you, they **will be filletted**
Past	I, he, she, it,	I, he, she, it **was filletted**
	we, you, they **filletted**	we, you, they **were filletted**
Past	I, he, she, it **was filletting**	I, he, she, it **was being filletted**
Prog.	we, you, they **were filletting**	we, you, they **were being filletted**
Past	I, he, she, it,	I, he, she, it,
Int.	we, you, they **did fillet**	we, you, they **did get filletted**
Pres.	I, we, you, they **have filletted**	I, we, you, they **have been filletted**
Perf.	he, she, it **has filletted**	he, she, it **has been filletted**
Past	I, he, she, it,	I, he, she, it,
Perf.	we, you, they **had filletted**	we, you, they **had been filletted**
Fut.	I, he, she, it, we, you, they	I, he, she, it, we, you, they
Perf.	**will have filletted**	**will have been filletted**

IMPERATIVE MOOD

fillet   **be filletted**

SUBJUNCTIVE MOOD

Pres.	if I, he, she, it,	if I, he, she, it,
	we, you, they **fillet**	we, you, they **be filletted**
Past	if I, he, she, it,	if I, he, she, it,
	we, you, they **filletted**	we, you, they **were filletted**
Fut.	if I, he, she, it,	if I, he, she, it,
	we, you, they **should fillet**	we, you, they **should be filletted**

An alternative French spelling of this verb is FILET. The "t" or "tt" is not pronounced.

My father always filleted the fish before he brought it home.
Was the salmon filleted on the ship or at the store?

find
(active voice)

be found
(passive voice)

INDICATIVE MOOD

Pres.	I, we, you, they **find**	I **am found**
		we, you, they **are found**
	he, she, it **finds**	he, she, it **is found**
Pres. *Prog.*	I **am finding**	I **am being found**
	we, you, they **are finding**	we, you, they **are being found**
	he, she, it **is finding**	he, she, it **is being found**
Pres. *Int.*	I, we, you, they **do find**	I, we, you, they **do get found**
	he, she, it **does find**	he, she, it **does get found**
Fut.	I, he, she, it,	I, he, she, it,
	we, you, they **will find**	we, you, they **will be found**
Past	I, he, she, it,	I, he, she, it **was found**
	we, you, they **found**	we, you, they **were found**
Past *Prog.*	I, he, she, it **was finding**	I, he, she, it **was being found**
	we, you, they **were finding**	we, you, they **were being found**
Past *Int.*	I, he, she, it,	I, he, she, it,
	we, you, they **did find**	we, you, they **did get found**
Pres. *Perf.*	I, we, you, they **have found**	I, we, you, they **have been found**
	he, she, it **has found**	he, she, it **has been found**
Past *Perf.*	I, he, she, it,	I, he, she, it,
	we, you, they **had found**	we, you, they **had been found**
Fut. *Perf.*	I, he, she, it, we, you, they	I, he, she, it, we, you, they
	will have found	**will have been found**

IMPERATIVE MOOD

find   **be found**

SUBJUNCTIVE MOOD

Pres.	if I, he, she, it,	if I, he, she, it,
	we, you, they **find**	we, you, they **be found**
Past	if I, he, she, it,	if I, he, she, it,
	we, you, they **found**	we, you, they **were found**
Fut.	if I, he, she, it,	if I, he, she, it,
	we, you, they **should find**	we, you, they **should be found**

This verb is normally transitive, except for the legal meaning, which uses the intransitive as in the following: "They **found** for the plaintiff, or the defendant."

He found the old photos in a trunk in the garage.
Her eyeglasses were found on the kitchen table.

AN ESSENTIAL 55 VERB

find

Examples

I find that tip very useful.

She finds coins on the street.

He found his wallet in his car.

She was found guilty of the crime.

We will find the time for a meeting.

Find it.

There are many treasures still waiting to be found.

It could be worth millions, if it were found.

I have found that exercise can reduce stress.

Do you think it will ever be found?

Words and expressions related to this verb

We'll have to find out.

I once was lost, but now I'm found.

Find time for the people you love.

You can't find me.

That can be found on the Internet.

We can find our way around with the map.

Note: *Don't confuse the past tense form* **found** *with the verb* **found,** *meaning* **to establish:**

He founds charitable trusts.

She founded a women's magazine.

The United States was founded on democratic principles.

Who founded this university?

finish
(active voice)

be finished
(passive voice)

F

INDICATIVE MOOD

Pres.	I, we, you, they **finish**	I **am finished**
		we, you, they **are finished**
	he, she, it **finishes**	he, she, it **is finished**
Pres.	I **am finishing**	I **am being finished**
Prog.	we, you, they **are finishing**	we, you, they **are being finished**
	he, she, it **is finishing**	he, she, it **is being finished**
Pres.	I, we, you, they **do finish**	I, we, you, they **do get finished**
Int.	he, she, it **does finish**	he, she, it **does get finished**
Fut.	I, he, she, it,	I, he, she, it,
	we, you, they **will finish**	we, you, they **will be finished**
Past	I, he, she, it,	I, he, she, it **was finished**
	we, you, they **finished**	we, you, they **were finished**
Past	I, he, she, it **was finishing**	I, he, she, it **was being finished**
Prog.	we, you, they **were finishing**	we, you, they **were being finished**
Past	I, he, she, it,	I, he, she, it,
Int.	we, you, they **did finish**	we, you, they **did get finished**
Pres.	I, we, you, they **have finished**	I, we, you, they **have been finished**
Perf.	he, she, it **has finished**	he, she, it **has been finished**
Past	I, he, she, it,	I, he, she, it,
Perf.	we, you, they **had finished**	we, you, they **had been finished**
Fut.	I, he, she, it, we, you, they	I, he, she, it, we, you, they
Perf.	**will have finished**	**will have been finished**

IMPERATIVE MOOD

finish   **be finished**

SUBJUNCTIVE MOOD

Pres.	if I, he, she, it,	if I, he, she, it,
	we, you, they **finish**	we, you, they **be finished**
Past	if I, he, she, it,	if I, he, she, it,
	we, you, they **finished**	we, you, they **were finished**
Fut.	if I, he, she, it,	if I, he, she, it,
	we, you, they **should finish**	we, you, they **should be finished**

Transitive and intransitive.

At this rate we will never finish the job.
When her homework was finished she was allowed to go out and play.

155

fit
(active voice)

be fitted
(passive voice)

INDICATIVE MOOD

Pres.	I, we, you, they **fit**	I **am fitted** we, you, they **are fitted**
	he, she, it **fits**	he, she, it **is fitted**
Pres. *Prog.*	I **am fitting** we, you, they **are fitting** he, she, it **is fitting**	I **am being fitted** we, you, they **are being fitted** he, she, it **is being fitted**
Pres. *Int.*	I, we, you, they **do fit** he, she, it **does fit**	I, we, you, they **do get fitted** he, she, it **does get fitted**
Fut.	I, he, she, it, we, you, they **will fit**	I, he, she, it, we, you, they **will be fitted**
Past	I, he, she, it, we, you, they **fitted/fit**	I, he, she, it **was fitted** we, you, they **were fitted**
Past *Prog.*	I, he, she, it **was fitting** we, you, they **were fitting**	I, he, she, it **was being fitted** we, you, they **were being fitted**
Past *Int.*	I, he, she, it, we, you, they **did fit**	I, he, she, it, we, you, they **did get fitted**
Pres. *Perf.*	I, we, you, they **have fitted** he, she, it **has fitted**	I, we, you, they **have been fitted** he, she, it **has been fitted**
Past *Perf.*	I, he, she, it, we, you, they **had fitted**	I, he, she, it, we, you, they **had been fitted**
Fut. *Perf.*	I, he, she, it, we, you, they **will have fitted**	I, he, she, it, we, you, they **will have been fitted**

IMPERATIVE MOOD

fit   **be fitted**

SUBJUNCTIVE MOOD

Pres.	if I, he, she, it, we, you, they **fit**	if I, he, she, it, we, you, they **be fitted**
Past	if I, he, she, it, we, you, they **fitted/fit**	if I, he, she, it, we, you, they **were fitted**
Fut.	if I, he, she, it, we, you, they **should fit**	if I, he, she, it, we, you, they **should be fitted**

The past tense has two forms, FITTED and FIT: "They fitted him for a suit"; "The shoes fit nicely."

These shoes fit perfectly.
Were the costumes fitted to the actors before the first dress rehearsal?

flee
(active voice)

be fled
(passive voice)

INDICATIVE MOOD

Pres.	I, we, you, they **flee**	I **am fled**
		we, you, they **are fled**
	he, she, it **flees**	he, she, it **is fled**
Pres.	I **am fleeing**	I **am being fled**
Prog.	we, you, they **are fleeing**	we, you, they **are being fled**
	he, she, it **is fleeing**	he, she, it **is being fled**
Pres.	I, we, you, they **do flee**	I, we, you, they **do get fled**
Int.	he, she, it **does flee**	he, she, it **does get fled**
Fut.	I, he, she, it,	I, he, she, it,
	we, you, they **will flee**	we, you, they **will be fled**
Past	I, he, she, it,	I, he, she, it **was fled**
	we, you, they **fled**	we, you, they **were fled**
Past	I, he, she, it **was fleeing**	I, he, she, it **was being fled**
Prog.	we, you, they **were fleeing**	we, you, they **were being fled**
Past	I, he, she, it,	I, he, she, it,
Int.	we, you, they **did flee**	we, you, they **did get fled**
Pres.	I, we, you, they **have fled**	I, we, you, they **have been fled**
Perf.	he, she, it **has fled**	he, she, it **has been fled**
Past	I, he, she, it,	I, he, she, it,
Perf.	we, you, they **had fled**	we, you, they **had been fled**
Fut.	I, he, she, it, we, you, they	I, he, she, it, we, you, they
Perf.	**will have fled**	**will have been fled**

IMPERATIVE MOOD

flee **be fled**

SUBJUNCTIVE MOOD

Pres.	if I, he, she, it,	if I, he, she, it,
	we, you, they **flee**	we, you, they **be fled**
Past	if I, he, she, it,	if I, he, she, it,
	we, you, they **fled**	we, you, they **were fled**
Fut.	if I, he, she, it,	if I, he, she, it,
	we, you, they **should flee**	we, you, they **should be fled**

Intransitive and transitive.

With no alternative they are fleeing the coast.
They fled as the fire grew ever closer.
The flooded area was fled by thousands.

fling
(active voice)

be flung
(passive voice)

INDICATIVE MOOD

Pres.	I, we, you, they **fling**	I **am flung**
		we, you, they **are flung**
	he, she, it **flings**	he, she, it **is flung**
Pres.	I **am flinging**	I **am being flung**
Prog.	we, you, they **are flinging**	we, you, they **are being flung**
	he, she, it **is flinging**	he, she, it **is being flung**
Pres.	I, we, you, they **do fling**	I, we, you, they **do get flung**
Int.	he, she, it **does fling**	he, she, it **does get flung**
Fut.	I, he, she, it,	I, he, she, it,
	we, you, they **will fling**	we, you, they **will be flung**
Past	I, he, she, it,	I, he, she, it **was flung**
	we, you, they **flung**	we, you, they **were flung**
Past	I, he, she, it **was flinging**	I, he, she, it **was being flung**
Prog.	we, you, they **were flinging**	we, you, they **were being flung**
Past	I, he, she, it,	I, he, she, it,
Int.	we, you, they **did fling**	we, you, they **did get flung**
Pres.	I, we, you, they **have flung**	I, we, you, they **have been flung**
Perf.	he, she, it **has flung**	he, she, it **has been flung**
Past	I, he, she, it,	I, he, she, it,
Perf.	we, you, they **had flung**	we, you, they **had been flung**
Fut.	I, he, she, it, we, you, they	I, he, she, it, we, you, they
Perf.	**will have flung**	**will have been flung**

IMPERATIVE MOOD

fling

be flung

SUBJUNCTIVE MOOD

Pres.	if I, he, she, it,	if I, he, she, it,
	we, you, they **fling**	we, you, they **be flung**
Past	if I, he, she, it,	if I, he, she, it,
	we, you, they **flung**	we, you, they **were flung**
Fut.	if I, he, she, it,	if I, he, she, it,
	we, you, they **should fling**	we, you, they **should be flung**

Transitive and intransitive.

The little boy flung himself onto the sofa.
The empty bottle was flung against the wall.

fly
(active voice)

be flown
(passive voice)

INDICATIVE MOOD

Pres.	I, we, you, they **fly**	I **am flown**
		we, you, they **are flown**
	he, she, it **flies**	he, she, it **is flown**
Pres.	I **am flying**	I **am being flown**
Prog.	we, you, they **are flying**	we, you, they **are being flown**
	he, she, it **is flying**	he, she, it **is being flown**
Pres.	I, we, you, they **do fly**	I, we, you, they **do get flown**
Int.	he, she, it **does fly**	he, she, it **does get flown**
Fut.	I, he, she, it,	I, he, she, it,
	we, you, they **will fly**	we, you, they **will be flown**
Past	I, he, she, it,	I, he, she, it **was flown**
	we, you, they **flew**	we, you, they **were flown**
Past	I, he, she, it **was flying**	I, he, she, it **was being flown**
Prog.	we, you, they **were flying**	we, you, they **were being flown**
Past	I, he, she, it,	I, he, she, it,
Int.	we, you, they **did fly**	we, you, they **did get flown**
Pres.	I, we, you, they **have flown**	I, we, you, they **have been flown**
Perf.	he, she, it **has flown**	he, she, it **has been flown**
Past	I, he, she, it,	I, he, she, it,
Perf.	we, you, they **had flown**	we, you, they **had been flown**
Fut.	I, he, she, it, we, you, they	I, he, she, it, we, you, they
Perf.	**will have flown**	**will have been flown**

F

IMPERATIVE MOOD

fly   **be flown**

SUBJUNCTIVE MOOD

Pres.	if I, he, she, it,	if I, he, she, it,
	we, you, they **fly**	we, you, they **be flown**
Past	if I, he, she, it,	if I, he, she, it,
	we, you, they **flew**	we, you, they **were flown**
Fut.	if I, he, she, it,	if I, he, she, it,
	we, you, they **should fly**	we, you, they **should be flown**

Intransitive and transitive. In baseball, the past tense is FLIED meaning "to hit a ball to the outfield": "He flied to center, left, or right."

I am flying almost every week.
Last week I flew to Japan.
This route has been flown since the early 1920s.
The batter flied out to the catcher.

focus
(active voice)

be focused/
focussed
(passive voice)

INDICATIVE MOOD

Pres.	I, we, you, they **focus**	I **am focused**
		we, you, they **are focused**
	he, she, it **focuses**	he, she, it **is focused**
Pres.	I **am focusing**	I **am being focused**
Prog.	we, you, they **are focusing**	we, you, they **are being focused**
	he, she, it **is focusing**	he, she, it **is being focused**
Pres.	I, we, you, they **do focus**	I, we, you, they **do get focused**
Int.	he, she, it **does focus**	he, she, it **does get focused**
Fut.	I, he, she, it,	I, he, she, it,
	we, you, they **will focus**	we, you, they **will be focused**
Past	I, he, she, it,	I, he, she, it **was focused**
	we, you, they **focused**	we, you, they **were focused**
Past	I, he, she, it **was focusing**	I, he, she, it **was being focused**
Prog.	we, you, they **were focusing**	we, you, they **were being focused**
Past	I, he, she, it,	I, he, she, it,
Int.	we, you, they **did focus**	we, you, they **did get focused**
Pres.	I, we, you, they **have focused**	I, we, you, they **have been focused**
Perf.	he, she, it **has focused**	he, she, it **has been focused**
Past	I, he, she, it,	I, he, she, it,
Perf.	we, you, they **had focused**	we, you, they **had been focused**
Fut.	I, he, she, it, we, you, they	I, he, she, it, we, you, they
Perf.	**will have focused**	**will have been focused**

IMPERATIVE MOOD

focus   **be focused**

SUBJUNCTIVE MOOD

Pres.	if I, he, she, it,	if I, he, she, it,
	we, you, they **focus**	we, you, they **be focused**
Past	if I, he, she, it,	if I, he, she, it,
	we, you, they **focused**	we, you, they **were focused**
Fut.	if I, he, she, it,	if I, he, she, it,
	we, you, they **should focus**	we, you, they **should be focused**

Transitive and intransitive. The past tense and participle forms may have either a single or double "s."

Unless we are focusing on our prime responsibility, we will be here all evening.
Their attention was focused on the acrobat high above the center ring.

follow	**PRINCIPAL PARTS: follows, following,**	be followed
(active voice)	**followed, followed**	(passive voice)

INDICATIVE MOOD

Pres.	I, we, you, they **follow**	I **am followed**
		we, you, they **are followed**
	he, she, it **follows**	he, she, it **is followed**
Pres.	I **am following**	I **am being followed**
Prog.	we, you, they **are following**	we, you, they **are being followed**
	he, she, it **is following**	he, she, it **is being followed**
Pres.	I, we, you, they **do follow**	I, we, you, they **do get followed**
Int.	he, she, it **does follow**	he, she, it **does get followed**
Fut.	I, he, she, it,	I, he, she, it,
	we, you, they **will follow**	we, you, they **will be followed**
Past	I, he, she, it,	I, he, she, it **was followed**
	we, you, they **followed**	we, you, they **were followed**
Past	I, he, she, it **was following**	I, he, she, it **was being followed**
Prog.	we, you, they **were following**	we, you, they **were being followed**
Past	I, he, she, it,	I, he, she, it,
Int.	we, you, they **did follow**	we, you, they **did get followed**
Pres.	I, we, you, they **have followed**	I, we, you, they **have been followed**
Perf.	he, she, it **has followed**	he, she, it **has been followed**
Past	I, he, she, it,	I, he, she, it,
Perf.	we, you, they **had followed**	we, you, they **had been followed**
Fut.	I, he, she, it, we, you, they	I, he, she, it, we, you, they
Perf.	**will have followed**	**will have been followed**

IMPERATIVE MOOD

follow	**be followed**

SUBJUNCTIVE MOOD

Pres.	if I, he, she, it,	if I, he, she, it,
	we, you, they **follow**	we, you, they **be followed**
Past	if I, he, she, it,	if I, he, she, it,
	we, you, they **followed**	we, you, they **were followed**
Fut.	if I, he, she, it,	if I, he, she, it,
	we, you, they **should follow**	we, you, they **should be followed**

Transitive and intransitive.

If I lead, will they follow?
The first act was followed by a ten-minute intermission.

AN ESSENTIAL
55 VERB

AN ESSENTIAL
55 VERB

follow

Examples

Who follows you in line?

I am following the most recent developments.

The politician was followed by several reporters.

Were you being followed?

They followed their leader.

His initial enthusiasm was followed by anxiety.

She will be followed by other performers.

Can anyone follow in his footsteps?

Follow me.

Dinner was followed by a coffee and conversation.

Words and expressions related to this verb

I will follow you.

Follow your heart.

We will follow up on our conversation next month.

The pitcher was failing to follow through.

May we follow along with the script?

She simply followed her conscience.

Follow the money.

I'll follow the sun.

He had not followed the directions.

To thine own self be true, and it must follow, as the night the day, thou canst not then be false to any man.

forbid
(active voice)

PRINCIPAL PARTS: **forbids, forbidding, forbade/forbad, forbidden/forbid**

be forbidden/forbid
(passive voice)

F

INDICATIVE MOOD

Pres.	I, we, you, they **forbid**	I **am forbidden**
		we, you, they **are forbidden**
	he, she, it **forbids**	he, she, it **is forbidden**
Pres.	I **am forbidding**	I **am being forbidden**
Prog.	we, you, they **are forbidding**	we, you, they **are being forbidden**
	he, she, it **is forbidding**	he, she, it **is being forbidden**
Pres.	I, we, you, they **do forbid**	I, we, you, they **do get forbidden**
Int.	he, she, it **does forbid**	he, she, it **does get forbidden**
Fut.	I, he, she, it,	I, he, she, it,
	we, you, they **will forbid**	we, you, they **will be forbidden**
Past	I, he, she, it,	I, he, she, it **was forbidden**
	we, you, they **forbade/forbad**	we, you, they **were forbidden**
Past	I, he, she, it **was forbidding**	I, he, she, it **was being forbidden**
Prog.	we, you, they **were forbidding**	we, you, they **were being forbidden**
Past	I, he, she, it,	I, he, she, it,
Int.	we, you, they **did forbid**	we, you, they **did get forbidden**
Pres.	I, we, you, they **have forbidden**	I, we, you, they **have been forbidden**
Perf.	he, she, it **has forbidden**	he, she, it **has been forbidden**
Past	I, he, she, it,	I, he, she, it,
Perf.	we, you, they **had forbidden**	we, you, they **had been forbidden**
Fut.	I, he, she, it, we, you, they	I, he, she, it, we, you, they
Perf.	**will have forbidden**	**will have been forbidden**

IMPERATIVE MOOD

forbid   **be forbidden**

SUBJUNCTIVE MOOD

Pres.	if I, he, she, it,	if I, he, she, it,
	we, you, they **forbid**	we, you, they **be forbidden**
Past	if I, he, she, it,	if I, he, she, it,
	we, you, they **forbade/forbad**	we, you, they **were forbidden**
Fut.	if I, he, she, it,	if I, he, she, it,
	we, you, they **should forbid**	we, you, they **should be forbidden**

In the past tense FORBADE and FORBAD are acceptable. The past participle may be FORBIDDEN or FORBID.

I am forbidding you to see him.
I forbade your father to ever speak of that again.
Many practices have been forbidden by well-intentioned patriots.

force
(active voice)

be forced
(passive voice)

INDICATIVE MOOD

Pres.	I, we, you, they **force**	I **am forced**
		we, you, they **are forced**
	he, she, it **forces**	he, she, it **is forced**
Pres.	I **am forcing**	I **am being forced**
Prog.	we, you, they **are forcing**	we, you, they **are being forced**
	he, she, it **is forcing**	he, she, it **is being forced**
Pres.	I, we, you, they **do force**	I, we, you, they **do get forced**
Int.	he, she, it **does force**	he, she, it **does get forced**
Fut.	I, he, she, it,	I, he, she, it,
	we, you, they **will force**	we, you, they **will be forced**
Past	I, he, she, it,	I, he, she, it **was forced**
	we, you, they **forced**	we, you, they **were forced**
Past	I, he, she, it **was forcing**	I, he, she, it **was being forced**
Prog.	we, you, they **were forcing**	we, you, they **were being forced**
Past	I, he, she, it,	I, he, she, it,
Int.	we, you, they **did force**	we, you, they **did get forced**
Pres.	I, we, you, they **have forced**	I, we, you, they **have been forced**
Perf.	he, she, it **has forced**	he, she, it **has been forced**
Past	I, he, she, it,	I, he, she, it,
Perf.	we, you, they **had forced**	we, you, they **had been forced**
Fut.	I, he, she, it, we, you, they	I, he, she, it, we, you, they
Perf.	**will have forced**	**will have been forced**

IMPERATIVE MOOD

force be forced

SUBJUNCTIVE MOOD

Pres.	if I, he, she, it,	if I, he, she, it,
	we, you, they **force**	we, you, they **be forced**
Past	if I, he, she, it,	if I, he, she, it,
	we, you, they **forced**	we, you, they **were forced**
Fut.	if I, he, she, it,	if I, he, she, it,
	we, you, they **should force**	we, you, they **should be forced**

There is always danger if someone is forcing his way into the meeting.
The hostage was forced to comply with their demands.

164

forecast
(active voice)

PRINCIPAL PARTS: forecasts, forecasting, forecast/forecasted, forecast/forecasted

be forecast/forecasted
(passive voice)

INDICATIVE MOOD

Pres.	I, we, you, they **forecast**	I **am forecast**
		we, you, they **are forecast**
	he, she, it **forecasts**	he, she, it **is forecast**
Pres.	I **am forecasting**	I **am being forecast**
Prog.	we, you, they **are forecasting**	we, you, they **are being forecast**
	he, she, it **is forecasting**	he, she, it **is being forecast**
Pres.	I, we, you, they **do forecast**	I, we, you, they **do get forecast**
Int.	he, she, it **does forecast**	he, she, it **does get forecast**
Fut.	I, he, she, it,	I, he, she, it,
	we, you, they **will forecast**	we, you, they **will be forecast**
Past	I, he, she, it,	I, he, she, it **was forecast**
	we, you, they **forecast**	we, you, they **were forecast**
Past	I, he, she, it **was forecasting**	I, he, she, it **was being forecast**
Prog.	we, you, they **were forecasting**	we, you, they **were being forecast**
Past	I, he, she, it,	I, he, she, it,
Int.	we, you, they **did forecast**	we, you, they **did get forecast**
Pres.	I, we, you, they **have forecast**	I, we, you, they **have been forecast**
Perf.	he, she, it **has forecast**	he, she, it **has been forecast**
Past	I, he, she, it,	I, he, she, it,
Perf.	we, you, they **had forecast**	we, you, they **had been forecast**
Fut.	I, he, she, it, we, you, they	I, he, she, it, we, you, they
Perf.	**will have forecast**	**will have been forecast**

IMPERATIVE MOOD

forecast · **be forecast**

SUBJUNCTIVE MOOD

Pres.	if I, he, she, it,	if I, he, she, it,
	we, you, they **forecast**	we, you, they **be forecast**
Past	if I, he, she, it,	if I, he, she, it,
	we, you, they **forecast**	we, you, they **were forecast**
Fut.	if I, he, she, it,	if I, he, she, it,
	we, you, they **should forecast**	we, you, they **should be forecast**

Transitive and intransitive. In the past and past participle forms, both FORECAST and FORECASTED are acceptable.

They are forecasting rain mixed with snow for tomorrow.
The blizzard was forecast well in advance of its arrival.

foresee
(active voice)

be foreseen
(passive voice)

INDICATIVE MOOD

Pres.	I, we, you, they **foresee**	I **am foreseen**
		we, you, they **are foreseen**
	he, she, it **foresees**	he, she, it **is foreseen**
Pres.	I **am foreseeing**	I **am being foreseen**
Prog.	we, you, they **are foreseeing**	we, you, they **are being foreseen**
	he, she, it **is foreseeing**	he, she, it **is being foreseen**
Pres.	I, we, you, they **do foresee**	I, we, you, they **do get foreseen**
Int.	he, she, it **does foresee**	he, she, it **does get foreseen**
Fut.	I, he, she, it,	I, he, she, it,
	we, you, they **will foresee**	we, you, they **will be foreseen**
Past	I, he, she, it,	I, he, she, it **was foreseen**
	we, you, they **foresaw**	we, you, they **were foreseen**
Past	I, he, she, it **was foreseeing**	I, he, she, it **was being foreseen**
Prog.	we, you, they **were foreseeing**	we, you, they **were being foreseen**
Past	I, he, she, it,	I, he, she, it,
Int.	we, you, they **did foresee**	we, you, they **did get foreseen**
Pres.	I, we, you, they **have foreseen**	I, we, you, they **have been foreseen**
Perf.	he, she, it **has foreseen**	he, she, it **has been foreseen**
Past	I, he, she, it,	I, he, she, it,
Perf.	we, you, they **had foreseen**	we, you, they **had been foreseen**
Fut.	I, he, she, it, we, you, they	I, he, she, it, we, you, they
Perf.	**will have foreseen**	**will have been foreseen**

IMPERATIVE MOOD

foresee   **be foreseen**

SUBJUNCTIVE MOOD

Pres.	if I, he, she, it,	if I, he, she, it,
	we, you, they **foresee**	we, you, they **be foreseen**
Past	if I, he, she, it,	if I, he, she, it,
	we, you, they **foresaw**	we, you, they **were foreseen**
Fut.	if I, he, she, it,	if I, he, she, it,
	we, you, they **should foresee**	we, you, they **should be foreseen**

No one is foreseeing all the consequences.
We foresaw none of the dangers.
Those complications should have been foreseen by a competent surgeon.

foretell
(active voice)

be foretold
(passive voice)

F

INDICATIVE MOOD

Pres.	I, we, you, they **foretell**	I **am foretold**
		we, you, they **are foretold**
	he, she, it **foretells**	he, she, it **is foretold**
Pres.	I **am foretelling**	I **am being foretold**
Prog.	we, you, they **are foretelling**	we, you, they **are being foretold**
	he, she, it **is foretelling**	he, she, it **is being foretold**
Pres.	I, we, you, they **do foretell**	I, we, you, they **do get foretold**
Int.	he, she, it **does foretell**	he, she, it **does get foretold**
Fut.	I, he, she, it,	I, he, she, it,
	we, you, they **will foretell**	we, you, they **will be foretold**
Past	I, he, she, it,	I, he, she, it **was foretold**
	we, you, they **foretold**	we, you, they **were foretold**
Past	I, he, she, it **was foretelling**	I, he, she, it **was being foretold**
Prog.	we, you, they **were foretelling**	we, you, they **were being foretold**
Past	I, he, she, it,	I, he, she, it,
Int.	we, you, they **did foretell**	we, you, they **did get foretold**
Pres.	I, we, you, they **have foretold**	I, we, you, they **have been foretold**
Perf.	he, she, it **has foretold**	he, she, it **has been foretold**
Past	I, he, she, it,	I, he, she, it,
Perf.	we, you, they **had foretold**	we, you, they **had been foretold**
Fut.	I, he, she, it, we, you, they	I, he, she, it, we, you, they
Perf.	**will have foretold**	**will have been foretold**

IMPERATIVE MOOD

foretell

be foretold

SUBJUNCTIVE MOOD

Pres.	if I, he, she, it,	if I, he, she, it,
	we, you, they **foretell**	we, you, they **be foretold**
Past	if I, he, she, it,	if I, he, she, it,
	we, you, they **foretold**	we, you, they **were foretold**
Fut.	if I, he, she, it,	if I, he, she, it,
	we, you, they **should foretell**	we, you, they **should be foretold**

Do you really believe he foretold the future?
They were convinced that the catastrophe had been foretold in his writings.

forget
(active voice)

be forgotten/forgot
(passive voice)

INDICATIVE MOOD

Pres.	I, we, you, they **forget**	I **am forgotten**
		we, you, they **are forgotten**
	he, she, it **forgets**	he, she, it **is forgotten**
Pres.	I **am forgetting**	I **am being forgotten**
Prog.	we, you, they **are forgetting**	we, you, they **are being forgotten**
	he, she, it **is forgetting**	he, she, it **is being forgotten**
Pres.	I, we, you, they **do forget**	I, we, you, they **do get forgotten**
Int.	he, she, it **does forget**	he, she, it **does get forgotten**
Fut.	I, he, she, it,	I, he, she, it,
	we, you, they **will forget**	we, you, they **will be forgotten**
Past	I, he, she, it,	I, he, she, it **was forgotten**
	we, you, they **forgot**	we, you, they **were forgotten**
Past	I, he, she, it **was forgetting**	I, he, she, it **was being forgotten**
Prog.	we, you, they **were forgetting**	we, you, they **were being forgotten**
Past	I, he, she, it,	I, he, she, it,
Int.	we, you, they **did forget**	we, you, they **did get forgotten**
Pres.	I, we, you, they **have forgotten**	I, we, you, they **have been forgotten**
Perf.	he, she, it **has forgotten**	he, she, it **has been forgotten**
Past	I, he, she, it,	I, he, she, it,
Perf.	we, you, they **had forgotten**	we, you, they **had been forgotten**
Fut.	I, he, she, it, we, you, they	I, he, she, it, we, you, they
Perf.	**will have forgotten**	**will have been forgotten**

IMPERATIVE MOOD

forget   **be forgotten**

SUBJUNCTIVE MOOD

Pres.	if I, he, she, it,	if I, he, she, it,
	we, you, they **forget**	we, you, they **be forgotten**
Past	if I, he, she, it,	if I, he, she, it,
	we, you, they **forgot**	we, you, they **were forgotten**
Fut.	if I, he, she, it,	if I, he, she, it,
	we, you, they **should forget**	we, you, they **should be forgotten**

Transitive and intransitive. The past participle form may be either FORGOTTEN or FORGOT.

This time we are not forgetting our duties.
I forgot to call Mom on her birthday.
No one and nothing will be forgotten.

forgive
(active voice)

PRINCIPAL PARTS: **forgives, forgiving, forgave, forgiven**

be forgiven
(passive voice)

F

INDICATIVE MOOD

Pres.	I, we, you, they **forgive**	I **am forgiven**
		we, you, they **are forgiven**
	he, she, it **forgives**	he, she, it **is forgiven**
Pres.	I **am forgiving**	I **am being forgiven**
Prog.	we, you, they **are forgiving**	we, you, they **are being forgiven**
	he, she, it **is forgiving**	he, she, it **is being forgiven**
Pres.	I, we, you, they **do forgive**	I, we, you, they **do get forgiven**
Int.	he, she, it **does forgive**	he, she, it **does get forgiven**
Fut.	I, he, she, it,	I, he, she, it,
	we, you, they **will forgive**	we, you, they **will be forgiven**
Past	I, he, she, it,	I, he, she, it **was forgiven**
	we, you, they **forgave**	we, you, they **were forgiven**
Past	I, he, she, it **was forgiving**	I, he, she, it **was being forgiven**
Prog.	we, you, they **were forgiving**	we, you, they **were being forgiven**
Past	I, he, she, it,	I, he, she, it,
Int.	we, you, they **did forgive**	we, you, they **did get forgiven**
Pres.	I, we, you, they **have forgiven**	I, we, you, they **have been forgiven**
Perf.	he, she, it **has forgiven**	he, she, it **has been forgiven**
Past	I, he, she, it,	I, he, she, it,
Perf.	we, you, they **had forgiven**	we, you, they **had been forgiven**
Fut.	I, he, she, it, we, you, they	I, he, she, it, we, you, they
Perf.	**will have forgiven**	**will have been forgiven**

IMPERATIVE MOOD

forgive   **be forgiven**

SUBJUNCTIVE MOOD

Pres.	if I, he, she, it,	if I, he, she, it,
	we, you, they **forgive**	we, you, they **be forgiven**
Past	if I, he, she, it,	if I, he, she, it,
	we, you, they **forgave**	we, you, they **were forgiven**
Fut.	if I, he, she, it,	if I, he, she, it,
	we, you, they **should forgive**	we, you, they **should be forgiven**

Transitive and intransitive.

A father is sometimes more forgiving than a mother.
He forgave his children long ago.
It is a relief to have had that debt forgiven.

PRINCIPAL PARTS: **forgoes, forgoing, forwent, forgone**

INDICATIVE MOOD

Pres.	I, we, you, they **forgo**	I **am forgone**
		we, you, they **are forgone**
	he, she, it **forgoes**	he, she, it **is forgone**
Pres.	I **am forgoing**	I **am being forgone**
Prog.	we, you, they **are forgoing**	we, you, they **are being forgone**
	he, she, it **is forgoing**	he, she, it **is being forgone**
Pres.	I, we, you, they **do forgo**	I, we, you, they **do get forgone**
Int.	he, she, it **does forgo**	he, she, it **does get forgone**
Fut.	I, he, she, it,	I, he, she, it,
	we, you, they **will forgo**	we, you, they **will be forgone**
Past	I, he, she, it,	I, he, she, it **was forgone**
	we, you, they **forwent**	we, you, they **were forgone**
Past	I, he, she, it **was forgoing**	I, he, she, it **was being forgone**
Prog.	we, you, they **were forgoing**	we, you, they **were being forgone**
Past	I, he, she, it,	I, he, she, it,
Int.	we, you, they **did forgo**	we, you, they **did get forgone**
Pres.	I, we, you, they **have forgone**	I, we, you, they **have been forgone**
Perf.	he, she, it **has forgone**	he, she, it **has been forgone**
Past	I, he, she, it,	I, he, she, it,
Perf.	we, you, they **had forgone**	we, you, they **had been forgone**
Fut.	I, he, she, it, we, you, they	I, he, she, it, we, you, they
Perf.	**will have forgone**	**will have been forgone**

IMPERATIVE MOOD

forgo   **be forgone**

SUBJUNCTIVE MOOD

Pres.	if I, he, she, it,	if I, he, she, it,
	we, you, they **forgo**	we, you, they **be forgone**
Past	if I, he, she, it,	if I, he, she, it,
	we, you, they **forwent**	we, you, they **were forgone**
Fut.	if I, he, she, it,	if I, he, she, it,
	we, you, they **should forgo**	we, you, they **should be forgone**

An alternate spelling of this verb, meaning "to abstain," is FOREGO, its past and past participle FOREWENT and FOREGONE. There is another verb FOREGO (past and past participle FOREWENT, FOREWENT), which means "to precede, come before something."

He often foregoes lunch at the office.
We are forgoing the formalities.
She forwent all chocolate for a whole week.
The introductions were forgone for the sake of brevity.

170

form
(active voice)

PRINCIPAL PARTS: **forms, forming, formed, formed**

br **formed**
(passive voice)

INDICATIVE MOOD

Pres. I, we, you, they **form**

he, she, it **forms**

I **am formed**
we, you, they **are formed**
he, she, it **is formed**

Pres. I **am forming**
Prog. we, you, they **are forming**
he, she, it **is forming**

I **am being formed**
we, you, they **are being formed**
he, she, it **is being formed**

Pres. I, we, you, they **do form**
Int. he, she, it **does form**

I, we, you, they **do get formed**
he, she, it **does get formed**

Fut. I, he, she, it,
we, you, they **will form**

I, he, she, it,
we, you, they **will be formed**

Past I, he, she, it,
we, you, they **formed**

I, he, she, it **was formed**
we, you, they **were formed**

Past I, he, she, it **was forming**
Prog. we, you, they **were forming**

I, he, she, it **was being formed**
we, you, they **were being formed**

Past I, he, she, it,
Int. we, you, they **did form**

I, he, she, it,
we, you, they **did get formed**

Pres. I, we, you, they **have formed**
Perf. he, she, it **has formed**

I, we, you, they **have been formed**
he, she, it **has been formed**

Past I, he, she, it,
Perf. we, you, they **had formed**

I, he, she, it,
we, you, they **had been formed**

Fut. I, he, she, it, we, you, they
Perf. **will have formed**

I, he, she, it, we, you, they
will have been formed

IMPERATIVE MOOD

form

be formed

SUBJUNCTIVE MOOD

Pres. if I, he, she, it,
we, you, they **form**

if I, he, she, it,
we, you, they **be formed**

Past if I, he, she, it,
we, you, they **formed**

if I, he, she, it,
we, you, they **were formed**

Fut. if I, he, she, it,
we, you, they **should form**

if I, he, she, it,
we, you, they **should be formed**

Transitive and intransitive.

The young women intend to form a new society.
The earth was formed millions of years ago.

171

format
(active voice)

be formatted
(passive voice)

INDICATIVE MOOD

Pres.	I, we, you, they **format**	I **am formatted**
		we, you, they **are formatted**
	he, she, it **formats**	he, she, it **is formatted**
Pres.	I **am formatting**	I **am being formatted**
Prog.	we, you, they **are formatting**	we, you, they **are being formatted**
	he, she, it **is formatting**	he, she, it **is being formatted**
Pres.	I, we, you, they **do format**	I, we, you, they **do get formatted**
Int.	he, she, it **does format**	he, she, it **does get formatted**
Fut.	I, he, she, it,	I, he, she, it,
	we, you, they **will format**	we, you, they **will be formatted**
Past	I, he, she, it,	I, he, she, it **was formatted**
	we, you, they **formatted**	we, you, they **were formatted**
Past	I, he, she, it **was formatting**	I, he, she, it **was being formatted**
Prog.	we, you, they **were formatting**	we, you, they **were being formatted**
Past	I, he, she, it,	I, he, she, it,
Int.	we, you, they **did format**	we, you, they **did get formatted**
Pres.	I, we, you, they **have formatted**	I, we, you, they **have been formatted**
Perf.	he, she, it **has formatted**	he, she, it **has been formatted**
Past	I, he, she, it,	I, he, she, it,
Perf.	we, you, they **had formatted**	we, you, they **had been formatted**
Fut.	I, he, she, it, we, you, they	I, he, she, it, we, you, they
Perf.	**will have formatted**	**will have been formatted**

IMPERATIVE MOOD

format   **be formatted**

SUBJUNCTIVE MOOD

Pres.	if I, he, she, it,	if I, he, she, it,
	we, you, they **format**	we, you, they **be formatted**
Past	if I, he, she, it,	if I, he, she, it,
	we, you, they **formatted**	we, you, they **were formatted**
Fut.	if I, he, she, it,	if I, he, she, it,
	we, you, they **should format**	we, you, they **should be formatted**

Are you still formatting the school newspaper?
They formatted the disks before they recorded them.
This CD has been properly formatted to copy that data.

forsake
(active voice)

PRINCIPAL PARTS: **forsakes, forsaking, forsook, forsaken**

be forsaken
(passive voice)

INDICATIVE MOOD

Pres.	I, we, you, they **forsake**	I **am forsaken**
		we, you, they **are forsaken**
	he, she, it **forsakes**	he, she, it **is forsaken**
Pres.	I **am forsaking**	I **am being forsaken**
Prog.	we, you, they **are forsaking**	we, you, they **are being forsaken**
	he, she, it **is forsaking**	he, she, it **is being forsaken**
Pres.	I, we, you, they **do forsake**	I, we, you, they **do get forsaken**
Int.	he, she, it **does forsake**	he, she, it **does get forsaken**
Fut.	I, he, she, it,	I, he, she, it,
	we, you, they **will forsake**	we, you, they **will be forsaken**
Past	I, he, she, it,	I, he, she, it **was forsaken**
	we, you, they **foresook**	we, you, they **were forsaken**
Past	I, he, she, it **was forsaking**	I, he, she, it **was being forsaken**
Prog.	we, you, they **were forsaking**	we, you, they **were being forsaken**
Past	I, he, she, it,	I, he, she, it,
Int.	we, you, they **did forsake**	we, you, they **did get forsaken**
Pres.	I, we, you, they **have forsaken**	I, we, you, they **have been forsaken**
Perf.	he, she, it **has forsaken**	he, she, it **has been forsaken**
Past	I, he, she, it,	I, he, she, it,
Perf.	we, you, they **had forsaken**	we, you, they **had been forsaken**
Fut.	I, he, she, it, we, you, they	I, he, she, it, we, you, they
Perf.	**will have forsaken**	**will have been forsaken**

IMPERATIVE MOOD

forsake

be forsaken

SUBJUNCTIVE MOOD

Pres.	if I, he, she, it,	if I, he, she, it,
	we, you, they **forsake**	we, you, they **be forsaken**
Past	if I, he, she, it,	if I, he, she, it,
	we, you, they **foresook**	we, you, they **were forsaken**
Fut.	if I, he, she, it,	if I, he, she, it,
	we, you, they **should forsake**	we, you, they **should be forsaken**

F

They used to sing, "Do not forsake me." But he is forsaking me.
He forsook his home and family to launch a new career.
I have never felt so forsaken.

found	PRINCIPAL PARTS: **founds, founding,**	be founded
(active voice)	**founded, founded**	(passive voice)

INDICATIVE MOOD

Pres.	I, we, you, they **found**	I **am founded**
		we, you, they **are founded**
	he, she, it **founds**	he, she, it **is founded**
Pres.	I **am founding**	I **am being founded**
Prog.	we, you, they **are founding**	we, you, they **are being founded**
	he, she, it **is founding**	he, she, it **is being founded**
Pres.	I, we, you, they **do found**	I, we, you, they **do get founded**
Int.	he, she, it **does found**	he, she, it **does get founded**
Fut.	I, he, she, it,	I, he, she, it,
	we, you, they **will found**	we, you, they **will be founded**
Past	I, he, she, it,	I, he, she, it **was founded**
	we, you, they **founded**	we, you, they **were founded**
Past	I, he, she, it **was founding**	I, he, she, it **was being founded**
Prog.	we, you, they **were founding**	we, you, they **were being founded**
Past	I, he, she, it,	I, he, she, it,
Int.	we, you, they **did found**	we, you, they **did get founded**
Pres.	I, we, you, they **have founded**	I, we, you, they **have been founded**
Perf.	he, she, it **has founded**	he, she, it **has been founded**
Past	I, he, she, it,	I, he, she, it,
Perf.	we, you, they **had founded**	we, you, they **had been founded**
Fut.	I, he, she, it, we, you, they	I, he, she, it, we, you, they
Perf.	**will have founded**	**will have been founded**

IMPERATIVE MOOD

found	**be founded**

SUBJUNCTIVE MOOD

Pres.	if I, he, she, it,	if I, he, she, it,
	we, you, they **found**	we, you, they **be founded**
Past	if I, he, she, it,	if I, he, she, it,
	we, you, they **founded**	we, you, they **were founded**
Fut.	if I, he, she, it,	if I, he, she, it,
	we, you, they **should found**	we, you, they **should be founded**

Transitive and intransitive.

The group founds new investment funds.
The new school was founded by a group of dedicated parents.

free
(active voice)

be freed
(passive voice)

F

INDICATIVE MOOD

Pres.	I, we, you, they **free**	I **am freed**
		we, you, they **are freed**
	he, she, it **frees**	he, she, it **is freed**
Pres.	I **am freeing**	I **am being freed**
Prog.	we, you, they **are freeing**	we, you, they **are being freed**
	he, she, it **is freeing**	he, she, it **is being freed**
Pres.	I, we, you, they **do free**	I, we, you, they **do get freed**
Int.	he, she, it **does free**	he, she, it **does get freed**
Fut.	I, he, she, it,	I, he, she, it,
	we, you, they **will free**	we, you, they **will be freed**
Past	I, he, she, it,	I, he, she, it **was freed**
	we, you, they **freed**	we, you, they **were freed**
Past	I, he, she, it **was freeing**	I, he, she, it **was being freed**
Prog.	we, you, they **were freeing**	we, you, they **were being freed**
Past	I, he, she, it,	I, he, she, it,
Int.	we, you, they **did free**	we, you, they **did get freed**
Pres.	I, we, you, they **have freed**	I, we, you, they **have been freed**
Perf.	he, she, it **has freed**	he, she, it **has been freed**
Past	I, he, she, it,	I, he, she, it,
Perf.	we, you, they **had freed**	we, you, they **had been freed**
Fut.	I, he, she, it, we, you, they	I, he, she, it, we, you, they
Perf.	**will have freed**	**will have been freed**

IMPERATIVE MOOD

free   **be freed**

SUBJUNCTIVE MOOD

Pres.	if I, he, she, it,	if I, he, she, it,
	we, you, they **free**	we, you, they **be freed**
Past	if I, he, she, it,	if I, he, she, it,
	we, you, they **freed**	we, you, they **were freed**
Fut.	if I, he, she, it,	if I, he, she, it,
	we, you, they **should free**	we, you, they **should be freed**

When are we freeing the dolphins?
He was freed from all his schoolwork until he felt better.

freeze
(active voice)

be frozen
(passive voice)

INDICATIVE MOOD

Pres.	I, we, you, they **freeze**	I **am frozen** we, you, they **are frozen**
	he, she, it **freezes**	he, she, it **is frozen**
Pres. *Prog.*	I **am freezing** we, you, they **are freezing** he, she, it **is freezing**	I **am being frozen** we, you, they **are being frozen** he, she, it **is being frozen**
Pres. *Int.*	I, we, you, they **do freeze** he, she, it **does freeze**	I, we, you, they **do get frozen** he, she, it **does get frozen**
Fut.	I, he, she, it, we, you, they **will freeze**	I, he, she, it, we, you, they **will be frozen**
Past	I, he, she, it, we, you, they **froze**	I, he, she, it **was frozen** we, you, they **were frozen**
Past *Prog.*	I, he, she, it **was freezing** we, you, they **were freezing**	I, he, she, it **was being frozen** we, you, they **were being frozen**
Past *Int.*	I, he, she, it, we, you, they **did freeze**	I, he, she, it, we, you, they **did get frozen**
Pres. *Perf.*	I, we, you, they **have frozen** he, she, it **has frozen**	I, we, you, they **have been frozen** he, she, it **has been frozen**
Past *Perf.*	I, he, she, it, we, you, they **had frozen**	I, he, she, it, we, you, they **had been frozen**
Fut. *Perf.*	I, he, she, it, we, you, they **will have frozen**	I, he, she, it, we, you, they **will have been frozen**

IMPERATIVE MOOD

freeze   **be frozen**

SUBJUNCTIVE MOOD

Pres.	if I, he, she, it, we, you, they **freeze**	if I, he, she, it, we, you, they **be frozen**
Past	if I, he, she, it, we, you, they **froze**	if I, he, she, it, we, you, they **were frozen**
Fut.	if I, he, she, it, we, you, they **should freeze**	if I, he, she, it, we, you, they **should be frozen**

Intransitive and transitive.

What does it mean "to freeze one's assets"?
They froze the client's account.
His finger tips were frozen after skiing for six hours.

frighten
(active voice)

PRINCIPAL PARTS: **frightens, frightening, frightened, frightened**

be frightened
(passive voice)

INDICATIVE MOOD

Pres.	I, we, you, they **frighten**	I **am frightened**
		we, you, they **are frightened**
	he, she, it **frightens**	he, she, it **is frightened**
Pres.	I **am frightening**	I **am being frightened**
Prog.	we, you, they **are frightening**	we, you, they **are being frightened**
	he, she, it **is frightening**	he, she, it **is being frightened**
Pres.	I, we, you, they **do frighten**	I, we, you, **do get frightened**
Int.	he, she, it **does frighten**	he, she, it **does get frightened**
Fut.	I, he, she, it,	I, he, she, it,
	we, you, they **will frighten**	we, you, they **will be frightened**
Past	I, he, she, it,	I, he, she, it **was frightened**
	we, you, they **frightened**	we, you, they **were frightened**
Past	I, he, she, it **was frightening**	I, he, she, it **was being frightened**
Prog.	we, you, they **were frightening**	we, you, they **were being frightened**
Past	I, he, she, it,	I, he, she, it, we, you, they
Int.	we, you, they **did frighten**	**did get frightened**
Pres.	I, we, you, they **have frightened**	I, we, you, they **have been frightened**
Perf.	he, she, it **has frightened**	he, she, it **has been frightened**
Past	I, he, she, it,	I, he, she, it,
Perf.	we, you, they **had frightened**	we, you, they **had been frightened**
Fut.	I, he, she, it, we, you, they	I, he, she, it, we, you, they
Perf.	**will have frightened**	**will have been frightened**

IMPERATIVE MOOD

frighten	**be frightened**

SUBJUNCTIVE MOOD

Pres.	if I, he, she, it,	if I, he, she, it,
	we, you, they **frighten**	we, you, they **be frightened**
Past	if I, he, she, it,	if I, he, she, it,
	we, you, they **frightened**	we, you, they **were frightened**
Fut.	if I, he, she, it,	if I, he, she, it,
	we, you, they **should frighten**	we, you, they **should be frightened**

The cat frightened the birds away.
I have never been so frightened by a movie.

INDICATIVE MOOD

Pres.	I, we, you, they **FTP**	I **am FTPed**
		we, you, they **are FTPed**
	he, she, it **FTPs**	he, she, it **is FTPed**
Pres.	I **am FTPing**	I **am being FTPed**
Prog.	we, you, they **are FTPing**	we, you, they **are being FTPed**
	he, she, it **is FTPing**	he, she, it **is being FTPed**
Pres.	I, we, you, they **do FTP**	I, we, you, they **do get FTPed**
Int.	he, she, it **does FTP**	he, she, it **does get FTPed**
Fut.	I, he, she, it,	I, he, she, it,
	we, you, they **will FTP**	we, you, they **will be FTPed**
Past	I, he, she, it,	I, he, she, it **was FTPed**
	we, you, they **FTPed**	we, you, they **were FTPed**
Past	I, he, she, it **was FTPing**	I, he, she, it **was being FTPed**
Prog.	we, you, they **were FTPing**	we, you, they **were being FTPed**
Past	I, he, she, it,	I, he, she, it, we, you, they
Int.	we, you, they **did FTP**	**did get FTPed**
Pres.	I, we, you, they **have FTPed**	I, we, you, they **have been FTPed**
Perf.	he, she, it **has FTPed**	he, she, it **has been FTPed**
Past	I, he, she, it,	I, he, she, it,
Perf.	we, you, they **had FTPed**	we, you, they **had been FTPed**
Fut.	I, he, she, it, we, you, they	I, he, she, it, we, you, they
Perf.	**will have FTPed**	**will have been FTPed**

IMPERATIVE MOOD

FTP **be FTPed**

SUBJUNCTIVE MOOD

Pres.	if I, he, she, it,	if I, he, she, it,
	we, you, they **FTP**	we, you, they **be FTPed**
Past	if I, he, she, it,	if I, he, she, it,
	we, you, they **FTPed**	we, you, they **were FTPed**
Fut.	if I, he, she, it,	if I, he, she, it,
	we, you, they **should FTP**	we, you, they **should be FTPed**

This verb is an abbreviation for "file transfer protocol." The letter "e" is normally omitted, when the word is written with an apostrophe after the "P": FTP'd. This verb can also be written in lower case, *ftp*.

You are FTPing that data to our server.
The budget was FTPed from headquarters to the CEO's laptop computer.

gamble
(active voice)

gambled
(passive voice)

INDICATIVE MOOD

Pres.	I, we, you, they **gamble**	I **am gambled**
		we, you, they **are gambled**
	he, she, it **gambles**	he, she, it **is gambled**
Pres.	I am **gambling**	I **am being gambled**
Prog.	we, you, they **are gambling**	we, you, they **are being gambled**
	he, she, it **is gambling**	he, she, it **is being gambled**
Pres.	I, we, you, they **do gamble**	I, we, you, they **do get gambled**
Int.	he, she, it **does gamble**	he, she, it **does get gambled**
Fut.	I, he, she, it,	I, he, she, it,
	we, you, they **will gamble**	we, you, they **will be gambled**
Past	I, he, she, it,	I, he, she, it **was gambled**
	we, you, they **gambled**	we, you, they **were gambled**
Past	I, he, she, it **was gambling**	I, he, she, it **was being gambled**
Prog.	we, you, they **were gambling**	we, you, they **were being gambled**
Past	I, he, she, it,	I, he, she, it,
Int.	we, you, they **did gamble**	we, you, they **did get gambled**
Pres.	I, we, you, they **have gambled**	I, we, you, they **have been gambled**
Perf.	he, she, it **has gambled**	he, she, it **has been gambled**
Past	I, he, she, it,	I, he, she, it,
Perf.	we, you, they **had gambled**	we, you, they **had been gambled**
Fut.	I, he, she, it, we, you, they	I, he, she, it, we, you, they
Perf.	**will have gambled**	**will have been gambled**

IMPERATIVE MOOD

gamble   **be gambled**

SUBJUNCTIVE MOOD

Pres.	if I, he, she, it,	if I, he, she, it,
	we, you, they **gamble**	we, you, they **be gambled**
Past	if I, he, she, it,	if I, he, she, it,
	we, you, they **gambled**	we, you, they **were gambled**
Fut.	if I, he, she, it,	if I, he, she, it,
	we, you, they **should gamble**	we, you, they **should be gambled**

G

He is gambling with the future of his family.
Unfortunately, the family's wealth was gambled away by their investment advisor.

get
(active voice)

PRINCIPAL PARTS: **gets, getting,**
got, gotten/got

be gotten/got
(passive voice)

INDICATIVE MOOD

Pres.	I, we, you, they **get**	I **am gotten**
		we, you, they **are gotten**
	he, she, it **gets**	he, she, it **is gotten**
Pres.	I **am getting**	I **am being gotten**
Prog.	we, you, they **are getting**	we, you, they **are being gotten**
	he, she, it **is getting**	he, she, it **is being gotten**
Pres.	I, we, you, they **do get**	I, we, you, they **do get gotten**
Int.	he, she, it **does get**	he, she, it **does get gotten**
Fut.	I, he, she, it,	I, he, she, it,
	we, you, they **will get**	we, you, they **will be gotten**
Past	I, he, she, it,	I, he, she, it **was gotten**
	we, you, they **got**	we, you, they **were gotten**
Past	I, he, she, it **was getting**	I, he, she, it **was being gotten**
Prog.	we, you, they **were getting**	we, you, they **were being gotten**
Past	I, he, she, it,	I, he, she, it,
Int.	we, you, they **did get**	we, you, they **did get gotten**
Pres.	I, we, you, they **have gotten**	I, we, you, they **have been gotten**
Perf.	he, she, it **has gotten**	he, she, it **has been gotten**
Past	I, he, she, it,	I, he, she, it,
Perf.	we, you, they **had gotten**	we, you, they **had been gotten**
Fut.	I, he, she, it, we, you, they	I, he, she, it, we, you, they
Perf.	**will have gotten**	**will have been gotten**

IMPERATIVE MOOD

get **be gotten**

SUBJUNCTIVE MOOD

Pres.	if I, he, she, it,	if I, he, she, it,
	we, you, they **get**	we, you, they **be gotten**
Past	if I, he, she, it,	if I, he, she, it,
	we, you, they **got**	we, you, they **were gotten**
Fut.	if I, he, she, it,	if I, he, she, it,
	we, you, they **should get**	we, you, they **should be gotten**

Transitive and intransitive. The past participle form may be either GOTTEN or GOT. The verb is used to make a passive statement, such as "I got elected." American English has both past participles, with GOT meaning "have" and GOTTEN meaning "obtained." The *Oxford Dictionary* prefers the past participle GOT. The archaic form of the past tense is GAT.

Where am I getting my information?
He got an earful of criticism.
The fortune was gotten by suspicious means.

180

Examples

I get it.

She gets the newspaper every day.

He gets her coffee.

We got the news from the radio.

Who will get the award?

Getting there is not easy.

I have gotten wet several times this week.

Get here before evening.

Who can get a car for the weekend?

She got a window seat for her flight.

Words and expressions related to this verb

G

Let's get together.

He must get his act together.

I've got you under my skin.

Get off at the next stop.

Can I get on the bus?

Get on the ball.

We have got to get going.

They got wet feet and decided to turn back.

He finally got it off his chest.

If you've got it, flaunt it.

Get on with your life.

You two must learn to get along with each other.

PRINCIPAL PARTS: **gives, giving, gave, given**

INDICATIVE MOOD

Pres.	I, we, you, they **give**	I **am given**
		we, you, they **are given**
	he, she, it **gives**	he, she, it **is given**
Pres.	I **am giving**	I **am being given**
Prog.	we, you, they **are giving**	we, you, they **are being given**
	he, she, it **is giving**	he, she, it **is being given**
Pres.	I, we, you, they **do give**	I, we, you, they **do get given**
Int.	he, she, it **does give**	he, she, it **does get given**
Fut.	I, he, she, it,	I, he, she, it,
	we, you, they **will give**	we, you, they **will be given**
Past	I, he, she, it,	I, he, she, it **was given**
	we, you, they **gave**	we, you, they **were given**
Past	I, he, she, it **was giving**	I, he, she, it **was being given**
Prog.	we, you, they **were giving**	we, you, they **were being given**
Past	I, he, she, it,	I, he, she, it,
Int.	we, you, they **did give**	we, you, they **did get given**
Pres.	I, we, you, they **have given**	I, we, you, they **have been given**
Perf.	he, she, it **has given**	he, she, it **has been given**
Past	I, he, she, it,	I, he, she, it,
Perf.	we, you, they **had given**	we, you, they **had been given**
Fut.	I, he, she, it, we, you, they	I, he, she, it, we, you, they
Perf.	**will have given**	**will have been given**

IMPERATIVE MOOD

give   **be given**

SUBJUNCTIVE MOOD

Pres.	if I, he, she, it,	if I, he, she, it,
	we, you, they **give**	we, you, they **be given**
Past	if I, he, she, it,	if I, he, she, it,
	we, you, they **gave**	we, you, they **were given**
Fut.	if I, he, she, it,	if I, he, she, it,
	we, you, they **should give**	we, you, they **should be given**

Transitive and intransitive.

I am not giving a donation at the office this year.
I already gave to that charity this year.
The flowers were given as a sign of his affection.

AN ESSENTIAL
55 VERB

give

Examples

She gives me everything I need.

I gave her the tapes.

She was given an award.

Who will give the address?

Have you been given the instructions?

Give me one more chance.

Given the evidence, he was justly convicted.

You give me hope.

What can you give to someone who has everything?

The acceptance speech was given by the chief executive officer.

Words and expressions related to this verb

Give up!

Don't give up.

It is better to give than to receive.

I will not give in.

I gave at the office.

She was given away by her father.

What gives?

Don't give me a hard time.

Give me liberty or give me death!

The satellite gives off a distinct signal.

The old motor finally gave out.

globalize
(active voice)

PRINCIPAL PARTS: **globalizes, globalizing, globalized, globalized**

be globalized
(passive voice)

INDICATIVE MOOD

Pres.	I, we, you, they **globalize**	I **am globalized** we, you, they **are globalized**
	he, she, it **globalizes**	he, she, it **is globalized**
Pres. *Prog.*	I am **globalizing** we, you, they **are globalizing** he, she, it **is globalizing**	I **am being globalized** we, you, they **are being globalized** he, she, it **is being globalized**
Pres. *Int.*	I, we, you, they **do globalize** he, she, it **does globalize**	I, we, you, they **do get globalized** he, she, it **does get globalized**
Fut.	I, he, she, it, we, you, they **will globalize**	I, he, she, it, we, you, they **will be globalized**
Past	I, he, she, it, we, you, they **globalized**	I, he, she, it **was globalized** we, you, they **were globalized**
Past *Prog.*	I, he, she, it **was globalizing** we, you, they **were globalizing**	I, he, she, it **was being globalized** we, you, they **were being globalized**
Past *Int.*	I, he, she, it, we, you, they **did globalize**	I, he, she, it, we, you, they **did get globalized**
Pres. *Perf.*	I, we, you, they **have globalized** he, she, it **has globalized**	I, we, you, they **have been globalized** he, she, it **has been globalized**
Past *Perf.*	I, he, she, it, we, you, they **had globalized**	I, he, she, it, we, you, they **had been globalized**
Fut. *Perf.*	I, he, she, it, we, you, they **will have globalized**	I, he, she, it, we, you, they **will have been globalized**

IMPERATIVE MOOD

globalize **be globalized**

SUBJUNCTIVE MOOD

Pres.	if I, he, she, it, we, you, they **globalize**	if I, he, she, it, we, you, they **be globalized**
Past	if I, he, she, it, we, you, they **globalized**	if I, he, she, it, we, you, they **were globalized**
Fut.	if I, he, she, it, we, you, they **should globalize**	if I, he, she, it, we, you, they **should be globalized**

Transitive and intransitive.

To expand our markets we are globalizing our distribution.
The financial operation has been completely globalized.

INDICATIVE MOOD

Pres.	I, we, you, they **go**	I **am gone** we, you, they **are gone**
	he, she, it **goes**	he, she, it **is gone**
Pres. *Prog.*	I **am going** we, you, they **are going** he, she, it **is going**	I **am being gone** we, you, they **are being gone** he, she, it **is being gone**
Pres. *Int.*	I, we, you, they **do go** he, she, it **does go**	I, we, you, they **do get gone** he, she, it **does get gone**
Fut.	I, he, she, it, we, you, they **will go**	I, he, she, it, we, you, they **will be gone**
Past	I, he, she, it, we, you, they **went**	I, he, she, it **was gone** we, you, they **were gone**
Past *Prog.*	I, he, she, it **was going** we, you, they **were going**	I, he, she, it **was being gone** we, you, they **were being gone**
Past *Int.*	I, he, she, it, we, you, they **did go**	I, he, she, it, we, you, they **did get gone**
Pres. *Perf.*	I, we, you, they **have gone** he, she, it **has gone**	I, we, you, they **have been gone** he, she, it **has been gone**
Past *Perf.*	I, he, she, it, we, you, they **had gone**	I, he, she, it, we, you, they **had been gone**
Fut. *Perf.*	I, he, she, it, we, you, they **will have gone**	I, he, she, it, we, you, they **will have been gone**

IMPERATIVE MOOD

go	**be gone**

SUBJUNCTIVE MOOD

Pres.	if I, he, she, it, we, you, they **go**	if I, he, she, it, we, you, they **be gone**
Past	if I, he, she, it, we, you, they **went**	if I, he, she, it, we, you, they **were gone**
Fut.	if I, he, she, it, we, you, they **should go**	if I, he, she, it, we, you, they **should be gone**

Intransitive and transitive.

Wherever she goes, I am going too.
We went to the circus with the children.
The time for hesitation has come and gone.

AN ESSENTIAL
55 VERB

185

go

Examples

He goes to the bookstore every Saturday.

I go fishing and hunting in Vermont.

She went home alone.

I would go to the concert if I had the money.

Go home.

They will go to visit him in the hospital.

We have gone there every summer.

Soon the summer will be gone.

I could have gone places.

You should have gone to law school.

Words and expressions related to this verb

That ball is going, going, gone.

He's been and gone.

You can't go home anymore.

The music goes on and on.

Life goes on.

The lights went out.

The cannon goes off at noon.

They simply go about their jobs.

He often goes off by himself.

We are going to get you.

She went off to sleep immediately.

google
(active voice)

be googled
(passive voice)

INDICATIVE MOOD

Pres.	I, we, you, they **google**	I **am googled**
		we, you, they **are googled**
	he, she, it **googles**	he, she, it **is googled**
Pres.	I am **googling**	I **am being googled**
Prog.	we, you, they **are googling**	we, you, they **are being googled**
	he, she, it **is googling**	he, she, it **is being googled**
Pres.	I, we, you, they **do google**	I, we, you, they **do get googled**
Int.	he, she, it **does google**	he, she, it **does get googled**
Fut.	I, he, she, it,	I, he, she, it,
	we, you, they **will google**	we, you, they **will be googled**
Past	I, he, she, it,	I, he, she, it **was googled**
	we, you, they **googled**	we, you, they **were googled**
Past	I, he, she, it **was googling**	I, he, she, it **was being googled**
Prog.	we, you, they **were googling**	we, you, they **were being googled**
Past	I, he, she, it,	I, he, she, it,
Int.	we, you, they **did google**	we, you, they **did get googled**
Pres.	I, we, you, they **have googled**	I, we, you, they **have been googled**
Perf.	he, she, it **has googled**	he, she, it **has been googled**
Past	I, he, she, it,	I, he, she, it,
Perf.	we, you, they **had googled**	we, you, they **had been googled**
Fut.	I, he, she, it, we, you, they	I, he, she, it, we, you, they
Perf.	**will have googled**	**will have been googled**

IMPERATIVE MOOD

google   **be googled**

SUBJUNCTIVE MOOD

Pres.	if I, he, she, it,	if I, he, she, it,
	we, you, they **google**	we, you, they **be googled**
Past	if I, he, she, it,	if I, he, she, it,
	we, you, they **googled**	we, you, they **were googled**
Fut.	if I, he, she, it,	if I, he, she, it,
	we, you, they **should google**	we, you, they **should be googled**

Transitive and intransitive.

You were googling almost every word.
I know people who keep a record of how often they themselves are googled.

G

grind
(active voice)

be ground
(passive voice)

INDICATIVE MOOD

Pres.	I, we, you, they **grind**	I **am ground** we, you, they **are ground**
	he, she, it **grinds**	he, she, it **is ground**
Pres. *Prog.*	I **am grinding** we, you, they **are grinding** he, she, it **is grinding**	I **am being ground** we, you, they **are being ground** he, she, it **is being ground**
Pres. *Int.*	I, we, you, they **do grind** he, she, it **does grind**	I, we, you, they **do get ground** he, she, it **does get ground**
Fut.	I, he, she, it, we, you, they **will grind**	I, he, she, it, we, you, they **will be ground**
Past	I, he, she, it, we, you, they **ground**	I, he, she, it **was ground** we, you, they **were ground**
Past *Prog.*	I, he, she, it **was grinding** we, you, they **were grinding**	I, he, she, it **was being ground** we, you, they **were being ground**
Past *Int.*	I, he, she, it, we, you, they **did grind**	I, he, she, it, we, you, they **did get ground**
Pres. *Perf.*	I, we, you, they **have ground** he, she, it **has ground**	I, we, you, they **have been ground** he, she, it **has been ground**
Past *Perf.*	I, he, she, it, we, you, they **had ground**	I, he, she, it, we, you, they **had been ground**
Fut. *Perf.*	I, he, she, it, we, you, they **will have ground**	I, he, she, it, we, you, they **will have been ground**

IMPERATIVE MOOD

grind be ground

be ground

SUBJUNCTIVE MOOD

Pres.	if I, he, she, it, we, you, they **grind**	if I, he, she, it, we, you, they **be ground**
Past	if I, he, she, it, we, you, they **ground**	if I, he, she, it, we, you, they **were ground**
Fut.	if I, he, she, it, we, you, they **should grind**	if I, he, she, it, we, you, they **should be ground**

Transitive and intransitive.

The shop grinds its coffee for every cup.
The coffee was ground extra fine.

grow	PRINCIPAL PARTS: grows, growing,	be grown
(active voice)	grew, grown	(passive voice)

INDICATIVE MOOD

Pres.   I, we, you, they **grow**   I **am grown**
we, you, they **are grown**
         he, she, it **grows**   he, she, it **is grown**

Pres.   I **am growing**   I **am being grown**
Prog.   we, you, they **are growing**   we, you, they **are being grown**
         he, she, it **is growing**   he, she, it **is being grown**

Pres.   I, we, you, they **do grow**   I, we, you, they **do get grown**
Int.   he, she, it **does grow**   he, she, it **does get grown**

Fut.   I, he, she, it,   I, he, she, it,
         we, you, they **will grow**   we, you, they **will be grown**

Past   I, he, she, it,   I, he, she, it **was grown**
         we, you, they **grew**   we, you, they **were grown**

Past   I, he, she, it **was growing**   I, he, she, it **was being grown**
Prog.   we, you, they **were growing**   we, you, they **were being grown**

Past   I, he, she, it,   I, he, she, it,
Int.   we, you, they **did grow**   we, you, they **did get grown**

Pres.   I, we, you, they **have grown**   I, we, you, they **have been grown**
Perf.   he, she, it **has grown**   he, she, it **has been grown**

Past   I, he, she, it,   I, he, she, it,
Perf.   we, you, they **had grown**   we, you, they **had been grown**

Fut.   I, he, she, it, we, you, they   I, he, she, it, we, you, they
Perf.   **will have grown**   **will have been grown**

IMPERATIVE MOOD

     grow   **be grown**

SUBJUNCTIVE MOOD

Pres.   if I, he, she, it,   if I, he, she, it,
         we, you, they **grow**   we, you, they **be grown**

Past   if I, he, she, it,   if I, he, she, it,
         we, you, they **grew**   we, you, they **were grown**

Fut.   if I, he, she, it,   if I, he, she, it,
         we, you, they **should grow**   we, you, they **should be grown**

G

Intransitive and transitive.

The young boy grew quite a bit in just a year.
I prefer fruits and vegetables that are grown locally.

| guess
(active voice) | PRINCIPAL PARTS: **guesses, guessing,**
guessed, guessed | be guessed
(passive voice) |

INDICATIVE MOOD

Pres.	I, we, you, they **guess**	I **am guessed** we, you, they **are guessed**
	he, she, it **guesses**	he, she, it **is guessed**
Pres. *Prog.*	I **am guessing** we, you, they **are guessing** he, she, it **is guessing**	I **am being guessed** we, you, they **are being guessed** he, she, it **is being guessed**
Pres. *Int.*	I, we, you, they **do guess** he, she, it **does guess**	I, we, you, they **do get guessed** he, she, it **does get guessed**
Fut.	I, he, she, it, we, you, they **will guess**	I, he, she, it, we, you, they **will be guessed**
Past	I, he, she, it, we, you, they **guessed**	I, he, she, it **was guessed** we, you, they **were guessed**
Past *Prog.*	I, he, she, it **was guessing** we, you, they **were guessing**	I, he, she, it **was being guessed** we, you, they **were being guessed**
Past *Int.*	I, he, she, it, we, you, they **did guess**	I, he, she, it, we, you, they **did get guessed**
Pres. *Perf.*	I, we, you, they **have guessed** he, she, it **has guessed**	I, we, you, they **have been guessed** he, she, it **has been guessed**
Past *Perf.*	I, he, she, it, we, you, they **had guessed**	I, he, she, it, we, you, they **had been guessed**
Fut. *Perf.*	I, he, she, it, we, you, they **will have guessed**	I, he, she, it, we, you, they **will have been guessed**

IMPERATIVE MOOD

guess	**be guessed**

SUBJUNCTIVE MOOD

Pres.	if I, he, she, it, we, you, they **guess**	if I, he, she, it, we, you, they **be guessed**
Past	if I, he, she, it, we, you, they **guessed**	if I, he, she, it, we, you, they **were guessed**
Fut.	if I, he, she, it, we, you, they **should guess**	if I, he, she, it, we, you, they **should be guessed**

Transitive and intransitive.

She guesses all the time.
I could never have guessed his age.
Choose a password that is not easily guessed.

190

hack
(active voice)

be hacked
(passive voice)

INDICATIVE MOOD

Pres.	I, we, you, they **hack**	I **am hacked**
		we, you, they **are hacked**
	he, she, it **hacks**	he, she, it **is hacked**
Pres.	I **am hacking**	I **am being hacked**
Prog.	we, you, they **are hacking**	we, you, they **are being hacked**
	he, she, it **is hacking**	he, she, it **is being hacked**
Pres.	I, we, you, they **do hack**	I, we, you, they **do get hacked**
Int.	he, she, it **does hack**	he, she, it **does get hacked**
Fut.	I, he, she, it,	I, he, she, it,
	we, you, they **will hack**	we, you, they **will be hacked**
Past	I, he, she, it,	I, he, she, it **was hacked**
	we, you, they **hacked**	we, you, they **were hacked**
Past	I, he, she, it **was hacking**	I, he, she, it **was being hacked**
Prog.	we, you, they **were hacking**	we, you, they **were being hacked**
Past	I, he, she, it,	I, he, she, it,
Int.	we, you, they **did hack**	we, you, they **did get hacked**
Pres.	I, we, you, they **have hacked**	I, we, you, they **have been hacked**
Perf.	he, she, it **has hacked**	he, she, it **has been hacked**
Past	I, he, she, it,	I, he, she, it,
Perf.	we, you, they **had hacked**	we, you, they **had been hacked**
Fut.	I, he, she, it, we, you, they	I, he, she, it, we, you, they
Perf.	**will have hacked**	**will have been hacked**

IMPERATIVE MOOD

hack   **be hacked**

SUBJUNCTIVE MOOD

Pres.	if I, he, she, it,	if I, he, she, it,
	we, you, they **hack**	we, you, they **be hacked**
Past	if I, he, she, it,	if I, he, she, it,
	we, you, they **hacked**	we, you, they **were hacked**
Fut.	if I, he, she, it,	if I, he, she, it,
	we, you, they **should hack**	we, you, they **should be hacked**

Transitive and intransitive.

They spent hours and hours and ultimately hacked into other computers.
After several hours a path had been hacked out of the wilderness.

PRINCIPAL PARTS: **handles, handling, handled, handled**

be handled
(passive voice)

INDICATIVE MOOD

Pres.	I, we, you, they **handle**	I **am handled**
		we, you, they **are handled**
	he, she, it **handles**	he, she, it **is handled**
Pres.	I **am handling**	I **am being handled**
Prog.	we, you, they **are handling**	we, you, they **are being handled**
	he, she, it **is handling**	he, she, it **is being handled**
Pres.	I, we, you, they **do handle**	I, we, you, they **do get handled**
Int.	he, she, it **does handle**	he, she, it **does get handled**
Fut.	I, he, she, it,	I, he, she, it,
	we, you, they **will handle**	we, you, they **will be handled**
Past	I, he, she, it,	I, he, she, it **was handled**
	we, you, they **handled**	we, you, they **were handled**
Past	I, he, she, it **was handling**	I, he, she, it **was being handled**
Prog.	we, you, they **were handling**	we, you, they **were being handled**
Past	I, he, she, it,	I, he, she, it,
Int.	we, you, they **did handle**	we, you, they **did get handled**
Pres.	I, we, you, they **have handled**	I, we, you, they **have been handled**
Perf.	he, she, it **has handled**	he, she, it **has been handled**
Past	I, he, she, it,	I, he, she, it,
Perf.	we, you, they **had handled**	we, you, they **had been handled**
Fut.	I, he, she, it, we, you, they	I, he, she, it, we, you, they
Perf.	**will have handled**	**will have been handled**

IMPERATIVE MOOD

handle   **be handled**

SUBJUNCTIVE MOOD

Pres.	if I, he, she, it,	if I, he, she, it,
	we, you, they **handle**	we, you, they **be handled**
Past	if I, he, she, it,	if I, he, she, it,
	we, you, they **handled**	we, you, they **were handled**
Fut.	if I, he, she, it,	if I, he, she, it,
	we, you, they **should handle**	we, you, they **should be handled**

Transitive and intransitive.

How well is he handling the new challenges?
The unruly guest was easily handled by the security guard.

PRINCIPAL PARTS: **hangs, hanging, hung, hung**

INDICATIVE MOOD

Pres.	I, we, you, they **hang**	I **am hung**
		we, you, they **are hung**
	he, she, it **hangs**	he, she, it **is hung**
Pres. *Prog.*	I **am hanging**	I **am being hung**
	we, you, they **are hanging**	we, you, they **are being hung**
	he, she, it **is hanging**	he, she, it **is being hung**
Pres. *Int.*	I, we, you, they **do hang**	I, we, you, they **do get hung**
	he, she, it **does hang**	he, she, it **does get hung**
Fut.	I, he, she, it,	I, he, she, it,
	we, you, they **will hang**	we, you, they **will be hung**
Past	I, he, she, it,	I, he, she, it **was hung**
	we, you, they **hung**	we, you, they **were hung**
Past *Prog.*	I, he, she, it **was hanging**	I, he, she, it **was being hung**
	we, you, they **were hanging**	we, you, they **were being hung**
Past *Int.*	I, he, she, it,	I, he, she, it,
	we, you, they **did hang**	we, you, they **did get hung**
Pres. *Perf.*	I, we, you, they **have hung**	I, we, you, they **have been hung**
	he, she, it **has hung**	he, she, it **has been hung**
Past *Perf.*	I, he, she, it,	I, he, she, it,
	we, you, they **had hung**	we, you, they **had been hung**
Fut. *Perf.*	I, he, she, it, we, you, they	I, he, she, it, we, you, they
	will have hung	**will have been hung**

IMPERATIVE MOOD

hang   **be hung**

SUBJUNCTIVE MOOD

Pres.	if I, he, she, it,	if I, he, she, it,
	we, you, they **hang**	we, you, they **be hung**
Past	if I, he, she, it,	if I, he, she, it,
	we, you, they **hung**	we, you, they **were hung**
Fut.	if I, he, she, it,	if I, he, she, it,
	we, you, they **should hang**	we, you, they **should be hung**

Transitive and intransitive. This means to "hang an object, fasten something."

Where was it that we hung this picture?
The stockings were hung by the chimney with care.

| hang
(active voice) | PRINCIPAL PARTS: **hangs, hanging,**
hanged, hanged | be hanged
(passive voice) |

INDICATIVE MOOD

Pres.	I, we, you, they **hang** he, she, it **hangs**	**I am hanged** we, you, they **are hanged** he, she, it **is hanged**
Pres. *Prog.*	**I am hanging** we, you, they **are hanging** he, she, it **is hanging**	**I am being hanged** we, you, they **are being hanged** he, she, it **is being hanged**
Pres. *Int.*	I, we, you, they **do hang** he, she, it **does hang**	I, we, you, they **do get hanged** he, she, it **does get hanged**
Fut.	I, he, she, it, we, you, they **will hang**	I, he, she, it, we, you, they **will be hanged**
Past	I, he, she, it, we, you, they **hanged**	I, he, she, it **was hanged** we, you, they **were hanged**
Past *Prog.*	I, he, she, it **was hanging** we, you, they **were hanging**	I, he, she, it **was being hanged** we, you, they **were being hanged**
Past *Int.*	I, he, she, it, we, you, they **did hang**	I, he, she, it, we, you, they **did get hanged**
Pres. *Perf.*	I, we, you, they **have hanged** he, she, it **has hanged**	I, we, you, they **have been hanged** he, she, it **has been hanged**
Past *Perf.*	I, he, she, it, we, you, they **had hanged**	I, he, she, it, we, you, they **had been hanged**
Fut. *Perf.*	I, he, she, it, we, you, they **will have hanged**	I, he, she, it, we, you, they **will have been hanged**

IMPERATIVE MOOD

hang	**be hanged**

SUBJUNCTIVE MOOD

Pres.	if I, he, she, it, we, you, they **hang**	if I, he, she, it, we, you, they **be hanged**
Past	if I, he, she, it, we, you, they **hanged**	if I, he, she, it, we, you, they **were hanged**
Fut.	if I, he, she, it, we, you, they **should hang**	if I, he, she, it, we, you, they **should be hanged**

Transitive and intransitive. This means to "execute a person by hanging" or to "express exasperation."

I thought they hanged Jesse James?
In the Old West outlaws were hanged.

INDICATIVE MOOD

Pres.   I, we, you, they **happen**

           he, she, it **happens**

Pres.   I **am happening**
Prog.   we, you, they **are happening**
           he, she, it **is happening**

Pres.   I, we, you, they **do happen**
Int.   he, she, it **does happen**

Fut.   I, he, she, it,
           we, you, they **will happen**

Past   I, he, she, it,
           we, you, they **happened**

Past   I, he, she, it **was happening**
Prog.   we, you, they **were happening**

Past   I, he, she, it,
Int.   we, you, they **did happen**

Pres.   I, we, you, they **have happened**
Perf.   he, she, it **has happened**

Past   I, he, she, it,
Perf.   we, you, they **had happened**

Fut.   I, he, she, it, we, you, they
Perf.   **will have happened**

IMPERATIVE MOOD

happen

SUBJUNCTIVE MOOD

Pres.   if I, he, she, it,
           we, you, they **happen**

Past   if I, he, she, it,
           we, you, they **happened**

Fut.   if I, he, she, it,
           we, you, they **should happen**

It often happens that the bus comes late.
Tell us how it happened.

AN ESSENTIAL
55 VERB

happen

Examples

She happens to like classical music.

What happened last night?

It was happening while we slept.

Where did the accident happen?

Do you happen to know his address?

He happens to be a physician.

What will happen with the children?

It should happen no later than next Monday.

Don't let any mistakes happen.

I remember that such an occurrence had happened once before.

| hate
(active voice) | PRINCIPAL PARTS: **hates, hating,
hated, hated** | **be hated**
(passive voice) |

INDICATIVE MOOD

Pres.	I, we, you, they **hate** he, she, it **hates**	I **am hated** we, you, they **are hated** he, she, it **is hated**
Pres. *Prog.*	I **am hating** we, you, they **are hating** he, she, it **is hating**	I **am being hated** we, you, they **are being hated** he, she, it **is being hated**
Pres. *Int.*	I, we, you, they **do hate** he, she, it **does hate**	I, we, you, they **do get hated** he, she, it **does get hated**
Fut.	I, he, she, it, we, you, they **will hate**	I, he, she, it, we, you, they **will be hated**
Past	I, he, she, it, we, you, they **hated**	I, he, she, it **was hated** we, you, they **were hated**
Past *Prog.*	I, he, she, it **was hating** we, you, they **were hating**	I, he, she, it **was being hated** we, you, they **were being hated**
Past *Int.*	I, he, she, it, we, you, they **did hate**	I, he, she, it, we, you, they **did get hated**
Pres. *Perf.*	I, we, you, they **have hated** he, she, it **has hated**	I, we, you, they **have been hated** he, she, it **has been hated**
Past *Perf.*	I, he, she, it, we, you, they **had hated**	I, he, she, it, we, you, they **had been hated**
Fut. *Perf.*	I, he, she, it, we, you, they **will have hated**	I, he, she, it, we, you, they **will have been hated**

IMPERATIVE MOOD

hate	**be hated**

SUBJUNCTIVE MOOD

Pres.	if I, he, she, it, we, you, they **hate**	if I, he, she, it, we, you, they **be hated**
Past	if I, he, she, it, we, you, they **hated**	if I, he, she, it, we, you, they **were hated**
Fut.	if I, he, she, it, we, you, they **should hate**	if I, he, she, it, we, you, they **should be hated**

Transitive and intransitive.

They are hating these cold mornings.
They say he was loved by few and hated by many.

have
(active voice)

PRINCIPAL PARTS: has, having,
had, had

be had
(passive voice)

INDICATIVE MOOD

Pres.	I, we, you, they **have**	I **am had**
		we, you, they **are had**
	he, she, it **has**	he, she, it **is had**
Pres. *Prog.*	I **am having**	I am being **had**
	we, you, they **are having**	we, you, they **are being had**
	he, she, it **is having**	he, she, it **is being had**
Pres. *Int.*	I, we, you, they **do have**	I, we, you, they **do get had**
	he, she, it **does have**	he, she, it **does get had**
Fut.	I, he, she, it, we, you, they **will have**	I, he, she, it, we, you, they **will be had**
Past	I, he, she, it, we, you, they **had**	I, he, she, it **was had** we, you, they **were had**
Past *Prog.*	I, he, she, it **was having** we, you, they **were having**	I, he, she, it **was being had** we, you, they **were being had**
Past *Int.*	I, he, she, it, we, you, they **did have**	I, he, she, it, we, you, they **did get had**
Pres. *Perf.*	I, we, you, they **have had** he, she, it **has had**	I, we, you, they **have been had** he, she, it **has been had**
Past *Perf.*	I, he, she, it, we, you, they **had had**	I, he, she, it, we, you, they **had been had**
Fut. *Perf.*	I, he, she, it, we, you, they **will have had**	I, he, she, it, we, you, they **will have been had**

IMPERATIVE MOOD

have	**be had**

SUBJUNCTIVE MOOD

Pres.	if I, he, she, it, we, you, they **have**	if I, he, she, it, we, you, they **be had**
Past	if I, he, she, it, we, you, they **had**	if I, he, she, it, we, you, they **were had**
Fut.	if I, he, she, it, we, you, they **should have**	if I, he, she, it, we, you, they **should be had**

As a transitive verb, HAVE means "possessing." It is also an auxiliary verb used to form the perfect tenses. It can be contracted: I have = I've, you have = you've, she has = she's, he has = he's, she had = she'd, he had = he'd; the negative contractions are haven't, hasn't, hadn't.

Who has a copy of that book?
Are you having a good time?
They had a very long and bumpy flight.
A good time was had by all.

AN ESSENTIAL
55 VERB

have

Examples

I have you, babe.

She has time and money.

He has expensive tastes.

You have no right to ask me that.

They have the right idea.

To have and to hold.

She had a bad day.

We will have lots of fun.

Are they having a baby?

Having you means everything to me.

I have had it with her.

Words and expressions related to this verb

I've lots of patience.

I have no money.

I haven't got the time.

She had no chance to win.

He hadn't a chance.

We've no problem with your offer.

I have to go.

She had to write a paper.

They will have to return tomorrow.

What did she have on last night?

hear	PRINCIPAL PARTS: hears, hearing,	be heard
(active voice)	heard, heard	(passive voice)

INDICATIVE MOOD

Pres.	I, we, you, they **hear**	I **am heard** we, you, they **are heard**
	he, she, it **hears**	he, she, it **is heard**
Pres. *Prog.*	I **am hearing** we, you, they **are hearing** he, she, it **is hearing**	I **am being heard** we, you, they **are being heard** he, she, it **is being heard**
Pres. *Int.*	I, we, you, they **do hear** he, she, it **does hear**	I, we, you, they **do get heard** he, she, it **does get heard**
Fut.	I, he, she, it, we, you, they **will hear**	I, he, she, it, we, you, they **will be heard**
Past	I, he, she, it, we, you, they **heard**	I, he, she, it **was heard** we, you, they **were heard**
Past *Prog.*	I, he, she, it **was hearing** we, you, they **were hearing**	I, he, she, it **was being heard** we, you, they **were being heard**
Past *Int.*	I, he, she, it, we, you, they **did hear**	I, he, she, it, we, you, they **did get heard**
Pres. *Perf.*	I, we, you, they **have heard** he, she, it **has heard**	I, we, you, they **have been heard** he, she, it **has been heard**
Past *Perf.*	I, he, she, it, we, you, they **had heard**	I, he, she, it, we, you, they **had been heard**
Fut. *Perf.*	I, he, she, it, we, you, they **will have heard**	I, he, she, it, we, you, they **will have been heard**

IMPERATIVE MOOD

hear	**be heard**

SUBJUNCTIVE MOOD

Pres.	if I, he, she, it, we, you, they **hear**	if I, he, she, it, we, you, they **be heard**
Past	if I, he, she, it, we, you, they **heard**	if I, he, she, it, we, you, they **were heard**
Fut.	if I, he, she, it, we, you, they **should hear**	if I, he, she, it, we, you, they **should be heard**

Transitive and intransitive.

Have you heard the latest news?
The shot was heard around the world.

AN ESSENTIAL
55 VERB

AN ESSENTIAL 55 VERB

Examples

He hears better with a hearing aid.

She had heard that lecture once before.

I hear excuses all day long.

Have you heard the news?

You will hear from us within a week.

You should have heard that concert.

Hear that note.

I am hearing a lot of static.

Nothing was heard from him for weeks.

I would like to hear your version of the events.

Words and expressions related to this verb

I hear the sound of music.

I've heard it all before.

Can you hear me now?

Which judge is hearing the case?

The shot was heard around the world.

You could hear a pin drop.

Let he who has ears hear.

Have you heard of the Beatles?

I simply will not hear of it.

Hear me out.

heave
(active voice)

be heaved
(passive voice)

INDICATIVE MOOD

Pres.	I, we, you, they **heave**	I **am heaved**
		we, you, they **are heaved**
	he, she, it **heaves**	he, she, it **is heaved**
Pres.	I **am heaving**	I **am being heaved**
Prog.	we, you, they **are heaving**	we, you, they **are being heaved**
	he, she, it **is heaving**	he, she, it **is being heaved**
Pres.	I, we, you, they **do heave**	I, we, you, they **do get heaved**
Int.	he, she, it **does heave**	he, she, it **does get heaved**
Fut.	I, he, she, it,	I, he, she, it,
	we, you, they **will heave**	we, you, they **will be heaved**
Past	I, he, she, it	I, he, she, it **was heaved**
	we, you, they **heaved**	we, you, they **were heaved**
Past	I, he, she, it **was heaving**	I, he, she, it **was being heaved**
Prog.	we, you, they **were heaving**	we, you, they **were being heaved**
Past	I, he, she, it,	I, he, she, it,
Int.	we, you, they **did heave**	we, you, they **did get heaved**
Pres.	I, we, you, they **have heaved**	I, we, you, they **have been heaved**
Perf.	he, she, it **has heaved**	he, she, it **has been heaved**
Past	I, he, she, it,	I, he, she, it,
Perf.	we, you, they **had heaved**	we, you, they **had been heaved**
Fut.	I, he, she, it, we, you, they	I, he, she, it, we, you, they
Perf.	**will have heaved**	**will have been heaved**

IMPERATIVE MOOD

heave | **be heaved**

SUBJUNCTIVE MOOD

Pres.	if I, he, she, it,	if I, he, she, it,
	we, you, they **heave**	we, you, they **be heaved**
Past	if I, he, she, it,	if I, he, she, it,
	we, you, they **heaved**	we, you, they **were heaved**
Fut.	if I, he, she, it,	if I, he, she, it,
	we, you, they **should heave**	we, you, they **should be heaved**

Transitive and intransitive. The past tense and past participle HOVE is used in nautical terminology meaning "move alongside, pull, or haul in rope or cable."

They heaved the line to the workman on the dock.
They were heaved out of the water by a pair of strong arms.
The smaller ship hove to on the captain's order.

AN ESSENTIAL 55 VERB

help

Examples

Can you help me?

She was always willing to help.

We helped them to move into the new house.

Their cause was helped by the publicity.

The mother helps her daughter with her homework.

Your comments are not helping the situation.

They helped the little boy up onto the chair.

They had always helped when asked.

She was helped off the stage.

I am helping out with the production.

Words and expressions related to this verb

Help the poor.

Help yourself.

Help! I need somebody.

Nothing helps.

Use your power to help people.

The gods help them that help themselves.

We are here to help, not to hinder you.

I couldn't help but wonder.

God help us.

Shouting does not help.

help
(active voice)

be helped
(passive voice)

INDICATIVE MOOD

Pres.	I, we, you, they **help**	I **am helped**
		we, you, they **are helped**
	he, she, it **helps**	he, she, it **is helped**
Pres.	I **am helping**	I **am being helped**
Prog.	we, you, they **are helping**	we, you, they **are being helped**
	he, she, it **is helping**	he, she, it **is being helped**
Pres.	I, we, you, they **do help**	I, we, you, they **do get helped**
Int.	he, she, it **does help**	he, she, it **does get helped**
Fut.	I, he, she, it,	I, he, she, it,
	we, you, they **will help**	we, you, they **will be helped**
Past	I, he, she, it,	I, he, she, it **was helped**
	we, you, they **helped**	we, you, they **were helped**
Past	I, he, she, it **was helping**	I, he, she, it **was being helped**
Prog.	we, you, they **were helping**	we, you, they **were being helped**
Past	I, he, she, it,	I, he, she, it,
Int.	we, you, they **did help**	we, you, they **did get helped**
Pres.	I, we, you, they **have helped**	I, we, you, they **have been helped**
Perf.	he, she, it **has helped**	he, she, it **has been helped**
Past	I, he, she, it,	I, he, she, it,
Perf.	we, you, they **had helped**	we, you, they **had been helped**
Fut.	I, he, she, it, we, you, they	I, he, she, it, we, you, they
Perf.	**will have helped**	**will have been helped**

IMPERATIVE MOOD

help   **be helped**

SUBJUNCTIVE MOOD

Pres.	if I, he, she, it,	if I, he, she, it,
	we, you, they **help**	we, you, they **be helped**
Past	if I, he, she, it,	if I, he, she, it,
	we, you, they **helped**	we, you, they **were helped**
Fut.	if I, he, she, it,	if I, he, she, it,
	we, you, they **should help**	we, you, they **should be helped**

Transitive and intransitive.

We helped them through difficult times.
I was often helped by my brother.

hide
(active voice)

be hidden/hid
(passive voice)

INDICATIVE MOOD

Pres.	I, we, you, they **hide**	I **am hidden**
		we, you, they **are hidden**
	he, she, it **hides**	he, she, it **is hidden**
Pres. *Prog.*	I **am hiding**	I **am being hidden**
	we, you, they **are hiding**	we, you, they **are being hidden**
	he, she, it **is hiding**	he, she, it **is being hidden**
Pres. *Int.*	I, we, you, they **do hide**	I, we, you, they **do get hidden**
	he, she, it **does hide**	he, she, it **does get hidden**
Fut.	I, he, she, it,	I, he, she, it,
	we, you, they **will hide**	we, you, they **will be hidden**
Past	I, he, she, it,	I, he, she, it **was hidden**
	we, you, they **hid**	we, you, they **were hidden**
Past *Prog.*	I, he, she, it **was hiding**	I, he, she, it **was being hidden**
	we, you, they **were hiding**	we, you, they **were being hidden**
Past *Int.*	I, he, she, it,	I, he, she, it,
	we, you, they **did hide**	we, you, they **did get hidden**
Pres. *Perf.*	I, we, you, they **have hidden**	I, we, you, they **have been hidden**
	he, she, it **has hidden**	he, she, it **has been hidden**
Past *Perf.*	I, he, she, it,	I, he, she, it,
	we, you, they **had hidden**	we, you, they **had been hidden**
Fut. *Perf.*	I, he, she, it, we, you, they	I, he, she, it, we, you, they
	will have hidden	**will have been hidden**

IMPERATIVE MOOD

hide   **be hidden**

SUBJUNCTIVE MOOD

Pres.	if I, he, she, it,	if I, he, she, it,
	we, you, they **hide**	we, you, they **be hidden**
Past	if I, he, she, it,	if I, he, she, it,
	we, you, they **hid**	we, you, they **were hidden**
Fut.	if I, he, she, it,	if I, he, she, it,
	we, you, they **should hide**	we, you, they **should be hidden**

Transitive and intransitive. The verb means to "be or put out of sight." The past participle may be either HIDDEN or HID. The *Oxford Dictionary* considers the past participle HID archaic. The verb HIDE, HIDES, HIDING, HIDED, HIDED means to "beat or flog."

Who is hiding in there?
They hid in a basement until the danger had passed.
The secret treasure was hidden in a cave.

| **hit** | PRINCIPAL PARTS: **hits, hitting,** | **be hit** |
| (active voice) | **hit, hit** | (passive voice) |

INDICATIVE MOOD

Pres.	I, we, you, they **hit**	I **am hit**
		we, you, they **are hit**
	he, she, it **hits**	he, she, it **is hit**
Pres.	I **am hitting**	I **am being hit**
Prog.	we, you, they **are hitting**	we, you, they **are being hit**
	he, she, it **is hitting**	he, she, it **is being hit**
Pres.	I, we, you, they **do hit**	I, we, you, they **do get hit**
Int.	he, she, it **does hit**	he, she, it **does get hit**
Fut.	I, he, she, it,	I, he, she, it,
	we, you, they **will hit**	we, you, they **will be hit**
Past	I, he, she, it,	I, he, she, it **was hit**
	we, you, they **hit**	we, you, they **were hit**
Past	I, he, she, it **was hitting**	I, he, she, it **was being hit**
Prog.	we, you, they **were hitting**	we, you, they **were being hit**
Past	I, he, she, it,	I, he, she, it,
Int.	we, you, they **did hit**	we, you, they **did get hit**
Pres.	I, we, you, they **have hit**	I, we, you, they **have been hit**
Perf.	he, she, it **has hit**	he, she, it **has been hit**
Past	I, he, she, it,	I, he, she, it,
Perf.	we, you, they **had hit**	we, you, they **had been hit**
Fut.	I, he, she, it, we, you, they	I, he, she, it, we, you, they
Perf.	**will have hit**	**will have been hit**

IMPERATIVE MOOD

hit　　　　　　　　　　**be hit**

SUBJUNCTIVE MOOD

Pres.	if I, he, she, it,	if I, he, she, it,
	we, you, they **hit**	we, you, they **be hit**
Past	if I, he, she, it,	if I, he, she, it,
	we, you, they **hit**	we, you, they **were hit**
Fut.	if I, he, she, it,	if I, he, she, it,
	we, you, they **should hit**	we, you, they **should be hit**

Transitive and intransitive.

She hits a golf ball further than her brother.
Who keeps hitting the ball out of bounds?
Yesterday he hit another car on the way to work.
The city was hit by several blizzards this winter.

hold	Principal Parts: **holds, holding,**	be held
(active voice)	**held, held**	(passive voice)

INDICATIVE MOOD

Pres.	I, we, you, they **hold**	I **am held**
		we, you, they **are held**
	he, she, it **holds**	he, she, it **is held**
Pres.	I **am holding**	I **am being held**
Prog.	we, you, they **are holding**	we, you, they **are being held**
	he, she, it **is holding**	he, she, it **is being held**
Pres.	I, we, you, they **do hold**	I, we, you, they **do get held**
Int.	he, she, it **does hold**	he, she, it **does get held**
Fut.	I, he, she, it,	I, he, she, it,
	we, you, they **will hold**	we, you, they **will be held**
Past	I, he, she, it,	I, he, she, it **was held**
	we, you, they **held**	we, you, they **were held**
Past	I, he, she, it **was holding**	I, he, she, it **was being held**
Prog.	we, you, they **were holding**	we, you, they **were being held**
Past	I, he, she, it,	I, he, she, it,
Int.	we, you, they **did hold**	we, you, they **did get held**
Pres.	I, we, you, they **have held**	I, we, you, they **have been held**
Perf.	he, she, it **has held**	he, she, it **has been held**
Past	I, he, she, it,	I, he, she, it,
Perf.	we, you, they **had held**	we, you, they **had been held**
Fut.	I, he, she, it, we, you, they	I, he, she, it, we, you, they
Perf.	**will have held**	**will have been held**

IMPERATIVE MOOD

hold   **be held**

SUBJUNCTIVE MOOD

Pres.	if I, he, she, it,	if I, he, she, it,
	we, you, they **hold**	we, you, they **be held**
Past	if I, he, she, it,	if I, he, she, it,
	we, you, they **held**	we, you, they **were held**
Fut.	if I, he, she, it,	if I, he, she, it,
	we, you, they **should hold**	we, you, they **should be held**

Transitive and intransitive.

They held onto their hope until the end.
They were both held in by their seat belts.

**AN ESSENTIAL
55 VERB**

Examples

The grandfather loves to hold the baby.

I am barely holding on.

Hold up your hands.

The charges were held over to the next month.

She held the hot dog over the fire.

I will hold your bag.

I need to hold onto the railing.

Hold on.

I have held up his application until it is complete.

The bank holds the title to the property.

Words and expressions related to this verb

Hold me tight.

Please hold while I take this other call.

The accident held up traffic for hours.

She holds all the cards.

The robbers held up the bank.

He didn't hold up his end of the deal.

The battery cannot hold a charge.

Hold onto my hand when we cross the street.

Hold your head up high.

Hold onto that thought.

Their flight was held up by the storm.

hop
(active voice)

be hopped
(passive voice)

INDICATIVE MOOD

Pres.	I, we, you, they **hop**	I **am hopped**
		we, you, they **are hopped**
	he, she, it **hops**	he, she, it **is hopped**
Pres.	I **am hopping**	I **am being hopped**
Prog.	we, you, they **are hopping**	we, you, they **are being hopped**
	he, she, it **is hopping**	he, she, it **is being hopped**
Pres.	I, we, you, they **do hop**	I, we, you, they **do get hopped**
Int.	he, she, it **does hop**	he, she, it **does get hopped**
Fut.	I, he, she, it,	I, he, she, it,
	we, you, they **will hop**	we, you, they **will be hopped**
Past	I, he, she, it,	I, he, she, it **was hopped**
	we, you, they **hopped**	we, you, they **were hopped**
Past	I, he, she, it **was hopping**	I, he, she, it **was being hopped**
Prog.	we, you, they **were hopping**	we, you, they **were being hopped**
Past	I, he, she, it,	I, he, she, it,
Int.	we, you, they **did hop**	we, you, they **did get hopped**
Pres.	I, we, you, they **have hopped**	I, we, you, they **have been hopped**
Perf.	he, she, it **has hopped**	he, she, it **has been hopped**
Past	I, he, she, it,	I, he, she, it,
Perf.	we, you, they **had hopped**	we, you, they **had been hopped**
Fut.	I, he, she, it, we, you, they	I, he, she, it, we, you, they
Perf.	**will have hopped**	**will have been hopped**

IMPERATIVE MOOD

hop   **be hopped**

SUBJUNCTIVE MOOD

Pres.	if I, he, she, it,	if I, he, she, it,
	we, you, they **hop**	we, you, they **be hopped**
Past	if I, he, she, it,	if I, he, she, it,
	we, you, they **hopped**	we, you, they **were hopped**
Fut.	if I, he, she, it,	if I, he, she, it,
	we, you, they **should hop**	we, you, they **should be hopped**

Intransitive and transitive.

Please stop hopping around.
They all hopped on the wagon.
That fence has been hopped by generations of schoolboys.

hope (active voice)	PRINCIPAL PARTS: hopes, hoping, hoped, hoped	be hoped (passive voice)

INDICATIVE MOOD

Pres.	I, we, you, they **hope** he, she, it **hopes**	I **am hoped** we, you, they **are hoped** he, she, it **is hoped**
Pres. *Prog.*	I **am hoping** we, you, they **are hoping** he, she, it **is hoping**	I **am being hoped** we, you, they **are being hoped** he, she, it **is being hoped**
Pres. *Int.*	I, we, you, they **do hope** he, she, it **does hope**	I, we, you, they **do get hoped** he, she, it **does get hoped**
Fut.	I, he, she, it, we, you, they **will hope**	I, he, she, it, we, you, they **will be hoped**
Past	I, he, she, it, we, you, they **hoped**	I, he, she, it **was hoped** we, you, they **were hoped**
Past *Prog.*	I, he, she, it **was hoping** we, you, they **were hoping**	I, he, she, it **was being hoped** we, you, they **were being hoped**
Past *Int.*	I, he, she, it, we, you, they **did hope**	I, he, she, it, we, you, they **did get hoped**
Pres. *Perf.*	I, we, you, they **have hoped** he, she, it **has hoped**	I, we, you, they **have been hoped** he, she, it **has been hoped**
Past *Perf.*	I, he, she, it, we, you, they **had hoped**	I, he, she, it, we, you, they **had been hoped**
Fut. *Perf.*	I, he, she, it, we, you, they **will have hoped**	I, he, she, it, we, you, they **will have been hoped**

IMPERATIVE MOOD

hope	**be hoped**

SUBJUNCTIVE MOOD

Pres.	if I, he, she, it, we, you, they **hope**	if I, he, she, it, we, you, they **be hoped**
Past	if I, he, she, it, we, you, they **hoped**	if I, he, she, it, we, you, they **were hoped**
Fut.	if I, he, she, it, we, you, they **should hope**	if I, he, she, it, we, you, they **should be hoped**

Intransitive and transitive.

We are hoping for better weather.
They finally received the praise they had hoped for.
His reward was the one that had been hoped for.

PRINCIPAL PARTS: **hosts, hosting,
hosted, hosted**

be hosted
(passive voice)

INDICATIVE MOOD

Pres.	I, we, you, they **host**	I **am host**
		we, you, they **are host**
	he, she, it **hosts**	he, she, it **is host**
Pres.	I **am hosting**	I **am being host**
Prog.	we, you, they **are hosting**	we, you, they **are being host**
	he, she, it **is hosting**	he, she, it **is being host**
Pres.	I, we, you, they **do host**	I, we, you, they **do get host**
Int.	he, she, it **does host**	he, she, it **does get host**
Fut.	I, he, she, it,	I, he, she, it,
	we, you, they **will host**	we, you, they **will be host**
Past	I, he, she, it,	I, he, she, it **was host**
	we, you, they **host**	we, you, they **were host**
Past	I, he, she, it **was hosting**	I, he, she, it **was being host**
Prog.	we, you, they **were hosting**	we, you, they **were being host**
Past	I, he, she, it,	I, he, she, it,
Int.	we, you, they **did host**	we, you, they **did get host**
Pres.	I, we, you, they **have host**	I, we, you, they **have been host**
Perf.	he, she, it **has host**	he, she, it **has been host**
Past	I, he, she, it,	I, he, she, it,
Perf.	we, you, they **had host**	we, you, they **had been host**
Fut.	I, he, she, it, we, you, they	I, he, she, it, we, you, they
Perf.	**will have host**	**will have been host**

IMPERATIVE MOOD

host   **be host**

SUBJUNCTIVE MOOD

Pres.	if I, he, she, it,	if I, he, she, it,
	we, you, they **host**	we, you, they **be host**
Past	if I, he, she, it,	if I, he, she, it,
	we, you, they **host**	we, you, they **were host**
Fut.	if I, he, she, it,	if I, he, she, it,
	we, you, they **should host**	we, you, they **should be host**

Transitive and intransitive.

It is our turn to host the annual office party.
The reception was hosted by the city officials.

hurt (active voice)	PRINCIPAL PARTS: **hurts, hurting,** **hurt, hurt**	be hurt (passive voice)

INDICATIVE MOOD

Pres.	I, we, you, they **hurt**	I **am hurt** we, you, they **are hurt** he, she, it **is hurt**
	he, she, it **hurts**	
Pres. *Prog.*	I **am hurting** we, you, they **are hurting** he, she, it **is hurting**	I **am being hurt** we, you, they **are being hurt** he, she, it **is being hurt**
Pres. *Int.*	I, we, you, they **do hurt** he, she, it **does hurt**	I, we, you, they **do get hurt** he, she, it **does get hurt**
Fut.	I, he, she, it, we, you, they **will hurt**	I, he, she, it, we, you, they **will be hurt**
Past	I, he, she, it, we, you, they **hurt**	I, he, she, it **was hurt** we, you, they **were hurt**
Past *Prog.*	I, he, she, it **was hurting** we, you, they **were hurting**	I, he, she, it **was being hurt** we, you, they **were being hurt**
Past *Int.*	I, he, she, it, we, you, they **did hurt**	I, he, she, it, we, you, they **did get hurt**
Pres. *Perf.*	I, we, you, they **have hurt** he, she, it **has hurt**	I, we, you, they **have been hurt** he, she, it **has been hurt**
Past *Perf.*	I, he, she, it, we, you, they **had hurt**	I, he, she, it, we, you, they **had been hurt**
Fut. *Perf.*	I, he, she, it, we, you, they **will have hurt**	I, he, she, it, we, you, they **will have been hurt**

IMPERATIVE MOOD

hurt	**be hurt**

SUBJUNCTIVE MOOD

Pres.	if I, he, she, it, we, you, they **hurt**	if I, he, she, it, we, you, they **be hurt**
Past	if I, he, she, it, we, you, they **hurt**	if I, he, she, it, we, you, they **were hurt**
Fut.	if I, he, she, it, we, you, they **should hurt**	if I, he, she, it, we, you, they **should be hurt**

Transitive and intransitive.

Mommy, it hurts.
Who hurt you?
They were hurt by flying sand.

IM
(active voice)

PRINCIPAL PARTS: **IM's, IM'ing,
IM'd, IM'd**

be IM'd
(passive voice)

INDICATIVE MOOD

Pres.	I, we, you, they **IM**	**I am IM'd**
		we, you, they **are IM'd**
	he, she, it **IM's**	he, she, it **is IM'd**
Pres.	**I am IM'ing**	**I am being IM'd**
Prog.	we, you, they **are IM'ing**	we, you, they **are being IM'd**
	he, she, it **is IM'ing**	he, she, it **is being IM'd**
Pres.	I, we, you, they **do IM**	I, we, you, they **do get IM'd**
Int.	he, she, it **does IM**	he, she, it **does get IM'd**
Fut.	I, he, she, it,	I, he, she, it,
	we, you, they **will IM**	we, you, they **will be IM'd**
Past	I, he, she, it,	I, he, she, it **was IM'd**
	we, you, they **IM'd**	we, you, they **were IM'd**
Past	I, he, she, it **was IM'ing**	I, he, she, it **was being IM'd**
Prog.	we, you, they **were IM'ing**	we, you, they **were being IM'd**
Past	I, he, she, it,	I, he, she, it,
Int.	we, you, they **did IM**	we, you, they **did get IM'd**
Pres.	I, we, you, they **have IM'd**	I, we, you, they **have been IM'd**
Perf.	he, she, it **has IM'd**	he, she, it **has been IM'd**
Past	I, he, she, it,	I, he, she, it,
Perf.	we, you, they **had IM'd**	we, you, they **had been IM'd**
Fut.	I, he, she, it, we, you, they	I, he, she, it, we, you, they
Perf.	**will have IM'd**	**will have been IM'd**

IMPERATIVE MOOD

IM   **be IM'd**

SUBJUNCTIVE MOOD

Pres.	if I, he, she, it,	if I, he, she, it,
	we, you, they **IM**	we, you, they **be IM'd**
Past	if I, he, she, it,	if I, he, she, it,
	we, you, they **IM'd**	we, you, they **were IM'd**
Fut.	if I, he, she, it,	if I, he, she, it,
	we, you, they **should IM**	we, you, they **should be IM'd**

Intransitive and transitive. This verb is an abbreviation for "instant messaging."

Is anyone IM'ing with you at this instant?
Our children IM'd all evening.
I was recently IM'd by an old classmate.

213

imagine
(active voice)

be imagined
(passive voice)

INDICATIVE MOOD

Pres.	I, we, you, they **imagine**	I **am imagined**
		we, you, they **are imagined**
	he, she, it **imagines**	he, she, it **is imagined**
Pres.	I **am imagining**	I **am being imagined**
Prog.	we, you, they **are imagining**	we, you, they **are being imagined**
	he, she, it **is imagining**	he, she, it **is being imagined**
Pres.	I, we, you, they **do imagine**	I, we, you, they **do get imagined**
Int.	he, she, it **does imagine**	he, she, it **does get imagined**
Fut.	I, he, she, it,	I, he, she, it,
	we, you, they **will imagine**	we, you, they **will be imagined**
Past	I, he, she, it,	I, he, she, it **was imagined**
	we, you, they **imagined**	we, you, they **were imagined**
Past	I, he, she, it **was imagining**	I, he, she, it **was being imagined**
Prog.	we, you, they **were imagining**	we, you, they **were being imagined**
Past	I, he, she, it,	I, he, she, it,
Int.	we, you, they **did imagine**	we, you, they **did get imagined**
Pres.	I, we, you, they **have imagined**	I, we, you, they **have been imagined**
Perf.	he, she, it **has imagined**	he, she, it **has been imagined**
Past	I, he, she, it,	I, he, she, it,
Perf.	we, you, they **had imagined**	we, you, they **had been imagined**
Fut.	I, he, she, it, we, you, they	I, he, she, it, we, you, they
Perf.	**will have imagined**	**will have been imagined**

IMPERATIVE MOOD

imagine   **be imagined**

SUBJUNCTIVE MOOD

Pres.	if I, he, she, it,	if I, he, she, it,
	we, you, they **imagine**	we, you, they **be imagined**
Past	if I, he, she, it,	if I, he, she, it,
	we, you, they **imagined**	we, you, they **were imagined**
Fut.	if I, he, she, it,	if I, he, she, it,
	we, you, they **should imagine**	we, you, they **should be imagined**

Transitive and intransitive.

We are imagining a much warmer reception.
Such an outcome could not have been imagined.

improve
(active voice)

PRINCIPAL PARTS: **improves, improving, improved, improved**

be improved
(passive voice)

INDICATIVE MOOD

Pres.	I, we, you, they **improve**	I **am improved**
		we, you, they **are improved**
	he, she, it **improves**	he, she, it **is improved**
Pres.	I **am improving**	I **am being improved**
Prog.	we, you, they **are improving**	we, you, they **are being improved**
	he, she, it **is improving**	he, she, it **is being improved**
Pres.	I, we, you, they **do improve**	I, we, you, they **do get improved**
Int.	he, she, it **does improve**	he, she, it **does get improved**
Fut.	I, he, she, it,	I, he, she, it,
	we, you, they **will improve**	we, you, they **will be improved**
Past	I, he, she, it,	I, he, she, it **was improved**
	we, you, they **improved**	we, you, they **were improved**
Past	I, he, she, it **was improving**	I, he, she, it **was being improved**
Prog.	we, you, they **were improving**	we, you, they **were being improved**
Past	I, he, she, it,	I, he, she, it,
Int.	we, you, they **did improve**	we, you, they **did get improved**
Pres.	I, we, you, they **have improved**	I, we, you, they **have been improved**
Perf.	he, she, it **has improved**	he, she, it **has been improved**
Past	I, he, she, it,	I, he, she, it,
Perf.	we, you, they **had improved**	we, you, they **had been improved**
Fut.	I, he, she, it, we, you, they	I, he, she, it, we, you, they
Perf.	**will have improved**	**will have been improved**

IMPERATIVE MOOD

improve   **be improved**

SUBJUNCTIVE MOOD

Pres.	if I, he, she, it,	if I, he, she, it,
	we, you, they **improve**	we, you, they **be improved**
Past	if I, he, she, it,	if I, he, she, it,
	we, you, they **improved**	we, you, they **were improved**
Fut.	if I, he, she, it,	if I, he, she, it,
	we, you, they **should improve**	we, you, they **should be improved**

Transitive and intransitive.

He is improving everyday with regular practice.
The group's performance was much improved.

include
(active voice)

be included
(passive voice)

INDICATIVE MOOD

Pres.	I, we, you, they **include**	I **am included**
		we, you, they **are included**
	he, she, it **includes**	he, she, it **is included**
Pres.	I **am including**	I **am being included**
Prog.	we, you, they **are including**	we, you, they **are being included**
	he, she, it **is including**	he, she, it **is being included**
Pres.	I, we, you, they **do include**	I, we, you, they **do get included**
Int.	he, she, it **does include**	he, she, it **does get included**
Fut.	I, he, she, it,	I, he, she, it,
	we, you, they **will include**	we, you, they **will be included**
Past	I, he, she, it,	I, he, she, it **was included**
	we, you, they **included**	we, you, they **were included**
Past	I, he, she, it **was including**	I, he, she, it **was being included**
Prog.	we, you, they **were including**	we, you, they **were being included**
Past	I, he, she, it,	I, he, she, it,
Int.	we, you, they **did include**	we, you, they **did get included**
Pres.	I, we, you, they **have included**	I, we, you, they **have been included**
Perf.	he, she, it **has included**	he, she, it **has been included**
Past	I, he, she, it,	I, he, she, it,
Perf.	we, you, they **had included**	we, you, they **had been included**
Fut.	I, he, she, it, we, you, they	I, he, she, it, we, you, they
Perf.	**will have included**	**will have been included**

IMPERATIVE MOOD

include   **be included**

SUBJUNCTIVE MOOD

Pres.	if I, he, she, it,	if I, he, she, it,
	we, you, they **include**	we, you, they **be included**
Past	if I, he, she, it,	if I, he, she, it,
	we, you, they **included**	we, you, they **were included**
Fut.	if I, he, she, it,	if I, he, she, it,
	we, you, they **should include**	we, you, they **should be included**

Many restaurants are automatically including a 10% gratuity.
Was her name included on the list?

Examples

I will include your name on the list.

She is often included, rarely excluded from our meetings.

What is included in the price?

They were not included in our original conversation.

She always includes her telephone number in her correspondence.

I certainly include you among my best friends.

The newspaper includes paid announcements.

Health care benefits are included.

They tried to include him in all their activities.

I want to be included in all your discussions.

Words and expressions related to this verb

All taxes and tips are included.

Please include me.

This new proposal includes your suggestions.

Don't forget to include some time for relaxation.

The menu includes vegetarian selections.

Her name can be included at a later time.

The book includes an index and a table of contents.

Her new computers did not include a set of instructions.

The course includes differing points of view.

Will anything else be included?

increase
(active voice)

Principal Parts: **increases, increasing,
increased, increased**

be increased
(passive voice)

INDICATIVE MOOD

Pres.	I, we, you, they **increase**	I **am increased**
		we, you, they **are increased**
	he, she, it **increases**	he, she, it **is increased**
Pres.	I **am increasing**	I **am being increased**
Prog.	we, you, they **are increasing**	we, you, they **are being increased**
	he, she, it **is increasing**	he, she, it **is being increased**
Pres.	I, we, you, they **do increase**	I, we, you, they **do get increased**
Int.	he, she, it **does increase**	he, she, it **does get increased**
Fut.	I, he, she, it,	I, he, she, it,
	we, you, they **will increase**	we, you, they **will be increased**
Past	I, he, she, it,	I, he, she, it **was increased**
	we, you, they **increased**	we, you, they **were increased**
Past	I, he, she, it **was increasing**	I, he, she, it **was being increased**
Prog.	we, you, they **were increasing**	we, you, they **were being increased**
Past	I, he, she, it,	I, he, she, it,
Int.	we, you, they **did increase**	we, you, they **did get increased**
Pres.	I, we, you, they **have increased**	I, we, you, they **have been increased**
Perf.	he, she, it **has increased**	he, she, it **has been increased**
Past	I, he, she, it,	I, he, she, it,
Perf.	we, you, they **had increased**	we, you, they **had been increased**
Fut.	I, he, she, it, we, you, they	I, he, she, it, we, you, they
Perf.	**will have increased**	**will have been increased**

IMPERATIVE MOOD

increase   **be increased**

SUBJUNCTIVE MOOD

Pres.	if I, he, she, it,	if I, he, she, it,
	we, you, they **increase**	we, you, they **be increased**
Past	if I, he, she, it,	if I, he, she, it,
	we, you, they **increased**	we, you, they **were increased**
Fut.	if I, he, she, it,	if I, he, she, it,
	we, you, they **should increase**	we, you, they **should be increased**

Intransitive and transitive.

Taxes on the property are increasing every year.
When were the prices on gasoline last increased?

indicate
(active voice)

be indicated
(passive voice)

INDICATIVE MOOD

Pres.	I, we, you, they **indicate**	I **am indicated**
		we, you, they **are indicated**
	he, she, it **indicates**	he, she, it **is indicated**
Pres.	I **am indicating**	I **am being indicated**
Prog.	we, you, they **are indicating**	we, you, they **are being indicated**
	he, she, it **is indicating**	he, she, it **is being indicated**
Pres.	I, we, you, they **do indicate**	I, we, you, they **do get indicated**
Int.	he, she, it **does indicate**	he, she, it **does get indicated**
Fut.	I, he, she, it,	I, he, she, it,
	we, you, they **will indicate**	we, you, they **will be indicated**
Past	I, he, she, it,	I, he, she, it **was indicated**
	we, you, they **indicated**	we, you, they **were indicated**
Past	I, he, she, it **was indicating**	I, he, she, it **was being indicated**
Prog.	we, you, they **were indicating**	we, you, they **were being indicated**
Past	I, he, she, it,	I, he, she, it,
Int.	we, you, they **did indicate**	we, you, they **did get indicated**
Pres.	I, we, you, they **have indicated**	I, we, you, they **have been indicated**
Perf.	he, she, it **has indicated**	he, she, it **has been indicated**
Past	I, he, she, it,	I, he, she, it,
Perf.	we, you, they **had indicated**	we, you, they **had been indicated**
Fut.	I, he, she, it, we, you, they	I, he, she, it, we, you, they
Perf.	**will have indicated**	**will have been indicated**

IMPERATIVE MOOD

indicate **be indicated**

SUBJUNCTIVE MOOD

Pres.	if I, he, she, it,	if I, he, she, it,
	we, you, they **indicate**	we, you, they **be indicated**
Past	if I, he, she, it,	if I, he, she, it,
	we, you, they **indicated**	we, you, they **were indicated**
Fut.	if I, he, she, it,	if I, he, she, it,
	we, you, they **should indicate**	we, you, they **should be indicated**

She is indicating her interest on her application.
The directions to the campus were clearly indicated on the map.

input
(active voice)

PRINCIPAL PARTS: **inputs, inputting,**
inputted/input, inputted/input

be inputted/input
(passive voice)

INDICATIVE MOOD

Pres.	I, we, you, they **input**	I **am inputted**
		we, you, they **are inputted**
	he, she, it **inputs**	he, she, it **is inputted**
Pres.	I **am inputting**	I **am being inputted**
Prog.	we, you, they **are inputting**	we, you, they **are being inputted**
	he, she, it **is inputting**	he, she, it **is being inputted**
Pres.	I, we, you, they **do input**	I, we, you, they **do get inputted**
Int.	he, she, it **does input**	he, she, it **does get inputted**
Fut.	I, he, she, it,	I, he, she, it,
	we, you, they **will input**	we, you, they **will be inputted**
Past	I, he, she, it,	I, he, she, it **was inputted**
	we, you, they **inputted**	we, you, they **were inputted**
Past	I, he, she, it **was inputting**	I, he, she, it **was being inputted**
Prog.	we, you, they **were inputting**	we, you, they **were being inputted**
Past	I, he, she, it,	I, he, she, it,
Int.	we, you, they **did input**	we, you, they **did get inputted**
Pres.	I, we, you, they **have inputted**	I, we, you, they **have been inputted**
Perf.	he, she, it **has inputted**	he, she, it **has been inputted**
Past	I, he, she, it,	I, he, she, it,
Perf.	we, you, they **had inputted**	we, you, they **had been inputted**
Fut.	I, he, she, it, we, you, they	I, he, she, it, we, you, they
Perf.	**will have inputted**	**will have been inputted**

IMPERATIVE MOOD

input   **be input**

SUBJUNCTIVE MOOD

Pres.	if I, he, she, it,	if I, he, she, it,
	we, you, they **input**	we, you, they **be inputted**
Past	if I, he, she, it,	if I, he, she, it,
	we, you, they **inputted**	we, you, they **were inputted**
Fut.	if I, he, she, it,	if I, he, she, it,
	we, you, they **should input**	we, you, they **should be inputted**

The past and past participle forms INPUTTED and INPUT are both acceptable.

We will want someone inputting the necessary coordinates.
Those figures were inputted by an automatic program.

220

inset
(active voice)

be inset
(passive voice)

INDICATIVE MOOD

Pres.	I, we, you, they **inset**	I **am inset**
		we, you, they **are inset**
	he, she, it **insets**	he, she, it **is inset**
Pres.	I **am insetting**	I **am being inset**
Prog.	we, you, they **are insetting**	we, you, they **are being inset**
	he, she, it **is insetting**	he, she, it **is being inset**
Pres.	I, we, you, they **do inset**	I, we, you, they **do get inset**
Int.	he, she, it **does inset**	he, she, it **does get inset**
Fut.	I, he, she, it,	I, he, she, it,
	we, you, they **will inset**	we, you, they **will be inset**
Past	I, he, she, it,	I, he, she, it **was inset**
	we, you, they **inset**	we, you, they **were inset**
Past	I, he, she, it **was insetting**	I, he, she, it **was being inset**
Prog.	we, you, they **were insetting**	we, you, they **were being inset**
Past	I, he, she, it,	I, he, she, it,
Int.	we, you, they **did inset**	we, you, they **did get inset**
Pres.	I, we, you, they **have inset**	I, we, you, they **have been inset**
Perf.	he, she, it **has inset**	he, she, it **has been inset**
Past	I, he, she, it,	I, he, she, it,
Perf.	we, you, they **had inset**	we, you, they **had been inset**
Fut.	I, he, she, it, we, you, they	I, he, she, it, we, you, they
Perf.	**will have inset**	**will have been inset**

IMPERATIVE MOOD

inset **be inset**

SUBJUNCTIVE MOOD

Pres.	if I, he, she, it,	if I, he, she, it,
	we, you, they **inset**	we, you, they **be inset**
Past	if I, he, she, it,	if I, he, she, it,
	we, you, they **inset**	we, you, they **were inset**
Fut.	if I, he, she, it,	if I, he, she, it,
	we, you, they **should inset**	we, you, they **should be inset**

The *Oxford Dictionary* and *Merriam Webster's* recognize INSETTED as an alternate past tense and past participle.

He is insetting a decorative piece between every second tile.
The time capsule was inset in the cornerstone 100 years ago.

INDICATIVE MOOD

Pres.   I, we, you, they **interface**

             he, she, it **interfaces**

Pres.   **I am interfacing**
Prog.   we, you, they **are interfacing**
             he, she, it **is interfacing**

Pres.   I, we, you, they **do interface**
Int.   he, she, it **does interface**

Fut.   I, he, she, it,
             we, you, they **will interface**

Past   I, he, she, it,
             we, you, they **interfaced**

Past   I, he, she, it **was interfacing**
Prog.   we, you, they **were interfacing**

Past   I, he, she, it,
Int.   we, you, they **did interface**

Pres.   I, we, you, they **have interfaced**
Perf.   he, she, it **has interfaced**

Past   I, he, she, it,
Perf.   we, you, they **had interfaced**

Fut.   I, he, she, it, we, you, they
Perf.   **will have interfaced**

IMPERATIVE MOOD

interface

SUBJUNCTIVE MOOD

Pres.   if I, he, she, it,
             we, you, they **interface**

Past   if I, he, she, it,
             we, you, they **interfaced**

Fut.   if I, he, she, it,
             we, you, they **should interface**

We are interfacing the two computers before inputting the data.
Were the machines properly interfaced?

involve
(active voice)

PRINCIPAL PARTS: **involves, involving, involved, involved**

be involved
(passive voice)

INDICATIVE MOOD

Pres.	I, we, you, they **involve**	I **am involved**
		we, you, they **are involved**
	he, she, it **involves**	he, she, it **is involved**
Pres.	I **am involving**	I **am being involved**
Prog.	we, you, they **are involving**	we, you, they **are being involved**
	he, she, it **is involving**	he, she, it **is being involved**
Pres.	I, we, you, they **do involve**	I, we, you, they **do get involved**
Int.	he, she, it **does involve**	he, she, it **does get involved**
Fut.	I, he, she, it,	I, he, she, it,
	we, you, they **will involve**	we, you, they **will be involved**
Past	I, he, she, it,	I, he, she, it **was involved**
	we, you, they **involved**	we, you, they **were involved**
Past	I, he, she, it **was involving**	I, he, she, it **was being involved**
Prog.	we, you, they **were involving**	we, you, they **were being involved**
Past	I, he, she, it,	I, he, she, it,
Int.	we, you, they **did involve**	we, you, they **did get involved**
Pres.	I, we, you, they **have involved**	I, we, you, they **have been involved**
Perf.	he, she, it **has involved**	he, she, it **has been involved**
Past	I, he, she, it,	I, he, she, it,
Perf.	we, you, they **had involved**	we, you, they **had been involved**
Fut.	I, he, she, it, we, you, they	I, he, she, it, we, you, they
Perf.	**will have involved**	**will have been involved**

IMPERATIVE MOOD

involve   **be involved**

SUBJUNCTIVE MOOD

Pres.	if I, he, she, it,	if I, he, she, it,
	we, you, they **involve**	we, you, they **be involved**
Past	if I, he, she, it,	if I, he, she, it,
	we, you, they **involved**	we, you, they **were involved**
Fut.	if I, he, she, it,	if I, he, she, it,
	we, you, they **should involve**	we, you, they **should be involved**

This is a matter involving both the child and his parents.
I was not involved in the decision-making process.

jet
(active voice)

PRINCIPAL PARTS: **jets, jetting,
jetted, jetted**

be jetted
(passive voice)

INDICATIVE MOOD

Pres.	I, we, you, they **jet**	I **am jetted**
		we, you, they **are jetted**
	he, she, it **jets**	he, she, it **is jetted**
Pres.	I **am jetting**	I **am being jetted**
Prog.	we, you, they **are jetting**	we, you, they **are being jetted**
	he, she, it **is jetting**	he, she, it **is being jetted**
Pres.	I, we, you, they **do jet**	I, we, you, they **do get jetted**
Int.	he, she, it **does jet**	he, she, it **does get jetted**
Fut.	I, he, she, it,	I, he, she, it,
	we, you, they **will jet**	we, you, they **will be jetted**
Past	I, he, she, it,	I, he, she, it **was jetted**
	we, you, they **jetted**	we, you, they **were jetted**
Past	I, he, she, it **was jetting**	I, he, she, it **was being jetted**
Prog.	we, you, they **were jetting**	we, you, they **were being jetted**
Past	I, he, she, it,	I, he, she, it,
Int.	we, you, they **did jet**	we, you, they **did get jetted**
Pres.	I, we, you, they **have jetted**	I, we, you, they **have been jetted**
Perf.	he, she, it **has jetted**	he, she, it **has been jetted**
Past	I, he, she, it,	I, he, she, it,
Perf.	we, you, they **had jetted**	we, you, they **had been jetted**
Fut.	I, he, she, it, we, you, they	I, he, she, it, we, you, they
Perf.	**will have jetted**	**will have been jetted**

IMPERATIVE MOOD

jet　　　　　　　　　**be jet**

SUBJUNCTIVE MOOD

Pres.	if I, he, she, it,	if I, he, she, it,
	we, you, they **jet**	we, you, they **be jetted**
Past	if I, he, she, it,	if I, he, she, it,
	we, you, they **jetted**	we, you, they **were jetted**
Fut.	if I, he, she, it,	if I, he, she, it,
	we, you, they **should jet**	we, you, they **should be jetted**

Intransitive and transitive. In the meaning to "travel by jet airplane," the verb is intransitive.

Lately she's been jetting from coast to coast weekly.
Water jetted from the leaking pipe.

jog
(active voice)

be jogged
(passive voice)

INDICATIVE MOOD

Pres.	I, we, you, they **jog**	I **am jogged**
		we, you, they **are jogged**
	he, she, it **jogs**	he, she, it **is jogged**
Pres.	I **am jogging**	I **am being jogged**
Prog.	we, you, they **are jogging**	we, you, they **are being jogged**
	he, she, it **is jogging**	he, she, it **is being jogged**
Pres.	I, we, you, they **do jog**	I, we, you, they **do get jogged**
Int.	he, she, it **does jog**	he, she, it **does get jogged**
Fut.	I, he, she, it,	I, he, she, it,
	we, you, they **will jog**	we, you, they **will be jogged**
Past	I, he, she, it,	I, he, she, it **was jogged**
	we, you, they **jogged**	we, you, they **were jogged**
Past	I, he, she, it **was jogging**	I, he, she, it **was being jogged**
Prog.	we, you, they **were jogging**	we, you, they **were being jogged**
Past	I, he, she, it,	I, he, she, it,
Int.	we, you, they **did jog**	we, you, they **did get jogged**
Pres.	I, we, you, they **have jogged**	I, we, you, they **have been jogged**
Perf.	he, she, it **has jogged**	he, she, it **has been jogged**
Past	I, he, she, it,	I, he, she, it,
Perf.	we, you, they **had jogged**	we, you, they **had been jogged**
Fut.	I, he, she, it, we, you, they	I, he, she, it, we, you, they
Perf.	**will have jogged**	**will have been jogged**

IMPERATIVE MOOD

jog   **be jog**

SUBJUNCTIVE MOOD

Pres.	if I, he, she, it,	if I, he, she, it,
	we, you, they **jog**	we, you, they **be jogged**
Past	if I, he, she, it,	if I, he, she, it,
	we, you, they **jogged**	we, you, they **were jogged**
Fut.	if I, he, she, it,	if I, he, she, it,
	we, you, they **should jog**	we, you, they **should be jogged**

Intransitive and transitive.

We are no longer jogging before or after work every day.
His memory was jogged by the sound of the whistle.

J

| join
(active voice) | PRINCIPAL PARTS: **joins, joining,
joined, joined** | be joined
(passive voice) |

INDICATIVE MOOD

Pres.	I, we, you, they **join** he, she, it **joins**	I **am joined** we, you, they **are joined** he, she, it **is joined**
Pres. *Prog.*	I **am joining** we, you, they **are joining** he, she, it **is joining**	I **am being joined** we, you, they **are being joined** he, she, it **is being joined**
Pres. *Int.*	I, we, you, they **do join** he, she, it **does join**	I, we, you, they **do get joined** he, she, it **does get joined**
Fut.	I, he, she, it, we, you, they **will join**	I, he, she, it, we, you, they **will be joined**
Past	I, he, she, it, we, you, they **joined**	I, he, she, it **was joined** we, you, they **were joined**
Past *Prog.*	I, he, she, it **was joining** we, you, they **were joining**	I, he, she, it **was being joined** we, you, they **were being joined**
Past *Int.*	I, he, she, it, we, you, they **did join**	I, he, she, it, we, you, they **did get joined**
Pres. *Perf.*	I, we, you, they **have joined** he, she, it **has joined**	I, we, you, they **have been joined** he, she, it **has been joined**
Past *Perf.*	I, he, she, it, we, you, they **had joined**	I, he, she, it, we, you, they **had been joined**
Fut. *Perf.*	I, he, she, it, we, you, they **will have joined**	I, he, she, it, we, you, they **will have been joined**

IMPERATIVE MOOD

join	**be joined**

SUBJUNCTIVE MOOD

Pres.	if I, he, she, it, we, you, they **join**	if I, he, she, it, we, you, they **be joined**
Past	if I, he, she, it, we, you, they **joined**	if I, he, she, it, we, you, they **were joined**
Fut.	if I, he, she, it, we, you, they **should join**	if I, he, she, it, we, you, they **should be joined**

Transitive and intransitive.

Join us for dinner this evening.
They were joined at their table by the restaurant owner.

keep
(active voice)

be kept
(passive voice)

INDICATIVE MOOD

Pres.	I, we, you, they **keep**	I **am kept**
		we, you, they **are kept**
	he, she, it **keeps**	he, she, it **is kept**
Pres.	I **am keeping**	I **am being kept**
Prog.	we, you, they **are keeping**	we, you, they **are being kept**
	he, she, it **is keeping**	he, she, it **is being kept**
Pres.	I, we, you, they **do keep**	I, we, you, they **do get kept**
Int.	he, she, it **does keep**	he, she, it **does get kept**
Fut.	I, he, she, it,	I, he, she, it,
	we, you, they **will keep**	we, you, they **will be kept**
Past	I, he, she, it,	I, he, she, it **was kept**
	we, you, they **kept**	we, you, they **were kept**
Past	I, he, she, it **was keeping**	I, he, she, it **was being kept**
Prog.	we, you, they **were keeping**	we, you, they **were being kept**
Past	I, he, she, it,	I, he, she, it,
Int.	we, you, they **did keep**	we, you, they **did get kept**
Pres.	I, we, you, they **have kept**	I, we, you, they **have been kept**
Perf.	he, she, it **has kept**	he, she, it **has been kept**
Past	I, he, she, it,	I, he, she, it,
Perf.	we, you, they **had kept**	we, you, they **had been kept**
Fut.	I, he, she, it, we, you, they	I, he, she, it, we, you, they
Perf.	**will have kept**	**will have been kept**

K

IMPERATIVE MOOD

keep   **be kept**

SUBJUNCTIVE MOOD

Pres.	if I, he, she, it,	if I, he, she, it,
	we, you, they **keep**	we, you, they **be kept**
Past	if I, he, she, it,	if I, he, she, it,
	we, you, they **kept**	we, you, they **were kept**
Fut.	if I, he, she, it,	if I, he, she, it,
	we, you, they **should keep**	we, you, they **should be kept**

Transitive and intransitive.

We kept all of our receipts for the trip.
The red wine was kept cool in the wine cellar.

AN ESSENTIAL
55 VERB

keep

Examples

Can I keep it?

Keep out the mosquitoes.

We need to keep the heat inside the house.

I am keeping a diary.

Who will keep the books for the business?

I kept her letter for years.

Those records weren't kept.

I couldn't keep up with the other runners.

She keeps everything.

He had kept the secret for over twenty years.

Words and expressions related to this verb

Keep calm.

She always keeps her word.

Keep your shirt on.

Keep it clean.

She was well kept for.

He wants to keep up with the Joneses.

I am trying to keep track of our expenses.

Coffee keeps me awake.

Keep off the grass.

Keep to the right side of the road.

He is trying to keep down his weight.

kill
(active voice)

PRINCIPAL PARTS: **kills, killing,
killed, killed**

be killed
(passive voice)

INDICATIVE MOOD

Pres.	I, we, you, they **kill** he, she, it **kills**	I **am killed** we, you, they **are killed** he, she, it **is killed**
Pres. *Prog.*	I **am killing** we, you, they **are killing** he, she, it **is killing**	I **am being killed** we, you, they **are being killed** he, she, it **is being killed**
Pres. *Int.*	I, we, you, they **do kill** he, she, it **does kill**	I, we, you, they **do get killed** he, she, it **does get killed**
Fut.	I, he, she, it, we, you, they **will kill**	I, he, she, it, we, you, they **will be killed**
Past	I, he, she, it, we, you, they **killed**	I, he, she, it **was killed** we, you, they **were killed**
Past *Prog.*	I, he, she, it **was killing** we, you, they **were killing**	I, he, she, it **was being killed** we, you, they **were being killed**
Past *Int.*	I, he, she, it, we, you, they **did kill**	I, he, she, it, we, you, they **did get killed**
Pres. *Perf.*	I, we, you, they **have killed** he, she, it **has killed**	I, we, you, they **have been killed** he, she, it **has been killed**
Past *Perf.*	I, he, she, it, we, you, they **had killed**	I, he, she, it, we, you, they **had been killed**
Fut. *Perf.*	I, he, she, it, we, you, they **will have killed**	I, he, she, it, we, you, they **will have been killed**

IMPERATIVE MOOD

kill   **be killed**

SUBJUNCTIVE MOOD

Pres.	if I, he, she, it, we, you, they **kill**	if I, he, she, it, we, you, they **be killed**
Past	if I, he, she, it, we, you, they **killed**	if I, he, she, it, we, you, they **were killed**
Fut.	if I, he, she, it, we, you, they **should kill**	if I, he, she, it, we, you, they **should be killed**

K

Transitive and intransitive.

Have you read To Kill a Mockingbird?
They were killed in the terrible flood.

PRINCIPAL PARTS: **kneels, kneeling, knelt/kneeled, knelt/kneeled**

INDICATIVE MOOD

Pres. I, we, you, they **kneel**

he, she, it **kneels**

Pres. I **am kneeling**
Prog. we, you, they **are kneeling**
he, she, it **is kneeling**

Pres. I, we, you, they **do kneel**
Int. he, she, it **does kneel**

Fut. I, he, she, it,
we, you, they **will kneel**

Past I, he, she, it,
we, you, they **knelt**

Past I, he, she, it **was kneeling**
Prog. we, you, they **were kneeling**

Past I, he, she, it,
Int. we, you, they **did kneel**

Pres. I, we, you, they **have knelt**
Perf. he, she, it **has knelt**

Past I, he, she, it,
Perf. we, you, they **had knelt**

Fut. I, he, she, it, we, you, they
Perf. **will have knelt**

IMPERATIVE MOOD

kneel

SUBJUNCTIVE MOOD

Pres. if I, he, she, it,
we, you, they **kneel**

Past if I, he, she, it,
we, you, they **knelt**

Fut. if I, he, she, it,
we, you, they **should kneel**

As I grow older I am kneeling down less and less.
In olden times one knelt before the king or queen.

| knit
(active voice) | PRINCIPAL PARTS: **knits, knitting,**
knit/knitted, knit/knitted | be knit/knitted
(passive voice) |

INDICATIVE MOOD

Pres.	I, we, you, they **knit**	I **am knit** we, you, they **are knit**
	he, she, it **knits**	he, she, it **is knit**
Pres. *Prog.*	I **am knitting** we, you, they **are knitting** he, she, it **is knitting**	I **am being knit** we, you, they **are being knit** he, she, it **is being knit**
Pres. *Int.*	I, we, you, they **do knit** he, she, it **does knit**	I, we, you, they **do get knit** he, she, it **does get knit**
Fut.	I, he, she, it, we, you, they **will knit**	I, he, she, it, we, you, they **will be knit**
Past	I, he, she, it, we, you, they **knit**	I, he, she, it **was knit** we, you, they **were knit**
Past *Prog.*	I, he, she, it **was knitting** we, you, they **were knitting**	I, he, she, it **was being knit** we, you, they **were being knit**
Past *Int.*	I, he, she, it, we, you, they **did knit**	I, he, she, it, we, you, they **did get knit**
Pres. *Perf.*	I, we, you, they **have knit** he, she, it **has knit**	I, we, you, they **have been knit** he, she, it **has been knit**
Past *Perf.*	I, he, she, it, we, you, they **had knit**	I, he, she, it, we, you, they **had been knit**
Fut. *Perf.*	I, he, she, it, we, you, they **will have knit**	I, he, she, it, we, you, they **will have been knit**

IMPERATIVE MOOD

knit	**be knit**

SUBJUNCTIVE MOOD

Pres.	if I, he, she, it, we, you, they **knit**	if I, he, she, it, we, you, they **be knit**
Past	if I, he, she, it, we, you, they **knit**	if I, he, she, it, we, you, they **were knit**
Fut.	if I, he, she, it, we, you, they **should knit**	if I, he, she, it, we, you, they **should be knit**

Transitive and intransitive. *Webster's* and the *Oxford Dictionary* list KNITTED as the first form for the past tense and past participle.

Grandma is knitting for an hour or two this afternoon.
She knit me a sweater for my birthday.
It is difficult to find something knit by hand in the stores.

knock
(active voice)

PRINCIPAL PARTS: knocks, knocking, knocked, knocked

be knocked
(passive voice)

INDICATIVE MOOD

Pres.	I, we, you, they **knock**	I **am knocked**
		we, you, they **are knocked**
	he, she, it **knocks**	he, she, it **is knocked**
Pres.	I **am knocking**	I **am being knocked**
Prog.	we, you, they **are knocking**	we, you, they **are being knocked**
	he, she, it **is knocking**	he, she, it **is being knocked**
Pres.	I, we, you, they **do knock**	I, we, you, they **do get knocked**
Int.	he, she, it **does knock**	he, she, it **does get knocked**
Fut.	I, he, she, it,	I, he, she, it,
	we, you, they **will knock**	we, you, they **will be knocked**
Past	I, he, she, it,	I, he, she, it **was knocked**
	we, you, they **knocked**	we, you, they **were knocked**
Past	I, he, she, it **was knocking**	I, he, she, it **was being knocked**
Prog.	we, you, they **were knocking**	we, you, they **were being knocked**
Past	I, he, she, it,	I, he, she, it,
Int.	we, you, they **did knock**	we, you, they **did get knocked**
Pres.	I, we, you, they **have knocked**	I, we, you, they **have been knocked**
Perf.	he, she, it **has knocked**	he, she, it **has been knocked**
Past	I, he, she, it,	I, he, she, it,
Perf.	we, you, they **had knocked**	we, you, they **had been knocked**
Fut.	I, he, she, it, we, you, they	I, he, she, it, we, you, they
Perf.	**will have knocked**	**will have been knocked**

IMPERATIVE MOOD

knock   **be knocked**

SUBJUNCTIVE MOOD

Pres.	if I, he, she, it,	if I, he, she, it,
	we, you, they **knock**	we, you, they **be knocked**
Past	if I, he, she, it,	if I, he, she, it,
	we, you, they **knocked**	we, you, they **were knocked**
Fut.	if I, he, she, it,	if I, he, she, it,
	we, you, they **should knock**	we, you, they **should be knocked**

Transitive and intransitive. In idiomatic expressions, the American and British variants differ significantly. To avoid embarrassment use this verb with caution. See Phrasal Verbs.

Who is knocking on my door?
The fireman knocked down the door to gain entrance to the room.
She was knocked over by the strong gust of wind.

know	PRINCIPAL PARTS: **knows, knowing,**	be known
(active voice)	**knew, known**	(passive voice)

INDICATIVE MOOD

Pres.	I, we, you, they **know**	I **am known**
		we, you, they **are known**
	he, she, it **knows**	he, she, it **is known**
Pres.	I **am knowing**	I **am being known**
Prog.	we, you, they **are knowing**	we, you, they **are being known**
	he, she, it **is knowing**	he, she, it **is being known**
Pres.	I, we, you, they **do know**	I, we, you, they **do get known**
Int.	he, she, it **does know**	he, she, it **does get known**
Fut.	I, he, she, it,	I, he, she, it,
	we, you, they **will know**	we, you, they **will be known**
Past	I, he, she, it,	I, he, she, it **was known**
	we, you, they **knew**	we, you, they **were known**
Past	I, he, she, it **was knowing**	I, he, she, it **was being known**
Prog.	we, you, they **were knowing**	we, you, they **were being known**
Past	I, he, she, it,	I, he, she, it,
Int.	we, you, they **did know**	we, you, they **did get known**
Pres.	I, we, you, they **have known**	I, we, you, they **have been known**
Perf.	he, she, it **has known**	he, she, it **has been known**
Past	I, he, she, it,	I, he, she, it,
Perf.	we, you, they **had known**	we, you, they **had been known**
Fut.	I, he, she, it, we, you, they	I, he, she, it, we, you, they
Perf.	**will have known**	**will have been known**

K

IMPERATIVE MOOD

know **be known**

SUBJUNCTIVE MOOD

Pres.	if I, he, she, it,	if I, he, she, it,
	we, you, they **know**	we, you, they **be known**
Past	if I, he, she, it,	if I, he, she, it,
	we, you, they **knew**	we, you, they **were known**
Fut.	if I, he, she, it,	if I, he, she, it,
	we, you, they **should know**	we, you, they **should be known**

Transitive and intransitive.

No one knew what he had experienced.
Some mysteries of life simply cannot be known.

AN ESSENTIAL
55 VERB

233

know

Examples

Who knows the combinations?

I once knew a man who could speak Turkish.

She knows his cell phone number.

He has known many famous persons.

If you only knew what I know.

Know your verb endings for tomorrow's test.

Soon we will know everything about her.

The secret recipe was known by only a select few.

It is impossible to know everything.

Know as much as you can.

Words and expressions related to this verb

Know thyself!

It takes one to know one.

If you knew Suzie, like I know Suzie.

Their identities were known to the authorities.

She has been known to do strange things.

You should have known better.

If only I had known!

You will be known to the whole world.

Who knew?

He knows more than he is telling us.

KO
(active voice)

be KO'd
(passive voice)

INDICATIVE MOOD

Pres.	I, we, you, they **KO**	I **am KO'd**
		we, you, they **are KO'ed**
	he, she, it **KO's**	he, she, it **is KO'ed**
Pres.	I **am KO'ing**	I **am being KO'ed**
Prog.	we, you, they **are KO'ing**	we, you, they **are being KO'ed**
	he, she, it **is KO'ing**	he, she, it **is being KO'ed**
Pres.	I, we, you, they **do KO**	I, we, you, they **do get KO'ed**
Int.	he, she, it **does KO**	he, she, it **does get KO'ed**
Fut.	I, he, she, it,	I, he, she, it,
	we, you, they **will KO**	we, you, they **will be KO'ed**
Past	I, he, she, it,	I, he, she, it **was KO'ed**
	we, you, they **KO'ed**	we, you, they **were KO'ed**
Past	I, he, she, it **was KO'ing**	I, he, she, it **was being KO'ed**
Prog.	we, you, they **were KO'ing**	we, you, they **were being KO'ed**
Past	I, he, she, it,	I, he, she, it,
Int.	we, you, they **did KO**	we, you, they **did get KO'ed**
Pres.	I, we, you, they **have KO'ed**	I, we, you, they **have been KO'ed**
Perf.	he, she, it **has KO'ed**	he, she, it **has been KO'ed**
Past	I, he, she, it,	I, he, she, it,
Perf.	we, you, they **had KO'ed**	we, you, they **had been KO'ed**
Fut.	I, he, she, it, we, you, they	I, he, she, it, we, you, they
Perf.	**will have KO'ed**	**will have been KO'ed**

K

IMPERATIVE MOOD

KO   be **KO'ed**

SUBJUNCTIVE MOOD

Pres.	if I, he, she, it,	if I, he, she, it,
	we, you, they **KO**	we, you, they **be KO'ed**
Past	if I, he, she, it,	if I, he, she, it,
	we, you, they **KO'ed**	we, you, they **were KO'ed**
Fut.	if I, he, she, it,	if I, he, she, it,
	we, you, they **should KO**	we, you, they **should be KO'ed**

The verb is an abbreviation for "knock out." The verb can also be written as KAYO, KAYOES, KAYOING, KAYOED.

The boxer KO's most of his opponents.
The champion was KO'd by the contender in the second round.

INDICATIVE MOOD

Pres.	I, we, you, they **lay**	I **am laid**
		we, you, they **are laid**
	he, she, it **lays**	he, she, it **is laid**
Pres.	I **am laying**	I **am being laid**
Prog.	we, you, they **are laying**	we, you, they **are being laid**
	he, she, it **is laying**	he, she, it **is being laid**
Pres.	I, we, you, they **do lay**	I, we, you, they **do get laid**
Int.	he, she, it **does lay**	he, she, it **does get laid**
Fut.	I, he, she, it,	I, he, she, it,
	we, you, they **will lay**	we, you, they **will be laid**
Past	I, he, she, it,	I, he, she, it **was laid**
	we, you, they **laid**	we, you, they **were laid**
Past	I, he, she, it **was laying**	I, he, she, it **was being laid**
Prog.	we, you, they **were laying**	we, you, they **were being laid**
Past	I, he, she, it,	I, he, she, it,
Int.	we, you, they **did lay**	we, you, they **did get laid**
Pres.	I, we, you, they **have laid**	I, we, you, they **have been laid**
Perf.	he, she, it **has laid**	he, she, it **has been laid**
Past	I, he, she, it,	I, he, she, it,
Perf.	we, you, they **had laid**	we, you, they **had been laid**
Fut.	I, he, she, it, we, you, they	I, he, she, it, we, you, they
Perf.	**will have laid**	**will have been laid**

IMPERATIVE MOOD

lay   **be laid**

SUBJUNCTIVE MOOD

Pres.	if I, he, she, it,	if I, he, she, it,
	we, you, they **lay**	we, you, they **be laid**
Past	if I, he, she, it,	if I, he, she, it,
	we, you, they **laid**	we, you, they **were laid**
Fut.	if I, he, she, it,	if I, he, she, it,
	we, you, they **should lay**	we, you, they **should be laid**

Transitive and intransitive. Do not confuse the verb LAY with the verb LIE.

Mama laid the infant in the cradle.
These bricks were laid by a master mason.

lead
(active voice)

be led
(passive voice)

INDICATIVE MOOD

Pres.	I, we, you, they **lead**	I **am led**
		we, you, they **are led**
	he, she, it **leads**	he, she, it **is led**
Pres.	I **am leading**	I **am being led**
Prog.	we, you, they **are leading**	we, you, they **are being led**
	he, she, it **is leading**	he, she, it **is being led**
Pres.	I, we, you, they **do lead**	I, we, you, they **do get led**
Int.	he, she, it **does lead**	he, she, it **does get led**
Fut.	I, he, she, it,	I, he, she, it,
	we, you, they **will lead**	we, you, they **will be led**
Past	I, he, she, it,	I, he, she, it **was led**
	we, you, they **led**	we, you, they **were led**
Past	I, he, she, it **was leading**	I, he, she, it **was being led**
Prog.	we, you, they **were leading**	we, you, they **were being led**
Past	I, he, she, it,	I, he, she, it,
Int.	we, you, they **did lead**	we, you, they **did get led**
Pres.	I, we, you, they **have led**	I, we, you, they **have been led**
Perf.	he, she, it **has led**	he, she, it **has been led**
Past	I, he, she, it,	I, he, she, it,
Perf.	we, you, they **had led**	we, you, they **had been led**
Fut.	I, he, she, it, we, you, they	I, he, she, it, we, you, they
Perf.	**will have led**	**will have been led**

IMPERATIVE MOOD

lead **be led**

SUBJUNCTIVE MOOD

Pres.	if I, he, she, it,	if I, he, she, it,
	we, you, they **lead**	we, you, they **be led**
Past	if I, he, she, it,	if I, he, she, it,
	we, you, they **led**	we, you, they **were led**
Fut.	if I, he, she, it,	if I, he, she, it,
	we, you, they **should lead**	we, you, they **should be led**

L

Transitive and intransitive.

Who led at the halfway marker?
They were led down the mountain by an experienced instructor.

AN ESSENTIAL
55 VERB

237

AN ESSENTIAL
55 VERB

lead

Examples

Who is leading the parade?

She led an exemplary life.

He leads the school band.

He was led through the jungle by an experienced guide.

I will lead a seminar at the conference.

She led that organization for a decade.

The excursion was lead by the museum director.

They were led to believe that they had inherited much money.

What courses had led to a degree in engineering?

Our team leads in the standings.

Words and expressions related to this verb

Lead the way.

He led her on for months.

They led off with a song.

She leads him around by the nose.

I was led astray by his promises.

One thing leads to another.

They were led on by the others in the group.

You can lead a horse to water, but you can't make him drink.

She is clearly leading the field.

Normally, the man leads in the waltz.

lean
(active voice)

PRINCIPAL PARTS: leans, leaning, leaned, leaned

be leaned
(passive voice)

INDICATIVE MOOD

Pres.	I, we, you, they **lean**	I **am leaned**
		we, you, they **are leaned**
	he, she, it **leans**	he, she, it **is leaned**
Pres.	I **am leaning**	I **am being leaned**
Prog.	we, you, they **are leaning**	we, you, they **are being leaned**
	he, she, it **is leaning**	he, she, it **is being leaned**
Pres.	I, we, you, they **do lean**	I, we, you, they **do get leaned**
Int.	he, she, it **does lean**	he, she, it **does get leaned**
Fut.	I, he, she, it,	I, he, she, it,
	we, you, they **will lean**	we, you, they **will be leaned**
Past	I, he, she, it,	I, he, she, it **was leaned**
	we, you, they **leaned**	we, you, they **were leaned**
Past	I, he, she, it **was leaning**	I, he, she, it **was being leaned**
Prog.	we, you, they **were leaning**	we, you, they **were being leaned**
Past	I, he, she, it,	I, he, she, it,
Int.	we, you, they **did lean**	we, you, they **did get leaned**
Pres.	I, we, you, they **have leaned**	I, we, you, they **have been leaned**
Perf.	he, she, it **has leaned**	he, she, it **has been leaned**
Past	I, he, she, it,	I, he, she, it,
Perf.	we, you, they **had leaned**	we, you, they **had been leaned**
Fut.	I, he, she, it, we, you, they	I, he, she, it, we, you, they
Perf.	**will have leaned**	**will have been leaned**

IMPERATIVE MOOD

lean   **be leaned**

SUBJUNCTIVE MOOD

Pres.	if I, he, she, it,	if I, he, she, it,
	we, you, they **lean**	we, you, they **be leaned**
Past	if I, he, she, it,	if I, he, she, it,
	we, you, they **leaned**	we, you, they **were leaned**
Fut.	if I, he, she, it,	if I, he, she, it,
	we, you, they **should lean**	we, you, they **should be leaned**

Intransitive and transitive. *Webster's* and the *Oxford Dictionary* recognize LEANT as an alternate past tense and past participle form, especially in British English.

He leaned against the railing.
I have been leaned on one time too many.

leap
(active voice)

PRINCIPAL PARTS: **leaps, leaping,**
leaped/leapt, leaped/leapt

be leaped/leapt
(passive voice)

INDICATIVE MOOD

Pres.	I, we, you, they **leap**	I **am leaped**
		we, you, they **are leaped**
	he, she, it **leaps**	he, she, it **is leaped**
Pres.	I **am leaping**	I **am being leaped**
Prog.	we, you, they **are leaping**	we, you, they **are being leaped**
	he, she, it **is leaping**	he, she, it **is being leaped**
Pres.	I, we, you, they **do leap**	I, we, you, they **do get leaped**
Int.	he, she, it **does leap**	he, she, it **does get leaped**
Fut.	I, he, she, it,	I, he, she, it,
	we, you, they **will leap**	we, you, they **will be leaped**
Past	I, he, she, it,	I, he, she, it **was leaped**
	we, you, they **leaped**	we, you, they **were leaped**
Past	I, he, she, it **was leaping**	I, he, she, it **was being leaped**
Prog.	we, you, they **were leaping**	we, you, they **were being leaped**
Past	I, he, she, it,	I, he, she, it,
Int.	we, you, they **did leap**	we, you, they **did get leaped**
Pres.	I, we, you, they **have leaped**	I, we, you, they **have been leaped**
Perf.	he, she, it **has leaped**	he, she, it **has been leaped**
Past	I, he, she, it,	I, he, she, it,
Perf.	we, you, they **had leaped**	we, you, they **had been leaped**
Fut.	I, he, she, it, we, you, they	I, he, she, it, we, you, they
Perf.	**will have leaped**	**will have been leaped**

IMPERATIVE MOOD

leap	**be leaped**

SUBJUNCTIVE MOOD

Pres.	if I, he, she, it,	if I, he, she, it,
	we, you, they **leap**	we, you, they **be leaped**
Past	if I, he, she, it,	if I, he, she, it,
	we, you, they **leaped**	we, you, they **were leaped**
Fut.	if I, he, she, it,	if I, he, she, it,
	we, you, they **should leap**	we, you, they **should be leaped**

Intransitive and transitive. *Webster's* lists LEAPT as the first form for the past tense and past participle and also recognizes the spelling LEPT.

In San Francisco we once leaped onto a cable car.
This hurdle can be easily leaped by all the runners.

learn
(active voice)

be learned/learnt
(passive voice)

INDICATIVE MOOD

Pres.	I, we, you, they **learn**	I **am learned**
		we, you, they **are learned**
	he, she, it **learns**	he, she, it **is learned**
Pres.	I **am learning**	I **am being learned**
Prog.	we, you, they **are learning**	we, you, they **are being learned**
	he, she, it **is learning**	he, she, it **is being learned**
Pres.	I, we, you, they **do learn**	I, we, you, they **do get learned**
Int.	he, she, it **does learn**	he, she, it **does get learned**
Fut.	I, he, she, it,	I, he, she, it,
	we, you, they **will learn**	we, you, they **will be learned**
Past	I, he, she, it,	I, he, she, it **was learned**
	we, you, they **learned**	we, you, they **were learned**
Past	I, he, she, it **was learning**	I, he, she, it **was being learned**
Prog.	we, you, they **were learning**	we, you, they **were being learned**
Past	I, he, she, it,	I, he, she, it,
Int.	we, you, they **did learn**	we, you, they **did get learned**
Pres.	I, we, you, they **have learned**	I, we, you, they **have been learned**
Perf.	he, she, it **has learned**	he, she, it **has been learned**
Past	I, he, she, it,	I, he, she, it,
Perf.	we, you, they **had learned**	we, you, they **had been learned**
Fut.	I, he, she, it, we, you, they	I, he, she, it, we, you, they
Perf.	**will have learned**	**will have been learned**

IMPERATIVE MOOD

learn   **be learned**

SUBJUNCTIVE MOOD

Pres.	if I, he, she, it,	if I, he, she, it,
	we, you, they **learn**	we, you, they **be learned**
Past	if I, he, she, it,	if I, he, she, it,
	we, you, they **learned**	we, you, they **were learned**
Fut.	if I, he, she, it,	if I, he, she, it,
	we, you, they **should learn**	we, you, they **should be learned**

Transitive and intransitive. The past tense and past participle have the forms LEARNED and LEARNT.

She learned the dance in a very short time.
The spelling words had to be learned by heart.

PRINCIPAL PARTS: **leaves, leaving,
left, left**

be left
(passive voice)

INDICATIVE MOOD

Pres.	I, we, you, they **leave**	I **am left**
		we, you, they **are left**
	he, she, it **leaves**	he, she, it **is left**
Pres.	I **am leaving**	I **am being left**
Prog.	we, you, they **are leaving**	we, you, they **are being left**
	he, she, it **is leaving**	he, she, it **is being left**
Pres.	I, we, you, they **do leave**	I, we, you, they **do get left**
Int.	he, she, it **does leave**	he, she, it **does get left**
Fut.	I, he, she, it,	I, he, she, it,
	we, you, they **will leave**	we, you, they **will be left**
Past	I, he, she, it,	I, he, she, it **was left**
	we, you, they **left**	we, you, they **were left**
Past	I, he, she, it **was leaving**	I, he, she, it **was being left**
Prog.	we, you, they **were leaving**	we, you, they **were being left**
Past	I, he, she, it,	I, he, she, it,
Int.	we, you, they **did leave**	we, you, they **did get left**
Pres.	I, we, you, they **have left**	I, we, you, they **have been left**
Perf.	he, she, it **has left**	he, she, it **has been left**
Past	I, he, she, it,	I, he, she, it,
Perf.	we, you, they **had left**	we, you, they **had been left**
Fut.	I, he, she, it, we, you, they	I, he, she, it, we, you, they
Perf.	**will have left**	**will have been left**

IMPERATIVE MOOD

leave

be left

SUBJUNCTIVE MOOD

Pres.	if I, he, she, it,	if I, he, she, it,
	we, you, they **leave**	we, you, they **be left**
Past	if I, he, she, it,	if I, he, she, it,
	we, you, they **left**	we, you, they **were left**
Fut.	if I, he, she, it,	if I, he, she, it,
	we, you, they **should leave**	we, you, they **should be left**

Transitive and intransitive. There is an intransitive verb LEAVE, with past and past participle LEAVED, meaning to bear leaves.

He is leaving at noon.
Her plane already left.
Was anything left after the dinner?

AN ESSENTIAL
55 VERB

AN ESSENTIAL 55 VERB

leave

Examples

Leave it on the table.

She leaves for Boston tonight.

He left his computer at home.

I will never leave you.

The mailman left the package at the front door.

Has she left him yet?

I have been leaving messages for you for over a week.

Ten voice mails had been left for her.

There was nothing left to do.

You can leave me at the airport.

Words and expressions related to this verb

Love me or leave me.

Leave it to me.

Where did we leave off?

Leave me alone.

You can leave your shoes on.

Nothing was left.

I'm leaving on a freight train.

He left them his entire estate.

Leave the dog inside the house.

Leave nothing out.

She was left behind.

lend
(active voice)

be lent
(passive voice)

INDICATIVE MOOD

Pres.	I, we, you, they **lend**	I **am lent**
		we, you, they **are lent**
	he, she, it **lends**	he, she, it **is lent**
Pres.	I **am lending**	I **am being lent**
Prog.	we, you, they **are lending**	we, you, they **are being lent**
	he, she, it **is lending**	he, she, it **is being lent**
Pres.	I, we, you, they **do lend**	I, we, you, they **do get lent**
Int.	he, she, it **does lend**	he, she, it **does get lent**
Fut.	I, he, she, it,	I, he, she, it,
	we, you, they **will lend**	we, you, they **will be lent**
Past	I, he, she, it,	I, he, she, it **was lent**
	we, you, they **lent**	we, you, they **were lent**
Past	I, he, she, it **was lending**	I, he, she, it **was being lent**
Prog.	we, you, they **were lending**	we, you, they **were being lent**
Past	I, he, she, it,	I, he, she, it,
Int.	we, you, they **did lend**	we, you, they **did get lent**
Pres.	I, we, you, they **have lent**	I, we, you, they **have been lent**
Perf.	he, she, it **has lent**	he, she, it **has been lent**
Past	I, he, she, it,	I, he, she, it,
Perf.	we, you, they **had lent**	we, you, they **had been lent**
Fut.	I, he, she, it, we, you, they	I, he, she, it, we, you, they
Perf.	**will have lent**	**will have been lent**

IMPERATIVE MOOD

lend　　　　　　　　　　**be lent**

SUBJUNCTIVE MOOD

Pres.	if I, he, she, it,	if I, he, she, it,
	we, you, they **lend**	we, you, they **be lent**
Past	if I, he, she, it,	if I, he, she, it,
	we, you, they **lent**	we, you, they **were lent**
Fut.	if I, he, she, it,	if I, he, she, it,
	we, you, they **should lend**	we, you, they **should be lent**

Transitive and intransitive.

Lend me a hand.
He lent his brother money to buy a car.
The books were lent for two weeks.

244

let
(active voice)

be let
(passive voice)

INDICATIVE MOOD

Pres.	I, we, you, they **let**	I **am let**
		we, you, they **are let**
	he, she, it **lets**	he, she, it **is let**
Pres.	I **am letting**	I **am being let**
Prog.	we, you, they **are letting**	we, you, they **are being let**
	he, she, it **is letting**	he, she, it **is being let**
Pres.	I, we, you, they **do let**	I, we, you, they **do get let**
Int.	he, she, it **does let**	he, she, it **does get let**
Fut.	I, he, she, it,	I, he, she, it,
	we, you, they **will let**	we, you, they **will be let**
Past	I, he, she, it,	I, he, she, it **was let**
	we, you, they **let**	we, you, they **were let**
Past	I, he, she, it **was letting**	I, he, she, it **was being let**
Prog.	we, you, they **were letting**	we, you, they **were being let**
Past	I, he, she, it,	I, he, she, it,
Int.	we, you, they **did let**	we, you, they **did get let**
Pres.	I, we, you, they **have let**	I, we, you, they **have been let**
Perf.	he, she, it **has let**	he, she, it **has been let**
Past	I, he, she, it,	I, he, she, it,
Perf.	we, you, they **had let**	we, you, they **had been let**
Fut.	I, he, she, it, we, you, they	I, he, she, it, we, you, they
Perf.	**will have let**	**will have been let**

IMPERATIVE MOOD

let **be let**

SUBJUNCTIVE MOOD

Pres.	if I, he, she, it,	if I, he, she, it,
	we, you, they **let**	we, you, they **be let**
Past	if I, he, she, it,	if I, he, she, it,
	we, you, they **let**	we, you, they **were let**
Fut.	if I, he, she, it,	if I, he, she, it,
	we, you, they **should let**	we, you, they **should be let**

Transitive and intransitive.

He is letting the children go to the movies alone.
Mother let them go alone last week.
That apartment was let last week.
He was let go from his position by the new administration.

INDICATIVE MOOD

Pres.   I, we, you, they **lie**

      he, she, it **lies**

Pres.   **I am lying**
Prog.   we, you, they **are lying**
      he, she, it **is lying**

Pres.   I, we, you, they **do lie**
Int.   he, she, it **does lie**

Fut.   I, he, she, it,
      we, you, they **will lie**

Past   I, he, she, it,
      we, you, they **lay**

Past   I, he, she, it **was lying**
Prog.   we, you, they **were lying**

Past   I, he, she, it,
Int.   we, you, they **did lie**

Pres.   I, we, you, they **have lain**
Perf.   he, she, it **has lain**

Past   I, he, she, it,
Perf.   we, you, they **had lain**

Fut.   I, he, she, it, we, you, they
Perf.   **will have lain**

IMPERATIVE MOOD

      lie

SUBJUNCTIVE MOOD

Pres.   if I, he, she, it,
      we, you, they **lie**

Past   if I, he, she, it,
      we, you, they **lay**

Fut.   if I, he, she, it,
      we, you, they **should lie**

The intransitive verb meaning to "be or place flat."

He is lying in the grass and enjoying the sunshine.
The dog lay on its side for at least an hour.
How long has she lain in that position?

246

lie
(active voice)

be lied
(passive voice)

INDICATIVE MOOD

Pres.	I, we, you, they **lie**	I **am lied**
		we, you, they **are lied**
	he, she, it **lies**	he, she, it **is lied**
Pres. *Prog.*	I **am lying**	I **am being lied**
	we, you, they **are lying**	we, you, they **are being lied**
	he, she, it **is lying**	he, she, it **is being lied**
Pres. *Int.*	I, we, you, they **do lie**	I, we, you, they **do get lied**
	he, she, it **does lie**	he, she, it **does get lied**
Fut.	I, he, she, it,	I, he, she, it,
	we, you, they **will lie**	we, you, they **will be lied**
Past	I, he, she, it	I, he, she, it **was lied**
	we, you, they **lied**	we, you, they **were lied**
Past *Prog.*	I, he, she, it **was lying**	I, he, she, it **was being lied**
	we, you, they **were lying**	we, you, they **were being lied**
Past *Int.*	I, he, she, it,	I, he, she, it,
	we, you, they **did lie**	we, you, they **did get lied**
Pres. *Perf.*	I, we, you, they **have lied**	I, we, you, they **have been lied**
	he, she, it **has lied**	he, she, it **has been lied**
Past *Perf.*	I, he, she, it,	I, he, she, it,
	we, you, they **had lied**	we, you, they **had been lied**
Fut. *Perf.*	I, he, she, it, we, you, they	I, he, she, it, we, you, they
	will have lied	**will have been lied**

IMPERATIVE MOOD

lie　　　　**be lied**

SUBJUNCTIVE MOOD

Pres.	if I, he, she, it,	if I, he, she, it,
	we, you, they **lie**	we, you, they **be lied**
Past	if I, he, she, it,	if I, he, she, it,
	we, you, they **lied**	we, you, they **were lied**
Fut.	if I, he, she, it,	if I, he, she, it,
	we, you, they **should lie**	we, you, they **should be lied**

Intransitive and transitive. This verb means to "tell something that is not true."

It is disturbing when a young child lies.
She is lying on the witness stand.
Have you ever lied or been lied to?

light
(active voice)

be lighted/lit
(passive voice)

INDICATIVE MOOD

Pres.	I, we, you, they **light**	I **am lighted**
		we, you, they **are lighted**
	he, she, it **lights**	he, she, it **is lighted**
Pres.	I **am lighting**	I **am being lighted**
Prog.	we, you, they **are lighting**	we, you, they **are being lighted**
	he, she, it **is lighting**	he, she, it **is being lighted**
Pres.	I, we, you, they **do light**	I, we, you, they **do get lighted**
Int.	he, she, it **does light**	he, she, it **does get lighted**
Fut.	I, he, she, it,	I, he, she, it,
	we, you, they **will light**	we, you, they **will be lighted**
Past	I, he, she, it,	I, he, she, it **was lighted**
	we, you, they **lighted**	we, you, they **were lighted**
Past	I, he, she, it **was lighting**	I, he, she, it **was being lighted**
Prog.	we, you, they **were lighting**	we, you, they **were being lighted**
Past	I, he, she, it,	I, he, she, it, we, you, they
Int.	we, you, they **did light**	**did get lighted**
Pres.	I, we, you, they **have lighted**	I, we, you, they **have been lighted**
Perf.	he, she, it **has lighted**	he, she, it **has been lighted**
Past	I, he, she, it,	I, he, she, it,
Perf.	we, you, they **had lighted**	we, you, they **had been lighted**
Fut.	I, he, she, it, we, you, they	I, he, she, it, we, you, they
Perf.	**will have lighted**	**will have been lighted**

IMPERATIVE MOOD

light   **be lighted**

SUBJUNCTIVE MOOD

Pres.	if I, he, she, it,	if I, he, she, it,
	we, you, they **light**	we, you, they **be lighted**
Past	if I, he, she, it,	if I, he, she, it,
	we, you, they **lighted**	we, you, they **were lighted**
Fut.	if I, he, she, it,	if I, he, she, it,
	we, you, they **should light**	we, you, they **should be lighted**

Transitive and intransitive. *Merriam Webster's* and the *Oxford Dictionary* list LIT as the first form for the past tense and past participle.

The moonshine lights our way.
He lighted the lantern in their cabin.
Their way was lighted by the stars.

248

lighten
(active voice)

be lightened
(passive voice)

INDICATIVE MOOD

Pres.	I, we, you, they **lighten**	I **am lightened**
		we, you, they **are lightened**
	he, she, it **lightens**	he, she, it **is lightened**
Pres.	I **am lightening**	I **am being lightened**
Prog.	we, you, they **are lightening**	we, you, they **are being lightened**
	he, she, it **is lightening**	he, she, it **is being lightened**
Pres.	I, we, you, they **do lighten**	I, we, you, they **do get lightened**
Int.	he, she, it **does lighten**	he, she, it **does get lightened**
Fut.	I, he, she, it,	I, he, she, it,
	we, you, they **will lighten**	we, you, they **will be lightened**
Past	I, he, she, it,	I, he, she, it **was lightened**
	we, you, they **lightened**	we, you, they **were lightened**
Past	I, he, she, it **was lightening**	I, he, she, it **was being lightened**
Prog.	we, you, they **were lightening**	we, you, they **were being lightened**
Past	I, he, she, it,	I, he, she, it,
Int.	we, you, they **did lighten**	we, you, they **did get lightened**
Pres.	I, we, you, they **have lightened**	I, we, you, they **have been lightened**
Perf.	he, she, it **has lightened**	he, she, it **has been lightened**
Past	I, he, she, it,	I, he, she, it,
Perf.	we, you, they **had lightened**	we, you, they **had been lightened**
Fut.	I, he, she, it, we, you, they	I, he, she, it, we, you, they
Perf.	**will have lightened**	**will have been lightened**

IMPERATIVE MOOD

lighten   **be lightened**

SUBJUNCTIVE MOOD

Pres.	if I, he, she, it,	if I, he, she, it,
	we, you, they **lighten**	we, you, they **be lightened**
Past	if I, he, she, it,	if I, he, she, it,
	we, you, they **lightened**	we, you, they **were lightened**
Fut.	if I, he, she, it,	if I, he, she, it,
	we, you, they **should lighten**	we, you, they **should be lightened**

Transitive and intransitive.

The stars can lighten the night.
We lightened the load by removing several objects.
The pathway was lightened by candles.
Our burden was lightened by news of his safe arrival.

249

like
(active voice)

PRINCIPAL PARTS: likes, liking, liked, liked

be liked
(passive voice)

INDICATIVE MOOD

Pres.	I, we, you, they **like**
	he, she, it **likes**

I am liked
we, you, they **are liked**
he, she, it **is liked**

Pres.	I **am liking**
Prog.	we, you, they **are liking**
	he, she, it **is liking**

I am being liked
we, you, they **are being liked**
he, she, it **is being liked**

Pres.	I, we, you, they **do like**
Int.	he, she, it **does like**

I, we, you, they **do get liked**
he, she, it **does get liked**

Fut.	I, he, she, it,
	we, you, they **will like**

I, he, she, it,
we, you, they **will be liked**

Past	I, he, she, it,
	we, you, they **liked**

I, he, she, it **was liked**
we, you, they **were liked**

Past	I, he, she, it **was liking**
Prog.	we, you, they **were liking**

I, he, she, it **was being liked**
we, you, they **were being liked**

Past	I, he, she, it,
Int.	we, you, they **did like**

I, he, she, it,
we, you, they **did get liked**

Pres.	I, we, you, they **have liked**
Perf.	he, she, it **has liked**

I, we, you, they **have been liked**
he, she, it **has been liked**

Past	I, he, she, it,
Perf.	we, you, they **had liked**

I, he, she, it,
we, you, they **had been liked**

Fut.	I, he, she, it, we, you, they
Perf.	**will have liked**

I, he, she, it, we, you, they
will have been liked

IMPERATIVE MOOD

like　　　　　　　　　　　**be liked**

SUBJUNCTIVE MOOD

Pres.	if I, he, she, it,
	we, you, they **like**

if I, he, she, it,
we, you, they **be liked**

Past	if I, he, she, it,
	we, you, they **liked**

if I, he, she, it,
we, you, they **were liked**

Fut.	if I, he, she, it,
	we, you, they **should like**

if I, he, she, it,
we, you, they **should be liked**

Transitive and intransitive.

How are you liking your new apartment?
The waitress liked serving large groups.
He was well liked by all his colleagues.

AN ESSENTIAL 55 VERB

like

Examples

She likes me.

I like ice cream.

Did anyone like that film?

They had always liked the outdoors.

The boss was liked by all her employees.

Do you think I will like a cruise?

I have always liked Russian novels.

She doesn't like to interfere.

I am liking this trip less and less.

I have never liked this cold weather.

Words and expressions related to this verb

Like it or not, here I come.

Like it or leave it.

How do you like that?

If you like her, you will love her sister.

I like your idea.

Would you like to dance?

He never liked his teachers.

She likes to do puzzles.

Would you like a refill on your drink?

What would you like to do?

limit
(active voice)

be limited
(passive voice)

INDICATIVE MOOD

Pres.	I, we, you, they **limit**	I **am limited**
		we, you, they **are limited**
	he, she, it **limits**	he, she, it **is limited**
Pres.	I **am limiting**	I **am being limited**
Prog.	we, you, they **are limiting**	we, you, they **are being limited**
	he, she, it **is limiting**	he, she, it **is being limited**
Pres.	I, we, you, they **do limit**	I, we, you, they **do get limited**
Int.	he, she, it **does limit**	he, she, it **does get limited**
Fut.	I, he, she, it,	I, he, she, it,
	we, you, they **will limit**	we, you, they **will be limited**
Past	I, he, she, it,	I, he, she, it **was limited**
	we, you, they **limited**	we, you, they **were limited**
Past	I, he, she, it **was limiting**	I, he, she, it **was being limited**
Prog.	we, you, they **were limiting**	we, you, they **were being limited**
Past	I, he, she, it,	I, he, she, it,
Int.	we, you, they **did limit**	we, you, they **did get limited**
Pres.	I, we, you, they **have limited**	I, we, you, they **have been limited**
Perf.	he, she, it **has limited**	he, she, it **has been limited**
Past	I, he, she, it,	I, he, she, it,
Perf.	we, you, they **had limited**	we, you, they **had been limited**
Fut.	I, he, she, it, we, you, they	I, he, she, it, we, you, they
Perf.	**will have limited**	**will have been limited**

IMPERATIVE MOOD

limit   **be limited**

SUBJUNCTIVE MOOD

Pres.	if I, he, she, it,	if I, he, she, it,
	we, you, they **limit**	we, you, they **be limited**
Past	if I, he, she, it,	if I, he, she, it,
	we, you, they **limited**	we, you, they **were limited**
Fut.	if I, he, she, it,	if I, he, she, it,
	we, you, they **should limit**	we, you, they **should be limited**

Transitive and intransitive.

They limited their consumption of fats for two weeks.
The speeches were limited to five minutes apiece.

252

link
(active voice)

be linked
(passive voice)

INDICATIVE MOOD

Pres.	I, we, you, they **link**	I **am linked**
		we, you, they **are linked**
	he, she, it **links**	he, she, it **is linked**
Pres.	I **am linking**	I **am being linked**
Prog.	we, you, they **are linking**	we, you, they **are being linked**
	he, she, it **is linking**	he, she, it **is being linked**
Pres.	I, we, you, they **do link**	I, we, you, they **do get linked**
Int.	he, she, it **does link**	he, she, it **does get linked**
Fut.	I, he, she, it,	I, he, she, it,
	we, you, they **will link**	we, you, they **will be linked**
Past	I, he, she, it,	I, he, she, it **was linked**
	we, you, they **linked**	we, you, they **were linked**
Past	I, he, she, it **was linking**	I, he, she, it **was being linked**
Prog.	we, you, they **were linking**	we, you, they **were being linked**
Past	I, he, she, it,	I, he, she, it,
Int.	we, you, they **did link**	we, you, they **did get linked**
Pres.	I, we, you, they **have linked**	I, we, you, they **have been linked**
Perf.	he, she, it **has linked**	he, she, it **has been linked**
Past	I, he, she, it,	I, he, she, it,
Perf.	we, you, they **had linked**	we, you, they **had been linked**
Fut.	I, he, she, it, we, you, they	I, he, she, it, we, you, they
Perf.	**will have linked**	**will have been linked**

L

IMPERATIVE MOOD

link   **be linked**

SUBJUNCTIVE MOOD

Pres.	if I, he, she, it,	if I, he, she, it,
	we, you, they **link**	we, you, they **be linked**
Past	if I, he, she, it,	if I, he, she, it,
	we, you, they **linked**	we, you, they **were linked**
Fut.	if I, he, she, it,	if I, he, she, it,
	we, you, they **should link**	we, you, they **should be linked**

Transitive and intransitive.

They linked their two computers together.
The family was linked electronically by e-mail.

PRINCIPAL PARTS: **listens, listening, listened, listened**

INDICATIVE MOOD

Pres.   I, we, you, they **listen**

he, she, it **listens**

Pres.   **I am listening**
Prog.   we, you, they **are listening**
he, she, it **is listening**

Pres.   I, we, you, they **do listen**
Int.   he, she, it **does listen**

Fut.   I, he, she, it,
we, you, they **will listen**

Past   I, he, she, it,
we, you, they **listened**

Past   I, he, she, it **was listening**
Prog.   we, you, they **were listening**

Past   I, he, she, it,
Int.   we, you, they **did listen**

Pres.   I, we, you, they **have listened**
Perf.   he, she, it **has listened**

Past   I, he, she, it,
Perf.   we, you, they **had listened**

Fut.   I, he, she, it, we, you, they
Perf.   **will have listened**

IMPERATIVE MOOD

listen

SUBJUNCTIVE MOOD

Pres.   if I, he, she, it,
we, you, they **listen**

Past   if I, he, she, it,
we, you, they **listened**

Fut.   if I, he, she, it,
we, you, they **should listen**

When we are listening, children, we do not speak.
The principal listened attentively as each student spoke.
The speech was listened to in both nations.

live
(active voice)

PRINCIPAL PARTS: **lives, living, lived, lived**

be lived
(passive voice)

INDICATIVE MOOD

Pres.	I, we, you, they **live**	I **am lived**
		we, you, they **are lived**
	he, she, it **lives**	he, she, it **is lived**
Pres.	I **am living**	I **am being lived**
Prog.	we, you, they **are living**	we, you, they **are being lived**
	he, she, it **is living**	he, she, it **is being lived**
Pres.	I, we, you, they **do live**	I, we, you, they **do get lived**
Int.	he, she, it **does live**	he, she, it **does get lived**
Fut.	I, he, she, it,	I, he, she, it,
	we, you, they **will live**	we, you, they **will be lived**
Past	I, he, she, it,	I, he, she, it **was lived**
	we, you, they **lived**	we, you, they **were lived**
Past	I, he, she, it **was living**	I, he, she, it **was being lived**
Prog.	we, you, they **were living**	we, you, they **were being lived**
Past	I, he, she, it,	I, he, she, it,
Int.	we, you, they **did live**	we, you, they **did get lived**
Pres.	I, we, you, they **have lived**	I, we, you, they **have been lived**
Perf.	he, she, it **has lived**	he, she, it **has been lived**
Past	I, he, she, it,	I, he, she, it,
Perf.	we, you, they **had lived**	we, you, they **had been lived**
Fut.	I, he, she, it, we, you, they	I, he, she, it, we, you, they
Perf.	**will have lived**	**will have been lived**

IMPERATIVE MOOD

live   **be lived**

SUBJUNCTIVE MOOD

Pres.	if I, he, she, it,	if I, he, she, it,
	we, you, they **live**	we, you, they **be lived**
Past	if I, he, she, it,	if I, he, she, it,
	we, you, they **lived**	we, you, they **were lived**
Fut.	if I, he, she, it,	if I, he, she, it,
	we, you, they **should live**	we, you, they **should be lived**

Transitive and intransitive.

He is living on a fixed income.
They lived in Florida for twenty years.
The teenage years must be lived to be appreciated.

255

Examples

Where do you live?

I live in town.

She lives across the river.

Has anyone lived abroad?

She had lived a long and fruitful life.

No one will live forever.

Live life to the fullest.

We lived through the flood.

Where is the best place to live?

He lives for his children.

Words and expressions related to this verb

Live it up.

He lives like a king.

Live and let live.

She could never live that mistake down.

They lived out their lives in peace.

They lived happily ever after.

Live by the rules.

He lived to fight another day.

She lived to tell about it.

Some legends have lived on for generations.

load
(active voice)

be loaded
(passive voice)

INDICATIVE MOOD

Pres.	I, we, you, they **load**	I **am loaded**
		we, you, they **are loaded**
	he, she, it **loads**	he, she, it **is loaded**
Pres.	I **am loading**	I **am being loaded**
Prog.	we, you, they **are loading**	we, you, they **are being loaded**
	he, she, it **is loading**	he, she, it **is being loaded**
Pres.	I, we, you, they **do load**	I, we, you, they **do get loaded**
Int.	he, she, it **does load**	he, she, it **does get loaded**
Fut.	I, he, she, it,	I, he, she, it,
	we, you, they **will load**	we, you, they **will be loaded**
Past	I, he, she, it,	I, he, she, it **was loaded**
	we, you, they **loaded**	we, you, they **were loaded**
Past	I, he, she, it **was loading**	I, he, she, it **was being loaded**
Prog.	we, you, they **were loading**	we, you, they **were being loaded**
Past	I, he, she, it,	I, he, she, it,
Int.	we, you, they **did load**	we, you, they **did get loaded**
Pres.	I, we, you, they **have loaded**	I, we, you, they **have been loaded**
Perf.	he, she, it **has loaded**	he, she, it **has been loaded**
Past	I, he, she, it,	I, he, she, it,
Perf.	we, you, they **had loaded**	we, you, they **had been loaded**
Fut.	I, he, she, it, we, you, they	I, he, she, it, we, you, they
Perf.	**will have loaded**	**will have been loaded**

IMPERATIVE MOOD

load **be loaded**

SUBJUNCTIVE MOOD

Pres.	if I, he, she, it,	if I, he, she, it,
	we, you, they **load**	we, you, they **be loaded**
Past	if I, he, she, it,	if I, he, she, it,
	we, you, they **loaded**	we, you, they **were loaded**
Fut.	if I, he, she, it,	if I, he, she, it,
	we, you, they **should load**	we, you, they **should be loaded**

Transitive and intransitive.

They loaded the car with suitcases.
The mailbox was loaded with flyers and bills.

look
(active voice)

PRINCIPAL PARTS: **looks, looking, looked, looked**

be looked
(passive voice)

INDICATIVE MOOD

Pres.	I, we, you, they **look**	I **am looked**
		we, you, they **are looked**
	he, she, it **looks**	he, she, it **is looked**
Pres.	I **am looking**	I **am being looked**
Prog.	we, you, they **are looking**	we, you, they **are being looked**
	he, she, it **is looking**	he, she, it **is being looked**
Pres.	I, we, you, they **do look**	I, we, you, they **do get looked**
Int.	he, she, it **does look**	he, she, it **does get looked**
Fut.	I, he, she, it,	I, he, she, it,
	we, you, they **will look**	we, you, they **will be looked**
Past	I, he, she, it,	I, he, she, it **was looked**
	we, you, they **looked**	we, you, they **were looked**
Past	I, he, she, it **was looking**	I, he, she, it **was being looked**
Prog.	we, you, they **were looking**	we, you, they **were being looked**
Past	I, he, she, it,	I, he, she, it,
Int.	we, you, they **did look**	we, you, they **did get looked**
Pres.	I, we, you, they **have looked**	I, we, you, they **have been looked**
Perf.	he, she, it **has looked**	he, she, it **has been looked**
Past	I, he, she, it,	I, he, she, it,
Perf.	we, you, they **had looked**	we, you, they **had been looked**
Fut.	I, he, she, it, we, you, they	I, he, she, it, we, you, they
Perf.	**will have looked**	**will have been looked**

IMPERATIVE MOOD

look　　　　　　　　　　**be looked**

SUBJUNCTIVE MOOD

Pres.	if I, he, she, it,	if I, he, she, it,
	we, you, they **look**	we, you, they **be looked**
Past	if I, he, she, it,	if I, he, she, it,
	we, you, they **looked**	we, you, they **were looked**
Fut.	if I, he, she, it,	if I, he, she, it,
	we, you, they **should look**	we, you, they **should be looked**

Intransitive and transitive.

She looked beautiful in her prom dress.
The case was looked at from many angles.

AN ESSENTIAL
55 VERB

look

Examples

Look both ways before you cross.

She looks great.

Look it up on the computer.

I look like my father.

He looked over the book last night.

They looked on as he crossed the finish line.

You have never looked better.

Have you looked under the bed?

Who will look for the key?

Look it over.

Words and expressions related to this verb

Don't look too closely.

Hey, look me over.

Here's looking at you.

You look marvelous.

What are you looking at?

No one is looking.

Look for it.

Look, but don't touch.

Look out!

The meat looks done.

I look up to both of my parents.

L

loose
(active voice)

be loosed
(passive voice)

INDICATIVE MOOD

Pres.	I, we, you, they **loose**	**I am loosed** we, you, they **are loosed**
	he, she, it **looses**	he, she, it **is loosed**
Pres. *Prog.*	**I am loosing** we, you, they **are loosing** he, she, it **is loosing**	**I am being loosed** we, you, they **are being loosed** he, she, it **is being loosed**
Pres. *Int.*	I, we, you, they **do loose** he, she, it **does loose**	I, we, you, they **do get loosed** he, she, it **does get loosed**
Fut.	I, he, she, it, we, you, they **will loose**	I, he, she, it, we, you, they **will be loosed**
Past	I, he, she, it, we, you, they **loosed**	I, he, she, it **was loosed** we, you, they **were loosed**
Past *Prog.*	I, he, she, it **was loosing** we, you, they **were loosing**	I, he, she, it **was being loosed** we, you, they **were being loosed**
Past *Int.*	I, he, she, it, we, you, they **did loose**	I, he, she, it, we, you, they **did get loosed**
Pres. *Perf.*	I, we, you, they **have loosed** he, she, it **has loosed**	I, we, you, they **have been loosed** he, she, it **has been loosed**
Past *Perf.*	I, he, she, it, we, you, they **had loosed**	I, he, she, it, we, you, they **had been loosed**
Fut. *Perf.*	I, he, she, it, we, you, they **will have loosed**	I, he, she, it, we, you, they **will have been loosed**

IMPERATIVE MOOD

loose   **be loosed**

SUBJUNCTIVE MOOD

Pres.	if I, he, she, it, we, you, they **loose**	if I, he, she, it, we, you, they **be loosed**
Past	if I, he, she, it, we, you, they **loosed**	if I, he, she, it, we, you, they **were loosed**
Fut.	if I, he, she, it, we, you, they **should loose**	if I, he, she, it, we, you, they **should be loosed**

Transitive and intransitive.

They are loosing the bonds.
They loosed the fish back into the pond.
The dog was loosed from its chain to run free.

260

loosen
(active voice)

be loosened
(passive voice)

INDICATIVE MOOD

Pres.	I, we, you, they **loosen**	I **am loosened**
		we, you, they **are loosened**
	he, she, it **loosens**	he, she, it **is loosened**
Pres.	I **am loosening**	I **am being loosened**
Prog.	we, you, they **are loosening**	we, you, they **are being loosened**
	he, she, it **is loosening**	he, she, it **is being loosened**
Pres.	I, we, you, they **do loosen**	I, we, you, they **do get loosened**
Int.	he, she, it **does loosen**	he, she, it **does get loosened**
Fut.	I, he, she, it, we, you, they **will loosen**	I, he, she, it, we, you, they **will be loosened**
Past	I, he, she, it, we, you, they **loosened**	I, he, she, it **was loosened** we, you, they **were loosened**
Past	I, he, she, it **was loosening**	I, he, she, it **was being loosened**
Prog.	we, you, they **were loosening**	we, you, they **were being loosened**
Past	I, he, she, it, we, you, they **did loosen**	I, he, she, it, we, you, they **did get loosened**
Int.		
Pres.	I, we, you, they **have loosened**	I, we, you, they **have been loosened**
Perf.	he, she, it **has loosened**	he, she, it **has been loosened**
Past	I, he, she, it, we, you, they **had loosened**	I, he, she, it, we, you, they **had been loosened**
Perf.		
Fut.	I, he, she, it, we, you, they	I, he, she, it, we, you, they
Perf.	**will have loosened**	**will have been loosened**

IMPERATIVE MOOD

loosen   **be loosened**

SUBJUNCTIVE MOOD

Pres.	if I, he, she, it, we, you, they **loosen**	if I, he, she, it, we, you, they **be loosened**
Past	if I, he, she, it, we, you, they **loosened**	if I, he, she, it, we, you, they **were loosened**
Fut.	if I, he, she, it, we, you, they **should loosen**	if I, he, she, it, we, you, they **should be loosened**

Transitive and intransitive.

I am loosening my belt after the second piece of cake.
The bolts were loosened and then tightened again.

lose (active voice)	PRINCIPAL PARTS: loses, losing, lost, lost	be lost (passive voice)

INDICATIVE MOOD

Pres.	I, we, you, they **lose** he, she, it **loses**	I **am lost** we, you, they **are lost** he, she, it **is lost**
Pres. *Prog.*	I **am losing** we, you, they **are losing** he, she, it **is losing**	I **am being lost** we, you, they **are being lost** he, she, it **is being lost**
Pres. *Int.*	I, we, you, they **do lose** he, she, it **does lose**	I, we, you, they **do get lost** he, she, it **does get lost**
Fut.	I, he, she, it, we, you, they **will lose**	I, he, she, it, we, you, they **will be lost**
Past	I, he, she, it, we, you, they **lost**	I, he, she, it **was lost** we, you, they **were lost**
Past *Prog.*	I, he, she, it **was losing** we, you, they **were losing**	I, he, she, it **was being lost** we, you, they **were being lost**
Past *Int.*	I, he, she, it, we, you, they **did lose**	I, he, she, it, we, you, they **did get lost**
Pres. *Perf.*	I, we, you, they **have lost** he, she, it **has lost**	I, we, you, they **have been lost** he, she, it **has been lost**
Past *Perf.*	I, he, she, it, we, you, they **had lost**	I, he, she, it, we, you, they **had been lost**
Fut. *Perf.*	I, he, she, it, we, you, they **will have lost**	I, he, she, it, we, you, they **will have been lost**

IMPERATIVE MOOD

lose	**be lost**

SUBJUNCTIVE MOOD

Pres.	if I, he, she, it, we, you, they **lose**	if I, he, she, it, we, you, they **be lost**
Past	if I, he, she, it, we, you, they **lost**	if I, he, she, it, we, you, they **were lost**
Fut.	if I, he, she, it, we, you, they **should lose**	if I, he, she, it, we, you, they **should be lost**

Transitive and intransitive.

We are losing the match.
They lost everything in the fire.
All is not lost.

love
(active voice)

be loved
(passive voice)

INDICATIVE MOOD

Pres.	I, we, you, they **love**	I **am loved**
		we, you, they **are loved**
	he, she, it **loves**	he, she, it **is loved**
Pres.	I **am loving**	I **am being loved**
Prog.	we, you, they **are loving**	we, you, they **are being loved**
	he, she, it **is loving**	he, she, it **is being loved**
Pres.	I, we, you, they **do love**	I, we, you, they **do get loved**
Int.	he, she, it **does love**	he, she, it **does get loved**
Fut.	I, he, she, it,	I, he, she, it,
	we, you, they **will love**	we, you, they **will be loved**
Past	I, he, she, it,	I, he, she, it **was loved**
	we, you, they **loved**	we, you, they **were loved**
Past	I, he, she, it **was loving**	I, he, she, it **was being loved**
Prog.	we, you, they **were loving**	we, you, they **were being loved**
Past	I, he, she, it,	I, he, she, it,
Int.	we, you, they **did love**	we, you, they **did get loved**
Pres.	I, we, you, they **have loved**	I, we, you, they **have been loved**
Perf.	he, she, it **has loved**	he, she, it **has been loved**
Past	I, he, she, it,	I, he, she, it,
Perf.	we, you, they **had loved**	we, you, they **had been loved**
Fut.	I, he, she, it, we, you, they	I, he, she, it, we, you, they
Perf.	**will have loved**	**will have been loved**

IMPERATIVE MOOD

love **be loved**

SUBJUNCTIVE MOOD

Pres.	if I, he, she, it,	if I, he, she, it,
	we, you, they **love**	we, you, they **be loved**
Past	if I, he, she, it,	if I, he, she, it,
	we, you, they **loved**	we, you, they **were loved**
Fut.	if I, he, she, it,	if I, he, she, it,
	we, you, they **should love**	we, you, they **should be loved**

Transitive and intransitive.

We are loving our new jobs.
They loved each other their whole lives.
A child is loved unconditionally.

maintain
(active voice)

INDICATIVE MOOD

Pres.	I, we, you, they **maintain**	I **am maintained**
		we, you, they **are maintained**
	he, she, it **maintains**	he, she, it **is maintained**
Pres.	I **am maintaining**	I **am being maintained**
Prog.	we, you, they **are maintaining**	we, you, they **are being maintained**
	he, she, it **is maintaining**	he, she, it **is being maintained**
Pres.	I, we, you, they **do maintain**	I, we, you, they **do get maintained**
Int.	he, she, it **does maintain**	he, she, it **does get maintained**
Fut.	I, he, she, it,	I, he, she, it,
	we, you, they **will maintain**	we, you, they **will be maintained**
Past	I, he, she, it,	I, he, she, it **was maintained**
	we, you, they **maintained**	we, you, they **were maintained**
Past	I, he, she, it **was maintaining**	I, he, she, it **was being maintained**
Prog.	we, you, they **were maintaining**	we, you, they **were being maintained**
Past	I, he, she, it,	I, he, she, it, we, you, they
Int.	we, you, they **did maintain**	**did get maintained**
Pres.	I, we, you, they **have maintained**	I, we, you, they **have been maintained**
Perf.	he, she, it **has maintained**	he, she, it **has been maintained**
Past	I, he, she, it,	I, he, she, it,
Perf.	we, you, they **had maintained**	we, you, they **had been maintained**
Fut.	I, he, she, it, we, you, they	I, he, she, it, we, you, they
Perf.	**will have maintained**	**will have been maintained**

IMPERATIVE MOOD

maintain **be maintained**

SUBJUNCTIVE MOOD

Pres.	if I, he, she, it,	if I, he, she, it,
	we, you, they **maintain**	we, you, they **be maintained**
Past	if I, he, she, it,	if I, he, she, it,
	we, you, they **maintained**	we, you, they **were maintained**
Fut.	if I, he, she, it,	if I, he, she, it,
	we, you, they **should maintain**	we, you, they **should be maintained**

They maintained contact even after graduation.
These facilities have to be maintained for future generations.

make
(active voice)

be made
(passive voice)

INDICATIVE MOOD

Pres.	I, we, you, they **make**	I **am made**
		we, you, they **are made**
	he, she, it **makes**	he, she, it **is made**
Pres.	I **am making**	I **am being made**
Prog.	we, you, they **are making**	we, you, they **are being made**
	he, she, it **is making**	he, she, it **is being made**
Pres.	I, we, you, they **do make**	I, we, you, they **do get made**
Int.	he, she, it **does make**	he, she, it **does get made**
Fut.	I, he, she, it,	I, he, she, it,
	we, you, they **will make**	we, you, they **will be made**
Past	I, he, she, it,	I, he, she, it **was made**
	we, you, they **made**	we, you, they **were made**
Past	I, he, she, it **was making**	I, he, she, it **was being made**
Prog.	we, you, they **were making**	we, you, they **were being made**
Past	I, he, she, it,	I, he, she, it,
Int.	we, you, they **did make**	we, you, they **did get made**
Pres.	I, we, you, they **have made**	I, we, you, they **have been made**
Perf.	he, she, it **has made**	he, she, it **has been made**
Past	I, he, she, it,	I, he, she, it,
Perf.	we, you, they **had made**	we, you, they **had been made**
Fut.	I, he, she, it, we, you, they	I, he, she, it, we, you, they
Perf.	**will have made**	**will have been made**

IMPERATIVE MOOD

make   **be made**

SUBJUNCTIVE MOOD

Pres.	if I, he, she, it,	if I, he, she, it,
	we, you, they **make**	we, you, they **be made**
Past	if I, he, she, it,	if I, he, she, it,
	we, you, they **made**	we, you, they **were made**
Fut.	if I, he, she, it,	if I, he, she, it,
	we, you, they **should make**	we, you, they **should be made**

Transitive and intransitive.

Dad is making dinner on the grill.
My sister made the birthday cake.
Several mistakes were made due to carelessness.

AN ESSENTIAL
55 VERB

make

Examples

Mom is making dinner.

He makes a good salary.

She made the cut.

We will make a good pair.

I have been making this trip for the past ten years.

We make twenty-eight flavors of ice cream.

Who made the bed?

They had a marriage made in heaven.

I would have made you a cake.

Did they make him an offer?

Maple syrup is made in Vermont.

Words and expressions related to this verb

He made me do it.

First you break up, then you make up.

How did she make out at the interview?

Let's make a deal.

He made off with the cash.

You made me love you.

She has it made in her new job.

They were made for each other.

Just you try and make me.

We made out well at the casino.

manage
(active voice)

PRINCIPAL PARTS: **manages, managing, managed, managed**

be managed
(passive voice)

INDICATIVE MOOD

Pres.	I, we, you, they **manage**	I **am managed**
		we, you, they **are managed**
	he, she, it **manages**	he, she, it **is managed**
Pres. *Prog.*	I **am managing**	I **am being managed**
	we, you, they **are managing**	we, you, they **are being managed**
	he, she, it **is managing**	he, she, it **is being managed**
Pres. *Int.*	I, we, you, they **do manage**	I, we, you, they **do get managed**
	he, she, it **does manage**	he, she, it **does get managed**
Fut.	I, he, she, it, we, you, they **will manage**	I, he, she, it, we, you, they **will be managed**
Past	I, he, she, it, we, you, they **managed**	I, he, she, it **was managed** we, you, they **were managed**
Past *Prog.*	I, he, she, it **was managing** we, you, they **were managing**	I, he, she, it **was being managed** we, you, they **were being managed**
Past *Int.*	I, he, she, it, we, you, they **did manage**	I, he, she, it, we, you, they **did get managed**
Pres. *Perf.*	I, we, you, they **have managed** he, she, it **has managed**	I, we, you, they **have been managed** he, she, it **has been managed**
Past *Perf.*	I, he, she, it, we, you, they **had managed**	I, he, she, it, we, you, they **had been managed**
Fut. *Perf.*	I, he, she, it, we, you, they **will have managed**	I, he, she, it, we, you, they **will have been managed**

IMPERATIVE MOOD

manage   **be managed**

SUBJUNCTIVE MOOD

Pres.	if I, he, she, it, we, you, they **manage**	if I, he, she, it, we, you, they **be managed**
Past	if I, he, she, it, we, you, they **managed**	if I, he, she, it, we, you, they **were managed**
Fut.	if I, he, she, it, we, you, they **should manage**	if I, he, she, it, we, you, they **should be managed**

Transitive and intransitive.

We are managing as best we can without her.
He managed several stores for the owners.
The team was managed by the same coach for twenty years.

Principal Parts: **marks, marking,
marked, marked**

be marked
(passive voice)

INDICATIVE MOOD

Pres.	I, we, you, they **mark**	**I am marked** we, you, they **are marked**
	he, she, it **marks**	he, she, it **is marked**
Pres. *Prog.*	**I am marking** we, you, they **are marking** he, she, it **is marking**	I am being marked we, you, they **are being marked** he, she, it **is being marked**
Pres. *Int.*	I, we, you, they **do mark** he, she, it **does mark**	I, we, you, they **do get marked** he, she, it **does get marked**
Fut.	I, he, she, it, we, you, they **will mark**	I, he, she, it, we, you, they **will be marked**
Past	I, he, she, it, we, you, they **marked**	I, he, she, it **was marked** we, you, they **were marked**
Past *Prog.*	I, he, she, it **was marking** we, you, they **were marking**	I, he, she, it **was being marked** we, you, they **were being marked**
Past *Int.*	I, he, she, it, we, you, they **did mark**	I, he, she, it, we, you, they **did get marked**
Pres. *Perf.*	I, we, you, they **have marked** he, she, it **has marked**	I, we, you, they **have been marked** he, she, it **has been marked**
Past *Perf.*	I, he, she, it, we, you, they **had marked**	I, he, she, it, we, you, they **had been marked**
Fut. *Perf.*	I, he, she, it, we, you, they **will have marked**	I, he, she, it, we, you, they **will have been marked**

IMPERATIVE MOOD

mark

be marked

SUBJUNCTIVE MOOD

Pres.	if I, he, she, it, we, you, they **mark**	if I, he, she, it, we, you, they **be marked**
Past	if I, he, she, it, we, you, they **marked**	if I, he, she, it, we, you, they **were marked**
Fut.	if I, he, she, it, we, you, they **should mark**	if I, he, she, it, we, you, they **should be marked**

Transitive and intransitive.

The device marked their position on the screen.
The priced was marked down for the sale.

market
(active voice)

PRINCIPAL PARTS: markets, marketing, marketed, marketed

be marketed
(passive voice)

INDICATIVE MOOD

Pres.	I, we, you, they **market**	I **am marketed**
		we, you, they **are marketed**
	he, she, it **markets**	he, she, it **is marketed**
Pres. *Prog.*	I **am marketing**	I **am being marketed**
	we, you, they **are marketing**	we, you, they **are being marketed**
	he, she, it **is marketing**	he, she, it **is being marketed**
Pres. *Int.*	I, we, you, they **do market**	I, we, you, they **do get marketed**
	he, she, it **does market**	he, she, it **does get marketed**
Fut.	I, he, she, it,	I, he, she, it,
	we, you, they **will market**	we, you, they **will be marketed**
Past	I, he, she, it,	I, he, she, it **was marketed**
	we, you, they **marketed**	we, you, they **were marketed**
Past *Prog.*	I, he, she, it **was marketing**	I, he, she, it **was being marketed**
	we, you, they **were marketing**	we, you, they **were being marketed**
Past *Int.*	I, he, she, it,	I, he, she, it,
	we, you, they **did market**	we, you, they **did get marketed**
Pres. *Perf.*	I, we, you, they **have marketed**	I, we, you, they **have been marketed**
	he, she, it **has marketed**	he, she, it **has been marketed**
Past *Perf.*	I, he, she, it,	I, he, she, it,
	we, you, they **had marketed**	we, you, they **had been marketed**
Fut. *Perf.*	I, he, she, it, we, you, they **will have marketed**	I, he, she, it, we, you, they **will have been marketed**

IMPERATIVE MOOD

market

be marketed

SUBJUNCTIVE MOOD

Pres.	if I, he, she, it, we, you, they **market**	if I, he, she, it, we, you, they **be marketed**
Past	if I, he, she, it, we, you, they **marketed**	if I, he, she, it, we, you, they **were marketed**
Fut.	if I, he, she, it, we, you, they **should market**	if I, he, she, it, we, you, they **should be marketed**

M

Transitive and intransitive.

He is marketing his skills at a job fair.
We marketed our cheese in major grocery stores.
Their coffee was marketed in the United States and Canada.

marry
(active voice)

be married
(passive voice)

INDICATIVE MOOD

Pres. I, we, you, they **marry**

he, she, it **marries**

I am married
we, you, they **are married**
he, she, it **is married**

Pres. I **am marrying**
Prog. we, you, they **are marrying**
he, she, it **is marrying**

I am being married
we, you, they **are being married**
he, she, it **is being married**

Pres. I, we, you, they **do marry**
Int. he, she, it **does marry**

I, we, you, they **do get married**
he, she, it **does get married**

Fut. I, he, she, it,
we, you, they **will marry**

I, he, she, it,
we, you, they **will be married**

Past I, he, she, it,
we, you, they **married**

I, he, she, it **was married**
we, you, they **were married**

Past I, he, she, it **was marrying**
Prog. we, you, they **were marrying**

I, he, she, it **was being married**
we, you, they **were being married**

Past I, he, she, it,
Int. we, you, they **did marry**

I, he, she, it,
we, you, they **did get married**

Pres. I, we, you, they **have married**
Perf. he, she, it **has married**

I, we, you, they **have been married**
he, she, it **has been married**

Past I, he, she, it,
Perf. we, you, they **had married**

I, he, she, it,
we, you, they **had been married**

Fut. I, he, she, it, we, you, they
Perf. **will have married**

I, he, she, it, we, you, they
will have been married

IMPERATIVE MOOD

marry

be married

SUBJUNCTIVE MOOD

Pres. if I, he, she, it,
we, you, they **marry**

if I, he, she, it,
we, you, they **be married**

Past if I, he, she, it,
we, you, they **married**

if I, he, she, it,
we, you, they **were married**

Fut. if I, he, she, it,
we, you, they **should marry**

if I, he, she, it,
we, you, they **should be married**

Transitive and intransitive.

We are marrying our daughter this June.
They married at a young age.
They were married in London.

mean (active voice)	PRINCIPAL PARTS: **means, meaning,** **meant, meant**	**be meant** (passive voice)

INDICATIVE MOOD

Pres.	I, we, you, they **mean**	I **am meant**
		we, you, they **are meant**
	he, she, it **means**	he, she, it **is meant**
Pres. *Prog.*	I **am meaning**	I **am being meant**
	we, you, they **are meaning**	we, you, they **are being meant**
	he, she, it **is meaning**	he, she, it **is being meant**
Pres. *Int.*	I, we, you, they **do mean**	I, we, you, they **do get meant**
	he, she, it **does mean**	he, she, it **does get meant**
Fut.	I, he, she, it,	I, he, she, it,
	we, you, they **will mean**	we, you, they **will be meant**
Past	I, he, she, it,	I, he, she, it **was meant**
	we, you, they **meant**	we, you, they **were meant**
Past *Prog.*	I, he, she, it **was meaning**	I, he, she, it **was being meant**
	we, you, they **were meaning**	we, you, they **were being meant**
Past *Int.*	I, he, she, it,	I, he, she, it,
	we, you, they **did mean**	we, you, they **did get meant**
Pres. *Perf.*	I, we, you, they **have meant**	I, we, you, they **have been meant**
	he, she, it **has meant**	he, she, it **has been meant**
Past *Perf.*	I, he, she, it,	I, he, she, it,
	we, you, they **had meant**	we, you, they **had been meant**
Fut. *Perf.*	I, he, she, it, we, you, they	I, he, she, it, we, you, they
	will have meant	**will have been meant**

IMPERATIVE MOOD

mean	**be meant**

SUBJUNCTIVE MOOD

Pres.	if I, he, she, it,	if I, he, she, it,
	we, you, they **mean**	we, you, they **be meant**
Past	if I, he, she, it,	if I, he, she, it,
	we, you, they **meant**	we, you, they **were meant**
Fut.	if I, he, she, it,	if I, he, she, it,
	we, you, they **should mean**	we, you, they **should be meant**

M

Transitive and intransitive.

He meant well.
What exactly was meant by that comment?

AN ESSENTIAL
55 VERB

Examples

She means well.

He meant to call.

We have been meaning to visit.

Do you mean to tell me you are not coming?

I did not mean to offend you.

You have to mean it.

What was meant by that gesture?

It could have meant so much more.

His gift was meant to please.

It was meant to send a signal.

Words and expressions related to this verb

Mean what you say and say what you mean.

I mean it.

They meant it.

She meant every word she said.

It was meant to be.

My mother meant the world to me.

It means nothing.

What do you mean?

I didn't mean to hurt you.

Do you know how much you mean to me?

I have been meaning to write.

PRINCIPAL PARTS: **measures, measuring,
measured, measured**

be measured
(passive voice)

INDICATIVE MOOD

Pres.	I, we, you, they **measure**	I **am measured**
		we, you, they **are measured**
	he, she, it **measures**	he, she, it **is measured**
Pres.	I **am measuring**	I **am being measured**
Prog.	we, you, they **are measuring**	we, you, they **are being measured**
	he, she, it **is measuring**	he, she, it **is being measured**
Pres.	I, we, you, they **do measure**	I, we, you, they **do get measured**
Int.	he, she, it **does measure**	he, she, it **does get measured**
Fut.	I, he, she, it,	I, he, she, it,
	we, you, they **will measure**	we, you, they **will be measured**
Past	I, he, she, it,	I, he, she, it **was measured**
	we, you, they **measured**	we, you, they **were measured**
Past	I, he, she, it **was measuring**	I, he, she, it **was being measured**
Prog.	we, you, they **were measuring**	we, you, they **were being measured**
Past	I, he, she, it,	I, he, she, it,
Int.	we, you, they **did measure**	we, you, they **did get measured**
Pres.	I, we, you, they **have measured**	I, we, you, they **have been measured**
Perf.	he, she, it **has measured**	he, she, it **has been measured**
Past	I, he, she, it,	I, he, she, it,
Perf.	we, you, they **had measured**	we, you, they **had been measured**
Fut.	I, he, she, it, we, you, they	I, he, she, it, we, you, they
Perf.	**will have measured**	**will have been measured**

IMPERATIVE MOOD

measure

be measured

SUBJUNCTIVE MOOD

Pres.	if I, he, she, it,	if I, he, she, it,
	we, you, they **measure**	we, you, they **be measured**
Past	if I, he, she, it,	if I, he, she, it,
	we, you, they **measured**	we, you, they **were measured**
Fut.	if I, he, she, it,	if I, he, she, it,
	we, you, they **should measure**	we, you, they **should be measured**

M

Transitive and intransitive.

The architect is measuring one more time.
The engineers measured the property.
Are the contents measured by weight or volume?

PRINCIPAL PARTS: **meets, meeting, met, met**

INDICATIVE MOOD

Pres.	I, we, you, they **meet**	I **am met** we, you, they **are met**
	he, she, it **meets**	he, she, it **is met**
Pres. *Prog.*	I **am meeting** we, you, they **are meeting** he, she, it **is meeting**	I **am being met** we, you, they **are being met** he, she, it **is being met**
Pres. *Int.*	I, we, you, they **do meet** he, she, it **does meet**	I, we, you, they **do get met** he, she, it **does get met**
Fut.	I, he, she, it, we, you, they **will meet**	I, he, she, it, we, you, they **will be met**
Past	I, he, she, it, we, you, they **met**	I, he, she, it **was met** we, you, they **were met**
Past *Prog.*	I, he, she, it **was meeting** we, you, they **were meeting**	I, he, she, it **was being met** we, you, they **were being met**
Past *Int.*	I, he, she, it, we, you, they **did meet**	I, he, she, it, we, you, they **did get met**
Pres. *Perf.*	I, we, you, they **have met** he, she, it **has met**	I, we, you, they **have been met** he, she, it **has been met**
Past *Perf.*	I, he, she, it, we, you, they **had met**	I, he, she, it, we, you, they **had been met**
Fut. *Perf.*	I, he, she, it, we, you, they **will have met**	I, he, she, it, we, you, they **will have been met**

IMPERATIVE MOOD

meet	**be met**

SUBJUNCTIVE MOOD

Pres.	if I, he, she, it, we, you, they **meet**	if I, he, she, it, we, you, they **be met**
Past	if I, he, she, it, we, you, they **met**	if I, he, she, it, we, you, they **were met**
Fut.	if I, he, she, it, we, you, they **should meet**	if I, he, she, it, we, you, they **should be met**

Transitive and intransitive.

Meet me in St. Louis.
They met for the first time at a school reunion.
The team was met by an enthusiastic group of supporters.

Examples

She meets the bus every afternoon.

I'll meet with you early next week.

They had met once before.

We need to meet our deadline.

She was met by an official representative.

They met at the airport.

We will be meeting once a month.

They had just met with the voters.

Several goals remained to be met.

I remember when I first met her.

Words and expressions related to this verb

Meet me in St. Louis.

Have we met?

She has been meeting regularly with her client.

I can meet you halfway.

She met her match in her husband.

There is more to that than meets the eye.

We are trying to make both ends meet.

We only part to meet again.

They met on the internet.

Never the twain shall meet.

M

mention
(active voice)

be mentioned
(passive voice)

INDICATIVE MOOD

Pres.	I, we, you, they **mention**	I **am mentioned**
		we, you, they **are mentioned**
	he, she, it **mentions**	he, she, it **is mentioned**
Pres.	I **am mentioning**	I **am being mentioned**
Prog.	we, you, they **are mentioning**	we, you, they **are being mentioned**
	he, she, it **is mentioning**	he, she, it **is being mentioned**
Pres.	I, we, you, they **do mention**	I, we, you, they **do get mentioned**
Int.	he, she, it **does mention**	he, she, it **does get mentioned**
Fut.	I, he, she, it,	I, he, she, it,
	we, you, they **will mention**	we, you, they **will be mentioned**
Past	I, he, she, it,	I, he, she, it **was mentioned**
	we, you, they **mentioned**	we, you, they **were mentioned**
Past	I, he, she, it **was mentioning**	I, he, she, it **was being mentioned**
Prog.	we, you, they **were mentioning**	we, you, they **were being mentioned**
Past	I, he, she, it,	I, he, she, it,
Int.	we, you, they **did mention**	we, you, they **did get mentioned**
Pres.	I, we, you, they **have mentioned**	I, we, you, they **have been mentioned**
Perf.	he, she, it **has mentioned**	he, she, it **has been mentioned**
Past	I, he, she, it,	I, he, she, it,
Perf.	we, you, they **had mentioned**	we, you, they **had been mentioned**
Fut.	I, he, she, it, we, you, they	I, he, she, it, we, you, they
Perf.	**will have mentioned**	**will have been mentioned**

IMPERATIVE MOOD

mention   **be mentioned**

SUBJUNCTIVE MOOD

Pres.	if I, he, she, it,	if I, he, she, it,
	we, you, they **mention**	we, you, they **be mentioned**
Past	if I, he, she, it,	if I, he, she, it,
	we, you, they **mentioned**	we, you, they **were mentioned**
Fut.	if I, he, she, it,	if I, he, she, it,
	we, you, they **should mention**	we, you, they **should be mentioned**

We mentioned his name only once.
That detail was mentioned in the newspaper.

mimic
(active voice)

PRINCIPAL PARTS: mimics, mimicking, mimicked, mimicked

be mimicked
(passive voice)

INDICATIVE MOOD

Pres.	I, we, you, they **mimic**	I **am mimicked**
	he, she, it **mimics**	we, you, they **are mimicked**
		he, she, it **is mimicked**
Pres. *Prog.*	I **am mimicking**	I **am being mimicked**
	we, you, they **are mimicking**	we, you, they **are being mimicked**
	he, she, it **is mimicking**	he, she, it **is being mimicked**
Pres. *Int.*	I, we, you, they **do mimic**	I, we, you, they **do get mimicked**
	he, she, it **does mimic**	he, she, it **does get mimicked**
Fut.	I, he, she, it, we, you, they **will mimic**	I, he, she, it, we, you, they **will be mimicked**
Past	I, he, she, it, we, you, they **mimicked**	I, he, she, it **was mimicked** we, you, they **were mimicked**
Past *Prog.*	I, he, she, it **was mimicking** we, you, they **were mimicking**	I, he, she, it **was being mimicked** we, you, they **were being mimicked**
Past *Int.*	I, he, she, it, we, you, they **did mimic**	I, he, she, it, we, you, they **did get mimicked**
Pres. *Perf.*	I, we, you, they **have mimicked** he, she, it **has mimicked**	I, we, you, they **have been mimicked** he, she, it **has been mimicked**
Past *Perf.*	I, he, she, it, we, you, they **had mimicked**	I, he, she, it, we, you, they **had been mimicked**
Fut. *Perf.*	I, he, she, it, we, you, they **will have mimicked**	I, he, she, it, we, you, they **will have been mimicked**

IMPERATIVE MOOD

mimic   **be mimicked**

SUBJUNCTIVE MOOD

Pres.	if I, he, she, it, we, you, they **mimic**	if I, he, she, it, we, you, they **be mimicked**
Past	if I, he, she, it, we, you, they **mimicked**	if I, he, she, it, we, you, they **were mimicked**
Fut.	if I, he, she, it, we, you, they **should mimic**	if I, he, she, it, we, you, they **should be mimicked**

M

Please stop mimicking your teacher.
He precisely mimicked the famous movie star.
Nature is often mimicked in architecture.

PRINCIPAL PARTS: **minds, minding, minded, minded**

INDICATIVE MOOD

Pres.	I, we, you, they **mind**	I **am minded**
		we, you, they **are minded**
	he, she, it **minds**	he, she, it **is minded**
Pres.	I **am minding**	I **am being minded**
Prog.	we, you, they **are minding**	we, you, they **are being minded**
	he, she, it **is minding**	he, she, it **is being minded**
Pres.	I, we, you, they **do mind**	I, we, you, they **do get minded**
Int.	he, she, it **does mind**	he, she, it **does get minded**
Fut.	I, he, she, it,	I, he, she, it,
	we, you, they **will mind**	we, you, they **will be minded**
Past	I, he, she, it,	I, he, she, it **was minded**
	we, you, they **minded**	we, you, they **were minded**
Past	I, he, she, it **was minding**	I, he, she, it **was being minded**
Prog.	we, you, they **were minding**	we, you, they **were being minded**
Past	I, he, she, it,	I, he, she, it,
Int.	we, you, they **did mind**	we, you, they **did get minded**
Pres.	I, we, you, they **have minded**	I, we, you, they **have been minded**
Perf.	he, she, it **has minded**	he, she, it **has been minded**
Past	I, he, she, it,	I, he, she, it,
Perf.	we, you, they **had minded**	we, you, they **had been minded**
Fut.	I, he, she, it, we, you, they	I, he, she, it, we, you, they
Perf.	**will have minded**	**will have been minded**

IMPERATIVE MOOD

mind **be minded**

SUBJUNCTIVE MOOD

Pres.	if I, he, she, it,	if I, he, she, it,
	we, you, they **mind**	we, you, they **be minded**
Past	if I, he, she, it,	if I, he, she, it,
	we, you, they **minded**	we, you, they **were minded**
Fut.	if I, he, she, it,	if I, he, she, it,
	we, you, they **should mind**	we, you, they **should be minded**

Transitive and intransitive.

The clerk minded the store during lunch time.
The shop was minded by two employees all through the night.

mislead
(active voice)

be misled
(passive voice)

INDICATIVE MOOD

Pres.	I, we, you, they **mislead**	I **am misled**
		we, you, they **are misled**
	he, she, it **misleads**	he, she, it **is misled**
Pres. *Prog.*	I **am misleading**	I **am being misled**
	we, you, they **are misleading**	we, you, they **are being misled**
	he, she, it **is misleading**	he, she, it **is being misled**
Pres. *Int.*	I, we, you, they **do mislead**	I, we, you, they **do get misled**
	he, she, it **does mislead**	he, she, it **does get misled**
Fut.	I, he, she, it,	I, he, she, it,
	we, you, they **will mislead**	we, you, they **will be misled**
Past	I, he, she, it,	I, he, she, it **was misled**
	we, you, they **misled**	we, you, they **were misled**
Past *Prog.*	I, he, she, it **was misleading**	I, he, she, it **was being misled**
	we, you, they **were misleading**	we, you, they **were being misled**
Past *Int.*	I, he, she, it,	I, he, she, it,
	we, you, they **did mislead**	we, you, they **did get misled**
Pres. *Perf.*	I, we, you, they **have misled**	I, we, you, they **have been misled**
	he, she, it **has misled**	he, she, it **has been misled**
Past *Perf.*	I, he, she, it,	I, he, she, it,
	we, you, they **had misled**	we, you, they **had been misled**
Fut. *Perf.*	I, he, she, it, we, you, they **will have misled**	I, he, she, it, we, you, they **will have been misled**

M

IMPERATIVE MOOD

mislead · **be misled**

SUBJUNCTIVE MOOD

Pres.	if I, he, she, it,	if I, he, she, it,
	we, you, they **mislead**	we, you, they **be misled**
Past	if I, he, she, it,	if I, he, she, it,
	we, you, they **misled**	we, you, they **were misled**
Fut.	if I, he, she, it,	if I, he, she, it,
	we, you, they **should mislead**	we, you, they **should be misled**

The information is misleading the searchers.
The attorney misled the opposing attorneys.
We were seriously misled on this matter.

misspell
(active voice)

be misspelled/
misspelt
(passive voice)

INDICATIVE MOOD

Pres.	I, we, you, they **misspell**	**I am misspelled** we, you, they **are misspelled**
	he, she, it **misspells**	he, she, it **is misspelled**
Pres. *Prog.*	**I am misspelling** we, you, they **are misspelling** he, she, it **is misspelling**	**I am being misspelled** we, you, they **are being misspelled** he, she, it **is being misspelled**
Pres. *Int.*	I, we, you, they **do misspell** he, she, it **does misspell**	I, we, you, they **do get misspelled** he, she, it **does get misspelled**
Fut.	I, he, she, it, we, you, they **will misspell**	I, he, she, it, we, you, they **will be misspelled**
Past	I, he, she, it, we, you, they **misspelled**	I, he, she, it **was misspelled** we, you, they **were misspelled**
Past *Prog.*	I, he, she, it **was misspelling** we, you, they **were misspelling**	I, he, she, it **was being misspelled** we, you, they **were being misspelled**
Past *Int.*	I, he, she, it, we, you, they **did misspell**	I, he, she, it, we, you, they **did get misspelled**
Pres. *Perf.*	I, we, you, they **have misspelled** he, she, it **has misspelled**	I, we, you, they **have been misspelled** he, she, it **has been misspelled**
Past *Perf.*	I, he, she, it, we, you, they **had misspelled**	I, he, she, it, we, you, they **had been misspelled**
Fut. *Perf.*	I, he, she, it, we, you, they **will have misspelled**	I, he, she, it, we, you, they **will have been misspelled**

IMPERATIVE MOOD

misspell　　　　　　　　　　**be misspelled**

SUBJUNCTIVE MOOD

Pres.	if I, he, she, it, we, you, they **misspell**	if I, he, she, it, we, you, they **be misspelled**
Past	if I, he, she, it, we, you, they **misspelled**	if I, he, she, it, we, you, they **were misspelled**
Fut.	if I, he, she, it, we, you, they **should misspell**	if I, he, she, it, we, you, they **should be misspelled**

The *Oxford Dictionary* lists MISSPELT first for the past tense and past participle forms.

I was embarrassed that I misspelled his name in my letter.
That word is often misspelled by native speakers.

mistake
(active voice)

PRINCIPAL PARTS: **mistakes, mistaking, mistook, mistaken**

be mistaken
(passive voice)

INDICATIVE MOOD

Pres.	I, we, you, they **mistake**	I **am mistaken** we, you, they **are mistaken**
	he, she, it **mistakes**	he, she, it **is mistaken**
Pres. *Prog.*	I **am mistaking** we, you, they **are mistaking** he, she, it **is mistaking**	I **am being mistaken** we, you, they **are being mistaken** he, she, it **is being mistaken**
Pres. *Int.*	I, we, you, they **do mistake** he, she, it **does mistake**	I, we, you, they **do get mistaken** he, she, it **does get mistaken**
Fut.	I, he, she, it, we, you, they **will mistake**	I, he, she, it, we, you, they **will be mistaken**
Past	I, he, she, it, we, you, they **mistook**	I, he, she, it **was mistaken** we, you, they **were mistaken**
Past *Prog.*	I, he, she, it **was mistaking** we, you, they **were mistaking**	I, he, she, it **was being mistaken** we, you, they **were being mistaken**
Past *Int.*	I, he, she, it, we, you, they **did mistake**	I, he, she, it, we, you, they **did get mistaken**
Pres. *Perf.*	I, we, you, they **have mistaken** he, she, it **has mistaken**	I, we, you, they **have been mistaken** he, she, it **has been mistaken**
Past *Perf.*	I, he, she, it, we, you, they **had mistaken**	I, he, she, it, we, you, they **had been mistaken**
Fut. *Perf.*	I, he, she, it, we, you, they **will have mistaken**	I, he, she, it, we, you, they **will have been mistaken**

IMPERATIVE MOOD

mistake   **be mistaken**

SUBJUNCTIVE MOOD

Pres.	if I, he, she, it, we, you, they **mistake**	if I, he, she, it, we, you, they **be mistaken**
Past	if I, he, she, it, we, you, they **mistook**	if I, he, she, it, we, you, they **were mistaken**
Fut.	if I, he, she, it, we, you, they **should mistake**	if I, he, she, it, we, you, they **should be mistaken**

M

Transitive and intransitive.

There can be no mistaking that voice.
She mistook the caller for a friend.
You are mistaken in your assumptions.

mop
(active voice)

be mopped
(passive voice)

INDICATIVE MOOD

Pres.	I, we, you, they **mop**	I **am mopped**
		we, you, they **are mopped**
	he, she, it **mops/mop**	he, she, it **is mopped**
Pres.	I **am mopping**	I **am being mopped**
Prog.	we, you, they **are mopping**	we, you, they **are being mopped**
	he, she, it **is mopping**	he, she, it **is being mopped**
Pres.	I, we, you, they **do mop**	I, we, you, they **do get mopped**
Int.	he, she, it **does mop**	he, she, it **does get mopped**
Fut.	I, he, she, it,	I, he, she, it,
	we, you, they **will mop**	we, you, they **will be mopped**
Past	I, he, she, it,	I, he, she, it **was mopped**
	we, you, they **mopped**	we, you, they **were mopped**
Past	I, he, she, it **was mopping**	I, he, she, it **was being mopped**
Prog.	we, you, they **were mopping**	we, you, they **were being mopped**
Past	I, he, she, it,	I, he, she, it,
Int.	we, you, they **did mop**	we, you, they **did get mopped**
Pres.	I, we, you, they **have mopped**	I, we, you, they **have been mopped**
Perf.	he, she, it **has mopped**	he, she, it **has been mopped**
Past	I, he, she, it,	I, he, she, it,
Perf.	we, you, they **had mopped**	we, you, they **had been mopped**
Fut.	I, he, she, it, we, you, they	I, he, she, it, we, you, they
Perf.	**will have mopped**	**will have been mopped**

IMPERATIVE MOOD

mop **be mopped**

SUBJUNCTIVE MOOD

Pres.	if I, he, she, it,	if I, he, she, it,
	we, you, they **mop**	we, you, they **be mopped**
Past	if I, he, she, it,	if I, he, she, it,
	we, you, they **mopped**	we, you, they **were mopped**
Fut.	if I, he, she, it,	if I, he, she, it,
	we, you, they **should mop**	we, you, they **should be mopped**

Who is mopping up the operation?
I mopped the floor and vacuumed the carpets.
This deck was mopped early this morning.

INDICATIVE MOOD

Pres.	I, we, you, they **move**	I **am moved**
		we, you, they **are moved**
	he, she, it **moves**	he, she, it **is moved**
Pres.	I **am moving**	I **am being moved**
Prog.	we, you, they **are moving**	we, you, they **are being moved**
	he, she, it **is moving**	he, she, it **is being moved**
Pres.	I, we, you, they **do move**	I, we, you, they **do get moved**
Int.	he, she, it **does move**	he, she, it **does get moved**
Fut.	I, he, she, it,	I, he, she, it,
	we, you, they **will move**	we, you, they **will be moved**
Past	I, he, she, it,	I, he, she, it **was moved**
	we, you, they **moved**	we, you, they **were moved**
Past	I, he, she, it **was moving**	I, he, she, it **was being moved**
Prog.	we, you, they **were moving**	we, you, they **were being moved**
Past	I, he, she, it,	I, he, she, it,
Int.	we, you, they **did move**	we, you, they **did get moved**
Pres.	I, we, you, they **have moved**	I, we, you, they **have been moved**
Perf.	he, she, it **has moved**	he, she, it **has been moved**
Past	I, he, she, it,	I, he, she, it,
Perf.	we, you, they **had moved**	we, you, they **had been moved**
Fut.	I, he, she, it, we, you, they	I, he, she, it, we, you, they
Perf.	**will have moved**	**will have been moved**

M

IMPERATIVE MOOD

move   **be moved**

SUBJUNCTIVE MOOD

Pres.	if I, he, she, it,	if I, he, she, it,
	we, you, they **move**	we, you, they **be moved**
Past	if I, he, she, it,	if I, he, she, it,
	we, you, they **moved**	we, you, they **were moved**
Fut.	if I, he, she, it,	if I, he, she, it,
	we, you, they **should move**	we, you, they **should be moved**

Intransitive and transitive.

They are moving to California.
We moved last year to this town.
My things are always moved by my wife.

**AN ESSENTIAL
55 VERB**

move

Examples

She always moves her chair for a better view.

I am moving next week.

Have those computers been moved into storage?

He will not move from his position.

They moved twice last year.

The dog had not moved from his post.

We will not be moved by tears.

If you move away, I will be very sad.

He is quickly moving up the corporate ladder.

The board member moved the motion and it was passed unanimously.

Words and expressions related to this verb

Move it!

Move over.

He can move mountains.

When are they moving out?

She decided it was time to move on with her life.

I was very moved by his speech.

We must move forward.

She moved back home after college.

He moved around until he found the ideal location.

They have already moved beyond their anger.

mow
(active voice)

be mowed/mown
(passive voice)

INDICATIVE MOOD

Pres.	I, we, you, they **mow**	I **am mowed**
		we, you, they **are mowed**
	he, she, it **mows**	he, she, it **is mowed**
Pres. *Prog.*	I **am mowing**	I **am being mowed**
	we, you, they **are mowing**	we, you, they **are being mowed**
	he, she, it **is mowing**	he, she, it **is being mowed**
Pres. *Int.*	I, we, you, they **do mow**	I, we, you, they **do get mowed**
	he, she, it **does mow**	he, she, it **does get mowed**
Fut.	I, he, she, it,	I, he, she, it,
	we, you, they **will mow**	we, you, they **will be mowed**
Past	I, he, she, it,	I, he, she, it **was mowed**
	we, you, they **mowed**	we, you, they **were mowed**
Past *Prog.*	I, he, she, it **was mowing**	I, he, she, it **was being mowed**
	we, you, they **were mowing**	we, you, they **were being mowed**
Past *Int.*	I, he, she, it,	I, he, she, it,
	we, you, they **did mow**	we, you, they **did get mowed**
Pres. *Perf.*	I, we, you, they **have mowed**	I, we, you, they **have been mowed**
	he, she, it **has mowed**	he, she, it **has been mowed**
Past *Perf.*	I, he, she, it,	I, he, she, it,
	we, you, they **had mowed**	we, you, they **had been mowed**
Fut. *Perf.*	I, he, she, it, we, you, they **will have mowed**	I, he, she, it, we, you, they **will have been mowed**

IMPERATIVE MOOD

mow **be mowed**

SUBJUNCTIVE MOOD

Pres.	if I, he, she, it,	if I, he, she, it,
	we, you, they **mow**	we, you, they **be mowed**
Past	if I, he, she, it,	if I, he, she, it,
	we, you, they **mowed**	we, you, they **were mowed**
Fut.	if I, he, she, it,	if I, he, she, it,
	we, you, they **should mow**	we, you, they **should be mowed**

Transitive and intransitive.

They mowed their lawn just yesterday.
The grass was not mowed for two weeks.

need
(active voice)

be needed
(passive voice)

INDICATIVE MOOD

Pres.	I, we, you, they **need**	I **am needed**
		we, you, they **are needed**
	he, she, it **needs/need***	he, she, it **is needed**
Pres.	I **am needing**	I **am being needed**
Prog.	we, you, they **are needing**	we, you, they **are being needed**
	he, she, it **is needing**	he, she, it **is being needed**
Pres.	I, we, you, they **do need**	I, we, you, they **do get needed**
Int.	he, she, it **does need**	he, she, it **does get needed**
Fut.	I, he, she, it,	I, he, she, it,
	we, you, they **will need**	we, you, they **will be needed**
Past	I, he, she, it,	I, he, she, it **was needed**
	we, you, they **needed**	we, you, they **were needed**
Past	I, he, she, it **was needing**	I, he, she, it **was being needed**
Prog.	we, you, they **were needing**	we, you, they **were being needed**
Past	I, he, she, it,	I, he, she, it,
Int.	we, you, they **did need**	we, you, they **did get needed**
Pres.	I, we, you, they **have needed**	I, we, you, they **have been needed**
Perf.	he, she, it **has needed**	he, she, it **has been needed**
Past	I, he, she, it,	I, he, she, it,
Perf.	we, you, they **had needed**	we, you, they **had been needed**
Fut.	I, he, she, it, we, you, they	I, he, she, it, we, you, they
Perf.	**will have needed**	**will have been needed**

IMPERATIVE MOOD

need **be needed**

SUBJUNCTIVE MOOD

Pres.	if I, he, she, it,	if I, he, she, it,
	we, you, they **need**	we, you, they **be needed**
Past	if I, he, she, it,	if I, he, she, it,
	we, you, they **needed**	we, you, they **were needed**
Fut.	if I, he, she, it,	if I, he, she, it,
	we, you, they **should need**	we, you, they **should be needed**

Transitive and intransitive. When used as an auxiliary verb, NEED has only one form even in the he-she-it form: "He need not apply."

He needed to know the correct address before forwarding the letter.
What was needed was greater dedication to the task.

**AN ESSENTIAL
55 VERB**

Examples

Who needs another drink?

I need to write a letter.

She needed to tell him that.

He had everything he needed for the trip.

Was that extra suitcase ever needed?

I will need for you to go to Chicago.

Do you need my help?

She felt that she was not needed.

She needs me as much as I need her.

He has never needed anyone or anything.

Words and expressions related to this verb

I need you, babe.

If ever she should need me, it wouldn't be in autumn.

I don't need your sympathy.

He needed her more than ever before.

Take as much as you need.

She needed to go.

I will need your signature.

If you need me, call me.

Everybody needs somebody.

We will get you whatever you need.

N

network
(active voice)

be networked
(passive voice)

INDICATIVE MOOD

Pres.	I, we, you, they **network**	I **am networked**
		we, you, they **are networked**
	he, she, it **networks**	he, she, it **is networked**
Pres.	I **am networking**	I **am being networked**
Prog.	we, you, they **are networking**	we, you, they **are being networked**
	he, she, it **is networking**	he, she, it **is being networked**
Pres.	I, we, you, they **do network**	I, we, you, they **do get networked**
Int.	he, she, it **does network**	he, she, it **does get networked**
Fut.	I, he, she, it,	I, he, she, it,
	we, you, they **will network**	we, you, they **will be networked**
Past	I, he, she, it,	I, he, she, it **was networked**
	we, you, they **networked**	we, you, they **were networked**
Past	I, he, she, it **was networking**	I, he, she, it **was being networked**
Prog.	we, you, they **were networking**	we, you, they **were being networked**
Past	I, he, she, it,	I, he, she, it,
Int.	we, you, they **did network**	we, you, they **did get networked**
Pres.	I, we, you, they **have networked**	I, we, you, they **have been networked**
Perf.	he, she, it **has networked**	he, she, it **has been networked**
Past	I, he, she, it,	I, he, she, it,
Perf.	we, you, they **had networked**	we, you, they **had been networked**
Fut.	I, he, she, it, we, you, they	I, he, she, it, we, you, they
Perf.	**will have networked**	**will have been networked**

IMPERATIVE MOOD

network　　　　　　　　**be networked**

SUBJUNCTIVE MOOD

Pres.	if I, he, she, it,	if I, he, she, it,
	we, you, they **network**	we, you, they **be networked**
Past	if I, he, she, it,	if I, he, she, it,
	we, you, they **networked**	we, you, they **were networked**
Fut.	if I, he, she, it,	if I, he, she, it,
	we, you, they **should network**	we, you, they **should be networked**

Transitive and intransitive.

They networked constantly as they were searching for a job.
He was networked to his clients via the Internet.

note
(active voice)

be noted
(passive voice)

INDICATIVE MOOD

Pres.	I, we, you, they **note**	I **am noted**
		we, you, they **are noted**
	he, she, it **notes**	he, she, it **is noted**
Pres.	I **am noting**	I **am being noted**
Prog.	we, you, they **are noting**	we, you, they **are being noted**
	he, she, it **is noting**	he, she, it **is being noted**
Pres.	I, we, you, they **do note**	I, we, you, they **do get noted**
Int.	he, she, it **does note**	he, she, it **does get noted**
Fut.	I, he, she, it,	I, he, she, it,
	we, you, they **will note**	we, you, they **will be noted**
Past	I, he, she, it,	I, he, she, it **was noted**
	we, you, they **noted**	we, you, they **were noted**
Past	I, he, she, it **was noting**	I, he, she, it **was being noted**
Prog.	we, you, they **were noting**	we, you, they **were being noted**
Past	I, he, she, it,	I, he, she, it,
Int.	we, you, they **did note**	we, you, they **did get noted**
Pres.	I, we, you, they **have noted**	I, we, you, they **have been noted**
Perf.	he, she, it **has noted**	he, she, it **has been noted**
Past	I, he, she, it,	I, he, she, it,
Perf.	we, you, they **had noted**	we, you, they **had been noted**
Fut.	I, he, she, it, we, you, they	I, he, she, it, we, you, they
Perf.	**will have noted**	**will have been noted**

N

IMPERATIVE MOOD

note **be noted**

SUBJUNCTIVE MOOD

Pres.	if I, he, she, it,	if I, he, she, it,
	we, you, they **note**	we, you, they **be noted**
Past	if I, he, she, it,	if I, he, she, it,
	we, you, they **noted**	we, you, they **were noted**
Fut.	if I, he, she, it,	if I, he, she, it,
	we, you, they **should note**	we, you, they **should be noted**

We noted the objections.
The key points in his speech were noted by several members of the audience.

notice
(active voice)

be noticed
(passive voice)

INDICATIVE MOOD

Pres.	I, we, you, they **notice**	I **am noticed**
		we, you, they **are noticed**
	he, she, it **notices**	he, she, it **is noticed**
Pres.	I **am noticing**	I **am being noticed**
Prog.	we, you, they **are noticing**	we, you, they **are being noticed**
	he, she, it **is noticing**	he, she, it **is being noticed**
Pres.	I, we, you, they **do notice**	I, we, you, they **do get noticed**
Int.	he, she, it **does notice**	he, she, it **does get noticed**
Fut.	I, he, she, it,	I, he, she, it,
	we, you, they **will notice**	we, you, they **will be noticed**
Past	I, he, she, it,	I, he, she, it **was noticed**
	we, you, they **noticed**	we, you, they **were noticed**
Past	I, he, she, it **was noticing**	I, he, she, it **was being noticed**
Prog.	we, you, they **were noticing**	we, you, they **were being noticed**
Past	I, he, she, it,	I, he, she, it,
Int.	we, you, they **did notice**	we, you, they **did get noticed**
Pres.	I, we, you, they **have noticed**	I, we, you, they **have been noticed**
Perf.	he, she, it **has noticed**	he, she, it **has been noticed**
Past	I, he, she, it,	I, he, she, it,
Perf.	we, you, they **had noticed**	we, you, they **had been noticed**
Fut.	I, he, she, it, we, you, they	I, he, she, it, we, you, they
Perf.	**will have noticed**	**will have been noticed**

IMPERATIVE MOOD

notice   **be noticed**

SUBJUNCTIVE MOOD

Pres.	if I, he, she, it,	if I, he, she, it,
	we, you, they **notice**	we, you, they **be noticed**
Past	if I, he, she, it,	if I, he, she, it,
	we, you, they **noticed**	we, you, they **were noticed**
Fut.	if I, he, she, it,	if I, he, she, it,
	we, you, they **should notice**	we, you, they **should be noticed**

We keep noticing new errors.
He noticed her immediately.
Do you think our sign was noticed by anyone?

observe
(active voice)

PRINCIPAL PARTS: **observes, observing, observed, observed**

be observed
(passive voice)

INDICATIVE MOOD

Pres.	I, we, you, they **observe**	I **am observed**
		we, you, they **are observed**
	he, she, it **observes**	he, she, it **is observed**
Pres.	I **am observing**	I **am being observed**
Prog.	we, you, they **are observing**	we, you, they **are being observed**
	he, she, it **is observing**	he, she, it **is being observed**
Pres.	I, we, you, they **do observe**	I, we, you, they **do get observed**
Int.	he, she, it **does observe**	he, she, it **does get observed**
Fut.	I, he, she, it,	I, he, she, it,
	we, you, they **will observe**	we, you, they **will be observed**
Past	I, he, she, it,	I, he, she, it **was observed**
	we, you, they **observed**	we, you, they **were observed**
Past	I, he, she, it **was observing**	I, he, she, it **was being observed**
Prog.	we, you, they **were observing**	we, you, they **were being observed**
Past	I, he, she, it,	I, he, she, it,
Int.	we, you, they **did observe**	we, you, they **did get observed**
Pres.	I, we, you, they **have observed**	I, we, you, they **have been observed**
Perf.	he, she, it **has observed**	he, she, it **has been observed**
Past	I, he, she, it,	I, he, she, it,
Perf.	we, you, they **had observed**	we, you, they **had been observed**
Fut.	I, he, she, it, we, you, they	I, he, she, it, we, you, they
Perf.	**will have observed**	**will have been observed**

O

IMPERATIVE MOOD

observe　　　　　　　　**be observed**

SUBJUNCTIVE MOOD

Pres.	if I, he, she, it,	if I, he, she, it,
	we, you, they **observe**	we, you, they **be observed**
Past	if I, he, she, it,	if I, he, she, it,
	we, you, they **observed**	we, you, they **were observed**
Fut.	if I, he, she, it,	if I, he, she, it,
	we, you, they **should observe**	we, you, they **should be observed**

Transitive and intransitive.

Are they supervisors observing her performance?
Who observed the eclipse?
Her practice performance was observed by all of the judges.

obtain
(active voice)

be obtained
(passive voice)

INDICATIVE MOOD

Pres.	I, we, you, they **obtain**	I **am obtained**
		we, you, they **are obtained**
	he, she, it **obtains**	he, she, it **is obtained**
Pres.	I **am obtaining**	I **am being obtained**
Prog.	we, you, they **are obtaining**	we, you, they **are being obtained**
	he, she, it **is obtaining**	he, she, it **is being obtained**
Pres.	I, we, you, they **do obtain**	I, we, you, they **do get obtained**
Int.	he, she, it **does obtain**	he, she, it **does get obtained**
Fut.	I, he, she, it,	I, he, she, it,
	we, you, they **will obtain**	we, you, they **will be obtained**
Past	I, he, she, it,	I, he, she, it **was obtained**
	we, you, they **obtained**	we, you, they **were obtained**
Past	I, he, she, it **was obtaining**	I, he, she, it **was being obtained**
Prog.	we, you, they **were obtaining**	we, you, they **were being obtained**
Past	I, he, she, it,	I, he, she, it,
Int.	we, you, they **did obtain**	we, you, they **did get obtained**
Pres.	I, we, you, they **have obtained**	I, we, you, they **have been obtained**
Perf.	he, she, it **has obtained**	he, she, it **has been obtained**
Past	I, he, she, it,	I, he, she, it,
Perf.	we, you, they **had obtained**	we, you, they **had been obtained**
Fut.	I, he, she, it, we, you, they	I, he, she, it, we, you, they
Perf.	**will have obtained**	**will have been obtained**

IMPERATIVE MOOD

obtain

be obtained

SUBJUNCTIVE MOOD

Pres.	if I, he, she, it,	if I, he, she, it,
	we, you, they **obtain**	we, you, they **be obtained**
Past	if I, he, she, it,	if I, he, she, it,
	we, you, they **obtained**	we, you, they **were obtained**
Fut.	if I, he, she, it,	if I, he, she, it,
	we, you, they **should obtain**	we, you, they **should be obtained**

Transitive and intransitive.

Of course, we obtained his permission to hunt on his land.
All the necessary signatures were obtained by the candidates.

292

INDICATIVE MOOD

Pres.	I, we, you, they **occur**
	he, she, it **occurs**
Pres.	I **am occurring**
Prog.	we, you, they **are occurring**
	he, she, it **is occurring**
Pres.	I, we, you, they **do occur**
Int.	he, she, it **does occur**
Fut.	I, he, she, it,
	we, you, they **will occur**
Past	I, he, she, it,
	we, you, they **occurred**
Past	I, he, she, it **was occurring**
Prog.	we, you, they **were occurring**
Past	I, he, she, it,
Int.	we, you, they **did occur**
Pres.	I, we, you, they **have occurred**
Perf.	he, she, it **has occurred**
Past	I, he, she, it,
Perf.	we, you, they **had occurred**
Fut.	I, he, she, it, we, you, they
Perf.	**will have occurred**

O

IMPERATIVE MOOD

occur

SUBJUNCTIVE MOOD

Pres.	if I, he, she, it,
	we, you, they **occur**
Past	if I, he, she, it,
	we, you, they **occurred**
Fut.	if I, he, she, it,
	we, you, they **should occur**

These flights are occurring more and more frequently.
The incident occurred during the early morning hours.

offer
(active voice)

be offered
(passive voice)

INDICATIVE MOOD

Pres.	I, we, you, they **offer**	I **am offered**
		we, you, they **are offered**
	he, she, it **offers**	he, she, it **is offered**
Pres.	I **am offering**	I **am being offered**
Prog.	we, you, they **are offering**	we, you, they **are being offered**
	he, she, it **is offering**	he, she, it **is being offered**
Pres.	I, we, you, they **do offer**	I, we, you, they **do get offered**
Int.	he, she, it **does offer**	he, she, it **does get offered**
Fut.	I, he, she, it,	I, he, she, it,
	we, you, they **will offer**	we, you, they **will be offered**
Past	I, he, she, it,	I, he, she, it **was offered**
	we, you, they **offered**	we, you, they **were offered**
Past	I, he, she, it **was offering**	I, he, she, it **was being offered**
Prog.	we, you, they **were offering**	we, you, they **were being offered**
Past	I, he, she, it,	I, he, she, it,
Int.	we, you, they **did offer**	we, you, they **did get offered**
Pres.	I, we, you, they **have offered**	I, we, you, they **have been offered**
Perf.	he, she, it **has offered**	he, she, it **has been offered**
Past	I, he, she, it,	I, he, she, it,
Perf.	we, you, they **had offered**	we, you, they **had been offered**
Fut.	I, he, she, it, we, you, they	I, he, she, it, we, you, they
Perf.	**will have offered**	**will have been offered**

IMPERATIVE MOOD

offer   **be offered**

SUBJUNCTIVE MOOD

Pres.	if I, he, she, it,	if I, he, she, it,
	we, you, they **offer**	we, you, they **be offered**
Past	if I, he, she, it,	if I, he, she, it,
	we, you, they **offered**	we, you, they **were offered**
Fut.	if I, he, she, it,	if I, he, she, it,
	we, you, they **should offer**	we, you, they **should be offered**

Transitive and intransitive.

He is offering a special discount.
Grandma offered to babysit for our children next Saturday.
The gifts were offered as a sign of goodwill.

offset
(active voice)

be offset
(passive voice)

INDICATIVE MOOD

Pres. I, we, you, they **offset**

he, she, it **offsets**

I **am offset**
we, you, they **are offset**
he, she, it **is offset**

Pres. I **am offsetting**
Prog. we, you, they **are offsetting**
he, she, it **is offsetting**

I **am being offset**
we, you, they **are being offset**
he, she, it **is being offset**

Pres. I, we, you, they **do offset**
Int. he, she, it **does offset**

I, we, you, they **do get offset**
he, she, it **does get offset**

Fut. I, he, she, it,
we, you, they **will offset**

I, he, she, it,
we, you, they **will be offset**

Past I, he, she, it,
we, you, they **offset**

I, he, she, it **was offset**
we, you, they **were offset**

Past I, he, she, it **was offsetting**
Prog. we, you, they **were offsetting**

I, he, she, it **was being offset**
we, you, they **were being offset**

Past I, he, she, it,
Int. we, you, they **did offset**

I, he, she, it,
we, you, they **did get offset**

Pres. I, we, you, they **have offset**
Perf. he, she, it **has offset**

I, we, you, they **have been offset**
he, she, it **has been offset**

Past I, he, she, it,
Perf. we, you, they **had offset**

I, he, she, it,
we, you, they **had been offset**

Fut. I, he, she, it, we, you, they
Perf. **will have offset**

I, he, she, it, we, you, they
will have been offset

IMPERATIVE MOOD

offset

be offset

SUBJUNCTIVE MOOD

Pres. if I, he, she, it,
we, you, they **offset**

if I, he, she, it,
we, you, they **be offset**

Past if I, he, she, it,
we, you, they **offset**

if I, he, she, it,
we, you, they **were offset**

Fut. if I, he, she, it,
we, you, they **should offset**

if I, he, she, it,
we, you, they **should be offset**

Transitive and intransitive.

His costs are offsetting his receipts.
The second story was offset by several feet.

open
(active voice)

be opened
(passive voice)

INDICATIVE MOOD

Pres.	I, we, you, they **open**	I **am opened**
		we, you, they **are opened**
	he, she, it **opens**	he, she, it **is opened**
Pres.	I **am opening**	I **am being opened**
Prog.	we, you, they **are opening**	we, you, they **are being opened**
	he, she, it **is opening**	he, she, it **is being opened**
Pres.	I, we, you, they **do open**	I, we, you, they **do get opened**
Int.	he, she, it **does open**	he, she, it **does get opened**
Fut.	I, he, she, it,	I, he, she, it,
	we, you, they **will open**	we, you, they **will be opened**
Past	I, he, she, it,	I, he, she, it **was opened**
	we, you, they **opened**	we, you, they **were opened**
Past	I, he, she, it **was opening**	I, he, she, it **was being opened**
Prog.	we, you, they **were opening**	we, you, they **were being opened**
Past	I, he, she, it,	I, he, she, it,
Int.	we, you, they **did open**	we, you, they **did get opened**
Pres.	I, we, you, they **have opened**	I, we, you, they **have been opened**
Perf.	he, she, it **has opened**	he, she, it **has been opened**
Past	I, he, she, it,	I, he, she, it,
Perf.	we, you, they **had opened**	we, you, they **had been opened**
Fut.	I, he, she, it, we, you, they	I, he, she, it, we, you, they
Perf.	**will have opened**	**will have been opened**

IMPERATIVE MOOD

open   **be opened**

SUBJUNCTIVE MOOD

Pres.	if I, he, she, it,	if I, he, she, it,
	we, you, they **open**	we, you, they **be opened**
Past	if I, he, she, it,	if I, he, she, it,
	we, you, they **opened**	we, you, they **were opened**
Fut.	if I, he, she, it,	if I, he, she, it,
	we, you, they **should open**	we, you, they **should be opened**

Transitive and intransitive.

He is opening a new store next year.
The letter had been opened before it was delivered to us.

operate
(active voice)

be operated
(passive voice)

INDICATIVE MOOD

Pres.	I, we, you, they **operate**	I **am operated**
		we, you, they **are operated**
	he, she, it **operates**	he, she, it **is operated**
Pres.	I **am operating**	I **am being operated**
Prog.	we, you, they **are operating**	we, you, they **are being operated**
	he, she, it **is operating**	he, she, it **is being operated**
Pres.	I, we, you, they **do operate**	I, we, you, they **do get operated**
Int.	he, she, it **does operate**	he, she, it **does get operated**
Fut.	I, he, she, it,	I, he, she, it,
	we, you, they **will operate**	we, you, they **will be operated**
Past	I, he, she, it,	I, he, she, it **was operated**
	we, you, they **operated**	we, you, they **were operated**
Past	I, he, she, it **was operating**	I, he, she, it **was being operated**
Prog.	we, you, they **were operating**	we, you, they **were being operated**
Past	I, he, she, it,	I, he, she, it,
Int.	we, you, they **did operate**	we, you, they **did get operated**
Pres.	I, we, you, they **have operated**	I, we, you, they **have been operated**
Perf.	he, she, it **has operated**	he, she, it **has been operated**
Past	I, he, she, it,	I, he, she, it,
Perf.	we, you, they **had operated**	we, you, they **had been operated**
Fut.	I, he, she, it, we, you, they	I, he, she, it, we, you, they
Perf.	**will have operated**	**will have been operated**

IMPERATIVE MOOD

operate   **be operated**

SUBJUNCTIVE MOOD

Pres.	if I, he, she, it,	if I, he, she, it,
	we, you, they **operate**	we, you, they **be operated**
Past	if I, he, she, it,	if I, he, she, it,
	we, you, they **operated**	we, you, they **were operated**
Fut.	if I, he, she, it,	if I, he, she, it,
	we, you, they **should operate**	we, you, they **should be operated**

Intransitive and transitive.

The doctor is operating on his leg this morning.
The crane was operated by an experienced worker.

O

order
(active voice)

PRINCIPAL PARTS: **orders, ordering,
ordered, ordered**

be ordered
(passive voice)

INDICATIVE MOOD

Pres.	I, we, you, they **order**	I **am ordered**
		we, you, they **are ordered**
	he, she, it **orders**	he, she, it **is ordered**
Pres.	I **am ordering**	I **am being ordered**
Prog.	we, you, they **are ordering**	we, you, they **are being ordered**
	he, she, it **is ordering**	he, she, it **is being ordered**
Pres.	I, we, you, they **do order**	I, we, you, they **do get ordered**
Int.	he, she, it **does order**	he, she, it **does get ordered**
Fut.	I, he, she, it,	I, he, she, it,
	we, you, they **will order**	we, you, they **will be ordered**
Past	I, he, she, it,	I, he, she, it **was ordered**
	we, you, they **ordered**	we, you, they **were ordered**
Past	I, he, she, it **was ordering**	I, he, she, it **was being ordered**
Prog.	we, you, they **were ordering**	we, you, they **were being ordered**
Past	I, he, she, it,	I, he, she, it,
Int.	we, you, they **did order**	we, you, they **did get ordered**
Pres.	I, we, you, they **have ordered**	I, we, you, they **have been ordered**
Perf.	he, she, it **has ordered**	he, she, it **has been ordered**
Past	I, he, she, it,	I, he, she, it,
Perf.	we, you, they **had ordered**	we, you, they **had been ordered**
Fut.	I, he, she, it, we, you, they	I, he, she, it, we, you, they
Perf.	**will have ordered**	**will have been ordered**

IMPERATIVE MOOD

order **be ordered**

SUBJUNCTIVE MOOD

Pres.	if I, he, she, it,	if I, he, she, it,
	we, you, they **order**	we, you, they **be ordered**
Past	if I, he, she, it,	if I, he, she, it,
	we, you, they **ordered**	we, you, they **were ordered**
Fut.	if I, he, she, it,	if I, he, she, it,
	we, you, they **should order**	we, you, they **should be ordered**

Transitive and intransitive.

He is ordering the vegetarian meal for you.
They were ordered to leave by the bartender.

INDICATIVE MOOD

Pres.	I, we, you, they **out**	I **am outed**
		we, you, they **are outed**
	he, she, it **outs**	he, she, it **is outed**
Pres.	I **am outing**	I **am being outed**
Prog.	we, you, they **are outing**	we, you, they **are being outed**
	he, she, it **is outing**	he, she, it **is being outed**
Pres.	I, we, you, they **do out**	I, we, you, they **do get outed**
Int.	he, she, it **does out**	he, she, it **does get outed**
Fut.	I, he, she, it,	I, he, she, it,
	we, you, they **will out**	we, you, they **will be outed**
Past	I, he, she, it,	I, he, she, it **was outed**
	we, you, they **outed**	we, you, they **were outed**
Past	I, he, she, it **was outing**	I, he, she, it **was being outed**
Prog.	we, you, they **were outing**	we, you, they **were being outed**
Past	I, he, she, it,	I, he, she, it,
Int.	we, you, they **did out**	we, you, they **did get outed**
Pres.	I, we, you, they **have outed**	I, we, you, they **have been outed**
Perf.	he, she, it **has outed**	he, she, it **has been outed**
Past	I, he, she, it,	I, he, she, it,
Perf.	we, you, they **had outed**	we, you, they **had been outed**
Fut.	I, he, she, it, we, you, they	I, he, she, it, we, you, they
Perf.	**will have outed**	**will have been outed**

IMPERATIVE MOOD

out   **be outed**

SUBJUNCTIVE MOOD

Pres.	if I, he, she, it,	if I, he, she, it,
	we, you, they **out**	we, you, they **be outed**
Past	if I, he, she, it,	if I, he, she, it,
	we, you, they **outed**	we, you, they **were outed**
Fut.	if I, he, she, it,	if I, he, she, it,
	we, you, they **should out**	we, you, they **should be outed**

Transitive and intransitive.

They outed all those who had not paid property taxes.

299

PRINCIPAL PARTS: **outbids, outbidding, outbid, outbidden/outbid**

INDICATIVE MOOD

Pres.	I, we, you, they **outbid**	I **am outbidden** we, you, they **are outbidden**
	he, she, it **outbids**	he, she, it **is outbidden**
Pres. *Prog.*	I **am outbidding** we, you, they **are outbidding** he, she, it **is outbidding**	I **am being outbidden** we, you, they **are being outbidden** he, she, it **is being outbidden**
Pres. *Int.*	I, we, you, they **do outbid** he, she, it **does outbid**	I, we, you, they **do get outbidden** he, she, it **does get outbidden**
Fut.	I, he, she, it, we, you, they **will outbid**	I, he, she, it, we, you, they **will be outbidden**
Past	I, he, she, it, we, you, they **outbid**	I, he, she, it **was outbidden** we, you, they **were outbidden**
Past *Prog.*	I, he, she, it **was outbidding** we, you, they **were outbidding**	I, he, she, it **was being outbidden** we, you, they **were being outbidden**
Past *Int.*	I, he, she, it, we, you, they **did outbid**	I, he, she, it, we, you, they **did get outbidden**
Pres. *Perf.*	I, we, you, they **have outbidden** he, she, it **has outbidden**	I, we, you, they **have been outbidden** he, she, it **has been outbidden**
Past *Perf.*	I, he, she, it, we, you, they **had outbidden**	I, he, she, it, we, you, they **had been outbidden**
Fut. *Perf.*	I, he, she, it, we, you, they **will have outbidden**	I, he, she, it, we, you, they **will have been outbidden**

IMPERATIVE MOOD

outbid	**be outbidden**

SUBJUNCTIVE MOOD

Pres.	if I, he, she, it, we, you, they **outbid**	if I, he, she, it, we, you, they **be outbidden**
Past	if I, he, she, it, we, you, they **outbid**	if I, he, she, it, we, you, they **were outbidden**
Fut.	if I, he, she, it, we, you, they **should outbid**	if I, he, she, it, we, you, they **should be outbidden**

The *Oxford Dictionary* and *Webster's* recognize only OUTBID as the past participle.

We are outbidding our competition.
They outbid us on the last job.
We promise never to be outbidden again.

outdo
(active voice)

be outdone
(passive voice)

INDICATIVE MOOD

Pres.	I, we, you, they **outdo**	I **am outdone**
		we, you, they **are outdone**
	he, she, it **outdoes**	he, she, it **is outdone**
Pres.	I **am outdoing**	I **am being outdone**
Prog.	we, you, they **are outdoing**	we, you, they **are being outdone**
	he, she, it **is outdoing**	he, she, it **is being outdone**
Pres.	I, we, you, they **do outdo**	I, we, you, they **do get outdone**
Int.	he, she, it **does outdo**	he, she, it **does get outdone**
Fut.	I, he, she, it,	I, he, she, it,
	we, you, they **will outdo**	we, you, they **will be outdone**
Past	I, he, she, it,	I, he, she, it **was outdone**
	we, you, they **outdid**	we, you, they **were outdone**
Past	I, he, she, it **was outdoing**	I, he, she, it **was being outdone**
Prog.	we, you, they **were outdoing**	we, you, they **were being outdone**
Past	I, he, she, it,	I, he, she, it,
Int.	we, you, they **did outdo**	we, you, they **did get outdone**
Pres.	I, we, you, they **have outdone**	I, we, you, they **have been outdone**
Perf.	he, she, it **has outdone**	he, she, it **has been outdone**
Past	I, he, she, it,	I, he, she, it,
Perf.	we, you, they **had outdone**	we, you, they **had been outdone**
Fut.	I, he, she, it, we, you, they	I, he, she, it, we, you, they
Perf.	**will have outdone**	**will have been outdone**

IMPERATIVE MOOD

outdo   **be outdone**

SUBJUNCTIVE MOOD

Pres.	if I, he, she, it,	if I, he, she, it,
	we, you, they **outdo**	we, you, they **be outdone**
Past	if I, he, she, it,	if I, he, she, it,
	we, you, they **outdid**	we, you, they **were outdone**
Fut.	if I, he, she, it,	if I, he, she, it,
	we, you, they **should outdo**	we, you, they **should be outdone**

He outdoes himself with every new challenge.
She is outdoing herself with this reception.
They outdid their previous efforts.
We cannot be outdone.

outrun
(active voice)

be outrun
(passive voice)

INDICATIVE MOOD

Pres. I, we, you, they **outrun**

I **am outrun**
we, you, they **are outrun**
he, she, it **outruns**
he, she, it **is outrun**

Pres. I **am outrunning**
Prog. we, you, they **are outrunning**
he, she, it **is outrunning**

I **am being outrun**
we, you, they **are being outrun**
he, she, it **is being outrun**

Pres. I, we, you, they **do outrun**
Int. he, she, it **does outrun**

I, we, you, they **do get outrun**
he, she, it **does get outrun**

Fut. I, he, she, it,
we, you, they **will outrun**

I, he, she, it,
we, you, they **will be outrun**

Past I, he, she, it,
we, you, they **outran**

I, he, she, it **was outrun**
we, you, they **were outrun**

Past I, he, she, it **was outrunning**
Prog. we, you, they **were outrunning**

I, he, she, it **was being outrun**
we, you, they **were being outrun**

Past I, he, she, it,
Int. we, you, they **did outrun**

I, he, she, it,
we, you, they **did get outrun**

Pres. I, we, you, they **have outrun**
Perf. he, she, it **has outrun**

I, we, you, they **have been outrun**
he, she, it **has been outrun**

Past I, he, she, it,
Perf. we, you, they **had outrun**

I, he, she, it,
we, you, they **had been outrun**

Fut. I, he, she, it, we, you, they
Perf. **will have outrun**

I, he, she, it, we, you, they
will have been outrun

IMPERATIVE MOOD

outrun

be outrun

SUBJUNCTIVE MOOD

Pres. if I, he, she, it,
we, you, they **outrun**

if I, he, she, it,
we, you, they **be outrun**

Past if I, he, she, it,
we, you, they **outran**

if I, he, she, it,
we, you, they **were outrun**

Fut. if I, he, she, it,
we, you, they **should outrun**

if I, he, she, it,
we, you, they **should be outrun**

He is outrunning and outjumping everyone this year.
Last year they outran and outjumped him.
Then he determined never to be outrun or outjumped by a classmate.

outsource
(active voice)

INDICATIVE MOOD

Pres.	I, we, you, they **outsource**	I **am outsourced**
		we, you, they **are outsourced**
	he, she, it **outsources**	he, she, it **is outsourced**
Pres.	I **am outsourcing**	I **am being outsourced**
Prog.	we, you, they **are outsourcing**	we, you, they **are being outsourced**
	he, she, it **is outsourcing**	he, she, it **is being outsourced**
Pres.	I, we, you, they **do outsource**	I, we, you, they **do get outsourced**
Int.	he, she, it **does outsource**	he, she, it **does get outsourced**
Fut.	I, he, she, it,	I, he, she, it,
	we, you, they **will outsource**	we, you, they **will be outsourced**
Past	I, he, she, it,	I, he, she, it **was outsourced**
	we, you, they **outsourced**	we, you, they **were outsourced**
Past	I, he, she, it **was outsourcing**	I, he, she, it **was being outsourced**
Prog.	we, you, they **were outsourcing**	we, you, they **were being outsourced**
Past	I, he, she, it,	I, he, she, it,
Int.	we, you, they **did outsource**	we, you, they **did get outsourced**
Pres.	I, we, you, they **have outsourced**	I, we, you, they **have been outsourced**
Perf.	he, she, it **has outsourced**	he, she, it **has been outsourced**
Past	I, he, she, it,	I, he, she, it,
Perf.	we, you, they **had outsourced**	we, you, they **had been outsourced**
Fut.	I, he, she, it, we, you, they	I, he, she, it, we, you, they
Perf.	**will have outsourced**	**will have been outsourced**

O

IMPERATIVE MOOD

outsource   **be outsourced**

SUBJUNCTIVE MOOD

Pres.	if I, he, she, it,	if I, he, she, it,
	we, you, they **outsource**	we, you, they **be outsourced**
Past	if I, he, she, it,	if I, he, she, it,
	we, you, they **outsourced**	we, you, they **were outsourced**
Fut.	if I, he, she, it,	if I, he, she, it,
	we, you, they **should outsource**	we, you, they **should be outsourced**

We are outsourcing all our production next year.
They complained when the company outsourced the work to another country.
Our customer service has been outsourced to save money.

| overcome
(active voice) | PRINCIPAL PARTS: **overcomes,
overcoming, overcame, overcome** | be overcome
(passive voice) |

INDICATIVE MOOD

Pres.	I, we, you, they **overcome**	I **am overcome**
		we, you, they **are overcome**
	he, she, it **overcomes**	he, she, it **is overcome**
Pres. *Prog.*	I **am overcoming** we, you, they **are overcoming** he, she, it **is overcoming**	I am being **overcome** we, you, they **are being overcome** he, she, it **is being overcome**
Pres. *Int.*	I, we, you, they **do overcome** he, she, it **does overcome**	I, we, you, **do get overcome** he, she, it **does get overcome**
Fut.	I, he, she, it, we, you, they **will overcome**	I, he, she, it, we, you, they **will be overcome**
Past	I, he, she, it, we, you, they **overcame**	I, he, she, it **was overcome** we, you, they **were overcome**
Past *Prog.*	I, he, she, it **was overcoming** we, you, they **were overcoming**	I, he, she, it **was being overcome** we, you, they **were being overcome**
Past *Int.*	I, he, she, it, we, you, they **did overcome**	I, he, she, it, we, you, they **did get overcome**
Pres. *Perf.*	I, we, you, they **have overcome** he, she, it **has overcome**	I, we, you, they **have been overcome** he, she, it **has been overcome**
Past *Perf.*	I, he, she, it, we, you, they **had overcome**	I, he, she, it, we, you, they **had been overcome**
Fut. *Perf.*	I, he, she, it, we, you, they **will have overcome**	I, he, she, it, we, you, they **will have been overcome**

IMPERATIVE MOOD

overcome	**be overcome**

SUBJUNCTIVE MOOD

Pres.	if I, he, she, it, we, you, they **overcome**	if I, he, she, it, we, you, they **be overcome**
Past	if I, he, she, it, we, you, they **overcame**	if I, he, she, it, we, you, they **were overcome**
Fut.	if I, he, she, it, we, you, they **should overcome**	if I, he, she, it, we, you, they **should be overcome**

Transitive and intransitive.

She is overcoming her shyness.
He overcame many difficulties on his road to political success.
They were overcome with smoke and ashes.

INDICATIVE MOOD

Pres.   I, we, you, they **overeat**

        he, she, it **overeats**

Pres.   I **am overeating**
Prog.   we, you, they **are overeating**
        he, she, it **is overeating**

Pres.   I, we, you, they **do overeat**
Int.   he, she, it **does overeat**

Fut.   I, he, she, it,
        we, you, they **will overeat**

Past   I, he, she, it,
        we, you, they **overate**

Past   I, he, she, it **was overeating**
Prog.   we, you, they **were overeating**

Past   I, he, she, it,
Int.   we, you, they **did overeat**

Pres.   I, we, you, they **have overeaten**
Perf.   he, she, it **has overeaten**

Past   I, he, she, it,
Perf.   we, you, they **had overeaten**

Fut.   I, he, she, it, we, you, they
Perf.   **will have overeaten**

IMPERATIVE MOOD

    overeat

SUBJUNCTIVE MOOD

Pres.   if I, he, she, it,
        we, you, they **overeat**

Past   if I, he, she, it,
        we, you, they **overate**

Fut.   if I, he, she, it,
        we, you, they **should overeat**

We all overate at the wedding feast.
I wish we had not overeaten last evening.

override
(active voice)

PRINCIPAL PARTS: **overrides, overriding, overrode, overridden**

be overridden
(passive voice)

INDICATIVE MOOD

Pres.	I, we, you, they **override**	I **am overridden**
		we, you, they **are overridden**
	he, she, it **overrides**	he, she, it **is overridden**
Pres.	I **am overriding**	I **am being overridden**
Prog.	we, you, they **are overriding**	we, you, they **are being overridden**
	he, she, it **is overriding**	he, she, it **is being overridden**
Pres.	I, we, you, they **do override**	I, we, you, they **do get overridden**
Int.	he, she, it **does override**	he, she, it **does get overridden**
Fut.	I, he, she, it,	I, he, she, it,
	we, you, they **will override**	we, you, they **will be overridden**
Past	I, he, she, it,	I, he, she, it **was overridden**
	we, you, they **overrode**	we, you, they **were overridden**
Past	I, he, she, it **was overriding**	I, he, she, it **was being overridden**
Prog.	we, you, they **were overriding**	we, you, they **were being overridden**
Past	I, he, she, it,	I, he, she, it,
Int.	we, you, they **did override**	we, you, they **did get overridden**
Pres.	I, we, you, they **have overridden**	I, we, you, they **have been overridden**
Perf.	he, she, it **has overridden**	he, she, it **has been overridden**
Past	I, he, she, it,	I, he, she, it,
Perf.	we, you, they **had overridden**	we, you, they **had been overridden**
Fut.	I, he, she, it, we, you, they	I, he, she, it, we, you, they
Perf.	**will have overridden**	**will have been overridden**

IMPERATIVE MOOD

override   **be overridden**

SUBJUNCTIVE MOOD

Pres.	if I, he, she, it,	if I, he, she, it,
	we, you, they **override**	we, you, they **be overridden**
Past	if I, he, she, it,	if I, he, she, it,
	we, you, they **overrode**	we, you, they **were overridden**
Fut.	if I, he, she, it,	if I, he, she, it,
	we, you, they **should override**	we, you, they **should be overridden**

These concerns are overriding our main interest.
The chairman overrode our decisions.
The committee's recommendation has been overridden.

| overrun
(active voice) | PRINCIPAL PARTS: **overruns,
overrunning, overran, overrun** | be overrun
(passive voice) |

INDICATIVE MOOD

Pres.	I, we, you, they **overrun**	I **am overrun** we, you, they **are overrun**
	he, she, it **overruns**	he, she, it **is overrun**
Pres. *Prog.*	I **am overrunning** we, you, they **are overrunning** he, she, it **is overrunning**	I **am being overrun** we, you, they **are being overrun** he, she, it **is being overrun**
Pres. *Int.*	I, we, you, they **do overrun** he, she, it **does overrun**	I, we, you, they **do get overrun** he, she, it **does get overrun**
Fut.	I, he, she, it, we, you, they **will overrun**	I, he, she, it, we, you, they **will be overrun**
Past	I, he, she, it, we, you, they **overran**	I, he, she, it **was overrun** we, you, they **were overrun**
Past *Prog.*	I, he, she, it **was overrunning** we, you, they **were overrunning**	I, he, she, it **was being overrun** we, you, they **were being overrun**
Past *Int.*	I, he, she, it, we, you, they **did overrun**	I, he, she, it, we, you, they **did get overrun**
Pres. *Perf.*	I, we, you, they **have overrun** he, she, it **has overrun**	I, we, you, they **have been overrun** he, she, it **has been overrun**
Past *Perf.*	I, he, she, it, we, you, they **had overrun**	I, he, she, it, we, you, they **had been overrun**
Fut. *Perf.*	I, he, she, it, we, you, they **will have overrun**	I, he, she, it, we, you, they **will have been overrun**

IMPERATIVE MOOD

overrun **be overrun**

SUBJUNCTIVE MOOD

Pres.	if I, he, she, it, we, you, they **overrun**	if I, he, she, it, we, you, they **be overrun**
Past	if I, he, she, it, we, you, they **overran**	if I, he, she, it, we, you, they **were overrun**
Fut.	if I, he, she, it, we, you, they **should overrun**	if I, he, she, it, we, you, they **should be overrun**

Transitive and intransitive.

Our costs are by far overrunning our receipts.
The bears overran their campsite.
Our camp was overrun with mosquitoes.

oversleep
(active voice)

be overslept
(passive voice)

INDICATIVE MOOD

Pres.	I, we, you, they **oversleep**	I **am overslept**
		we, you, they **are overslept**
	he, she, it **oversleeps**	he, she, it **is overslept**
Pres.	I **am oversleeping**	I **am being overslept**
Prog.	we, you, they **are oversleeping**	we, you, they **are being overslept**
	he, she, it **is oversleeping**	he, she, it **is being overslept**
Pres.	I, we, you, they **do oversleep**	I, we, you, they **do get overslept**
Int.	he, she, it **does oversleep**	he, she, it **does get overslept**
Fut.	I, he, she, it,	I, he, she, it,
	we, you, they **will oversleep**	we, you, they **will be overslept**
Past	I, he, she, it,	I, he, she, it **was overslept**
	we, you, they **overslept**	we, you, they **were overslept**
Past	I, he, she, it **was oversleeping**	I, he, she, it **was being overslept**
Prog.	we, you, they **were oversleeping**	we, you, they **were being overslept**
Past	I, he, she, it,	I, he, she, it,
Int.	we, you, they **did oversleep**	we, you, they **did get overslept**
Pres.	I, we, you, they **have overslept**	I, we, you, they **have been overslept**
Perf.	he, she, it **has overslept**	he, she, it **has been overslept**
Past	I, he, she, it,	I, he, she, it,
Perf.	we, you, they **had overslept**	we, you, they **had been overslept**
Fut.	I, he, she, it, we, you, they	I, he, she, it, we, you, they
Perf.	**will have overslept**	**will have been overslept**

IMPERATIVE MOOD

oversleep   **be overslept**

SUBJUNCTIVE MOOD

Pres.	if I, he, she, it,	if I, he, she, it,
	we, you, they **oversleep**	we, you, they **be overslept**
Past	if I, he, she, it,	if I, he, she, it,
	we, you, they **overslept**	we, you, they **were overslept**
Fut.	if I, he, she, it,	if I, he, she, it,
	we, you, they **should oversleep**	we, you, they **should be overslept**

Intransitive and transitive.

She overslept and missed her plane.
The dentist appointment was overslept by the boy on purpose.

overtake
(active voice)

PRINCIPAL PARTS: **overtakes, overtaking, overtook, overtaken**

be overtaken
(passive voice)

INDICATIVE MOOD

Pres. I, we, you, they **overtake**

he, she, it **overtakes**

I **am overtaken**
we, you, they **are overtaken**
he, she, it **is overtaken**

Pres. I **am overtaking**
Prog. we, you, they **are overtaking**
he, she, it **is overtaking**

I **am being overtaken**
we, you, they **are being overtaken**
he, she, it **is being overtaken**

Pres. I, we, you, they **do overtake**
Int. he, she, it **does overtake**

I, we, you, they **do get overtaken**
he, she, it **does get overtaken**

Fut. I, he, she, it,
we, you, they **will overtake**

I, he, she, it,
we, you, they **will be overtaken**

Past I, he, she, it,
we, you, they **overtook**

I, he, she, it **was overtaken**
we, you, they **were overtaken**

Past I, he, she, it **was overtaking**
Prog. we, you, they **were overtaking**

I, he, she, it **was being overtaken**
we, you, they **were being overtaken**

Past I, he, she, it,
Int. we, you, they **did overtake**

I, he, she, it,
we, you, they **did get overtaken**

Pres. I, we, you, they **have overtaken**
Perf. he, she, it **has overtaken**

I, we, you, they **have been overtaken**
he, she, it **has been overtaken**

Past I, he, she, it,
Perf. we, you, they **had overtaken**

I, he, she, it,
we, you, they **had been overtaken**

Fut. I, he, she, it, we, you, they
Perf. **will have overtaken**

I, he, she, it, we, you, they
will have been overtaken

IMPERATIVE MOOD

overtake

be overtaken

SUBJUNCTIVE MOOD

Pres. if I, he, she, it,
we, you, they **overtake**

if I, he, she, it,
we, you, they **be overtaken**

Past if I, he, she, it,
we, you, they **overtook**

if I, he, she, it,
we, you, they **were overtaken**

Fut. if I, he, she, it,
we, you, they **should overtake**

if I, he, she, it,
we, you, they **should be overtaken**

The second-place car is overtaking the leader.
We overtook the other ship in the last few seconds of the race.
The runner was overtaken in the last mile of the marathon.

INDICATIVE MOOD

Pres.	I, we, you, they **overthrow**	I **am overthrown**
		we, you, they **are overthrown**
	he, she, it **overthrows**	he, she, it **is overthrown**
Pres.	I **am overthrowing**	I **am being overthrown**
Prog.	we, you, they **are overthrowing**	we, you, they **are being overthrown**
	he, she, it **is overthrowing**	he, she, it **is being overthrown**
Pres.	I, we, you, they **do overthrow**	I, we, you, they **do get overthrown**
Int.	he, she, it **does overthrow**	he, she, it **does get overthrown**
Fut.	I, he, she, it,	I, he, she, it,
	we, you, they **will overthrow**	we, you, they **will be overthrown**
Past	I, he, she, it,	I, he, she, it **was overthrown**
	we, you, they **overthrew**	we, you, they **were overthrown**
Past	I, he, she, it **was overthrowing**	I, he, she, it **was being overthrown**
Prog.	we, you, they **were overthrowing**	we, you, they **were being overthrown**
Past	I, he, she, it,	I, he, she, it,
Int.	we, you, they **did overthrow**	we, you, they **did get overthrown**
Pres.	I, we, you, they **have overthrown**	I, we, you, they **have been overthrown**
Perf.	he, she, it **has overthrown**	he, she, it **has been overthrown**
Past	I, he, she, it,	I, he, she, it,
Perf.	we, you, they **had overthrown**	we, you, they **had been overthrown**
Fut.	I, he, she, it, we, you, they	I, he, she, it, we, you, they
Perf.	**will have overthrown**	**will have been overthrown**

IMPERATIVE MOOD

overthrow	**be overthrown**

SUBJUNCTIVE MOOD

Pres.	if I, he, she, it,	if I, he, she, it,
	we, you, they **overthrow**	we, you, they **be overthrown**
Past	if I, he, she, it,	if I, he, she, it,
	we, you, they **overthrew**	we, you, they **were overthrown**
Fut.	if I, he, she, it,	if I, he, she, it,
	we, you, they **should overthrow**	we, you, they **should be overthrown**

They overthrew the dictatorship during their revolution.
What are the consequences now that he has been overthrown?

INDICATIVE MOOD

Pres.	I, we, you, they **panic**	I **am panicked**
		we, you, they **are panicked**
	he, she, it **panics**	he, she, it **is panicked**
Pres.	I **am panicking**	I **am being panicked**
Prog.	we, you, they **are panicking**	we, you, they **are being panicked**
	he, she, it **is panicking**	he, she, it **is being panicked**
Pres.	I, we, you, they **do panic**	I, we, you, they **do get panicked**
Int.	he, she, it **does panic**	he, she, it **does get panicked**
Fut.	I, he, she, it,	I, he, she, it,
	we, you, they **will panic**	we, you, they **will be panicked**
Past	I, he, she, it,	I, he, she, it **was panicked**
	we, you, they **panicked**	we, you, they **were panicked**
Past	I, he, she, it **was panicking**	I, he, she, it **was being panicked**
Prog.	we, you, they **were panicking**	we, you, they **were being panicked**
Past	I, he, she, it,	I, he, she, it,
Int.	we, you, they **did panic**	we, you, they **did get panicked**
Pres.	I, we, you, they **have panicked**	I, we, you, they **have been panicked**
Perf.	he, she, it **has panicked**	he, she, it **has been panicked**
Past	I, he, she, it,	I, he, she, it,
Perf.	we, you, they **had panicked**	we, you, they **had been panicked**
Fut.	I, he, she, it, we, you, they	I, he, she, it, we, you, they
Perf.	**will have panicked**	**will have been panicked**

IMPERATIVE MOOD

panic   **be panicked**

SUBJUNCTIVE MOOD

Pres.	if I, he, she, it,	if I, he, she, it,
	we, you, they **panic**	we, you, they **be panicked**
Past	if I, he, she, it,	if I, he, she, it,
	we, you, they **panicked**	we, you, they **were panicked**
Fut.	if I, he, she, it,	if I, he, she, it,
	we, you, they **should panic**	we, you, they **should be panicked**

Transitive and intransitive.

They are panicking even as we speak.
The boy panicked and ran at the sight of the snake.
The market was panicked by rumors of oil shortages.

partake
(active voice)

be partaken
(passive voice)

INDICATIVE MOOD

Pres.	I, we, you, they **partake**	I **am partaken**
		we, you, they **are partaken**
	he, she, it **partakes**	he, she, it **is partaken**
Pres.	I **am partaking**	I **am being partaken**
Prog.	we, you, they **are partaking**	we, you, they **are being partaken**
	he, she, it **is partaking**	he, she, it **is being partaken**
Pres.	I, we, you, they **do partake**	I, we, you, they **do get partaken**
Int.	he, she, it **does partake**	he, she, it **does get partaken**
Fut.	I, he, she, it,	I, he, she, it,
	we, you, they **will partake**	we, you, they **will be partaken**
Past	I, he, she, it,	I, he, she, it **was partaken**
	we, you, they **partook**	we, you, they **were partaken**
Past	I, he, she, it **was partaking**	I, he, she, it **was being partaken**
Prog.	we, you, they **were partaking**	we, you, they **were being partaken**
Past	I, he, she, it,	I, he, she, it,
Int.	we, you, they **did partake**	we, you, they **did get partaken**
Pres.	I, we, you, they **have partaken**	I, we, you, they **have been partaken**
Perf.	he, she, it **has partaken**	he, she, it **has been partaken**
Past	I, he, she, it,	I, he, she, it,
Perf.	we, you, they **had partaken**	we, you, they **had been partaken**
Fut.	I, he, she, it, we, you, they	I, he, she, it, we, you, they
Perf.	**will have partaken**	**will have been partaken**

IMPERATIVE MOOD

partake   **be partaken**

SUBJUNCTIVE MOOD

Pres.	if I, he, she, it,	if I, he, she, it,
	we, you, they **partake**	we, you, they **be partaken**
Past	if I, he, she, it,	if I, he, she, it,
	we, you, they **partook**	we, you, they **were partaken**
Fut.	if I, he, she, it,	if I, he, she, it,
	we, you, they **should partake**	we, you, they **should be partaken**

Intransitive and transitive.

They enjoy partaking in their weekly ritual.
We both partook of the ceremonial wine.
The secret rite can be partaken only by the initiated.

pass
(active voice)

be passed
(passive voice)

INDICATIVE MOOD

Pres.	I, we, you, they **pass**	I am **passed**
		we, you, they **are passed**
	he, she, it **passes**	he, she, it **is passed**
Pres.	I **am passing**	I **am being passed**
Prog.	we, you, they **are passing**	we, you, they **are being passed**
	he, she, it **is passing**	he, she, it **is being passed**
Pres.	I, we, you, they **do pass**	I, we, you, they **do get passed**
Int.	he, she, it **does pass**	he, she, it **does get passed**
Fut.	I, he, she, it,	I, he, she, it,
	we, you, they **will pass**	we, you, they **will be passed**
Past	I, he, she, it,	I, he, she, it **was passed**
	we, you, they **passed**	we, you, they **were passed**
Past	I, he, she, it **was passing**	I, he, she, it **was being passed**
Prog.	we, you, they **were passing**	we, you, they **were being passed**
Past	I, he, she, it,	I, he, she, it,
Int.	we, you, they **did pass**	we, you, they **did get passed**
Pres.	I, we, you, they **have passed**	I, we, you, they **have been passed**
Perf.	he, she, it **has passed**	he, she, it **has been passed**
Past	I, he, she, it,	I, he, she, it,
Perf.	we, you, they **had passed**	we, you, they **had been passed**
Fut.	I, he, she, it, we, you, they	I, he, she, it, we, you, they
Perf.	**will have passed**	**will have been passed**

IMPERATIVE MOOD

pass   **be passed**

SUBJUNCTIVE MOOD

Pres.	if I, he, she, it,	if I, he, she, it,
	we, you, they **pass**	we, you, they **be passed**
Past	if I, he, she, it,	if I, he, she, it,
	we, you, they **passed**	we, you, they **were passed**
Fut.	if I, he, she, it,	if I, he, she, it,
	we, you, they **should pass**	we, you, they **should be passed**

P

Intransitive and transitive.

He passed the ball to the other player.
The bill was passed by the legislative body on Thursday.

PRINCIPAL PARTS: **pays, paying, paid, paid**

INDICATIVE MOOD

Pres.	I, we, you, they **pay**	I **am paid** we, you, they **are paid**
	he, she, it **pays**	he, she, it **is paid**
Pres. *Prog.*	I **am paying** we, you, they **are paying** he, she, it **is paying**	I **am being paid** we, you, they **are being paid** he, she, it **is being paid**
Pres. *Int.*	I, we, you, they **do pay** he, she, it **does pay**	I, we, you, they **do get paid** he, she, it **does get paid**
Fut.	I, he, she, it, we, you, they **will pay**	I, he, she, it, we, you, they **will be paid**
Past	I, he, she, it, we, you, they **paid**	I, he, she, it **was paid** we, you, they **were paid**
Past *Prog.*	I, he, she, it **was paying** we, you, they **were paying**	I, he, she, it **was being paid** we, you, they **were being paid**
Past *Int.*	I, he, she, it, we, you, they **did pay**	I, he, she, it, we, you, they **did get paid**
Pres. *Perf.*	I, we, you, they **have paid** he, she, it **has paid**	I, we, you, they **have been paid** he, she, it **has been paid**
Past *Perf.*	I, he, she, it, we, you, they **had paid**	I, he, she, it, we, you, they **had been paid**
Fut. *Perf.*	I, he, she, it, we, you, they **will have paid**	I, he, she, it, we, you, they **will have been paid**

IMPERATIVE MOOD

pay	**be paid**

SUBJUNCTIVE MOOD

Pres.	if I, he, she, it, we, you, they **pay**	if I, he, she, it, we, you, they **be paid**
Past	if I, he, she, it, we, you, they **paid**	if I, he, she, it, we, you, they **were paid**
Fut.	if I, he, she, it, we, you, they **should pay**	if I, he, she, it, we, you, they **should be paid**

Transitive and intransitive.

Dad paid for the family vacation.
The parking ticket was paid before the car was released.

pay

Examples

He always pays with cash.

She paid her bills on time.

I will pay you back tomorrow.

The car was paid for by her mother.

Pay at the checkout counter.

He hadn't been paid for two months.

She has been paying for her braces.

It's time to pay up.

You couldn't pay me to do that.

This account pays interest.

Words and expressions related to this verb

Buy now, pay later.

Pay me now or pay me later.

You will pay for that.

He has paid his dues.

You will have to pay your own way.

She never pays her fair share.

One always has to pay for one's mistakes.

His account is all paid up.

They never paid off their debt.

Crime does not pay.

P

pen	PRINCIPAL PARTS: pens, penning,	be penned
(active voice)	penned, penned	(passive voice)

INDICATIVE MOOD

Pres.   I, we, you, they **pen**

        he, she, it **pens**

Pres.   I am **penning**
Prog.   we, you, they **are penning**
        he, she, it **is penning**

Pres.   I, we, you, they **do pen**
Int.   he, she, it **does pen**

Fut.   I, he, she, it,
        we, you, they **will pen**

Past   I, he, she, it,
        we, you, they **penned**

Past   I, he, she, it **was penning**
Prog.   we, you, they **were penning**

Past   I, he, she, it,
Int.   we, you, they **did pen**

Pres.   I, we, you, they **have penned**
Perf.   he, she, it **has penned**

Past   I, he, she, it,
Perf.   we, you, they **had penned**

Fut.   I, he, she, it, we, you, they
Perf.   **will have penned**

I am **penned**
we, you, they **are penned**
he, she, it **is penned**

I am **being penned**
we, you, they **are being penned**
he, she, it **is being penned**

I, we, you, they **do get penned**
he, she, it **does get penned**

I, he, she, it,
we, you, they **will be penned**

I, he, she, it **was penned**
we, you, they **were penned**

I, he, she, it **was being penned**
we, you, they **were being penned**

I, he, she, it,
we, you, they **did get penned**

I, we, you, they **have been penned**
he, she, it **has been penned**

I, he, she, it,
we, you, they **had been penned**

I, he, she, it, we, you, they
will have been penned

IMPERATIVE MOOD

pen   **be penned**

SUBJUNCTIVE MOOD

Pres.   if I, he, she, it,
        we, you, they **pen**

Past   if I, he, she, it,
        we, you, they **penned**

Fut.   if I, he, she, it,
        we, you, they **should pen**

if I, he, she, it,
we, you, they **be penned**

if I, he, she, it,
we, you, they **were penned**

if I, he, she, it,
we, you, they **should be penned**

PEN, PENNED means "write or compose." There is another verb PEN, PENNED, or PENT meaning to "confine in a pen."

They are penning in the animals for the night.
The author penned a carefully worded reply.
The horses were penned in the corral.

permit
(active voice)

PRINCIPAL PARTS: **permits, permitting, permitted, permitted**

be permitted
(passive voice)

INDICATIVE MOOD

Pres.	I, we, you, they **permit**	**I am permitted** we, you, they **are permitted**
	he, she, it **permits**	he, she, it **is permitted**
Pres. *Prog.*	**I am permitting** we, you, they **are permitting** he, she, it **is permitting**	**I am being permitted** we, you, they **are being permitted** he, she, it **is being permitted**
Pres. *Int.*	I, we, you, they **do permit** he, she, it **does permit**	I, we, you, they **do get permitted** he, she, it **does get permitted**
Fut.	I, he, she, it, we, you, they **will permit**	I, he, she, it, we, you, they **will be permitted**
Past	I, he, she, it, we, you, they **permitted**	I, he, she, it **was permitted** we, you, they **were permitted**
Past *Prog.*	I, he, she, it **was permitting** we, you, they **were permitting**	I, he, she, it **was being permitted** we, you, they **were being permitted**
Past *Int.*	I, he, she, it, we, you, they **did permit**	I, he, she, it, we, you, they **did get permitted**
Pres. *Perf.*	I, we, you, they **have permitted** he, she, it **has permitted**	I, we, you, they **have been permitted** he, she, it **has been permitted**
Past *Perf.*	I, he, she, it, we, you, they **had permitted**	I, he, she, it, we, you, they **had been permitted**
Fut. *Perf.*	I, he, she, it, we, you, they **will have permitted**	I, he, she, it, we, you, they **will have been permitted**

IMPERATIVE MOOD

permit

be permitted

SUBJUNCTIVE MOOD

Pres.	if I, he, she, it, we, you, they **permit**	if I, he, she, it, we, you, they **be permitted**
Past	if I, he, she, it, we, you, they **permitted**	if I, he, she, it, we, you, they **were permitted**
Fut.	if I, he, she, it, we, you, they **should permit**	if I, he, she, it, we, you, they **should be permitted**

Transitive and intransitive.

They are not permitting us to dance on Saturday.
We permitted the opening of the show after the fire inspection.
Smoking is not permitted in airports.

| pick | PRINCIPAL PARTS: **picks, picking,** | be picked |
| (active voice) | **picked, picked** | (passive voice) |

INDICATIVE MOOD

Pres. I, we, you, they **pick**

I am picked
we, you, they **are picked**
he, she, it **picks**
he, she, it **is picked**

Pres. **I am picking**
Prog. we, you, they **are picking**
he, she, it **is picking**

I am being picked
we, you, they **are being picked**
he, she, it **is being picked**

Pres. I, we, you, they **do pick**
Int. he, she, it **does pick**

I, we, you, they **do get picked**
he, she, it **does get picked**

Fut. I, he, she, it,
we, you, they **will pick**

I, he, she, it,
we, you, they **will be picked**

Past I, he, she, it,
we, you, they **picked**

I, he, she, it **was picked**
we, you, they **were picked**

Past I, he, she, it **was picking**
Prog. we, you, they **were picking**

I, he, she, it **was being picked**
we, you, they **were being picked**

Past I, he, she, it,
Int. we, you, they **did pick**

I, he, she, it,
we, you, they **did get picked**

Pres. I, we, you, they **have picked**
Perf. he, she, it **has picked**

I, we, you, they **have been picked**
he, she, it **has been picked**

Past I, he, she, it,
Perf. we, you, they **had picked**

I, he, she, it,
we, you, they **had been picked**

Fut. I, he, she, it, we, you, they
Perf. **will have picked**

I, he, she, it, we, you, they
will have been picked

IMPERATIVE MOOD

pick **be picked**

SUBJUNCTIVE MOOD

Pres. if I, he, she, it,
we, you, they **pick**

if I, he, she, it,
we, you, they **be picked**

Past if I, he, she, it,
we, you, they **picked**

if I, he, she, it,
we, you, they **were picked**

Fut. if I, he, she, it,
we, you, they **should pick**

if I, he, she, it,
we, you, they **should be picked**

Transitive and intransitive.

We picked several pounds of strawberries.
He was picked to win by most of the experts.

place
(active voice)

be placed
(passive voice)

INDICATIVE MOOD

Pres.	I, we, you, they **place**	I **am placed**
		we, you, they **are placed**
	he, she, it **places**	he, she, it **is placed**
Pres.	I **am placing**	I **am being placed**
Prog.	we, you, they **are placing**	we, you, they **are being placed**
	he, she, it **is placing**	he, she, it **is being placed**
Pres.	I, we, you, they **do place**	I, we, you, they **do get placed**
Int.	he, she, it **does place**	he, she, it **does get placed**
Fut.	I, he, she, it,	I, he, she, it,
	we, you, they **will place**	we, you, they **will be placed**
Past	I, he, she, it,	I, he, she, it **was placed**
	we, you, they **placed**	we, you, they **were placed**
Past	I, he, she, it **was placing**	I, he, she, it **was being placed**
Prog.	we, you, they **were placing**	we, you, they **were being placed**
Past	I, he, she, it,	I, he, she, it,
Int.	we, you, they **did place**	we, you, they **did get placed**
Pres.	I, we, you, they **have placed**	I, we, you, they **have been placed**
Perf.	he, she, it **has placed**	he, she, it **has been placed**
Past	I, he, she, it,	I, he, she, it,
Perf.	we, you, they **had placed**	we, you, they **had been placed**
Fut.	I, he, she, it, we, you, they	I, he, she, it, we, you, they
Perf.	**will have placed**	**will have been placed**

IMPERATIVE MOOD

place

be placed

SUBJUNCTIVE MOOD

Pres.	if I, he, she, it,	if I, he, she, it,
	we, you, they **place**	we, you, they **be placed**
Past	if I, he, she, it,	if I, he, she, it,
	we, you, they **placed**	we, you, they **were placed**
Fut.	if I, he, she, it,	if I, he, she, it,
	we, you, they **should place**	we, you, they **should be placed**

Transitive and intransitive.

We are placing our bets on the best horse.
They placed their boots in their lockers.
The stockings were placed by the chimney with care.

P

| plan
(active voice) | PRINCIPAL PARTS: **plans, planning,**
planned, planned | be planned
(passive voice) |

INDICATIVE MOOD

Pres.	I, we, you, they **plan** he, she, it **plans**	I **am planned** we, you, they **are planned** he, she, it **is planned**
Pres. *Prog.*	I **am planning** we, you, they **are planning** he, she, it **is planning**	I **am being planned** we, you, they **are being planned** he, she, it **is being planned**
Pres. *Int.*	I, we, you, they **do plan** he, she, it **does plan**	I, we, you, they **do get planned** he, she, it **does get planned**
Fut.	I, he, she, it, we, you, they **will plan**	I, he, she, it, we, you, they **will be planned**
Past	I, he, she, it, we, you, they **planned**	I, he, she, it **was planned** we, you, they **were planned**
Past *Prog.*	I, he, she, it **was planning** we, you, they **were planning**	I, he, she, it **was being planned** we, you, they **were being planned**
Past *Int.*	I, he, she, it, we, you, they **did plan**	I, he, she, it, we, you, they **did get planned**
Pres. *Perf.*	I, we, you, they **have planned** he, she, it **has planned**	I, we, you, they **have been planned** he, she, it **has been planned**
Past *Perf.*	I, he, she, it, we, you, they **had planned**	I, he, she, it, we, you, they **had been planned**
Fut. *Perf.*	I, he, she, it, we, you, they **will have planned**	I, he, she, it, we, you, they **will have been planned**

IMPERATIVE MOOD

plan	**be planned**

SUBJUNCTIVE MOOD

Pres.	if I, he, she, it, we, you, they **plan**	if I, he, she, it, we, you, they **be planned**
Past	if I, he, she, it, we, you, they **planned**	if I, he, she, it, we, you, they **were planned**
Fut.	if I, he, she, it, we, you, they **should plan**	if I, he, she, it, we, you, they **should be planned**

Transitive and intransitive.

Are you planning for the next snowstorm?
They planned the party as a complete surprise.
The meeting was planned months ago.

play
(active voice)

PRINCIPAL PARTS: **plays, playing,
played, played**

be played
(passive voice)

INDICATIVE MOOD

Pres.	I, we, you, they **play**	I **am played**
		we, you, they **are played**
	he, she, it **plays**	he, she, it **is played**
Pres.	I **am playing**	I **am being played**
Prog.	we, you, they **are playing**	we, you, they **are being played**
	he, she, it **is playing**	he, she, it **is being played**
Pres.	I, we, you, they **do play**	I, we, you, they **do get played**
Int.	he, she, it **does play**	he, she, it **does get played**
Fut.	I, he, she, it,	I, he, she, it,
	we, you, they **will play**	we, you, they **will be played**
Past	I, he, she, it,	I, he, she, it **was played**
	we, you, they **played**	we, you, they **were played**
Past	I, he, she, it **was playing**	I, he, she, it **was being played**
Prog.	we, you, they **were playing**	we, you, they **were being played**
Past	I, he, she, it,	I, he, she, it,
Int.	we, you, they **did play**	we, you, they **did get played**
Pres.	I, we, you, they **have played**	I, we, you, they **have been played**
Perf.	he, she, it **has played**	he, she, it **has been played**
Past	I, he, she, it,	I, he, she, it,
Perf.	we, you, they **had played**	we, you, they **had been played**
Fut.	I, he, she, it, we, you, they	I, he, she, it, we, you, they
Perf.	**will have played**	**will have been played**

P

IMPERATIVE MOOD

play **be played**

SUBJUNCTIVE MOOD

Pres.	if I, he, she, it,	if I, he, she, it,
	we, you, they **play**	we, you, they **be played**
Past	if I, he, she, it,	if I, he, she, it,
	we, you, they **played**	we, you, they **were played**
Fut.	if I, he, she, it,	if I, he, she, it,
	we, you, they **should play**	we, you, they **should be played**

Transitive and intransitive.

*Mother always played the piano at our family gatherings.
There is a growing market for games that have already
been played.*

AN ESSENTIAL
55 VERB

AN ESSENTIAL 55 VERB

play

She plays computer games on weekends.

Do you play in an orchestra?

The musical is playing on Broadway.

The games were played in the rain.

Who played that role in the movie?

You will play in the next period.

He never got to play on a team.

Play a song for us.

What's playing this evening?

He plays both the piano and guitar.

Words and expressions related to this verb

They are playing for high stakes.

Go play outside.

Let's play for keeps.

Play a simple little melody.

And the band played on.

He is playing with fire.

Please play back that song.

He is playing her for her money.

You should play up your previous experience.

He plays to win.

plead
(active voice)

PRINCIPAL PARTS: **pleads, pleading, pleaded/pled, pleaded/pled**

be pleaded/pled
(passive voice)

INDICATIVE MOOD

Pres.	I, we, you, they **plead**	I **am pleaded**
		we, you, they **are pleaded**
	he, she, it **pleads**	he, she, it **is pleaded**
Pres.	I **am pleading**	I **am being pleaded**
Prog.	we, you, they **are pleading**	we, you, they **are being pleaded**
	he, she, it **is pleading**	he, she, it **is being pleaded**
Pres.	I, we, you, they **do plead**	I, we, you, they **do get pleaded**
Int.	he, she, it **does plead**	he, she, it **does get pleaded**
Fut.	I, he, she, it,	I, he, she, it,
	we, you, they **will plead**	we, you, they **will be pleaded**
Past	I, he, she, it,	I, he, she, it **was pleaded**
	we, you, they **pleaded**	we, you, they **were pleaded**
Past	I, he, she, it **was pleading**	I, he, she, it **was being pleaded**
Prog.	we, you, they **were pleading**	we, you, they **were being pleaded**
Past	I, he, she, it,	I, he, she, it,
Int.	we, you, they **did plead**	we, you, they **did get pleaded**
Pres.	I, we, you, they **have pleaded**	I, we, you, they **have been pleaded**
Perf.	he, she, it **has pleaded**	he, she, it **has been pleaded**
Past	I, he, she, it,	I, he, she, it,
Perf.	we, you, they **had pleaded**	we, you, they **had been pleaded**
Fut.	I, he, she, it, we, you, they	I, he, she, it, we, you, they
Perf.	**will have pleaded**	**will have been pleaded**

IMPERATIVE MOOD

plead

be pleaded

SUBJUNCTIVE MOOD

Pres.	if I, he, she, it,	if I, he, she, it,
	we, you, they **plead**	we, you, they **be pleaded**
Past	if I, he, she, it,	if I, he, she, it,
	we, you, they **pleaded**	we, you, they **were pleaded**
Fut.	if I, he, she, it,	if I, he, she, it,
	we, you, they **should plead**	we, you, they **should be pleaded**

Intransitive and transitive. The *Oxford Dictionary* accepts the past tense and past participle form PLED as American English. *Merriam Webster's* and *Webster's* recognize the alternate spelling PLEAD.

We pleaded with her to stay home that evening.
His case was pleaded by a court-appointed attorney.

please (active voice)	PRINCIPAL PARTS: **pleases, pleasing,** **pleased, pleased**	be pleased (passive voice)

INDICATIVE MOOD

Pres.	I, we, you, they **please**	**I am pleased** we, you, they **are pleased**
	he, she, it **pleases**	he, she, it **is pleased**
Pres. *Prog.*	**I am pleasing** we, you, they **are pleasing** he, she, it **is pleasing**	**I am being pleased** we, you, they **are being pleased** he, she, it **is being pleased**
Pres. *Int.*	I, we, you, they **do please** he, she, it **does please**	I, we, you, they **do get pleased** he, she, it **does get pleased**
Fut.	I, he, she, it, we, you, they **will please**	I, he, she, it, we, you, they **will be pleased**
Past	I, he, she, it, we, you, they **pleased**	I, he, she, it **was pleased** we, you, they **were pleased**
Past *Prog.*	I, he, she, it **was pleasing** we, you, they **were pleasing**	I, he, she, it **was being pleased** we, you, they **were being pleased**
Past *Int.*	I, he, she, it, we, you, they **did please**	I, he, she, it, we, you, they **did get pleased**
Pres. *Perf.*	I, we, you, they **have pleased** he, she, it **has pleased**	I, we, you, they **have been pleased** he, she, it **has been pleased**
Past *Perf.*	I, he, she, it, we, you, they **had pleased**	I, he, she, it, we, you, they **had been pleased**
Fut. *Perf.*	I, he, she, it, we, you, they **will have pleased**	I, he, she, it, we, you, they **will have been pleased**

IMPERATIVE MOOD

please	**be pleased**

SUBJUNCTIVE MOOD

Pres.	if I, he, she, it, we, you, they **please**	if I, he, she, it, we, you, they **be pleased**
Past	if I, he, she, it, we, you, they **pleased**	if I, he, she, it, we, you, they **were pleased**
Fut.	if I, he, she, it, we, you, they **should please**	if I, he, she, it, we, you, they **should be pleased**

Transitive and intransitive.

That perfume is very pleasing to most men.
Your thoughtful gift of flowers pleased her immensely.
They were pleased by the large attendance.

point
(active voice)

be pointed
(passive voice)

INDICATIVE MOOD

Pres.	I, we, you, they **point**	I **am pointed**
		we, you, they **are pointed**
	he, she, it **points**	he, she, it **is pointed**
Pres.	I **am pointing**	I **am being pointed**
Prog.	we, you, they **are pointing**	we, you, they **are being pointed**
	he, she, it **is pointing**	he, she, it **is being pointed**
Pres.	I, we, you, they **do point**	I, we, you, they **do get pointed**
Int.	he, she, it **does point**	he, she, it **does get pointed**
Fut.	I, he, she, it,	I, he, she, it,
	we, you, they **will point**	we, you, they **will be pointed**
Past	I, he, she, it,	I, he, she, it **was pointed**
	we, you, they **pointed**	we, you, they **were pointed**
Past	I, he, she, it **was pointing**	I, he, she, it **was being pointed**
Prog.	we, you, they **were pointing**	we, you, they **were being pointed**
Past	I, he, she, it,	I, he, she, it,
Int.	we, you, they **did point**	we, you, they **did get pointed**
Pres.	I, we, you, they **have pointed**	I, we, you, they **have been pointed**
Perf.	he, she, it **has pointed**	he, she, it **has been pointed**
Past	I, he, she, it,	I, he, she, it,
Perf.	we, you, they **had pointed**	we, you, they **had been pointed**
Fut.	I, he, she, it, we, you, they	I, he, she, it, we, you, they
Perf.	**will have pointed**	**will have been pointed**

IMPERATIVE MOOD

point   **be pointed**

SUBJUNCTIVE MOOD

Pres.	if I, he, she, it,	if I, he, she, it,
	we, you, they **point**	we, you, they **be pointed**
Past	if I, he, she, it,	if I, he, she, it,
	we, you, they **pointed**	we, you, they **were pointed**
Fut.	if I, he, she, it,	if I, he, she, it,
	we, you, they **should point**	we, you, they **should be pointed**

Transitive and intransitive.

The passerby pointed us in the right direction.
Was his gun pointed at you?

325

precede
(active voice)

PRINCIPAL PARTS: **precedes, preceding, preceded, preceded**

be preceded
(passive voice)

INDICATIVE MOOD

Pres.	I, we, you, they **precede**	I **am preceded**
		we, you, they **are preceded**
	he, she, it **precedes**	he, she, it **is preceded**
Pres.	I **am preceding**	I **am being preceded**
Prog.	we, you, they **are preceding**	we, you, they **are being preceded**
	he, she, it **is preceding**	he, she, it **is being preceded**
Pres.	I, we, you, they **do precede**	I, we, you, they **do get preceded**
Int.	he, she, it **does precede**	he, she, it **does get preceded**
Fut.	I, he, she, it,	I, he, she, it,
	we, you, they **will precede**	we, you, they **will be preceded**
Past	I, he, she, it,	I, he, she, it **was preceded**
	we, you, they **preceded**	we, you, they **were preceded**
Past	I, he, she, it **was preceding**	I, he, she, it **was being preceded**
Prog.	we, you, they **were preceding**	we, you, they **were being preceded**
Past	I, he, she, it,	I, he, she, it,
Int.	we, you, they **did precede**	we, you, they **did get preceded**
Pres.	I, we, you, they **have preceded**	I, we, you, they **have been preceded**
Perf.	he, she, it **has preceded**	he, she, it **has been preceded**
Past	I, he, she, it,	I, he, she, it,
Perf.	we, you, they **had preceded**	we, you, they **had been preceded**
Fut.	I, he, she, it, we, you, they	I, he, she, it, we, you, they
Perf.	**will have preceded**	**will have been preceded**

IMPERATIVE MOOD

precede   **be preceded**

SUBJUNCTIVE MOOD

Pres.	if I, he, she, it,	if I, he, she, it,
	we, you, they **precede**	we, you, they **be preceded**
Past	if I, he, she, it,	if I, he, she, it,
	we, you, they **preceded**	we, you, they **were preceded**
Fut.	if I, he, she, it,	if I, he, she, it,
	we, you, they **should precede**	we, you, they **should be preceded**

Transitive and intransitive.

We are preceding the dancers on the program.
In France the main dish often preceded the salad.
His arrival was preceded by an advance team of agents.

prefer
(active voice)

be preferred
(passive voice)

INDICATIVE MOOD

Pres.	I, we, you, they **prefer**	I **am preferred**
		we, you, they **are preferred**
	he, she, it **prefers**	he, she, it **is preferred**
Pres.	I **am preferring**	I **am being preferred**
Prog.	we, you, they **are preferring**	we, you, they **are being preferred**
	he, she, it **is preferring**	he, she, it **is being preferred**
Pres.	I, we, you, they **do prefer**	I, we, you, they **do get preferred**
Int.	he, she, it **does prefer**	he, she, it **does get preferred**
Fut.	I, he, she, it,	I, he, she, it,
	we, you, they **will prefer**	we, you, they **will be preferred**
Past	I, he, she, it,	I, he, she, it **was preferred**
	we, you, they **preferred**	we, you, they **were preferred**
Past	I, he, she, it **was preferring**	I, he, she, it **was being preferred**
Prog.	we, you, they **were preferring**	we, you, they **were being preferred**
Past	I, he, she, it,	I, he, she, it,
Int.	we, you, they **did prefer**	we, you, they **did get preferred**
Pres.	I, we, you, they **have preferred**	I, we, you, they **have been preferred**
Perf.	he, she, it **has preferred**	he, she, it **has been preferred**
Past	I, he, she, it,	I, he, she, it,
Perf.	we, you, they **had preferred**	we, you, they **had been preferred**
Fut.	I, he, she, it, we, you, they	I, he, she, it, we, you, they
Perf.	**will have preferred**	**will have been preferred**

IMPERATIVE MOOD

prefer **be preferred**

SUBJUNCTIVE MOOD

Pres.	if I, he, she, it,	if I, he, she, it,
	we, you, they **prefer**	we, you, they **be preferred**
Past	if I, he, she, it,	if I, he, she, it,
	we, you, they **preferred**	we, you, they **were preferred**
Fut.	if I, he, she, it,	if I, he, she, it,
	we, you, they **should prefer**	we, you, they **should be preferred**

Is anyone preferring the red wine?
We preferred the late seating for dinner.
This brand is preferred over all others.

prepare
(active voice)

PRINCIPAL PARTS: **prepares, preparing, prepared, prepared**

be prepared
(passive voice)

INDICATIVE MOOD

Pres.	I, we, you, they **prepare**	I **am prepared** we, you, they **are prepared**
	he, she, it **prepares**	he, she, it **is prepared**
Pres. *Prog.*	I **am preparing** we, you, they **are preparing** he, she, it **is preparing**	I **am being prepared** we, you, they **are being prepared** he, she, it **is being prepared**
Pres. *Int.*	I, we, you, they **do prepare** he, she, it **does prepare**	I, we, you, they **do get prepared** he, she, it **does get prepared**
Fut.	I, he, she, it, we, you, they **will prepare**	I, he, she, it, we, you, they **will be prepared**
Past	I, he, she, it, we, you, they **prepared**	I, he, she, it **was prepared** we, you, they **were prepared**
Past *Prog.*	I, he, she, it **was preparing** we, you, they **were preparing**	I, he, she, it **was being prepared** we, you, they **were being prepared**
Past *Int.*	I, he, she, it, we, you, they **did prepare**	I, he, she, it, we, you, they **did get prepared**
Pres. *Perf.*	I, we, you, they **have prepared** he, she, it **has prepared**	I, we, you, they **have been prepared** he, she, it **has been prepared**
Past *Perf.*	I, he, she, it, we, you, they **had prepared**	I, he, she, it, we, you, they **had been prepared**
Fut. *Perf.*	I, he, she, it, we, you, they **will have prepared**	I, he, she, it, we, you, they **will have been prepared**

IMPERATIVE MOOD

prepare   **be prepared**

SUBJUNCTIVE MOOD

Pres.	if I, he, she, it, we, you, they **prepare**	if I, he, she, it, we, you, they **be prepared**
Past	if I, he, she, it, we, you, they **prepared**	if I, he, she, it, we, you, they **were prepared**
Fut.	if I, he, she, it, we, you, they **should prepare**	if I, he, she, it, we, you, they **should be prepared**

Transitive and intransitive.

Is anyone preparing a gift for him?
They prepared all evening for their exams.
Dinner was prepared by two famous chefs.

present
(active voice)

be presented
(passive voice)

INDICATIVE MOOD

Pres.	I, we, you, they **present**	I **am presented**
		we, you, they **are presented**
	he, she, it **presents**	he, she, it **is presented**
Pres.	I **am presenting**	I **am being presented**
Prog.	we, you, they **are presenting**	we, you, they **are being presented**
	he, she, it **is presenting**	he, she, it **is being presented**
Pres.	I, we, you, they **do present**	I, we, you, they **do get presented**
Int.	he, she, it **does present**	he, she, it **does get presented**
Fut.	I, he, she, it,	I, he, she, it,
	we, you, they **will present**	we, you, they **will be presented**
Past	I, he, she, it,	I, he, she, it **was presented**
	we, you, they **presented**	we, you, they **were presented**
Past	I, he, she, it **was presenting**	I, he, she, it **was being presented**
Prog.	we, you, they **were presenting**	we, you, they **were being presented**
Past	I, he, she, it,	I, he, she, it,
Int.	we, you, they **did present**	we, you, they **did get presented**
Pres.	I, we, you, they **have presented**	I, we, you, they **have been presented**
Perf.	he, she, it **has presented**	he, she, it **has been presented**
Past	I, he, she, it,	I, he, she, it,
Perf.	we, you, they **had presented**	we, you, they **had been presented**
Fut.	I, he, she, it, we, you, they	I, he, she, it, we, you, they
Perf.	**will have presented**	**will have been presented**

IMPERATIVE MOOD

present   **be presented**

SUBJUNCTIVE MOOD

Pres.	if I, he, she, it,	if I, he, she, it,
	we, you, they **present**	we, you, they **be presented**
Past	if I, he, she, it,	if I, he, she, it,
	we, you, they **presented**	we, you, they **were presented**
Fut.	if I, he, she, it,	if I, he, she, it,
	we, you, they **should present**	we, you, they **should be presented**

They presented their credentials to the authorities.
The trophies were presented at the awards banquet.

prevent
(active voice)

be prevented
(passive voice)

INDICATIVE MOOD

Pres.	I, we, you, they **prevent**	I **am prevented**
		we, you, they **are prevented**
	he, she, it **prevents**	he, she, it **is prevented**
Pres.	I **am preventing**	I **am being prevented**
Prog.	we, you, they **are preventing**	we, you, they **are being prevented**
	he, she, it **is preventing**	he, she, it **is being prevented**
Pres.	I, we, you, they **do prevent**	I, we, you, they **do get prevented**
Int.	he, she, it **does prevent**	he, she, it **does get prevented**
Fut.	I, he, she, it,	I, he, she, it,
	we, you, they **will prevent**	we, you, they **will be prevented**
Past	I, he, she, it,	I, he, she, it **was prevented**
	we, you, they **prevented**	we, you, they **were prevented**
Past	I, he, she, it **was preventing**	I, he, she, it **was being prevented**
Prog.	we, you, they **were preventing**	we, you, they **were being prevented**
Past	I, he, she, it,	I, he, she, it,
Int.	we, you, they **did prevent**	we, you, they **did get prevented**
Pres.	I, we, you, they **have prevented**	I, we, you, they **have been prevented**
Perf.	he, she, it **has prevented**	he, she, it **has been prevented**
Past	I, he, she, it,	I, he, she, it,
Perf.	we, you, they **had prevented**	we, you, they **had been prevented**
Fut.	I, he, she, it, we, you, they	I, he, she, it, we, you, they
Perf.	**will have prevented**	**will have been prevented**

IMPERATIVE MOOD

prevent   **be prevented**

SUBJUNCTIVE MOOD

Pres.	if I, he, she, it,	if I, he, she, it,
	we, you, they **prevent**	we, you, they **be prevented**
Past	if I, he, she, it,	if I, he, she, it,
	we, you, they **prevented**	we, you, they **were prevented**
Fut.	if I, he, she, it,	if I, he, she, it,
	we, you, they **should prevent**	we, you, they **should be prevented**

Transitive and intransitive.

A quick response prevented any further damage.
Most fires could be prevented.

INDICATIVE MOOD

Pres.　I, we, you, they **proceed**

　　　he, she, it **proceeds**

Pres.　I **am proceeding**
Prog.　we, you, they **are proceeding**
　　　he, she, it **is proceeding**

Pres.　I, we, you, they **do proceed**
Int.　he, she, it **does proceed**

Fut.　I, he, she, it,
　　　we, you, they **will proceed**

Past　I, he, she, it,
　　　we, you, they **proceeded**

Past　I, he, she, it **was proceeding**
Prog.　we, you, they **were proceeding**

Past　I, he, she, it,
Int.　we, you, they **did proceed**

Pres.　I, we, you, they **have proceeded**
Perf.　he, she, it **has proceeded**

Past　I, he, she, it,
Perf.　we, you, they **had proceeded**

Fut.　I, he, she, it, we, you, they
Perf.　**will have proceeded**

IMPERATIVE MOOD

proceed

SUBJUNCTIVE MOOD

Pres.　if I, he, she, it,
　　　we, you, they **proceed**

Past　if I, he, she, it,
　　　we, you, they **proceeded**

Fut.　if I, he, she, it,
　　　we, you, they **should proceed**

We are proceeding very cautiously.
His points proceeded logically one from the other.

331

produce
(active voice)

be produced
(passive voice)

INDICATIVE MOOD

Pres.	I, we, you, they **produce**	I **am produced** we, you, they **are produced**
	he, she, it **produces**	he, she, it **is produced**
Pres. *Prog.*	I **am producing** we, you, they **are producing** he, she, it **is producing**	I **am being produced** we, you, they **are being produced** he, she, it **is being produced**
Pres. *Int.*	I, we, you, they **do produce** he, she, it **does produce**	I, we, you, they **do get produced** he, she, it **does get produced**
Fut.	I, he, she, it, we, you, they **will produce**	I, he, she, it, we, you, they **will be produced**
Past	I, he, she, it, we, you, they **produced**	I, he, she, it **was produced** we, you, they **were produced**
Past *Prog.*	I, he, she, it **was producing** we, you, they **were producing**	I, he, she, it **was being produced** we, you, they **were being produced**
Past *Int.*	I, he, she, it, we, you, they **did produce**	I, he, she, it, we, you, they **did get produced**
Pres. *Perf.*	I, we, you, they **have produced** he, she, it **has produced**	I, we, you, they **have been produced** he, she, it **has been produced**
Past *Perf.*	I, he, she, it, we, you, they **had produced**	I, he, she, it, we, you, they **had been produced**
Fut. *Perf.*	I, he, she, it, we, you, they **will have produced**	I, he, she, it, we, you, they **will have been produced**

IMPERATIVE MOOD

produce   **be produced**

SUBJUNCTIVE MOOD

Pres.	if I, he, she, it, we, you, they **produce**	if I, he, she, it, we, you, they **be produced**
Past	if I, he, she, it, we, you, they **produced**	if I, he, she, it, we, you, they **were produced**
Fut.	if I, he, she, it, we, you, they **should produce**	if I, he, she, it, we, you, they **should be produced**

Transitive and intransitive.

They are producing our new line of sporting goods.
The harvest produced a record crop of lettuce.
These cell phones are produced in the United Kingdom.

program
(active voice)

be programmed/
programed
(passive voice)

INDICATIVE MOOD

Pres.	I, we, you, they **program**	I **am programmed**
		we, you, they **are programmed**
	he, she, it **programs**	he, she, it **is programmed**
Pres.	I **am programming**	I **am being programmed**
Prog.	we, you, they **are programming**	we, you, they **are being programmed**
	he, she, it **is programming**	he, she, it **is being programmed**
Pres.	I, we, you, they **do program**	I, we, you, they **do get programmed**
Int.	he, she, it **does program**	he, she, it **does get programmed**
Fut.	I, he, she, it,	I, he, she, it,
	we, you, they **will program**	we, you, they **will be programmed**
Past	I, he, she, it,	I, he, she, it **was programmed**
	we, you, they **programmed**	we, you, they **were programmed**
Past	I, he, she, it **was programming**	I, he, she, it **was being programmed**
Prog.	we, you, they **were programming**	we, you, they **were being programmed**
Past	I, he, she, it,	I, he, she, it, we, you, they
Int.	we, you, they **did program**	**did get programmed**
Pres.	I, we, you, they **have programmed**	I, we, you, they **have been programmed**
Perf.	he, she, it **has programmed**	he, she, it **has been programmed**
Past	I, he, she, it,	I, he, she, it, we, you, they
Perf.	we, you, they **had programmed**	**had been programmed**
Fut.	I, he, she, it, we, you, they	I, he, she, it, we, you, they
Perf.	**will have programmed**	**will have been programmed**

IMPERATIVE MOOD

program   **be programmed**

SUBJUNCTIVE MOOD

Pres.	if I, he, she, it,	if I, he, she, it,
	we, you, they **program**	we, you, they **be programmed**
Past	if I, he, she, it,	if I, he, she, it,
	we, you, they **programmed**	we, you, they **were programmed**
Fut.	if I, he, she, it,	if I, he, she, it, we, you, they
	we, you, they **should program**	**should be programmed**

The British variant of this word can also be spelled PROGRAMME. The spelling with the single "m" is accepted in American English by *American Heritage* and *Merriam Webster's Dictionaries*.

She is programming our new home entertainment system.
He programmed their computer after it was repaired.
The rocket was programmed to explode if it strayed off course.

prove
(active voice)

be proved/proven
(passive voice)

INDICATIVE MOOD

Pres.	I, we, you, they **prove**	I **am proved** we, you, they **are proved**
	he, she, it **proves**	he, she, it **is proved**
Pres. *Prog.*	I **am proving** we, you, they **are proving** he, she, it **is proving**	I **am being proved** we, you, they **are being proved** he, she, it **is being proved**
Pres. *Int.*	I, we, you, they **do prove** he, she, it **does prove**	I, we, you, they **do get proved** he, she, it **does get proved**
Fut.	I, he, she, it, we, you, they **will prove**	I, he, she, it, we, you, they **will be proved**
Past	I, he, she, it, we, you, they **proved**	I, he, she, it **was proved** we, you, they **were proved**
Past *Prog.*	I, he, she, it **was proving** we, you, they **were proving**	I, he, she, it **was being proved** we, you, they **were being proved**
Past *Int.*	I, he, she, it, we, you, they **did prove**	I, he, she, it, we, you, they **did get proved**
Pres. *Perf.*	I, we, you, they **have proved** he, she, it **has proved**	I, we, you, they **have been proved** he, she, it **has been proved**
Past *Perf.*	I, he, she, it, we, you, they **had proved**	I, he, she, it, we, you, they **had been proved**
Fut. *Perf.*	I, he, she, it, we, you, they **will have proved**	I, he, she, it, we, you, they **will have been proved**

IMPERATIVE MOOD

prove

be proved

SUBJUNCTIVE MOOD

Pres.	if I, he, she, it, we, you, they **prove**	if I, he, she, it, we, you, they **be proved**
Past	if I, he, she, it, we, you, they **proved**	if I, he, she, it, we, you, they **were proved**
Fut.	if I, he, she, it, we, you, they **should prove**	if I, he, she, it, we, you, they **should be proved**

Transitive and intransitive.

We are proving our abilities on the playing field.
They proved that the leak was the contractor's responsibility.
This has been proven over and over again.

334

provide
(active voice)

be provided
(passive voice)

INDICATIVE MOOD

Pres.   I, we, you, they **provide**   I **am provided**
     we, you, they **are provided**

he, she, it **provides**   he, she, it **is provided**

Pres.   I **am providing**   I **am being provided**
Prog.   we, you, they **are providing**   we, you, they **are being provided**
     he, she, it **is providing**   he, she, it **is being provided**

Pres.   I, we, you, they **do provide**   I, we, you, they **do get provided**
Int.   he, she, it **does provide**   he, she, it **does get provided**

Fut.   I, he, she, it,   I, he, she, it,
     we, you, they **will provide**   we, you, they **will be provided**

Past   I, he, she, it,   I, he, she, it **was provided**
     we, you, they **provided**   we, you, they **were provided**

Past   I, he, she, it **was providing**   I, he, she, it **was being provided**
Prog.   we, you, they **were providing**   we, you, they **were being provided**

Past   I, he, she, it,   I, he, she, it,
Int.   we, you, they **did provide**   we, you, they **did get provided**

Pres.   I, we, you, they **have provided**   I, we, you, they **have been provided**
Perf.   he, she, it **has provided**   he, she, it **has been provided**

Past   I, he, she, it,   I, he, she, it,
Perf.   we, you, they **had provided**   we, you, they **had been provided**

Fut.   I, he, she, it, we, you, they   I, he, she, it, we, you, they
Perf.   **will have provided**   **will have been provided**

IMPERATIVE MOOD

provide   **be provided**

SUBJUNCTIVE MOOD

Pres.   if I, he, she, it,   if I, he, she, it,
     we, you, they **provide**   we, you, they **be provided**

Past   if I, he, she, it,   if I, he, she, it,
     we, you, they **provided**   we, you, they **were provided**

Fut.   if I, he, she, it,   if I, he, she, it,
     we, you, they **should provide**   we, you, they **should be provided**

Transitive and intransitive.

The school is providing all the necessary financial support.
They provided airfare and hotel accommodations.
Pens and paper are provided in your welcome kits.

AN ESSENTIAL
55 VERB

Examples

The college provides medical insurance.

Do they provide for emergencies?

I will provide the snacks.

Maps and directions have been provided.

Blankets were provided by the Red Cross.

He provides for his sick parents.

The school children are provided with pencil and paper.

We haven't provided for the unexpected.

Provide for the poor.

What are you providing for the picnic?

Words and expressions related to this verb

Lunch will be provided.

Their needs were well provided for.

Who provides your Internet connection?

Meals are no longer provided on airlines.

No instructions were provided.

Do you provide towels?

The state must provide for the common defense.

You have to believe that the universe will provide.

Each day provides its own gifts.

His education provided him with wonderful opportunities.

pull
(active voice)

be pulled
(passive voice)

INDICATIVE MOOD

Pres.	I, we, you, they **pull**	**I am pulled**
		we, you, they **are pulled**
	he, she, it **pulls**	he, she, it **is pulled**
Pres.	**I am pulling**	I am being pulled
Prog.	we, you, they **are pulling**	we, you, they **are being pulled**
	he, she, it **is pulling**	he, she, it **is being pulled**
Pres.	I, we, you, they **do pull**	I, we, you, they **do get pulled**
Int.	he, she, it **does pull**	he, she, it **does get pulled**
Fut.	I, he, she, it,	I, he, she, it,
	we, you, they **will pull**	we, you, they **will be pulled**
Past	I, he, she, it,	I, he, she, it **was pulled**
	we, you, they **pulled**	we, you, they **were pulled**
Past	I, he, she, it **was pulling**	I, he, she, it **was being pulled**
Prog.	we, you, they **were pulling**	we, you, they **were being pulled**
Past	I, he, she, it,	I, he, she, it,
Int.	we, you, they **did pull**	we, you, they **did get pulled**
Pres.	I, we, you, they **have pulled**	I, we, you, they **have been pulled**
Perf.	he, she, it **has pulled**	he, she, it **has been pulled**
Past	I, he, she, it,	I, he, she, it,
Perf.	we, you, they **had pulled**	we, you, they **had been pulled**
Fut.	I, he, she, it, we, you, they	I, he, she, it, we, you, they
Perf.	**will have pulled**	**will have been pulled**

IMPERATIVE MOOD

pull   **be pulled**

SUBJUNCTIVE MOOD

Pres.	if I, he, she, it,	if I, he, she, it,
	we, you, they **pull**	we, you, they **be pulled**
Past	if I, he, she, it,	if I, he, she, it,
	we, you, they **pulled**	we, you, they **were pulled**
Fut.	if I, he, she, it,	if I, he, she, it,
	we, you, they **should pull**	we, you, they **should be pulled**

Transitive and intransitive.

He pulled the team together at the last minute.
They were being pulled in opposite directions.

PRINCIPAL PARTS: **puts, putting, put, put**

INDICATIVE MOOD

Pres.	I, we, you, they **put**	I **am put**
		we, you, they **are put**
	he, she, it **puts**	he, she, it **is put**
Pres. *Prog.*	I **am putting**	I **am being put**
	we, you, they **are putting**	we, you, they **are being put**
	he, she, it **is putting**	he, she, it **is being put**
Pres. *Int.*	I, we, you, they **do put**	I, we, you, they **do get put**
	he, she, it **does put**	he, she, it **does get put**
Fut.	I, he, she, it, we, you, they **will put**	I, he, she, it, we, you, they **will be put**
Past	I, he, she, it, we, you, they **put**	I, he, she, it **was put** we, you, they **were put**
Past *Prog.*	I, he, she, it **was putting** we, you, they **were putting**	I, he, she, it **was being put** we, you, they **were being put**
Past *Int.*	I, he, she, it, we, you, they **did put**	I, he, she, it, we, you, they **did get put**
Pres. *Perf.*	I, we, you, they **have put** he, she, it **has put**	I, we, you, they **have been put** he, she, it **has been put**
Past *Perf.*	I, he, she, it, we, you, they **had put**	I, he, she, it, we, you, they **had been put**
Fut. *Perf.*	I, he, she, it, we, you, they **will have put**	I, he, she, it, we, you, they **will have been put**

IMPERATIVE MOOD

put   **be put**

SUBJUNCTIVE MOOD

Pres.	if I, he, she, it, we, you, they **put**	if I, he, she, it, we, you, they **be put**
Past	if I, he, she, it, we, you, they **put**	if I, he, she, it, we, you, they **were put**
Fut.	if I, he, she, it, we, you, they **should put**	if I, he, she, it, we, you, they **should be put**

Transitive and intransitive.

She always puts the potatoes in the pan with the meat.
This contest is putting us on the map.
He put his money in your wallet.
The diploma was put on the wall next to her certificate of merit.

AN ESSENTIAL 55 VERB

put

Examples

I put my money in the bank.

He puts his credit cards in his wallet.

He put his shirt in the suitcase.

Who put the butter in the refrigerator?

Who will put the candles on the cake?

He was put in prison for his crime.

Where did I put my eyeglasses?

They are putting the last coat of paint on today.

Just put it anywhere.

In which classes should you have been put?

Words and expressions related to this verb

Do not put off to tomorrow what you can do today.

Put your hat on.

We were put off by his explanation.

He must put in forty hours a week.

Put out the trash.

I was put on hold by the operator.

Put your money where your mouth is.

Firemen put their lives on the line.

I can no longer put up with him.

She is trying to put something over on our client.

Put it down in writing.

P

quarrel

INDICATIVE MOOD

Pres.   I, we, you, they **quarrel**

he, she, it **quarrels**

Pres.   I **am quarreling**
Prog.   we, you, they **are quarreling**
he, she, it **is quarreling**

Pres.   I, we, you, they **do quarrel**
Int.   he, she, it **does quarrel**

Fut.   I, he, she, it,
we, you, they **will quarrel**

Past   I, he, she, it,
we, you, they **quarreled**

Past   I, he, she, it **was quarreling**
Prog.   we, you, they **were quarreling**

Past   I, he, she, it,
Int.   we, you, they **did quarrel**

Pres.   I, we, you, they **have quarreled**
Perf.   he, she, it **has quarreled**

Past   I, he, she, it,
Perf.   we, you, they **had quarreled**

Fut.   I, he, she, it, we, you, they
Perf.   **will have quarreled**

IMPERATIVE MOOD

quarrel

SUBJUNCTIVE MOOD

Pres.   if I, he, she, it,
we, you, they **quarrel**

Past   if I, he, she, it,
we, you, they **quarreled**

Fut.   if I, he, she, it,
we, you, they **should quarrel**

The *Oxford Dictionary* prefers the double "ll" in the present and past participles: QUARRELLING, QUARRELLED.

The couple is always quarreling.
They quarreled over the smallest details.
This is not the first time we have quarreled.

quit
(active voice)

be quit/quitted
(passive voice)

INDICATIVE MOOD

Pres.	I, we, you, they **quit**	I **am quit**
we, you, they **are quit**
	he, she, it **quits**	he, she, it **is quit**
Pres.
Prog.	I **am quitting**
we, you, they **are quitting**
he, she, it **is quitting**	I **am being quit**
we, you, they **are being quit**
he, she, it **is being quit**
Pres.
Int.	I, we, you, they **do quit**
he, she, it **does quit**	I, we, you, they **do get quit**
he, she, it **does get quit**
Fut.	I, he, she, it,
we, you, they **will quit**	I, he, she, it,
we, you, they **will be quit**
Past	I, he, she, it,
we, you, they **quit**	I, he, she, it **was quit**
we, you, they **were quit**
Past
Prog.	I, he, she, it **was quitting**
we, you, they **were quitting**	I, he, she, it **was being quit**
we, you, they **were being quit**
Past
Int.	I, he, she, it,
we, you, they **did quit**	I, he, she, it,
we, you, they **did get quit**
Pres.
Perf.	I, we, you, they **have quit**
he, she, it **has quit**	I, we, you, they **have been quit**
he, she, it **has been quit**
Past
Perf.	I, he, she, it,
we, you, they **had quit**	I, he, she, it,
we, you, they **had been quit**
Fut.
Perf.	I, he, she, it, we, you, they
will have quit	I, he, she, it, we, you, they
will have been quit

IMPERATIVE MOOD

quit | **be quit**

SUBJUNCTIVE MOOD

Pres.	if I, he, she, it,
we, you, they **quit**	if I, he, she, it,
we, you, they **be quit**
Past	if I, he, she, it,
we, you, they **quit**	if I, he, she, it,
we, you, they **were quit**
Fut.	if I, he, she, it,
we, you, they **should quit**	if I, he, she, it,
we, you, they **should be quit**

Transitive and intransitive.

He quits smoking once a year.
We are quitting the club at the end of the month.
Last year he quit for two months.
The job was quit on the last day of the year.

Q

341

quiz
(active voice)

be quizzed
(passive voice)

INDICATIVE MOOD

Pres.	I, we, you, they **quiz**	I **am quizzed**
		we, you, they **are quizzed**
	he, she, it **quizzes**	he, she, it **is quizzed**
Pres.	I **am quizzing**	I **am being quizzed**
Prog.	we, you, they **are quizzing**	we, you, they **are being quizzed**
	he, she, it **is quizzing**	he, she, it **is being quizzed**
Pres.	I, we, you, they **do quiz**	I, we, you, they **do get quizzed**
Int.	he, she, it **does quiz**	he, she, it **does get quizzed**
Fut.	I, he, she, it,	I, he, she, it,
	we, you, they **will quiz**	we, you, they **will be quizzed**
Past	I, he, she, it,	I, he, she, it **was quizzed**
	we, you, they **quizzed**	we, you, they **were quizzed**
Past	I, he, she, it **was quizzing**	I, he, she, it **was being quizzed**
Prog.	we, you, they **were quizzing**	we, you, they **were being quizzed**
Past	I, he, she, it,	I, he, she, it,
Int.	we, you, they **did quiz**	we, you, they **did get quizzed**
Pres.	I, we, you, they **have quizzed**	I, we, you, they **have been quizzed**
Perf.	he, she, it **has quizzed**	he, she, it **has been quizzed**
Past	I, he, she, it,	I, he, she, it,
Perf.	we, you, they **had quizzed**	we, you, they **had been quizzed**
Fut.	I, he, she, it, we, you, they	I, he, she, it, we, you, they
Perf.	**will have quizzed**	**will have been quizzed**

IMPERATIVE MOOD

quiz   **be quizzed**

SUBJUNCTIVE MOOD

Pres.	if I, he, she, it,	if I, he, she, it,
	we, you, they **quiz**	we, you, they **be quizzed**
Past	if I, he, she, it,	if I, he, she, it,
	we, you, they **quizzed**	we, you, they **were quizzed**
Fut.	if I, he, she, it,	if I, he, she, it,
	we, you, they **should quiz**	we, you, they **should be quizzed**

The officer is quizzing the two drivers about the accident.
Their dad quizzed them on their homework.
We were quizzed for over an hour.

radio
(active voice)

be radioed
(passive voice)

INDICATIVE MOOD

Pres.	I, we, you, they **radio**	I **am radioed**
		we, you, they **are radioed**
	he, she, it **radios**	he, she, it **is radioed**
Pres.	I **am radioing**	I **am being radioed**
Prog.	we, you, they **are radioing**	we, you, they **are being radioed**
	he, she, it **is radioing**	he, she, it **is being radioed**
Pres.	I, we, you, they **do radio**	I, we, you, they **do get radioed**
Int.	he, she, it **does radio**	he, she, it **does get radioed**
Fut.	I, he, she, it,	I, he, she, it,
	we, you, they **will radio**	we, you, they **will be radioed**
Past	I, he, she, it,	I, he, she, it **was radioed**
	we, you, they **radioed**	we, you, they **were radioed**
Past	I, he, she, it **was radioing**	I, he, she, it **was being radioed**
Prog.	we, you, they **were radioing**	we, you, they **were being radioed**
Past	I, he, she, it,	I, he, she, it,
Int.	we, you, they **did radio**	we, you, they **did get radioed**
Pres.	I, we, you, they **have radioed**	I, we, you, they **have been radioed**
Perf.	he, she, it **has radioed**	he, she, it **has been radioed**
Past	I, he, she, it,	I, he, she, it,
Perf.	we, you, they **had radioed**	we, you, they **had been radioed**
Fut.	I, he, she, it, we, you, they	I, he, she, it, we, you, they
Perf.	**will have radioed**	**will have been radioed**

IMPERATIVE MOOD

radio **be radioed**

SUBJUNCTIVE MOOD

Pres.	if I, he, she, it,	if I, he, she, it,
	we, you, they **radio**	we, you, they **be radioed**
Past	if I, he, she, it,	if I, he, she, it,
	we, you, they **radioed**	we, you, they **were radioed**
Fut.	if I, he, she, it,	if I, he, she, it,
	we, you, they **should radio**	we, you, they **should be radioed**

Transitive and intransitive.

The pilot is radioing for a new course.
The pilot radioed for landing instructions.
The position of the ship was radioed to all other ships in the area.

raise
(active voice)

PRINCIPAL PARTS: **raises, raising, raised, raised**

be raised
(passive voice)

INDICATIVE MOOD

Pres.	I, we, you, they **raise**	I **am raised**
		we, you, they **are raised**
	he, she, it **raises**	he, she, it **is raised**
Pres.	I **am raising**	I **am being raised**
Prog.	we, you, they **are raising**	we, you, they **are being raised**
	he, she, it **is raising**	he, she, it **is being raised**
Pres.	I, we, you, they **do raise**	I, we, you, they **do get raised**
Int.	he, she, it **does raise**	he, she, it **does get raised**
Fut.	I, he, she, it,	I, he, she, it,
	we, you, they **will raise**	we, you, they **will be raised**
Past	I, he, she, it,	I, he, she, it **was raised**
	we, you, they **raised**	we, you, they **were raised**
Past	I, he, she, it **was raising**	I, he, she, it **was being raised**
Prog.	we, you, they **were raising**	we, you, they **were being raised**
Past	I, he, she, it,	I, he, she, it,
Int.	we, you, they **did raise**	we, you, they **did get raised**
Pres.	I, we, you, they **have raised**	I, we, you, they **have been raised**
Perf.	he, she, it **has raised**	he, she, it **has been raised**
Past	I, he, she, it,	I, he, she, it,
Perf.	we, you, they **had raised**	we, you, they **had been raised**
Fut.	I, he, she, it, we, you, they	I, he, she, it, we, you, they
Perf.	**will have raised**	**will have been raised**

IMPERATIVE MOOD

raise

be raised

SUBJUNCTIVE MOOD

Pres.	if I, he, she, it,	if I, he, she, it,
	we, you, they **raise**	we, you, they **be raised**
Past	if I, he, she, it,	if I, he, she, it,
	we, you, they **raised**	we, you, they **were raised**
Fut.	if I, he, she, it,	if I, he, she, it,
	we, you, they **should raise**	we, you, they **should be raised**

Transitive and intransitive.

They are raising their children very strictly.
We raised the bar on our hiring requirements.
He was raised by his grandparents to respect his elders.

rap
(active voice)

be rapped/rapt
(passive voice)

INDICATIVE MOOD

Pres.	I, we, you, they **rap**	**I am rapped** we, you, they **are rapped**
	he, she, it **raps**	he, she, it **is rapped**
Pres. *Prog.*	**I am rapping** we, you, they **are rapping** he, she, it **is rapping**	**I am being rapped** we, you, they **are being rapped** he, she, it **is being rapped**
Pres. *Int.*	I, we, you, they **do rap** he, she, it **does rap**	I, we, you, they **do get rapped** he, she, it **does get rapped**
Fut.	I, he, she, it, we, you, they **will rap**	I, he, she, it, we, you, they **will be rapped**
Past	I, he, she, it, we, you, they **rapped**	I, he, she, it **was rapped** we, you, they **were rapped**
Past *Prog.*	I, he, she, it **was rapping** we, you, they **were rapping**	I, he, she, it **was being rapped** we, you, they **were being rapped**
Past *Int.*	I, he, she, it, we, you, they **did rap**	I, he, she, it, we, you, they **did get rapped**
Pres. *Perf.*	I, we, you, they **have rapped** he, she, it **has rapped**	I, we, you, they **have been rapped** he, she, it **has been rapped**
Past *Perf.*	I, he, she, it, we, you, they **had rapped**	I, he, she, it, we, you, they **had been rapped**
Fut. *Perf.*	I, he, she, it, we, you, they **will have rapped**	I, he, she, it, we, you, they **will have been rapped**

R

IMPERATIVE MOOD

rap | **be rapped**

SUBJUNCTIVE MOOD

Pres.	if I, he, she, it, we, you, they **rap**	if I, he, she, it, we, you, they **be rapped**
Past	if I, he, she, it, we, you, they **rapped**	if I, he, she, it, we, you, they **were rapped**
Fut.	if I, he, she, it, we, you, they **should rap**	if I, he, she, it, we, you, they **should be rapped**

Transitive and intransitive. There are actually three verbs. The first RAP, RAPPED means to hit sharply. The second takes the past tense and past participle form RAPT, meaning "seized with rapture." The third is intransitive meaning to RAP, as in music.

They are rapping the pipe to listen for imperfections.
The students rapped all night.
A hundred years ago kids were rapped on the knuckles to get their attention.

reach (active voice)	PRINCIPAL PARTS: **reaches, reaching,** **reached, reached**	be reached (passive voice)

INDICATIVE MOOD

Pres.	I, we, you, they **reach**	I **am reached** we, you, they **are reached**
	he, she, it **reaches**	he, she, it **is reached**
Pres. *Prog.*	I **am reaching** we, you, they **are reaching** he, she, it **is reaching**	I **am being reached** we, you, they **are being reached** he, she, it **is being reached**
Pres. *Int.*	I, we, you, they **do reach** he, she, it **does reach**	I, we, you, they **do get reached** he, she, it **does get reached**
Fut.	I, he, she, it, we, you, they **will reach**	I, he, she, it, we, you, they **will be reached**
Past	I, he, she, it, we, you, they **reached**	I, he, she, it **was reached** we, you, they **were reached**
Past *Prog.*	I, he, she, it **was reaching** we, you, they **were reaching**	I, he, she, it **was being reached** we, you, they **were being reached**
Past *Int.*	I, he, she, it, we, you, they **did reach**	I, he, she, it, we, you, they **did get reached**
Pres. *Perf.*	I, we, you, they **have reached** he, she, it **has reached**	I, we, you, they **have been reached** he, she, it **has been reached**
Past *Perf.*	I, he, she, it, we, you, they **had reached**	I, he, she, it, we, you, they **had been reached**
Fut. *Perf.*	I, he, she, it, we, you, they **will have reached**	I, he, she, it, we, you, they **will have been reached**

IMPERATIVE MOOD

reach	**be reached**

SUBJUNCTIVE MOOD

Pres.	if I, he, she, it, we, you, they **reach**	if I, he, she, it, we, you, they **be reached**
Past	if I, he, she, it, we, you, they **reached**	if I, he, she, it, we, you, they **were reached**
Fut.	if I, he, she, it, we, you, they **should reach**	if I, he, she, it, we, you, they **should be reached**

Transitive and intransitive.

The jury reached a verdict in two hours.
The summit was reached after a two-week climb.

react
(active voice)

be reacted
(passive voice)

INDICATIVE MOOD

Pres.	I, we, you, they **react**	I **am reacted**
		we, you, they **are reacted**
	he, she, it **reacts**	he, she, it **is reacted**
Pres.	I **am reacting**	I **am being reacted**
Prog.	we, you, they **are reacting**	we, you, they **are being reacted**
	he, she, it **is reacting**	he, she, it **is being reacted**
Pres.	I, we, you, they **do react**	I, we, you, they **do get reacted**
Int.	he, she, it **does react**	he, she, it **does get reacted**
Fut.	I, he, she, it,	I, he, she, it,
	we, you, they **will react**	we, you, they **will be reacted**
Past	I, he, she, it,	I, he, she, it **was reacted**
	we, you, they **reacted**	we, you, they **were reacted**
Past	I, he, she, it **was reacting**	I, he, she, it **was being reacted**
Prog.	we, you, they **were reacting**	we, you, they **were being reacted**
Past	I, he, she, it,	I, he, she, it,
Int.	we, you, they **did react**	we, you, they **did get reacted**
Pres.	I, we, you, they **have reacted**	I, we, you, they **have been reacted**
Perf.	he, she, it **has reacted**	he, she, it **has been reacted**
Past	I, he, she, it,	I, he, she, it,
Perf.	we, you, they **had reacted**	we, you, they **had been reacted**
Fut.	I, he, she, it, we, you, they	I, he, she, it, we, you, they
Perf.	**will have reacted**	**will have been reacted**

R

IMPERATIVE MOOD

react 　　　　　　**be reacted**

SUBJUNCTIVE MOOD

Pres.	if I, he, she, it,	if I, he, she, it,
	we, you, they **react**	we, you, they **be reacted**
Past	if I, he, she, it,	if I, he, she, it,
	we, you, they **reacted**	we, you, they **were reacted**
Fut.	if I, he, she, it,	if I, he, she, it,
	we, you, they **should react**	we, you, they **should be reacted**

Transitive and intransitive.

They reacted to the news with disbelief.
The chemicals in the tube were reacted with a small amount of the agent.

read
(active voice)

be read
(passive voice)

INDICATIVE MOOD

Pres.	I, we, you, they **read**	I **am read**
		we, you, they **are read**
	he, she, it **reads**	he, she, it **is read**
Pres.	I **am reading**	I **am being read**
Prog.	we, you, they **are reading**	we, you, they **are being read**
	he, she, it **is reading**	he, she, it **is being read**
Pres.	I, we, you, they **do read**	I, we, you, they **do get read**
Int.	he, she, it **does read**	he, she, it **does get read**
Fut.	I, he, she, it,	I, he, she, it,
	we, you, they **will read**	we, you, they **will be read**
Past	I, he, she, it,	I, he, she, it **was read**
	we, you, they **read**	we, you, they **were read**
Past	I, he, she, it **was reading**	I, he, she, it **was being read**
Prog.	we, you, they **were reading**	we, you, they **were being read**
Past	I, he, she, it,	I, he, she, it,
Int.	we, you, they **did read**	we, you, they **did get read**
Pres.	I, we, you, they **have read**	I, we, you, they **have been read**
Perf.	he, she, it **has read**	he, she, it **has been read**
Past	I, he, she, it,	I, he, she, it,
Perf.	we, you, they **had read**	we, you, they **had been read**
Fut.	I, he, she, it, we, you, they	I, he, she, it, we, you, they
Perf.	**will have read**	**will have been read**

IMPERATIVE MOOD

read   **be read**

SUBJUNCTIVE MOOD

Pres.	if I, he, she, it,	if I, he, she, it,
	we, you, they **read**	we, you, they **be read**
Past	if I, he, she, it,	if I, he, she, it,
	we, you, they **read**	we, you, they **were read**
Fut.	if I, he, she, it,	if I, he, she, it,
	we, you, they **should read**	we, you, they **should be read**

Transitive and intransitive. Note the pronunciation of the past tense and past participle as "red."

He reads the news every day.
Yesterday she read about the new medical discovery.
That story has been read by generations of children.

348

realize
(active voice)

be realized
(passive voice)

INDICATIVE MOOD

Pres.	I, we, you, they **realize**
	he, she, it **realizes**

I **am realized**
we, you, they **are realized**
he, she, it **is realized**

Pres.	I **am realizing**
Prog.	we, you, they **are realizing**
	he, she, it **is realizing**

I **am being realized**
we, you, they **are being realized**
he, she, it **is being realized**

Pres.	I, we, you, they **do realize**
Int.	he, she, it **does realize**

I, we, you, they **do get realized**
he, she, it **does get realized**

Fut.	I, he, she, it,
	we, you, they **will realize**

I, he, she, it,
we, you, they **will be realized**

Past	I, he, she, it,
	we, you, they **realized**

I, he, she, it **was realized**
we, you, they **were realized**

Past	I, he, she, it **was realizing**
Prog.	we, you, they **were realizing**

I, he, she, it **was being realized**
we, you, they **were being realized**

Past	I, he, she, it,
Int.	we, you, they **did realize**

I, he, she, it,
we, you, they **did get realized**

Pres.	I, we, you, they **have realized**
Perf.	he, she, it **has realized**

I, we, you, they **have been realized**
he, she, it **has been realized**

Past	I, he, she, it,
Perf.	we, you, they **had realized**

I, he, she, it,
we, you, they **had been realized**

Fut.	I, he, she, it, we, you, they
Perf.	**will have realized**

I, he, she, it, we, you, they
will have been realized

R

IMPERATIVE MOOD

realize   **be realized**

SUBJUNCTIVE MOOD

Pres.	if I, he, she, it,
	we, you, they **realize**

if I, he, she, it,
we, you, they **be realized**

Past	if I, he, she, it,
	we, you, they **realized**

if I, he, she, it,
we, you, they **were realized**

Fut.	if I, he, she, it,
	we, you, they **should realize**

if I, he, she, it,
we, you, they **should be realized**

Transitive and intransitive.

The new recruits are realizing the difficulty of the physical requirements.
We realized our mistake only after the fact.
Gains were realized in all four quarters.

rebound
(active voice)

PRINCIPAL PARTS: **rebounds, rebounding, be rebounded
rebounded, rebounded** (passive voice)

INDICATIVE MOOD

Pres.	I, we, you, they **rebound**	**I am rebounded** we, you, they **are rebounded**
	he, she, it **rebounds**	he, she, it **is rebounded**
Pres. *Prog.*	**I am rebounding** we, you, they **are rebounding** he, she, it **is rebounding**	**I am being rebounded** we, you, they **are being rebounded** he, she, it **is being rebounded**
Pres. *Int.*	I, we, you, they **do rebound** he, she, it **does rebound**	I, we, you, they **do get rebounded** he, she, it **does get rebounded**
Fut.	I, he, she, it, we, you, they **will rebound**	I, he, she, it, we, you, they **will be rebounded**
Past	I, he, she, it, we, you, they **rebounded**	I, he, she, it **was rebounded** we, you, they **were rebounded**
Past *Prog.*	I, he, she, it **was rebounding** we, you, they **were rebounding**	I, he, she, it **was being rebounded** we, you, they **were being rebounded**
Past *Int.*	I, he, she, it, we, you, they **did rebound**	I, he, she, it, we, you, they **did get rebounded**
Pres. *Perf.*	I, we, you, they **have rebounded** he, she, it **has rebounded**	I, we, you, they **have been rebounded** he, she, it **has been rebounded**
Past *Perf.*	I, he, she, it, we, you, they **had rebounded**	I, he, she, it, we, you, they **had been rebounded**
Fut. *Perf.*	I, he, she, it, we, you, they **will have rebounded**	I, he, she, it, we, you, they **will have been rebounded**

IMPERATIVE MOOD

rebound   **be rebounded**

SUBJUNCTIVE MOOD

Pres.	if I, he, she, it, we, you, they **rebound**	if I, he, she, it, we, you, they **be rebounded**
Past	if I, he, she, it, we, you, they **rebounded**	if I, he, she, it, we, you, they **were rebounded**
Fut.	if I, he, she, it, we, you, they **should rebound**	if I, he, she, it, we, you, they **should be rebounded**

Intransitive and transitive.

The stock market rebounded after several days of losses.
The shot off the rim was rebounded by the smallest player on the team.

350

rebuild
(active voice)

be rebuilt
(passive voice)

INDICATIVE MOOD

Pres.	I, we, you, they **rebuild**	I **am rebuilt**
		we, you, they **are rebuilt**
	he, she, it **rebuilds**	he, she, it **is rebuilt**
Pres.	I **am rebuilding**	I **am being rebuilt**
Prog.	we, you, they **are rebuilding**	we, you, they **are being rebuilt**
	he, she, it **is rebuilding**	he, she, it **is being rebuilt**
Pres.	I, we, you, they **do rebuild**	I, we, you, they **do get rebuilt**
Int.	he, she, it **does rebuild**	he, she, it **does get rebuilt**
Fut.	I, he, she, it,	I, he, she, it,
	we, you, they **will rebuild**	we, you, they **will be rebuilt**
Past	I, he, she, it,	I, he, she, it **was rebuilt**
	we, you, they **rebuilt**	we, you, they **were rebuilt**
Past	I, he, she, it **was rebuilding**	I, he, she, it **was being rebuilt**
Prog.	we, you, they **were rebuilding**	we, you, they **were being rebuilt**
Past	I, he, she, it,	I, he, she, it,
Int.	we, you, they **did rebuild**	we, you, they **did get rebuilt**
Pres.	I, we, you, they **have rebuilt**	I, we, you, they **have been rebuilt**
Perf.	he, she, it **has rebuilt**	he, she, it **has been rebuilt**
Past	I, he, she, it,	I, he, she, it,
Perf.	we, you, they **had rebuilt**	we, you, they **had been rebuilt**
Fut.	I, he, she, it, we, you, they	I, he, she, it, we, you, they
Perf.	**will have rebuilt**	**will have been rebuilt**

IMPERATIVE MOOD

rebuild

be rebuilt

SUBJUNCTIVE MOOD

Pres.	if I, he, she, it,	if I, he, she, it,
	we, you, they **rebuild**	we, you, they **be rebuilt**
Past	if I, he, she, it,	if I, he, she, it,
	we, you, they **rebuilt**	we, you, they **were rebuilt**
Fut.	if I, he, she, it,	if I, he, she, it,
	we, you, they **should rebuild**	we, you, they **should be rebuilt**

Transitive and intransitive.

The community rebuilt the family's damaged house over the summer.
Our town was rebuilt after the Revolutionary War.

R

receive
(active voice)

be received
(passive voice)

INDICATIVE MOOD

Pres.	I, we, you, they **receive**	I **am received**
		we, you, they **are received**
	he, she, it **receives**	he, she, it **is received**
Pres.	I **am receiving**	I **am being received**
Prog.	we, you, they **are receiving**	we, you, they **are being received**
	he, she, it **is receiving**	he, she, it **is being received**
Pres.	I, we, you, they **do receive**	I, we, you, they **do get received**
Int.	he, she, it **does receive**	he, she, it **does get received**
Fut.	I, he, she, it,	I, he, she, it,
	we, you, they **will receive**	we, you, they **will be received**
Past	I, he, she, it,	I, he, she, it **was received**
	we, you, they **received**	we, you, they **were received**
Past	I, he, she, it **was receiving**	I, he, she, it **was being received**
Prog.	we, you, they **were receiving**	we, you, they **were being received**
Past	I, he, she, it,	I, he, she, it,
Int.	we, you, they **did receive**	we, you, they **did get received**
Pres.	I, we, you, they **have received**	I, we, you, they **have been received**
Perf.	he, she, it **has received**	he, she, it **has been received**
Past	I, he, she, it,	I, he, she, it,
Perf.	we, you, they **had received**	we, you, they **had been received**
Fut.	I, he, she, it, we, you, they	I, he, she, it, we, you, they
Perf.	**will have received**	**will have been received**

IMPERATIVE MOOD

receive	**be received**

SUBJUNCTIVE MOOD

Pres.	if I, he, she, it,	if I, he, she, it,
	we, you, they **receive**	we, you, they **be received**
Past	if I, he, she, it,	if I, he, she, it,
	we, you, they **received**	we, you, they **were received**
Fut.	if I, he, she, it,	if I, he, she, it,
	we, you, they **should receive**	we, you, they **should be received**

Transitive and intransitive.

She is receiving an award for her robot design.
We received the flowers yesterday.
The new ambassador was received with great ceremony.

| **recognize**
(active voice) | PRINCIPAL PARTS: **recognizes,**
recognizing, recognized, recognized | **be recognized**
(passive voice) |

INDICATIVE MOOD

Pres.	I, we, you, they **recognize**	I **am recognized** we, you, they **are recognized**
	he, she, it **recognizes**	he, she, it **is recognized**
Pres. *Prog.*	I **am recognizing** we, you, they **are recognizing** he, she, it **is recognizing**	I **am being recognized** we, you, they **are being recognized** he, she, it **is being recognized**
Pres. *Int.*	I, we, you, they **do recognize** he, she, it **does recognize**	I, we, you, they **do get recognized** he, she, it **does get recognized**
Fut.	I, he, she, it, we, you, they **will recognize**	I, he, she, it, we, you, they **will be recognized**
Past	I, he, she, it, we, you, they **recognized**	I, he, she, it **was recognized** we, you, they **were recognized**
Past *Prog.*	I, he, she, it **was recognizing** we, you, they **were recognizing**	I, he, she, it **was being recognized** we, you, they **were being recognized**
Past *Int.*	I, he, she, it, we, you, they **did recognize**	I, he, she, it, we, you, they **did get recognized**
Pres. *Perf.*	I, we, you, they **have recognized** he, she, it **has recognized**	I, we, you, they **have been recognized** he, she, it **has been recognized**
Past *Perf.*	I, he, she, it, we, you, they **had recognized**	I, he, she, it, we, you, they **had been recognized**
Fut. *Perf.*	I, he, she, it, we, you, they **will have recognized**	I, he, she, it, we, you, they **will have been recognized**

IMPERATIVE MOOD

recognize	**be recognized**

SUBJUNCTIVE MOOD

Pres.	if I, he, she, it, we, you, they **recognize**	if I, he, she, it, we, you, they **be recognized**
Past	if I, he, she, it, we, you, they **recognized**	if I, he, she, it, we, you, they **were recognized**
Fut.	if I, he, she, it, we, you, they **should recognize**	if I, he, she, it, we, you, they **should be recognized**

R

He is just now recognizing the potential consequences.
No one recognized him in his mask and costume.
The danger of pollution has been recognized by all nations.

redo
(active voice)

PRINCIPAL PARTS: **redoes, redoing,
redid, redone**

be redone
(passive voice)

INDICATIVE MOOD

Pres.	I, we, you, they **redo**	I **am redone**
		we, you, they **are redone**
	he, she, it **redoes**	he, she, it **is redone**
Pres.	I **am redoing**	I **am being redone**
Prog.	we, you, they **are redoing**	we, you, they **are being redone**
	he, she, it **is redoing**	he, she, it **is being redone**
Pres.	I, we, you, they **do redo**	I, we, you, they **do get redone**
Int.	he, she, it **does redo**	he, she, it **does get redone**
Fut.	I, he, she, it,	I, he, she, it,
	we, you, they **will redo**	we, you, they **will be redone**
Past	I, he, she, it,	I, he, she, it **was redone**
	we, you, they **redid**	we, you, they **were redone**
Past	I, he, she, it **was redoing**	I, he, she, it **was being redone**
Prog.	we, you, they **were redoing**	we, you, they **were being redone**
Past	I, he, she, it,	I, he, she, it,
Int.	we, you, they **did redo**	we, you, they **did get redone**
Pres.	I, we, you, they **have redone**	I, we, you, they **have been redone**
Perf.	he, she, it **has redone**	he, she, it **has been redone**
Past	I, he, she, it,	I, he, she, it,
Perf.	we, you, they **had redone**	we, you, they **had been redone**
Fut.	I, he, she, it, we, you, they	I, he, she, it, we, you, they
Perf.	**will have redone**	**will have been redone**

IMPERATIVE MOOD

redo **be redone**

SUBJUNCTIVE MOOD

Pres.	if I, he, she, it,	if I, he, she, it,
	we, you, they **redo**	we, you, they **be redone**
Past	if I, he, she, it,	if I, he, she, it,
	we, you, they **redid**	we, you, they **were redone**
Fut.	if I, he, she, it,	if I, he, she, it,
	we, you, they **should redo**	we, you, they **should be redone**

The carpenter redoes old cabinets and tables.
We are redoing our kitchen.
We redid our notebooks for extra credit.
The musical was redone for its Broadway premiere.

reduce
(active voice)

be reduced
(passive voice)

INDICATIVE MOOD

Pres.	I, we, you, they **reduce**	I **am reduced**
		we, you, they **are reduced**
	he, she, it **reduces**	he, she, it **is reduced**
Pres.	I **am reducing**	I **am being reduced**
Prog.	we, you, they **are reducing**	we, you, they **are being reduced**
	he, she, it **is reducing**	he, she, it **is being reduced**
Pres.	I, we, you, they **do reduce**	I, we, you, they **do get reduced**
Int.	he, she, it **does reduce**	he, she, it **does get reduced**
Fut.	I, he, she, it,	I, he, she, it,
	we, you, they **will reduce**	we, you, they **will be reduced**
Past	I, he, she, it,	I, he, she, it **was reduced**
	we, you, they **reduced**	we, you, they **were reduced**
Past	I, he, she, it **was reducing**	I, he, she, it **was being reduced**
Prog.	we, you, they **were reducing**	we, you, they **were being reduced**
Past	I, he, she, it,	I, he, she, it,
Int.	we, you, they **did reduce**	we, you, they **did get reduced**
Pres.	I, we, you, they **have reduced**	I, we, you, they **have been reduced**
Perf.	he, she, it **has reduced**	he, she, it **has been reduced**
Past	I, he, she, it,	I, he, she, it,
Perf.	we, you, they **had reduced**	we, you, they **had been reduced**
Fut.	I, he, she, it, we, you, they	I, he, she, it, we, you, they
Perf.	**will have reduced**	**will have been reduced**

R

IMPERATIVE MOOD

reduce   **be reduced**

SUBJUNCTIVE MOOD

Pres.	if I, he, she, it,	if I, he, she, it,
	we, you, they **reduce**	we, you, they **be reduced**
Past	if I, he, she, it,	if I, he, she, it,
	we, you, they **reduced**	we, you, they **were reduced**
Fut.	if I, he, she, it,	if I, he, she, it,
	we, you, they **should reduce**	we, you, they **should be reduced**

Transitive and intransitive.

We are reducing our mortgage rates after April 1.
She reduced her gasoline expenses by riding a bicycle two days a week.
The amount of reading was reduced by the instructor.

refer
(active voice)

be referred
(passive voice)

INDICATIVE MOOD

Pres.	I, we, you, they **refer**	I **am referred**
		we, you, they **are referred**
	he, she, it **refers**	he, she, it **is referred**
Pres.	I **am referring**	I **am being referred**
Prog.	we, you, they **are referring**	we, you, they **are being referred**
	he, she, it **is referring**	he, she, it **is being referred**
Pres.	I, we, you, they **do refer**	I, we, you, they **do get referred**
Int.	he, she, it **does refer**	he, she, it **does get referred**
Fut.	I, he, she, it,	I, he, she, it,
	we, you, they **will refer**	we, you, they **will be referred**
Past	I, he, she, it,	I, he, she, it **was referred**
	we, you, they **referred**	we, you, they **were referred**
Past	I, he, she, it **was referring**	I, he, she, it **was being referred**
Prog.	we, you, they **were referring**	we, you, they **were being referred**
Past	I, he, she, it,	I, he, she, it,
Int.	we, you, they **did refer**	we, you, they **did get referred**
Pres.	I, we, you, they **have referred**	I, we, you, they **have been referred**
Perf.	he, she, it **has referred**	he, she, it **has been referred**
Past	I, he, she, it,	I, he, she, it,
Perf.	we, you, they **had referred**	we, you, they **had been referred**
Fut.	I, he, she, it, we, you, they	I, he, she, it, we, you, they
Perf.	**will have referred**	**will have been referred**

IMPERATIVE MOOD

refer   **be referred**

SUBJUNCTIVE MOOD

Pres.	if I, he, she, it,	if I, he, she, it,
	we, you, they **refer**	we, you, they **be referred**
Past	if I, he, she, it,	if I, he, she, it,
	we, you, they **referred**	we, you, they **were referred**
Fut.	if I, he, she, it,	if I, he, she, it,
	we, you, they **should refer**	we, you, they **should be referred**

Transitive and intransitive.

He was referring to his earlier statements.
They referred her to counseling.
We were referred to you by our good friends.

356

PRINCIPAL PARTS: **regrets, regretting, regretted, regretted**

INDICATIVE MOOD

Pres.	I, we, you, they **regret**	I **am regretted**
		we, you, they **are regretted**
	he, she, it **regrets**	he, she, it **is regretted**
Pres.	I **am regretting**	I **am being regretted**
Prog.	we, you, they **are regretting**	we, you, they **are being regretted**
	he, she, it **is regretting**	he, she, it **is being regretted**
Pres.	I, we, you, they **do regret**	I, we, you, they **do get regretted**
Int.	he, she, it **does regret**	he, she, it **does get regretted**
Fut.	I, he, she, it,	I, he, she, it,
	we, you, they **will regret**	we, you, they **will be regretted**
Past	I, he, she, it,	I, he, she, it **was regretted**
	we, you, they **regretted**	we, you, they **were regretted**
Past	I, he, she, it **was regretting**	I, he, she, it **was being regretted**
Prog.	we, you, they **were regretting**	we, you, they **were being regretted**
Past	I, he, she, it,	I, he, she, it,
Int.	we, you, they **did regret**	we, you, they **did get regretted**
Pres.	I, we, you, they **have regretted**	I, we, you, they **have been regretted**
Perf.	he, she, it **has regretted**	he, she, it **has been regretted**
Past	I, he, she, it,	I, he, she, it,
Perf.	we, you, they **had regretted**	we, you, they **had been regretted**
Fut.	I, he, she, it, we, you, they	I, he, she, it, we, you, they
Perf.	**will have regretted**	**will have been regretted**

R

IMPERATIVE MOOD

regret   **be regretted**

SUBJUNCTIVE MOOD

Pres.	if I, he, she, it,	if I, he, she, it,
	we, you, they **regret**	we, you, they **be regretted**
Past	if I, he, she, it,	if I, he, she, it,
	we, you, they **regretted**	we, you, they **were regretted**
Fut.	if I, he, she, it,	if I, he, she, it,
	we, you, they **should regret**	we, you, they **should be regretted**

Transitive and intransitive.

Just now am I regretting that decision.
She regretted not going to his concert.
The omission was regretted by the organizers.

relate
(active voice)

be related
(passive voice)

INDICATIVE MOOD

Pres.	I, we, you, they **relate**	I **am related**
		we, you, they **are related**
	he, she, it **relates**	he, she, it **is related**
Pres.	I **am relating**	I **am being related**
Prog.	we, you, they **are relating**	we, you, they **are being related**
	he, she, it **is relating**	he, she, it **is being related**
Pres.	I, we, you, they **do relate**	I, we, you, they **do get related**
Int.	he, she, it **does relate**	he, she, it **does get related**
Fut.	I, he, she, it,	I, he, she, it,
	we, you, they **will relate**	we, you, they **will be related**
Past	I, he, she, it,	I, he, she, it **was related**
	we, you, they **related**	we, you, they **were related**
Past	I, he, she, it **was relating**	I, he, she, it **was being related**
Prog.	we, you, they **were relating**	we, you, they **were being related**
Past	I, he, she, it,	I, he, she, it,
Int.	we, you, they **did relate**	we, you, they **did get related**
Pres.	I, we, you, they **have related**	I, we, you, they **have been related**
Perf.	he, she, it **has related**	he, she, it **has been related**
Past	I, he, she, it,	I, he, she, it,
Perf.	we, you, they **had related**	we, you, they **had been related**
Fut.	I, he, she, it, we, you, they	I, he, she, it, we, you, they
Perf.	**will have related**	**will have been related**

IMPERATIVE MOOD

relate　　　　　　　　　　**be related**

SUBJUNCTIVE MOOD

Pres.	if I, he, she, it,	if I, he, she, it,
	we, you, they **relate**	we, you, they **be related**
Past	if I, he, she, it,	if I, he, she, it,
	we, you, they **related**	we, you, they **were related**
Fut.	if I, he, she, it,	if I, he, she, it,
	we, you, they **should relate**	we, you, they **should be related**

Transitive and intransitive.

The two pandas are relating well to one another.
She related well to her co-workers.
We are related by marriage.

re-lay
(active voice)

be re-laid
(passive voice)

INDICATIVE MOOD

Pres.	I, we, you, they **re-lay**	I **am re-laid**
		we, you, they **are re-laid**
	he, she, it **re-lays**	he, she, it **is re-laid**
Pres.	I **am re-laying**	I **am being re-laid**
Prog.	we, you, they **are re-laying**	we, you, they **are being re-laid**
	he, she, it **is re-laying**	he, she, it **is being re-laid**
Pres.	I, we, you, they **do re-lay**	I, we, you, they **do get re-laid**
Int.	he, she, it **does re-lay**	he, she, it **does get re-laid**
Fut.	I, he, she, it,	I, he, she, it,
	we, you, they **will re-lay**	we, you, they **will be re-laid**
Past	I, he, she, it,	I, he, she, it **was re-laid**
	we, you, they **re-laid**	we, you, they **were re-laid**
Past	I, he, she, it **was re-laying**	I, he, she, it **was being re-laid**
Prog.	we, you, they **were re-laying**	we, you, they **were being re-laid**
Past	I, he, she, it,	I, he, she, it,
Int.	we, you, they **did re-lay**	we, you, they **did get re-laid**
Pres.	I, we, you, they **have re-laid**	I, we, you, they **have been re-laid**
Perf.	he, she, it **has re-laid**	he, she, it **has been re-laid**
Past	I, he, she, it,	I, he, she, it,
Perf.	we, you, they **had re-laid**	we, you, they **had been re-laid**
Fut.	I, he, she, it, we, you, they	I, he, she, it, we, you, they
Perf.	**will have re-laid**	**will have been re-laid**

IMPERATIVE MOOD

re-lay **be re-laid**

SUBJUNCTIVE MOOD

Pres.	if I, he, she, it,	if I, he, she, it,
	we, you, they **re-lay**	we, you, they **be re-laid**
Past	if I, he, she, it,	if I, he, she, it,
	we, you, they **re-laid**	we, you, they **were re-laid**
Fut.	if I, he, she, it,	if I, he, she, it,
	we, you, they **should re-lay**	we, you, they **should be re-laid**

Transitive and intransitive. This verb means to "install something again."

We are re-laying the tile in our bathroom.
She re-laid the returned books on the shelf.
The floor was re-laid by the original contractor.

relay
(active voice)

be relayed
(passive voice)

INDICATIVE MOOD

Pres.	I, we, you, they **relay**	I **am relayed**
		we, you, they **are relayed**
	he, she, it **relays**	he, she, it **is relayed**
Pres.	I **am relaying**	I **am being relayed**
Prog.	we, you, they **are relaying**	we, you, they **are being relayed**
	he, she, it **is relaying**	he, she, it **is being relayed**
Pres.	I, we, you, they **do relay**	I, we, you, they **do get relayed**
Int.	he, she, it **does relay**	he, she, it **does get relayed**
Fut.	I, he, she, it,	I, he, she, it,
	we, you, they **will relay**	we, you, they **will be relayed**
Past	I, he, she, it,	I, he, she, it **was relayed**
	we, you, they **relayed**	we, you, they **were relayed**
Past	I, he, she, it **was relaying**	I, he, she, it **was being relayed**
Prog.	we, you, they **were relaying**	we, you, they **were being relayed**
Past	I, he, she, it,	I, he, she, it,
Int.	we, you, they **did relay**	we, you, they **did get relayed**
Pres.	I, we, you, they **have relayed**	I, we, you, they **have been relayed**
Perf.	he, she, it **has relayed**	he, she, it **has been relayed**
Past	I, he, she, it,	I, he, she, it,
Perf.	we, you, they **had relayed**	we, you, they **had been relayed**
Fut.	I, he, she, it, we, you, they	I, he, she, it, we, you, they
Perf.	**will have relayed**	**will have been relayed**

IMPERATIVE MOOD

relay   **be relayed**

SUBJUNCTIVE MOOD

Pres.	if I, he, she, it,	if I, he, she, it,
	we, you, they **relay**	we, you, they **be relayed**
Past	if I, he, she, it,	if I, he, she, it,
	we, you, they **relayed**	we, you, they **were relayed**
Fut.	if I, he, she, it,	if I, he, she, it,
	we, you, they **should relay**	we, you, they **should be relayed**

We are relaying his complaint to our service department.
He relayed the news to his editor.
The notice was relayed via e-mail to all the workers.

remain

INDICATIVE MOOD

Pres. I, we, you, they **remain**

he, she, it **remains**

Pres.
Prog. I **am remaining**
we, you, they **are remaining**
he, she, it **is remaining**

Pres.
Int. I, we, you, they **do remain**
he, she, it **does remain**

Fut. I, he, she, it,
we, you, they **will remain**

Past I, he, she, it,
we, you, they **remained**

Past
Prog. I, he, she, it **was remaining**
we, you, they **were remaining**

Past
Int. I, he, she, it,
we, you, they **did remain**

Pres.
Perf. I, we, you, they **have remained**
he, she, it **has remained**

Past
Perf. I, he, she, it,
we, you, they **had remained**

Fut.
Perf. I, he, she, it, we, you, they
will have remained

R

IMPERATIVE MOOD

remain

SUBJUNCTIVE MOOD

Pres. if I, he, she, it,
we, you, they **remain**

Past if I, he, she, it,
we, you, they **remained**

Fut. if I, he, she, it,
we, you, they **should remain**

Who remained to clean up after the party?
Nothing had remained undamaged.

remember
(active voice)

be remembered
(passive voice)

INDICATIVE MOOD

Pres.	I, we, you, they **remember**	I **am remembered**
		we, you, they **are remembered**
	he, she, it **remembers**	he, she, it **is remembered**
Pres.	I **am remembering**	I **am being remembered**
Prog.	we, you, they **are remembering**	we, you, they **are being remembered**
	he, she, it **is remembering**	he, she, it **is being remembered**
Pres.	I, we, you, they **do remember**	I, we, you, they **do get remembered**
Int.	he, she, it **does remember**	he, she, it **does get remembered**
Fut.	I, he, she, it,	I, he, she, it,
	we, you, they **will remember**	we, you, they **will be remembered**
Past	I, he, she, it,	I, he, she, it **was remembered**
	we, you, they **remembered**	we, you, they **were remembered**
Past	I, he, she, it **was remembering**	I, he, she, it **was being remembered**
Prog.	we, you, they **were remembering**	we, you, they **were being remembered**
Past	I, he, she, it,	I, he, she, it,
Int.	we, you, they **did remember**	we, you, they **did get remembered**
Pres.	I, we, you, they **have remembered**	I, we, you, they **have been remembered**
Perf.	he, she, it **has remembered**	he, she, it **has been remembered**
Past	I, he, she, it,	I, he, she, it,
Perf.	we, you, they **had remembered**	we, you, they **had been remembered**
Fut.	I, he, she, it, we, you, they	I, he, she, it, we, you, they
Perf.	**will have remembered**	**will have been remembered**

IMPERATIVE MOOD

remember   **be remembered**

SUBJUNCTIVE MOOD

Pres.	if I, he, she, it,	if I, he, she, it,
	we, you, they **remember**	we, you, they **be remembered**
Past	if I, he, she, it,	if I, he, she, it,
	we, you, they **remembered**	we, you, they **were remembered**
Fut.	if I, he, she, it,	if I, he, she, it, we, you, they
	we, you, they **should remember**	**should be remembered**

Transitive and intransitive.

Grandma remembered when we were babies.
He was remembered at a memorial service.

remove
(active voice)

be removed
(passive voice)

INDICATIVE MOOD

Pres.	I, we, you, they **remove**	I **am removed**
		we, you, they **are removed**
	he, she, it **removes**	he, she, it **is removed**
Pres.	I **am removing**	I **am being removed**
Prog.	we, you, they **are removing**	we, you, they **are being removed**
	he, she, it **is removing**	he, she, it **is being removed**
Pres.	I, we, you, they **do remove**	I, we, you, they **do get removed**
Int.	he, she, it **does remove**	he, she, it **does get removed**
Fut.	I, he, she, it,	I, he, she, it,
	we, you, they **will remove**	we, you, they **will be removed**
Past	I, he, she, it,	I, he, she, it **was removed**
	we, you, they **removed**	we, you, they **were removed**
Past	I, he, she, it **was removing**	I, he, she, it **was being removed**
Prog.	we, you, they **were removing**	we, you, they **were being removed**
Past	I, he, she, it,	I, he, she, it,
Int.	we, you, they **did remove**	we, you, they **did get removed**
Pres.	I, we, you, they **have removed**	I, we, you, they **have been removed**
Perf.	he, she, it **has removed**	he, she, it **has been removed**
Past	I, he, she, it,	I, he, she, it,
Perf.	we, you, they **had removed**	we, you, they **had been removed**
Fut.	I, he, she, it, we, you, they	I, he, she, it, we, you, they
Perf.	**will have removed**	**will have been removed**

IMPERATIVE MOOD

remove　　　　　　　**be removed**

SUBJUNCTIVE MOOD

Pres.	if I, he, she, it,	if I, he, she, it,
	we, you, they **remove**	we, you, they **be removed**
Past	if I, he, she, it,	if I, he, she, it,
	we, you, they **removed**	we, you, they **were removed**
Fut.	if I, he, she, it,	if I, he, she, it,
	we, you, they **should remove**	we, you, they **should be removed**

R

Transitive and intransitive.

Are you removing the old paint first?
They removed their coats before they entered the theater.
The ants were removed by boiling water.

rend
(active voice)

be rent/rended
(passive voice)

INDICATIVE MOOD

Pres.	I, we, you, they **rend**	I **am rent**
		we, you, they **are rent**
	he, she, it **rends**	he, she, it **is rent**
Pres.	I **am rending**	I **am being rent**
Prog.	we, you, they **are rending**	we, you, they **are being rent**
	he, she, it **is rending**	he, she, it **is being rent**
Pres.	I, we, you, they **do rend**	I, we, you, they **do get rent**
Int.	he, she, it **does rend**	he, she, it **does get rent**
Fut.	I, he, she, it,	I, he, she, it,
	we, you, they **will rend**	we, you, they **will be rent**
Past	I, he, she, it,	I, he, she, it **was rent**
	we, you, they **rent**	we, you, they **were rent**
Past	I, he, she, it **was rending**	I, he, she, it **was being rent**
Prog.	we, you, they **were rending**	we, you, they **were being rent**
Past	I, he, she, it,	I, he, she, it,
Int.	we, you, they **did rend**	we, you, they **did get rent**
Pres.	I, we, you, they **have rent**	I, we, you, they **have been rent**
Perf.	he, she, it **has rent**	he, she, it **has been rent**
Past	I, he, she, it,	I, he, she, it,
Perf.	we, you, they **had rent**	we, you, they **had been rent**
Fut.	I, he, she, it, we, you, they	I, he, she, it, we, you, they
Perf.	**will have rent**	**will have been rent**

IMPERATIVE MOOD

rend

be rent

SUBJUNCTIVE MOOD

Pres.	if I, he, she, it,	if I, he, she, it,
	we, you, they **rend**	we, you, they **be rent**
Past	if I, he, she, it,	if I, he, she, it,
	we, you, they **rent**	we, you, they **were rent**
Fut.	if I, he, she, it,	if I, he, she, it,
	we, you, they **should rend**	we, you, they **should be rent**

Transitive and intransitive. The *American Heritage* and *Merriam Webster's* accept for the past tense and past participle both RENT and RENDED.

The children rended the pillow into shreds.
Her new dress was rent in pieces by the washing machine.

rent	PRINCIPAL PARTS: rents, renting,	be rented
(active voice)	rented, rented	(passive voice)

Pres. I, we, you, they **rent**

I am rented
we, you, they **are rented**
he, she, it **rents**
he, she, it **is rented**

Pres. **I am renting**
Prog. we, you, they **are renting**
he, she, it **is renting**

I am being rented
we, you, they **are being rented**
he, she, it **is being rented**

Pres. I, we, you, they **do rent**
Int. he, she, it **does rent**

I, we, you, they **do get rented**
he, she, it **does get rented**

Fut. I, he, she, it,
we, you, they **will rent**

I, he, she, it,
we, you, they **will be rented**

Past I, he, she, it,
we, you, they **rented**

I, he, she, it **was rented**
we, you, they **were rented**

Past I, he, she, it **was renting**
Prog. we, you, they **were renting**

I, he, she, it **was being rented**
we, you, they **were being rented**

Past I, he, she, it,
Int. we, you, they **did rent**

I, he, she, it,
we, you, they **did get rented**

Pres. I, we, you, they **have rented**
Perf. he, she, it **has rented**

I, we, you, they **have been rented**
he, she, it **has been rented**

Past I, he, she, it,
Perf. we, you, they **had rented**

I, he, she, it,
we, you, they **had been rented**

Fut. I, he, she, it, we, you, they
Perf. **will have rented**

I, he, she, it, we, you, they
will have been rented

R

IMPERATIVE MOOD

rent

be rented

SUBJUNCTIVE MOOD

Pres. if I, he, she, it,
we, you, they **rent**

if I, he, she, it,
we, you, they **be rented**

Past if I, he, she, it,
we, you, they **rented**

if I, he, she, it,
we, you, they **were rented**

Fut. if I, he, she, it,
we, you, they **should rent**

if I, he, she, it,
we, you, they **should be rented**

Transitive and intransitive.

We rented an apartment in the city for the summer.
All of the hotel rooms were rented for the summer.

repay
(active voice)

be repaid
(passive voice)

INDICATIVE MOOD

Pres.	I, we, you, they **repay**	I **am repaid** we, you, they **are repaid**
	he, she, it **repays**	he, she, it **is repaid**
Pres. *Prog.*	I **am repaying** we, you, they **are repaying** he, she, it **is repaying**	I **am being repaid** we, you, they **are being repaid** he, she, it **is being repaid**
Pres. *Int.*	I, we, you, they **do repay** he, she, it **does repay**	I, we, you, they **do get repaid** he, she, it **does get repaid**
Fut.	I, he, she, it, we, you, they **will repay**	I, he, she, it, we, you, they **will be repaid**
Past	I, he, she, it, we, you, they **repaid**	I, he, she, it **was repaid** we, you, they **were repaid**
Past *Prog.*	I, he, she, it **was repaying** we, you, they **were repaying**	I, he, she, it **was being repaid** we, you, they **were being repaid**
Past *Int.*	I, he, she, it, we, you, they **did repay**	I, he, she, it, we, you, they **did get repaid**
Pres. *Perf.*	I, we, you, they **have repaid** he, she, it **has repaid**	I, we, you, they **have been repaid** he, she, it **has been repaid**
Past *Perf.*	I, he, she, it, we, you, they **had repaid**	I, he, she, it, we, you, they **had been repaid**
Fut. *Perf.*	I, he, she, it, we, you, they **will have repaid**	I, he, she, it, we, you, they **will have been repaid**

IMPERATIVE MOOD

repay   **be repaid**

SUBJUNCTIVE MOOD

Pres.	if I, he, she, it, we, you, they **repay**	if I, he, she, it, we, you, they **be repaid**
Past	if I, he, she, it, we, you, they **repaid**	if I, he, she, it, we, you, they **were repaid**
Fut.	if I, he, she, it, we, you, they **should repay**	if I, he, she, it, we, you, they **should be repaid**

Transitive and intransitive.

I repaid my college loans over twenty years.
The debt was repaid and the account was closed.

366

reply
(active voice)

be replied
(passive voice)

INDICATIVE MOOD

Pres.	I, we, you, they **reply**	I **am replied**
		we, you, they **are replied**
	he, she, it **replies**	he, she, it **is replied**
Pres. *Prog.*	I **am replying** we, you, they **are replying** he, she, it **is replying**	I **am being replied** we, you, they **are being replied** he, she, it **is being replied**
Pres. *Int.*	I, we, you, they **do reply** he, she, it **does reply**	I, we, you, they **do get replied** he, she, it **does get replied**
Fut.	I, he, she, it, we, you, they **will reply**	I, he, she, it, we, you, they **will be replied**
Past	I, he, she, it, we, you, they **replied**	I, he, she, it **was replied** we, you, they **were replied**
Past *Prog.*	I, he, she, it **was replying** we, you, they **were replying**	I, he, she, it **was being replied** we, you, they **were being replied**
Past *Int.*	I, he, she, it, we, you, they **did reply**	I, he, she, it, we, you, they **did get replied**
Pres. *Perf.*	I, we, you, they **have replied** he, she, it **has replied**	I, we, you, they **have been replied** he, she, it **has been replied**
Past *Perf.*	I, he, she, it, we, you, they **had replied**	I, he, she, it, we, you, they **had been replied**
Fut. *Perf.*	I, he, she, it, we, you, they **will have replied**	I, he, she, it, we, you, they **will have been replied**

IMPERATIVE MOOD

reply   **be replied**

SUBJUNCTIVE MOOD

Pres.	if I, he, she, it, we, you, they **reply**	if I, he, she, it, we, you, they **be replied**
Past	if I, he, she, it, we, you, they **replied**	if I, he, she, it, we, you, they **were replied**
Fut.	if I, he, she, it, we, you, they **should reply**	if I, he, she, it, we, you, they **should be replied**

Transitive and intransitive.

He always replies within a week.
They replied promptly to our demands.
Our requests were replied to only two months later.

report
(active voice)

PRINCIPAL PARTS: reports, reporting, reported, reported

be reported
(passive voice)

INDICATIVE MOOD

Pres.	I, we, you, they **report**	I **am reported**
		we, you, they **are reported**
	he, she, it **reports**	he, she, it **is reported**
Pres.	I **am reporting**	I **am being reported**
Prog.	we, you, they **are reporting**	we, you, they **are being reported**
	he, she, it **is reporting**	he, she, it **is being reported**
Pres.	I, we, you, they **do report**	I, we, you, they **do get reported**
Int.	he, she, it **does report**	he, she, it **does get reported**
Fut.	I, he, she, it,	I, he, she, it,
	we, you, they **will report**	we, you, they **will be reported**
Past	I, he, she, it,	I, he, she, it **was reported**
	we, you, they **reported**	we, you, they **were reported**
Past	I, he, she, it **was reporting**	I, he, she, it **was being reported**
Prog.	we, you, they **were reporting**	we, you, they **were being reported**
Past	I, he, she, it,	I, he, she, it,
Int.	we, you, they **did report**	we, you, they **did get reported**
Pres.	I, we, you, they **have reported**	I, we, you, they **have been reported**
Perf.	he, she, it **has reported**	he, she, it **has been reported**
Past	I, he, she, it,	I, he, she, it,
Perf.	we, you, they **had reported**	we, you, they **had been reported**
Fut.	I, he, she, it, we, you, they	I, he, she, it, we, you, they
Perf.	**will have reported**	**will have been reported**

IMPERATIVE MOOD

report   **be reported**

SUBJUNCTIVE MOOD

Pres.	if I, he, she, it,	if I, he, she, it,
	we, you, they **report**	we, you, they **be reported**
Past	if I, he, she, it,	if I, he, she, it,
	we, you, they **reported**	we, you, they **were reported**
Fut.	if I, he, she, it,	if I, he, she, it,
	we, you, they **should report**	we, you, they **should be reported**

Transitive and intransitive.

They reported the loss of several million gallons of oil.
The accident was reported in the local press.

represent
(active voice)

PRINCIPAL PARTS: represents, representing, represented, represented

be represented
(passive voice)

INDICATIVE MOOD

Pres.	I, we, you, they **represent**	I **am represented**
		we, you, they **are represented**
	he, she, it **represents**	he, she, it **is represented**
Pres.	I **am representing**	I **am being represented**
Prog.	we, you, they **are representing**	we, you, they **are being represented**
	he, she, it **is representing**	he, she, it **is being represented**
Pres.	I, we, you, they **do represent**	I, we, you, they **do get represented**
Int.	he, she, it **does represent**	he, she, it **does get represented**
Fut.	I, he, she, it,	I, he, she, it,
	we, you, they **will represent**	we, you, they **will be represented**
Past	I, he, she, it,	I, he, she, it **was represented**
	we, you, they **represented**	we, you, they **were represented**
Past	I, he, she, it **was representing**	I, he, she, it **was being represented**
Prog.	we, you, they **were representing**	we, you, they **were being represented**
Past	I, he, she, it,	I, he, she, it,
Int.	we, you, they **did represent**	we, you, they **did get represented**
Pres.	I, we, you, they **have represented**	I, we, you, they **have been represented**
Perf.	he, she, it **has represented**	he, she, it **has been represented**
Past	I, he, she, it,	I, he, she, it,
Perf.	we, you, they **had represented**	we, you, they **had been represented**
Fut.	I, he, she, it, we, you, they	I, he, she, it, we, you, they
Perf.	**will have represented**	**will have been represented**

IMPERATIVE MOOD

represent   **be represented**

SUBJUNCTIVE MOOD

Pres.	if I, he, she, it,	if I, he, she, it,
	we, you, they **represent**	we, you, they **be represented**
Past	if I, he, she, it,	if I, he, she, it,
	we, you, they **represented**	we, you, they **were represented**
Fut.	if I, he, she, it,	if I, he, she, it, we, you, they
	we, you, they **should represent**	**should be represented**

He represented himself at the open meeting.
They were represented by legal counsel.

require
(active voice)

be required
(passive voice)

INDICATIVE MOOD

Pres.	I, we, you, they **require**	I **am required**
		we, you, they **are required**
	he, she, it **requires**	he, she, it **is required**
Pres.	I **am requiring**	I **am being required**
Prog.	we, you, they **are requiring**	we, you, they **are being required**
	he, she, it **is requiring**	he, she, it **is being required**
Pres.	I, we, you, they **do require**	I, we, you, they **do get required**
Int.	he, she, it **does require**	he, she, it **does get required**
Fut.	I, he, she, it,	I, he, she, it,
	we, you, they **will require**	we, you, they **will be required**
Past	I, he, she, it,	I, he, she, it **was required**
	we, you, they **required**	we, you, they **were required**
Past	I, he, she, it **was requiring**	I, he, she, it **was being required**
Prog.	we, you, they **were requiring**	we, you, they **were being required**
Past	I, he, she, it,	I, he, she, it,
Int.	we, you, they **did require**	we, you, they **did get required**
Pres.	I, we, you, they **have required**	I, we, you, they **have been required**
Perf.	he, she, it **has required**	he, she, it **has been required**
Past	I, he, she, it,	I, he, she, it,
Perf.	we, you, they **had required**	we, you, they **had been required**
Fut.	I, he, she, it, we, you, they	I, he, she, it, we, you, they
Perf.	**will have required**	**will have been required**

IMPERATIVE MOOD

require   **be required**

SUBJUNCTIVE MOOD

Pres.	if I, he, she, it,	if I, he, she, it,
	we, you, they **require**	we, you, they **be required**
Past	if I, he, she, it,	if I, he, she, it,
	we, you, they **required**	we, you, they **were required**
Fut.	if I, he, she, it,	if I, he, she, it,
	we, you, they **should require**	we, you, they **should be required**

Transitive and intransitive.

We are requiring a composition from all prospective students.
They required no letters of recommendation.
Payment of all fees is required before registration.

rescue
(active voice)

be rescued
(passive voice)

INDICATIVE MOOD

Pres.	I, we, you, they **rescue**	I **am rescued**
		we, you, they **are rescued**
	he, she, it **rescues**	he, she, it **is rescued**
Pres.	I **am rescuing**	I **am being rescued**
Prog.	we, you, they **are rescuing**	we, you, they **are being rescued**
	he, she, it **is rescuing**	he, she, it is being rescued
Pres.	I, we, you, they **do rescue**	I, we, you, they **do get rescued**
Int.	he, she, it **does rescue**	he, she, it **does get rescued**
Fut.	I, he, she, it,	I, he, she, it,
	we, you, they **will rescue**	we, you, they **will be rescued**
Past	I, he, she, it,	I, he, she, it **was rescued**
	we, you, they **rescued**	we, you, they **were rescued**
Past	I, he, she, it **was rescuing**	I, he, she, it **was being rescued**
Prog.	we, you, they **were rescuing**	we, you, they **were being rescued**
Past	I, he, she, it,	I, he, she, it,
Int.	we, you, they **did rescue**	we, you, they **did get rescued**
Pres.	I, we, you, they **have rescued**	I, we, you, they **have been rescued**
Perf.	he, she, it **has rescued**	he, she, it **has been rescued**
Past	I, he, she, it,	I, he, she, it,
Perf.	we, you, they **had rescued**	we, you, they **had been rescued**
Fut.	I, he, she, it, we, you, they	I, he, she, it, we, you, they
Perf.	**will have rescued**	**will have been rescued**

IMPERATIVE MOOD

rescue   **be rescued**

SUBJUNCTIVE MOOD

Pres.	if I, he, she, it,	if I, he, she, it,
	we, you, they **rescue**	we, you, they **be rescued**
Past	if I, he, she, it,	if I, he, she, it,
	we, you, they **rescued**	we, you, they **were rescued**
Fut.	if I, he, she, it,	if I, he, she, it,
	we, you, they **should rescue**	we, you, they **should be rescued**

The fireman is rescuing that cat from a tree.
They rescued all of their digital photographs.
Their data was rescued by a good backup system.

PRINCIPAL PARTS: **rests, resting,
rested, rested**

be rested
(passive voice)

INDICATIVE MOOD

Pres.	I, we, you, they **rest**	I **am rested** we, you, they **are rested**
	he, she, it **rests**	he, she, it **is rested**
Pres. *Prog.*	I **am resting** we, you, they **are resting** he, she, it **is resting**	I **am being rested** we, you, they **are being rested** he, she, it **is being rested**
Pres. *Int.*	I, we, you, they **do rest** he, she, it **does rest**	I, we, you, they **do get rested** he, she, it **does get rested**
Fut.	I, he, she, it, we, you, they **will rest**	I, he, she, it, we, you, they **will be rested**
Past	I, he, she, it, we, you, they **rested**	I, he, she, it **was rested** we, you, they **were rested**
Past *Prog.*	I, he, she, it **was resting** we, you, they **were resting**	I, he, she, it **was being rested** we, you, they **were being rested**
Past *Int.*	I, he, she, it, we, you, they **did rest**	I, he, she, it, we, you, they **did get rested**
Pres. *Perf.*	I, we, you, they **have rested** he, she, it **has rested**	I, we, you, they **have been rested** he, she, it **has been rested**
Past *Perf.*	I, he, she, it, we, you, they **had rested**	I, he, she, it, we, you, they **had been rested**
Fut. *Perf.*	I, he, she, it, we, you, they **will have rested**	I, he, she, it, we, you, they **will have been rested**

IMPERATIVE MOOD

rest

be rested

SUBJUNCTIVE MOOD

Pres.	if I, he, she, it, we, you, they **rest**	if I, he, she, it, we, you, they **be rested**
Past	if I, he, she, it, we, you, they **rested**	if I, he, she, it, we, you, they **were rested**
Fut.	if I, he, she, it, we, you, they **should rest**	if I, he, she, it, we, you, they **should be rested**

Transitive and intransitive.

They rested for a few minutes before marching on.
The trophies were rested on the top shelf of the case.

INDICATIVE MOOD

Pres. I, we, you, they **result**

he, she, it **results**

Pres. I **am resulting**
Prog. we, you, they **are resulting**
he, she, it **is resulting**

Pres. I, we, you, they **do result**
Int. he, she, it **does result**

Fut. I, he, she, it,
we, you, they **will result**

Past I, he, she, it,
we, you, they **resulted**

Past I, he, she, it **was resulting**
Prog. we, you, they **were resulting**

Past I, he, she, it,
Int. we, you, they **did result**

Pres. I, we, you, they **have resulted**
Perf. he, she, it **has resulted**

Past I, he, she, it,
Perf. we, you, they **had resulted**

Fut. I, he, she, it, we, you, they
Perf. **will have resulted**

IMPERATIVE MOOD

result

SUBJUNCTIVE MOOD

Pres. if I, he, she, it,
we, you, they **result**

Past if I, he, she, it,
we, you, they **resulted**

Fut. if I, he, she, it,
we, you, they **should result**

Their actions resulted in serious damage to the building.
The flood had resulted from inadequate preparations.

INDICATIVE MOOD

Pres.	I, we, you, they **retell**	**I am retold**
		we, you, they **are retold**
	he, she, it **retells**	he, she, it **is retold**
Pres.	**I am retelling**	I am being retold
Prog.	we, you, they **are retelling**	we, you, they **are being retold**
	he, she, it **is retelling**	he, she, it **is being retold**
Pres.	I, we, you, they **do retell**	I, we, you, they **do get retold**
Int.	he, she, it **does retell**	he, she, it **does get retold**
Fut.	I, he, she, it,	I, he, she, it,
	we, you, they **will retell**	we, you, they **will be retold**
Past	I, he, she, it,	I, he, she, it **was retold**
	we, you, they **retold**	we, you, they **were retold**
Past	I, he, she, it **was retelling**	I, he, she, it **was being retold**
Prog.	we, you, they **were retelling**	we, you, they **were being retold**
Past	I, he, she, it,	I, he, she, it,
Int.	we, you, they **did retell**	we, you, they **did get retold**
Pres.	I, we, you, they **have retold**	I, we, you, they **have been retold**
Perf.	he, she, it **has retold**	he, she, it **has been retold**
Past	I, he, she, it,	I, he, she, it,
Perf.	we, you, they **had retold**	we, you, they **had been retold**
Fut.	I, he, she, it, we, you, they	I, he, she, it, we, you, they
Perf.	**will have retold**	**will have been retold**

IMPERATIVE MOOD

retell **be retold**

SUBJUNCTIVE MOOD

Pres.	if I, he, she, it,	if I, he, she, it,
	we, you, they **retell**	we, you, they **be retold**
Past	if I, he, she, it,	if I, he, she, it,
	we, you, they **retold**	we, you, they **were retold**
Fut.	if I, he, she, it,	if I, he, she, it,
	we, you, they **should retell**	we, you, they **should be retold**

She retold the story over and over for the children.
A version of that tale has been retold to generations of candidates.

return
(active voice)

be returned
(passive voice)

INDICATIVE MOOD

Pres.	I, we, you, they **return**	I **am returned**
		we, you, they **are returned**
	he, she, it **returns**	he, she, it **is returned**
Pres.	I **am returning**	I **am being returned**
Prog.	we, you, they **are returning**	we, you, they **are being returned**
	he, she, it **is returning**	he, she, it **is being returned**
Pres.	I, we, you, they **do return**	I, we, you, they **do get returned**
Int.	he, she, it **does return**	he, she, it **does get returned**
Fut.	I, he, she, it,	I, he, she, it,
	we, you, they **will return**	we, you, they **will be returned**
Past	I, he, she, it,	I, he, she, it **was returned**
	we, you, they **returned**	we, you, they **were returned**
Past	I, he, she, it **was returning**	I, he, she, it **was being returned**
Prog.	we, you, they **were returning**	we, you, they **were being returned**
Past	I, he, she, it,	I, he, she, it,
Int.	we, you, they **did return**	we, you, they **did get returned**
Pres.	I, we, you, they **have returned**	I, we, you, they **have been returned**
Perf.	he, she, it **has returned**	he, she, it **has been returned**
Past	I, he, she, it,	I, he, she, it,
Perf.	we, you, they **had returned**	we, you, they **had been returned**
Fut.	I, he, she, it, we, you, they	I, he, she, it, we, you, they
Perf.	**will have returned**	**will have been returned**

IMPERATIVE MOOD

return   **be returned**

SUBJUNCTIVE MOOD

Pres.	if I, he, she, it,	if I, he, she, it,
	we, you, they **return**	we, you, they **be returned**
Past	if I, he, she, it,	if I, he, she, it,
	we, you, they **returned**	we, you, they **were returned**
Fut.	if I, he, she, it,	if I, he, she, it,
	we, you, they **should return**	we, you, they **should be returned**

Intransitive and transitive.

The patron returned all the books to the library.
The letter was returned to the sender for more postage.

rewrite
(active voice)

PRINCIPAL PARTS: **rewrites, rewriting, rewrote, rewritten**

be rewritten
(passive voice)

INDICATIVE MOOD

Pres.	I, we, you, they **rewrite**	I **am rewritten**
		we, you, they **are rewritten**
	he, she, it **rewrites**	he, she, it **is rewritten**
Pres.	I **am rewriting**	I **am being rewritten**
Prog.	we, you, they **are rewriting**	we, you, they **are being rewritten**
	he, she, it **is rewriting**	he, she, it **is being rewritten**
Pres.	I, we, you, they **do rewrite**	I, we, you, they **do get rewritten**
Int.	he, she, it **does rewrite**	he, she, it **does get rewritten**
Fut.	I, he, she, it,	I, he, she, it,
	we, you, they **will rewrite**	we, you, they **will be rewritten**
Past	I, he, she, it,	I, he, she, it **was rewritten**
	we, you, they **rewrote**	we, you, they **were rewritten**
Past	I, he, she, it **was rewriting**	I, he, she, it **was being rewritten**
Prog.	we, you, they **were rewriting**	we, you, they **were being rewritten**
Past	I, he, she, it,	I, he, she, it,
Int.	we, you, they **did rewrite**	we, you, they **did get rewritten**
Pres.	I, we, you, they **have rewritten**	I, we, you, they **have been rewritten**
Perf.	he, she, it **has rewritten**	he, she, it **has been rewritten**
Past	I, he, she, it,	I, he, she, it,
Perf.	we, you, they **had rewritten**	we, you, they **had been rewritten**
Fut.	I, he, she, it, we, you, they	I, he, she, it, we, you, they
Perf.	**will have rewritten**	**will have been rewritten**

IMPERATIVE MOOD

rewrite   **be rewritten**

SUBJUNCTIVE MOOD

Pres.	if I, he, she, it,	if I, he, she, it,
	we, you, they **rewrite**	we, you, they **be rewritten**
Past	if I, he, she, it,	if I, he, she, it,
	we, you, they **rewrote**	we, you, they **were rewritten**
Fut.	if I, he, she, it,	if I, he, she, it,
	we, you, they **should rewrite**	we, you, they **should be rewritten**

Transitive and intransitive.

We are rewriting our papers for extra credit.
The author rewrote the introduction several times.
The composition was rewritten on the basis of her teacher's corrections.

376

rid
(active voice)

PRINCIPAL PARTS: **rids, ridding,**
rid/ridded, rid/ridded

be rid/ridded
(passive voice)

INDICATIVE MOOD

Pres.	I, we, you, they **rid**	I **am rid**
		we, you, they **are rid**
	he, she, it **rids**	he, she, it **is rid**
Pres.	I **am ridding**	I **am being rid**
Prog.	we, you, they **are ridding**	we, you, they **are being rid**
	he, she, it **is ridding**	he, she, it **is being rid**
Pres.	I, we, you, they **do rid**	I, we, you, they **do get rid**
Int.	he, she, it **does rid**	he, she, it **does get rid**
Fut.	I, he, she, it,	I, he, she, it,
	we, you, they **will rid**	we, you, they **will be rid**
Past	I, he, she, it,	I, he, she, it **was rid**
	we, you, they **rid**	we, you, they **were rid**
Past	I, he, she, it **was ridding**	I, he, she, it **was being rid**
Prog.	we, you, they **were ridding**	we, you, they **were being rid**
Past	I, he, she, it,	I, he, she, it,
Int.	we, you, they **did rid**	we, you, they **did get rid**
Pres.	I, we, you, they **have rid**	I, we, you, they **have been rid**
Perf.	he, she, it **has rid**	he, she, it **has been rid**
Past	I, he, she, it,	I, he, she, it,
Perf.	we, you, they **had rid**	we, you, they **had been rid**
Fut.	I, he, she, it, we, you, they	I, he, she, it, we, you, they
Perf.	**will have rid**	**will have been rid**

IMPERATIVE MOOD

rid

be rid

SUBJUNCTIVE MOOD

Pres.	if I, he, she, it,	if I, he, she, it,
	we, you, they **rid**	we, you, they **be rid**
Past	if I, he, she, it,	if I, he, she, it,
	we, you, they **rid**	we, you, they **were rid**
Fut.	if I, he, she, it,	if I, he, she, it,
	we, you, they **should rid**	we, you, they **should be rid**

The *Oxford Dictionary* classifies RIDDED as archaic.

They are ridding their garden of all the weeds.
He rid his shed of a pile of junk.
The language of his paper was rid of mistakes before it was submitted.

ride
(active voice)

be ridden
(passive voice)

INDICATIVE MOOD

Pres.	I, we, you, they **ride** he, she, it **rides**	I **am ridden** we, you, they **are ridden** he, she, it **is ridden**
Pres. *Prog.*	I **am riding** we, you, they **are riding** he, she, it **is riding**	I **am being ridden** we, you, they **are being ridden** he, she, it **is being ridden**
Pres. *Int.*	I, we, you, they **do ride** he, she, it **does ride**	I, we, you, they **do get ridden** he, she, it **does get ridden**
Fut.	I, he, she, it, we, you, they **will ride**	I, he, she, it, we, you, they **will be ridden**
Past	I, he, she, it, we, you, they **rode**	I, he, she, it **was ridden** we, you, they **were ridden**
Past *Prog.*	I, he, she, it **was riding** we, you, they **were riding**	I, he, she, it **was being ridden** we, you, they **were being ridden**
Past *Int.*	I, he, she, it, we, you, they **did ride**	I, he, she, it, we, you, they **did get ridden**
Pres. *Perf.*	I, we, you, they **have ridden** he, she, it **has ridden**	I, we, you, they **have been ridden** he, she, it **has been ridden**
Past *Perf.*	I, he, she, it, we, you, they **had ridden**	I, he, she, it, we, you, they **had been ridden**
Fut. *Perf.*	I, he, she, it, we, you, they **will have ridden**	I, he, she, it, we, you, they **will have been ridden**

IMPERATIVE MOOD

ride   **be ridden**

SUBJUNCTIVE MOOD

Pres.	if I, he, she, it, we, you, they **ride**	if I, he, she, it, we, you, they **be ridden**
Past	if I, he, she, it, we, you, they **rode**	if I, he, she, it, we, you, they **were ridden**
Fut.	if I, he, she, it, we, you, they **should ride**	if I, he, she, it, we, you, they **should be ridden**

Intransitive and transitive.

The children are out riding their scooters.
The mayor rode the subway to work.
The Moscow metro system is ridden by millions of passengers a day.

rig
(active voice)

PRINCIPAL PARTS: **rigs, rigging, rigged, rigged**

be rigged
(passive voice)

INDICATIVE MOOD

Pres.	I, we, you, they **rig**	I **am rigged**
		we, you, they **are rigged**
	he, she, it **rigs**	he, she, it **is rigged**
Pres.	I **am rigging**	I **am being rigged**
Prog.	we, you, they **are rigging**	we, you, they **are being rigged**
	he, she, it **is rigging**	he, she, it **is being rigged**
Pres.	I, we, you, they **do rig**	I, we, you, they **do get rigged**
Int.	he, she, it **does rig**	he, she, it **does get rigged**
Fut.	I, he, she, it,	I, he, she, it,
	we, you, they **will rig**	we, you, they **will be rigged**
Past	I, he, she, it,	I, he, she, it **was rigged**
	we, you, they **rigged**	we, you, they **were rigged**
Past	I, he, she, it **was rigging**	I, he, she, it **was being rigged**
Prog.	we, you, they **were rigging**	we, you, they **were being rigged**
Past	I, he, she, it,	I, he, she, it,
Int.	we, you, they **did rig**	we, you, they **did get rigged**
Pres.	I, we, you, they **have rigged**	I, we, you, they **have been rigged**
Perf.	he, she, it **has rigged**	he, she, it **has been rigged**
Past	I, he, she, it,	I, he, she, it,
Perf.	we, you, they **had rigged**	we, you, they **had been rigged**
Fut.	I, he, she, it, we, you, they	I, he, she, it, we, you, they
Perf.	**will have rigged**	**will have been rigged**

R

IMPERATIVE MOOD

rig

be rigged

SUBJUNCTIVE MOOD

Pres.	if I, he, she, it,	if I, he, she, it,
	we, you, they **rig**	we, you, they **be rigged**
Past	if I, he, she, it,	if I, he, she, it,
	we, you, they **rigged**	we, you, they **were rigged**
Fut.	if I, he, she, it,	if I, he, she, it,
	we, you, they **should rig**	we, you, they **should be rigged**

They are rigging a backup system for their network.
They rigged the ship for stormy weather.
The truck was rigged for heavy-duty driving in snow and mud.

INDICATIVE MOOD

Pres.	I, we, you, they **ring**	I **am rung**
		we, you, they **are rung**
	he, she, it **rings**	he, she, it **is rung**
Pres.	I **am ringing**	I **am being rung**
Prog.	we, you, they **are ringing**	we, you, they **are being rung**
	he, she, it **is ringing**	he, she, it **is being rung**
Pres.	I, we, you, they **do ring**	I, we, you, they **do get rung**
Int.	he, she, it **does ring**	he, she, it **does get rung**
Fut.	I, he, she, it,	I, he, she, it,
	we, you, they **will ring**	we, you, they **will be rung**
Past	I, he, she, it,	I, he, she, it **was rung**
	we, you, they **rang**	we, you, they **were rung**
Past	I, he, she, it **was ringing**	I, he, she, it **was being rung**
Prog.	we, you, they **were ringing**	we, you, they **were being rung**
Past	I, he, she, it,	I, he, she, it,
Int.	we, you, they **did ring**	we, you, they **did get rung**
Pres.	I, we, you, they **have rung**	I, we, you, they **have been rung**
Perf.	he, she, it **has rung**	he, she, it **has been rung**
Past	I, he, she, it,	I, he, she, it,
Perf.	we, you, they **had rung**	we, you, they **had been rung**
Fut.	I, he, she, it, we, you, they	I, he, she, it, we, you, they
Perf.	**will have rung**	**will have been rung**

IMPERATIVE MOOD

ring **be rung**

SUBJUNCTIVE MOOD

Pres.	if I, he, she, it,	if I, he, she, it,
	we, you, they **ring**	we, you, they **be rung**
Past	if I, he, she, it,	if I, he, she, it,
	we, you, they **rang**	we, you, they **were rung**
Fut.	if I, he, she, it,	if I, he, she, it,
	we, you, they **should ring**	we, you, they **should be rung**

Intransitive and transitive.

The teacher rings the bell at the beginning of class.
The telephone rang early this morning.
The bell was rung to summon the patients.

380

ring
(active voice)

be ringed
(passive voice)

INDICATIVE MOOD

Pres.	I, we, you, they **ring**	I **am ringed**
		we, you, they **are ringed**
	he, she, it **rings**	he, she, it **is ringed**
Pres.	I **am ringing**	I **am being ringed**
Prog.	we, you, they **are ringing**	we, you, they **are being ringed**
	he, she, it **is ringing**	he, she, it **is being ringed**
Pres.	I, we, you, they **do ring**	I, we, you, they **do get ringed**
Int.	he, she, it **does ring**	he, she, it **does get ringed**
Fut.	I, he, she, it,	I, he, she, it,
	we, you, they **will ring**	we, you, they **will be ringed**
Past	I, he, she, it,	I, he, she, it **was ringed**
	we, you, they **ringed**	we, you, they **were ringed**
Past	I, he, she, it **was ringing**	I, he, she, it **was being ringed**
Prog.	we, you, they **were ringing**	we, you, they **were being ringed**
Past	I, he, she, it,	I, he, she, it,
Int.	we, you, they **did ring**	we, you, they **did get ringed**
Pres.	I, we, you, they **have ringed**	I, we, you, they **have been ringed**
Perf.	he, she, it **has ringed**	he, she, it **has been ringed**
Past	I, he, she, it,	I, he, she, it,
Perf.	we, you, they **had ringed**	we, you, they **had been ringed**
Fut.	I, he, she, it, we, you, they	I, he, she, it, we, you, they
Perf.	**will have ringed**	**will have been ringed**

IMPERATIVE MOOD

ring

be ringed

SUBJUNCTIVE MOOD

Pres.	if I, he, she, it,	if I, he, she, it,
	we, you, they **ring**	we, you, they **be ringed**
Past	if I, he, she, it,	if I, he, she, it,
	we, you, they **ringed**	we, you, they **were ringed**
Fut.	if I, he, she, it,	if I, he, she, it,
	we, you, they **should ring**	we, you, they **should be ringed**

R

Transitive and intransitive. This verb means to "encircle." Do not confuse it with the verb meaning to "ring a bell."

They are ringing off the area.
The police ringed off the bank.
The singer was ringed by screaming fans.

rip
(active voice)

be ripped
(passive voice)

INDICATIVE MOOD

Pres.	I, we, you, they **rip**	I **am ripped**
		we, you, they **are ripped**
	he, she, it **rips**	he, she, it **is ripped**
Pres.	I **am ripping**	I **am being ripped**
Prog.	we, you, they **are ripping**	we, you, they **are being ripped**
	he, she, it **is ripping**	he, she, it **is being ripped**
Pres.	I, we, you, they **do rip**	I, we, you, they **do get ripped**
Int.	he, she, it **does rip**	he, she, it **does get ripped**
Fut.	I, he, she, it,	I, he, she, it,
	we, you, they **will rip**	we, you, they **will be ripped**
Past	I, he, she, it,	I, he, she, it **was ripped**
	we, you, they **ripped**	we, you, they **were ripped**
Past	I, he, she, it **was ripping**	I, he, she, it **was being ripped**
Prog.	we, you, they **were ripping**	we, you, they **were being ripped**
Past	I, he, she, it,	I, he, she, it,
Int.	we, you, they **did rip**	we, you, they **did get ripped**
Pres.	I, we, you, they **have ripped**	I, we, you, they **have been ripped**
Perf.	he, she, it **has ripped**	he, she, it **has been ripped**
Past	I, he, she, it,	I, he, she, it,
Perf.	we, you, they **had ripped**	we, you, they **had been ripped**
Fut.	I, he, she, it, we, you, they	I, he, she, it, we, you, they
Perf.	**will have ripped**	**will have been ripped**

IMPERATIVE MOOD

rip　　　　**be ripped**

SUBJUNCTIVE MOOD

Pres.	if I, he, she, it,	if I, he, she, it,
	we, you, they **rip**	we, you, they **be ripped**
Past	if I, he, she, it,	if I, he, she, it,
	we, you, they **ripped**	we, you, they **were ripped**
Fut.	if I, he, she, it,	if I, he, she, it,
	we, you, they **should rip**	we, you, they **should be ripped**

Transitive and intransitive.

They are ripping up the pavement this afternoon.
They ripped the CD to make a copy of a song.
The film was ripped from an original copy.

rise
(active voice)

be risen
(passive voice)

INDICATIVE MOOD

Pres.	I, we, you, they **rise**	I **am risen**
		we, you, they **are risen**
	he, she, it **rises**	he, she, it **is risen**
Pres.	I **am rising**	I **am being risen**
Prog.	we, you, they **are rising**	we, you, they **are being risen**
	he, she, it **is rising**	he, she, it **is being risen**
Pres.	I, we, you, they **do rise**	I, we, you, they **do get risen**
Int.	he, she, it **does rise**	he, she, it **does get risen**
Fut.	I, he, she, it,	I, he, she, it,
	we, you, they **will rise**	we, you, they **will be risen**
Past	I, he, she, it,	I, he, she, it **was risen**
	we, you, they **rose**	we, you, they **were risen**
Past	I, he, she, it **was rising**	I, he, she, it **was being risen**
Prog.	we, you, they **were rising**	we, you, they **were being risen**
Past	I, he, she, it,	I, he, she, it,
Int.	we, you, they **did rise**	we, you, they **did get risen**
Pres.	I, we, you, they **have risen**	I, we, you, they **have been risen**
Perf.	he, she, it **has risen**	he, she, it **has been risen**
Past	I, he, she, it,	I, he, she, it,
Perf.	we, you, they **had risen**	we, you, they **had been risen**
Fut.	I, he, she, it, we, you, they	I, he, she, it, we, you, they
Perf.	**will have risen**	**will have been risen**

IMPERATIVE MOOD

rise   **be risen**

SUBJUNCTIVE MOOD

Pres.	if I, he, she, it,	if I, he, she, it,
	we, you, they **rise**	we, you, they **be risen**
Past	if I, he, she, it,	if I, he, she, it,
	we, you, they **rose**	we, you, they **were risen**
Fut.	if I, he, she, it,	if I, he, she, it,
	we, you, they **should rise**	we, you, they **should be risen**

R

Intransitive and transitive.

The sun is rising earlier each morning.
She rose from her chair with difficulty.
A cry of anguish has risen in the camp.

| **rob**
 (active voice) | PRINCIPAL PARTS: **robs, robbing,**
 robbed, robbed | **be robbed**
 (passive voice) |

INDICATIVE MOOD

Pres.	I, we, you, they **rob** he, she, it **robs**	I **am robbed** we, you, they **are robbed** he, she, it **is robbed**
Pres. *Prog.*	I **am robbing** we, you, they **are robbing** he, she, it **is robbing**	I **am being robbed** we, you, they **are being robbed** he, she, it **is being robbed**
Pres. *Int.*	I, we, you, they **do rob** he, she, it **does rob**	I, we, you, they **do get robbed** he, she, it **does get robbed**
Fut.	I, he, she, it, we, you, they **will rob**	I, he, she, it, we, you, they **will be robbed**
Past	I, he, she, it, we, you, they **robbed**	I, he, she, it **was robbed** we, you, they **were robbed**
Past *Prog.*	I, he, she, it **was robbing** we, you, they **were robbing**	I, he, she, it **was being robbed** we, you, they **were being robbed**
Past *Int.*	I, he, she, it, we, you, they **did rob**	I, he, she, it, we, you, they **did get robbed**
Pres. *Perf.*	I, we, you, they **have robbed** he, she, it **has robbed**	I, we, you, they **have been robbed** he, she, it **has been robbed**
Past *Perf.*	I, he, she, it, we, you, they **had robbed**	I, he, she, it, we, you, they **had been robbed**
Fut. *Perf.*	I, he, she, it, we, you, they **will have robbed**	I, he, she, it, we, you, they **will have been robbed**

IMPERATIVE MOOD

rob	**be robbed**

SUBJUNCTIVE MOOD

Pres.	if I, he, she, it, we, you, they **rob**	if I, he, she, it, we, you, they **be robbed**
Past	if I, he, she, it, we, you, they **robbed**	if I, he, she, it, we, you, they **were robbed**
Fut.	if I, he, she, it, we, you, they **should rob**	if I, he, she, it, we, you, they **should be robbed**

Intransitive and transitive.

Someone is robbing our newspaper every morning.
The thieves robbed several major works of art.
She was robbed of first place by poor officiating.

rout
(active voice)

be routed
(passive voice)

INDICATIVE MOOD

Pres.	I, we, you, they **rout**	I **am routed**
		we, you, they **are routed**
	he, she, it **routs**	he, she, it **is routed**
Pres.	I **am routing**	I **am being routed**
Prog.	we, you, they **are routing**	we, you, they **are being routed**
	he, she, it **is routing**	he, she, it **is being routed**
Pres.	I, we, you, they **do rout**	I, we, you, they **do get routed**
Int.	he, she, it **does rout**	he, she, it **does get routed**
Fut.	I, he, she, it,	I, he, she, it,
	we, you, they **will rout**	we, you, they **will be routed**
Past	I, he, she, it,	I, he, she, it **was routed**
	we, you, they **routed**	we, you, they **were routed**
Past	I, he, she, it **was routing**	I, he, she, it **was being routed**
Prog.	we, you, they **were routing**	we, you, they **were being routed**
Past	I, he, she, it,	I, he, she, it,
Int.	we, you, they **did rout**	we, you, they **did get routed**
Pres.	I, we, you, they **have routed**	I, we, you, they **have been routed**
Perf.	he, she, it **has routed**	he, she, it **has been routed**
Past	I, he, she, it,	I, he, she, it,
Perf.	we, you, they **had routed**	we, you, they **had been routed**
Fut.	I, he, she, it, we, you, they	I, he, she, it, we, you, they
Perf.	**will have routed**	**will have been routed**

IMPERATIVE MOOD

rout

be routed

SUBJUNCTIVE MOOD

Pres.	if I, he, she, it,	if I, he, she, it,
	we, you, they **rout**	we, you, they **be routed**
Past	if I, he, she, it,	if I, he, she, it,
	we, you, they **routed**	we, you, they **were routed**
Fut.	if I, he, she, it,	if I, he, she, it,
	we, you, they **should rout**	we, you, they **should be routed**

The transitive verb ROUT means to "force into retreat or defeat." There is also an intransitive and transitive verb meaning to "dig."

They are routing the enemy forces.
They routed their opponents 15 to 1.
The incumbent was routed by the challenger.

route
(active voice)

be routed
(passive voice)

INDICATIVE MOOD

Pres.	I, we, you, they **route**	I **am routed**
		we, you, they **are routed**
	he, she, it **routes**	he, she, it **is routed**
Pres.	I **am routing**	I **am being routed**
Prog.	we, you, they **are routing**	we, you, they **are being routed**
	he, she, it **is routing**	he, she, it **is being routed**
Pres.	I, we, you, they **do route**	I, we, you, they **do get routed**
Int.	he, she, it **does route**	he, she, it **does get routed**
Fut.	I, he, she, it,	I, he, she, it,
	we, you, they **will route**	we, you, they **will be routed**
Past	I, he, she, it,	I, he, she, it **was routed**
	we, you, they **routed**	we, you, they **were routed**
Past	I, he, she, it **was routing**	I, he, she, it **was being routed**
Prog.	we, you, they **were routing**	we, you, they **were being routed**
Past	I, he, she, it,	I, he, she, it,
Int.	we, you, they **did route**	we, you, they **did get routed**
Pres.	I, we, you, they **have routed**	I, we, you, they **have been routed**
Perf.	he, she, it **has routed**	he, she, it **has been routed**
Past	I, he, she, it,	I, he, she, it,
Perf.	we, you, they **had routed**	we, you, they **had been routed**
Fut.	I, he, she, it, we, you, they	I, he, she, it, we, you, they
Perf.	**will have routed**	**will have been routed**

IMPERATIVE MOOD

route   **be routed**

SUBJUNCTIVE MOOD

Pres.	if I, he, she, it,	if I, he, she, it,
	we, you, they **route**	we, you, they **be routed**
Past	if I, he, she, it,	if I, he, she, it,
	we, you, they **routed**	we, you, they **were routed**
Fut.	if I, he, she, it,	if I, he, she, it,
	we, you, they **should rout**	we, you, they **should be routed**

This verb means to "send by a specific route."

The airline is routing us through Cleveland.
We routed you first to New York and then to Frankfurt.
The truck was routed to the pickup point by an onboard computer.

ruin
(active voice)

PRINCIPAL PARTS: **ruins, ruining,
ruined, ruined**

be ruined
(passive voice)

INDICATIVE MOOD

Pres.	I, we, you, they **ruin**	I **am ruined** we, you, they **are ruined**
	he, she, it **ruins**	he, she, it **is ruined**
Pres. *Prog.*	I **am ruining** we, you, they **are ruining** he, she, it **is ruining**	I **am being ruined** we, you, they **are being ruined** he, she, it **is being ruined**
Pres. *Int.*	I, we, you, they **do ruin** he, she, it **does ruin**	I, we, you, they **do get ruined** he, she, it **does get ruined**
Fut.	I, he, she, it, we, you, they **will ruin**	I, he, she, it, we, you, they **will be ruined**
Past	I, he, she, it, we, you, they **ruined**	I, he, she, it **was ruined** we, you, they **were ruined**
Past *Prog.*	I, he, she, it **was ruining** we, you, they **were ruining**	I, he, she, it **was being ruined** we, you, they **were being ruined**
Past *Int.*	I, he, she, it, we, you, they **did ruin**	I, he, she, it, we, you, they **did get ruined**
Pres. *Perf.*	I, we, you, they **have ruined** he, she, it **has ruined**	I, we, you, they **have been ruined** he, she, it **has been ruined**
Past *Perf.*	I, he, she, it, we, you, they **had ruined**	I, he, she, it, we, you, they **had been ruined**
Fut. *Perf.*	I, he, she, it, we, you, they **will have ruined**	I, he, she, it, we, you, they **will have been ruined**

IMPERATIVE MOOD

ruin   **be ruined**

SUBJUNCTIVE MOOD

Pres.	if I, he, she, it, we, you, they **ruin**	if I, he, she, it, we, you, they **be ruined**
Past	if I, he, she, it, we, you, they **ruined**	if I, he, she, it, we, you, they **were ruined**
Fut.	if I, he, she, it, we, you, they **should ruin**	if I, he, she, it, we, you, they **should be ruined**

Transitive and intransitive.

The laundry ruined my new blouse.
The picnic was ruined by rain.

R

| run
(active voice) | PRINCIPAL PARTS: **runs, running,**
ran, run | be run
(passive voice) |

INDICATIVE MOOD

Pres.	I, we, you, they **run**	I **am run** we, you, they **are run**
	he, she, it **runs**	he, she, it **is run**
Pres. *Prog.*	I **am running** we, you, they **are running** he, she, it **is running**	I **am being run** we, you, they **are being run** he, she, it **is being run**
Pres. *Int.*	I, we, you, they **do run** he, she, it **does run**	I, we, you, they **do get run** he, she, it **does get run**
Fut.	I, he, she, it, we, you, they **will run**	I, he, she, it, we, you, they **will be run**
Past	I, he, she, it, we, you, they **ran**	I, he, she, it **was run** we, you, they **were run**
Past *Prog.*	I, he, she, it **was running** we, you, they **were running**	I, he, she, it **was being run** we, you, they **were being run**
Past *Int.*	I, he, she, it, we, you, they **did run**	I, he, she, it, we, you, they **did get run**
Pres. *Perf.*	I, we, you, they **have run** he, she, it **has run**	I, we, you, they **have been run** he, she, it **has been run**
Past *Perf.*	I, he, she, it, we, you, they **had run**	I, he, she, it, we, you, they **had been run**
Fut. *Perf.*	I, he, she, it, we, you, they **will have run**	I, he, she, it, we, you, they **will have been run**

IMPERATIVE MOOD

run	**be run**

SUBJUNCTIVE MOOD

Pres.	if I, he, she, it, we, you, they **run**	if I, he, she, it, we, you, they **be run**
Past	if I, he, she, it, we, you, they **ran**	if I, he, she, it, we, you, they **were run**
Fut.	if I, he, she, it, we, you, they **should run**	if I, he, she, it, we, you, they **should be run**

Intransitive and transitive.

She is finally running for office.
They ran ten miles yesterday.
The race was run for exercise and to raise money for charity.

AN ESSENTIAL
55 VERB

run

Examples

She runs fast.

We are running next week in the marathon.

I will run the figures for our meeting.

He ran the meeting very smoothly.

The skunk was run over in the night.

Let's run across the bridge.

The engine is still running.

He had already run ten miles.

Who will run for the position?

A train runs on tracks.

Words and expressions related to this verb

We ran out of money.

He ran off with the books.

Run for your lives.

Run along now.

We run into her often.

He ran a red light.

The melting snow ran off into the stream.

Run this by him.

You run the risk of losing.

You can run, but you can't hide.

R

save
(active voice)

PRINCIPAL PARTS: saves, saving, saved, saved

be saved
(passive voice)

INDICATIVE MOOD

Pres.	I, we, you, they **save**	I **am saved**
		we, you, they **are saved**
	he, she, it **saves**	he, she, it **is saved**

Pres.	I **am saving**	I **am being saved**
Prog.	we, you, they **are saving**	we, you, they **are being saved**
	he, she, it **is saving**	he, she, it **is being saved**

| *Pres.* | I, we, you, they **do save** | I, we, you, they **do get saved** |
| *Int.* | he, she, it **does save** | he, she, it **does get saved** |

| *Fut.* | I, he, she, it, | I, he, she, it, |
| | we, you, they **will save** | we, you, they **will be saved** |

| *Past* | I, he, she, it, | I, he, she, it **was saved** |
| | we, you, they **saved** | we, you, they **were saved** |

| *Past* | I, he, she, it **was saving** | I, he, she, it **was being saved** |
| *Prog.* | we, you, they **were saving** | we, you, they **were being saved** |

| *Past* | I, he, she, it, | I, he, she, it, |
| *Int.* | we, you, they **did save** | we, you, they **did get saved** |

| *Pres.* | I, we, you, they **have saved** | I, we, you, they **have been saved** |
| *Perf.* | he, she, it **has saved** | he, she, it **has been saved** |

| *Past* | I, he, she, it, | I, he, she, it, |
| *Perf.* | we, you, they **had saved** | we, you, they **had been saved** |

| *Fut.* | I, he, she, it, we, you, they | I, he, she, it, we, you, they |
| *Perf.* | **will have saved** | **will have been saved** |

IMPERATIVE MOOD

save   **be saved**

SUBJUNCTIVE MOOD

| *Pres.* | if I, he, she, it, | if I, he, she, it, |
| | we, you, they **save** | we, you, they **be saved** |

| *Past* | if I, he, she, it, | if I, he, she, it, |
| | we, you, they **saved** | we, you, they **were saved** |

| *Fut.* | if I, he, she, it, | if I, he, she, it, |
| | we, you, they **should save** | we, you, they **should be saved** |

Transitive and intransitive.

We are saving our money for a rainy day.
They saved the whales off their coast.
We were saved by the bell.

saw (active voice)	Principal Parts: **saws, sawing, sawed, sawed/sawn**	be sawed/ sawn (passive voice)

INDICATIVE MOOD

Pres.	I, we, you, they **saw** he, she, it **saws**	I am **sawed** we, you, they **are sawed** he, she, it **is sawed**
Pres. *Prog.*	I **am sawing** we, you, they **are sawing** he, she, it **is sawing**	I **am being sawed** we, you, they **are being sawed** he, she, it **is being sawed**
Pres. *Int.*	I, we, you, they **do saw** he, she, it **does saw**	I, we, you, they **do get sawed** he, she, it **does get sawed**
Fut.	I, he, she, it, we, you, they **will saw**	I, he, she, it, we, you, they **will be sawed**
Past	I, he, she, it, we, you, they **sawed**	I, he, she, it **was sawed** we, you, they **were sawed**
Past *Prog.*	I, he, she, it **was sawing** we, you, they **were sawing**	I, he, she, it **was being sawed** we, you, they **were being sawed**
Past *Int.*	I, he, she, it, we, you, they **did saw**	I, he, she, it, we, you, they **did get sawed**
Pres. *Perf.*	I, we, you, they **have sawed** he, she, it **has sawed**	I, we, you, they **have been sawed** he, she, it **has been sawed**
Past *Perf.*	I, he, she, it, we, you, they **had sawed**	I, he, she, it, we, you, they **had been sawed**
Fut. *Perf.*	I, he, she, it, we, you, they **will have sawed**	I, he, she, it, we, you, they **will have been sawed**

IMPERATIVE MOOD

saw	**be sawed**

SUBJUNCTIVE MOOD

Pres.	if I, he, she, it, we, you, they **saw**	if I, he, she, it, we, you, they **be sawed**
Past	if I, he, she, it, we, you, they **sawed**	if I, he, she, it, we, you, they **were sawed**
Fut.	if I, he, she, it, we, you, they **should saw**	if I, he, she, it, we, you, they **should be sawed**

Transitive and intransitive.

She sawed all of their firewood.
The wood was sawed at the mill.

S

say (active voice)	PRINCIPAL PARTS: **says, saying,** **said, said**	be said (passive voice)

INDICATIVE MOOD

Pres.	I, we, you, they **say**	I **am said** we, you, they **are said**
	he, she, it **says**	he, she, it **is said**
Pres. *Prog.*	I **am saying** we, you, they **are saying** he, she, it **is saying**	I **am being said** we, you, they **are being said** he, she, it **is being said**
Pres. *Int.*	I, we, you, they **do say** he, she, it **does say**	I, we, you, they **do get said** he, she, it **does get said**
Fut.	I, he, she, it, we, you, they **will say**	I, he, she, it, we, you, they **will be said**
Past	I, he, she, it, we, you, they **said**	I, he, she, it **was said** we, you, they **were said**
Past *Prog.*	I, he, she, it **was saying** we, you, they **were saying**	I, he, she, it **was being said** we, you, they **were being said**
Past *Int.*	I, he, she, it, we, you, they **did say**	I, he, she, it, we, you, they **did get said**
Pres. *Perf.*	I, we, you, they **have said** he, she, it **has said**	I, we, you, they **have been said** he, she, it **has been said**
Past *Perf.*	I, he, she, it, we, you, they **had said**	I, he, she, it, we, you, they **had been said**
Fut. *Perf.*	I, he, she, it, we, you, they **will have said**	I, he, she, it, we, you, they **will have been said**

IMPERATIVE MOOD

	say	**be said**

SUBJUNCTIVE MOOD

Pres.	if I, he, she, it, we, you, they **say**	if I, he, she, it, we, you, they **be said**
Past	if I, he, she, it, we, you, they **said**	if I, he, she, it, we, you, they **were said**
Fut.	if I, he, she, it, we, you, they **should say**	if I, he, she, it, we, you, they **should be said**

Transitive and intransitive.

Who said you cannot come?
It has been said that all good things must end.

AN ESSENTIAL
55 VERB

392

AN ESSENTIAL
55 VERB

say

Examples

I say my prayers every day.

You say you really need me.

She says that she cares.

We said the right things.

They will say whatever is necessary.

To say you are sorry is not enough.

I wish you had not said that.

How can I say what I feel?

What more is there to say?

Did he really mean what he said?

Words and expressions related to this verb

I'll say!

Never say never.

You can say that again.

Say cheese!

Say you'll never leave me.

Need I say more?

You said it!

Easier said than done.

When all is said and done, we will still have the problem.

Enough said.

No sooner said than done.

You know what they say about him.

S

seat (active voice)	PRINCIPAL PARTS: seats, seating, seated, seated	be seated (passive voice)

INDICATIVE MOOD

Pres.	I, we, you, they **seat**	I **am seated** we, you, they **are seated**
	he, she, it **seats**	he, she, it **is seated**
Pres. *Prog.*	I **am seating** we, you, they **are seating** he, she, it **is seating**	I **am being seated** we, you, they **are being seated** he, she, it **is being seated**
Pres. *Int.*	I, we, you, they **do seat** he, she, it **does seat**	I, we, you, they **do get seated** he, she, it **does get seated**
Fut.	I, he, she, it, we, you, they **will seat**	I, he, she, it, we, you, they **will be seated**
Past	I, he, she, it, we, you, they **seated**	I, he, she, it **was seated** we, you, they **were seated**
Past *Prog.*	I, he, she, it **was seating** we, you, they **were seating**	I, he, she, it **was being seated** we, you, they **were being seated**
Past *Int.*	I, he, she, it, we, you, they **did seat**	I, he, she, it, we, you, they **did get seated**
Pres. *Perf.*	I, we, you, they **have seated** he, she, it **has seated**	I, we, you, they **have been seated** he, she, it **has been seated**
Past *Perf.*	I, he, she, it, we, you, they **had seated**	I, he, she, it, we, you, they **had been seated**
Fut. *Perf.*	I, he, she, it, we, you, they **will have seated**	I, he, she, it, we, you, they **will have been seated**

IMPERATIVE MOOD

seat	**be seated**

SUBJUNCTIVE MOOD

Pres.	if I, he, she, it, we, you, they **seat**	if I, he, she, it, we, you, they **be seated**
Past	if I, he, she, it, we, you, they **seated**	if I, he, she, it, we, you, they **were seated**
Fut.	if I, he, she, it, we, you, they **should seat**	if I, he, she, it, we, you, they **should be seated**

Transitive and intransitive.

They seated the guests of honor in the first row.
We were seated at the captain's table.

see (active voice)	PRINCIPAL PARTS: sees, seeing, saw, seen	be seen (passive voice)

INDICATIVE MOOD

Pres.	I, we, you, they **see**	I **am seen** we, you, they **are seen**
	he, she, it **sees**	he, she, it **is seen**
Pres. *Prog.*	I **am seeing** we, you, they **are seeing** he, she, it **is seeing**	I **am being seen** we, you, they **are being seen** he, she, it **is being seen**
Pres. *Int.*	I, we, you, they **do see** he, she, it **does see**	I, we, you, they **do get seen** he, she, it **does get seen**
Fut.	I, he, she, it, we, you, they **will see**	I, he, she, it, we, you, they **will be seen**
Past	I, he, she, it, we, you, they **saw**	I, he, she, it **was seen** we, you, they **were seen**
Past *Prog.*	I, he, she, it **was seeing** we, you, they **were seeing**	I, he, she, it **was being seen** we, you, they **were being seen**
Past *Int.*	I, he, she, it, we, you, they **did see**	I, he, she, it, we, you, they **did get seen**
Pres. *Perf.*	I, we, you, they **have seen** he, she, it **has seen**	I, we, you, they **have been seen** he, she, it **has been seen**
Past *Perf.*	I, he, she, it, we, you, they **had seen**	I, he, she, it, we, you, they **had been seen**
Fut. *Perf.*	I, he, she, it, we, you, they **will have seen**	I, he, she, it, we, you, they **will have been seen**

IMPERATIVE MOOD

see	**be seen**

SUBJUNCTIVE MOOD

Pres.	if I, he, she, it, we, you, they **see**	if I, he, she, it, we, you, they **be seen**
Past	if I, he, she, it, we, you, they **saw**	if I, he, she, it, we, you, they **were seen**
Fut.	if I, he, she, it, we, you, they **should see**	if I, he, she, it, we, you, they **should be seen**

Transitive and intransitive.

This evening we are seeing Swan Lake.
They saw the car too late to avoid the accident.
People claim that strange aircraft have been seen in
the night sky.

AN ESSENTIAL
55 VERB

Examples

I see her every day at work.

She sees her son once a month.

Who saw the new movie?

They will see a musical in New York City.

A comet was seen on the East Coast.

I have never seen a ghost.

Can you see land?

She is seeing her doctor next week.

Some things are so small they can be seen only with a microscope.

See that building!

Words and expressions related to this verb

Children should be seen, not heard.

We shall see what we shall see.

They had been seeing each other for months.

See to it!

They saw them off last evening.

The waiter saw them to their table.

The hostess saw them out.

Haven't I seen you somewhere before?

To see is to believe.

If you could only see me now.

We will see this thing through to the end.

seek
(active voice)

be sought
(passive voice)

INDICATIVE MOOD

Pres.	I, we, you, they **seek**	I **am sought** we, you, they **are sought**
	he, she, it **seeks**	he, she, it **is sought**
Pres. *Prog.*	I **am seeking** we, you, they **are seeking** he, she, it **is seeking**	I **am being sought** we, you, they **are being sought** he, she, it **is being sought**
Pres. *Int.*	I, we, you, they **do seek** he, she, it **does seek**	I, we, you, they **do get sought** he, she, it **does get sought**
Fut.	I, he, she, it, we, you, they **will seek**	I, he, she, it, we, you, they **will be sought**
Past	I, he, she, it, we, you, they **sought**	I, he, she, it **was sought** we, you, they **were sought**
Past *Prog.*	I, he, she, it **was seeking** we, you, they **were seeking**	I, he, she, it **was being sought** we, you, they **were being sought**
Past *Int.*	I, he, she, it, we, you, they **did seek**	I, he, she, it, we, you, they **did get sought**
Pres. *Perf.*	I, we, you, they **have sought** he, she, it **has sought**	I, we, you, they **have been sought** he, she, it **has been sought**
Past *Perf.*	I, he, she, it, we, you, they **had sought**	I, he, she, it, we, you, they **had been sought**
Fut. *Perf.*	I, he, she, it, we, you, they **will have sought**	I, he, she, it, we, you, they **will have been sought**

IMPERATIVE MOOD

seek　　　　　　　　**be sought**

SUBJUNCTIVE MOOD

Pres.	if I, he, she, it, we, you, they **seek**	if I, he, she, it, we, you, they **be sought**
Past	if I, he, she, it, we, you, they **sought**	if I, he, she, it, we, you, they **were sought**
Fut.	if I, he, she, it, we, you, they **should seek**	if I, he, she, it, we, you, they **should be sought**

Transitive and intransitive.

They sought help from a local agency.
He is being sought for questioning by the authorities.

PRINCIPAL PARTS: **seems, seeming**
seemed, seemed

INDICATIVE MOOD

Pres.	I, we, you, they **seem**
	he, she, it **seems**
Pres. *Prog.*	I **am seeming** we, you, they **are seeming** he, she, it **is seeming**
Pres. *Int.*	I, we, you, they **do seem** he, she, it **does seem**
Fut.	I, he, she, it, we, you, they **will seem**
Past	I, he, she, it, we, you, they **seemed**
Past *Prog.*	I, he, she, it **was seeming** we, you, they **were seeming**
Past *Int.*	I, he, she, it, we, you, they **did seem**
Pres. *Perf.*	I, we, you, they **have seemed** he, she, it **has seemed**
Past *Perf.*	I, he, she, it, we, you, they **had seemed**
Fut. *Perf.*	I, he, she, it, we, you, they **will have seemed**

IMPERATIVE MOOD

seem

SUBJUNCTIVE MOOD

Pres.	if I, he, she, it, we, you, they **seem**
Past	if I, he, she, it, we, you, they **seemed**
Fut.	if I, he, she, it, we, you, they **should seem**

He seemed preoccupied with another thought.
It has often seemed to me that she is extremely graceful.

AN ESSENTIAL
55 VERB

Examples

She seems very nice.

He seemed preoccupied.

Everything seemed just right.

For the first few minutes it will seem strange.

He has always seemed distant.

I seem to remember meeting you somewhere before.

He could not have seemed more relaxed.

Doesn't that seem strange to you?

It should have seemed natural.

They do seem very upset.

Words and expressions related to this verb

Things aren't always as they seem.

It seems to me that you are mistaken.

What seems to be the trouble?

All seems well.

He seemed out of place.

She seemed right at home.

It's not what it seems.

The meat seems done to me.

It is a profitable thing, if one is wise, to seem foolish.

All that we see or seem is but a dream inside a dream.

S

sell
(active voice)

be sold
(passive voice)

INDICATIVE MOOD

Pres.	I, we, you, they **sell**	I **am sold**
		we, you, they **are sold**
	he, she, it **sells**	he, she, it **is sold**
Pres.	I **am selling**	I **am being sold**
Prog.	we, you, they **are selling**	we, you, they **are being sold**
	he, she, it **is selling**	he, she, it **is being sold**
Pres.	I, we, you, they **do sell**	I, we, you, they **do get sold**
Int.	he, she, it **does sell**	he, she, it **does get sold**
Fut.	I, he, she, it,	I, he, she, it,
	we, you, they **will sell**	we, you, they **will be sold**
Past	I, he, she, it,	I, he, she, it **was sold**
	we, you, they **sold**	we, you, they **were sold**
Past	I, he, she, it **was selling**	I, he, she, it **was being sold**
Prog.	we, you, they **were selling**	we, you, they **were being sold**
Past	I, he, she, it,	I, he, she, it,
Int.	we, you, they **did sell**	we, you, they **did get sold**
Pres.	I, we, you, they **have sold**	I, we, you, they **have been sold**
Perf.	he, she, it **has sold**	he, she, it **has been sold**
Past	I, he, she, it,	I, he, she, it,
Perf.	we, you, they **had sold**	we, you, they **had been sold**
Fut.	I, he, she, it, we, you, they	I, he, she, it, we, you, they
Perf.	**will have sold**	**will have been sold**

IMPERATIVE MOOD

sell

be sold

SUBJUNCTIVE MOOD

Pres.	if I, he, she, it,	if I, he, she, it,
	we, you, they **sell**	we, you, they **be sold**
Past	if I, he, she, it,	if I, he, she, it,
	we, you, they **sold**	we, you, they **were sold**
Fut.	if I, he, she, it,	if I, he, she, it,
	we, you, they **should sell**	we, you, they **should be sold**

Transitive and intransitive.

My wife sold her old clothes on the Internet.
More books were sold on the Internet than in bookstores last year.

send
(active voice)

PRINCIPAL PARTS: **sends, sending, sent, sent**

be sent
(passive voice)

INDICATIVE MOOD

Pres.	I, we, you, they **send**	I **am sent**
		we, you, they **are sent**
	he, she, it **sends**	he, she, it **is sent**
Pres.	I **am sending**	I **am being sent**
Prog.	we, you, they **are sending**	we, you, they **are being sent**
	he, she, it **is sending**	he, she, it **is being sent**
Pres.	I, we, you, they **do send**	I, we, you, they **do get sent**
Int.	he, she, it **does send**	he, she, it **does get sent**
Fut.	I, he, she, it,	I, he, she, it,
	we, you, they **will send**	we, you, they **will be sent**
Past	I, he, she, it,	I, he, she, it **was sent**
	we, you, they **sent**	we, you, they **were sent**
Past	I, he, she, it **was sending**	I, he, she, it **was being sent**
Prog.	we, you, they **were sending**	we, you, they **were being sent**
Past	I, he, she, it,	I, he, she, it,
Int.	we, you, they **did send**	we, you, they **did get sent**
Pres.	I, we, you, they **have sent**	I, we, you, they **have been sent**
Perf.	he, she, it **has sent**	he, she, it **has been sent**
Past	I, he, she, it,	I, he, she, it,
Perf.	we, you, they **had sent**	we, you, they **had been sent**
Fut.	I, he, she, it, we, you, they	I, he, she, it, we, you, they
Perf.	**will have sent**	**will have been sent**

S

IMPERATIVE MOOD

send **be sent**

SUBJUNCTIVE MOOD

Pres.	if I, he, she, it,	if I, he, she, it,
	we, you, they **send**	we, you, they **be sent**
Past	if I, he, she, it,	if I, he, she, it,
	we, you, they **sent**	we, you, they **were sent**
Fut.	if I, he, she, it,	if I, he, she, it,
	we, you, they **should send**	we, you, they **should be sent**

Transitive and intransitive.

He sent her a present of flowers for her birthday.
The e-mail to all employees was sent this morning.

serve
(active voice)

be served
(passive voice)

INDICATIVE MOOD

Pres.	I, we, you, they **serve**	I **am served**
		we, you, they **are served**
	he, she, it **serves**	he, she, it **is served**
Pres.	I **am serving**	I **am being served**
Prog.	we, you, they **are serving**	we, you, they **are being served**
	he, she, it **is serving**	he, she, it **is being served**
Pres.	I, we, you, they **do serve**	I, we, you, they **do get served**
Int.	he, she, it **does serve**	he, she, it **does get served**
Fut.	I, he, she, it,	I, he, she, it,
	we, you, they **will serve**	we, you, they **will be served**
Past	I, he, she, it,	I, he, she, it **was served**
	we, you, they **served**	we, you, they **were served**
Past	I, he, she, it **was serving**	I, he, she, it **was being served**
Prog.	we, you, they **were serving**	we, you, they **were being served**
Past	I, he, she, it,	I, he, she, it,
Int.	we, you, they **did serve**	we, you, they **did get served**
Pres.	I, we, you, they **have served**	I, we, you, they **have been served**
Perf.	he, she, it **has served**	he, she, it **has been served**
Past	I, he, she, it,	I, he, she, it,
Perf.	we, you, they **had served**	we, you, they **had been served**
Fut.	I, he, she, it, we, you, they	I, he, she, it, we, you, they
Perf.	**will have served**	**will have been served**

IMPERATIVE MOOD

serve   **be served**

SUBJUNCTIVE MOOD

Pres.	if I, he, she, it,	if I, he, she, it,
	we, you, they **serve**	we, you, they **be served**
Past	if I, he, she, it,	if I, he, she, it,
	we, you, they **served**	we, you, they **were served**
Fut.	if I, he, she, it,	if I, he, she, it,
	we, you, they **should serve**	we, you, they **should be served**

Transitive and intransitive.

Are you serving a vegetarian alternative meal?
They served their country for two years of military service.
The wives were served by their husbands.

set (active voice)	PRINCIPAL PARTS: sets, setting, set, set	be set (passive voice)

INDICATIVE MOOD

Pres.	I, we, you, they **set**	I **am set** we, you, they **are set**
	he, she, it **sets**	he, she, it **is set**
Pres. *Prog.*	I **am setting** we, you, they **are setting** he, she, it **is setting**	I **am being set** we, you, they **are being set** he, she, it **is being set**
Pres. *Int.*	I, we, you, they **do set** he, she, it **does set**	I, we, you, they **do get set** he, she, it **does get set**
Fut.	I, he, she, it, we, you, they **will set**	I, he, she, it, we, you, they **will be set**
Past	I, he, she, it, we, you, they **set**	I, he, she, it **was set** we, you, they **were set**
Past *Prog.*	I, he, she, it **was setting** we, you, they **were setting**	I, he, she, it **was being set** we, you, they **were being set**
Past *Int.*	I, he, she, it, we, you, they **did set**	I, he, she, it, we, you, they **did get set**
Pres. *Perf.*	I, we, you, they **have set** he, she, it **has set**	I, we, you, they **have been set** he, she, it **has been set**
Past *Perf.*	I, he, she, it, we, you, they **had set**	I, he, she, it, we, you, they **had been set**
Fut. *Perf.*	I, he, she, it, we, you, they **will have set**	I, he, she, it, we, you, they **will have been set**

IMPERATIVE MOOD

set	**be set**

SUBJUNCTIVE MOOD

Pres.	if I, he, she, it, we, you, they **set**	if I, he, she, it, we, you, they **be set**
Past	if I, he, she, it, we, you, they **set**	if I, he, she, it, we, you, they **were set**
Fut.	if I, he, she, it, we, you, they **should set**	if I, he, she, it, we, you, they **should be set**

Transitive and intransitive.

Mother always sets the table on Sundays.
They are setting the pin further back for the match.
The surgeon set the broken bone without complication.
The flowers were set on the tables before the guests arrived.

AN ESSENTIAL
55 VERB

403

set

Examples

Who usually sets the table?

Mother set the table.

The sun sets in the west.

Please set the package on the table.

The time had been set by the administrator.

We will set the conditions after we have consulted our attorney.

The flower was set on the window sill.

The diamond was set into a gold ring.

The broken bone was set by the surgeon.

Let's set up the tent.

Words and expressions related to this verb

He is set in his ways.

The alarm was set off by the smoke.

The accident set back his progress.

Her performance set her apart from her peers.

She set down the plane on the runway without incident.

I am setting off tomorrow for a long journey.

Set him straight on the facts.

He was set up for failure by his supposed friends.

They were set free by their captors.

Set yourself realistic goals.

sew
(active voice)

be sewn/sewed
(passive voice)

INDICATIVE MOOD

Pres.	I, we, you, they **sew**	I **am sewn**
		we, you, they **are sewn**
	he, she, it **sews**	he, she, it **is sewn**
Pres.	I **am sewing**	I **am being sewn**
Prog.	we, you, they **are sewing**	we, you, they **are being sewn**
	he, she, it **is sewing**	he, she, it **is being sewn**
Pres.	I, we, you, they **do sew**	I, we, you, they **do get sewn**
Int.	he, she, it **does sew**	he, she, it **does get sewn**
Fut.	I, he, she, it,	I, he, she, it,
	we, you, they **will sew**	we, you, they **will be sewn**
Past	I, he, she, it,	I, he, she, it **was sewn**
	we, you, they **sewed**	we, you, they **were sewn**
Past	I, he, she, it **was sewing**	I, he, she, it **was being sewn**
Prog.	we, you, they **were sewing**	we, you, they **were being sewn**
Past	I, he, she, it,	I, he, she, it,
Int.	we, you, they **did sew**	we, you, they **did get sewn**
Pres.	I, we, you, they **have sewn**	I, we, you, they **have been sewn**
Perf.	he, she, it **has sewn**	he, she, it **has been sewn**
Past	I, he, she, it,	I, he, she, it,
Perf.	we, you, they **had sewn**	we, you, they **had been sewn**
Fut.	I, he, she, it, we, you, they	I, he, she, it, we, you, they
Perf.	**will have sewn**	**will have been sewn**

S

IMPERATIVE MOOD

sew

be sewn

SUBJUNCTIVE MOOD

Pres.	if I, he, she, it,	if I, he, she, it,
	we, you, they **sew**	we, you, they **be sewn**
Past	if I, he, she, it,	if I, he, she, it,
	we, you, they **sewed**	we, you, they **were sewn**
Fut.	if I, he, she, it,	if I, he, she, it,
	we, you, they **should sew**	we, you, they **should be sewn**

Transitive and intransitive.

My mother sewed all of our costumes.
The name tags are sewn onto the uniforms.

shake
(active voice)

be shaken
(passive voice)

INDICATIVE MOOD

Pres.	I, we, you, they **shake**	I **am shaken**
		we, you, they **are shaken**
	he, she, it **shakes**	he, she, it **is shaken**
Pres.	I **am shaking**	I **am being shaken**
Prog.	we, you, they **are shaking**	we, you, they **are being shaken**
	he, she, it **is shaking**	he, she, it **is being shaken**
Pres.	I, we, you, they **do shake**	I, we, you, they **do get shaken**
Int.	he, she, it **does shake**	he, she, it **does get shaken**
Fut.	I, he, she, it,	I, he, she, it,
	we, you, they **will shake**	we, you, they **will be shaken**
Past	I, he, she, it,	I, he, she, it **was shaken**
	we, you, they **shook**	we, you, they **were shaken**
Past	I, he, she, it **was shaking**	I, he, she, it **was being shaken**
Prog.	we, you, they **were shaking**	we, you, they **were being shaken**
Past	I, he, she, it,	I, he, she, it,
Int.	we, you, they **did shake**	we, you, they **did get shaken**
Pres.	I, we, you, they **have shaken**	I, we, you, they **have been shaken**
Perf.	he, she, it **has shaken**	he, she, it **has been shaken**
Past	I, he, she, it,	I, he, she, it,
Perf.	we, you, they **had shaken**	we, you, they **had been shaken**
Fut.	I, he, she, it, we, you, they	I, he, she, it, we, you, they
Perf.	**will have shaken**	**will have been shaken**

IMPERATIVE MOOD

shake **be shaken**

SUBJUNCTIVE MOOD

Pres.	if I, he, she, it,	if I, he, she, it,
	we, you, they **shake**	we, you, they **be shaken**
Past	if I, he, she, it,	if I, he, she, it,
	we, you, they **shook**	we, you, they **were shaken**
Fut.	if I, he, she, it,	if I, he, she, it,
	we, you, they **should shake**	we, you, they **should be shaken**

Transitive and intransitive.

The politician is shaking hands with his supporters.
The child shook with fever.
They were shaken by the bad news.

406

shampoo
(active voice)

be shampooed
(passive voice)

INDICATIVE MOOD

Pres.	I, we, you, they **shampoo**	I **am shampooed**
		we, you, they **are shampooed**
	he, she, it **shampoos**	he, she, it **is shampooed**
Pres.	I **am shampooing**	I **am being shampooed**
Prog.	we, you, they **are shampooing**	we, you, they **are being shampooed**
	he, she, it **is shampooing**	he, she, it **is being shampooed**
Pres.	I, we, you, they **do shampoo**	I, we, you, they **do get shampooed**
Int.	he, she, it **does shampoo**	he, she, it **does get shampooed**
Fut.	I, he, she, it,	I, he, she, it,
	we, you, they **will shampoo**	we, you, they **will be shampooed**
Past	I, he, she, it,	I, he, she, it **was shampooed**
	we, you, they **shampooed**	we, you, they **were shampooed**
Past	I, he, she, it **was shampooing**	I, he, she, it **was being shampooed**
Prog.	we, you, they **were shampooing**	we, you, they **were being shampooed**
Past	I, he, she, it,	I, he, she, it,
Int.	we, you, they **did shampoo**	we, you, they **did get shampooed**
Pres.	I, we, you, they **have shampooed**	I, we, you, they **have been shampooed**
Perf.	he, she, it **has shampooed**	he, she, it **has been shampooed**
Past	I, he, she, it,	I, he, she, it,
Perf.	we, you, they **had shampooed**	we, you, they **had been shampooed**
Fut.	I, he, she, it, we, you, they	I, he, she, it, we, you, they
Perf.	**will have shampooed**	**will have been shampooed**

IMPERATIVE MOOD

shampoo   **be shampooed**

SUBJUNCTIVE MOOD

Pres.	if I, he, she, it,	if I, he, she, it,
	we, you, they **shampoo**	we, you, they **be shampooed**
Past	if I, he, she, it,	if I, he, she, it,
	we, you, they **shampooed**	we, you, they **were shampooed**
Fut.	if I, he, she, it,	if I, he, she, it,
	we, you, they **should shampoo**	we, you, they **should be shampooed**

Transitive and intransitive.

She shampoos her long hair twice a week.
They are shampooing the baby's hair in warm water.
Can you believe that she shampooed her dogs?
I was shampooed by the nurses when I was in the hospital.

S

shape
(active voice)

be shaped
(passive voice)

INDICATIVE MOOD

Pres.	I, we, you, they **shape**	I **am shaped**
		we, you, they **are shaped**
	he, she, it **shapes**	he, she, it **is shaped**
Pres. *Prog.*	I **am shaping**	I **am being shaped**
	we, you, they **are shaping**	we, you, they **are being shaped**
	he, she, it **is shaping**	he, she, it **is being shaped**
Pres. *Int.*	I, we, you, they **do shape**	I, we, you, they **do get shaped**
	he, she, it **does shape**	he, she, it **does get shaped**
Fut.	I, he, she, it,	I, he, she, it,
	we, you, they **will shape**	we, you, they **will be shaped**
Past	I, he, she, it,	I, he, she, it **was shaped**
	we, you, they **shaped**	we, you, they **were shaped**
Past *Prog.*	I, he, she, it **was shaping**	I, he, she, it **was being shaped**
	we, you, they **were shaping**	we, you, they **were being shaped**
Past *Int.*	I, he, she, it,	I, he, she, it,
	we, you, they **did shape**	we, you, they **did get shaped**
Pres. *Perf.*	I, we, you, they **have shaped**	I, we, you, they **have been shaped**
	he, she, it **has shaped**	he, she, it **has been shaped**
Past *Perf.*	I, he, she, it,	I, he, she, it,
	we, you, they **had shaped**	we, you, they **had been shaped**
Fut. *Perf.*	I, he, she, it, we, you, they	I, he, she, it, we, you, they
	will have shaped	**will have been shaped**

IMPERATIVE MOOD

shape　　　　　　　　**be shaped**

SUBJUNCTIVE MOOD

Pres.	if I, he, she, it,	if I, he, she, it,
	we, you, they **shape**	we, you, they **be shaped**
Past	if I, he, she, it,	if I, he, she, it,
	we, you, they **shaped**	we, you, they **were shaped**
Fut.	if I, he, she, it,	if I, he, she, it,
	we, you, they **should shape**	we, you, they **should be shaped**

Transitive and intransitive.

They are shaping the ice into an igloo.
He shaped his argument to his audience's interests.
Our vote was shaped by public comment.

shave
(active voice)

Principal Parts: shaves, shaving, shaved, shaved/shaven

be shaved/shaven
(passive voice)

INDICATIVE MOOD

Pres.	I, we, you, they **shave**	I **am shaved**
		we, you, they **are shaved**
	he, she, it **shaves**	he, she, it **is shaved**
Pres.	I **am shaving**	I **am being shaved**
Prog.	we, you, they **are shaving**	we, you, they **are being shaved**
	he, she, it **is shaving**	he, she, it **is being shaved**
Pres.	I, we, you, they **do shave**	I, we, you, they **do get shaved**
Int.	he, she, it **does shave**	he, she, it **does get shaved**
Fut.	I, he, she, it,	I, he, she, it,
	we, you, they **will shave**	we, you, they **will be shaved**
Past	I, he, she, it,	I, he, she, it **was shaved**
	we, you, they **shaved**	we, you, they **were shaved**
Past	I, he, she, it **was shaving**	I, he, she, it **was being shaved**
Prog.	we, you, they **were shaving**	we, you, they **were being shaved**
Past	I, he, she, it,	I, he, she, it,
Int.	we, you, they **did shave**	we, you, they **did get shaved**
Pres.	I, we, you, they **have shaved**	I, we, you, they **have been shaved**
Perf.	he, she, it **has shaved**	he, she, it **has been shaved**
Past	I, he, she, it,	I, he, she, it,
Perf.	we, you, they **had shaved**	we, you, they **had been shaved**
Fut.	I, he, she, it, we, you, they	I, he, she, it, we, you, they
Perf.	**will have shaved**	**will have been shaved**

IMPERATIVE MOOD

shave

be shaved

SUBJUNCTIVE MOOD

Pres.	if I, he, she, it,	if I, he, she, it,
	we, you, they **shave**	we, you, they **be shaved**
Past	if I, he, she, it,	if I, he, she, it,
	we, you, they **shaved**	we, you, they **were shaved**
Fut.	if I, he, she, it,	if I, he, she, it,
	we, you, they **should shave**	we, you, they **should be shaved**

Transitive and intransitive.

Are you shaving before we go out?
I shaved this morning.
The heads of the recruits were shaved with an electric razor.

S

PRINCIPAL PARTS: **sheds, shedding, shed, shed**

INDICATIVE MOOD

Pres.	I, we, you, they **shed**	**I am shed** we, you, they **are shed**
	he, she, it **sheds**	he, she, it **is shed**
Pres. *Prog.*	I **am shedding** we, you, they **are shedding** he, she, it **is shedding**	**I am being shed** we, you, they **are being shed** he, she, it **is being shed**
Pres. *Int.*	I, we, you, they **do shed** he, she, it **does shed**	I, we, you, they **do get shed** he, she, it **does get shed**
Fut.	I, he, she, it, we, you, they **will shed**	I, he, she, it, we, you, they **will be shed**
Past	I, he, she, it, we, you, they **shed**	I, he, she, it **was shed** we, you, they **were shed**
Past *Prog.*	I, he, she, it **was shedding** we, you, they **were shedding**	I, he, she, it **was being shed** we, you, they **were being shed**
Past *Int.*	I, he, she, it, we, you, they **did shed**	I, he, she, it, we, you, they **did get shed**
Pres. *Perf.*	I, we, you, they **have shed** he, she, it **has shed**	I, we, you, they **have been shed** he, she, it **has been shed**
Past *Perf.*	I, he, she, it, we, you, they **had shed**	I, he, she, it, we, you, they **had been shed**
Fut. *Perf.*	I, he, she, it, we, you, they **will have shed**	I, he, she, it, we, you, they **will have been shed**

IMPERATIVE MOOD

shed   **be shed**

SUBJUNCTIVE MOOD

Pres.	if I, he, she, it, we, you, they **shed**	if I, he, she, it, we, you, they **be shed**
Past	if I, he, she, it, we, you, they **shed**	if I, he, she, it, we, you, they **were shed**
Fut.	if I, he, she, it, we, you, they **should shed**	if I, he, she, it, we, you, they **should be shed**

Transitive and intransitive.

He is shedding a few pounds a month.
That snake shed its skin five times last year.
Her fears and clothes having been shed, she plunged into the cold water.

shine
(active voice)

PRINCIPAL PARTS: shines, shining, shone/shined, shone/shined

be shone/shined
(passive voice)

INDICATIVE MOOD

Pres.	I, we, you, they **shine**	I **am shone**
	he, she, it **shines**	we, you, they **are shone**
		he, she, it **is shone**
Pres.	I **am shining**	I **am being shone**
Prog.	we, you, they **are shining**	we, you, they **are being shone**
	he, she, it **is shining**	he, she, it **is being shone**
Pres.	I, we, you, they **do shine**	I, we, you, they **do get shone**
Int.	he, she, it **does shine**	he, she, it **does get shone**
Fut.	I, he, she, it,	I, he, she, it,
	we, you, they **will shine**	we, you, they **will be shone**
Past	I, he, she, it,	I, he, she, it **was shone**
	we, you, they **shone**	we, you, they **were shone**
Past	I, he, she, it **was shining**	I, he, she, it **was being shone**
Prog.	we, you, they **were shining**	we, you, they **were being shone**
Past	I, he, she, it,	I, he, she, it,
Int.	we, you, they **did shine**	we, you, they **did get shone**
Pres.	I, we, you, they **have shone**	I, we, you, they **have been shone**
Perf.	he, she, it **has shone**	he, she, it **has been shone**
Past	I, he, she, it,	I, he, she, it,
Perf.	we, you, they **had shone**	we, you, they **had been shone**
Fut.	I, he, she, it, we, you, they	I, he, she, it, we, you, they
Perf.	**will have shone**	**will have been shone**

IMPERATIVE MOOD

shine   **be shone**

SUBJUNCTIVE MOOD

Pres.	if I, he, she, it,	if I, he, she, it,
	we, you, they **shine**	we, you, they **be shone**
Past	if I, he, she, it,	if I, he, she, it,
	we, you, they **shone**	we, you, they **were shone**
Fut.	if I, he, she, it,	if I, he, she, it,
	we, you, they **should shine**	we, you, they **should be shone**

Intransitive or transitive. Past tense and past participle may be either SHONE or SHINED. In the meaning of "polishing" only SHINED is used for the past tense and past participle.

The sun is shining brightly.
They shone a light on the fuse box.
Any light that could be shone on this matter would be helpful.

shoot
(active voice)

be shot
(passive voice)

INDICATIVE MOOD

Pres.	I, we, you, they **shoot**	I **am shot**
		we, you, they **are shot**
	he, she, it **shoots**	he, she, it **is shot**
Pres.	I **am shooting**	I **am being shot**
Prog.	we, you, they **are shooting**	we, you, they **are being shot**
	he, she, it **is shooting**	he, she, it **is being shot**
Pres.	I, we, you, they **do shoot**	I, we, you, they **do get shot**
Int.	he, she, it **does shoot**	he, she, it **does get shot**
Fut.	I, he, she, it,	I, he, she, it,
	we, you, they **will shoot**	we, you, they **will be shot**
Past	I, he, she, it,	I, he, she, it **was shot**
	we, you, they **shot**	we, you, they **were shot**
Past	I, he, she, it **was shooting**	I, he, she, it **was being shot**
Prog.	we, you, they **were shooting**	we, you, they **were being shot**
Past	I, he, she, it,	I, he, she, it,
Int.	we, you, they **did shoot**	we, you, they **did get shot**
Pres.	I, we, you, they **have shot**	I, we, you, they **have been shot**
Perf.	he, she, it **has shot**	he, she, it **has been shot**
Past	I, he, she, it,	I, he, she, it,
Perf.	we, you, they **had shot**	we, you, they **had been shot**
Fut.	I, he, she, it, we, you, they	I, he, she, it, we, you, they
Perf.	**will have shot**	**will have been shot**

IMPERATIVE MOOD

shoot   **be shot**

SUBJUNCTIVE MOOD

Pres.	if I, he, she, it,	if I, he, she, it,
	we, you, they **shoot**	we, you, they **be shot**
Past	if I, he, she, it,	if I, he, she, it,
	we, you, they **shot**	we, you, they **were shot**
Fut.	if I, he, she, it,	if I, he, she, it,
	we, you, they **should shoot**	we, you, they **should be shot**

Transitive and intransitive.

He shot a rifle for the first time in basic military training.
The fireworks were shot into the air by professionals.

shop
(active voice)

be shopped
(passive voice)

INDICATIVE MOOD

Pres.	I, we, you, they **shop**	I **am shopped**
		we, you, they **are shopped**
	he, she, it **shops**	he, she, it **is shopped**
Pres.	I **am shopping**	I **am being shopped**
Prog.	we, you, they **are shopping**	we, you, they **are being shopped**
	he, she, it **is shopping**	he, she, it **is being shopped**
Pres.	I, we, you, they **do shop**	I, we, you, they **do get shopped**
Int.	he, she, it **does shop**	he, she, it **does get shopped**
Fut.	I, he, she, it,	I, he, she, it,
	we, you, they **will shop**	we, you, they **will be shopped**
Past	I, he, she, it,	I, he, she, it **was shopped**
	we, you, they **shopped**	we, you, they **were shopped**
Past	I, he, she, it **was shopping**	I, he, she, it **was being shopped**
Prog.	we, you, they **were shopping**	we, you, they **were being shopped**
Past	I, he, she, it,	I, he, she, it,
Int.	we, you, they **did shop**	we, you, they **did get shopped**
Pres.	I, we, you, they **have shopped**	I, we, you, they **have been shopped**
Perf.	he, she, it **has shopped**	he, she, it **has been shopped**
Past	I, he, she, it,	I, he, she, it,
Perf.	we, you, they **had shopped**	we, you, they **had been shopped**
Fut.	I, he, she, it, we, you, they	I, he, she, it, we, you, they
Perf.	**will have shopped**	**will have been shopped**

S

IMPERATIVE MOOD

shop **be shopped**

SUBJUNCTIVE MOOD

Pres.	if I, he, she, it,	if I, he, she, it,
	we, you, they **shop**	we, you, they **be shopped**
Past	if I, he, she, it,	if I, he, she, it,
	we, you, they **shopped**	we, you, they **were shopped**
Fut.	if I, he, she, it,	if I, he, she, it,
	we, you, they **should shop**	we, you, they **should be shopped**

Intransitive and transitive.

The girls are shopping with their mother.
They shopped until they dropped.
The shelves were shopped clean before the storm arrived.

short	**PRINCIPAL PARTS: shorts, shorting,**	be shorted
(active voice)	**shorted, shorted**	(passive voice)

INDICATIVE MOOD

Pres.	I, we, you, they **short**	**I am shorted**
		we, you, they **are shorted**
	he, she, it **shorts**	he, she, it **is shorted**
Pres.	**I am shorting**	**I am being shorted**
Prog.	we, you, they **are shorting**	we, you, they **are being shorted**
	he, she, it **is shorting**	he, she, it **is being shorted**
Pres.	I, we, you, they **do short**	I, we, you, they **do get shorted**
Int.	he, she, it **does short**	he, she, it **does get shorted**
Fut.	I, he, she, it,	I, he, she, it,
	we, you, they **will short**	we, you, they **will be shorted**
Past	I, he, she, it,	I, he, she, it **was shorted**
	we, you, they **shorted**	we, you, they **were shorted**
Past	I, he, she, it **was shorting**	I, he, she, it **was being shorted**
Prog.	we, you, they **were shorting**	we, you, they **were being shorted**
Past	I, he, she, it,	I, he, she, it,
Int.	we, you, they **did short**	we, you, they **did get shorted**
Pres.	I, we, you, they **have shorted**	I, we, you, they **have been shorted**
Perf.	he, she, it **has shorted**	he, she, it **has been shorted**
Past	I, he, she, it,	I, he, she, it,
Perf.	we, you, they **had shorted**	we, you, they **had been shorted**
Fut.	I, he, she, it, we, you, they	I, he, she, it, we, you, they
Perf.	**will have shorted**	**will have been shorted**

IMPERATIVE MOOD

short   **be shorted**

SUBJUNCTIVE MOOD

Pres.	if I, he, she, it,	if I, he, she, it,
	we, you, they **short**	we, you, they **be shorted**
Past	if I, he, she, it,	if I, he, she, it,
	we, you, they **shorted**	we, you, they **were shorted**
Fut.	if I, he, she, it,	if I, he, she, it,
	we, you, they **should short**	we, you, they **should be shorted**

Transitive and intransitive.

The hair dryer shorted the circuit.
The garage door opener was shorted by an electric surge.

shorten
(active voice)

be shortened
(passive voice)

INDICATIVE MOOD

Pres.	I, we, you, they **shorten**	I **am shortened**
		we, you, they **are shortened**
	he, she, it **shortens**	he, she, it **is shortened**
Pres.	I **am shortening**	I **am being shortened**
Prog.	we, you, they **are shortening**	we, you, they **are being shortened**
	he, she, it **is shortening**	he, she, it **is being shortened**
Pres.	I, we, you, they **do shorten**	I, we, you, they **do get shortened**
Int.	he, she, it **does shorten**	he, she, it **does get shortened**
Fut.	I, he, she, it,	I, he, she, it,
	we, you, they **will shorten**	we, you, they **will be shortened**
Past	I, he, she, it,	I, he, she, it **was shortened**
	we, you, they **shortened**	we, you, they **were shortened**
Past	I, he, she, it **was shortening**	I, he, she, it **was being shortened**
Prog.	we, you, they **were shortening**	we, you, they **were being shortened**
Past	I, he, she, it,	I, he, she, it,
Int.	we, you, they **did shorten**	we, you, they **did get shortened**
Pres.	I, we, you, they **have shortened**	I, we, you, they **have been shortened**
Perf.	he, she, it **has shortened**	he, she, it **has been shortened**
Past	I, he, she, it,	I, he, she, it,
Perf.	we, you, they **had shortened**	we, you, they **had been shortened**
Fut.	I, he, she, it, we, you, they	I, he, she, it, we, you, they
Perf.	**will have shortened**	**will have been shortened**

IMPERATIVE MOOD

shorten   **be shortened**

SUBJUNCTIVE MOOD

Pres.	if I, he, she, it,	if I, he, she, it,
	we, you, they **shorten**	we, you, they **be shortened**
Past	if I, he, she, it,	if I, he, she, it,
	we, you, they **shortened**	we, you, they **were shortened**
Fut.	if I, he, she, it,	if I, he, she, it,
	we, you, they **should shorten**	we, you, they **should be shortened**

Transitive and intransitive.

He shortened his routine to fit the required time limits.
Her toenails were shortened before she donned her pointe shoes.

shovel
(active voice)

Principal Parts: shovels, shoveling/
shovelling, shoveled/shovelled,
shoveled/shovelled

be shoveled/
shovelled
(passive voice)

INDICATIVE MOOD

Pres.	I, we, you, they **shovel**	I **am shoveled** we, you, they **are shoveled**
	he, she, it **shovels**	he, she, it **is shoveled**
Pres. *Prog.*	I **am shoveling** we, you, they **are shoveling** he, she, it **is shoveling**	I **am being shoveled** we, you, they **are being shoveled** he, she, it **is being shoveled**
Pres. *Int.*	I, we, you, they **do shovel** he, she, it **does shovel**	I, we, you, they **do get shoveled** he, she, it **does get shoveled**
Fut.	I, he, she, it, we, you, they **will shovel**	I, he, she, it, we, you, they **will be shoveled**
Past	I, he, she, it, we, you, they **shoveled**	I, he, she, it **was shoveled** we, you, they **were shoveled**
Past *Prog.*	I, he, she, it **was shoveling** we, you, they **were shoveling**	I, he, she, it **was being shoveled** we, you, they **were being shoveled**
Past *Int.*	I, he, she, it, we, you, they **did shovel**	I, he, she, it, we, you, they **did get shoveled**
Pres. *Perf.*	I, we, you, they **have shoveled** he, she, it **has shoveled**	I, we, you, they **have been shoveled** he, she, it **has been shoveled**
Past *Perf.*	I, he, she, it, we, you, they **had shoveled**	I, he, she, it, we, you, they **had been shoveled**
Fut. *Perf.*	I, he, she, it, we, you, they **will have shoveled**	I, he, she, it, we, you, they **will have been shoveled**

IMPERATIVE MOOD

shovel   **be shoveled**

SUBJUNCTIVE MOOD

Pres.	if I, he, she, it, we, you, they **shovel**	if I, he, she, it, we, you, they **be shoveled**
Past	if I, he, she, it, we, you, they **shoveled**	if I, he, she, it, we, you, they **were shoveled**
Fut.	if I, he, she, it, we, you, they **should shovel**	if I, he, she, it, we, you, they **should be shoveled**

Transitive and intransitive. The *Oxford Dictionary* prefers the spellings with "ll": SHOVELLING, SHOVELLED.

Papa is shoveling the driveway after our big snowstorm.
They shoveled the topsoil throughout the garden.
This sidewalk is shoveled by the town.

| show
(active voice) | PRINCIPAL PARTS: **shows, showing,
showed, shown/showed** | be shown/showed
(passive voice) |

INDICATIVE MOOD

Pres.	I, we, you, they **show**	I **am shown**
		we, you, they **are shown**
	he, she, it **shows**	he, she, it **is shown**
Pres. *Prog.*	I **am showing**	I **am being shown**
	we, you, they **are showing**	we, you, they **are being shown**
	he, she, it **is showing**	he, she, it **is being shown**
Pres. *Int.*	I, we, you, they **do show**	I, we, you, they **do get shown**
	he, she, it **does show**	he, she, it **does get shown**
Fut.	I, he, she, it, we, you, they **will show**	I, he, she, it, we, you, they **will be shown**
Past	I, he, she, it, we, you, they **showed**	I, he, she, it **was shown** we, you, they **were shown**
Past *Prog.*	I, he, she, it **was showing** we, you, they **were showing**	I, he, she, it **was being shown** we, you, they **were being shown**
Past *Int.*	I, he, she, it, we, you, they **did show**	I, he, she, it, we, you, they **did get shown**
Pres. *Perf.*	I, we, you, they **have shown** he, she, it **has shown**	I, we, you, they **have been shown** he, she, it **has been shown**
Past *Perf.*	I, he, she, it, we, you, they **had shown**	I, he, she, it, we, you, they **had been shown**
Fut. *Perf.*	I, he, she, it, we, you, they **will have shown**	I, he, she, it, we, you, they **will have been shown**

S

IMPERATIVE MOOD

show	**be shown**

SUBJUNCTIVE MOOD

Pres.	if I, he, she, it, we, you, they **show**	if I, he, she, it, we, you, they **be shown**
Past	if I, he, she, it, we, you, they **showed**	if I, he, she, it, we, you, they **were shown**
Fut.	if I, he, she, it, we, you, they **should show**	if I, he, she, it, we, you, they **should be shown**

Transitive and intransitive.

He showed us all his pictures.
This film has been shown before on television.

AN ESSENTIAL
55 VERB

show

Examples

Show me.

He showed her the new furniture.

Passports must be shown at the airport counter.

We were shown in to his office.

I want to be shown the exits.

What movie is showing downtown?

Your hem is showing.

I am showing you my finest selection.

The pictures are being shown for the first time.

The attorney will be shown all the evidence against her client.

Words and expressions related to this verb

Show me your stuff.

Show me what you can do.

He was shown to the door.

He is always showing off.

They showed up late.

It just showed up on my screen.

The realtor is showing our house today.

When are you showing your dog?

He was shown up by a newcomer.

I will show you around the campus.

shred
(active voice)

be shredded/shred
(passive voice)

INDICATIVE MOOD

Pres.	I, we, you, they **shred**	I **am shredded**
		we, you, they **are shredded**
	he, she, it **shreds**	he, she, it **is shredded**
Pres.	I **am shredding**	I **am being shredded**
Prog.	we, you, they **are shredding**	we, you, they **are being shredded**
	he, she, it **is shredding**	he, she, it **is being shredded**
Pres.	I, we, you, they **do shred**	I, we, you, they **do get shredded**
Int.	he, she, it **does shred**	he, she, it **does get shredded**
Fut.	I, he, she, it,	I, he, she, it,
	we, you, they **will shred**	we, you, they **will be shredded**
Past	I, he, she, it,	I, he, she, it **was shredded**
	we, you, they **shredded**	we, you, they **were shredded**
Past	I, he, she, it **was shredding**	I, he, she, it **was being shredded**
Prog.	we, you, they **were shredding**	we, you, they **were being shredded**
Past	I, he, she, it,	I, he, she, it,
Int.	we, you, they **did shred**	we, you, they **did get shredded**
Pres.	I, we, you, they **have shredded**	I, we, you, they **have been shredded**
Perf.	he, she, it **has shredded**	he, she, it **has been shredded**
Past	I, he, she, it,	I, he, she, it,
Perf.	we, you, they **had shredded**	we, you, they **had been shredded**
Fut.	I, he, she, it, we, you, they	I, he, she, it, we, you, they
Perf.	**will have shredded**	**will have been shredded**

IMPERATIVE MOOD

shred

be shredded

SUBJUNCTIVE MOOD

Pres.	if I, he, she, it,	if I, he, she, it,
	we, you, they **shred**	we, you, they **be shredded**
Past	if I, he, she, it,	if I, he, she, it,
	we, you, they **shredded**	we, you, they **were shredded**
Fut.	if I, he, she, it,	if I, he, she, it,
	we, you, they **should shred**	we, you, they **should be shredded**

They are shredding the confidential documents.
He shredded the carrots for a salad.
Have all the copies been shredded?

shrink
(active voice)

PRINCIPAL PARTS: shrinks, shrinking, shrank/shrunk, shrunk/shrunken

be shrunk/shrunken
(passive voice)

INDICATIVE MOOD

Pres.	I, we, you, they **shrink**		I **am shrunk**
			we, you, they **are shrunk**
	he, she, it **shrinks**		he, she, it **is shrunk**
Pres.	I **am shrinking**		I **am being shrunk**
Prog.	we, you, they **are shrinking**		we, you, they **are being shrunk**
	he, she, it **is shrinking**		he, she, it **is being shrunk**
Pres.	I, we, you, they **do shrink**		I, we, you, they **do get shrunk**
Int.	he, she, it **does shrink**		he, she, it **does get shrunk**
Fut.	I, he, she, it,		I, he, she, it,
	we, you, they **will shrink**		we, you, they **will be shrunk**
Past	I, he, she, it,		I, he, she, it **was shrunk**
	we, you, they **shrank**		we, you, they **were shrunk**
Past	I, he, she, it **was shrinking**		I, he, she, it **was being shrunk**
Prog.	we, you, they **were shrinking**		we, you, they **were being shrunk**
Past	I, he, she, it,		I, he, she, it,
Int.	we, you, they **did shrink**		we, you, they **did get shrunk**
Pres.	I, we, you, they **have shrunk**		I, we, you, they **have been shrunk**
Perf.	he, she, it **has shrunk**		he, she, it **has been shrunk**
Past	I, he, she, it,		I, he, she, it,
Perf.	we, you, they **had shrunk**		we, you, they **had been shrunk**
Fut.	I, he, she, it, we, you, they		I, he, she, it, we, you, they
Perf.	**will have shrunk**		**will have been shrunk**

IMPERATIVE MOOD

shrink

be shrunk

SUBJUNCTIVE MOOD

Pres.	if I, he, she, it,		if I, he, she, it,
	we, you, they **shrink**		we, you, they **be shrunk**
Past	if I, he, she, it,		if I, he, she, it,
	we, you, they **shrank**		we, you, they **were shrunk**
Fut.	if I, he, she, it,		if I, he, she, it,
	we, you, they **should shrink**		we, you, they **should be shrunk**

Intransitive and transitive. The past tense may be either SHRANK or SHRUNK. The past participle is either SHRUNK or SHRUNKEN.

They shrank the size of the files for storage.
The digital photos were shrunk to half their original size.

shut
(active voice)

be shut
(passive voice)

INDICATIVE MOOD

Pres.	I, we, you, they **shut**	I **am shut**
		we, you, they **are shut**
	he, she, it **shuts**	he, she, it **is shut**
Pres.	I **am shutting**	I **am being shut**
Prog.	we, you, they **are shutting**	we, you, they **are being shut**
	he, she, it **is shutting**	he, she, it **is being shut**
Pres.	I, we, you, they **do shut**	I, we, you, they **do get shut**
Int.	he, she, it **does shut**	he, she, it **does get shut**
Fut.	I, he, she, it,	I, he, she, it,
	we, you, they **will shut**	we, you, they **will be shut**
Past	I, he, she, it,	I, he, she, it **was shut**
	we, you, they **shut**	we, you, they **were shut**
Past	I, he, she, it **was shutting**	I, he, she, it **was being shut**
Prog.	we, you, they **were shutting**	we, you, they **were being shut**
Past	I, he, she, it,	I, he, she, it,
Int.	we, you, they **did shut**	we, you, they **did get shut**
Pres.	I, we, you, they **have shut**	I, we, you, they **have been shut**
Perf.	he, she, it **has shut**	he, she, it **has been shut**
Past	I, he, she, it,	I, he, she, it,
Perf.	we, you, they **had shut**	we, you, they **had been shut**
Fut.	I, he, she, it, we, you, they	I, he, she, it, we, you, they
Perf.	**will have shut**	**will have been shut**

IMPERATIVE MOOD

shut   **be shut**

SUBJUNCTIVE MOOD

Pres.	if I, he, she, it,	if I, he, she, it,
	we, you, they **shut**	we, you, they **be shut**
Past	if I, he, she, it,	if I, he, she, it,
	we, you, they **shut**	we, you, they **were shut**
Fut.	if I, he, she, it,	if I, he, she, it,
	we, you, they **should shut**	we, you, they **should be shut**

Transitive and intransitive.

She shuts her windows every night.
We are shutting down the camp for the winter.
He shut down his computer for the weekend.
The store was shut for the holidays.

421

sing
(active voice)

PRINCIPAL PARTS: **sings, singing,
sang/sung, sung**

be sung
(passive voice)

INDICATIVE MOOD

Pres.	I, we, you, they **sing**	**I am sung** we, you, they **are sung**
	he, she, it **sings**	he, she, it **is sung**
Pres. *Prog.*	**I am singing** we, you, they **are singing** he, she, it **is singing**	**I am being sung** we, you, they **are being sung** he, she, it **is being sung**
Pres. *Int.*	I, we, you, they **do sing** he, she, it **does sing**	I, we, you, they **do get sung** he, she, it **does get sung**
Fut.	I, he, she, it, we, you, they **will sing**	I, he, she, it, we, you, they **will be sung**
Past	I, he, she, it, we, you, they **sang**	I, he, she, it **was sung** we, you, they **were sung**
Past *Prog.*	I, he, she, it **was singing** we, you, they **were singing**	I, he, she, it **was being sung** we, you, they **were being sung**
Past *Int.*	I, he, she, it, we, you, they **did sing**	I, he, she, it, we, you, they **did get sung**
Pres. *Perf.*	I, we, you, they **have sung** he, she, it **has sung**	I, we, you, they **have been sung** he, she, it **has been sung**
Past *Perf.*	I, he, she, it, we, you, they **had sung**	I, he, she, it, we, you, they **had been sung**
Fut. *Perf.*	I, he, she, it, we, you, they **will have sung**	I, he, she, it, we, you, they **will have been sung**

IMPERATIVE MOOD

sing

be sung

SUBJUNCTIVE MOOD

Pres.	if I, he, she, it, we, you, they **sing**	if I, he, she, it, we, you, they **be sung**
Past	if I, he, she, it, we, you, they **sang**	if I, he, she, it, we, you, they **were sung**
Fut.	if I, he, she, it, we, you, they **should sing**	if I, he, she, it, we, you, they **should be sung**

Intransitive and transitive. The *Oxford Dictionary* and *Webster's* do not list the past tense form
SUNG.

She sang like a bird.
Their song has been sung at weddings for ages.

singe
(active voice)

be singed
(passive voice)

INDICATIVE MOOD

Pres.	I, we, you, they **singe**	I **am singed**
		we, you, they **are singed**
	he, she, it **singes**	he, she, it **is singed**
Pres.	I **am singeing**	I **am being singed**
Prog.	we, you, they **are singeing**	we, you, they **are being singed**
	he, she, it **is singeing**	he, she, it **is being singed**
Pres.	I, we, you, they **do singe**	I, we, you, they **do get singed**
Int.	he, she, it **does singe**	he, she, it **does get singed**
Fut.	I, he, she, it,	I, he, she, it,
	we, you, they **will singe**	we, you, they **will be singed**
Past	I, he, she, it,	I, he, she, it **was singed**
	we, you, they **singed**	we, you, they **were singed**
Past	I, he, she, it **was singeing**	I, he, she, it **was being singed**
Prog.	we, you, they **were singeing**	we, you, they **were being singed**
Past	I, he, she, it,	I, he, she, it,
Int.	we, you, they **did singe**	we, you, they **did get singed**
Pres.	I, we, you, they **have singed**	I, we, you, they **have been singed**
Perf.	he, she, it **has singed**	he, she, it **has been singed**
Past	I, he, she, it,	I, he, she, it,
Perf.	we, you, they **had singed**	we, you, they **had been singed**
Fut.	I, he, she, it, we, you, they	I, he, she, it, we, you, they
Perf.	**will have singed**	**will have been singed**

IMPERATIVE MOOD

singe **be singed**

SUBJUNCTIVE MOOD

Pres.	if I, he, she, it,	if I, he, she, it,
	we, you, they **singe**	we, you, they **be singed**
Past	if I, he, she, it,	if I, he, she, it,
	we, you, they **singed**	we, you, they **were singed**
Fut.	if I, he, she, it,	if I, he, she, it,
	we, you, they **should singe**	we, you, they **should be singed**

That hot iron is singeing the skirt.
She singed her hair with the curling iron.
Only the very tips of her fingers were singed by the fire.

sink
(active voice)

be sunk
(passive voice)

INDICATIVE MOOD

Pres.	I, we, you, they **sink**	I **am sunk**
		we, you, they **are sunk**
	he, she, it **sinks**	he, she, it **is sunk**
Pres.	I **am sinking**	I **am being sunk**
Prog.	we, you, they **are sinking**	we, you, they **are being sunk**
	he, she, it **is sinking**	he, she, it **is being sunk**
Pres.	I, we, you, they **do sink**	I, we, you, they **do get sunk**
Int.	he, she, it **does sink**	he, she, it **does get sunk**
Fut.	I, he, she, it,	I, he, she, it,
	we, you, they **will sink**	we, you, they **will be sunk**
Past	I, he, she, it,	I, he, she, it **was sunk**
	we, you, they **sank**	we, you, they **were sunk**
Past	I, he, she, it **was sinking**	I, he, she, it **was being sunk**
Prog.	we, you, they **were sinking**	we, you, they **were being sunk**
Past	I, he, she, it,	I, he, she, it,
Int.	we, you, they **did sink**	we, you, they **did get sunk**
Pres.	I, we, you, they **have sunk**	I, we, you, they **have been sunk**
Perf.	he, she, it **has sunk**	he, she, it **has been sunk**
Past	I, he, she, it,	I, he, she, it,
Perf.	we, you, they **had sunk**	we, you, they **had been sunk**
Fut.	I, he, she, it, we, you, they	I, he, she, it, we, you, they
Perf.	**will have sunk**	**will have been sunk**

IMPERATIVE MOOD

sink

be sunk

SUBJUNCTIVE MOOD

Pres.	if I, he, she, it,	if I, he, she, it,
	we, you, they **sink**	we, you, they **be sunk**
Past	if I, he, she, it,	if I, he, she, it,
	we, you, they **sank**	we, you, they **were sunk**
Fut.	if I, he, she, it,	if I, he, she, it,
	we, you, they **should sink**	we, you, they **should be sunk**

Intransitive and transitive. The past tense may be either SANK or SUNK.

The family sank its entire savings into bonds.
The ship was sunk by a huge wave.

424

sit
(active voice)

PRINCIPAL PARTS: **sits, sitting, sat, sat**

be sat
(passive voice)

INDICATIVE MOOD

Pres.	I, we, you, they **sit**	I **am sat**
		we, you, they **are sat**
	he, she, it **sits**	he, she, it **is sat**
Pres.	I **am sitting**	I **am being sat**
Prog.	we, you, they **are sitting**	we, you, they **are being sat**
	he, she, it **is sitting**	he, she, it **is being sat**
Pres.	I, we, you, they **do sit**	I, we, you, they **do get sat**
Int.	he, she, it **does sit**	he, she, it **does get sat**
Fut.	I, he, she, it,	I, he, she, it,
	we, you, they **will sit**	we, you, they **will be sat**
Past	I, he, she, it,	I, he, she, it **was sat**
	we, you, they **sat**	we, you, they **were sat**
Past	I, he, she, it **was sitting**	I, he, she, it **was being sat**
Prog.	we, you, they **were sitting**	we, you, they **were being sat**
Past	I, he, she, it,	I, he, she, it,
Int.	we, you, they **did sit**	we, you, they **did get sat**
Pres.	I, we, you, they **have sat**	I, we, you, they **have been sat**
Perf.	he, she, it **has sat**	he, she, it **has been sat**
Past	I, he, she, it,	I, he, she, it,
Perf.	we, you, they **had sat**	we, you, they **had been sat**
Fut.	I, he, she, it, we, you, they	I, he, she, it, we, you, they
Perf.	**will have sat**	**will have been sat**

IMPERATIVE MOOD

sit

be sat

SUBJUNCTIVE MOOD

Pres.	if I, he, she, it,	if I, he, she, it,
	we, you, they **sit**	we, you, they **be sat**
Past	if I, he, she, it,	if I, he, she, it,
	we, you, they **sat**	we, you, they **were sat**
Fut.	if I, he, she, it,	if I, he, she, it,
	we, you, they **should sit**	we, you, they **should be sat**

Intransitive and transitive.

He is sitting at the top of the stadium.
She sat there lost in thought.
The misbehaving child was sat in the corner for ten minutes.

ski
(active voice)

PRINCIPAL PARTS: **skis, skiing,**
skied, skied

be skied
(passive voice)

INDICATIVE MOOD

Pres.	I, we, you, they **ski**	I **am skied**
		we, you, they **are skied**
	he, she, it **skis**	he, she, it **is skied**
Pres.	I **am skiing**	I **am being skied**
Prog.	we, you, they **are skiing**	we, you, they **are being skied**
	he, she, it **is skiing**	he, she, it **is being skied**
Pres.	I, we, you, they **do ski**	I, we, you, they **do get skied**
Int.	he, she, it **does ski**	he, she, it **does get skied**
Fut.	I, he, she, it,	I, he, she, it,
	we, you, they **will ski**	we, you, they **will be skied**
Past	I, he, she, it,	I, he, she, it **was skied**
	we, you, they **skied**	we, you, they **were skied**
Past	I, he, she, it **was skiing**	I, he, she, it **was being skied**
Prog.	we, you, they **were skiing**	we, you, they **were being skied**
Past	I, he, she, it,	I, he, she, it,
Int.	we, you, they **did ski**	we, you, they **did get skied**
Pres.	I, we, you, they **have skied**	I, we, you, they **have been skied**
Perf.	he, she, it **has skied**	he, she, it **has been skied**
Past	I, he, she, it,	I, he, she, it,
Perf.	we, you, they **had skied**	we, you, they **had been skied**
Fut.	I, he, she, it, we, you, they	I, he, she, it, we, you, they
Perf.	**will have skied**	**will have been skied**

IMPERATIVE MOOD

ski   be skied

SUBJUNCTIVE MOOD

Pres.	if I, he, she, it,	if I, he, she, it,
	we, you, they **ski**	we, you, they **be skied**
Past	if I, he, she, it,	if I, he, she, it,
	we, you, they **skied**	we, you, they **were skied**
Fut.	if I, he, she, it,	if I, he, she, it,
	we, you, they **should ski**	we, you, they **should be skied**

Intransitive and transitive.

We are skiing on the expert trails today.
She skied every weekend as a young girl.
These trails have almost never been skied in competition.

| slay
(active voice) | PRINCIPAL PARTS: slays, slaying,
slew, slain | be slain
(passive voice) |

INDICATIVE MOOD

Pres.	I, we, you, they **slay**	I **am slain** we, you, they **are slain**
	he, she, it **slays**	he, she, it **is slain**
Pres. *Prog.*	I **am slaying** we, you, they **are slaying** he, she, it **is slaying**	I **am being slain** we, you, they **are being slain** he, she, it **is being slain**
Pres. *Int.*	I, we, you, they **do slay** he, she, it **does slay**	I, we, you, they **do get slain** he, she, it **does get slain**
Fut.	I, he, she, it, we, you, they **will slay**	I, he, she, it, we, you, they **will be slain**
Past	I, he, she, it, we, you, they **slew**	I, he, she, it **was slain** we, you, they **were slain**
Past *Prog.*	I, he, she, it **was slaying** we, you, they **were slaying**	I, he, she, it **was being slain** we, you, they **were being slain**
Past *Int.*	I, he, she, it, we, you, they **did slay**	I, he, she, it, we, you, they **did get slain**
Pres. *Perf.*	I, we, you, they **have slain** he, she, it **has slain**	I, we, you, they **have been slain** he, she, it **has been slain**
Past *Perf.*	I, he, she, it, we, you, they **had slain**	I, he, she, it, we, you, they **had been slain**
Fut. *Perf.*	I, he, she, it, we, you, they **will have slain**	I, he, she, it, we, you, they **will have been slain**

IMPERATIVE MOOD

slay	**be slain**

SUBJUNCTIVE MOOD

Pres.	if I, he, she, it, we, you, they **slay**	if I, he, she, it, we, you, they **be slain**
Past	if I, he, she, it, we, you, they **slew**	if I, he, she, it, we, you, they **were slain**
Fut.	if I, he, she, it, we, you, they **should slay**	if I, he, she, it, we, you, they **should be slain**

S

The prince slew the dragon.
The warriors were slain by the opposing army's arrows.

sleep
(active voice)

be slept
(passive voice)

INDICATIVE MOOD

Pres.	I, we, you, they **sleep**	I **am slept**
		we, you, they **are slept**
	he, she, it **sleeps**	he, she, it **is slept**
Pres.	I **am sleeping**	I **am being slept**
Prog.	we, you, they **are sleeping**	we, you, they **are being slept**
	he, she, it **is sleeping**	he, she, it **is being slept**
Pres.	I, we, you, they **do sleep**	I, we, you, they **do get slept**
Int.	he, she, it **does sleep**	he, she, it **does get slept**
Fut.	I, he, she, it,	I, he, she, it,
	we, you, they **will sleep**	we, you, they **will be slept**
Past	I, he, she, it,	I, he, she, it **was slept**
	we, you, they **slept**	we, you, they **were slept**
Past	I, he, she, it **was sleeping**	I, he, she, it **was being slept**
Prog.	we, you, they **were sleeping**	we, you, they **were being slept**
Past	I, he, she, it,	I, he, she, it,
Int.	we, you, they **did sleep**	we, you, they **did get slept**
Pres.	I, we, you, they **have slept**	I, we, you, they **have been slept**
Perf.	he, she, it **has slept**	he, she, it **has been slept**
Past	I, he, she, it,	I, he, she, it,
Perf.	we, you, they **had slept**	we, you, they **had been slept**
Fut.	I, he, she, it, we, you, they	I, he, she, it, we, you, they
Perf.	**will have slept**	**will have been slept**

IMPERATIVE MOOD

sleep   **be slept**

SUBJUNCTIVE MOOD

Pres.	if I, he, she, it,	if I, he, she, it,
	we, you, they **sleep**	we, you, they **be slept**
Past	if I, he, she, it,	if I, he, she, it,
	we, you, they **slept**	we, you, they **were slept**
Fut.	if I, he, she, it,	if I, he, she, it,
	we, you, they **should sleep**	we, you, they **should be slept**

Intransitive and transitive.

I slept through the entire lecture.
The early morning hours were slept away by the partygoers.

slide
(active voice)

be slid
(passive voice)

INDICATIVE MOOD

Pres.	I, we, you, they **slide**	I **am slid**
		we, you, they **are slid**
	he, she, it **slides**	he, she, it **is slid**
Pres.	I **am sliding**	I **am being slid**
Prog.	we, you, they **are sliding**	we, you, they **are being slid**
	he, she, it **is sliding**	he, she, it **is being slid**
Pres.	I, we, you, they **do slide**	I, we, you, they **do get slid**
Int.	he, she, it **does slide**	he, she, it **does get slid**
Fut.	I, he, she, it,	I, he, she, it,
	we, you, they **will slide**	we, you, they **will be slid**
Past	I, he, she, it,	I, he, she, it **was slid**
	we, you, they **slid**	we, you, they **were slid**
Past	I, he, she, it **was sliding**	I, he, she, it **was being slid**
Prog.	we, you, they **were sliding**	we, you, they **were being slid**
Past	I, he, she, it,	I, he, she, it,
Int.	we, you, they **did slide**	we, you, they **did get slid**
Pres.	I, we, you, they **have slid**	I, we, you, they **have been slid**
Perf.	he, she, it **has slid**	he, she, it **has been slid**
Past	I, he, she, it,	I, he, she, it,
Perf.	we, you, they **had slid**	we, you, they **had been slid**
Fut.	I, he, she, it, we, you, they	I, he, she, it, we, you, they
Perf.	**will have slid**	**will have been slid**

IMPERATIVE MOOD

slide　　　　　　　**be slid**

SUBJUNCTIVE MOOD

Pres.	if I, he, she, it,	if I, he, she, it,
	we, you, they **slide**	we, you, they **be slid**
Past	if I, he, she, it,	if I, he, she, it,
	we, you, they **slid**	we, you, they **were slid**
Fut.	if I, he, she, it,	if I, he, she, it,
	we, you, they **should slide**	we, you, they **should be slid**

Intransitive and transitive.

The soap keeps sliding from my hands.
He slid the plate with his cake across the table.
The tray was carefully slid into the hot oven.

S

INDICATIVE MOOD

Pres.	I, we, you, they **sling**	I **am slung**
		we, you, they **are slung**
	he, she, it **slings**	he, she, it **is slung**
Pres.	I **am slinging**	I **am being slung**
Prog.	we, you, they **are slinging**	we, you, they **are being slung**
	he, she, it **is slinging**	he, she, it **is being slung**
Pres.	I, we, you, they **do sling**	I, we, you, they **do get slung**
Int.	he, she, it **does sling**	he, she, it **does get slung**
Fut.	I, he, she, it,	I, he, she, it,
	we, you, they **will sling**	we, you, they **will be slung**
Past	I, he, she, it,	I, he, she, it **was slung**
	we, you, they **slung**	we, you, they **were slung**
Past	I, he, she, it **was slinging**	I, he, she, it **was being slung**
Prog.	we, you, they **were slinging**	we, you, they **were being slung**
Past	I, he, she, it,	I, he, she, it,
Int.	we, you, they **did sling**	we, you, they **did get slung**
Pres.	I, we, you, they **have slung**	I, we, you, they **have been slung**
Perf.	he, she, it **has slung**	he, she, it **has been slung**
Past	I, he, she, it,	I, he, she, it,
Perf.	we, you, they **had slung**	we, you, they **had been slung**
Fut.	I, he, she, it, we, you, they	I, he, she, it, we, you, they
Perf.	**will have slung**	**will have been slung**

IMPERATIVE MOOD

sling   **be slung**

SUBJUNCTIVE MOOD

Pres.	if I, he, she, it,	if I, he, she, it,
	we, you, they **sling**	we, you, they **be slung**
Past	if I, he, she, it,	if I, he, she, it,
	we, you, they **slung**	we, you, they **were slung**
Fut.	if I, he, she, it,	if I, he, she, it,
	we, you, they **should sling**	we, you, they **should be slung**

He slung the backpack over his shoulder.
Her purse was slung on her arm.

slip
(active voice)

be slipped
(passive voice)

INDICATIVE MOOD

Pres.	I, we, you, they **slip**	I **am slipped** we, you, they **are slipped**
	he, she, it **slips**	he, she, it **is slipped**
Pres. *Prog.*	I **am slipping** we, you, they **are slipping** he, she, it **is slipping**	I **am being slipped** we, you, they **are being slipped** he, she, it **is being slipped**
Pres. *Int.*	I, we, you, they **do slip** he, she, it **does slip**	I, we, you **do get slipped** he, she, it **does get slipped**
Fut.	I, he, she, it, we, you, they **will slip**	I, he, she, it, we, you, they **will be slipped**
Past	I, he, she, it, we, you, they **slipped**	I, he, she, it **was slipped** we, you, they **were slipped**
Past *Prog.*	I, he, she, it **was slipping** we, you, they **were slipping**	I, he, she, it **was being slipped** we, you, they **were being slipped**
Past *Int.*	I, he, she, it, we, you, they **did slip**	I, he, she, it, we, you, they **did get slipped**
Pres. *Perf.*	I, we, you, they **have slipped** he, she, it **has slipped**	I, we, you, they **have been slipped** he, she, it **has been slipped**
Past *Perf.*	I, he, she, it, we, you, they **had slipped**	I, he, she, it, we, you, they **had been slipped**
Fut. *Perf.*	I, he, she, it, we, you, they **will have slipped**	I, he, she, it, we, you, they **will have been slipped**

IMPERATIVE MOOD

slip   **be slipped**

SUBJUNCTIVE MOOD

Pres.	if I, he, she, it, we, you, they **slip**	if I, he, she, it, we, you, they **be slipped**
Past	if I, he, she, it, we, you, they **slipped**	if I, he, she, it, we, you, they **were slipped**
Fut.	if I, he, she, it, we, you, they **should slip**	if I, he, she, it, we, you, they **should be slipped**

Intransitive and transitive.

The boat is slipping into its berth.
She slipped and fell on the ice.
The money was slipped quietly into his waiting hand.

431

PRINCIPAL PARTS: **slits, slitting, slit, slit**

INDICATIVE MOOD

Pres.	I, we, you, they **slit**	I **am slit**
		we, you, they **are slit**
	he, she, it **slits**	he, she, it **is slit**
Pres.	I **am slitting**	I **am being slit**
Prog.	we, you, they **are slitting**	we, you, they **are being slit**
	he, she, it **is slitting**	he, she, it **is being slit**
Pres.	I, we, you, they **do slit**	I, we, you, they **do get slit**
Int.	he, she, it **does slit**	he, she, it **does get slit**
Fut.	I, he, she, it,	I, he, she, it,
	we, you, they **will slit**	we, you, they **will be slit**
Past	I, he, she, it,	I, he, she, it **was slit**
	we, you, they **slit**	we, you, they **were slit**
Past	I, he, she, it **was slitting**	I, he, she, it **was being slit**
Prog.	we, you, they **were slitting**	we, you, they **were being slit**
Past	I, he, she, it,	I, he, she, it,
Int.	we, you, they **did slit**	we, you, they **did get slit**
Pres.	I, we, you, they **have slit**	I, we, you, they **have been slit**
Perf.	he, she, it **has slit**	he, she, it **has been slit**
Past	I, he, she, it,	I, he, she, it,
Perf.	we, you, they **had slit**	we, you, they **had been slit**
Fut.	I, he, she, it, we, you, they	I, he, she, it, we, you, they
Perf.	**will have slit**	**will have been slit**

IMPERATIVE MOOD

slit

be slit

SUBJUNCTIVE MOOD

Pres.	if I, he, she, it,	if I, he, she, it,
	we, you, they **slit**	we, you, they **be slit**
Past	if I, he, she, it,	if I, he, she, it,
	we, you, they **slit**	we, you, they **were slit**
Fut.	if I, he, she, it,	if I, he, she, it,
	we, you, they **should slit**	we, you, they **should be slit**

She first slits a hole for the button and then sews it up.
He slit his finger on a piece of glass.
The pants were slit down the middle.

smell
(active voice)

be smelled/smelt
(passive voice)

INDICATIVE MOOD

Pres.	I, we, you, they **smell**	I **am smelled**
		we, you, they **are smelled**
	he, she, it **smells**	he, she, it **is smelled**
Pres.	I **am smelling**	I **am being smelled**
Prog.	we, you, they **are smelling**	we, you, they **are being smelled**
	he, she, it **is smelling**	he, she, it **is being smelled**
Pres.	I, we, you, they **do smell**	I, we, you, they **do get smelled**
Int.	he, she, it **does smell**	he, she, it **does get smelled**
Fut.	I, he, she, it,	I, he, she, it,
	we, you, they **will smell**	we, you, they **will be smelled**
Past	I, he, she, it,	I, he, she, it **was smelled**
	we, you, they **smelled**	we, you, they **were smelled**
Past	I, he, she, it **was smelling**	I, he, she, it **was being smelled**
Prog.	we, you, they **were smelling**	we, you, they **were being smelled**
Past	I, he, she, it,	I, he, she, it,
Int.	we, you, they **did smell**	we, you, they **did get smelled**
Pres.	I, we, you, they **have smelled**	I, we, you, they **have been smelled**
Perf.	he, she, it **has smelled**	he, she, it **has been smelled**
Past	I, he, she, it,	I, he, she, it,
Perf.	we, you, they **had smelled**	we, you, they **had been smelled**
Fut.	I, he, she, it, we, you, they	I, he, she, it, we, you, they
Perf.	**will have smelled**	**will have been smelled**

IMPERATIVE MOOD

smell **be smelled**

SUBJUNCTIVE MOOD

Pres.	if I, he, she, it,	if I, he, she, it,
	we, you, they **smell**	we, you, they **be smelled**
Past	if I, he, she, it,	if I, he, she, it,
	we, you, they **smelled**	we, you, they **were smelled**
Fut.	if I, he, she, it,	if I, he, she, it,
	we, you, they **should smell**	we, you, they **should be smelled**

Transitive and intransitive. The *Oxford Dictionary* lists SMELT as the first form for the past tense and past participle.

I smelled the skunk before I saw it.
The wines were carefully smelled by the experts for their rating.

433

PRINCIPAL PARTS: **smiles, smiling, smiled, smiled**

INDICATIVE MOOD

Pres.	I, we, you, they **smile**	I **am smiled**
		we, you, they **are smiled**
	he, she, it **smiles**	he, she, it **is smiled**
Pres.	I **am smiling**	I **am being smiled**
Prog.	we, you, they **are smiling**	we, you, they **are being smiled**
	he, she, it **is smiling**	he, she, it **is being smiled**
Pres.	I, we, you, they **do smile**	I, we, you, they **do get smiled**
Int.	he, she, it **does smile**	he, she, it **does get smiled**
Fut.	I, he, she, it,	I, he, she, it,
	we, you, they **will smile**	we, you, they **will be smiled**
Past	I, he, she, it,	I, he, she, it **was smiled**
	we, you, they **smiled**	we, you, they **were smiled**
Past	I, he, she, it **was smiling**	I, he, she, it **was being smiled**
Prog.	we, you, they **were smiling**	we, you, they **were being smiled**
Past	I, he, she, it,	I, he, she, it,
Int.	we, you, they **did smile**	we, you, they **did get smiled**
Pres.	I, we, you, they **have smiled**	I, we, you, they **have been smiled**
Perf.	he, she, it **has smiled**	he, she, it **has been smiled**
Past	I, he, she, it,	I, he, she, it,
Perf.	we, you, they **had smiled**	we, you, they **had been smiled**
Fut.	I, he, she, it, we, you, they	I, he, she, it, we, you, they
Perf.	**will have smiled**	**will have been smiled**

IMPERATIVE MOOD

smile   **be smiled**

SUBJUNCTIVE MOOD

Pres.	if I, he, she, it,	if I, he, she, it,
	we, you, they **smile**	we, you, they **be smiled**
Past	if I, he, she, it,	if I, he, she, it,
	we, you, they **smiled**	we, you, they **were smiled**
Fut.	if I, he, she, it,	if I, he, she, it,
	we, you, they **should smile**	we, you, they **should be smiled**

Intransitive and transitive.

When Irish eyes are smiling, all the world is bright and gay.
She smiled at him as she waved good-bye.
The juggler's efforts were smiled at by the crowd.

434

sneak
(active voice)

PRINCIPAL PARTS: **sneaks, sneaking,**
sneaked/snuck, sneaked/snuck

be sneaked/snuck
(passive voice)

INDICATIVE MOOD

Pres.	I, we, you, they **sneak**	I **am sneaked** we, you, they **are sneaked**
	he, she, it **sneaks**	he, she, it **is sneaked**
Pres. *Prog.*	I **am sneaking** we, you, they **are sneaking** he, she, it **is sneaking**	I **am being sneaked** we, you, they **are being sneaked** he, she, it **is being sneaked**
Pres. *Int.*	I, we, you, they **do sneak** he, she, it **does sneak**	I, we, you, they **do get sneaked** he, she, it **does get sneaked**
Fut.	I, he, she, it, we, you, they **will sneak**	I, he, she, it, we, you, they **will be sneaked**
Past	I, he, she, it, we, you, they **sneaked**	I, he, she, it **was sneaked** we, you, they **were sneaked**
Past *Prog.*	I, he, she, it **was sneaking** we, you, they **were sneaking**	I, he, she, it **was being sneaked** we, you, they **were being sneaked**
Past *Int.*	I, he, she, it, we, you, they **did sneak**	I, he, she, it, we, you, they **did get sneaked**
Pres. *Perf.*	I, we, you, they **have sneaked** he, she, it **has sneaked**	I, we, you, they **have been sneaked** he, she, it **has been sneaked**
Past *Perf.*	I, he, she, it, we, you, they **had sneaked**	I, he, she, it, we, you, they **had been sneaked**
Fut. *Perf.*	I, he, she, it, we, you, they **will have sneaked**	I, he, she, it, we, you, they **will have been sneaked**

S

IMPERATIVE MOOD

sneak   **be sneaked**

SUBJUNCTIVE MOOD

Pres.	if I, he, she, it, we, you, they **sneak**	if I, he, she, it, we, you, they **be sneaked**
Past	if I, he, she, it, we, you, they **sneaked**	if I, he, she, it, we, you, they **were sneaked**
Fut.	if I, he, she, it, we, you, they **should sneak**	if I, he, she, it, we, you, they **should be sneaked**

Intransitive and transitive. The *Oxford Dictionary* lists as colloquial the past tense and past participle SNUCK.

They sneaked into the movie theater.
Their friends were sneaked in by a relative.

snowboard
(active voice)

INDICATIVE MOOD

Pres.   I, we, you, they **snowboard**

he, she, it **snowboards**

Pres.   I **am snowboarding**
Prog.   we, you, they **are snowboarding**
he, she, it **is snowboarding**

Pres.   I, we, you, they **do snowboard**
Int.   he, she, it **does snowboard**

Fut.   I, he, she, it,
we, you, they **will snowboard**

Past   I, he, she, it,
we, you, they **snowboarded**

Past   I, he, she, it **was snowboarding**
Prog.   we, you, they **were snowboarding**

Past   I, he, she, it,
Int.   we, you, they **did snowboard**

Pres.   I, we, you, they **have snowboarded**
Perf.   he, she, it **has snowboarded**

Past   I, he, she, it,
Perf.   we, you, they **had snowboarded**

Fut.   I, he, she, it, we, you, they
Perf.   **will have snowboarded**

IMPERATIVE MOOD

snowboard

SUBJUNCTIVE MOOD

Pres.   if I, he, she, it,
we, you, they **snowboard**

Past   if I, he, she, it,
we, you, they **snowboarded**

Fut.   if I, he, she, it,
we, you, they **should snowboard**

We snowboarded down two or three awesome trails today.
That mountain was one of the first to have been snowboarded.

sound
(active voice)

PRINCIPAL PARTS: sounds, sounding, sounded, sounded

be sounded
(passive voice)

INDICATIVE MOOD

Pres.	I, we, you, they **sound**	**I am sounded**
		we, you, they **are sounded**
	he, she, it **sounds**	he, she, it **is sounded**
Pres.	**I am sounding**	I am being sounded
Prog.	we, you, they **are sounding**	we, you, they **are being sounded**
	he, she, it **is sounding**	he, she, it **is being sounded**
Pres.	I, we, you, they **do sound**	I, we, you, they **do get sounded**
Int.	he, she, it **does sound**	he, she, it **does get sounded**
Fut.	I, he, she, it,	I, he, she, it,
	we, you, they **will sound**	we, you, they **will be sounded**
Past	I, he, she, it,	I, he, she, it **was sounded**
	we, you, they **sounded**	we, you, they **were sounded**
Past	I, he, she, it **was sounding**	I, he, she, it **was being sounded**
Prog.	we, you, they **were sounding**	we, you, they **were being sounded**
Past	I, he, she, it,	I, he, she, it,
Int.	we, you, they **did sound**	we, you, they **did get sounded**
Pres.	I, we, you, they **have sounded**	I, we, you, they **have been sounded**
Perf.	he, she, it **has sounded**	he, she, it **has been sounded**
Past	I, he, she, it,	I, he, she, it,
Perf.	we, you, they **had sounded**	we, you, they **had been sounded**
Fut.	I, he, she, it, we, you, they	I, he, she, it, we, you, they
Perf.	**will have sounded**	**will have been sounded**

S

IMPERATIVE MOOD

sound   **be sounded**

SUBJUNCTIVE MOOD

Pres.	if I, he, she, it,	if I, he, she, it,
	we, you, they **sound**	we, you, they **be sounded**
Past	if I, he, she, it,	if I, he, she, it,
	we, you, they **sounded**	we, you, they **were sounded**
Fut.	if I, he, she, it,	if I, he, she, it,
	we, you, they **should sound**	we, you, they **should be sounded**

Transitive and intransitive.

That sounded like thunder.
The alarm was sounded by the watchman.

437

sow
(active voice)

PRINCIPAL PARTS: sows, sowing,
sowed, sown/sowed

be sown/sowed
(passive voice)

INDICATIVE MOOD

Pres.	I, we, you, they **sow**	I **am sown**
		we, you, they **are sown**
	he, she, it **sows**	he, she, it **is sown**
Pres.	I **am sowing**	I **am being sown**
Prog.	we, you, they **are sowing**	we, you, they **are being sown**
	he, she, it **is sowing**	he, she, it **is being sown**
Pres.	I, we, you, they **do sow**	I, we, you, they **do get sown**
Int.	he, she, it **does sow**	he, she, it **does get sown**
Fut.	I, he, she, it,	I, he, she, it,
	we, you, they **will sow**	we, you, they **will be sown**
Past	I, he, she, it,	I, he, she, it **was sown**
	we, you, they **sowed**	we, you, they **were sown**
Past	I, he, she, it **was sowing**	I, he, she, it **was being sown**
Prog.	we, you, they **were sowing**	we, you, they **were being sown**
Past	I, he, she, it,	I, he, she, it,
Int.	we, you, they **did sow**	we, you, they **did get sown**
Pres.	I, we, you, they **have sown**	I, we, you, they **have been sown**
Perf.	he, she, it **has sown**	he, she, it **has been sown**
Past	I, he, she, it,	I, he, she, it,
Perf.	we, you, they **had sown**	we, you, they **had been sown**
Fut.	I, he, she, it, we, you, they	I, he, she, it, we, you, they
Perf.	**will have sown**	**will have been sown**

IMPERATIVE MOOD

sow　　　　　　　　　　　　　　**be sown**

SUBJUNCTIVE MOOD

Pres.	if I, he, she, it,	if I, he, she, it,
	we, you, they **sow**	we, you, they **be sown**
Past	if I, he, she, it,	if I, he, she, it,
	we, you, they **sowed**	we, you, they **were sown**
Fut.	if I, he, she, it,	if I, he, she, it,
	we, you, they **should sow**	we, you, they **should be sown**

Transitive and intransitive.

You reap what you sowed.
The seeds were sown just after the thaw.

spam
(active voice)

be spammed
(passive voice)

INDICATIVE MOOD

Pres.   I, we, you, they **spam**   I **am spammed**
                                  we, you, they **are spammed**
        he, she, it **spams**   he, she, it **is spammed**

Pres.   I **am spamming**   I **am being spammed**
Prog.   we, you, they **are spamming**   we, you, they **are being spammed**
        he, she, it **is spamming**   he, she, it **is being spammed**

Pres.   I, we, you, they **do spam**   I, we, you, they **do get spammed**
Int.   he, she, it **does spam**   he, she, it **does get spammed**

Fut.   I, he, she, it,   I, he, she, it,
        we, you, they **will spam**   we, you, they **will be spammed**

Past   I, he, she, it,   I, he, she, it **was spammed**
        we, you, they **spammed**   we, you, they **were spammed**

Past   I, he, she, it **was spamming**   I, he, she, it **was being spammed**
Prog.   we, you, they **were spamming**   we, you, they **were being spammed**

Past   I, he, she, it,   I, he, she, it,
Int.   we, you, they **did spam**   we, you, they **did get spammed**

Pres.   I, we, you, they **have spammed**   I, we, you, they **have been spammed**
Perf.   he, she, it **has spammed**   he, she, it **has been spammed**

Past   I, he, she, it,   I, he, she, it,
Perf.   we, you, they **had spammed**   we, you, they **had been spammed**

Fut.   I, he, she, it, we, you, they   I, he, she, it, we, you, they
Perf.   **will have spammed**   **will have been spammed**

IMPERATIVE MOOD

         spam   **be spammed**

SUBJUNCTIVE MOOD

Pres.   if I, he, she, it,   if I, he, she, it,
        we, you, they **spam**   we, you, they **be spammed**

Past   if I, he, she, it,   if I, he, she, it,
        we, you, they **spammed**   we, you, they **were spammed**

Fut.   if I, he, she, it,   if I, he, she, it,
        we, you, they **should spam**   we, you, they **should be spammed**

S

They are spamming us with tons of junk mail.
He spammed the others just to upset them.
Our users have been spammed repeatedly in the past week.

speak
(active voice)

PRINCIPAL PARTS: **speaks, speaking, spoke, spoken**

be spoken
(passive voice)

INDICATIVE MOOD

Pres.	I, we, you, they **speak**	I **am spoken**
		we, you, they **are spoken**
	he, she, it **speaks**	he, she, it **is spoken**
Pres.	I **am speaking**	I **am being spoken**
Prog.	we, you, they **are speaking**	we, you, they **are being spoken**
	he, she, it **is speaking**	he, she, it **is being spoken**
Pres.	I, we, you, they **do speak**	I, we, you, they **do get spoken**
Int.	he, she, it **does speak**	he, she, it **does get spoken**
Fut.	I, he, she, it,	I, he, she, it,
	we, you, they **will speak**	we, you, they **will be spoken**
Past	I, he, she, it,	I, he, she, it **was spoken**
	we, you, they **spoke**	we, you, they **were spoken**
Past	I, he, she, it **was speaking**	I, he, she, it **was being spoken**
Prog.	we, you, they **were speaking**	we, you, they **were being spoken**
Past	I, he, she, it,	I, he, she, it,
Int.	we, you, they **did speak**	we, you, they **did get spoken**
Pres.	I, we, you, they **have spoken**	I, we, you, they **have been spoken**
Perf.	he, she, it **has spoken**	he, she, it **has been spoken**
Past	I, he, she, it,	I, he, she, it,
Perf.	we, you, they **had spoken**	we, you, they **had been spoken**
Fut.	I, he, she, it, we, you, they	I, he, she, it, we, you, they
Perf.	**will have spoken**	**will have been spoken**

IMPERATIVE MOOD

speak   **be spoken**

SUBJUNCTIVE MOOD

Pres.	if I, he, she, it,	if I, he, she, it,
	we, you, they **speak**	we, you, they **be spoken**
Past	if I, he, she, it,	if I, he, she, it,
	we, you, they **spoke**	we, you, they **were spoken**
Fut.	if I, he, she, it,	if I, he, she, it,
	we, you, they **should speak**	we, you, they **should be spoken**

Intransitive and transitive.

We spoke of times gone by.
Too many harsh words have already been spoken on this topic.

speed
(active voice)

be sped/speeded
(passive voice)

INDICATIVE MOOD

Pres.	I, we, you, they **speed**	I **am sped**
		we, you, they **are sped**
	he, she, it **speeds**	he, she, it **is sped**
Pres.	I **am speeding**	I **am being sped**
Prog.	we, you, they **are speeding**	we, you, they **are being sped**
	he, she, it **is speeding**	he, she, it **is being sped**
Pres.	I, we, you, they **do speed**	I, we, you, they **do get sped**
Int.	he, she, it **does speed**	he, she, it **does get sped**
Fut.	I, he, she, it,	I, he, she, it,
	we, you, they **will speed**	we, you, they **will be sped**
Past	I, he, she, it,	I, he, she, it **was sped**
	we, you, they **sped**	we, you, they **were sped**
Past	I, he, she, it **was speeding**	I, he, she, it **was being sped**
Prog.	we, you, they **were speeding**	we, you, they **were being sped**
Past	I, he, she, it,	I, he, she, it,
Int.	we, you, they **did speed**	we, you, they **did get sped**
Pres.	I, we, you, they **have sped**	I, we, you, they **have been sped**
Perf.	he, she, it **has sped**	he, she, it **has been sped**
Past	I, he, she, it,	I, he, she, it,
Perf.	we, you, they **had sped**	we, you, they **had been sped**
Fut.	I, he, she, it, we, you, they	I, he, she, it, we, you, they
Perf.	**will have sped**	**will have been sped**

IMPERATIVE MOOD

speed **be sped**

SUBJUNCTIVE MOOD

Pres.	if I, he, she, it,	if I, he, she, it,
	we, you, they **speed**	we, you, they **be sped**
Past	if I, he, she, it,	if I, he, she, it,
	we, you, they **sped**	we, you, they **were sped**
Fut.	if I, he, she, it,	if I, he, she, it,
	we, you, they **should speed**	we, you, they **should be sped**

Transitive and intransitive.

He sped by the police car at high speed.
The reply was sped to all the interested parties.

S

spell
(active voice)

PRINCIPAL PARTS: **spells, spelling,
spelled/spelt, spelled/spelt**

be spelled/spelt
(passive voice)

INDICATIVE MOOD

Pres.	I, we, you, they **spell**	I **am spelled**
		we, you, they **are spelled**
	he, she, it **spells**	he, she, it **is spelled**
Pres.	I **am spelling**	I **am being spelled**
Prog.	we, you, they **are spelling**	we, you, they **are being spelled**
	he, she, it **is spelling**	he, she, it **is being spelled**
Pres.	I, we, you, they **do spell**	I, we, you, they **do get spelled**
Int.	he, she, it **does spell**	he, she, it **does get spelled**
Fut.	I, he, she, it,	I, he, she, it,
	we, you, they **will spell**	we, you, they **will be spelled**
Past	I, he, she, it,	I, he, she, it **was spelled**
	we, you, they **spelled**	we, you, they **were spelled**
Past	I, he, she, it **was spelling**	I, he, she, it **was being spelled**
Prog.	we, you, they **were spelling**	we, you, they **were being spelled**
Past	I, he, she, it,	I, he, she, it,
Int.	we, you, they **did spell**	we, you, they **did get spelled**
Pres.	I, we, you, they **have spelled**	I, we, you, they **have been spelled**
Perf.	he, she, it **has spelled**	he, she, it **has been spelled**
Past	I, he, she, it,	I, he, she, it,
Perf.	we, you, they **had spelled**	we, you, they **had been spelled**
Fut.	I, he, she, it, we, you, they	I, he, she, it, we, you, they
Perf.	**will have spelled**	**will have been spelled**

IMPERATIVE MOOD

spell   **be spelled**

SUBJUNCTIVE MOOD

Pres.	if I, he, she, it,	if I, he, she, it,
	we, you, they **spell**	we, you, they **be spelled**
Past	if I, he, she, it,	if I, he, she, it,
	we, you, they **spelled**	we, you, they **were spelled**
Fut.	if I, he, she, it,	if I, he, she, it,
	we, you, they **should spell**	we, you, they **should be spelled**

Transitive and intransitive. When the verb refers to "spelling a word" the past tense and past participle may be SPELLED or SPELT. When it means to "relieve someone by taking turns or to cast a spell on someone" only the form SPELLED is permitted.

He spelled all fifty words correctly.
That word has been spelled wrong at least a dozen times in your paper.

spend
(active voice)

be spent
(passive voice)

INDICATIVE MOOD

Pres.	I, we, you, they **spend**	I **am spent**
		we, you, they **are spent**
	he, she, it **spends**	he, she, it **is spent**
Pres.	I **am spending**	I **am being spent**
Prog.	we, you, they **are spending**	we, you, they **are being spent**
	he, she, it **is spending**	he, she, it **is being spent**
Pres.	I, we, you, they **do spend**	I, we, you, they **do get spent**
Int.	he, she, it **does spend**	he, she, it **does get spent**
Fut.	I, he, she, it,	I, he, she, it,
	we, you, they **will spend**	we, you, they **will be spent**
Past	I, he, she, it,	I, he, she, it **was spent**
	we, you, they **spent**	we, you, they **were spent**
Past	I, he, she, it **was spending**	I, he, she, it **was being spent**
Prog.	we, you, they **were spending**	we, you, they **were being spent**
Past	I, he, she, it,	I, he, she, it,
Int.	we, you, they **did spend**	we, you, they **did get spent**
Pres.	I, we, you, they **have spent**	I, we, you, they **have been spent**
Perf.	he, she, it **has spent**	he, she, it **has been spent**
Past	I, he, she, it,	I, he, she, it,
Perf.	we, you, they **had spent**	we, you, they **had been spent**
Fut.	I, he, she, it, we, you, they	I, he, she, it, we, you, they
Perf.	**will have spent**	**will have been spent**

S

IMPERATIVE MOOD

spend   **be spent**

SUBJUNCTIVE MOOD

Pres.	if I, he, she, it,	if I, he, she, it,
	we, you, they **spend**	we, you, they **be spent**
Past	if I, he, she, it,	if I, he, she, it,
	we, you, they **spent**	we, you, they **were spent**
Fut.	if I, he, she, it,	if I, he, she, it,
	we, you, they **should spend**	we, you, they **should be spent**

Transitive and intransitive.

She spent his money on chocolate.
Their savings were spent on a new home.

443

spill
(active voice)

PRINCIPAL PARTS: **spills, spilling, spilled/spilt, spilled/spilt**

be spilled/spilt
(passive voice)

INDICATIVE MOOD

Pres.	I, we, you, they **spill**	I **am spilled**
		we, you, they **are spilled**
	he, she, it **spills**	he, she, it **is spilled**
Pres.	I **am spilling**	I **am being spilled**
Prog.	we, you, they **are spilling**	we, you, they **are being spilled**
	he, she, it **is spilling**	he, she, it **is being spilled**
Pres.	I, we, you, they **do spill**	I, we, you, they **do get spilled**
Int.	he, she, it **does spill**	he, she, it **does get spilled**
Fut.	I, he, she, it,	I, he, she, it,
	we, you, they **will spill**	we, you, they **will be spilled**
Past	I, he, she, it,	I, he, she, it **was spilled**
	we, you, they **spilled**	we, you, they **were spilled**
Past	I, he, she, it **was spilling**	I, he, she, it **was being spilled**
Prog.	we, you, they **were spilling**	we, you, they **were being spilled**
Past	I, he, she, it,	I, he, she, it,
Int.	we, you, they **did spill**	we, you, they **did get spilled**
Pres.	I, we, you, they **have spilled**	I, we, you, they **have been spilled**
Perf.	he, she, it **has spilled**	he, she, it **has been spilled**
Past	I, he, she, it,	I, he, she, it,
Perf.	we, you, they **had spilled**	we, you, they **had been spilled**
Fut.	I, he, she, it, we, you, they	I, he, she, it, we, you, they
Perf.	**will have spilled**	**will have been spilled**

IMPERATIVE MOOD

spill   **be spilled**

SUBJUNCTIVE MOOD

Pres.	if I, he, she, it,	if I, he, she, it,
	we, you, they **spill**	we, you, they **be spilled**
Past	if I, he, she, it,	if I, he, she, it,
	we, you, they **spilled**	we, you, they **were spilled**
Fut.	if I, he, she, it,	if I, he, she, it,
	we, you, they **should spill**	we, you, they **should be spilled**

Transitive and intransitive. The *Oxford Dictionary* prefers the form SPILT for the past tense and past participle.

The child spilled her milk on the floor.
We monitor any oil that has been spilled accidentally.

444

spin
(active voice)

be spun
(passive voice)

INDICATIVE MOOD

Pres.	I, we, you, they **spin**	I **am spun**
		we, you, they **are spun**
	he, she, it **spins**	he, she, it **is spun**
Pres.	I **am spinning**	I **am being spun**
Prog.	we, you, they **are spinning**	we, you, they **are being spun**
	he, she, it **is spinning**	he, she, it **is being spun**
Pres.	I, we, you, they **do spin**	I, we, you, they **do get spun**
Int.	he, she, it **does spin**	he, she, it **does get spun**
Fut.	I, he, she, it,	I, he, she, it,
	we, you, they **will spin**	we, you, they **will be spun**
Past	I, he, she, it,	I, he, she, it **was spun**
	we, you, they **spun**	we, you, they **were spun**
Past	I, he, she, it **was spinning**	I, he, she, it **was being spun**
Prog.	we, you, they **were spinning**	we, you, they **were being spun**
Past	I, he, she, it,	I, he, she, it,
Int.	we, you, they **did spin**	we, you, they **did get spun**
Pres.	I, we, you, they **have spun**	I, we, you, they **have been spun**
Perf.	he, she, it **has spun**	he, she, it **has been spun**
Past	I, he, she, it,	I, he, she, it,
Perf.	we, you, they **had spun**	we, you, they **had been spun**
Fut.	I, he, she, it, we, you, they	I, he, she, it, we, you, they
Perf.	**will have spun**	**will have been spun**

IMPERATIVE MOOD

spin   **be spun**

SUBJUNCTIVE MOOD

Pres.	if I, he, she, it,	if I, he, she, it,
	we, you, they **spin**	we, you, they **be spun**
Past	if I, he, she, it,	if I, he, she, it,
	we, you, they **spun**	we, you, they **were spun**
Fut.	if I, he, she, it,	if I, he, she, it,
	we, you, they **should spin**	we, you, they **should be spun**

Transitive and intransitive. The *Oxford Dictionary* lists SPAN as an alternate past tense form.

The top is spinning on the table.
She spun the wheel and hoped for a winning number.
The little ship was spun about on the sea by the wind.

PRINCIPAL PARTS: **spits, spitting, spat/spit, spat/spit**

INDICATIVE MOOD

Pres.	I, we, you, they **spit**	I **am spat**
		we, you, they **are spat**
	he, she, it **spits**	he, she, it **is spat**
Pres.	I **am spitting**	I **am being spat**
Prog.	we, you, they **are spitting**	we, you, they **are being spat**
	he, she, it **is spitting**	he, she, it **is being spat**
Pres.	I, we, you, they **do spit**	I, we, you, they **do get spat**
Int.	he, she, it **does spit**	he, she, it **does get spat**
Fut.	I, he, she, it,	I, he, she, it,
	we, you, they **will spit**	we, you, they **will be spat**
Past	I, he, she, it,	I, he, she, it **was spat**
	we, you, they **spat**	we, you, they **were spat**
Past	I, he, she, it **was spitting**	I, he, she, it **was being spat**
Prog.	we, you, they **were spitting**	we, you, they **were being spat**
Past	I, he, she, it,	I, he, she, it,
Int.	we, you, they **did spit**	we, you, they **did get spat**
Pres.	I, we, you, they **have spat**	I, we, you, they **have been spat**
Perf.	he, she, it **has spat**	he, she, it **has been spat**
Past	I, he, she, it,	I, he, she, it,
Perf.	we, you, they **had spat**	we, you, they **had been spat**
Fut.	I, he, she, it, we, you, they	I, he, she, it, we, you, they
Perf.	**will have spat**	**will have been spat**

IMPERATIVE MOOD

spit **be spat**

SUBJUNCTIVE MOOD

Pres.	if I, he, she, it,	if I, he, she, it,
	we, you, they **spit**	we, you, they **be spat**
Past	if I, he, she, it,	if I, he, she, it,
	we, you, they **spat**	we, you, they **were spat**
Fut.	if I, he, she, it,	if I, he, she, it,
	we, you, they **should spit**	we, you, they **should be spat**

Transitive or intransitive. For the past and past participle there are two forms, SPAT or SPIT. The verb with the past tense and past participle SPITTED means to "impale on something, as on a spit."

They are spitting out the pits.
She spat out the seeds of her grapes.
The challenge was spat out with contempt.

split
(active voice)

be split
(passive voice)

INDICATIVE MOOD

Pres.	I, we, you, they **split**	I **am split** we, you, they **are split**
	he, she, it **splits**	he, she, it **is split**
Pres. *Prog.*	I **am splitting** we, you, they **are splitting** he, she, it **is splitting**	I **am being split** we, you, they **are being split** he, she, it **is being split**
Pres. *Int.*	I, we, you, they **do split** he, she, it **does split**	I, we, you, they **do get split** he, she, it **does get split**
Fut.	I, he, she, it, we, you, they **will split**	I, he, she, it, we, you, they **will be split**
Past	I, he, she, it, we, you, they **split**	I, he, she, it **was split** we, you, they **were split**
Past *Prog.*	I, he, she, it **was splitting** we, you, they **were splitting**	I, he, she, it **was being split** we, you, they **were being split**
Past *Int.*	I, he, she, it, we, you, they **did split**	I, he, she, it, we, you, they **did get split**
Pres. *Perf.*	I, we, you, they **have split** he, she, it **has split**	I, we, you, they **have been split** he, she, it **has been split**
Past *Perf.*	I, he, she, it, we, you, they **had split**	I, he, she, it, we, you, they **had been split**
Fut. *Perf.*	I, he, she, it, we, you, they **will have split**	I, he, she, it, we, you, they **will have been split**

IMPERATIVE MOOD

split **be split**

SUBJUNCTIVE MOOD

Pres.	if I, he, she, it, we, you, they **split**	if I, he, she, it, we, you, they **be split**
Past	if I, he, she, it, we, you, they **split**	if I, he, she, it, we, you, they **were split**
Fut.	if I, he, she, it, we, you, they **should split**	if I, he, she, it, we, you, they **should be split**

Transitive and intransitive.

He splits his lunch with his friend.
She split her winnings.
The experts were split in their opinions.

spoil
(active voice)

PRINCIPAL PARTS: **spoils, spoiling, spoiled/spoilt, spoiled/spoilt**

be spoiled/spoilt
(passive voice)

INDICATIVE MOOD

Pres.	I, we, you, they **spoil**	I **am spoiled**
		we, you, they **are spoiled**
	he, she, it **spoils**	he, she, it **is spoiled**
Pres.	I **am spoiling**	I **am being spoiled**
Prog.	we, you, they **are spoiling**	we, you, they **are being spoiled**
	he, she, it **is spoiling**	he, she, it **is being spoiled**
Pres.	I, we, you, they **do spoil**	I, we, you, they **do get spoiled**
Int.	he, she, it **does spoil**	he, she, it **does get spoiled**
Fut.	I, he, she, it,	I, he, she, it,
	we, you, they **will spoil**	we, you, they **will be spoiled**
Past	I, he, she, it,	I, he, she, it **was spoiled**
	we, you, they **spoiled**	we, you, they **were spoiled**
Past	I, he, she, it **was spoiling**	I, he, she, it **was being spoiled**
Prog.	we, you, they **were spoiling**	we, you, they **were being spoiled**
Past	I, he, she, it,	I, he, she, it,
Int.	we, you, they **did spoil**	we, you, they **did get spoiled**
Pres.	I, we, you, they **have spoiled**	I, we, you, they **have been spoiled**
Perf.	he, she, it **has spoiled**	he, she, it **has been spoiled**
Past	I, he, she, it,	I, he, she, it,
Perf.	we, you, they **had spoiled**	we, you, they **had been spoiled**
Fut.	I, he, she, it, we, you, they	I, he, she, it, we, you, they
Perf.	**will have spoiled**	**will have been spoiled**

IMPERATIVE MOOD

spoil   **be spoiled**

SUBJUNCTIVE MOOD

Pres.	if I, he, she, it,	if I, he, she, it,
	we, you, they **spoil**	we, you, they **be spoiled**
Past	if I, he, she, it,	if I, he, she, it,
	we, you, they **spoiled**	we, you, they **were spoiled**
Fut.	if I, he, she, it,	if I, he, she, it,
	we, you, they **should spoil**	we, you, they **should be spoiled**

Transitive and intransitive. The *Oxford Dictionary* prefers the past tense and past participle form SPOILT.

Too many cooks spoiled the broth.
The barbecue was spoiled by cold and rainy weather.

spread	PRINCIPAL PARTS: spreads, spreading,	be spread
(active voice)	spread, spread	(passive voice)

Pres.	I, we, you, they **spread**	I **am spread**
		we, you, they **are spread**
	he, she, it **spreads**	he, she, it **is spread**
Pres.	I **am spreading**	I **am being spread**
Prog.	we, you, they **are spreading**	we, you, they **are being spread**
	he, she, it **is spreading**	he, she, it **is being spread**
Pres.	I, we, you, they **do spread**	I, we, you, they **do get spread**
Int.	he, she, it **does spread**	he, she, it **does get spread**
Fut.	I, he, she, it,	I, he, she, it,
	we, you, they **will spread**	we, you, they **will be spread**
Past	I, he, she, it,	I, he, she, it **was spread**
	we, you, they **spread**	we, you, they **were spread**
Past	I, he, she, it **was spreading**	I, he, she, it **was being spread**
Prog.	we, you, they **were spreading**	we, you, they **were being spread**
Past	I, he, she, it,	I, he, she, it,
Int.	we, you, they **did spread**	we, you, they **did get spread**
Pres.	I, we, you, they **have spread**	I, we, you, they **have been spread**
Perf.	he, she, it **has spread**	he, she, it **has been spread**
Past	I, he, she, it,	I, he, she, it,
Perf.	we, you, they **had spread**	we, you, they **had been spread**
Fut.	I, he, she, it, we, you, they	I, he, she, it, we, you, they
Perf.	**will have spread**	**will have been spread**

S

spread	**be spread**

Pres.	if I, he, she, it,	if I, he, she, it,
	we, you, they **spread**	we, you, they **be spread**
Past	if I, he, she, it,	if I, he, she, it,
	we, you, they **spread**	we, you, they **were spread**
Fut.	if I, he, she, it,	if I, he, she, it,
	we, you, they **should spread**	we, you, they **should be spread**

Transitive and intransitive.

He spreads his butter with a knife.
The disease spread without warning.
The flu was spread by birds.

| spring
(active voice) | Principal Parts: **springs, springing,
sprang/sprung, sprung** | be sprung
(passive voice) |

INDICATIVE MOOD

Pres.	I, we, you, they **spring**	I **am sprung**
		we, you, they **are sprung**
	he, she, it **springs**	he, she, it **is sprung**
Pres. *Prog.*	I **am springing** we, you, they **are springing** he, she, it **is springing**	I **am being sprung** we, you, they **are being sprung** he, she, it **is being sprung**
Pres. *Int.*	I, we, you, they **do spring** he, she, it **does spring**	I, we, you, they **do get sprung** he, she, it **does get sprung**
Fut.	I, he, she, it, we, you, they **will spring**	I, he, she, it, we, you, they **will be sprung**
Past	I, he, she, it, we, you, they **sprang**	I, he, she, it **was sprung** we, you, they **were sprung**
Past *Prog.*	I, he, she, it **was springing** we, you, they **were springing**	I, he, she, it **was being sprung** we, you, they **were being sprung**
Past *Int.*	I, he, she, it, we, you, they **did spring**	I, he, she, it, we, you, they **did get sprung**
Pres. *Perf.*	I, we, you, they **have sprung** he, she, it **has sprung**	I, we, you, they **have been sprung** he, she, it **has been sprung**
Past *Perf.*	I, he, she, it, we, you, they **had sprung**	I, he, she, it, we, you, they **had been sprung**
Fut. *Perf.*	I, he, she, it, we, you, they **will have sprung**	I, he, she, it, we, you, they **will have been sprung**

IMPERATIVE MOOD

spring	**be sprung**

SUBJUNCTIVE MOOD

Pres.	if I, he, she, it, we, you, they **spring**	if I, he, she, it, we, you, they **be sprung**
Past	if I, he, she, it, we, you, they **sprang**	if I, he, she, it, we, you, they **were sprung**
Fut.	if I, he, she, it, we, you, they **should spring**	if I, he, she, it, we, you, they **should be sprung**

Intransitive and transitive.

The little boy sprang up with the correct answer.
The quiz was sprung on them with no warning.

stalk	PRINCIPAL PARTS: **stalks, stalking,**	be stalked
(active voice)	**stalked, stalked**	(passive voice)

INDICATIVE MOOD

Pres.	I, we, you, they **stalk**	**I am stalked**
		we, you, they **are stalked**
	he, she, it **stalks**	he, she, it **is stalked**
Pres.	**I am stalking**	**I am being stalked**
Prog.	we, you, they **are stalking**	we, you, they **are being stalked**
	he, she, it **is stalking**	he, she, it **is being stalked**
Pres.	I, we, you, they **do stalk**	I, we, you, they **do get stalked**
Int.	he, she, it **does stalk**	he, she, it **does get stalked**
Fut.	I, he, she, it,	I, he, she, it,
	we, you, they **will stalk**	we, you, they **will be stalked**
Past	I, he, she, it,	I, he, she, it **was stalked**
	we, you, they **stalked**	we, you, they **were stalked**
Past	I, he, she, it **was stalking**	I, he, she, it **was being stalked**
Prog.	we, you, they **were stalking**	we, you, they **were being stalked**
Past	I, he, she, it,	I, he, she, it,
Int.	we, you, they **did stalk**	we, you, they **did get stalked**
Pres.	I, we, you, they **have stalked**	I, we, you, they **have been stalked**
Perf.	he, she, it **has stalked**	he, she, it **has been stalked**
Past	I, he, she, it,	I, he, she, it,
Perf.	we, you, they **had stalked**	we, you, they **had been stalked**
Fut.	I, he, she, it, we, you, they	I, he, she, it, we, you, they
Perf.	**will have stalked**	**will have been stalked**

IMPERATIVE MOOD

stalk	**be stalked**

SUBJUNCTIVE MOOD

Pres.	if I, he, she, it,	if I, he, she, it,
	we, you, they **stalk**	we, you, they **be stalked**
Past	if I, he, she, it,	if I, he, she, it,
	we, you, they **stalked**	we, you, they **were stalked**
Fut.	if I, he, she, it,	if I, he, she, it,
	we, you, they **should stalk**	we, you, they **should be stalked**

S

Transitive and intransitive.

They stalked the deer for over a mile.
The enemy failed to realize he was being stalked.

stand
(active voice)

be stood
(passive voice)

INDICATIVE MOOD

Pres.	I, we, you, they **stand**	I **am stood** we, you, they **are stood**
	he, she, it **stands**	he, she, it **is stood**
Pres. *Prog.*	I **am standing** we, you, they **are standing** he, she, it **is standing**	I **am being stood** we, you, they **are being stood** he, she, it **is being stood**
Pres. *Int.*	I, we, you, they **do stand** he, she, it **does stand**	I, we, you, they **do get stood** he, she, it **does get stood**
Fut.	I, he, she, it, we, you, they **will stand**	I, he, she, it, we, you, they **will be stood**
Past	I, he, she, it, we, you, they **stood**	I, he, she, it **was stood** we, you, they **were stood**
Past *Prog.*	I, he, she, it **was standing** we, you, they **were standing**	I, he, she, it **was being stood** we, you, they **were being stood**
Past *Int.*	I, he, she, it, we, you, they **did stand**	I, he, she, it, we, you, they **did get stood**
Pres. *Perf.*	I, we, you, they **have stood** he, she, it **has stood**	I, we, you, they **have been stood** he, she, it **has been stood**
Past *Perf.*	I, he, she, it, we, you, they **had stood**	I, he, she, it, we, you, they **had been stood**
Fut. *Perf.*	I, he, she, it, we, you, they **will have stood**	I, he, she, it, we, you, they **will have been stood**

IMPERATIVE MOOD

stand   **be stood**

SUBJUNCTIVE MOOD

Pres.	if I, he, she, it, we, you, they **stand**	if I, he, she, it, we, you, they **be stood**
Past	if I, he, she, it, we, you, they **stood**	if I, he, she, it, we, you, they **were stood**
Fut.	if I, he, she, it, we, you, they **should stand**	if I, he, she, it, we, you, they **should be stood**

Intransitive and transitive.

He stood in the doorway and looked at the sleeping child.
The flowers were stood in the window to attract more customers.

AN ESSENTIAL
55 VERB

Examples

Where should I stand?

Stand over there.

She stands at the head of the line.

I stood for over eight hours yesterday.

Who will stand up for our rights?

Where does he stand on the issues?

The winner is the last person who is standing.

We have stood in the rain for hours.

She knows what she stands for.

They stood off to the side.

Words and expressions related to this verb

You must learn to stand on your own two feet.

Stand by me.

She was stood up by her boyfriend.

I cannot stand it any longer.

Stand by for an important announcement.

She stands out in any crowd.

It stands to reason.

You should try to stand for something.

That will not stand the test of time.

It is time to stand up and be counted.

S

start	PRINCIPAL PARTS: **starts, starting,**	be started
(active voice)	**started, started**	(passive voice)

INDICATIVE MOOD

Pres.	I, we, you, they **start**	I **am started**
		we, you, they **are started**
	he, she, it **starts**	he, she, it **is started**
Pres.	I **am starting**	I **am being started**
Prog.	we, you, they **are starting**	we, you, they **are being started**
	he, she, it **is starting**	he, she, it **is being started**
Pres.	I, we, you, they **do start**	I, we, you, they **do get started**
Int.	he, she, it **does start**	he, she, it **does get started**
Fut.	I, he, she, it,	I, he, she, it,
	we, you, they **will start**	we, you, they **will be started**
Past	I, he, she, it,	I, he, she, it **was started**
	we, you, they **started**	we, you, they **were started**
Past	I, he, she, it **was starting**	I, he, she, it **was being started**
Prog.	we, you, they **were starting**	we, you, they **were being started**
Past	I, he, she, it,	I, he, she, it,
Int.	we, you, they **did start**	we, you, they **did get started**
Pres.	I, we, you, they **have started**	I, we, you, they **have been started**
Perf.	he, she, it **has started**	he, she, it **has been started**
Past	I, he, she, it,	I, he, she, it,
Perf.	we, you, they **had started**	we, you, they **had been started**
Fut.	I, he, she, it, we, you, they	I, he, she, it, we, you, they
Perf.	**will have started**	**will have been started**

IMPERATIVE MOOD

start   **be started**

SUBJUNCTIVE MOOD

Pres.	if I, he, she, it,	if I, he, she, it,
	we, you, they **start**	we, you, they **be started**
Past	if I, he, she, it,	if I, he, she, it,
	we, you, they **started**	we, you, they **were started**
Fut.	if I, he, she, it,	if I, he, she, it,
	we, you, they **should start**	we, you, they **should be started**

Intransitive and transitive.

We started late, but we finished on time.
The race was started with the traditional green flag.

AN ESSENTIAL
55 VERB

start

Examples

Who wants to start?

She always starts her lectures with a joke.

I start my day with a healthy breakfast.

She started learning dance at a young age.

The company was started by two young entrepreneurs.

We like to start on time.

We may have started a trend.

Tomorrow we will start all over again.

Don't start until I give the command.

They had already started before we arrived.

Words and expressions related to this verb

Who started it?

Start your engines.

Let's start at the very beginning.

They are starting over.

We started out two hours ago.

We will start with an appetizer.

You must start somewhere.

Finish what you start.

The military doesn't start wars. Politicians start wars.

Start acting your age.

S

| state | PRINCIPAL PARTS: states, stating, | be stated |
| (active voice) | stated, stated | (passive voice) |

INDICATIVE MOOD

Pres.	I, we, you, they **state**	I **am stated**
		we, you, they **are stated**
	he, she, it **states**	he, she, it **is stated**
Pres.	I **am stating**	I **am being stated**
Prog.	we, you, they **are stating**	we, you, they **are being stated**
	he, she, it **is stating**	he, she, it **is being stated**
Pres.	I, we, you, they **do state**	I, we, you, they **do get stated**
Int.	he, she, it **does state**	he, she, it **does get stated**
Fut.	I, he, she, it,	I, he, she, it,
	we, you, they **will state**	we, you, they **will be stated**
Past	I, he, she, it,	I, he, she, it **was stated**
	we, you, they **stated**	we, you, they **were stated**
Past	I, he, she, it **was stating**	I, he, she, it **was being stated**
Prog.	we, you, they **were stating**	we, you, they **were being stated**
Past	I, he, she, it,	I, he, she, it,
Int.	we, you, they **did state**	we, you, they **did get stated**
Pres.	I, we, you, they **have stated**	I, we, you, they **have been stated**
Perf.	he, she, it **has stated**	he, she, it **has been stated**
Past	I, he, she, it,	I, he, she, it,
Perf.	we, you, they **had stated**	we, you, they **had been stated**
Fut.	I, he, she, it, we, you, they	I, he, she, it, we, you, they
Perf.	**will have stated**	**will have been stated**

IMPERATIVE MOOD

state	**be stated**

SUBJUNCTIVE MOOD

Pres.	if I, he, she, it,	if I, he, she, it,
	we, you, they **state**	we, you, they **be stated**
Past	if I, he, she, it,	if I, he, she, it,
	we, you, they **stated**	we, you, they **were stated**
Fut.	if I, he, she, it,	if I, he, she, it,
	we, you, they **should state**	we, you, they **should be stated**

He is stating their case this afternoon.
They stated their objections before the committee.
Our concerns were clearly stated in our letter.

stay
(active voice)

PRINCIPAL PARTS: **stays, staying, stayed, stayed**

be stayed
(passive voice)

INDICATIVE MOOD

Pres.	I, we, you, they **stay**	I **am stayed**
		we, you, they **are stayed**
	he, she, it **stays**	he, she, it **is stayed**
Pres.	I **am staying**	I **am being stayed**
Prog.	we, you, they **are staying**	we, you, they **are being stayed**
	he, she, it **is staying**	he, she, it **is being stayed**
Pres.	I, we, you, they **do stay**	I, we, you, they **do get stayed**
Int.	he, she, it **does stay**	he, she, it **does get stayed**
Fut.	I, he, she, it,	I, he, she, it,
	we, you, they **will stay**	we, you, they **will be stayed**
Past	I, he, she, it,	I, he, she, it **was stayed**
	we, you, they **stayed**	we, you, they **were stayed**
Past	I, he, she, it **was staying**	I, he, she, it **was being stayed**
Prog.	we, you, they **were staying**	we, you, they **were being stayed**
Past	I, he, she, it,	I, he, she, it,
Int.	we, you, they **did stay**	we, you, they **did get stayed**
Pres.	I, we, you, they **have stayed**	I, we, you, they **have been stayed**
Perf.	he, she, it **has stayed**	he, she, it **has been stayed**
Past	I, he, she, it,	I, he, she, it,
Perf.	we, you, they **had stayed**	we, you, they **had been stayed**
Fut.	I, he, she, it, we, you, they	I, he, she, it, we, you, they
Perf.	**will have stayed**	**will have been stayed**

IMPERATIVE MOOD

stay   **be stayed**

SUBJUNCTIVE MOOD

Pres.	if I, he, she, it,	if I, he, she, it,
	we, you, they **stay**	we, you, they **be stayed**
Past	if I, he, she, it,	if I, he, she, it,
	we, you, they **stayed**	we, you, they **were stayed**
Fut.	if I, he, she, it,	if I, he, she, it,
	we, you, they **should stay**	we, you, they **should be stayed**

Intransitive and transitive.

He stayed for the entire lecture.
The verdict was stayed by the Appeals Court.

| steal
(active voice) | PRINCIPAL PARTS: steals, stealing,
stole, stolen | be stolen
(passive voice) |

INDICATIVE MOOD

Pres.	I, we, you, they **steal**	I **am stolen** we, you, they **are stolen**
	he, she, it **steals**	he, she, it **is stolen**
Pres. *Prog.*	I **am stealing** we, you, they **are stealing** he, she, it **is stealing**	I **am being stolen** we, you, they **are being stolen** he, she, it **is being stolen**
Pres. *Int.*	I, we, you, they **do steal** he, she, it **does steal**	I, we, you, they **do get stolen** he, she, it **does get stolen**
Fut.	I, he, she, it, we, you, they **will steal**	I, he, she, it, we, you, they **will be stolen**
Past	I, he, she, it, we, you, they **stole**	I, he, she, it **was stolen** we, you, they **were stolen**
Past *Prog.*	I, he, she, it **was stealing** we, you, they **were stealing**	I, he, she, it **was being stolen** we, you, they **were being stolen**
Past *Int.*	I, he, she, it, we, you, they **did steal**	I, he, she, it, we, you, they **did get stolen**
Pres. *Perf.*	I, we, you, they **have stolen** he, she, it **has stolen**	I, we, you, they **have been stolen** he, she, it **has been stolen**
Past *Perf.*	I, he, she, it, we, you, they **had stolen**	I, he, she, it, we, you, they **had been stolen**
Fut. *Perf.*	I, he, she, it, we, you, they **will have stolen**	I, he, she, it, we, you, they **will have been stolen**

IMPERATIVE MOOD

steal	**be stolen**

SUBJUNCTIVE MOOD

Pres.	if I, he, she, it, we, you, they **steal**	if I, he, she, it, we, you, they **be stolen**
Past	if I, he, she, it, we, you, they **stole**	if I, he, she, it, we, you, they **were stolen**
Fut.	if I, he, she, it, we, you, they **should steal**	if I, he, she, it, we, you, they **should be stolen**

Transitive and intransitive.

Someone stole our newspaper this morning.
The paintings were stolen by the victors.

stick
(active voice)

PRINCIPAL PARTS: **sticks, sticking, stuck/sticked, stuck/sticked**

be stuck/sticked
(passive voice)

INDICATIVE MOOD

Pres.	I, we, you, they **stick**	I **am stuck**
		we, you, they **are stuck**
	he, she, it **sticks**	he, she, it **is stuck**
Pres.	I **am sticking**	I **am being stuck**
Prog.	we, you, they **are sticking**	we, you, they **are being stuck**
	he, she, it **is sticking**	he, she, it **is being stuck**
Pres.	I, we, you, they **do stick**	I, we, you, they **do get stuck**
Int.	he, she, it **does stick**	he, she, it **does get stuck**
Fut.	I, he, she, it,	I, he, she, it,
	we, you, they **will stick**	we, you, they **will be stuck**
Past	I, he, she, it,	I, he, she, it **was stuck**
	we, you, they **stuck**	we, you, they **were stuck**
Past	I, he, she, it **was sticking**	I, he, she, it **was being stuck**
Prog.	we, you, they **were sticking**	we, you, they **were being stuck**
Past	I, he, she, it,	I, he, she, it,
Int.	we, you, they **did stick**	we, you, they **did get stuck**
Pres.	I, we, you, they **have stuck**	I, we, you, they **have been stuck**
Perf.	he, she, it **has stuck**	he, she, it **has been stuck**
Past	I, he, she, it,	I, he, she, it,
Perf.	we, you, they **had stuck**	we, you, they **had been stuck**
Fut.	I, he, she, it, we, you, they	I, he, she, it, we, you, they
Perf.	**will have stuck**	**will have been stuck**

IMPERATIVE MOOD

stick **be stuck**

SUBJUNCTIVE MOOD

Pres.	if I, he, she, it,	if I, he, she, it,
	we, you, they **stick**	we, you, they **be stuck**
Past	if I, he, she, it,	if I, he, she, it,
	we, you, they **stuck**	we, you, they **were stuck**
Fut.	if I, he, she, it,	if I, he, she, it,
	we, you, they **should stick**	we, you, they **should be stuck**

Transitive and intransitive. The past and past participle form STICKED is used in the sense of "propping something up with a stick." It is also used in the printing profession meaning to "set type on a stick."

I stuck two stamps on the letter.
The truck was stuck in the deep snow.

S

sting
(active voice)

be stung
(passive voice)

INDICATIVE MOOD

Pres.	I, we, you, they **sting**	I **am stung** we, you, they **are stung**
	he, she, it **stings**	he, she, it **is stung**
Pres. *Prog.*	I **am stinging** we, you, they **are stinging** he, she, it **is stinging**	I **am being stung** we, you, they **are being stung** he, she, it **is being stung**
Pres. *Int.*	I, we, you, they **do sting** he, she, it **does sting**	I, we, you, they **do get stung** he, she, it **does get stung**
Fut.	I, he, she, it, we, you, they **will sting**	I, he, she, it, we, you, they **will be stung**
Past	I, he, she, it, we, you, they **stung**	I, he, she, it **was stung** we, you, they **were stung**
Past *Prog.*	I, he, she, it **was stinging** we, you, they **were stinging**	I, he, she, it **was being stung** we, you, they **were being stung**
Past *Int.*	I, he, she, it, we, you, they **did sting**	I, he, she, it, we, you, they **did get stung**
Pres. *Perf.*	I, we, you, they **have stung** he, she, it **has stung**	I, we, you, they **have been stung** he, she, it **has been stung**
Past *Perf.*	I, he, she, it, we, you, they **had stung**	I, he, she, it, we, you, they **had been stung**
Fut. *Perf.*	I, he, she, it, we, you, they **will have stung**	I, he, she, it, we, you, they **will have been stung**

IMPERATIVE MOOD

sting　　　　　　　　　　**be stung**

SUBJUNCTIVE MOOD

Pres.	if I, he, she, it, we, you, they **sting**	if I, he, she, it, we, you, they **be stung**
Past	if I, he, she, it, we, you, they **stung**	if I, he, she, it, we, you, they **were stung**
Fut.	if I, he, she, it, we, you, they **should sting**	if I, he, she, it, we, you, they **should be stung**

Transitive and intransitive.

The injection stung for just a second.
Have you ever been stung by a bee?

stink
(active voice)

be stunk
(passive voice)

INDICATIVE MOOD

Pres.	I, we, you, they **stink**
	he, she, it **stinks**

I **am stunk**
we, you, they **are stunk**
he, she, it **is stunk**

Pres.	I **am stinking**
Prog.	we, you, they **are stinking**
	he, she, it **is stinking**

I **am being stunk**
we, you, they **are being stunk**
he, she, it **is being stunk**

Pres.	I, we, you, they **do stink**
Int.	he, she, it **does stink**

I, we, you, they **do get stunk**
he, she, it **does get stunk**

Fut.	I, he, she, it,
	we, you, they **will stink**

I, he, she, it,
we, you, they **will be stunk**

Past	I, he, she, it,
	we, you, they **stank**

I, he, she, it **was stunk**
we, you, they **were stunk**

Past	I, he, she, it **was stinking**
Prog.	we, you, they **were stinking**

I, he, she, it **was being stunk**
we, you, they **were being stunk**

Past	I, he, she, it,
Int.	we, you, they **did stink**

I, he, she, it,
we, you, they **did get stunk**

Pres.	I, we, you, they **have stunk**
Perf.	he, she, it **has stunk**

I, we, you, they **have been stunk**
he, she, it **has been stunk**

Past	I, he, she, it,
Perf.	we, you, they **had stunk**

I, he, she, it,
we, you, they **had been stunk**

Fut.	I, he, she, it, we, you, they
Perf.	**will have stunk**

I, he, she, it, we, you, they
will have been stunk

IMPERATIVE MOOD

stink

be stunk

SUBJUNCTIVE MOOD

Pres.	if I, he, she, it,
	we, you, they **stink**

if I, he, she, it,
we, you, they **be stunk**

Past	if I, he, she, it,
	we, you, they **stank**

if I, he, she, it,
we, you, they **were stunk**

Fut.	if I, he, she, it,
	we, you, they **should stink**

if I, he, she, it,
we, you, they **should be stunk**

Intransitive and transitive.

The manure pile stank especially on damp days.
The dead skunk had stunk for more than a day.

S

stop
(active voice)

be stopped
(passive voice)

INDICATIVE MOOD

Pres.	I, we, you, they **stop**	I **am stopped**
		we, you, they **are stopped**
	he, she, it **stops**	he, she, it **is stopped**
Pres.	I **am stopping**	I **am being stopped**
Prog.	we, you, they **are stopping**	we, you, they **are being stopped**
	he, she, it **is stopping**	he, she, it **is being stopped**
Pres.	I, we, you, they **do stop**	I, we, you, they **do get stopped**
Int.	he, she, it **does stop**	he, she, it **does get stopped**
Fut.	I, he, she, it,	I, he, she, it,
	we, you, they **will stop**	we, you, they **will be stopped**
Past	I, he, she, it,	I, he, she, it **was stopped**
	we, you, they **stopped**	we, you, they **were stopped**
Past	I, he, she, it **was stopping**	I, he, she, it **was being stopped**
Prog.	we, you, they **were stopping**	we, you, they **were being stopped**
Past	I, he, she, it,	I, he, she, it,
Int.	we, you, they **did stop**	we, you, they **did get stopped**
Pres.	I, we, you, they **have stopped**	I, we, you, they **have been stopped**
Perf.	he, she, it **has stopped**	he, she, it **has been stopped**
Past	I, he, she, it,	I, he, she, it,
Perf.	we, you, they **had stopped**	we, you, they **had been stopped**
Fut.	I, he, she, it, we, you, they	I, he, she, it, we, you, they
Perf.	**will have stopped**	**will have been stopped**

IMPERATIVE MOOD

stop   **be stopped**

SUBJUNCTIVE MOOD

Pres.	if I, he, she, it,	if I, he, she, it,
	we, you, they **stop**	we, you, they **be stopped**
Past	if I, he, she, it,	if I, he, she, it,
	we, you, they **stopped**	we, you, they **were stopped**
Fut.	if I, he, she, it,	if I, he, she, it,
	we, you, they **should stop**	we, you, they **should be stopped**

Transitive and intransitive.

We are stopping our subscription after the next issue.
He stopped for the red light.
She was stopped by a tourist asking for directions.

strategize

INDICATIVE MOOD

Pres.	I, we, you, they **strategize**
	he, she, it **strategizes**
Pres. *Prog.*	I **am strategizing** we, you, they **are strategizing** he, she, it **is strategizing**
Pres. *Int.*	I, we, you, they **do strategize** he, she, it **does strategize**
Fut.	I, he, she, it, we, you, they **will strategize**
Past	I, he, she, it, we, you, they **strategized**
Past *Prog.*	I, he, she, it **was strategizing** we, you, they **were strategizing**
Past *Int.*	I, he, she, it, we, you, they **did strategize**
Pres. *Perf.*	I, we, you, they **have strategized** he, she, it **has strategized**
Past *Perf.*	I, he, she, it, we, you, they **had strategized**
Fut. *Perf.*	I, he, she, it, we, you, they **will have strategized**

S

IMPERATIVE MOOD

strategize

SUBJUNCTIVE MOOD

Pres.	if I, he, she, it, we, you, they **strategize**
Past	if I, he, she, it, we, you, they **strategized**
Fut.	if I, he, she, it, we, you, they **should strategize**

They are strategizing now for next year's budget.
The technicians strategized a new approach to the problem.
One possible solution had been strategized by a set of consultants.

strew
(active voice)

PRINCIPAL PARTS: **strews, strewing, strewed, strewn/strewed**

be strewn/strewed
(passive voice)

INDICATIVE MOOD

Pres.	I, we, you, they **strew**	I **am strewn**
		we, you, they **are strewn**
	he, she, it **strews**	he, she, it **is strewn**
Pres.	I **am strewing**	I **am being strewn**
Prog.	we, you, they **are strewing**	we, you, they **are being strewn**
	he, she, it **is strewing**	he, she, it **is being strewn**
Pres.	I, we, you, they **do strew**	I, we, you, they **do get strewn**
Int.	he, she, it **does strew**	he, she, it **does get strewn**
Fut.	I, he, she, it,	I, he, she, it,
	we, you, they **will strew**	we, you, they **will be strewn**
Past	I, he, she, it,	I, he, she, it **was strewn**
	we, you, they **strewed**	we, you, they **were strewn**
Past	I, he, she, it **was strewing**	I, he, she, it **was being strewn**
Prog.	we, you, they **were strewing**	we, you, they **were being strewn**
Past	I, he, she, it,	I, he, she, it,
Int.	we, you, they **did strew**	we, you, they **did get strewn**
Pres.	I, we, you, they **have strewn**	I, we, you, they **have been strewn**
Perf.	he, she, it **has strewn**	he, she, it **has been strewn**
Past	I, he, she, it,	I, he, she, it,
Perf.	we, you, they **had strewn**	we, you, they **had been strewn**
Fut.	I, he, she, it, we, you, they	I, he, she, it, we, you, they
Perf.	**will have strewn**	**will have been strewn**

IMPERATIVE MOOD

strew　　　　　　　　　　**be strewn**

SUBJUNCTIVE MOOD

Pres.	if I, he, she, it,	if I, he, she, it,
	we, you, they **strew**	we, you, they **be strewn**
Past	if I, he, she, it,	if I, he, she, it,
	we, you, they **strewed**	we, you, they **were strewn**
Fut.	if I, he, she, it,	if I, he, she, it,
	we, you, they **should strew**	we, you, they **should be strewn**

They strewed hay over the new grass seed.
The street was strewn with posters for the candidate.

464

stride
(active voice)

PRINCIPAL PARTS: **strides, striding, strode, stridden**

be stridden
(passive voice)

INDICATIVE MOOD

Pres.	I, we, you, they **stride**	I **am stridden**
		we, you, they **are stridden**
	he, she, it **strides**	he, she, it **is stridden**
Pres.	I **am striding**	I **am being stridden**
Prog.	we, you, they **are striding**	we, you, they **are being stridden**
	he, she, it **is striding**	he, she, it **is being stridden**
Pres.	I, we, you, they **do stride**	I, we, you, they **do get stridden**
Int.	he, she, it **does stride**	he, she, it **does get stridden**
Fut.	I, he, she, it,	I, he, she, it,
	we, you, they **will stride**	we, you, they **will be stridden**
Past	I, he, she, it,	I, he, she, it **was stridden**
	we, you, they **strode**	we, you, they **were stridden**
Past	I, he, she, it **was striding**	I, he, she, it **was being stridden**
Prog.	we, you, they **were striding**	we, you, they **were being stridden**
Past	I, he, she, it,	I, he, she, it,
Int.	we, you, they **did stride**	we, you, they **did get stridden**
Pres.	I, we, you, they **have stridden**	I, we, you, they **have been stridden**
Perf.	he, she, it **has stridden**	he, she, it **has been stridden**
Past	I, he, she, it,	I, he, she, it,
Perf.	we, you, they **had stridden**	we, you, they **had been stridden**
Fut.	I, he, she, it, we, you, they	I, he, she, it, we, you, they
Perf.	**will have stridden**	**will have been stridden**

IMPERATIVE MOOD

stride

be stridden

SUBJUNCTIVE MOOD

Pres.	if I, he, she, it,	if I, he, she, it,
	we, you, they **stride**	we, you, they **be stridden**
Past	if I, he, she, it,	if I, he, she, it,
	we, you, they **strode**	we, you, they **were stridden**
Fut.	if I, he, she, it,	if I, he, she, it,
	we, you, they **should stride**	we, you, they **should be stridden**

S

Intransitive and transitive.

The new model is striding with confidence down the walkway.
He strode into the meeting with authority.
So many obstacles had been stridden over in achieving success.

strike (active voice)	PRINCIPAL PARTS: **strikes, striking, struck, struck/stricken**	be struck/stricken (passive voice)

INDICATIVE MOOD

Pres.	I, we, you, they **strike**	I **am struck** we, you, they **are struck**
	he, she, it **strikes**	he, she, it **is struck**
Pres. *Prog.*	I **am striking** we, you, they **are striking** he, she, it **is striking**	I **am being struck** we, you, they **are being struck** he, she, it **is being struck**
Pres. *Int.*	I, we, you, they **do strike** he, she, it **does strike**	I, we, you, they **do get struck** he, she, it **does get struck**
Fut.	I, he, she, it, we, you, they **will strike**	I, he, she, it, we, you, they **will be struck**
Past	I, he, she, it, we, you, they **struck**	I, he, she, it **was struck** we, you, they **were struck**
Past *Prog.*	I, he, she, it **was striking** we, you, they **were striking**	I, he, she, it **was being struck** we, you, they **were being struck**
Past *Int.*	I, he, she, it, we, you, they **did strike**	I, he, she, it, we, you, they **did get struck**
Pres. *Perf.*	I, we, you, they **have struck** he, she, it **has struck**	I, we, you, they **have been struck** he, she, it **has been struck**
Past *Perf.*	I, he, she, it, we, you, they **had struck**	I, he, she, it, we, you, they **had been struck**
Fut. *Perf.*	I, he, she, it, we, you, they **will have struck**	I, he, she, it, we, you, they **will have been struck**

IMPERATIVE MOOD

strike	**be struck**

SUBJUNCTIVE MOOD

Pres.	if I, he, she, it, we, you, they **strike**	if I, he, she, it, we, you, they **be struck**
Past	if I, he, she, it, we, you, they **struck**	if I, he, she, it, we, you, they **were struck**
Fut.	if I, he, she, it, we, you, they **should strike**	if I, he, she, it, we, you, they **should be struck**

Transitive and intransitive. The *Oxford Dictionary* lists as archaic the past participle form STRICKEN.

The workers are striking for higher pay.
He struck the tree with his ax.
He was struck by her comments.

466

string
(active voice)

be strung
(passive voice)

INDICATIVE MOOD

Pres.	I, we, you, they **string**	I **am strung**
		we, you, they **are strung**
	he, she, it **strings**	he, she, it **is strung**
Pres.	I **am stringing**	I **am being strung**
Prog.	we, you, they **are stringing**	we, you, they **are being strung**
	he, she, it **is stringing**	he, she, it **is being strung**
Pres.	I, we, you, they **do string**	I, we, you, they **do get strung**
Int.	he, she, it **does string**	he, she, it **does get strung**
Fut.	I, he, she, it,	I, he, she, it,
	we, you, they **will string**	we, you, they **will be strung**
Past	I, he, she, it,	I, he, she, it **was strung**
	we, you, they **strung**	we, you, they **were strung**
Past	I, he, she, it **was stringing**	I, he, she, it **was being strung**
Prog.	we, you, they **were stringing**	we, you, they **were being strung**
Past	I, he, she, it,	I, he, she, it,
Int.	we, you, they **did string**	we, you, they **did get strung**
Pres.	I, we, you, they **have strung**	I, we, you, they **have been strung**
Perf.	he, she, it **has strung**	he, she, it **has been strung**
Past	I, he, she, it,	I, he, she, it,
Perf.	we, you, they **had strung**	we, you, they **had been strung**
Fut.	I, he, she, it, we, you, they	I, he, she, it, we, you, they
Perf.	**will have strung**	**will have been strung**

S

IMPERATIVE MOOD

string   **be strung**

SUBJUNCTIVE MOOD

Pres.	if I, he, she, it,	if I, he, she, it,
	we, you, they **string**	we, you, they **be strung**
Past	if I, he, she, it,	if I, he, she, it,
	we, you, they **strung**	we, you, they **were strung**
Fut.	if I, he, she, it,	if I, he, she, it,
	we, you, they **should string**	we, you, they **should be strung**

Transitive and intransitive.

They strung lights from the tree.
The stockings were strung from the chimney with care.

INDICATIVE MOOD

Pres.   I, we, you, they **strive**

            he, she, it **strives**

Pres.   **I am striving**
Prog.   we, you, they **are striving**
            he, she, it **is striving**

Pres.   I, we, you, they **do strive**
Int.   he, she, it **does strive**

Fut.   I, he, she, it,
            we, you, they **will strive**

Past   I, he, she, it,
            we, you, they **strove**

Past   I, he, she, it **was striving**
Prog.   we, you, they **were striving**

Past   I, he, she, it,
Int.   we, you, they **did strive**

Pres.   I, we, you, they **have striven**
Perf.   he, she, it **has striven**

Past   I, he, she, it,
Perf.   we, you, they **had striven**

Fut.   I, he, she, it, we, you, they
Perf.   **will have striven**

IMPERATIVE MOOD

            strive

SUBJUNCTIVE MOOD

Pres.   if I, he, she, it,
            we, you, they **strive**

Past   if I, he, she, it,
            we, you, they **strove**

Fut.   if I, he, she, it,
            we, you, they **should strive**

The past may be STROVE or STRIVED; the past participle is STRIVEN or STRIVED.

We are always striving to do our best.
She strove to pass her exams.
They had striven to win the competition.

stroke
(active voice)

PRINCIPAL PARTS: **strokes, stroking, stroked, stroked**

be stroked
(passive voice)

INDICATIVE MOOD

Pres.	I, we, you, they **stroke**	**I am stroked**
		we, you, they **are stroked**
	he, she, it **strokes**	he, she, it **is stroked**
Pres.	**I am stroking**	**I am being stroked**
Prog.	we, you, they **are stroking**	we, you, they **are being stroked**
	he, she, it **is stroking**	he, she, it **is being stroked**
Pres.	I, we, you, they **do stroke**	I, we, you, they **do get stroked**
Int.	he, she, it **does stroke**	he, she, it **does get stroked**
Fut.	I, he, she, it,	I, he, she, it,
	we, you, they **will stroke**	we, you, they **will be stroked**
Past	I, he, she, it,	I, he, she, it **was stroked**
	we, you, they **stroked**	we, you, they **were stroked**
Past	I, he, she, it **was stroking**	I, he, she, it **was being stroked**
Prog.	we, you, they **were stroking**	we, you, they **were being stroked**
Past	I, he, she, it,	I, he, she, it,
Int.	we, you, they **did stroke**	we, you, they **did get stroked**
Pres.	I, we, you, they **have stroked**	I, we, you, they **have been stroked**
Perf.	he, she, it **has stroked**	he, she, it **has been stroked**
Past	I, he, she, it,	I, he, she, it,
Perf.	we, you, they **had stroked**	we, you, they **had been stroked**
Fut.	I, he, she, it, we, you, they	I, he, she, it, we, you, they
Perf.	**will have stroked**	**will have been stroked**

IMPERATIVE MOOD

stroke   **be stroked**

SUBJUNCTIVE MOOD

Pres.	if I, he, she, it,	if I, he, she, it,
	we, you, they **stroke**	we, you, they **be stroked**
Past	if I, he, she, it,	if I, he, she, it,
	we, you, they **stroked**	we, you, they **were stroked**
Fut.	if I, he, she, it,	if I, he, she, it,
	we, you, they **should stroke**	we, you, they **should be stroked**

Transitive and intransitive.

He is stroking his boss for the new position.
She softly stroked the baby's head.
My hand was gently stroked by my wife as we watched the children.

study
(active voice)

be studied
(passive voice)

INDICATIVE MOOD

Pres.	I, we, you, they **study**	I **am studied** we, you, they **are studied**
	he, she, it **studies**	he, she, it **is studied**
Pres. *Prog.*	I **am studying** we, you, they **are studying** he, she, it **is studying**	I **am being studied** we, you, they **are being studied** he, she, it **is being studied**
Pres. *Int.*	I, we, you, they **do study** he, she, it **does study**	I, we, you, they **do get studied** he, she, it **does get studied**
Fut.	I, he, she, it, we, you, they **will study**	I, he, she, it, we, you, they **will be studied**
Past	I, he, she, it, we, you, they **studied**	I, he, she, it **was studied** we, you, they **were studied**
Past *Prog.*	I, he, she, it **was studying** we, you, they **were studying**	I, he, she, it **was being studied** we, you, they **were being studied**
Past *Int.*	I, he, she, it, we, you, they **did study**	I, he, she, it, we, you, they **did get studied**
Pres. *Perf.*	I, we, you, they **have studied** he, she, it **has studied**	I, we, you, they **have been studied** he, she, it **has been studied**
Past *Perf.*	I, he, she, it, we, you, they **had studied**	I, he, she, it, we, you, they **had been studied**
Fut. *Perf.*	I, he, she, it, we, you, they **will have studied**	I, he, she, it, we, you, they **will have been studied**

IMPERATIVE MOOD

study   **be studied**

SUBJUNCTIVE MOOD

Pres.	if I, he, she, it, we, you, they **study**	if I, he, she, it, we, you, they **be studied**
Past	if I, he, she, it, we, you, they **studied**	if I, he, she, it, we, you, they **were studied**
Fut.	if I, he, she, it, we, you, they **should study**	if I, he, she, it, we, you, they **should be studied**

Transitive and intransitive.

We did study yesterday!
Those strange objects should be studied.
I was studying when she came.

470

PRINCIPAL PARTS: sues, suing,
sued, sued

INDICATIVE MOOD

Pres.	I, we, you, they **sue**	I **am sued**
		we, you, they **are sued**
	he, she, it **sues**	he, she, it **is sued**
Pres.	I **am suing**	I **am being sued**
Prog.	we, you, they **are suing**	we, you, they **are being sued**
	he, she, it **is suing**	he, she, it **is being sued**
Pres.	I, we, you, they **do sue**	I, we, you, they **do get sued**
Int.	he, she, it **does sue**	he, she, it **does get sued**
Fut.	I, he, she, it,	I, he, she, it,
	we, you, they **will sue**	we, you, they **will be sued**
Past	I, he, she, it,	I, he, she, it **was sued**
	we, you, they **sued**	we, you, they **were sued**
Past	I, he, she, it **was suing**	I, he, she, it **was being sued**
Prog.	we, you, they **were suing**	we, you, they **were being sued**
Past	I, he, she, it,	I, he, she, it,
Int.	we, you, they **did sue**	we, you, they **did get sued**
Pres.	I, we, you, they **have sued**	I, we, you, they **have been sued**
Perf.	he, she, it **has sued**	he, she, it **has been sued**
Past	I, he, she, it,	I, he, she, it,
Perf.	we, you, they **had sued**	we, you, they **had been sued**
Fut.	I, he, she, it, we, you, they	I, he, she, it, we, you, they
Perf.	**will have sued**	**will have been sued**

IMPERATIVE MOOD

sue   **be sued**

SUBJUNCTIVE MOOD

Pres.	if I, he, she, it,	if I, he, she, it,
	we, you, they **sue**	we, you, they **be sued**
Past	if I, he, she, it,	if I, he, she, it,
	we, you, they **sued**	we, you, they **were sued**
Fut.	if I, he, she, it,	if I, he, she, it,
	we, you, they **should sue**	we, you, they **should be sued**

S

Transitive and intransitive.

Are you suing them?
They sued for damages.
That company had been sued several times in the past year.

| suggest (active voice) | PRINCIPAL PARTS: **suggests, suggesting, suggested, suggested** | be suggested (passive voice) |

INDICATIVE MOOD

Pres.	I, we, you, they **suggest**	I **am suggested**
		we, you, they **are suggested**
	he, she, it **suggests**	he, she, it **is suggested**
Pres.	I **am suggesting**	I **am being suggested**
Prog.	we, you, they **are suggesting**	we, you, they **are being suggested**
	he, she, it **is suggesting**	he, she, it **is being suggested**
Pres.	I, we, you, they **do suggest**	I, we, you, they **do get suggested**
Int.	he, she, it **does suggest**	he, she, it **does get suggested**
Fut.	I, he, she, it,	I, he, she, it,
	we, you, they **will suggest**	we, you, they **will be suggested**
Past	I, he, she, it,	I, he, she, it **was suggested**
	we, you, they **suggested**	we, you, they **were suggested**
Past	I, he, she, it **was suggesting**	I, he, she, it **was being suggested**
Prog.	we, you, they **were suggesting**	we, you, they **were being suggested**
Past	I, he, she, it,	I, he, she, it,
Int.	we, you, they **did suggest**	we, you, they **did get suggested**
Pres.	I, we, you, they **have suggested**	I, we, you, they **have been suggested**
Perf.	he, she, it **has suggested**	he, she, it **has been suggested**
Past	I, he, she, it,	I, he, she, it,
Perf.	we, you, they **had suggested**	we, you, they **had been suggested**
Fut.	I, he, she, it, we, you, they	I, he, she, it, we, you, they
Perf.	**will have suggested**	**will have been suggested**

IMPERATIVE MOOD

suggest	**be suggested**

SUBJUNCTIVE MOOD

Pres.	if I, he, she, it,	if I, he, she, it,
	we, you, they **suggest**	we, you, they **be suggested**
Past	if I, he, she, it,	if I, he, she, it,
	we, you, they **suggested**	we, you, they **were suggested**
Fut.	if I, he, she, it,	if I, he, she, it,
	we, you, they **should suggest**	we, you, they **should be suggested**

You suggested that we cancel the meeting.
The alternative had been suggested at the last moment.

472

PRINCIPAL PARTS: **supports, supporting, supported, supported**

INDICATIVE MOOD

Pres.	I, we, you, they **support**	I **am supported**
		we, you, they **are supported**
	he, she, it **supports**	he, she, it **is supported**
Pres.	I **am supporting**	I **am being supported**
Prog.	we, you, they **are supporting**	we, you, they **are being supported**
	he, she, it **is supporting**	he, she, it **is being supported**
Pres.	I, we, you, they **do support**	I, we, you, they **do get supported**
Int.	he, she, it **does support**	he, she, it **does get supported**
Fut.	I, he, she, it,	I, he, she, it,
	we, you, they **will support**	we, you, they **will be supported**
Past	I, he, she, it,	I, he, she, it **was supported**
	we, you, they **supported**	we, you, they **were supported**
Past	I, he, she, it **was supporting**	I, he, she, it **was being supported**
Prog.	we, you, they **were supporting**	we, you, they **were being supported**
Past	I, he, she, it,	I, he, she, it,
Int.	we, you, they **did support**	we, you, they **did get supported**
Pres.	I, we, you, they **have supported**	I, we, you, they **have been supported**
Perf.	he, she, it **has supported**	he, she, it **has been supported**
Past	I, he, she, it,	I, he, she, it,
Perf.	we, you, they **had supported**	we, you, they **had been supported**
Fut.	I, he, she, it, we, you, they	I, he, she, it, we, you, they
Perf.	**will have supported**	**will have been supported**

IMPERATIVE MOOD

support   **be supported**

SUBJUNCTIVE MOOD

Pres.	if I, he, she, it,	if I, he, she, it,
	we, you, they **support**	we, you, they **be supported**
Past	if I, he, she, it,	if I, he, she, it,
	we, you, they **supported**	we, you, they **were supported**
Fut.	if I, he, she, it,	if I, he, she, it,
	we, you, they **should support**	we, you, they **should be supported**

He supports our schools in his newspaper.
The old man was supported by his granddaughters.

suppose
(active voice)

PRINCIPAL PARTS: **supposes, supposing, supposed, supposed**

be supposed
(passive voice)

INDICATIVE MOOD

Pres.	I, we, you, they **suppose**	**I am supposed** we, you, they **are supposed**
	he, she, it **supposes**	he, she, it **is supposed**
Pres. *Prog.*	**I am supposing** we, you, they **are supposing** he, she, it **is supposing**	**I am being supposed** we, you, they **are being supposed** he, she, it **is being supposed**
Pres. *Int.*	I, we, you, they **do suppose** he, she, it **does suppose**	I, we, you, they **do get supposed** he, she, it **does get supposed**
Fut.	I, he, she, it, we, you, they **will suppose**	I, he, she, it, we, you, they **will be supposed**
Past	I, he, she, it, we, you, they **supposed**	I, he, she, it **was supposed** we, you, they **were supposed**
Past *Prog.*	I, he, she, it **was supposing** we, you, they **were supposing**	I, he, she, it **was being supposed** we, you, they **were being supposed**
Past *Int.*	I, he, she, it, we, you, they **did suppose**	I, he, she, it, we, you, they **did get supposed**
Pres. *Perf.*	I, we, you, they **have supposed** he, she, it **has supposed**	I, we, you, they **have been supposed** he, she, it **has been supposed**
Past *Perf.*	I, he, she, it, we, you, they **had supposed**	I, he, she, it, we, you, they **had been supposed**
Fut. *Perf.*	I, he, she, it, we, you, they **will have supposed**	I, he, she, it, we, you, they **will have been supposed**

IMPERATIVE MOOD

suppose **be supposed**

SUBJUNCTIVE MOOD

Pres.	if I, he, she, it, we, you, they **suppose**	if I, he, she, it, we, you, they **be supposed**
Past	if I, he, she, it, we, you, they **supposed**	if I, he, she, it, we, you, they **were supposed**
Fut.	if I, he, she, it, we, you, they **should suppose**	if I, he, she, it, we, you, they **should be supposed**

Transitive and intransitive.

I supposed that you would be a member of our team.
A significant contribution had been supposed by the development officer.

474

surf
(active voice)

be surfed
(passive voice)

INDICATIVE MOOD

Pres.	I, we, you, they **surf**	I **am surfed**
		we, you, they **are surfed**
	he, she, it **surfs**	he, she, it **is surfed**
Pres.	I **am surfing**	I **am being surfed**
Prog.	we, you, they **are surfing**	we, you, they **are being surfed**
	he, she, it **is surfing**	he, she, it **is being surfed**
Pres.	I, we, you, they **do surf**	I, we, you, **do get surfed**
Int.	he, she, it **does surf**	he, she, it **does get surfed**
Fut.	I, he, she, it,	I, he, she, it,
	we, you, they **will surf**	we, you, they **will be surfed**
Past	I, he, she, it,	I, he, she, it **was surfed**
	we, you, they **surfed**	we, you, they **were surfed**
Past	I, he, she, it **was surfing**	I, he, she, it **was being surfed**
Prog.	we, you, they **were surfing**	we, you, they **were being surfed**
Past	I, he, she, it,	I, he, she, it,
Int.	we, you, they **did surf**	we, you, they **did get surfed**
Pres.	I, we, you, they **have surfed**	I, we, you, they **have been surfed**
Perf.	he, she, it **has surfed**	he, she, it **has been surfed**
Past	I, he, she, it,	I, he, she, it,
Perf.	we, you, they **had surfed**	we, you, they **had been surfed**
Fut.	I, he, she, it, we, you, they	I, he, she, it, we, you, they
Perf.	**will have surfed**	**will have been surfed**

S

IMPERATIVE MOOD

surf

be surfed

SUBJUNCTIVE MOOD

Pres.	if I, he, she, it,	if I, he, she, it,
	we, you, they **surf**	we, you, they **be surfed**
Past	if I, he, she, it,	if I, he, she, it,
	we, you, they **surfed**	we, you, they **were surfed**
Fut.	if I, he, she, it,	if I, he, she, it,
	we, you, they **should surf**	we, you, they **should be surfed**

Transitive and intransitive.

He surfed the waves all afternoon.
The Internet is surfed in almost every corner of the earth.

PRINCIPAL PARTS: **surprises, surprising, surprised, surprised**

INDICATIVE MOOD

Pres.	I, we, you, they **surprise**	I **am surprised** we, you, they **are surprised**
	he, she, it **surprises**	he, she, it **is surprised**
Pres. *Prog.*	I **am surprising** we, you, they **are surprising** he, she, it **is surprising**	I **am being surprised** we, you, they **are being surprised** he, she, it **is being surprised**
Pres. *Int.*	I, we, you, they **do surprise** he, she, it **does surprise**	I, we, you, they **do get surprised** he, she, it **does get surprised**
Fut.	I, he, she, it, we, you, they **will surprise**	I, he, she, it, we, you, they **will be surprised**
Past	I, he, she, it, we, you, they **surprised**	I, he, she, it **was surprised** we, you, they **were surprised**
Past *Prog.*	I, he, she, it **was surprising** we, you, they **were surprising**	I, he, she, it **was being surprised** we, you, they **were being surprised**
Past *Int.*	I, he, she, it, we, you, they **did surprise**	I, he, she, it, we, you, they **did get surprised**
Pres. *Perf.*	I, we, you, they **have surprised** he, she, it **has surprised**	I, we, you, they **have been surprised** he, she, it **has been surprised**
Past *Perf.*	I, he, she, it, we, you, they **had surprised**	I, he, she, it, we, you, they **had been surprised**
Fut. *Perf.*	I, he, she, it, we, you, they **will have surprised**	I, he, she, it, we, you, they **will have been surprised**

IMPERATIVE MOOD

surprise   **be surprised**

SUBJUNCTIVE MOOD

Pres.	if I, he, she, it, we, you, they **surprise**	if I, he, she, it, we, you, they **be surprised**
Past	if I, he, she, it, we, you, they **surprised**	if I, he, she, it, we, you, they **were surprised**
Fut.	if I, he, she, it, we, you, they **should surprise**	if I, he, she, it, we, you, they **should be surprised**

He is surprising his employees this week with his resignation.
She surprised us with her visit.
We were surprised by the size of the deficit.

swear
(active voice)

PRINCIPAL PARTS: **swears, swearing,
swore, sworn**

be sworn
(passive voice)

INDICATIVE MOOD

Pres.	I, we, you, they **swear**	I **am sworn**
		we, you, they **are sworn**
	he, she, it **swears**	he, she, it **is sworn**
Pres.	I **am swearing**	I **am being sworn**
Prog.	we, you, they **are swearing**	we, you, they **are being sworn**
	he, she, it **is swearing**	he, she, it **is being sworn**
Pres.	I, we, you, they **do swear**	I, we, you, they **do get sworn**
Int.	he, she, it **does swear**	he, she, it **does get sworn**
Fut.	I, he, she, it,	I, he, she, it,
	we, you, they **will swear**	we, you, they **will be sworn**
Past	I, he, she, it,	I, he, she, it **was sworn**
	we, you, they **swore**	we, you, they **were sworn**
Past	I, he, she, it **was swearing**	I, he, she, it **was being sworn**
Prog.	we, you, they **were swearing**	we, you, they **were being sworn**
Past	I, he, she, it,	I, he, she, it,
Int.	we, you, they **did swear**	we, you, they **did get sworn**
Pres.	I, we, you, they **have sworn**	I, we, you, they **have been sworn**
Perf.	he, she, it **has sworn**	he, she, it **has been sworn**
Past	I, he, she, it,	I, he, she, it,
Perf.	we, you, they **had sworn**	we, you, they **had been sworn**
Fut.	I, he, she, it, we, you, they	I, he, she, it, we, you, they
Perf.	**will have sworn**	**will have been sworn**

IMPERATIVE MOOD

swear

be sworn

SUBJUNCTIVE MOOD

Pres.	if I, he, she, it,	if I, he, she, it,
	we, you, they **swear**	we, you, they **be sworn**
Past	if I, he, she, it,	if I, he, she, it,
	we, you, they **swore**	we, you, they **were sworn**
Fut.	if I, he, she, it,	if I, he, she, it,
	we, you, they **should swear**	we, you, they **should be sworn**

Intransitive and transitive.

He swore never to speed again.
We were all sworn to secrecy in the matter.

sweat
(active voice)

PRINCIPAL PARTS: **sweats, sweating,
sweated/sweat, sweated/sweat**

be sweated/sweat
(passive voice)

INDICATIVE MOOD

Pres.	I, we, you, they **sweat**	I **am sweated**
		we, you, they **are sweated**
	he, she, it **sweats**	he, she, it **is sweated**
Pres.	I **am sweating**	I **am being sweated**
Prog.	we, you, they **are sweating**	we, you, they **are being sweated**
	he, she, it **is sweating**	he, she, it **is being sweated**
Pres.	I, we, you, they **do sweat**	I, we, you, they **do get sweated**
Int.	he, she, it **does sweat**	he, she, it **does get sweated**
Fut.	I, he, she, it,	I, he, she, it,
	we, you, they **will sweat**	we, you, they **will be sweated**
Past	I, he, she, it,	I, he, she, it **was sweated**
	we, you, they **sweated**	we, you, they **were sweated**
Past	I, he, she, it **was sweating**	I, he, she, it **was being sweated**
Prog.	we, you, they **were sweating**	we, you, they **were being sweated**
Past	I, he, she, it,	I, he, she, it,
Int.	we, you, they **did sweat**	we, you, they **did get sweated**
Pres.	I, we, you, they **have sweated**	I, we, you, they **have been sweated**
Perf.	he, she, it **has sweated**	he, she, it **has been sweated**
Past	I, he, she, it,	I, he, she, it,
Perf.	we, you, they **had sweated**	we, you, they **had been sweated**
Fut.	I, he, she, it, we, you, they	I, he, she, it, we, you, they
Perf.	**will have sweated**	**will have been sweated**

IMPERATIVE MOOD

sweat   **be sweated**

SUBJUNCTIVE MOOD

Pres.	if I, he, she, it,	if I, he, she, it,
	we, you, they **sweat**	we, you, they **be sweated**
Past	if I, he, she, it,	if I, he, she, it,
	we, you, they **sweated**	we, you, they **were sweated**
Fut.	if I, he, she, it,	if I, he, she, it,
	we, you, they **should sweat**	we, you, they **should be sweated**

Intransitive or transitive. The *Oxford Dictionary* classifies as an Americanism the past tense and past participle SWEAT.

She always sweats during her dance workout.
Last night we sweated even in our air-conditioned home.
The prisoners were sweated to the bone by the hard labor.

sweep (active voice)	PRINCIPAL PARTS: sweeps, sweeping, swept, swept	be swept (passive voice)

INDICATIVE MOOD

Pres.	I, we, you, they **sweep**	I am **swept**
		we, you, they **are swept**
	he, she, it **sweeps**	he, she, it **is swept**
Pres.	I **am sweeping**	I am **being swept**
Prog.	we, you, they **are sweeping**	we, you, they **are being swept**
	he, she, it **is sweeping**	he, she, it **is being swept**
Pres.	I, we, you, they **do sweep**	I, we, you, they **do get swept**
Int.	he, she, it **does sweep**	he, she, it **does get swept**
Fut.	I, he, she, it,	I, he, she, it,
	we, you, they **will sweep**	we, you, they **will be swept**
Past	I, he, she, it,	I, he, she, it **was swept**
	we, you, they **swept**	we, you, they **were swept**
Past	I, he, she, it **was sweeping**	I, he, she, it **was being swept**
Prog.	we, you, they **were sweeping**	we, you, they **were being swept**
Past	I, he, she, it,	I, he, she, it,
Int.	we, you, they **did sweep**	we, you, they **did get swept**
Pres.	I, we, you, they **have swept**	I, we, you, they **have been swept**
Perf.	he, she, it **has swept**	he, she, it **has been swept**
Past	I, he, she, it,	I, he, she, it,
Perf.	we, you, they **had swept**	we, you, they **had been swept**
Fut.	I, he, she, it, we, you, they	I, he, she, it, we, you, they
Perf.	**will have swept**	**will have been swept**

IMPERATIVE MOOD

sweep	**be swept**

SUBJUNCTIVE MOOD

Pres.	if I, he, she, it,	if I, he, she, it,
	we, you, they **sweep**	we, you, they **be swept**
Past	if I, he, she, it,	if I, he, she, it,
	we, you, they **swept**	we, you, they **were swept**
Fut.	if I, he, she, it,	if I, he, she, it,
	we, you, they **should sweep**	we, you, they **should be swept**

S

Transitive and intransitive.

Your sister swept the driveway last time.
The slate was swept clean with one admission.

swell
(active voice)

PRINCIPAL PARTS: **swells, swelling,
swelled, swelled/swollen**

be swelled/swollen
(passive voice)

INDICATIVE MOOD

Pres.	I, we, you, they **swell**	I **am swelled** we, you, they **are swelled**
	he, she, it **swells**	he, she, it **is swelled**
Pres. *Prog.*	I **am swelling** we, you, they **are swelling** he, she, it **is swelling**	I **am being swelled** we, you, they **are being swelled** he, she, it **is being swelled**
Pres. *Int.*	I, we, you, they **do swell** he, she, it **does swell**	I, we, you, they **do get swelled** he, she, it **does get swelled**
Fut.	I, he, she, it, we, you, they **will swell**	I, he, she, it, we, you, they **will be swelled**
Past	I, he, she, it, we, you, they **swelled**	I, he, she, it **was swelled** we, you, they **were swelled**
Past *Prog.*	I, he, she, it **was swelling** we, you, they **were swelling**	I, he, she, it **was being swelled** we, you, they **were being swelled**
Past *Int.*	I, he, she, it, we, you, they **did swell**	I, he, she, it, we, you, they **did get swelled**
Pres. *Perf.*	I, we, you, they **have swelled** he, she, it **has swelled**	I, we, you, they **have been swelled** he, she, it **has been swelled**
Past *Perf.*	I, he, she, it, we, you, they **had swelled**	I, he, she, it, we, you, they **had been swelled**
Fut. *Perf.*	I, he, she, it, we, you, they **will have swelled**	I, he, she, it, we, you, they **will have been swelled**

IMPERATIVE MOOD

swell **be swelled**

SUBJUNCTIVE MOOD

Pres.	if I, he, she, it, we, you, they **swell**	if I, he, she, it, we, you, they **be swelled**
Past	if I, he, she, it, we, you, they **swelled**	if I, he, she, it, we, you, they **were swelled**
Fut.	if I, he, she, it, we, you, they **should swell**	if I, he, she, it, we, you, they **should be swelled**

Intransitive and transitive. The *Oxford Dictionary* prefers the past participle SWOLLEN.

The waves swelled over his head.
His head was swelled by the praise.

swim
(active voice)

be swum
(passive voice)

INDICATIVE MOOD

Pres.	I, we, you, they **swim**	I **am swum**
		we, you, they **are swum**
	he, she, it **swims**	he, she, it **is swum**
Pres.	I **am swimming**	I **am being swum**
Prog.	we, you, they **are swimming**	we, you, they **are being swum**
	he, she, it **is swimming**	he, she, it **is being swum**
Pres.	I, we, you, they **do swim**	I, we, you, they **do get swum**
Int.	he, she, it **does swim**	he, she, it **does get swum**
Fut.	I, he, she, it,	I, he, she, it,
	we, you, they **will swim**	we, you, they **will be swum**
Past	I, he, she, it,	I, he, she, it **was swum**
	we, you, they **swam**	we, you, they **were swum**
Past	I, he, she, it **was swimming**	I, he, she, it **was being swum**
Prog.	we, you, they **were swimming**	we, you, they **were being swum**
Past	I, he, she, it,	I, he, she, it,
Int.	we, you, they **did swim**	we, you, they **did get swum**
Pres.	I, we, you, they **have swum**	I, we, you, they **have been swum**
Perf.	he, she, it **has swum**	he, she, it **has been swum**
Past	I, he, she, it,	I, he, she, it,
Perf.	we, you, they **had swum**	we, you, they **had been swum**
Fut.	I, he, she, it, we, you, they	I, he, she, it, we, you, they
Perf.	**will have swum**	**will have been swum**

S

IMPERATIVE MOOD

swim   **be swum**

SUBJUNCTIVE MOOD

Pres.	if I, he, she, it,	if I, he, she, it,
	we, you, they **swim**	we, you, they **be swum**
Past	if I, he, she, it,	if I, he, she, it,
	we, you, they **swam**	we, you, they **were swum**
Fut.	if I, he, she, it,	if I, he, she, it,
	we, you, they **should swim**	we, you, they **should be swum**

Intransitive and transitive.

We are swimming at the lake today.
He swam across the English Channel.
The meet was swum by swimmers from ten different countries.

PRINCIPAL PARTS: **swings, swinging, swung, swung**

INDICATIVE MOOD

Pres.	I, we, you, they **swing**	I **am swung**
		we, you, they **are swung**
	he, she, it **swings**	he, she, it **is swung**
Pres.	I **am swinging**	I **am being swung**
Prog.	we, you, they **are swinging**	we, you, they **are being swung**
	he, she, it **is swinging**	he, she, it **is being swung**
Pres.	I, we, you, they **do swing**	I, we, you, they **do get swung**
Int.	he, she, it **does swing**	he, she, it **does get swung**
Fut.	I, he, she, it,	I, he, she, it,
	we, you, they **will swing**	we, you, they **will be swung**
Past	I, he, she, it,	I, he, she, it **was swung**
	we, you, they **swung**	we, you, they **were swung**
Past	I, he, she, it **was swinging**	I, he, she, it **was being swung**
Prog.	we, you, they **were swinging**	we, you, they **were being swung**
Past	I, he, she, it,	I, he, she, it,
Int.	we, you, they **did swing**	we, you, they **did get swung**
Pres.	I, we, you, they **have swung**	I, we, you, they **have been swung**
Perf.	he, she, it **has swung**	he, she, it **has been swung**
Past	I, he, she, it,	I, he, she, it,
Perf.	we, you, they **had swung**	we, you, they **had been swung**
Fut.	I, he, she, it, we, you, they	I, he, she, it, we, you, they
Perf.	**will have swung**	**will have been swung**

IMPERATIVE MOOD

swing   **be swung**

SUBJUNCTIVE MOOD

Pres.	if I, he, she, it,	if I, he, she, it,
	we, you, they **swing**	we, you, they **be swung**
Past	if I, he, she, it,	if I, he, she, it,
	we, you, they **swung**	we, you, they **were swung**
Fut.	if I, he, she, it,	if I, he, she, it,
	we, you, they **should swing**	we, you, they **should be swung**

Intransitive and transitive.

The child swung back and forth for hours.
The cargo was swung over to the other ship.

sync(h)
(active voice)

be sync(h)ed
(passive voice)

INDICATIVE MOOD

Pres.	I, we, you, they **sync(h)**	I **am sync(h)ed**
		we, you, they **are sync(h)ed**
	he, she, it **sync(h)s**	he, she, it **is sync(h)ed**
Pres. *Prog.*	I **am sync(h)ing**	I **am being sync(h)ed**
	we, you, they **are sync(h)ing**	we, you, they **are being sync(h)ed**
	he, she, it **is sync(h)ing**	he, she, it **is being sync(h)ed**
Pres. *Int.*	I, we, you, they **do sync(h)**	I, we, you, they **do get sync(h)ed**
	he, she, it **does sync(h)**	he, she, it **does get sync(h)ed**
Fut.	I, he, she, it,	I, he, she, it,
	we, you, they **will sync(h)**	we, you, they **will be sync(h)ed**
Past	I, he, she, it,	I, he, she, it **was sync(h)ed**
	we, you, they **sync(h)ed**	we, you, they **were sync(h)ed**
Past *Prog.*	I, he, she, it **was sync(h)ing**	I, he, she, it **was being sync(h)ed**
	we, you, they **were sync(h)ing**	we, you, they **were being sync(h)ed**
Past *Int.*	I, he, she, it,	I, he, she, it,
	we, you, they **did sync(h)**	we, you, they **did get sync(h)ed**
Pres. *Perf.*	I, we, you, they **have sync(h)ed**	I, we, you, they **have been sync(h)ed**
	he, she, it **has sync(h)ed**	he, she, it **has been sync(h)ed**
Past *Perf.*	I, he, she, it,	I, he, she, it,
	we, you, they **had sync(h)ed**	we, you, they **had been sync(h)ed**
Fut. *Perf.*	I, he, she, it, we, you, they	I, he, she, it, we, you, they
	will have sync(h)ed	**will have been sync(h)ed**

S

IMPERATIVE MOOD

sync(h)   be sync(h)ed

SUBJUNCTIVE MOOD

Pres.	if I, he, she, it,	if I, he, she, it,
	we, you, they **sync(h)**	we, you, they **be sync(h)ed**
Past	if I, he, she, it,	if I, he, she, it,
	we, you, they **sync(h)ed**	we, you, they **were sync(h)ed**
Fut.	if I, he, she, it,	if I, he, she, it,
	we, you, they **should sync(h)**	we, you, they **should be sync(h)ed**

Transitive and intransitive. This verb derived from "synchronize" can be spelled either as SYNC or SYNCH.

We are syncing our watches for the race.
They synced their computers.
The files were synced on all the office machines.

take (active voice)	PRINCIPAL PARTS: **takes, taking,** **took, taken**	**be taken** (passive voice)

INDICATIVE MOOD

	Active	Passive
Pres.	I, we, you, they **take** he, she, it **takes**	I **am taken** we, you, they **are taken** he, she, it **is taken**
Pres. *Prog.*	I **am taking** we, you, they **are taking** he, she, it **is taking**	I **am being taken** we, you, they **are being taken** he, she, it **is being taken**
Pres. *Int.*	I, we, you, they **do take** he, she, it **does take**	I, we, you, they **do get taken** he, she, it **does get taken**
Fut.	I, he, she, it, we, you, they **will take**	I, he, she, it, we, you, they **will be taken**
Past	I, he, she, it, we, you, they **took**	I, he, she, it **was taken** we, you, they **were taken**
Past *Prog.*	I, he, she, it **was taking** we, you, they **were taking**	I, he, she, it **was being taken** we, you, they **were being taken**
Past *Int.*	I, he, she, it, we, you, they **did take**	I, he, she, it, we, you, they **did get taken**
Pres. *Perf.*	I, we, you, they **have taken** he, she, it **has taken**	I, we, you, they **have been taken** he, she, it **has been taken**
Past *Perf.*	I, he, she, it, we, you, they **had taken**	I, he, she, it, we, you, they **had been taken**
Fut. *Perf.*	I, he, she, it, we, you, they **will have taken**	I, he, she, it, we, you, they **will have been taken**

IMPERATIVE MOOD

	take	**be taken**

SUBJUNCTIVE MOOD

	Active	Passive
Pres.	if I, he, she, it, we, you, they **take**	if I, he, she, it, we, you, they **be taken**
Past	if I, he, she, it, we, you, they **took**	if I, he, she, it, we, you, they **were taken**
Fut.	if I, he, she, it, we, you, they **should take**	if I, he, she, it, we, you, they **should be taken**

Transitive and intransitive.

I am taking medicine for my cough.
He took a wrong turn and was lost.
What had taken them so long?

AN ESSENTIAL
55 VERB

take

Examples

Please take the trash out.

I took him to the dentist this afternoon.

The little girl always takes the dog out for a walk.

Who will take a chance on him?

Mom would take you if she could.

Take a ticket and wait until your number is called.

He is taking a course in self-defense.

I have taken all my required exams.

You should have taken the left turn.

I'll take this one and you can take the next one.

Words and expressions related to this verb

It is time to take a break.

Take me out to the ballgame.

Take time for yourself.

He was taken for the ride of his life.

Is this seat taken?

Do not take yourself so seriously.

It took a long time.

The bank robbers took off with the money.

You can take off your jacket.

They will take on a major assignment.

She takes over control of the company tomorrow.

T

talk
(active voice)

be talked
(passive voice)

INDICATIVE MOOD

Pres.   I, we, you, they **talk**

he, she, it **talks**

I **am talked**
we, you, they **are talked**
he, she, it **is talked**

Pres.   I **am talking**
Prog.   we, you, they **are talking**
he, she, it **is talking**

I **am being talked**
we, you, they **are being talked**
he, she, it **is being talked**

Pres.   I, we, you, they **do talk**
Int.   he, she, it **does talk**

I, we, you, they **do get talked**
he, she, it **does get talked**

Fut.   I, he, she, it,
we, you, they **will talk**

I, he, she, it,
we, you, they **will be talked**

Past   I, he, she, it,
we, you, they **talked**

I, he, she, it **was talked**
we, you, they **were talked**

Past   I, he, she, it **was talking**
Prog.   we, you, they **were talking**

I, he, she, it **was being talked**
we, you, they **were being talked**

Past   I, he, she, it,
Int.   we, you, they **did talk**

I, he, she, it,
we, you, they **did get talked**

Pres.   I, we, you, they **have talked**
Perf.   he, she, it **has talked**

I, we, you, they **have been talked**
he, she, it **has been talked**

Past   I, he, she, it,
Perf.   we, you, they **had talked**

I, he, she, it,
we, you, they **had been talked**

Fut.   I, he, she, it, we, you, they
Perf.   **will have talked**

I, he, she, it, we, you, they
will have been talked

IMPERATIVE MOOD

talk

be talked

SUBJUNCTIVE MOOD

Pres.   if I, he, she, it,
we, you, they **talk**

if I, he, she, it,
we, you, they **be talked**

Past   if I, he, she, it,
we, you, they **talked**

if I, he, she, it,
we, you, they **were talked**

Fut.   if I, he, she, it,
we, you, they **should talk**

if I, he, she, it,
we, you, they **should be talked**

Transitive and intransitive.

We talked all evening.
She was talked into going with them to the show.

taxi
(active voice)

be taxied
(passive voice)

INDICATIVE MOOD

Pres.	I, we, you, they **taxi**	I **am taxied**
		we, you, they **are taxied**
	he, she, it **taxis**	he, she, it **is taxied**
Pres.	I **am taxiing**	I **am being taxied**
Prog.	we, you, they **are taxiing**	we, you, they **are being taxied**
	he, she, it **is taxiing**	he, she, it **is being taxied**
Pres.	I, we, you, they **do taxi**	I, we, you, they **do get taxied**
Int.	he, she, it **does taxi**	he, she, it **does get taxied**
Fut.	I, he, she, it,	I, he, she, it,
	we, you, they **will taxi**	we, you, they **will be taxied**
Past	I, he, she, it,	I, he, she, it **was taxied**
	we, you, they **taxied**	we, you, they **were taxied**
Past	I, he, she, it **was taxiing**	I, he, she, it **was being taxied**
Prog.	we, you, they **were taxiing**	we, you, they **were being taxied**
Past	I, he, she, it,	I, he, she, it,
Int.	we, you, they **did taxi**	we, you, they **did get taxied**
Pres.	I, we, you, they **have taxied**	I, we, you, they **have been taxied**
Perf.	he, she, it **has taxied**	he, she, it **has been taxied**
Past	I, he, she, it,	I, he, she, it,
Perf.	we, you, they **had taxied**	we, you, they **had been taxied**
Fut.	I, he, she, it, we, you, they	I, he, she, it, we, you, they
Perf.	**will have taxied**	**will have been taxied**

IMPERATIVE MOOD

taxi   **be taxied**

SUBJUNCTIVE MOOD

Pres.	if I, he, she, it,	if I, he, she, it,
	we, you, they **taxi**	we, you, they **be taxied**
Past	if I, he, she, it,	if I, he, she, it,
	we, you, they **taxied**	we, you, they **were taxied**
Fut.	if I, he, she, it,	if I, he, she, it,
	we, you, they **should taxi**	we, you, they **should be taxied**

Intransitive and transitive.

He taxies people back and forth to work.
We are taxiing the guests to the hotel.
The huge plane taxied onto the runway.
The official visitors were taxied to the palace.

T

487

INDICATIVE MOOD

Pres.	I, we, you, they **teach**	I **am taught**
		we, you, they **are taught**
	he, she, it **teaches**	he, she, it **is taught**
Pres.	I **am teaching**	I **am being taught**
Prog.	we, you, they **are teaching**	we, you, they **are being taught**
	he, she, it **is teaching**	he, she, it **is being taught**
Pres.	I, we, you, they **do teach**	I, we, you, they **do get taught**
Int.	he, she, it **does teach**	he, she, it **does get taught**
Fut.	I, he, she, it,	I, he, she, it,
	we, you, they **will teach**	we, you, they **will be taught**
Past	I, he, she, it,	I, he, she, it **was taught**
	we, you, they **taught**	we, you, they **were taught**
Past	I, he, she, it **was teaching**	I, he, she, it **was being taught**
Prog.	we, you, they **were teaching**	we, you, they **were being taught**
Past	I, he, she, it,	I, he, she, it,
Int.	we, you, they **did teach**	we, you, they **did get taught**
Pres.	I, we, you, they **have taught**	I, we, you, they **have been taught**
Perf.	he, she, it **has taught**	he, she, it **has been taught**
Past	I, he, she, it,	I, he, she, it,
Perf.	we, you, they **had taught**	we, you, they **had been taught**
Fut.	I, he, she, it, we, you, they	I, he, she, it, we, you, they
Perf.	**will have taught**	**will have been taught**

IMPERATIVE MOOD

teach   **be taught**

SUBJUNCTIVE MOOD

Pres.	if I, he, she, it,	if I, he, she, it,
	we, you, they **teach**	we, you, they **be taught**
Past	if I, he, she, it,	if I, he, she, it,
	we, you, they **taught**	we, you, they **were taught**
Fut.	if I, he, she, it,	if I, he, she, it,
	we, you, they **should teach**	we, you, they **should be taught**

Transitive and intransitive.

He teaches in an elementary school.
My grandpa taught me how to tie my shoes.
They were taught by master craftsmen.

tear
(active voice)

be torn
(passive voice)

INDICATIVE MOOD

Pres.	I, we, you, they **tear**	I **am torn**
		we, you, they **are torn**
	he, she, it **tears**	he, she, it **is torn**
Pres.	I **am tearing**	I **am being torn**
Prog.	we, you, they **are tearing**	we, you, they **are being torn**
	he, she, it **is tearing**	he, she, it **is being torn**
Pres.	I, we, you, they **do tear**	I, we, you, they **do get torn**
Int.	he, she, it **does tear**	he, she, it **does get torn**
Fut.	I, he, she, it,	I, he, she, it,
	we, you, they **will tear**	we, you, they **will be torn**
Past	I, he, she, it,	I, he, she, it **was torn**
	we, you, they **tore**	we, you, they **were torn**
Past	I, he, she, it **was tearing**	I, he, she, it **was being torn**
Prog.	we, you, they **were tearing**	we, you, they **were being torn**
Past	I, he, she, it,	I, he, she, it,
Int.	we, you, they **did tear**	we, you, they **did get torn**
Pres.	I, we, you, they **have torn**	I, we, you, they **have been torn**
Perf.	he, she, it **has torn**	he, she, it **has been torn**
Past	I, he, she, it,	I, he, she, it,
Perf.	we, you, they **had torn**	we, you, they **had been torn**
Fut.	I, he, she, it, we, you, they	I, he, she, it, we, you, they
Perf.	**will have torn**	**will have been torn**

IMPERATIVE MOOD

tear   **be torn**

SUBJUNCTIVE MOOD

Pres.	if I, he, she, it,	if I, he, she, it,
	we, you, they **tear**	we, you, they **be torn**
Past	if I, he, she, it,	if I, he, she, it,
	we, you, they **tore**	we, you, they **were torn**
Fut.	if I, he, she, it,	if I, he, she, it,
	we, you, they **should tear**	we, you, they **should be torn**

Transitive and intransitive. The verb TEAR meaning to "fill with tears" is intransitive and has the past tense and past participle form TEARED.

She tore the receipts in half.
The shutters were torn from the house by the high winds.

tell	**PRINCIPAL PARTS: tells, telling,**	be told
(active voice)	**told, told**	(passive voice)

INDICATIVE MOOD

Pres.	I, we, you, they **tell**	I **am told**
		we, you, they **are told**
	he, she, it **tells**	he, she, it **is told**
Pres.	I **am telling**	I **am being told**
Prog.	we, you, they **are telling**	we, you, they **are being told**
	he, she, it **is telling**	he, she, it **is being told**
Pres.	I, we, you, they **do tell**	I, we, you, they **do get told**
Int.	he, she, it **does tell**	he, she, it **does get told**
Fut.	I, he, she, it,	I, he, she, it,
	we, you, they **will tell**	we, you, they **will be told**
Past	I, he, she, it,	I, he, she, it **was told**
	we, you, they **told**	we, you, they **were told**
Past	I, he, she, it **was telling**	I, he, she, it **was being told**
Prog.	we, you, they **were telling**	we, you, they **were being told**
Past	I, he, she, it,	I, he, she, it,
Int.	we, you, they **did tell**	we, you, they **did get told**
Pres.	I, we, you, they **have told**	I, we, you, they **have been told**
Perf.	he, she, it **has told**	he, she, it **has been told**
Past	I, he, she, it,	I, he, she, it,
Perf.	we, you, they **had told**	we, you, they **had been told**
Fut.	I, he, she, it, we, you, they	I, he, she, it, we, you, they
Perf.	**will have told**	**will have been told**

IMPERATIVE MOOD

tell	**be told**

SUBJUNCTIVE MOOD

Pres.	if I, he, she, it,	if I, he, she, it,
	we, you, they **tell**	we, you, they **be told**
Past	if I, he, she, it,	if I, he, she, it,
	we, you, they **told**	we, you, they **were told**
Fut.	if I, he, she, it,	if I, he, she, it,
	we, you, they **should tell**	we, you, they **should be told**

Transitive and intransitive.

She told me her life story.
They were told to remain in their cabins until the
storm subsided.

490

Examples

I tell them what they want to hear.

She tells him everything.

They told their story to the judge.

That story has been told for generations.

Who will tell?

I have told you everything I remember.

He wasn't told of her letter.

The policeman told him he had been speeding.

That story could never be told.

Tell the truth.

Words and expressions related to this verb

Don't ask, don't tell.

I cannot tell a lie.

Time will tell.

I told you so.

Tell all.

Never tell everything at once.

She certainly told him off.

We were told of his good fortune.

Tell me that you love me.

She isn't telling the truth.

T

text (active voice)	PRINCIPAL PARTS: **texts, texting,** **texted, texted**	be texted (passive voice)

INDICATIVE MOOD

Pres.	I, we, you, they **text**	I **am texted**
		we, you, they **are texted**
	he, she, it **texts**	he, she, it **is texted**
Pres. *Prog.*	I **am texting** we, you, they **are texting** he, she, it **is texting**	I **am being texted** we, you, they **are being texted** he, she, it **is being texted**
Pres. *Int.*	I, we, you, they **do text** he, she, it **does text**	I, we, you, they **do get texted** he, she, it **does get texted**
Fut.	I, he, she, it, we, you, they **will text**	I, he, she, it, we, you, they **will be texted**
Past	I, he, she, it, we, you, they **texted**	I, he, she, it **was texted** we, you, they **were texted**
Past *Prog.*	I, he, she, it **was texting** we, you, they **were texting**	I, he, she, it **was being texted** we, you, they **were being texted**
Past *Int.*	I, he, she, it, we, you, they **did text**	I, he, she, it, we, you, they **did get texted**
Pres. *Perf.*	I, we, you, they **have texted** he, she, it **has texted**	I, we, you, they **have been texted** he, she, it **has been texted**
Past *Perf.*	I, he, she, it, we, you, they **had texted**	I, he, she, it, we, you, they **had been texted**
Fut. *Perf.*	I, he, she, it, we, you, they **will have texted**	I, he, she, it, we, you, they **will have been texted**

IMPERATIVE MOOD

	text	**be texted**

SUBJUNCTIVE MOOD

Pres.	if I, he, she, it, we, you, they **text**	if I, he, she, it, we, you, they **be texted**
Past	if I, he, she, it, we, you, they **texted**	if I, he, she, it, we, you, they **were texted**
Fut.	if I, he, she, it, we, you, they **should text**	if I, he, she, it, we, you, they **should be texted**

I texted my friends about the party.
The news of his arrival was texted to all the students.

think
(active voice)

be thought
(passive voice)

INDICATIVE MOOD

Pres.	I, we, you, they **think**	I **am thought**
		we, you, they **are thought**
	he, she, it **thinks**	he, she, it **is thought**
Pres.	I **am thinking**	I **am being thought**
Prog.	we, you, they **are thinking**	we, you, they **are being thought**
	he, she, it **is thinking**	he, she, it **is being thought**
Pres.	I, we, you, they **do think**	I, we, you, they **do get thought**
Int.	he, she, it **does think**	he, she, it **does get thought**
Fut.	I, he, she, it,	I, he, she, it,
	we, you, they **will think**	we, you, they **will be thought**
Past	I, he, she, it,	I, he, she, it **was thought**
	we, you, they **thought**	we, you, they **were thought**
Past	I, he, she, it **was thinking**	I, he, she, it **was being thought**
Prog.	we, you, they **were thinking**	we, you, they **were being thought**
Past	I, he, she, it,	I, he, she, it,
Int.	we, you, they **did think**	we, you, they **did get thought**
Pres.	I, we, you, they **have thought**	I, we, you, they **have been thought**
Perf.	he, she, it **has thought**	he, she, it **has been thought**
Past	I, he, she, it,	I, he, she, it,
Perf.	we, you, they **had thought**	we, you, they **had been thought**
Fut.	I, he, she, it, we, you, they	I, he, she, it, we, you, they
Perf.	**will have thought**	**will have been thought**

IMPERATIVE MOOD

think

be thought

SUBJUNCTIVE MOOD

Pres.	if I, he, she, it,	if I, he, she, it,
	we, you, they **think**	we, you, they **be thought**
Past	if I, he, she, it,	if I, he, she, it,
	we, you, they **thought**	we, you, they **were thought**
Fut.	if I, he, she, it,	if I, he, she, it,
	we, you, they **should think**	we, you, they **should be thought**

Transitive and intransitive.

We thought the ballerina looked tired.
The relics were thought to be from ancient Greece.

AN ESSENTIAL
55 VERB

AN ESSENTIAL 55 VERB

Examples

I think that is a great idea.

What do you think?

She thinks that she can do it by this evening.

I thought you knew.

He was very well thought of in the community.

He was thought to be out of the country.

Have you ever thought of becoming an actress?

Think it over.

What could he be thinking?

Who could have thought that we would meet again?

Words and expressions related to this verb

I think, therefore I am.

Think of me.

Who do you think I am?

I never thought of that.

Their move was not very well thought out.

Think before you speak.

We'll think about it.

He thought of her often.

Think it through.

She does not care what I think.

INDICATIVE MOOD

Pres.	I, we, you, they **thread**	I **am threaded**
		we, you, they **are threaded**
	he, she, it **threads**	he, she, it **is threaded**
Pres.	I **am threading**	I **am being threaded**
Prog.	we, you, they **are threading**	we, you, they **are being threaded**
	he, she, it **is threading**	he, she, it **is being threaded**
Pres.	I, we, you, they **do thread**	I, we, you, they **do get threaded**
Int.	he, she, it **does thread**	he, she, it **does get threaded**
Fut.	I, he, she, it,	I, he, she, it,
	we, you, they **will thread**	we, you, they **will be threaded**
Past	I, he, she, it,	I, he, she, it **was threaded**
	we, you, they **threaded**	we, you, they **were threaded**
Past	I, he, she, it **was threading**	I, he, she, it **was being threaded**
Prog.	we, you, they **were threading**	we, you, they **were being threaded**
Past	I, he, she, it,	I, he, she, it,
Int.	we, you, they **did thread**	we, you, they **did get threaded**
Pres.	I, we, you, they **have threaded**	I, we, you, they **have been threaded**
Perf.	he, she, it **has threaded**	he, she, it **has been threaded**
Past	I, he, she, it,	I, he, she, it,
Perf.	we, you, they **had threaded**	we, you, they **had been threaded**
Fut.	I, he, she, it, we, you, they	I, he, she, it, we, you, they
Perf.	**will have threaded**	**will have been threaded**

IMPERATIVE MOOD

thread **be threaded**

SUBJUNCTIVE MOOD

Pres.	if I, he, she, it,	if I, he, she, it,
	we, you, they **thread**	we, you, they **be threaded**
Past	if I, he, she, it,	if I, he, she, it,
	we, you, they **threaded**	we, you, they **were threaded**
Fut.	if I, he, she, it,	if I, he, she, it,
	we, you, they **should thread**	we, you, they **should be threaded**

T

Transitive and intransitive.

He threaded his car into the parking spot.
The needles in the emergency kit were already threaded.

INDICATIVE MOOD

Pres.	I, we, you, they **thrive** he, she, it **thrives**
Pres. *Prog.*	**I am thriving** we, you, they **are thriving** he, she, it **is thriving**
Pres. *Int.*	I, we, you, they **do thrive** he, she, it **does thrive**
Fut.	I, he, she, it, we, you, they **will thrive**
Past	I, he, she, it, we, you, they **thrived**
Past *Prog.*	I, he, she, it **was thriving** we, you, they **were thriving**
Past *Int.*	I, he, she, it, we, you, they **did thrive**
Pres. *Perf.*	I, we, you, they **have thrived** he, she, it **has thrived**
Past *Perf.*	I, he, she, it, we, you, they **had thrived**
Fut. *Perf.*	I, he, she, it, we, you, they **will have thrived**

IMPERATIVE MOOD

thrive

SUBJUNCTIVE MOOD

Pres.	if I, he, she, it, we, you, they **thrive**
Past	if I, he, she, it, we, you, they **thrived**
Fut.	if I, he, she, it, we, you, they **should thrive**

Intransitive verb. The *Oxford Dictionary* prefers THROVE for the past tense and THRIVEN for the past participle.

The children are thriving now that the weather is warmer.
The new plant thrived in his living room.
Our children have thrived on the fresh fruits and vegetables.

throw
(active voice)

be thrown
(passive voice)

INDICATIVE MOOD

Pres.	I, we, you, they **throw**	I **am thrown**
		we, you, they **are thrown**
	he, she, it **throws**	he, she, it **is thrown**
Pres.	I **am throwing**	I **am being thrown**
Prog.	we, you, they **are throwing**	we, you, they **are being thrown**
	he, she, it **is throwing**	he, she, it **is being thrown**
Pres.	I, we, you, they **do throw**	I, we, you, they **do get thrown**
Int.	he, she, it **does throw**	he, she, it **does get thrown**
Fut.	I, he, she, it,	I, he, she, it,
	we, you, they **will throw**	we, you, they **will be thrown**
Past	I, he, she, it,	I, he, she, it **was thrown**
	we, you, they **threw**	we, you, they **were thrown**
Past	I, he, she, it **was throwing**	I, he, she, it **was being thrown**
Prog.	we, you, they **were throwing**	we, you, they **were being thrown**
Past	I, he, she, it,	I, he, she, it,
Int.	we, you, they **did throw**	we, you, they **did get thrown**
Pres.	I, we, you, they **have thrown**	I, we, you, they **have been thrown**
Perf.	he, she, it **has thrown**	he, she, it **has been thrown**
Past	I, he, she, it,	I, he, she, it,
Perf.	we, you, they **had thrown**	we, you, they **had been thrown**
Fut.	I, he, she, it, we, you, they	I, he, she, it, we, you, they
Perf.	**will have thrown**	**will have been thrown**

IMPERATIVE MOOD

throw

be thrown

SUBJUNCTIVE MOOD

Pres.	if I, he, she, it,	if I, he, she, it,
	we, you, they **throw**	we, you, they **be thrown**
Past	if I, he, she, it,	if I, he, she, it,
	we, you, they **threw**	we, you, they **were thrown**
Fut.	if I, he, she, it,	if I, he, she, it,
	we, you, they **should throw**	we, you, they **should be thrown**

T

Transitive and intransitive.

He threw out the first ball.
The check was thrown out with the trash.

497

thrust
(active voice)

be thrust
(passive voice)

INDICATIVE MOOD

Pres.	I, we, you, they **thrust**	I **am thrust**
		we, you, they **are thrust**
	he, she, it **thrusts**	he, she, it **is thrust**
Pres.	I **am thrusting**	I **am being thrust**
Prog.	we, you, they **are thrusting**	we, you, they **are being thrust**
	he, she, it **is thrusting**	he, she, it **is being thrust**
Pres.	I, we, you, they **do thrust**	I, we, you, they **do get thrust**
Int.	he, she, it **does thrust**	he, she, it **does get thrust**
Fut.	I, he, she, it,	I, he, she, it,
	we, you, they **will thrust**	we, you, they **will be thrust**
Past	I, he, she, it,	I, he, she, it **was thrust**
	we, you, they **thrust**	we, you, they **were thrust**
Past	I, he, she, it **was thrusting**	I, he, she, it **was being thrust**
Prog.	we, you, they **were thrusting**	we, you, they **were being thrust**
Past	I, he, she, it,	I, he, she, it,
Int.	we, you, they **did thrust**	we, you, they **did get thrust**
Pres.	I, we, you, they **have thrust**	I, we, you, they **have been thrust**
Perf.	he, she, it **has thrust**	he, she, it **has been thrust**
Past	I, he, she, it,	I, he, she, it,
Perf.	we, you, they **had thrust**	we, you, they **had been thrust**
Fut.	I, he, she, it, we, you, they	I, he, she, it, we, you, they
Perf.	**will have thrust**	**will have been thrust**

IMPERATIVE MOOD

thrust   **be thrust**

SUBJUNCTIVE MOOD

Pres.	if I, he, she, it,	if I, he, she, it,
	we, you, they **thrust**	we, you, they **be thrust**
Past	if I, he, she, it,	if I, he, she, it,
	we, you, they **thrust**	we, you, they **were thrust**
Fut.	if I, he, she, it,	if I, he, she, it,
	we, you, they **should thrust**	we, you, they **should be thrust**

Transitive and intransitive.

She thrusts as quickly as any man.
He thrust his sword at his opponent.
They were thrust into the spotlight by the success of their book.

tie
(active voice)

PRINCIPAL PARTS: **ties, tying, tied, tied**

be tied
(passive voice)

INDICATIVE MOOD

Pres.	I, we, you, they **tie**	I **am tied**
		we, you, they **are tied**
	he, she, it **ties**	he, she, it **is tied**
Pres.	I **am tying**	I **am being tied**
Prog.	we, you, they **are tying**	we, you, they **are being tied**
	he, she, it **is tying**	he, she, it **is being tied**
Pres.	I, we, you, they **do tie**	I, we, you, they **do get tied**
Int.	he, she, it **does tie**	he, she, it **does get tied**
Fut.	I, he, she, it,	I, he, she, it,
	we, you, they **will tie**	we, you, they **will be tied**
Past	I, he, she, it,	I, he, she, it **was tied**
	we, you, they **tied**	we, you, they **were tied**
Past	I, he, she, it **was tying**	I, he, she, it **was being tied**
Prog.	we, you, they **were tying**	we, you, they **were being tied**
Past	I, he, she, it,	I, he, she, it,
Int.	we, you, they **did tie**	we, you, they **did get tied**
Pres.	I, we, you, they **have tied**	I, we, you, they **have been tied**
Perf.	he, she, it **has tied**	he, she, it **has been tied**
Past	I, he, she, it,	I, he, she, it,
Perf.	we, you, they **had tied**	we, you, they **had been tied**
Fut.	I, he, she, it, we, you, they	I, he, she, it, we, you, they
Perf.	**will have tied**	**will have been tied**

IMPERATIVE MOOD

tie   **be tied**

SUBJUNCTIVE MOOD

Pres.	if I, he, she, it,	if I, he, she, it,
	we, you, they **tie**	we, you, they **be tied**
Past	if I, he, she, it,	if I, he, she, it,
	we, you, they **tied**	we, you, they **were tied**
Fut.	if I, he, she, it,	if I, he, she, it,
	we, you, they **should tie**	we, you, they **should be tied**

Transitive and intransitive.

I am tying our son's tie.
They tied the score.
The gifts were tied with fancy ribbon.

train
(active voice)

PRINCIPAL PARTS: **trains, training,**
trained, trained

be trained
(passive voice)

INDICATIVE MOOD

Pres.	I, we, you, they **train**	I **am trained**
		we, you, they **are trained**
	he, she, it **trains**	he, she, it **is trained**
Pres.	I **am training**	I **am being trained**
Prog.	we, you, they **are training**	we, you, they **are being trained**
	he, she, it **is training**	he, she, it **is being trained**
Pres.	I, we, you, they **do train**	I, we, you, they **do get trained**
Int.	he, she, it **does train**	he, she, it **does get trained**
Fut.	I, he, she, it,	I, he, she, it,
	we, you, they **will train**	we, you, they **will be trained**
Past	I, he, she, it,	I, he, she, it **was trained**
	we, you, they **trained**	we, you, they **were trained**
Past	I, he, she, it **was training**	I, he, she, it **was being trained**
Prog.	we, you, they **were training**	we, you, they **were being trained**
Past	I, he, she, it,	I, he, she, it,
Int.	we, you, they **did train**	we, you, they **did get trained**
Pres.	I, we, you, they **have trained**	I, we, you, they **have been trained**
Perf.	he, she, it **has trained**	he, she, it **has been trained**
Past	I, he, she, it,	I, he, she, it,
Perf.	we, you, they **had trained**	we, you, they **had been trained**
Fut.	I, he, she, it, we, you, they	I, he, she, it, we, you, they
Perf.	**will have trained**	**will have been trained**

IMPERATIVE MOOD

train   **be trained**

SUBJUNCTIVE MOOD

Pres.	if I, he, she, it,	if I, he, she, it,
	we, you, they **train**	we, you, they **be trained**
Past	if I, he, she, it,	if I, he, she, it,
	we, you, they **trained**	we, you, they **were trained**
Fut.	if I, he, she, it,	if I, he, she, it,
	we, you, they **should train**	we, you, they **should be trained**

Transitive and intransitive.

We trained a new generation of scholars.
I was trained by one of the best.

transfer
(active voice)

be transferred
(passive voice)

INDICATIVE MOOD

Pres.	I, we, you, they **transfer**	I **am transferred**
		we, you, they **are transferred**
	he, she, it **transfers**	he, she, it **is transferred**
Pres.	I **am transferring**	I **am being transferred**
Prog.	we, you, they **are transferring**	we, you, they **are being transferred**
	he, she, it **is transferring**	he, she, it **is being transferred**
Pres.	I, we, you, they **do transfer**	I, we, you, they **do get transferred**
Int.	he, she, it **does transfer**	he, she, it **does get transferred**
Fut.	I, he, she, it,	I, he, she, it,
	we, you, they **will transfer**	we, you, they **will be transferred**
Past	I, he, she, it,	I, he, she, it **was transferred**
	we, you, they **transferred**	we, you, they **were transferred**
Past	I, he, she, it **was transferring**	I, he, she, it **was being transferred**
Prog.	we, you, they **were transferring**	we, you, they **were being transferred**
Past	I, he, she, it,	I, he, she, it,
Int.	we, you, they **did transfer**	we, you, they **did get transferred**
Pres.	I, we, you, they **have transferred**	I, we, you, they **have been transferred**
Perf.	he, she, it **has transferred**	he, she, it **has been transferred**
Past	I, he, she, it,	I, he, she, it,
Perf.	we, you, they **had transferred**	we, you, they **had been transferred**
Fut.	I, he, she, it, we, you, they	I, he, she, it, we, you, they
Perf.	**will have transferred**	**will have been transferred**

IMPERATIVE MOOD

transfer   **be transferred**

SUBJUNCTIVE MOOD

Pres.	if I, he, she, it,	if I, he, she, it,
	we, you, they **transfer**	we, you, they **be transferred**
Past	if I, he, she, it,	if I, he, she, it,
	we, you, they **transferred**	we, you, they **were transferred**
Fut.	if I, he, she, it,	if I, he, she, it,
	we, you, they **should transfer**	we, you, they **should be transferred**

Transitive and intransitive.

We are transferring to a new school in September.
He transferred his funds to the new bank account.
They were transferred to other positions in the company.

transmit
(active voice)

(passive voice)

INDICATIVE MOOD

Pres.	I, we, you, they **transmit**	I **am transmitted**
		we, you, they **are transmitted**
	he, she, it **transmits**	he, she, it **is transmitted**
Pres.	I **am transmitting**	I **am being transmitted**
Prog.	we, you, they **are transmitting**	we, you, they **are being transmitted**
	he, she, it **is transmitting**	he, she, it **is being transmitted**
Pres.	I, we, you, they **do transmit**	I, we, you, they **do get transmitted**
Int.	he, she, it **does transmit**	he, she, it **does get transmitted**
Fut.	I, he, she, it,	I, he, she, it,
	we, you, they **will transmit**	we, you, they **will be transmitted**
Past	I, he, she, it,	I, he, she, it **was transmitted**
	we, you, they **transmitted**	we, you, they **were transmitted**
Past	I, he, she, it **was transmitting**	I, he, she, it **was being transmitted**
Prog.	we, you, they **were transmitting**	we, you, they **were being transmitted**
Past	I, he, she, it,	I, he, she, it,
Int.	we, you, they **did transmit**	we, you, they **did get transmitted**
Pres.	I, we, you, they **have transmitted**	I, we, you, they **have been transmitted**
Perf.	he, she, it **has transmitted**	he, she, it **has been transmitted**
Past	I, he, she, it,	I, he, she, it,
Perf.	we, you, they **had transmitted**	we, you, they **had been transmitted**
Fut.	I, he, she, it, we, you, they	I, he, she, it, we, you, they
Perf.	**will have transmitted**	**will have been transmitted**

IMPERATIVE MOOD

transmit   **be transmitted**

SUBJUNCTIVE MOOD

Pres.	if I, he, she, it,	if I, he, she, it,
	we, you, they **transmit**	we, you, they **be transmitted**
Past	if I, he, she, it,	if I, he, she, it,
	we, you, they **transmitted**	we, you, they **were transmitted**
Fut.	if I, he, she, it,	if I, he, she, it,
	we, you, they **should transmit**	we, you, they **should be transmitted**

Transitive and intransitive.

The station is transmitting only classical music.
We transmitted our coordinates to headquarters.
The data was transmitted over fiber optic cables.

502

tread
(active voice)

be trodden/trod
(passive voice)

INDICATIVE MOOD

Pres.	I, we, you, they **tread**	I **am trodden**
		we, you, they **are trodden**
	he, she, it **treads**	he, she, it **is trodden**
Pres.	I **am treading**	I **am being trodden**
Prog.	we, you, they **are treading**	we, you, they **are being trodden**
	he, she, it **is treading**	he, she, it **is being trodden**
Pres.	I, we, you, they **do tread**	I, we, you, they **do get trodden**
Int.	he, she, it **does tread**	he, she, it **does get trodden**
Fut.	I, he, she, it,	I, he, she, it,
	we, you, they **will tread**	we, you, they **will be trodden**
Past	I, he, she, it,	I, he, she, it **was trodden**
	we, you, they **trod**	we, you, they **were trodden**
Past	I, he, she, it **was treading**	I, he, she, it **was being trodden**
Prog.	we, you, they **were treading**	we, you, they **were being trodden**
Past	I, he, she, it,	I, he, she, it,
Int.	we, you, they **did tread**	we, you, they **did get trodden**
Pres.	I, we, you, they **have trodden**	I, we, you, they **have been trodden**
Perf.	he, she, it **has trodden**	he, she, it **has been trodden**
Past	I, he, she, it,	I, he, she, it,
Perf.	we, you, they **had trodden**	we, you, they **had been trodden**
Fut.	I, he, she, it, we, you, they	I, he, she, it, we, you, they
Perf.	**will have trodden**	**will have been trodden**

IMPERATIVE MOOD

tread　　　　　　　　　**be trodden**

SUBJUNCTIVE MOOD

Pres.	if I, he, she, it,	if I, he, she, it,
	we, you, they **tread**	we, you, they **be trodden**
Past	if I, he, she, it,	if I, he, she, it,
	we, you, they **trod**	we, you, they **were trodden**
Fut.	if I, he, she, it,	if I, he, she, it,
	we, you, they **should tread**	we, you, they **should be trodden**

Transitive and intransitive.

They trod softly through the forest.
This path has been trodden for generations.

treat
(active voice)

be treated
(passive voice)

INDICATIVE MOOD

Pres.	I, we, you, they **treat**	I **am treated**
		we, you, they **are treated**
	he, she, it **treats**	he, she, it **is treated**
Pres.	I **am treating**	I **am being treated**
Prog.	we, you, they **are treating**	we, you, they **are being treated**
	he, she, it **is treating**	he, she, it **is being treated**
Pres.	I, we, you, they **do treat**	I, we, you, they **do get treated**
Int.	he, she, it **does treat**	he, she, it **does get treated**
Fut.	I, he, she, it,	I, he, she, it,
	we, you, they **will treat**	we, you, they **will be treated**
Past	I, he, she, it,	I, he, she, it **was treated**
	we, you, they **treated**	we, you, they **were treated**
Past	I, he, she, it **was treating**	I, he, she, it **was being treated**
Prog.	we, you, they **were treating**	we, you, they **were being treated**
Past	I, he, she, it,	I, he, she, it,
Int.	we, you, they **did treat**	we, you, they **did get treated**
Pres.	I, we, you, they **have treated**	I, we, you, they **have been treated**
Perf.	he, she, it **has treated**	he, she, it **has been treated**
Past	I, he, she, it,	I, he, she, it,
Perf.	we, you, they **had treated**	we, you, they **had been treated**
Fut.	I, he, she, it, we, you, they	I, he, she, it, we, you, they
Perf.	**will have treated**	**will have been treated**

IMPERATIVE MOOD

treat   **be treated**

SUBJUNCTIVE MOOD

Pres.	if I, he, she, it,	if I, he, she, it,
	we, you, they **treat**	we, you, they **be treated**
Past	if I, he, she, it,	if I, he, she, it,
	we, you, they **treated**	we, you, they **were treated**
Fut.	if I, he, she, it,	if I, he, she, it,
	we, you, they **should treat**	we, you, they **should be treated**

Transitive and intransitive.

They treated themselves to chocolates.
We were treated at the hospital for frostbite.

try	PRINCIPAL PARTS: **tries, trying,**	**be tried**
(active voice)	**tried, tried**	(passive voice)

INDICATIVE MOOD

Pres.	I, we, you, they **try**	I **am tried**
		we, you, they **are tried**
	he, she, it **tries**	he, she, it **is tried**
Pres.	I **am trying**	I **am being tried**
Prog.	we, you, they **are trying**	we, you, they **are being tried**
	he, she, it **is trying**	he, she, it **is being tried**
Pres.	I, we, you, they **do try**	I, we, you, they **do get tried**
Int.	he, she, it **does try**	he, she, it **does get tried**
Fut.	I, he, she, it,	I, he, she, it,
	we, you, they **will try**	we, you, they **will be tried**
Past	I, he, she, it,	I, he, she, it **was tried**
	we, you, they **tried**	we, you, they **were tried**
Past	I, he, she, it **was trying**	I, he, she, it **was being tried**
Prog.	we, you, they **were trying**	we, you, they **were being tried**
Past	I, he, she, it,	I, he, she, it,
Int.	we, you, they **did try**	we, you, they **did get tried**
Pres.	I, we, you, they **have tried**	I, we, you, they **have been tried**
Perf.	he, she, it **has tried**	he, she, it **has been tried**
Past	I, he, she, it,	I, he, she, it,
Perf.	we, you, they **had tried**	we, you, they **had been tried**
Fut.	I, he, she, it, we, you, they	I, he, she, it, we, you, they
Perf.	**will have tried**	**will have been tried**

IMPERATIVE MOOD

try	**be tried**

SUBJUNCTIVE MOOD

Pres.	if I, he, she, it,	if I, he, she, it,
	we, you, they **try**	we, you, they **be tried**
Past	if I, he, she, it,	if I, he, she, it,
	we, you, they **tried**	we, you, they **were tried**
Fut.	if I, he, she, it,	if I, he, she, it,
	we, you, they **should try**	we, you, they **should be tried**

Transitive and intransitive.

She always tries to look her best.
He tried to open the jar.
They were tried in a court of public opinion.

AN ESSENTIAL
55 VERB

AN ESSENTIAL 55 VERB

try

Examples

You should try it.

He already tried it.

She'll try anything.

She tried on everything in the store.

He was tried and convicted.

Try on the new shoes.

Try to understand.

Try not to make a mistake.

Try it, you'll like it.

I will try to make it up to you.

Words and expressions related to this verb

Try to remember.

These are times that try men's souls.

Try me.

If at first you don't succeed, try, try again.

That has been tried before.

Have you tried the red wine?

He tried his best.

Let's try again.

She is trying out for the team.

You can make it if you try.

turn
(active voice)

PRINCIPAL PARTS: **turns, turning, turned, turned**

be turned
(passive voice)

INDICATIVE MOOD

Pres.	I, we, you, they **turn**	I **am turned**
		we, you, they **are turned**
	he, she, it **turns**	he, she, it **is turned**
Pres.	I **am turning**	I **am being turned**
Prog.	we, you, they **are turning**	we, you, they **are being turned**
	he, she, it **is turning**	he, she, it **is being turned**
Pres.	I, we, you, they **do turn**	I, we, you, they **do get turned**
Int.	he, she, it **does turn**	he, she, it **does get turned**
Fut.	I, he, she, it,	I, he, she, it,
	we, you, they **will turn**	we, you, they **will be turned**
Past	I, he, she, it,	I, he, she, it **was turned**
	we, you, they **turned**	we, you, they **were turned**
Past	I, he, she, it **was turning**	I, he, she, it **was being turned**
Prog.	we, you, they **were turning**	we, you, they **were being turned**
Past	I, he, she, it,	I, he, she, it,
Int.	we, you, they **did turn**	we, you, they **did get turned**
Pres.	I, we, you, they **have turned**	I, we, you, they **have been turned**
Perf.	he, she, it **has turned**	he, she, it **has been turned**
Past	I, he, she, it,	I, he, she, it,
Perf.	we, you, they **had turned**	we, you, they **had been turned**
Fut.	I, he, she, it, we, you, they	I, he, she, it, we, you, they
Perf.	**will have turned**	**will have been turned**

IMPERATIVE MOOD

turn   **be turned**

SUBJUNCTIVE MOOD

Pres.	if I, he, she, it,	if I, he, she, it,
	we, you, they **turn**	we, you, they **be turned**
Past	if I, he, she, it,	if I, he, she, it,
	we, you, they **turned**	we, you, they **were turned**
Fut.	if I, he, she, it,	if I, he, she, it,
	we, you, they **should turn**	we, you, they **should be turned**

Transitive and intransitive.

He turned to face his accuser.
They were turned toward the window when the lightning struck.

AN ESSENTIAL
55 VERB

507

turn

Examples

Turn right at the next light.

We will have to turn around.

Turn the chicken on the grill after three minutes.

The wheel turns too slowly.

Turn your clocks back one hour.

You will have to turn the plant around.

Can I turn on the radio?

Where can we turn to go in the opposite direction?

Having turned the corner, they saw their hotel.

They had turned too soon.

Words and expressions related to this verb

Please turn off the lights.

He turned on his computer.

She turned over in her sleep.

Turn the page.

The battle turned the tide in their favor.

She has turned over a new page.

That new music turns me off.

That really turns me on.

Turn, turn, turn.

Please turn up the volume.

If I could turn back time.

uncover
(active voice)

PRINCIPAL PARTS: **uncovers, uncovering, uncovered, uncovered**

be uncovered
(passive voice)

INDICATIVE MOOD

Pres.	I, we, you, they **uncover**	I **am uncovered**
		we, you, they **are uncovered**
	he, she, it **uncovers**	he, she, it **is uncovered**
Pres.	I **am uncovering**	I **am being uncovered**
Prog.	we, you, they **are uncovering**	we, you, they **are being uncovered**
	he, she, it **is uncovering**	he, she, it **is being uncovered**
Pres.	I, we, you, they **do uncover**	I, we, you, they **do get uncovered**
Int.	he, she, it **does uncover**	he, she, it **does get uncovered**
Fut.	I, he, she, it,	I, he, she, it,
	we, you, they **will uncover**	we, you, they **will be uncovered**
Past	I, he, she, it,	I, he, she, it **was uncovered**
	we, you, they **uncovered**	we, you, they **were uncovered**
Past	I, he, she, it **was uncovering**	I, he, she, it **was being uncovered**
Prog.	we, you, they **were uncovering**	we, you, they **were being uncovered**
Past	I, he, she, it,	I, he, she, it,
Int.	we, you, they **did uncover**	we, you, they **did get uncovered**
Pres.	I, we, you, they **have uncovered**	I, we, you, they **have been uncovered**
Perf.	he, she, it **has uncovered**	he, she, it **has been uncovered**
Past	I, he, she, it,	I, he, she, it,
Perf.	we, you, they **had uncovered**	we, you, they **had been uncovered**
Fut.	I, he, she, it, we, you, they	I, he, she, it, we, you, they
Perf.	**will have uncovered**	**will have been uncovered**

IMPERATIVE MOOD

uncover

be uncovered

SUBJUNCTIVE MOOD

Pres.	if I, he, she, it,	if I, he, she, it,
	we, you, they **uncover**	we, you, they **be uncovered**
Past	if I, he, she, it,	if I, he, she, it,
	we, you, they **uncovered**	we, you, they **were uncovered**
Fut.	if I, he, she, it,	if I, he, she, it,
	we, you, they **should uncover**	we, you, they **should be uncovered**

Transitive and intransitive.

They uncovered the mistake by accident.
Their secret was uncovered by the journalist.

undergo
(active voice)

INDICATIVE MOOD

Pres.	I, we, you, they **undergo**	I **am undergone**
		we, you, they **are undergone**
	he, she, it **undergoes**	he, she, it **is undergone**
Pres.	I **am undergoing**	I **am being undergone**
Prog.	we, you, they **are undergoing**	we, you, they **are being undergone**
	he, she, it **is undergoing**	he, she, it **is being undergone**
Pres.	I, we, you, they **do undergo**	I, we, you, they **do get undergone**
Int.	he, she, it **does undergo**	he, she, it **does get undergone**
Fut.	I, he, she, it,	I, he, she, it,
	we, you, they **will undergo**	we, you, they **will be undergone**
Past	I, he, she, it,	I, he, she, it **was undergone**
	we, you, they **underwent**	we, you, they **were undergone**
Past	I, he, she, it **was undergoing**	I, he, she, it **was being undergone**
Prog.	we, you, they **were undergoing**	we, you, they **were being undergone**
Past	I, he, she, it,	I, he, she, it,
Int.	we, you, they **did undergo**	we, you, they **did get undergone**
Pres.	I, we, you, they **have undergone**	I, we, you, they **have been undergone**
Perf.	he, she, it **has undergone**	he, she, it **has been undergone**
Past	I, he, she, it,	I, he, she, it,
Perf.	we, you, they **had undergone**	we, you, they **had been undergone**
Fut.	I, he, she, it, we, you, they	I, he, she, it, we, you, they
Perf.	**will have undergone**	**will have been undergone**

IMPERATIVE MOOD

undergo   **be undergone**

SUBJUNCTIVE MOOD

Pres.	if I, he, she, it,	if I, he, she, it,
	we, you, they **undergo**	we, you, they **be undergone**
Past	if I, he, she, it,	if I, he, she, it,
	we, you, they **underwent**	we, you, they **were undergone**
Fut.	if I, he, she, it,	if I, he, she, it,
	we, you, they **should undergo**	we, you, they **should be undergone**

She undergoes a series of tests.
He is undergoing surgery tomorrow.
He underwent three harsh winters.
The same obstacles have been undergone by your predecessors.

510

PRINCIPAL PARTS: **understands,
understanding, understood, understood**

INDICATIVE MOOD

Pres.	I, we, you, they **understand**
	he, she, it **understands**

I **am understood**
we, you, they **are understood**
he, she, it **is understood**

Pres. *Prog.*	I **am understanding** we, you, they **are understanding** he, she, it **is understanding**

I **am being understood**
we, you, they **are being understood**
he, she, it **is being understood**

Pres. *Int.*	I, we, you, they **do understand** he, she, it **does understand**

I, we, you, they **do get understood**
he, she, it **does get understood**

Fut.	I, he, she, it, we, you, they **will understand**

I, he, she, it,
we, you, they **will be understood**

Past	I, he, she, it, we, you, they **understood**

I, he, she, it **was understood**
we, you, they **were understood**

Past *Prog.*	I, he, she, it **was understanding** we, you, they **were understanding**

I, he, she, it **was being understood**
we, you, they **were being understood**

Past *Int.*	I, he, she, it, we, you, they **did understand**

I, he, she, it,
we, you, they **did get understood**

Pres. *Perf.*	I, we, you, they **have understood** he, she, it **has understood**

I, we, you, they **have been understood**
he, she, it **has been understood**

Past *Perf.*	I, he, she, it, we, you, they **had understood**

I, he, she, it,
we, you, they **had been understood**

Fut. *Perf.*	I, he, she, it, we, you, they **will have understood**

I, he, she, it, we, you, they
will have been understood

IMPERATIVE MOOD

understand   **be understood**

SUBJUNCTIVE MOOD

Pres.	if I, he, she, it, we, you, they **understand**

if I, he, she, it,
we, you, they **be understood**

Past	if I, he, she, it, we, you, they **understood**

if I, he, she, it,
we, you, they **were understood**

Fut.	if I, he, she, it, we, you, they **should understand**

if I, he, she, it,
we, you, they **should be understood**

U

Transitive and intransitive.

I understood the directions the second time I heard them.
The speaker could barely be understood past the first few rows.

undertake
(active voice)

PRINCIPAL PARTS: **undertakes,
undertaking, undertook, undertaken**

be undertaken
(passive voice)

INDICATIVE MOOD

Pres.	I, we, you, they **undertake**	I **am undertaken**
		we, you, they **are undertaken**
	he, she, it **undertakes**	he, she, it **is undertaken**
Pres.	I **am undertaking**	I **am being undertaken**
Prog.	we, you, they **are undertaking**	we, you, they **are being undertaken**
	he, she, it **is undertaking**	he, she, it **is being undertaken**
Pres.	I, we, you, they **do undertake**	I, we, you, they **do get undertaken**
Int.	he, she, it **does undertake**	he, she, it **does get undertaken**
Fut.	I, he, she, it,	I, he, she, it,
	we, you, they **will undertake**	we, you, they **will be undertaken**
Past	I, he, she, it,	I, he, she, it **was undertaken**
	we, you, they **undertook**	we, you, they **were undertaken**
Past	I, he, she, it **was undertaking**	I, he, she, it **was being undertaken**
Prog.	we, you, they **were undertaking**	we, you, they **were being undertaken**
Past	I, he, she, it,	I, he, she, it,
Int.	we, you, they **did undertake**	we, you, they **did get undertaken**
Pres.	I, we, you, they **have undertaken**	I, we, you, they **have been undertaken**
Perf.	he, she, it **has undertaken**	he, she, it **has been undertaken**
Past	I, he, she, it,	I, he, she, it,
Perf.	we, you, they **had undertaken**	we, you, they **had been undertaken**
Fut.	I, he, she, it, we, you, they	I, he, she, it, we, you, they
Perf.	**will have undertaken**	**will have been undertaken**

IMPERATIVE MOOD

undertake   **be undertaken**

SUBJUNCTIVE MOOD

Pres.	if I, he, she, it,	if I, he, she, it,
	we, you, they **undertake**	we, you, they **be undertaken**
Past	if I, he, she, it,	if I, he, she, it,
	we, you, they **undertook**	we, you, they **were undertaken**
Fut.	if I, he, she, it,	if I, he, she, it,
	we, you, they **should undertake**	we, you, they **should be undertaken**

We are undertaking this challenge to prove ourselves.
She undertook a rigorous exercise program.
The tasks were undertaken by a select group of recruits.

undo
(active voice)

Principal Parts: undoes, undoing, undid, undone

be undone
(passive voice)

INDICATIVE MOOD

Pres.	I, we, you, they **undo**	I **am undone**
		we, you, they **are undone**
	he, she, it **undoes**	he, she, it **is undone**
Pres.	I **am undoing**	I **am being undone**
Prog.	we, you, they **are undoing**	we, you, they **are being undone**
	he, she, it **is undoing**	he, she, it **is being undone**
Pres.	I, we, you, they **do undo**	I, we, you, they **did get undone**
Int.	he, she, it **does undo**	he, she, it **does get undone**
Fut.	I, he, she, it,	I, he, she, it,
	we, you, they **will undo**	we, you, they **will be undone**
Past	I, he, she, it,	I, he, she, it **was undone**
	we, you, they **undid**	we, you, they **were undone**
Past	I, he, she, it **was undoing**	I, he, she, it **was being undone**
Prog.	we, you, they **were undoing**	we, you, they **were being undone**
Past	I, he, she, it,	I, he, she, it,
Int.	we, you, they **did undo**	we, you, they **did get undone**
Pres.	I, we, you, they **have undone**	I, we, you, they **have been undone**
Perf.	he, she, it **has undone**	he, she, it **has been undone**
Past	I, he, she, it,	I, he, she, it,
Perf.	we, you, they **had undone**	we, you, they **had been undone**
Fut.	I, he, she, it, we, you, they	I, he, she, it, we, you, they
Perf.	**will have undone**	**will have been undone**

IMPERATIVE MOOD

undo	**be undone**

SUBJUNCTIVE MOOD

Pres.	if I, he, she, it,	if I, he, she, it,
	we, you, they **undo**	we, you, they **be undone**
Past	if I, he, she, it,	if I, he, she, it,
	we, you, they **undid**	we, you, they **were undone**
Fut.	if I, he, she, it,	if I, he, she, it,
	we, you, they **should undo**	we, you, they **should be undone**

Transitive and intransitive.

Who undoes the damage if we fail?
The little girl is undoing the laces on her shoes.
He undid the knot and cast off.
Their good work was undone by the rumors.

513

unite	PRINCIPAL PARTS: **unites, uniting,**	be united
(active voice)	**united, united**	(passive voice)

INDICATIVE MOOD

Pres.	I, we, you, they **unite**	I **am united**
		we, you, they **are united**
	he, she, it **unites**	he, she, it **is united**
Pres.	I **am uniting**	I **am being united**
Prog.	we, you, they **are uniting**	we, you, they **are being united**
	he, she, it **is uniting**	he, she, it **is being united**
Pres.	I, we, you, they **do unite**	I, we, you, they **do get united**
Int.	he, she, it **does unite**	he, she, it **does get united**
Fut.	I, he, she, it,	I, he, she, it,
	we, you, they **will unite**	we, you, they **will be united**
Past	I, he, she, it,	I, he, she, it **was united**
	we, you, they **united**	we, you, they **were united**
Past	I, he, she, it **was uniting**	I, he, she, it **was being united**
Prog.	we, you, they **were uniting**	we, you, they **were being united**
Past	I, he, she, it,	I, he, she, it,
Int.	we, you, they **did unite**	we, you, they **did get united**
Pres.	I, we, you, they **have united**	I, we, you, they **have been united**
Perf.	he, she, it **has united**	he, she, it **has been united**
Past	I, he, she, it,	I, he, she, it,
Perf.	we, you, they **had united**	we, you, they **had been united**
Fut.	I, he, she, it, we, you, they	I, he, she, it, we, you, they
Perf.	**will have united**	**will have been united**

IMPERATIVE MOOD

unite	**be united**

SUBJUNCTIVE MOOD

Pres.	if I, he, she, it,	if I, he, she, it,
	we, you, they **unite**	we, you, they **be united**
Past	if I, he, she, it,	if I, he, she, it,
	we, you, they **united**	we, you, they **were united**
Fut.	if I, he, she, it,	if I, he, she, it,
	we, you, they **should unite**	we, you, they **should be united**

Transitive and intransitive.

We are uniting our resources.
They united their two companies in the merger.
We are united in our resolve to do a better job.

PRINCIPAL PARTS: **upholds, upholding, upheld, upheld**

INDICATIVE MOOD

Pres.	I, we, you, they **uphold**	I **am upheld**
		we, you, they **are upheld**
	he, she, it **upholds**	he, she, it **is upheld**
Pres.	I **am upholding**	I **am being upheld**
Prog.	we, you, they **are upholding**	we, you, they **are being upheld**
	he, she, it **is upholding**	he, she, it **is being upheld**
Pres.	I, we, you, they **do uphold**	I, we, you, they **do get upheld**
Int.	he, she, it **does uphold**	he, she, it **does get upheld**
Fut.	I, he, she, it,	I, he, she, it,
	we, you, they **will uphold**	we, you, they **will be upheld**
Past	I, he, she, it,	I, he, she, it **was upheld**
	we, you, they **upheld**	we, you, they **were upheld**
Past	I, he, she, it **was upholding**	I, he, she, it **was being upheld**
Prog.	we, you, they **were upholding**	we, you, they **were being upheld**
Past	I, he, she, it,	I, he, she, it,
Int.	we, you, they **did uphold**	we, you, they **did get upheld**
Pres.	I, we, you, they **have upheld**	I, we, you, they **have been upheld**
Perf.	he, she, it **has upheld**	he, she, it **has been upheld**
Past	I, he, she, it,	I, he, she, it,
Perf.	we, you, they **had upheld**	we, you, they **had been upheld**
Fut.	I, he, she, it, we, you, they	I, he, she, it, we, you, they
Perf.	**will have upheld**	**will have been upheld**

IMPERATIVE MOOD

uphold   **be upheld**

SUBJUNCTIVE MOOD

Pres.	if I, he, she, it,	if I, he, she, it,
	we, you, they **uphold**	we, you, they **be upheld**
Past	if I, he, she, it,	if I, he, she, it,
	we, you, they **upheld**	we, you, they **were upheld**
Fut.	if I, he, she, it,	if I, he, she, it,
	we, you, they **should uphold**	we, you, they **should be upheld**

They upheld their end of the bargain.
The original decision was upheld upon appeal.

INDICATIVE MOOD

Pres.	I, we, you, they **upset**	I **am upset** we, you, they **are upset**
	he, she, it **upsets**	he, she, it **is upset**
Pres. *Prog.*	I **am upsetting** we, you, they **are upsetting** he, she, it **is upsetting**	I **am being upset** we, you, they **are being upset** he, she, it **is being upset**
Pres. *Int.*	I, we, you, they **do upset** he, she, it **does upset**	I, we, you, they **do get upset** he, she, it **does get upset**
Fut.	I, he, she, it, we, you, they **will upset**	I, he, she, it, we, you, they **will be upset**
Past	I, he, she, it, we, you, they **upset**	I, he, she, it **was upset** we, you, they **were upset**
Past *Prog.*	I, he, she, it **was upsetting** we, you, they **were upsetting**	I, he, she, it **was being upset** we, you, they **were being upset**
Past *Int.*	I, he, she, it, we, you, they **did upset**	I, he, she, it, we, you, they **did get upset**
Pres. *Perf.*	I, we, you, they **have upset** he, she, it **has upset**	I, we, you, they **have been upset** he, she, it **has been upset**
Past *Perf.*	I, he, she, it, we, you, they **had upset**	I, he, she, it, we, you, they **had been upset**
Fut. *Perf.*	I, he, she, it, we, you, they **will have upset**	I, he, she, it, we, you, they **will have been upset**

IMPERATIVE MOOD

upset　　　　　　**be upset**

SUBJUNCTIVE MOOD

Pres.	if I, he, she, it, we, you, they **upset**	if I, he, she, it, we, you, they **be upset**
Past	if I, he, she, it, we, you, they **upset**	if I, he, she, it, we, you, they **were upset**
Fut.	if I, he, she, it, we, you, they **should upset**	if I, he, she, it, we, you, they **should be upset**

Transitive and intransitive.

His visit always upsets his parents.
Why is she upsetting us so?
She upset her mother with her choice of a man.
We were upset by our child's teacher.

516

use (active voice)	PRINCIPAL PARTS: uses, using, used, used	be used (passive voice)

INDICATIVE MOOD

Pres.	I, we, you, they **use**	I **am used** we, you, they **are used**
	he, she, it **uses**	he, she, it **is used**
Pres. *Prog.*	I **am using** we, you, they **are using** he, she, it **is using**	I **am being used** we, you, they **are being used** he, she, it **is being used**
Pres. *Int.*	I, we, you, they **do use** he, she, it **does use**	I, we, you, they **do get used** he, she, it **does get used**
Fut.	I, he, she, it, we, you, they **will use**	I, he, she, it, we, you, they **will be used**
Past	I, he, she, it, we, you, they **used**	I, he, she, it **was used** we, you, they **were used**
Past *Prog.*	I, he, she, it **was using** we, you, they **were using**	I, he, she, it **was being used** we, you, they **were being used**
Past *Int.*	I, he, she, it, we, you, they **did use**	I, he, she, it, we, you, they **did get used**
Pres. *Perf.*	I, we, you, they **have used** he, she, it **has used**	I, we, you, they **have been used** he, she, it **has been used**
Past *Perf.*	I, he, she, it, we, you, they **had used**	I, he, she, it, we, you, they **had been used**
Fut. *Perf.*	I, he, she, it, we, you, they **will have used**	I, he, she, it, we, you, they **will have been used**

IMPERATIVE MOOD

use	**be used**

SUBJUNCTIVE MOOD

Pres.	if I, he, she, it, we, you, they **use**	if I, he, she, it, we, you, they **be used**
Past	if I, he, she, it, we, you, they **used**	if I, he, she, it, we, you, they **were used**
Fut.	if I, he, she, it, we, you, they **should use**	if I, he, she, it, we, you, they **should be used**

USED TO can form the past tense meaning "a former custom, or activity."

Are you using the new program?
I used the drill very rarely last year.
The program was used by millions of computers.

AN ESSENTIAL 55 VERB

Examples

Use it wisely.

I have used this detergent before.

She uses only the most expensive perfumes.

Use it at your own risk.

What have you been using?

They have already used their allotment.

We could have used your expertise.

Can you use this more than once?

Who is able to use his computer?

The leftovers were all used in the stew.

Words and expressions related to this verb

Use it or lose it.

Use it up.

Don't use too much.

I cannot use your services.

I used all the milk for the cake.

It was used over and over again.

Can a password be used more than once?

He used me.

She uses people.

What credit card will you be using?

vary (active voice)	PRINCIPAL PARTS: **varies, varying, varied, varied**	**be varied** (passive voice)

INDICATIVE MOOD

Pres.	I, we, you, they **vary**	I **am varied**
		we, you, they **are varied**
	he, she, it **varies**	he, she, it **is varied**
Pres.	I **am varying**	I **am being varied**
Prog.	we, you, they **are varying**	we, you, they **are being varied**
	he, she, it **is varying**	he, she, it **is being varied**
Pres.	I, we, you, they **do vary**	I, we, you, they **do get varied**
Int.	he, she, it **does vary**	he, she, it **does get varied**
Fut.	I, he, she, it,	I, he, she, it,
	we, you, they **will vary**	we, you, they **will be varied**
Past	I, he, she, it,	I, he, she, it **was varied**
	we, you, they **varied**	we, you, they **were varied**
Past	I, he, she, it **was varying**	I, he, she, it **was being varied**
Prog.	we, you, they **were varying**	we, you, they **were being varied**
Past	I, he, she, it,	I, he, she, it,
Int.	we, you, they **did vary**	we, you, they **did get varied**
Pres.	I, we, you, they **have varied**	I, we, you, they **have been varied**
Perf.	he, she, it **has varied**	he, she, it **has been varied**
Past	I, he, she, it,	I, he, she, it,
Perf.	we, you, they **had varied**	we, you, they **had been varied**
Fut.	I, he, she, it, we, you, they	I, he, she, it, we, you, they
Perf.	**will have varied**	**will have been varied**

IMPERATIVE MOOD

vary	**be varied**

SUBJUNCTIVE MOOD

Pres.	if I, he, she, it,	if I, he, she, it,
	we, you, they **vary**	we, you, they **be varied**
Past	if I, he, she, it,	if I, he, she, it,
	we, you, they **varied**	we, you, they **were varied**
Fut.	if I, he, she, it,	if I, he, she, it,
	we, you, they **should vary**	we, you, they **should be varied**

V

Transitive and intransitive.

The quality of the apples varies from year to year.
We are varying our arrival times.
They varied the formula in search of a winner.
The temperature was varied for each patron.

| visit
(active voice) | PRINCIPAL PARTS: **visits, visiting,
visited, visited** | be visited
(passive voice) |

INDICATIVE MOOD

Pres.	I, we, you, they **visit**	I **am visited** we, you, they **are visited**
	he, she, it **visits**	he, she, it **is visited**
Pres. *Prog.*	I **am visiting** we, you, they **are visiting**	I **am being visited** we, you, they **are being visited**
	he, she, it **is visiting**	he, she, it **is being visited**
Pres. *Int.*	I, we, you, they **do visit** he, she, it **does visit**	I, we, you, they **do get visited** he, she, it **does get visited**
Fut.	I, he, she, it, we, you, they **will visit**	I, he, she, it, we, you, they **will be visited**
Past	I, he, she, it we, you, they **visited**	I, he, she, it **was visited** we, you, they **were visited**
Past *Prog.*	I, he, she, it **was visiting** we, you, they **were visiting**	I, he, she, it **was being visited** we, you, they **were being visited**
Past *Int.*	I, he, she, it, we, you, they **did visit**	I, he, she, it, we, you, they **did get visited**
Pres. *Perf.*	I, we, you, they **have visited** he, she, it **has visited**	I, we, you, they **have been visited** he, she, it **has been visited**
Past *Perf.*	I, he, she, it, we, you, they **had visited**	I, he, she, it, we, you, they **had been visited**
Fut. *Perf.*	I, he, she, it, we, you, they **will have visited**	I, he, she, it, we, you, they **will have been visited**

IMPERATIVE MOOD

visit	**be visited**

SUBJUNCTIVE MOOD

Pres.	if I, he, she, it, we, you, they **visit**	if I, he, she, it, we, you, they **be visited**
Past	if I, he, she, it, we, you, they **visited**	if I, he, she, it, we, you, they **were visited**
Fut.	if I, he, she, it, we, you, they **should visit**	if I, he, she, it, we, you, they **should be visited**

Transitive and intransitive.

We visited your country last year.
He was visited by an official delegation.

wait
(active voice)

be waited
(passive voice)

INDICATIVE MOOD

Pres.	I, we, you, they **wait**	I **am waited**
		we, you, they **are waited**
	he, she, it **waits**	he, she, it **is waited**
Pres. *Prog.*	I **am waiting**	I **am being waited**
	we, you, they **are waiting**	we, you, they **are being waited**
	he, she, it **is waiting**	he, she, it **is being waited**
Pres. *Int.*	I, we, you, they **do wait**	I, we, you, they **do get waited**
	he, she, it **does wait**	he, she, it **does get waited**
Fut.	I, he, she, it,	I, he, she, it,
	we, you, they **will wait**	we, you, they **will be waited**
Past	I, he, she, it,	I, he, she, it **was waited**
	we, you, they **waited**	we, you, they **were waited**
Past *Prog.*	I, he, she, it **was waiting**	I, he, she, it **was being waited**
	we, you, they **were waiting**	we, you, they **were being waited**
Past *Int.*	I, he, she, it,	I, he, she, it,
	we, you, they **did wait**	we, you, they **did get waited**
Pres. *Perf.*	I, we, you, they **have waited**	I, we, you, they **have been waited**
	he, she, it **has waited**	he, she, it **has been waited**
Past *Perf.*	I, he, she, it,	I, he, she, it,
	we, you, they **had waited**	we, you, they **had been waited**
Fut. *Perf.*	I, he, she, it, we, you, they	I, he, she, it, we, you, they
	will have waited	**will have been waited**

IMPERATIVE MOOD

wait   **be waited**

SUBJUNCTIVE MOOD

Pres.	if I, he, she, it,	if I, he, she, it,
	we, you, they **wait**	we, you, they **be waited**
Past	if I, he, she, it,	if I, he, she, it,
	we, you, they **waited**	we, you, they **were waited**
Fut.	if I, he, she, it,	if I, he, she, it,
	we, you, they **should wait**	we, you, they **should be waited**

W
X
Y
Z

Intransitive and transitive.

We waited too long before we called.
The table was waited on by the new waitress.

wake
(active voice)

PRINCIPAL PARTS: wakes, waking, woke/waked, waked/woken

be waked/woken
(passive voice)

INDICATIVE MOOD

Pres.	I, we, you, they **wake**	I **am waked**
		we, you, they **are waked**
	he, she, it **wakes**	he, she, it **is waked**
Pres.	I **am waking**	I **am being waked**
Prog.	we, you, they **are waking**	we, you, they **are being waked**
	he, she, it **is waking**	he, she, it **is being waked**
Pres.	I, we, you, they **do wake**	I, we, you, they **do get waked**
Int.	he, she, it **does wake**	he, she, it **does get waked**
Fut.	I, he, she, it,	I, he, she, it,
	we, you, they **will wake**	we, you, they **will be waked**
Past	I, he, she, it	I, he, she, it **was waked**
	we, you, they **woke**	we, you, they **were waked**
Past	I, he, she, it **was waking**	I, he, she, it **was being waked**
Prog.	we, you, they **were waking**	we, you, they **were being waked**
Past	I, he, she, it,	I, he, she, it,
Int.	we, you, they **did wake**	we, you, they **did get waked**
Pres.	I, we, you, they **have waked**	I, we, you, they **have been waked**
Perf.	he, she, it **has waked**	he, she, it **has been waked**
Past	I, he, she, it,	I, he, she, it,
Perf.	we, you, they **had waked**	we, you, they **had been waked**
Fut.	I, he, she, it, we, you, they	I, he, she, it, we, you, they
Perf.	**will have waked**	**will have been waked**

IMPERATIVE MOOD

wake   **be waked**

SUBJUNCTIVE MOOD

Pres.	if I, he, she, it,	if I, he, she, it,
	we, you, they **wake**	we, you, they **be waked**
Past	if I, he, she, it,	if I, he, she, it,
	we, you, they **woke**	we, you, they **were waked**
Fut.	if I, he, she, it,	if I, he, she, it,
	we, you, they **should wake**	we, you, they **should be waked**

Intransitive and transitive. The *Oxford Dictionary* prefers the past participle WOKEN. *Webster's* also lists as a past participle WOKE.

She is waking now.
He woke with a splitting headache.
They were woken to the storm by the pounding rain.

INDICATIVE MOOD

Pres.	I, we, you, they **waken**	I **am wakened**
		we, you, they **are wakened**
	he, she, it **wakens**	he, she, it **is wakened**
Pres.	I **am wakening**	I **am being wakened**
Prog.	we, you, they **are wakening**	we, you, they **are being wakened**
	he, she, it **is wakening**	he, she, it **is being wakened**
Pres.	I, we, you, they **do waken**	I, we, you, they **do get wakened**
Int.	he, she, it **does waken**	he, she, it **does get wakened**
Fut.	I, he, she, it,	I, he, she, it,
	we, you, they **will waken**	we, you, they **will be wakened**
Past	I, he, she, it,	I, he, she, it **was wakened**
	we, you, they **wakened**	we, you, they **were wakened**
Past	I, he, she, it **was wakening**	I, he, she, it **was being wakened**
Prog.	we, you, they **were wakening**	we, you, they **were being wakened**
Past	I, he, she, it,	I, he, she, it,
Int.	we, you, they **did waken**	we, you, they **did get wakened**
Pres.	I, we, you, they **have wakened**	I, we, you, they **have been wakened**
Perf.	he, she, it **has wakened**	he, she, it **has been wakened**
Past	I, he, she, it,	I, he, she, it,
Perf.	we, you, they **had wakened**	we, you, they **had been wakened**
Fut.	I, he, she, it, we, you, they	I, he, she, it, we, you, they
Perf.	**will have wakened**	**will have been wakened**

IMPERATIVE MOOD

waken	**be wakened**

SUBJUNCTIVE MOOD

Pres.	if I, he, she, it,	if I, he, she, it,
	we, you, they **waken**	we, you, they **be wakened**
Past	if I, he, she, it,	if I, he, she, it,
	we, you, they **wakened**	we, you, they **were wakened**
Fut.	if I, he, she, it,	if I, he, she, it,
	we, you, they **should waken**	we, you, they **should be wakened**

W
X
Y
Z

Transitive and intransitive.

We wakened to the sight of fresh snow.
The boy was wakened by his little brother.

523

walk	PRINCIPAL PARTS: **walks, walking,**	be walked
(active voice)	**walked, walked**	(passive voice)

INDICATIVE MOOD

Pres.	I, we, you, they **walk**	I **am walked**
		we, you, they **are walked**
	he, she, it **walks**	he, she, it **is walked**
Pres.	I **am walking**	I **am being walked**
Prog.	we, you, they **are walking**	we, you, they **are being walked**
	he, she, it **is walking**	he, she, it **is being walked**
Pres.	I, we, you, they **do walk**	I, we, you, they **do get walked**
Int.	he, she, it **does walk**	he, she, it **does get walked**
Fut.	I, he, she, it,	I, he, she, it,
	we, you, they **will walk**	we, you, they **will be walked**
Past	I, he, she, it,	I, he, she, it **was walked**
	we, you, they **walked**	we, you, they **were walked**
Past	I, he, she, it **was walking**	I, he, she, it **was being walked**
Prog.	we, you, they **were walking**	we, you, they **were being walked**
Past	I, he, she, it,	I, he, she, it,
Int.	we, you, they **did walk**	we, you, they **did get walked**
Pres.	I, we, you, they **have walked**	I, we, you, they **have been walked**
Perf.	he, she, it **has walked**	he, she, it **has been walked**
Past	I, he, she, it,	I, he, she, it,
Perf.	we, you, they **had walked**	we, you, they **had been walked**
Fut.	I, he, she, it, we, you, they	I, he, she, it, we, you, they
Perf.	**will have walked**	**will have been walked**

IMPERATIVE MOOD

walk	**be walked**

SUBJUNCTIVE MOOD

Pres.	if I, he, she, it,	if I, he, she, it,
	we, you, they **walk**	we, you, they **be walked**
Past	if I, he, she, it,	if I, he, she, it,
	we, you, they **walked**	we, you, they **were walked**
Fut.	if I, he, she, it,	if I, he, she, it,
	we, you, they **should walk**	we, you, they **should be walked**

Intransitive and transitive.

You walked twenty five miles!
The trail was walked by a group of hikers.

want (active voice)	PRINCIPAL PARTS: **wants, wanting** **wanted, wanted**	be wanted (passive voice)

INDICATIVE MOOD

Pres.	I, we, you, they **want**	I **am wanted**
		we, you, they **are wanted**
	he, she, it **wants**	he, she, it **is wanted**
Pres.	I **am wanting**	I **am being wanted**
Prog.	we, you, they **are wanting**	we, you, they **are being wanted**
	he, she, it **is wanting**	he, she, it **is being wanted**
Pres.	I, we, you, they **do want**	I, we, you, they **do get wanted**
Int.	he, she, it **does want**	he, she, it **does get wanted**
Fut.	I, he, she, it,	I, he, she, it,
	we, you, they **will want**	we, you, they **will be wanted**
Past	I, he, she, it,	I, he, she, it **was wanted**
	we, you, they **wanted**	we, you, they **were wanted**
Past	I, he, she, it **was wanting**	I, he, she, it **was being wanted**
Prog.	we, you, they **were wanting**	we, you, they **were being wanted**
Past	I, he, she, it,	I, he, she, it,
Int.	we, you, they **did want**	we, you, they **did get wanted**
Pres.	I, we, you, they **have wanted**	I, we, you, they **have been wanted**
Perf.	he, she, it **has wanted**	he, she, it **has been wanted**
Past	I, he, she, it,	I, he, she, it,
Perf.	we, you, they **had wanted**	we, you, they **had been wanted**
Fut.	I, he, she, it, we, you, they	I, he, she, it, we, you, they
Perf.	**will have wanted**	**will have been wanted**

IMPERATIVE MOOD

want	**be wanted**

SUBJUNCTIVE MOOD

Pres.	if I, he, she, it,	if I, he, she, it,
	we, you, they **want**	we, you, they **be wanted**
Past	if I, he, she, it,	if I, he, she, it,
	we, you, they **wanted**	we, you, they **were wanted**
Fut.	if I, he, she, it,	if I, he, she, it,
	we, you, they **should want**	we, you, they **should be wanted**

Transitive and intransitive.

She wanted a better life.
The outlaw was wanted in three states.

AN ESSENTIAL
55 VERB

AN ESSENTIAL 55 VERB

want

Examples

Who wants ice cream?

I want to go home.

They wanted a new life.

He was wanted by the authorities.

What will they want to do here?

It is okay to want a better life.

We have been wanting a grandchild for years.

Her presence was not wanted.

He really does want to see you.

Want less.

| **watch**
(active voice) | PRINCIPAL PARTS: **watches, watching,**
watched, watched | **be watched**
(passive voice) |

INDICATIVE MOOD

Pres.	I, we, you, they **watch** he, she, it **watches**	I **am watched** we, you, they **are watched** he, she, it **is watched**
Pres. *Prog.*	I **am watching** we, you, they **are watching** he, she, it **is watching**	I **am being watched** we, you, they **are being watched** he, she, it **is being watched**
Pres. *Int.*	I, we, you, they **do watch** he, she, it **does watch**	I, we, you, they **do get watched** he, she, it **does get watched**
Fut.	I, he, she, it, we, you, they **will watch**	I, he, she, it, we, you, they **will be watched**
Past	I, he, she, it, we, you, they **watched**	I, he, she, it **was watched** we, you, they **were watched**
Past *Prog.*	I, he, she, it **was watching** we, you, they **were watching**	I, he, she, it **was being watched** we, you, they **were being watched**
Past *Int.*	I, he, she, it, we, you, they **did watch**	I, he, she, it, we, you, they **did get watched**
Pres. *Perf.*	I, we, you, they **have watched** he, she, it **has watched**	I, we, you, they **have been watched** he, she, it **has been watched**
Past *Perf.*	I, he, she, it, we, you, they **had watched**	I, he, she, it, we, you, they **had been watched**
Fut. *Perf.*	I, he, she, it, we, you, they **will have watched**	I, he, she, it, we, you, they **will have been watched**

IMPERATIVE MOOD

watch	**be watched**

SUBJUNCTIVE MOOD

Pres.	if I, he, she, it, we, you, they **watch**	if I, he, she, it, we, you, they **be watched**
Past	if I, he, she, it, we, you, **watched**	if I, he, she, it, we, you, they **were watched**
Fut.	if I, he, she, it, we, you, they **should watch**	if I, he, she, it, we, you, they **should be watched**

W
X
Y
Z

Intransitive and transitive.

He watches her every time she dances.
We watched the Olympics in our hotel.
The suspect was watched on surveillance cameras.

INDICATIVE MOOD

Pres.	I, we, you, they **waylay**	I **am waylaid** we, you, they **are waylaid**
	he, she, it **waylays**	he, she, it **is waylaid**
Pres. *Prog.*	I **am waylaying** we, you, they **are waylaying** he, she, it **is waylaying**	I **am being waylaid** we, you, they **are being waylaid** he, she, it **is being waylaid**
Pres. *Int.*	I, we, you, they **do waylay** he, she, it **does waylay**	I, we, you, they **do get waylaid** he, she, it **does get waylaid**
Fut.	I, he, she, it, we, you, they **will waylay**	I, he, she, it, we, you, they **will be waylaid**
Past	I, he, she, it, we, you, they **waylaid**	I, he, she, it **was waylaid** we, you, they **were waylaid**
Past *Prog.*	I, he, she, it **was waylaying** we, you, they **were waylaying**	I, he, she, it **was being waylaid** we, you, they **were being waylaid**
Past *Int.*	I, he, she, it, we, you, they **did waylay**	I, he, she, it, we, you, they **did get waylaid**
Pres. *Perf.*	I, we, you, they **have waylaid** he, she, it **has waylaid**	I, we, you, they **have been waylaid** he, she, it **has been waylaid**
Past *Perf.*	I, he, she, it, we, you, they **had waylaid**	I, he, she, it, we, you, they **had been waylaid**
Fut. *Perf.*	I, he, she, it, we, you, they **will have waylaid**	I, he, she, it, we, you, they **will have been waylaid**

IMPERATIVE MOOD

waylay **be waylaid**

SUBJUNCTIVE MOOD

Pres.	if I, he, she, it, we, you, they **waylay**	if I, he, she, it, we, you, they **be waylaid**
Past	if I, he, she, it, we, you, they **waylaid**	if I, he, she, it, we, you, they **were waylaid**
Fut.	if I, he, she, it, we, you, they **should waylay**	if I, he, she, it, we, you, they **should be waylaid**

He waylaid me as I was going to my room.
The actor was waylaid by photographers.

wear
(active voice)

PRINCIPAL PARTS: **wears, wearing, wore, worn**

be worn
(passive voice)

INDICATIVE MOOD

Pres.	I, we, you, they **wear**	I **am worn**
		we, you, they **are worn**
	he, she, it **wears**	he, she, it **is worn**
Pres.	I **am wearing**	I **am being worn**
Prog.	we, you, they **are wearing**	we, you, they **are being worn**
	he, she, it **is wearing**	he, she, it **is being worn**
Pres.	I, we, you, they **do wear**	I, we, you, they **do get worn**
Int.	he, she, it **does wear**	he, she, it **does get worn**
Fut.	I, he, she, it,	I, he, she, it,
	we, you, they **will wear**	we, you, they **will be worn**
Past	I, he, she, it,	I, he, she, it **was worn**
	we, you, they **wore**	we, you, they **were worn**
Past	I, he, she, it **was wearing**	I, he, she, it **was being worn**
Prog.	we, you, they **were wearing**	we, you, they **were being worn**
Past	I, he, she, it,	I, he, she, it,
Int.	we, you, they **did wear**	we, you, they **did get worn**
Pres.	I, we, you, they **have worn**	I, we, you, they **have been worn**
Perf.	he, she, it **has worn**	he, she, it **has been worn**
Past	I, he, she, it,	I, he, she, it,
Perf.	we, you, they **had worn**	we, you, they **had been worn**
Fut.	I, he, she, it, we, you, they	I, he, she, it, we, you, they
Perf.	**will have worn**	**will have been worn**

IMPERATIVE MOOD

wear

be worn

SUBJUNCTIVE MOOD

Pres.	if I, he, she, it,	if I, he, she, it,
	we, you, they **wear**	we, you, they **be worn**
Past	if I, he, she, it,	if I, he, she, it,
	we, you, they **wore**	we, you, they **were worn**
Fut.	if I, he, she, it,	if I, he, she, it,
	we, you, they **should wear**	we, you, they **should be worn**

W
X
Y
Z

Transitive and intransitive.

She wore a yellow ribbon in her hair.
The jeans were worn on the hips.

weave (active voice)	PRINCIPAL PARTS: **weaves, weaving,** **wove/weaved, woven/weaved**	be woven/weaved (passive voice)

INDICATIVE MOOD

Pres.	I, we, you, they **weave**	I **am woven** we, you, they **are woven**
	he, she, it **weaves**	he, she, it **is woven**
Pres. *Prog.*	I **am weaving** we, you, they **are weaving** he, she, it **is weaving**	I **am being woven** we, you, they **are being woven** he, she, it **is being woven**
Pres. *Int.*	I, we, you, they **do weave** he, she, it **does weave**	I, we, you, they **do get woven** he, she, it **does get woven**
Fut.	I, he, she, it, we, you, they **will weave**	I, he, she, it, we, you, they **will be woven**
Past	I, he, she, it, we, you, they **wove**	I, he, she, it **was woven** we, you, they **were woven**
Past *Prog.*	I, he, she, it **was weaving** we, you, they **were weaving**	I, he, she, it **was being woven** we, you, they **were being woven**
Past *Int.*	I, he, she, it, we, you, they **did weave**	I, he, she, it, we, you, they **did get woven**
Pres. *Perf.*	I, we, you, they **have woven** he, she, it **has woven**	I, we, you, they **have been woven** he, she, it **has been woven**
Past *Perf.*	I, he, she, it, we, you, they **had woven**	I, he, she, it, we, you, they **had been woven**
Fut. *Perf.*	I, he, she, it, we, you, they **will have woven**	I, he, she, it, we, you, they **will have been woven**

IMPERATIVE MOOD

weave	**be woven**

SUBJUNCTIVE MOOD

Pres.	if I, he, she, it, we, you, they **weave**	if I, he, she, it, we, you, they **be woven**
Past	if I, he, she, it, we, you, they **wove**	if I, he, she, it, we, you, they **were woven**
Fut.	if I, he, she, it, we, you, they **should weave**	if I, he, she, it, we, you, they **should be woven**

The transitive verb with the forms WOVE and WOVEN has to do with making cloth. The transitive and intransitive verb with the past tense and past participle WEAVED means "moving from side to side as through traffic." The *Oxford Dictionary* lists WOVE as an alternate form of the past participle.

He is weaving a web of deception.
The driver wove in and out of the traffic.
The school's crest was woven onto their jackets.

530

wed
(active voice)

PRINCIPAL PARTS: **weds, wedding,
wedded, wed/wedded**

be wed/wedded
(passive voice)

INDICATIVE MOOD

Pres.	I, we, you, they **wed**	I **am wed**
		we, you, they **are wed**
	he, she, it **weds**	he, she, it **is wed**
Pres.	I **am wedding**	I **am being wed**
Prog.	we, you, they **are wedding**	we, you, they **are being wed**
	he, she, it **is wedding**	he, she, it **is being wed**
Pres.	I, we, you, they **do wed**	I, we, you, they **do get wed**
Int.	he, she, it **does wed**	he, she, it **does get wed**
Fut.	I, he, she, it,	I, he, she, it,
	we, you, they **will wed**	we, you, they **will be wed**
Past	I, he, she, it,	I, he, she, it **was wed**
	we, you, they **wedded**	we, you, they **were wed**
Past	I, he, she, it **was wedding**	I, he, she, it **was being wed**
Prog.	we, you, they **were wedding**	we, you, they **were being wed**
Past	I, he, she, it,	I, he, she, it,
Int.	we, you, they **did wed**	we, you, they **did get wed**
Pres.	I, we, you, they **have wed**	I, we, you, they **have been wed**
Perf.	he, she, it **has wed**	he, she, it **has been wed**
Past	I, he, she, it,	I, he, she, it,
Perf.	we, you, they **had wed**	we, you, they **had been wed**
Fut.	I, he, she, it, we, you, they	I, he, she, it, we, you, they
Perf.	**will have wed**	**will have been wed**

IMPERATIVE MOOD

wed	**be wed**

SUBJUNCTIVE MOOD

Pres.	if I, he, she, it,	if I, he, she, it,
	we, you, they **wed**	we, you, they **be wed**
Past	if I, he, she, it,	if I, he, she, it,
	we, you, they **wedded**	we, you, they **were wed**
Fut.	if I, he, she, it,	if I, he, she, it,
	we, you, they **should wed**	we, you, they **should be wed**

**W
X
Y
Z**

Transitive and intransitive.

The town clerk weds dozens of couples each year.
He is wedding her on Saturday.
She wedded in March of last year.
We were wed in a modest ceremony for family and friends.

weep
(active voice)

be wept
(passive voice)

INDICATIVE MOOD

Pres.	I, we, you, they **weep**	I **am wept** we, you, they **are wept** he, she, it **is wept**
	he, she, it **weeps**	
Pres. *Prog.*	I **am weeping** we, you, they **are weeping** he, she, it **is weeping**	I **am being wept** we, you, they **are being wept** he, she, it **is being wept**
Pres. *Int.*	I, we, you, they **do weep** he, she, it **does weep**	I, we, you, they **do get wept** he, she, it **does get wept**
Fut.	I, he, she, it, we, you, they **will weep**	I, he, she, it, we, you, they **will be wept**
Past	I, he, she, it, we, you, they **wept**	I, he, she, it **was wept** we, you, they **were wept**
Past *Prog.*	I, he, she, it **was weeping** we, you, they **were weeping**	I, he, she, it **was being wept** we, you, they **were being wept**
Past *Int.*	I, he, she, it, we, you, they **did weep**	I, he, she, it, we, you, they **did get wept**
Pres. *Perf.*	I, we, you, they **have wept** he, she, it **has wept**	I, we, you, they **have been wept** he, she, it **has been wept**
Past *Perf.*	I, he, she, it, we, you, they **had wept**	I, he, she, it, we, you, they **had been wept**
Fut. *Perf.*	I, he, she, it, we, you, they **will have wept**	I, he, she, it, we, you, they **will have been wept**

IMPERATIVE MOOD

weep

be wept

SUBJUNCTIVE MOOD

Pres.	if I, he, she, it, we, you, they **weep**	if I, he, she, it, we, you, they **be wept**
Past	if I, he, she, it, we, you, they **wept**	if I, he, she, it, we, you, they **were wept**
Fut.	if I, he, she, it, we, you, they **should weep**	if I, he, she, it, we, you, they **should be wept**

Transitive and intransitive.

She wept for the loss of her husband.
Tears were wept in joy and sorrow that day.

wet
(active voice)

be wet/wetted
(passive voice)

INDICATIVE MOOD

Pres.	I, we, you, they **wet**	I **am wet**
		we, you, they **are wet**
	he, she, it **wets**	he, she, it **is wet**
Pres.	I **am wetting**	I **am being wet**
Prog.	we, you, they **are wetting**	we, you, they **are being wet**
	he, she, it **is wetting**	he, she, it **is being wet**
Pres.	I, we, you, they **do wet**	I, we, you, they **do get wet**
Int.	he, she, it **does wet**	he, she, it **does get wet**
Fut.	I, he, she, it,	I, he, she, it,
	we, you, they **will wet**	we, you, they **will be wet**
Past	I, he, she, it,	I, he, she, it **was wet**
	we, you, they **wet**	we, you, they **were wet**
Past	I, he, she, it **was wetting**	I, he, she, it **was being wet**
Prog.	we, you, they **were wetting**	we, you, they **were being wet**
Past	I, he, she, it,	I, he, she, it,
Int.	we, you, they **did wet**	we, you, they **did get wet**
Pres.	I, we, you, they **have wet**	I, we, you, they **have been wet**
Perf.	he, she, it **has wet**	he, she, it **has been wet**
Past	I, he, she, it,	I, he, she, it,
Perf.	we, you, they **had wet**	we, you, they **had been wet**
Fut.	I, he, she, it, we, you, they	I, he, she, it, we, you, they
Perf.	**will have wet**	**will have been wet**

IMPERATIVE MOOD

wet **be wet**

SUBJUNCTIVE MOOD

Pres.	if I, he, she, it,	if I, he, she, it,
	we, you, they **wet**	we, you, they **be wet**
Past	if I, he, she, it,	if I, he, she, it,
	we, you, they **wet**	we, you, they **were wet**
Fut.	if I, he, she, it,	if I, he, she, it,
	we, you, they **should wet**	we, you, they **should be wet**

W X Y Z

Transitive and intransitive.

The baker wets his hands before working with the dough.
The spray is wetting the newly seeded lawn.
She wet her rag and began cleaning.
His hair was wet from the rain.

whip
(active voice)

be whipped/whipt
(passive voice)

INDICATIVE MOOD

Pres.	I, we, you, they **whip**	I **am whipped** we, you, they **are whipped**
	he, she, it **whips**	he, she, it **is whipped**
Pres. *Prog.*	I **am whipping** we, you, they **are whipping** he, she, it **is whipping**	I **am being whipped** we, you, they **are being whipped** he, she, it **is being whipped**
Pres. *Int.*	I, we, you, they **do whip** he, she, it **does whip**	I, we, you, they **do get whipped** he, she, it **does get whipped**
Fut.	I, he, she, it, we, you, they **will whip**	I, he, she, it, we, you, they **will be whipped**
Past	I, he, she, it, we, you, they **whipped**	I, he, she, it **was whipped** we, you, they **were whipped**
Past *Prog.*	I, he, she, it **was whipping** we, you, they **were whipping**	I, he, she, it **was being whipped** we, you, they **were being whipped**
Past *Int.*	I, he, she, it, we, you, they **did whip**	I, he, she, it, we, you, they **did get whipped**
Pres. *Perf.*	I, we, you, they **have whipped** he, she, it **has whipped**	I, we, you, they **have been whipped** he, she, it **has been whipped**
Past *Perf.*	I, he, she, it, we, you, they **had whipped**	I, he, she, it, we, you, they **had been whipped**
Fut. *Perf.*	I, he, she, it, we, you, they **will have whipped**	I, he, she, it, we, you, they **will have been whipped**

IMPERATIVE MOOD

whip   **be whipped**

SUBJUNCTIVE MOOD

Pres.	if I, he, she, it, we, you, they **whip**	if I, he, she, it, we, you, they **be whipped**
Past	if I, he, she, it, we, you, they **whipped**	if I, he, she, it, we, you, they **were whipped**
Fut.	if I, he, she, it, we, you, they **should whip**	if I, he, she, it, we, you, they **should be whipped**

Transitive and intransitive. The *Oxford Dictionary* prefers the form WHIPT for the past tense and past participle.

Grandpa is whipping the cream.
Mom whipped up a delicious dinner.
The cream was whipped with an electric mixer.

will
(active voice)

PRINCIPAL PARTS: wills, willing, willed, willed

be willed
(passive voice)

INDICATIVE MOOD

Pres.	I, we, you, they **will**	I **am willed**
		we, you, they **are willed**
	he, she, it **wills**	he, she, it **is willed**
Pres.	I **am willing**	I **am being willed**
Prog.	we, you, they **are willing**	we, you, they **are being willed**
	he, she, it **is willing**	he, she, it **is being willed**
Pres.	I, we, you, they **do will**	I, we, you, they **do get willed**
Int.	he, she, it **does will**	he, she, it **does get willed**
Fut.	I, he, she, it,	I, he, she, it,
	we, you, they **will will**	we, you, they **will be willed**
Past	I, he, she, it,	I, he, she, it **was willed**
	we, you, they **willed**	we, you, they **were willed**
Past	I, he, she, it **was willing**	I, he, she, it **was being willed**
Prog.	we, you, they **were willing**	we, you, they **were being willed**
Past	I, he, she, it,	I, he, she, it,
Int.	we, you, they **did will**	we, you, they **did get willed**
Pres.	I, we, you, they **have willed**	I, we, you, they **have been willed**
Perf.	he, she, it **has willed**	he, she, it **has been willed**
Past	I, he, she, it,	I, he, she, it,
Perf.	we, you, they **had willed**	we, you, they **had been willed**
Fut.	I, he, she, it, we, you, they	I, he, she, it, we, you, they
Perf.	**will have willed**	**will have been willed**

IMPERATIVE MOOD

will **be willed**

SUBJUNCTIVE MOOD

Pres.	if I, he, she, it,	if I, he, she, it,
	we, you, they **will**	we, you, they **be willed**
Past	if I, he, she, it,	if I, he, she, it,
	we, you, they **willed**	we, you, they **were willed**
Fut.	if I, he, she, it,	if I, he, she, it,
	we, you, they **should will**	we, you, they **should be willed**

W
X
Y
Z

Transitive and intransitive. As an auxiliary verb WILL has only two forms: WILL for the present and WOULD for the past.

I will you my books.
I am willing them my belongings.
He willed them into being.
The unwanted thoughts were willed into oblivion.

535

win (active voice)	PRINCIPAL PARTS: **wins, winning, won, won**	be won (passive voice)

INDICATIVE MOOD

Pres.	I, we, you, they **win**	I **am won** we, you, they **are won**
	he, she, it **wins**	he, she, it **is won**
Pres.	I **am winning**	I **am being won**
Prog.	we, you, they **are winning**	we, you, they **are being won**
	he, she, it **is winning**	he, she, it **is being won**
Pres.	I, we, you, they **do win**	I, we, you, they **do get won**
Int.	he, she, it **does win**	he, she, it **does get won**
Fut.	I, he, she, it,	I, he, she, it,
	we, you, they **will win**	we, you, they **will be won**
Past	I, he, she, it,	I, he, she, it **was won**
	we, you, they **won**	we, you, they **were won**
Past	I, he, she, it **was winning**	I, he, she, it **was being won**
Prog.	we, you, they **were winning**	we, you, they **were being won**
Past	I, he, she, it,	I, he, she, it,
Int.	we, you, they **did win**	we, you, they **did get won**
Pres.	I, we, you, they **have won**	I, we, you, they **have been won**
Perf.	he, she, it **has won**	he, she, it **has been won**
Past	I, he, she, it,	I, he, she, it,
Perf.	we, you, they **had won**	we, you, they **had been won**
Fut.	I, he, she, it, we, you, they	I, he, she, it, we, you, they
Perf.	**will have won**	**will have been won**

IMPERATIVE MOOD

win	**be won**

SUBJUNCTIVE MOOD

Pres.	if I, he, she, it,	if I, he, she, it,
	we, you, they **win**	we, you, they **be won**
Past	if I, he, she, it,	if I, he, she, it,
	we, you, they **won**	we, you, they **were won**
Fut.	if I, he, she, it,	if I, he, she, it,
	we, you, they **should win**	we, you, they **should be won**

Intransitive and transitive.

We are winning every match this year.
Our team won the state championship.
The lottery was won by a group of deserving individuals.

536

wind (active voice)	PRINCIPAL PARTS: **winds, winding,** **wound, wound**	**be wound** (passive voice)

INDICATIVE MOOD

Pres.	I, we, you, they **wind**	I **am wound** we, you, they **are wound**
	he, she, it **winds**	he, she, it **is wound**
Pres. *Prog.*	I **am winding** we, you, they **are winding** he, she, it **is winding**	I **am being wound** we, you, they **are being wound** he, she, it **is being wound**
Pres. *Int.*	I, we, you, they **do wind** he, she, it **does wind**	I, we, you, they **do get wound** he, she, it **does get wound**
Fut.	I, he, she, it, we, you, they **will wind**	I, he, she, it, we, you, they **will be wound**
Past	I, he, she, it, we, you, they **wound**	I, he, she, it **was wound** we, you, they **were wound**
Past *Prog.*	I, he, she, it **was winding** we, you, they **were winding**	I, he, she, it **was being wound** we, you, they **were being wound**
Past *Int.*	I, he, she, it, we, you, they **did wind**	I, he, she, it, we, you, they **did get wound**
Pres. *Perf.*	I, we, you, they **have wound** he, she, it **has wound**	I, we, you, they **have been wound** he, she, it **has been wound**
Past *Perf.*	I, he, she, it, we, you, they **had wound**	I, he, she, it, we, you, they **had been wound**
Fut. *Perf.*	I, he, she, it, we, you, they **will have wound**	I, he, she, it, we, you, they **will have been wound**

IMPERATIVE MOOD

wind	**be wound**

SUBJUNCTIVE MOOD

Pres.	if I, he, she, it, we, you, they **wind**	if I, he, she, it, we, you, they **be wound**
Past	if I, he, she, it, we, you, they **wound**	if I, he, she, it, we, you, they **were wound**
Fut.	if I, he, she, it, we, you, they **should wind**	if I, he, she, it, we, you, they **should be wound**

W
X
Y
Z

Transitive and intransitive. This verb means to "turn or twirl around, like a watch."
The verb WIND, WINDS, WINDING, WINDED, WINDED means to "expose to the air, be short of breath."

He wound the clock once a week.
The cord was wound around the telephone.

wish
(active voice)

be wished
(passive voice)

INDICATIVE MOOD

Pres.	I, we, you, they **wish**	I **am wished**
		we, you, they **are wished**
	he, she, it **wishes**	he, she, it **is wished**
Pres.	I **am wishing**	I **am being wished**
Prog.	we, you, they **are wishing**	we, you, they **are being wished**
	he, she, it **is wishing**	he, she, it **is being wished**
Pres.	I, we, you, they **do wish**	I, we, you, **do get wished**
Int.	he, she, it **does wish**	he, she, it **does get wished**
Fut.	I, he, she, it,	I, he, she, it,
	we, you, they **will wish**	we, you, they **will be wished**
Past	I, he, she, it,	I, he, she, it **was wished**
	we, you, they **wished**	we, you, they **were wished**
Past	I, he, she, it **was wishing**	I, he, she, it **was being wished**
Prog.	we, you, they **were wishing**	we, you, they **were being wished**
Past	I, he, she, it,	I, he, she, it,
Int.	we, you, they **did wish**	we, you, they **did get wished**
Pres.	I, we, you, they **have wished**	I, we, you, they **have been wished**
Perf.	he, she, it **has wished**	he, she, it **has been wished**
Past	I, he, she, it,	I, he, she, it,
Perf.	we, you, they **had wished**	we, you, they **had been wished**
Fut.	I, he, she, it, we, you, they	I, he, she, it, we, you, they
Perf.	**will have wished**	**will have been wished**

IMPERATIVE MOOD

wish

be wished

SUBJUNCTIVE MOOD

Pres.	if I, he, she, it,	if I, he, she, it,
	we, you, they **wish**	we, you, they **be wished**
Past	if I, he, she, it,	if I, he, she, it,
	we, you, they **wished**	we, you, they **were wished**
Fut.	if I, he, she, it,	if I, he, she, it,
	we, you, they **should wish**	we, you, they **should be wished**

Transitive and intransitive.

He wishes you all the best in the coming year.
We wished them a happy holiday.
They were wished a happy anniversary by their parents.

withhold
(active voice)

PRINCIPAL PARTS: withholds, withholding, withheld, withheld

be withheld
(passive voice)

INDICATIVE MOOD

Pres.	I, we, you, they **withhold**	I **am withheld**
		we, you, they **are withheld**
	he, she, it **withholds**	he, she, it **is withheld**
Pres.	I **am withholding**	I **am being withheld**
Prog.	we, you, they **are withholding**	we, you, they **are being withheld**
	he, she, it **is withholding**	he, she, it **is being withheld**
Pres.	I, we, you, they **do withhold**	I, we, you, they **do get withheld**
Int.	he, she, it **does withhold**	he, she, it **does get withheld**
Fut.	I, he, she, it,	I, he, she, it,
	we, you, they **will withhold**	we, you, they **will be withheld**
Past	I, he, she, it,	I, he, she, it **was withheld**
	we, you, they **withheld**	we, you, they **were withheld**
Past	I, he, she, it **was withholding**	I, he, she, it **was being withheld**
Prog.	we, you, they **were withholding**	we, you, they **were being withheld**
Past	I, he, she, it,	I, he, she, it,
Int.	we, you, they **did withhold**	we, you, they **did get withheld**
Pres.	I, we, you, they **have withheld**	I, we, you, they **have been withheld**
Perf.	he, she, it **has withheld**	he, she, it **has been withheld**
Past	I, he, she, it,	I, he, she, it,
Perf.	we, you, they **had withheld**	we, you, they **had been withheld**
Fut.	I, he, she, it, we, you, they	I, he, she, it, we, you, they
Perf.	**will have withheld**	**will have been withheld**

IMPERATIVE MOOD

withhold

be withheld

SUBJUNCTIVE MOOD

Pres.	if I, he, she, it,	if I, he, she, it,
	we, you, they **withhold**	we, you, they **be withheld**
Past	if I, he, she, it,	if I, he, she, it,
	we, you, they **withheld**	we, you, they **were withheld**
Fut.	if I, he, she, it,	if I, he, she, it,
	we, you, they **should withhold**	we, you, they **should be withheld**

W
X
Y
Z

Transitive and intransitive.

I withheld the document until I consulted my attorney.
Any evidence withheld cannot be submitted later.

| withstand
(active voice) | PRINCIPAL PARTS: withstands,
withstanding, withstood, withstood | be withstood
(passive voice) |

INDICATIVE MOOD

Pres.	I, we, you, they **withstand**	I **am withstood** we, you, they **are withstood**
	he, she, it **withstands**	he, she, it **is withstood**
Pres. *Prog.*	I **am withstanding** we, you, they **are withstanding** he, she, it **is withstanding**	I **am being withstood** we, you, they **are being withstood** he, she, it **is being withstood**
Pres. *Int.*	I, we, you, they **do withstand** he, she, it **does withstand**	I, we, you, they **do get withstood** he, she, it **does get withstood**
Fut.	I, he, she, it, we, you, they **will withstand**	I, he, she, it, we, you, they **will be withstood**
Past	I, he, she, it, we, you, they **withstood**	I, he, she, it **was withstood** we, you, they **were withstood**
Past *Prog.*	I, he, she, it **was withstanding** we, you, they **were withstanding**	I, he, she, it **was being withstood** we, you, they **were being withstood**
Past *Int.*	I, he, she, it, we, you, they **did withstand**	I, he, she, it, we, you, they **did get withstood**
Pres. *Perf.*	I, we, you, they **have withstood** he, she, it **has withstood**	I, we, you, they **have been withstood** he, she, it **has been withstood**
Past *Perf.*	I, he, she, it, we, you, they **had withstood**	I, he, she, it, we, you, they **had been withstood**
Fut. *Perf.*	I, he, she, it, we, you, they **will have withstood**	I, he, she, it, we, you, they **will have been withstood**

IMPERATIVE MOOD

withstand	**be withstood**

SUBJUNCTIVE MOOD

Pres.	if I, he, she, it, we, you, they **withstand**	if I, he, she, it, we, you, they **be withstood**
Past	if I, he, she, it, we, you, they **withstood**	if I, he, she, it, we, you, they **were withstood**
Fut.	if I, he, she, it, we, you, they **should withstand**	if I, he, she, it, we, you, they **should be withstood**

Transitive and intransitive.

He withstood the criticism without flinching.
Worse abuse has been withstood by the inhabitants of that country.

PRINCIPAL PARTS: wonders,
wondering, wondered, wondered

be wondered
(passive voice)

INDICATIVE MOOD

Pres.	I, we, you, they **wonder**	I **am wondered**
		we, you, they **are wondered**
	he, she, it **wonders**	he, she, it **is wondered**
Pres.	I **am wondering**	I **am being wondered**
Prog.	we, you, they **are wondering**	we, you, they **are being wondered**
	he, she, it **is wondering**	he, she, it **is being wondered**
Pres.	I, we, you, they **do wonder**	I, we, you, they **do get wondered**
Int.	he, she, it **does wonder**	he, she, it **does get wondered**
Fut.	I, he, she, it,	I, he, she, it,
	we, you, they **will wonder**	we, you, they **will be wondered**
Past	I, he, she, it,	I, he, she, it **was wondered**
	we, you, they **wondered**	we, you, they **were wondered**
Past	I, he, she, it **was wondering**	I, he, she, it **was being wondered**
Prog.	we, you, they **were wondering**	we, you, they **were being wondered**
Past	I, he, she, it,	I, he, she, it,
Int.	we, you, they **did wonder**	we, you, they **did get wondered**
Pres.	I, we, you, they **have wondered**	I, we, you, they **have been wondered**
Perf.	he, she, it **has wondered**	he, she, it **has been wondered**
Past	I, he, she, it,	I, he, she, it,
Perf.	we, you, they **had wondered**	we, you, they **had been wondered**
Fut.	I, he, she, it, we, you, they	I, he, she, it, we, you, they
Perf.	**will have wondered**	**will have been wondered**

IMPERATIVE MOOD

wonder **be wondered**

SUBJUNCTIVE MOOD

Pres.	if I, he, she, it,	if I, he, she, it,
	we, you, they **wonder**	we, you, they **be wondered**
Past	if I, he, she, it,	if I, he, she, it,
	we, you, they **wondered**	we, you, they **were wondered**
Fut.	if I, he, she, it,	if I, he, she, it,
	we, you, they **should wonder**	we, you, they **should be wondered**

W
X
Y
Z

Intransitive and transitive.

We wondered what had happened to her.
His invention was wondered at by dozens of scientists.

work (active voice)	**PRINCIPAL PARTS: works, working,** **worked/wrought, worked/wrought**	**be worked/wrought** (passive voice)

INDICATIVE MOOD

Pres.	I, we, you, they **work**	I **am worked** we, you, they **are worked**
	he, she, it **works**	he, she, it **is worked**
Pres. *Prog.*	I **am working** we, you, they **are working** he, she, it **is working**	I **am being worked** we, you, they **are being worked** he, she, it **is being worked**
Pres. *Int.*	I, we, you, they **do work** he, she, it **does work**	I, we, you, they **do get worked** he, she, it **does get worked**
Fut.	I, he, she, it, we, you, they **will work**	I, he, she, it, we, you, they **will be worked**
Past	I, he, she, it, we, you, they **worked**	I, he, she, it **was worked** we, you, they **were worked**
Past *Prog.*	I, he, she, it **was working** we, you, they **were working**	I, he, she, it **was being worked** we, you, they **were being worked**
Past *Int.*	I, he, she, it, we, you, they **did work**	I, he, she, it, we, you, they **did get worked**
Pres. *Perf.*	I, we, you, they **have worked** he, she, it **has worked**	I, we, you, they **have been worked** he, she, it **has been worked**
Past *Perf.*	I, he, she, it, we, you, they **had worked**	I, he, she, it, we, you, they **had been worked**
Fut. *Perf.*	I, he, she, it, we, you, they **will have worked**	I, he, she, it, we, you, they **will have been worked**

IMPERATIVE MOOD

work	**be worked**

SUBJUNCTIVE MOOD

Pres.	if I, he, she, it, we, you, they **work**	if I, he, she, it, we, you, they **be worked**
Past	if I, he, she, it, we, you, they **worked**	if I, he, she, it, we, you, they **were worked**
Fut.	if I, he, she, it, we, you, they **should work**	if I, he, she, it, we, you, they **should be worked**

Intransitive and transitive. The past tense and past participle can be WORKED or WROUGHT.

She worked the night shift.
That old painting has been worked on by several restorers.
"What Blogs have Wrought?" is a strange-sounding title.

AN ESSENTIAL 55 VERB

AN ESSENTIAL 55 VERB

work

Examples

I work on a farm.

She works for fun.

He worked in China for five years.

The watch worked fine until yesterday.

They worked on a project together.

That approach worked once.

This pen doesn't work.

Are you working this weekend?

Work hard.

Are they working on my car yet?

Words and expressions related to this verb

I've been working on the railroad.

We can work it out.

He was worked over.

I am working off my debt.

That works for me.

Work on it.

She is working at home this week.

Is it working?

How does it work?

Whistle while you work.

She works out every evening.

W
X
Y
Z

worry
(active voice)

PRINCIPAL PARTS: **worries, worrying, worried, worried**

be worried
(passive voice)

INDICATIVE MOOD

Pres.	I, we, you, they **worry**	I **am worried**
		we, you, they **are worried**
	he, she, it **worries**	he, she, it **is worried**
Pres.	I **am worrying**	I **am being worried**
Prog.	we, you, they **are worrying**	we, you, they **are being worried**
	he, she, it **is worrying**	he, she, it **is being worried**
Pres.	I, we, you, they **do worry**	I, we, you, they **do get worried**
Int.	he, she, it **does worry**	he, she, it **does get worried**
Fut.	I, he, she, it,	I, he, she, it,
	we, you, they **will worry**	we, you, they **will be worried**
Past	I, he, she, it,	I, he, she, it **was worried**
	we, you, they **worried**	we, you, they **were worried**
Past	I, he, she, it **was worrying**	I, he, she, it **was being worried**
Prog.	we, you, they **were worrying**	we, you, they **were being worried**
Past	I, he, she, it,	I, he, she, it,
Int.	we, you, they **did worry**	we, you, they **did get worried**
Pres.	I, we, you, they **have worried**	I, we, you, they **have been worried**
Perf.	he, she, it **has worried**	he, she, it **has been worried**
Past	I, he, she, it,	I, he, she, it,
Perf.	we, you, they **had worried**	we, you, they **had been worried**
Fut.	I, he, she, it, we, you, they	I, he, she, it, we, you, they
Perf.	**will have worried**	**will have been worried**

IMPERATIVE MOOD

worry	**be worried**

SUBJUNCTIVE MOOD

Pres.	if I, he, she, it,	if I, he, she, it,
	we, you, they **worry**	we, you, they **be worried**
Past	if I, he, she, it,	if I, he, she, it,
	we, you, they **worried**	we, you, they **were worried**
Fut.	if I, he, she, it,	if I, he, she, it,
	we, you, they **should worry**	we, you, they **should be worried**

Intransitive and transitive.

He worries too much.
She worried me half to death.
We were all worried for her safety.

worship
(active voice)

PRINCIPAL PARTS: worships, worshiping/ worshipping, worshiped/worshipped, worshiped/worshipped

be worshiped/ worshipped
(passive voice)

INDICATIVE MOOD

Pres.	I, we, you, they **worship**	I **am worshiped**
		we, you, they **are worshiped**
	he, she, it **worships**	he, she, it **is worshiped**
Pres.	I **am worshiping**	I **am being worshiped**
Prog.	we, you, they **are worshiping**	we, you, they **are being worshiped**
	he, she, it **is worshiping**	he, she, it **is being worshiped**
Pres.	I, we, you, they **do worship**	I, we, you, they **do get worshiped**
Int.	he, she, it **does worship**	he, she, it **does get worshiped**
Fut.	I, he, she, it,	I, he, she, it,
	we, you, they **will worship**	we, you, they **will be worshiped**
Past	I, he, she, it,	I, he, she, it **was worshiped**
	we, you, they **worshiped**	we, you, they **were worshiped**
Past	I, he, she, it **was worshiping**	I, he, she, it **was being worshiped**
Prog.	we, you, they **were worshiping**	we, you, they **were being worshiped**
Past	I, he, she, it,	I, he, she, it,
Int.	we, you, they **did worship**	we, you, they **did get worshiped**
Pres.	I, we, you, they **have worshiped**	I, we, you, they **have been worshiped**
Perf.	he, she, it **has worshiped**	he, she, it **has been worshiped**
Past	I, he, she, it,	I, he, she, it,
Perf.	we, you, they **had worshiped**	we, you, they **had been worshiped**
Fut.	I, he, she, it, we, you, they	I, he, she, it, we, you, they
Perf.	**will have worshiped**	**will have been worshiped**

IMPERATIVE MOOD

worship **be worshiped**

SUBJUNCTIVE MOOD

Pres.	if I, he, she, it,	if I, he, she, it,
	we, you, they **worship**	we, you, they **be worshiped**
Past	if I, he, she, it,	if I, he, she, it,
	we, you, they **worshiped**	we, you, they **were worshiped**
Fut.	if I, he, she, it,	if I, he, she, it,
	we, you, they **should worship**	we, you, they **should be worshiped**

W
X
Y
Z

Transitive and intransitive. The *Oxford Dictionary* prefers the spelling with the double "pp" for the past tense and participles: WORSHIPPING, WORSHIPPED.

Each is worshiping in his or her own way.
They worshiped the sun in days gone by.
Natural phenomena were worshiped by primitive peoples.

wound
(active voice)

be wounded
(passive voice)

INDICATIVE MOOD

Pres.	I, we, you, they **wound**	I **am wounded**
		we, you, they **are wounded**
	he, she, it **wounds**	he, she, it **is wounded**
Pres.	I **am wounding**	I **am being wounded**
Prog.	we, you, they **are wounding**	we, you, they **are being wounded**
	he, she, it **is wounding**	he, she, it **is being wounded**
Pres.	I, we, you, they **do wound**	I, we, you, they **do get wounded**
Int.	he, she, it **does wound**	he, she, it **does get wounded**
Fut.	I, he, she, it,	I, he, she, it,
	we, you, they **will wound**	we, you, they **will be wounded**
Past	I, he, she, it,	I, he, she, it **was wounded**
	we, you, they **wounded**	we, you, they **were wounded**
Past	I, he, she, it **was wounding**	I, he, she, it **was being wounded**
Prog.	we, you, they **were wounding**	we, you, they **were being wounded**
Past	I, he, she, it,	I, he, she, it,
Int.	we, you, they **did wound**	we, you, they **did get wounded**
Pres.	I, we, you, they **have wounded**	I, we, you, they **have been wounded**
Perf.	he, she, it **has wounded**	he, she, it **has been wounded**
Past	I, he, she, it,	I, he, she, it,
Perf.	we, you, they **had wounded**	we, you, they **had been wounded**
Fut.	I, he, she, it, we, you, they	I, he, she, it, we, you, they
Perf.	**will have wounded**	**will have been wounded**

IMPERATIVE MOOD

wound　　　　　　**be wounded**

SUBJUNCTIVE MOOD

Pres.	if I, he, she, it,	if I, he, she, it,
	we, you, they **wound**	we, you, they **be wounded**
Past	if I, he, she, it,	if I, he, she, it,
	we, you, they **wounded**	we, you, they **were wounded**
Fut.	if I, he, she, it,	if I, he, she, it,
	we, you, they **should wound**	we, you, they **should be wounded**

Transitive and intransitive.

He wounded his enemy in the shoulder.
He was not wounded in the engagement.

546

wrap
(active voice)

be wrapped/wrapt
(passive voice)

INDICATIVE MOOD

Pres.	I, we, you, they **wrap**	I am **wrapped**
		we, you, they **are wrapped**
	he, she, it **wraps**	he, she, it **is wrapped**
Pres.	I **am wrapping**	I **am being wrapped**
Prog.	we, you, they **are wrapping**	we, you, they **are being wrapped**
	he, she, it **is wrapping**	he, she, it **is being wrapped**
Pres.	I, we, you, they **do wrap**	I, we, you, they **do get wrapped**
Int.	he, she, it **does wrap**	he, she, it **does get wrapped**
Fut.	I, he, she, it,	I, he, she, it,
	we, you, they **will wrap**	we, you, they **will be wrapped**
Past	I, he, she, it,	I, he, she, it **was wrapped**
	we, you, they **wrapped**	we, you, they **were wrapped**
Past	I, he, she, it **was wrapping**	I, he, she, it **was being wrapped**
Prog.	we, you, they **were wrapping**	we, you, they **were being wrapped**
Past	I, he, she, it,	I, he, she, it,
Int.	we, you, they **did wrap**	we, you, they **did get wrapped**
Pres.	I, we, you, they **have wrapped**	I, we, you, they **have been wrapped**
Perf.	he, she, it **has wrapped**	he, she, it **has been wrapped**
Past	I, he, she, it,	I, he, she, it,
Perf.	we, you, they **had wrapped**	we, you, they **had been wrapped**
Fut.	I, he, she, it, we, you, they	I, he, she, it, we, you, they
Perf.	**will have wrapped**	**will have been wrapped**

IMPERATIVE MOOD

wrap   **be wrapped**

SUBJUNCTIVE MOOD

Pres.	if I, he, she, it,	if I, he, she, it,
	we, you, they **wrap**	we, you, they **be wrapped**
Past	if I, he, she, it,	if I, he, she, it,
	we, you, they **wrapped**	we, you, they **were wrapped**
Fut.	if I, he, she, it,	if I, he, she, it,
	we, you, they **should wrap**	we, you, they **should be wrapped**

W
X
Y
Z

Transitive and intransitive.

We are wrapping our gifts ourselves.
She wrapped the fish in newspaper.
The package was wrapped for shipment.

wreck
(active voice)

be wrecked
(passive voice)

INDICATIVE MOOD

Pres.	I, we, you, they **wreck**	I **am wrecked**
		we, you, they **are wrecked**
	he, she, it **wrecks**	he, she, it **is wrecked**
Pres.	I **am wrecking**	I **am being wrecked**
Prog.	we, you, they **are wrecking**	we, you, they **are being wrecked**
	he, she, it **is wrecking**	he, she, it **is being wrecked**
Pres.	I, we, you, they **do wreck**	I, we, you, they **do get wrecked**
Int.	he, she, it **does wreck**	he, she, it **does get wrecked**
Fut.	I, he, she, it,	I, he, she, it,
	we, you, they **will wreck**	we, you, they **will be wrecked**
Past	I, he, she, it,	I, he, she, it **was wrecked**
	we, you, they **wrecked**	we, you, they **were wrecked**
Past	I, he, she, it **was wrecking**	I, he, she, it **was being wrecked**
Prog.	we, you, they **were wrecking**	we, you, they **were being wrecked**
Past	I, he, she, it,	I, he, she, it,
Int.	we, you, they **did wreck**	we, you, they **did get wrecked**
Pres.	I, we, you, they **have wrecked**	I, we, you, they **have been wrecked**
Perf.	he, she, it **has wrecked**	he, she, it **has been wrecked**
Past	I, he, she, it,	I, he, she, it,
Perf.	we, you, they **had wrecked**	we, you, they **had been wrecked**
Fut.	I, he, she, it, we, you, they	I, he, she, it, we, you, they
Perf.	**will have wrecked**	**will have been wrecked**

IMPERATIVE MOOD

wreck

be wrecked

SUBJUNCTIVE MOOD

Pres.	if I, he, she, it,	if I, he, she, it,
	we, you, they **wreck**	we, you, they **be wrecked**
Past	if I, he, she, it,	if I, he, she, it,
	we, you, they **wrecked**	we, you, they **were wrecked**
Fut.	if I, he, she, it,	if I, he, she, it,
	we, you, they **should wreck**	we, you, they **should be wrecked**

Transitive and intransitive.

I wrecked my car last weekend.
The ship was wrecked at sea.

wring
(active voice)

PRINCIPAL PARTS: **wrings, wringing, wrung, wrung**

be wrung
(passive voice)

INDICATIVE MOOD

Pres.	I, we, you, they **wring**	I **am wrung**
		we, you, they **are wrung**
	he, she, it **wrings**	he, she, it **is wrung**
Pres.	I **am wringing**	I **am being wrung**
Prog.	we, you, they **are wringing**	we, you, they **are being wrung**
	he, she, it **is wringing**	he, she, it **is being wrung**
Pres.	I, we, you, they **do wring**	I, we, you, they **do get wrung**
Int.	he, she, it **does wring**	he, she, it **does get wrung**
Fut.	I, he, she, it,	I, he, she, it,
	we, you, they **will wring**	we, you, they **will be wrung**
Past	I, he, she, it,	I, he, she, it **was wrung**
	we, you, they **wrung**	we, you, they **were wrung**
Past	I, he, she, it **was wringing**	I, he, she, it **was being wrung**
Prog.	we, you, they **were wringing**	we, you, they **were being wrung**
Past	I, he, she, it,	I, he, she, it,
Int.	we, you, they **did wring**	we, you, they **did get wrung**
Pres.	I, we, you, they **have wrung**	I, we, you, they **have been wrung**
Perf.	he, she, it **has wrung**	he, she, it **has been wrung**
Past	I, he, she, it,	I, he, she, it,
Perf.	we, you, they **had wrung**	we, you, they **had been wrung**
Fut.	I, he, she, it, we, you, they	I, he, she, it, we, you, they
Perf.	**will have wrung**	**will have been wrung**

IMPERATIVE MOOD

wring　　　　　　　　　　**be wrung**

SUBJUNCTIVE MOOD

Pres.	if I, he, she, it,	if I, he, she, it,
	we, you, they **wring**	we, you, they **be wrung**
Past	if I, he, she, it,	if I, he, she, it,
	we, you, they **wrung**	we, you, they **were wrung**
Fut.	if I, he, she, it,	if I, he, she, it,
	we, you, they **should wring**	we, you, they **should be wrung**

W
X
Y
Z

Transitive and intransitive.

My mother wrung her laundry by hand.
The bathing suits were wrung out and hung on the line.

write (active voice)	PRINCIPAL PARTS: **writes, writing,** **wrote, written**	**be written** (passive voice)

INDICATIVE MOOD

Pres.	I, we, you, they **write**	I **am written** we, you, they **are written**
	he, she, it **writes**	he, she, it **is written**
Pres. *Prog.*	I **am writing** we, you, they **are writing** he, she, it **is writing**	I **am being written** we, you, they **are being written** he, she, it **is being written**
Pres. *Int.*	I, we, you, they **do write** he, she, it **does write**	I, we, you, they **do get written** he, she, it **does get written**
Fut.	I, he, she, it, we, you, they **will write**	I, he, she, it, we, you, they **will be written**
Past	I, he, she, it, we, you, they **wrote**	I, he, she, it **was written** we, you, they **were written**
Past *Prog.*	I, he, she, it **was writing** we, you, they **were writing**	I, he, she, it **was being written** we, you, they **were being written**
Past *Int.*	I, he, she, it, we, you, they **did write**	I, he, she, it, we, you, they **did get written**
Pres. *Perf.*	I, we, you, they **have written** he, she, it **has written**	I, we, you, they **have been written** he, she, it **has been written**
Past *Perf.*	I, he, she, it, we, you, they **had written**	I, he, she, it, we, you, they **had been written**
Fut. *Perf.*	I, he, she, it, we, you, they **will have written**	I, he, she, it, we, you, they **will have been written**

IMPERATIVE MOOD

write	**be written**

SUBJUNCTIVE MOOD

Pres.	if I, he, she, it, we, you, they **write**	if I, he, she, it, we, you, they **be written**
Past	if I, he, she, it, we, you, they **wrote**	if I, he, she, it, we, you, they **were written**
Fut.	if I, he, she, it, we, you, they **should write**	if I, he, she, it, we, you, they **should be written**

Transitive and intransitive.

She is writing to her mother.
He wrote me just last spring.
The words were written in a time of great stress.

550

AN ESSENTIAL
55 VERB

write

Examples

He writes so well!

Who wrote that letter?

I write a little every day.

You should write and complain about the poor service.

He had not written a letter in over a year.

The poem was written in a single evening.

Please write me a note when you are settled in.

Don't forget to write.

Have you written your will?

Who will write the opening remarks?

Words and expressions related to this verb

Write it out in full.

I'm going to sit right down and write myself a letter.

You can write off those expenses against your taxes.

They just wrote him off as a candidate.

The police officer wrote up his report.

I've written some poetry I don't understand myself.

Either write something worth reading or do something worth writing.

The regulations are not written in stone.

Who wrote that book?

He wrote the book on procrastination.

W
X
Y
Z

x-ray
(active voice)

PRINCIPAL PARTS: **x-rays, x-raying,
x-rayed, x-rayed**

be x-rayed
(passive voice)

INDICATIVE MOOD

Pres.	I, we, you, they **x-ray**	I **am x-rayed**
		we, you, they **are x-rayed**
	he, she, it **x-rays**	he, she, it **is x-rayed**
Pres.	I **am x-raying**	I **am being x-rayed**
Prog.	we, you, they **are x-raying**	we, you, they **are being x-rayed**
	he, she, it **is x-raying**	he, she, it **is being x-rayed**
Pres.	I, we, you, they **do x-ray**	I, we, you, they **do get x-rayed**
Int.	he, she, it **does x-ray**	he, she, it **does get x-rayed**
Fut.	I, he, she, it,	I, he, she, it,
	we, you, they **will x-ray**	we, you, they **will be x-rayed**
Past	I, he, she, it,	I, he, she, it **was x-rayed**
	we, you, they **x-rayed**	we, you, they **were x-rayed**
Past	I, he, she, it **was x-raying**	I, he, she, it **was being x-rayed**
Prog.	we, you, they **were x-raying**	we, you, they **were being x-rayed**
Past	I, he, she, it,	I, he, she, it,
Int.	we, you, they **did x-ray**	we, you, they **did get x-rayed**
Pres.	I, we, you, they **have x-rayed**	I, we, you, they **have been x-rayed**
Perf.	he, she, it **has x-rayed**	he, she, it **has been x-rayed**
Past	I, he, she, it,	I, he, she, it,
Perf.	we, you, they **had x-rayed**	we, you, they **had been x-rayed**
Fut.	I, he, she, it, we, you, they	I, he, she, it, we, you, they
Perf.	**will have x-rayed**	**will have been x-rayed**

IMPERATIVE MOOD

x-ray **be x-rayed**

SUBJUNCTIVE MOOD

Pres.	if I, he, she, it,	if I, he, she, it,
	we, you, they **x-ray**	we, you, they **be x-rayed**
Past	if I, he, she, it,	if I, he, she, it,
	we, you, they **x-rayed**	we, you, they **were x-rayed**
Fut.	if I, he, she, it,	if I, he, she, it,
	we, you, they **should x-ray**	we, you, they **should be x-rayed**

They x-rayed all baggage before clearing it.
I have been x-rayed at the dentist and at the hospital.

xerox
(active voice)

be xeroxed
(passive voice)

INDICATIVE MOOD

Pres.	I, we, you, they **xerox**	I **am xeroxed**
		we, you, they **are xeroxed**
	he, she, it **xeroxes**	he, she, it **is xeroxed**
Pres.	I **am xeroxing**	I **am being xeroxed**
Prog.	we, you, they **are xeroxing**	we, you, they **are being xeroxed**
	he, she, it **is xeroxing**	he, she, it **is being xeroxed**
Pres.	I, we, you, they **do xerox**	I, we, you, they **do get xeroxed**
Int.	he, she, it **does xerox**	he, she, it **does get xeroxed**
Fut.	I, he, she, it,	I, he, she, it,
	we, you, they **will xerox**	we, you, they **will be xeroxed**
Past	I, he, she, it,	I, he, she, it **was xeroxed**
	we, you, they **xeroxed**	we, you, they **were xeroxed**
Past	I, he, she, it **was xeroxing**	I, he, she, it **was being xeroxed**
Prog.	we, you, they **were xeroxing**	we, you, they **were being xeroxed**
Past	I, he, she, it,	I, he, she, it,
Int.	we, you, they **did xerox**	we, you, they **did get xeroxed**
Pres.	I, we, you, they **have xeroxed**	I, we, you, they **have been xeroxed**
Perf.	he, she, it **has xeroxed**	he, she, it **has been xeroxed**
Past	I, he, she, it,	I, he, she, it,
Perf.	we, you, they **had xeroxed**	we, you, they **had been xeroxed**
Fut.	I, he, she, it, we, you, they	I, he, she, it, we, you, they
Perf.	**will have xeroxed**	**will have been xeroxed**

IMPERATIVE MOOD

xerox   **be xeroxed**

SUBJUNCTIVE MOOD

Pres.	if I, he, she, it,	if I, he, she, it,
	we, you, they **xerox**	we, you, they **be xeroxed**
Past	if I, he, she, it,	if I, he, she, it,
	we, you, they **xeroxed**	we, you, they **were xeroxed**
Fut.	if I, he, she, it,	if I, he, she, it,
	we, you, they **should xerox**	we, you, they **should be xeroxed**

W
X
Y
Z

Transitive and intransitive.

He xeroxes hundreds of pages a week.
We xeroxed several copies for the board meeting.
Those copies were xeroxed in town.

yes
(active voice)

PRINCIPAL PARTS: **yeses, yessing,
yessed, yessed**

be yessed
(passive voice)

INDICATIVE MOOD

Pres.	I, we, you, they **yes**	I **am yessed**
		we, you, they **are yessed**
	he, she, it **yeses**	he, she, it **is yessed**
Pres.	I **am yessing**	I **am being yessed**
Prog.	we, you, they **are yessing**	we, you, they **are being yessed**
	he, she, it **is yessing**	he, she, it **is being yessed**
Pres.	I, we, you, they **do yes**	I, we, you, they **do get yessed**
Int.	he, she, it **does yes**	he, she, it **does get yessed**
Fut.	I, he, she, it,	I, he, she, it,
	we, you, they **will yes**	we, you, they **will be yessed**
Past	I, he, she, it,	I, he, she, it **was yessed**
	we, you, they **yessed**	we, you, they **were yessed**
Past	I, he, she, it **was yessing**	I, he, she, it **was being yessed**
Prog.	we, you, they **were yessing**	we, you, they **were being yessed**
Past	I, he, she, it,	I, he, she, it,
Int.	we, you, they **did yes**	we, you, they **did get yessed**
Pres.	I, we, you, they **have yessed**	I, we, you, they **have been yessed**
Perf.	he, she, it **has yessed**	he, she, it **has been yessed**
Past	I, he, she, it,	I, he, she, it,
Perf.	we, you, they **had yessed**	we, you, they **had been yessed**
Fut.	I, he, she, it, we, you, they	I, he, she, it, we, you, they
Perf.	**will have yessed**	**will have been yessed**

IMPERATIVE MOOD

yes   **be yessed**

SUBJUNCTIVE MOOD

Pres.	if I, he, she, it,	if I, he, she, it,
	we, you, they **yes**	we, you, they **be yessed**
Past	if I, he, she, it,	if I, he, she, it,
	we, you, they **yessed**	we, you, they **were yessed**
Fut.	if I, he, she, it,	if I, he, she, it,
	we, you, they **should yes**	we, you, they **should be yessed**

They yessed the boss until he left.
I have been yessed by my students until I agreed to their requests.

zero
(active voice)

be zeroed
(passive voice)

INDICATIVE MOOD

Pres.	I, we, you, they **zero**	I **am zeroed**
		we, you, they **are zeroed**
	he, she, it **zeroes**	he, she, it **is zeroed**
Pres.	I **am zeroing**	I **am being zeroed**
Prog.	we, you, they **are zeroing**	we, you, they **are being zeroed**
	he, she, it **is zeroing**	he, she, it **is being zeroed**
Pres.	I, we, you, they **do zero**	I, we, you, they **do get zeroed**
Int.	he, she, it **does zero**	he, she, it **does get zeroed**
Fut.	I, he, she, it,	I, he, she, it,
	we, you, they **will zero**	we, you, they **will be zeroed**
Past	I, he, she, it,	I, he, she, it **was zeroed**
	we, you, they **zeroed**	we, you, they **were zeroed**
Past	I, he, she, it **was zeroing**	I, he, she, it **was being zeroed**
Prog.	we, you, they **were zeroing**	we, you, they **were being zeroed**
Past	I, he, she, it,	I, he, she, it,
Int.	we, you, they **did zero**	we, you, they **did get zeroed**
Pres.	I, we, you, they **have zeroed**	I, we, you, they **have been zeroed**
Perf.	he, she, it **has zeroed**	he, she, it **has been zeroed**
Past	I, he, she, it,	I, he, she, it,
Perf.	we, you, they **had zeroed**	we, you, they **had been zeroed**
Fut.	I, he, she, it, we, you, they	I, he, she, it, we, you, they
Perf.	**will have zeroed**	**will have been zeroed**

IMPERATIVE MOOD

zero　　　　　　　　　　　　　　**be zeroed**

SUBJUNCTIVE MOOD

Pres.	if I, he, she, it,	if I, he, she, it,
	we, you, they **zero**	we, you, they **be zeroed**
Past	if I, he, she, it,	if I, he, she, it,
	we, you, they **zeroed**	we, you, they **were zeroed**
Fut.	if I, he, she, it,	if I, he, she, it,
	we, you, they **should zero**	we, you, they **should be zeroed**

W
X
Y
Z

A great marksman always zeroes her rifle at the start of a match.
We are zeroing in on the truth.
The pilots zeroed in on the runway.
The target was zeroed in on by laser.

zip (active voice)	PRINCIPAL PARTS: zips, zipping, zipped, zipped	be zippd (passive voice)

INDICATIVE MOOD

Pres.	I, we, you, they **zip**	**I am zipped** we, you, they **are zipped**
	he, she, it **zips**	he, she, it **is zipped**
Pres. *Prog.*	**I am zipping** we, you, they **are zipping** he, she, it **is zipping**	**I am being zipped** we, you, they **are being zipped** he, she, it **is being zipped**
Pres. *Int.*	I, we, you, they **do zip** he, she, it **does zip**	I, we, you, they **do get zipped** he, she, it **does get zipped**
Fut.	I, he, she, it, we, you, they **will zip**	I, he, she, it, we, you, they **will be zipped**
Past	I, he, she, it, we, you, they **zipped**	I, he, she, it **was zipped** we, you, they **were zipped**
Past *Prog.*	I, he, she, it **was zipping** we, you, they **were zipping**	I, he, she, it **was being zipped** we, you, they **were being zipped**
Past *Int.*	I, he, she, it, we, you, they **did zip**	I, he, she, it, we, you, they **did get zipped**
Pres. *Perf.*	I, we, you, they **have zipped** he, she, it **has zipped**	I, we, you, they **have been zipped** he, she, it **has been zipped**
Past *Perf.*	I, he, she, it, we, you, they **had zipped**	I, he, she, it, we, you, they **had been zipped**
Fut. *Perf.*	I, he, she, it, we, you, they **will have zipped**	I, he, she, it, we, you, they **will have been zipped**

IMPERATIVE MOOD

zip	**be zipped**

SUBJUNCTIVE MOOD

Pres.	if I, he, she, it, we, you, they **zip**	if I, he, she, it, we, you, they **be zipped**
Past	if I, he, she, it, we, you, they **zipped**	if I, he, she, it, we, you, they **were zipped**
Fut.	if I, he, she, it, we, you, they **should zip**	if I, he, she, it, we, you, they **should be zipped**

Transitive and intransitive.

Dad is zipping up her jacket.
He zipped the files before sending them.
His jacket was zipped by the kind teacher.

Appendixes

Phrasal Verbs

Many English verbs occur with one or more prepositions or adverbs where the meaning is not readily apparent from the different elements. Here is a list of many of these combinations for the verbs conjugated in *501 English Verbs*. I have omitted most of the forms considered slang. In assembling the list I have relied primarily on the *American Heritage Dictionary of the English Language*.

Abide by: comply with, conform to
> *You should abide by your parents' wishes.*

Act out: dramatize
> *John and Sara acted out the dialogue.*

Act up: misbehave
> *Joe continues to act up during class.*

Act up: begin to bother
> *My old war injury started to act up again.*

Add up: be logical, make sense
> *Their main points in the discussion simply did not add up.*

Add up to be: amount to
> *Their arguments all added up to be a reasonable conclusion.*

Allow for: make provision for
> *We allowed for a slight overage in our calculations.*

Ask after: inquire about someone
> *He asked after you last evening.*

Ask for it (trouble): continue an action in spite of likely punishment
> *The kids were finally punished by their mother, who simply said: "They asked for it."*

Ask out: invite (as on a date)
> *I'm so happy that George asked me out to the prom.*

Be about: occupy self with
> *You should be about your business.*

Bear down: apply maximum effort
> *It's time for us to bear down and get this job completed.*

Bear down on: harm
> *The financial pressures are already beginning to bear down on him.*

Bear out: confirm
> *The results of the experiment bore out our worst fears.*

Bear up: withstand the pressure
> *Given all of the commotion, it is a wonder how well he is bearing up.*

Bear with: endure, persevere
> *Bear with me for just a minute as I try to explain.*

Beat off: repel
> *They ultimately beat off their attackers.*

Beat it: leave quickly
> *He beat it when the police arrived.*

Beat out: arrive first

>*He beat out the other candidate by just two votes.*

Become of: happen to

>*What becomes of a broken heart?*

Beg off: ask to be excused

>*Given the constraints on his time, he begged off the assignment.*

Bid up: force a price higher

>*They bid up the price of the painting to over a million dollars.*

Bind over: to hold someone on bail or bond

>*The prisoner was bound over for trial.*

Blow away: overwhelm

>*His performance blew me away.*

Blow off: release

>*Let him blow off some steam.*

Blow out: extinguish

>*Please don't forget to blow out the candles.*

Blow over: pass by (like a storm)

>*We're hoping the controversy will blow over with time.*

Blow up: enlarge

>*Can you blow up these photos?*

Blow up: explode

>*If you're not careful, you'll blow up the whole neighborhood with that explosive charge.*

Boot up: turn on a computer.

>*After you boot up, open the program.*

Break down: cause to collapse

>*The elevator is always breaking down.*

Break down: become distressed

>*When confronted with the evidence the suspect broke down and cried.*

Break even: gain back the original investment

>*After many years of hard work they finally broke even.*

Break in: train

>*They were trying to break in the new horse.*

Break in: adapt for a purpose

>*He used the oil to break in his new baseball glove.*

Break in: enter illegally

>*The burglars broke in last evening.*

Break in/into: interrupt

>*The secretary broke into our conversation with an important message.*

Break into: enter a profession

>*He broke into the major leagues in 1947.*

Break off: cease

>*They broke off negotiations after the last round of talks.*

Break out: skin eruption
>*He broke out in a rash after eating just a few peanuts.*

Break out: escape
>*Last evening two criminals broke out of a maximum security prison.*

Break out: begin
>*Fighting broke out in the streets of Jerusalem.*

Break up: separate
>*The couple broke up after the argument on their last date.*

Bring around: convince one to adopt an opinion
>*The shop foreman finally brought the workers around to management's point of view.*

Bring around: restore to consciousness
>*They used smelling salts to bring her around.*

Bring back: recall to mind
>*Those songs bring back such fond memories.*

Bring down: cause to fall
>*The Russian Revolution brought down the Romanov dynasty.*

Bring forth: propose
>*They brought forth a series of new proposals at our meeting this morning.*

Bring forth: give birth
>*And she brought forth a son.*

Bring in: render a verdict
>*The jury brought in a verdict of "not guilty."*

Bring off: accomplish
>*I don't see how we can bring that off without help.*

Bring on: cause to appear
>*You can bring on the dancers.*

Bring out: reveal or expose
>*The lecture brought out the best and worst in him.*

Bring to: restore to consciousness
>*The doctor brought him to.*

Bring up: raise
>*I didn't want to bring this up, but since you mentioned it, I feel I must.*

Build in: include as an integral part
>*The car stereo is built in.*

Build on: use as a basis
>*These proposals finally give us something to build on.*

Build up: increase gradually
>*The errors continued to build up until they harmed his performance.*

Burn out: wear out from exhaustion
>*Toward the end of the race he felt like he was burning out.*

Burn up: make very angry
>*Your attitude really burns me up.*

Burst out: begin suddenly
>*They burst out laughing at the speaker.*

Buy into: buy a stock of
I bought into IBM when it was just beginning.
Buy into: give credence to
He never bought into the company's philosophy.
Buy off: bribe
They bought off the politician with a large contribution to her campaign.
Buy out: purchase all the shares
The larger company bought them out.
Buy up: purchase all that is available
The speculator keeps buying up the plots in that old neighborhood.

Call back: ask to return
The workers were called back to the job as the strike vote was being counted.
Call for: arrive to meet
The young gentlemen called for his new found friend.
Call for: requires
That calls for a celebration.
Call forth: evoke
Their attack called forth an immediate response.
Call in: summon
A heart specialist was called in to review the diagnosis.
Call in: use the telephone to communicate
Has the salesman called in yet?
Call off: cancel
The ball game was called off on account of rain.
Call up: summon to military duty
The reserves were called up during the Gulf War.
Call upon: require
I call upon you to take up your arms in the defense of liberty.
Call upon: visit
When can I call upon you to discuss this matter?

Care for: provide for
I cared for the children while their Mom was away.

Carry away: excite
She was carried away by the sound of his voice.
Carry off: cause the death of
The entire population of the village was carried off by a new strain of the virus.
Carry on: continue
The officer was pleased with the inspection and told his men to carry on with their duties.
Carry out: put into practice
They carried out his orders without hesitation.
Carry through: persevere to a goal or conclusion
He rarely carries through on his promises.

Cast about: search for
He kept casting about for the answers.
Cast around: search about for something
She was casting around for a friend.

Cast off: throw away
>She loves to cast off last year's fashions.

Cast off: launch a boat
>They cast off for the next destination.

Cast out: expel
>An exorcist casts out devils.

Catch on: become popular
>It didn't take long for colored hair to catch on with the younger generation.

Catch up: overtake from behind
>How do you ever expect me to catch up if you walk so fast?

Change off: alternate performing tasks
>We can change off in an hour or so if you get tired.

Close down: discontinue, go out of business
>The clothing store closed down after the Christmas season.

Close in: advance, surround
>The enemy used the darkness of night to close in on our positions.

Close up: block up or shut down
>They closed up the entrance to the cave.

Close out: dispose, terminate
>We must close out this particular product at the end of the month.

Come about: happen
>It just came about.

Come across: find, meet
>I was lucky to come across just the perfect gift.

Come along: go with someone else
>You may come along if you wish.

Come around (round): regain consciousness
>The boxer finally came around in the dressing room.

Come at: approach
>You can come at that problem from a number of angles.

Come back: regain past state
>He came back quickly after the knee operation.

Come by: acquire
>How did you come by this money?

Come down: lose position, money, standing
>He has certainly come down in the opinion polls.

Come in: arrive
>The new spring fashions have just come in.

Come into: acquire or inherit
>My brother recently came into a small fortune.

Come off: happen, occur
>The concert came off without any problems.

Come on: show an interest in
>He came on to her all evening at the party.

Come out: make known
>They finally came out with the official statement.

Come through: deliver on a promise
I am so happy he finally came through with his contribution.
Come to: regain consciousness
He came to an hour after the operation.
Come over: drop by for a visit
Why don't you come over this evening?
Come to pass: happen
And so it came to pass that they parted as friends.
Come up: appear
Everything is coming up on the screen as we expected.
Come upon: discover
I came upon the evidence quite by accident.

Cover up: conceal after the fact
They tried to cover up their wrongdoing.

Cry down: belittle someone
The speaker was cried down by the unruly audience.
Cry out: exclaim
The wounded soldier cried out in pain.

Cut back: reduce
We are cutting back production as of next Monday.
Cut down: kill
He was cut down by a stray bullet on the street last evening.
Cut down: reduce
You should cut down on the amount of fat in your diet.
Cut in: break into a line
It is rude to cut in, when we have been standing here over an hour.
Cut off: stop
I am afraid that I must cut off this discussion right now.
Cut off: separate
They were cut off from the exit by the progress of the fire.
Cut out: form or shape by cutting
Little children love to cut out paper dolls.
Cut out: exclude
Let's cut her out of the final decision.
Cut out: suited for
He is not cut out to be a doctor.
Cut short: interrupt
Our trip was cut short by my wife's accident.
Cut up: clown about
The little boy loves to cut up when the teacher turns his back.
Cut up: destroy completely
The division was cut up by the air attack.

Dial in: access by telephone or modem
He often dials in from home to check his e-mail.
Dial out: access a telephone line for a phone call
How can I dial out from this phone?

Die down: subside

>The controversy died down after a month.

Die off: decline dramatically

>The tribal members died off.

Die out: become extinct

>The tigers in India are dying out.

Dig in: hold on stubbornly

>Let's dig in and meet the challenge.

Dig in: begin to eat

>Let's dig in, guys. I'm so hungry I could eat a horse.

Do in: ruin or kill

>He was done in by his fellow inmates.

Do up: dress elaborately

>The little girl was all done up for her school play.

Do without: manage in spite of a lack of something

>The kids can't do without television.

Drag on: go on for a long time

>The hours seem to drag on endlessly.

Drag out: extend

>I can't understand why they are dragging this matter out so long.

Draw away: pull ahead

>We must continue drawing away from the other colleges.

Draw back: retreat

>Let's draw back and regroup.

Draw down: deplete resources

>We will have to draw down on our grain supplies.

Draw out: prolong

>Just how long can she draw out the committee meeting?

Draw up: compose

>Let's just draw up a contract.

Dream up: invent

>Who dreamed up that idea?

Drink in: listen closely

>He drank in her every word.

Drink to: raise a toast

>Let's drink to days gone by.

Drive at: hint, lead in a direction

>What are you driving at?

Drop behind: fall behind

>The little kids kept dropping behind their parents on the walk.

Drop by: stop in for a visit

>Don't forget to drop by when you are in town.

Drop off: go to sleep
I finally dropped off at midnight.
Drop out: withdraw from school
Continue your studies. Don't drop out of school.

Dwell on/upon: write, speak, or think at length
We have been dwelling on this topic for over a week.

Eat into: deplete
The number of returns began to eat into their profits.
Eat out: dine in a restaurant
Do you eat out often?
Eat up: enjoy enormously
She ate up the evening's entertainment.

End up: reach a place
I don't know how, but I ended up in Cleveland.

Enter into: take an active role in
He entered into politics late in life.
Enter on/upon: set out, begin
Today we enter on the new phase of our project.

Explain away: minimize
He kept trying to explain away the illegal contributions.

Face down: confront and overcome
He faced down his opponent in the first match.
Face off: start or resume play in hockey, lacrosse and other games
They faced off in their opponents' zone.
Face off: take sides against one another
The two warring factions had faced off at the first meeting.
Face up: deal with an issue
It's time for you to face up to your obligations.

Fall apart: break down
After his wife's death he completely fell apart.
Fall back: lag behind
The others fell back after the first mile of the hike.
Fall back on: rely on
What can I fall back on if this doesn't work?
Fall behind: fail to pay on time
When he lost his job, they fell behind in their mortgage payments.
Fall down: fail to meet expectations
Unfortunately the new boss fell down on the job.
Fall for: succumb to, fall in love
He fell for her at first glance.
Fall for: be deceived
He fell for the con artist's scam.

Fall in: take a place
>All of the principal investors fell in after the initial presentation.

Fall off: decrease
>The interest in foreign languages has been gradually falling off.

Fall on: attack
>Those waiting in ambush fell on the unsuspecting soldiers.

Fall out: leave military formation
>The sergeant roared, "Company, fall out!"

Fall through: fail
>The deal fell through at the last moment.

Fall to: approach energetically
>The new maid fell to the cleaning.

Fall short: fail to obtain
>His efforts to earn a million dollars fell short.

Feel like: wish or want to
>I feel like taking a walk.

Feel out: try to find out something indirectly
>Could you feel out the opposition before we meet next week?

Feel up to: be prepared for
>I don't really feel up to a five mile run.

Fight back: suppress one's feeling
>He fought back tears at the announcement.

Fight off: repel an attack
>They fought off the attackers until their ammunition ran out.

Figure in: include
>Be sure to figure in the extra expenses.

Figure on: depend upon someone
>I never thought we could figure on their support.

Figure on: consider
>Figure on at least a one-hour delay in your flight.

Figure out: resolve
>Now how are we going to figure that out?

Fill in: provide with new information
>Could you fill me in on the latest news?

Fill in: substitute for
>He filled in for her when she was on vacation.

Fill out: complete a form or application
>Be sure to fill out both sides of the form.

Find out: learn or discover
>Let's see what we can find out about tigers.

Finish off: end or complete
>Let's finish off for the evening.

Finish off: destroy or kill
>He finished them off with a hunting knife.

Finish up: conclude, bring to an end
>He finished up at midnight.

Fit in: be compatible
> *He doesn't fit in with that crowd.*

Fly at: attack someone
> *He flew at him in a rage.*

Follow along: move in unison with
> *The others just followed along with the song.*

Follow through: pursue something to completion
> *We simply have to follow through on our commitments.*

Follow through: complete the motion of a baseball, golf, or tennis swing
> *When you hit the ball, be sure to follow through.*

Follow out: comply with
> *They followed out his instructions precisely.*

Follow up: check the progress
> *Did you ever follow up on those sales leads?*

Freeze out: exclude
> *They froze him out of the negotiations.*

Get about: walk again
> *It was a week before he could get about.*

Get across: make something comprehensible
> *I keep trying to get the same point across to you.*

Get after: encourage, follow up
> *It's time to get after those kids again.*

Get along: co-exist
> *Can't you find a way to get along with one another?*

Get around: avoid
> *There is no way we can get around this situation.*

Get at: reach successfully
> *Put the cookies where the children can't get at them.*

Get at: suggest
> *What are you trying to get at with that question?*

Get back: receive
> *Did you ever get your money back?*

Get back at: exact revenge
> *He tried unsuccessfully to get back at his enemies.*

Get by: go past
> *Excuse me, can I get by here?*

Get by: barely succeed
> *He did just enough homework to get by.*

Get down: descend
> *Please get down from the table.*

Get down: devote your attention
> *Let's get down to work.*

Get down: discourage
> *Don't let her criticism get you down.*

Get in: enter
> *We were lucky to get in before they closed the doors.*

Get in: succeed in accomplishing
> *They got the game in before the rain.*

Get into: become involved
> *I really can get into this assignment.*

Get off: depart
> *Did he ever get off last evening?*

Get off: fire a shot
> *Try to get off a shot if he appears.*

Get off: send a message
> *He got off a quick note before he left the office.*

Get off: escape punishment
> *He got off with only two years.*

Get off: finish the work day
> *When do you get off?*

Get on: continue on good terms
> *They seem to be getting on well together.*

Get on: make progress
> *Let's get on with it. Time is money.*

Get out: escape
> *How did the bird get out of its cage?*

Get out: publish a newspaper
> *They got the paper out last evening.*

Get over: prevail
> *How will they ever get over the loss of their home?*

Get over: recover from difficult experience
> *He never got over the death of his son.*

Get through: make contact
> *I tried calling, but I couldn't get through.*

Get to: make contact with
> *How can we get to the head of the corporation?*

Get to: affect
> *The strain of the job finally got to him.*

Get together: gather
> *We should all get together on Friday morning.*

Get up: arise from bed
> *It's six o'clock and time to get up.*

Get up: initiate
> *He got up a petition against the property tax.*

Give away: present at a wedding
> *The father gave his daughter away with a tear in his eye.*

Give away: reveal accidentally
> *He gave away the secret in the press conference.*

Give back: return
> *Don't forget to give me the book back.*

Give in: surrender
> *Don't give in—regardless of the pressure.*

Give of: devote
> *He gave generously of himself in the cause of peace.*

Give off: emit

    The lawn mower was giving off strange smells.

Give out: distribute

    The company representative was giving out free samples.

Give out: stop functioning

    His heart gave out last night.

Give over: place in another's care

    He gave over his assets to his attorney for safekeeping.

Give over: devote oneself

    He gave himself over to helping humanity.

Give over: surrender oneself

    He gave himself over to her with his heart and soul.

Give up: surrender, desist, lose hope

    Don't give up, try again.

Go about: continue

    He should go about his business.

Go along: agree

    They will go along with whatever we suggest.

Go at: attack

    He went at his opponent determined to prevail.

Go at: approach

    How many ways can we go at this problem?

Go by: elapse

    As time goes by we grow wiser.

Go by: pay a short visit

    They went by the new neighbors' house to say hello.

Go down: set

    The sun goes down very early in winter.

Go down: fall to ground

    The boxer went down after being hit on the chin.

Go down: lose

    They went down to defeat.

Go down: be recorded

    This will go down as a very important event of the decade.

Go for: like, have an urge for

    I could go for an ice cream.

Go in for: participate

    He goes in for tennis and swimming.

Go off: explode

    The bomb went off on a deserted street.

Go off: depart

    He went off to the navy after high school.

Go on: happen

    What's going on here?

Go on: continue

    Life goes on.

Go on: keep on doing

    He went on reading even after the sun went down.

Go out: become extinguished
>   *The fire went out.*
Go out: go outdoors
>   *Mommy, can we go out?*
Go out: partake in social life
>   *Since her husband died, she never goes out anymore.*
Go over: review
>   *Can we go over these figures one more time?*
Go over: gain acceptance
>   *The presentation went over very well.*
Go through: examine carefully
>   *We have to go through the clothes and papers.*
Go through: experience
>   *I hope I never have to go through that again.*
Go through: perform
>   *He went through his lines like a professional actor.*
Go under: fail
>   *The business went under after only six months of mismanagement.*
Go under: lose consciousness to anesthesia
>   *The patient wanted to see her before he went under.*
Go with: date regularly
>   *Sally has been going with John since eighth grade.*

Grind out: produce by hard work
>   *He keeps grinding out those articles for the newspaper.*

Grow into: develop
>   *He is growing into a handsome young man.*
Grow on: become acceptable
>   *That music grows on you.*
Grow out of: become too mature for something
>   *He grew out of those children's books.*
Grow out of: come into existence
>   *This project grew out of preliminary discussions last year.*
Grow up: become an adult
>   *When will you grow up?*

Hang around: loiter
>   *Why does he hang around with those kids every afternoon?*
Hang back: hold back
>   *Be sure to hang back at the start of the match.*
Hang in: persevere
>   *You just have to hang in there with him.*
Hang on: persevere
>   *We must hang on until the rescue helicopter arrives.*
Hang together: be united
>   *Let's hang together in the salary negotiations.*
Hang up: end a telephone conversation
>   *Don't you dare hang up on me.*

Hang up: hinder
>*What's hanging up the parade?*

Have on: wear
>*What did he have on when you saw him?*

Have to: must
>*I just have to see that movie.*

Hear from: be notified
>*When will we hear from you about the application?*

Hear from: be reprimanded
>*He certainly will hear from his superiors about that error.*

Hear of: be aware of
>*Have you heard of the new family in town?*

Hear out: listen fully
>*I would like you to hear me out on this matter before you proceed.*

Heave to: turn into the wind or to the seas before a storm
>*With the storm approaching, the captain gave the order to heave to.*

Hide out: conceal yourself
>*He hid out for two months in the hills.*

Hold back: restrain oneself
>*All evening I held back my applause.*

Hold down: restrict
>*Please hold down the noise.*

Hold forth: talk at length
>*The president held forth on international relations all during dinner.*

Hold off: withstand
>*Can anyone hold off the invaders?*

Hold on: persist
>*We will just hold on until our wish is granted.*

Hold out: last
>*The supplies held out for two months.*

Hold over: delay
>*The sale has been held over one more week.*

Hold to: remain loyal
>*He held to his promises.*

Hold up: delay
>*What is holding up the construction?*

Hold up: rob
>*He held up a bank in Chicago.*

Hold with: agree
>*No one seriously holds with his opinions.*

Join in: participate
>*They joined in at the end of the first verse.*

Keep at: persevere
> *Just keep at it and you'll succeed.*

Keep down: restrain
> *They kept the cost of college education down as long as they could.*

Keep off: stay away from
> *Keep off the grass!*

Keep to: stay with
> *Let's keep to the main idea.*

Keep up: maintain properly
> *You must keep up your dues to remain a member in good standing.*

Kill off: eliminate
> *All the rats were killed off by the poison.*

Knock around: be rough with someone
> *You won't be able to knock her around any more.*

Knock around: travel
> *They knocked around California for a month.*

Knock back: gulp down
> *They both knocked back the vodka in true Russian style.*

Knock down: topple
> *The little girl knocked down the sand castle her father had just completed.*

Knock off: stop work
> *Let's knock off today at four.*

Knock off: kill
> *They knocked off the drug dealer in a back alley.*

Knock out: render unconscious
> *That last punch knocked him out for two minutes.*

Knock out: be confined by illness or injury
> *The flu really knocked him out for a week.*

Knock together: make something quickly
> *Let's see if we can knock this table together before evening.*

Knock up: wake or summon by knocking at the door (British English)
> *Don't forget to knock me up tomorrow.*

Knock up: make pregnant (American English—crude and vulgar)

Lay aside: give up
> *Lay aside your arms and come out.*

Lay away: reserve for the future
> *Be sure to lay away some extra funds for a vacation.*

Lay in: store for the future
> *It's time to lay in some seed for the spring.*

Lay into: reprimand
> *The boss is really laying into the new employee.*

Lay off: terminate one's employment
> *Ten thousand people are scheduled to be laid off tomorrow.*

Lay on: prepare
> *They laid on a reception for fifty people.*

Lay out: present

    Can you lay out your intentions for us?

Lay out: clothe a corpse

    She was laid out in her finest dress.

Lay over: make a stopover

    We will have to lay over in Moscow enroute to Siberia.

Lead off: start

    Johnny will lead off the discussion.

Lead on: entice, encourage, deceive

    The young man led her on for almost two years.

Lean on: apply pressure

    I want you to lean on him until his performance improves.

Leave alone: refrain from disturbing

    Please leave me alone. I'm busy.

Leave go: relax one's grasp

    She left go of the girl's hand.

Leave off: cease doing something

    She left off in the middle of the sentence.

Leave out: omit

    She left out two answers.

Lend itself to: be suitable for

    That story lends itself well to a screen adaptation.

Let down: disappoint

    In the end his friends let him down.

Let on: admit knowing

    We finally had to let on to the fact that we had known all along.

Let out: end

    School let out at 2:00 PM.

Let up: diminish

    The rain did not let up for two hours.

Lie down: do little

    He keeps lying down on the job.

Lie with: depend upon

    The final word lies with you.

Light into: attack

    Did you see how she lit into him?

Light out: depart hastily

    He certainly lit out after work.

Light up: become animated

    Whenever he started talking, her face lit up.

Light up: start smoking

    They both lit up after the play.

Listen in: eavesdrop
> *The teacher tried to listen into the conversation at the next table.*

Listen in: tune in to a radio broadcast
> *They listened in to the show every Sunday morning.*

Live down: overcome the shame
> *Can he ever live down that disgraceful performance?*

Live it up: enjoy life in an extravagant fashion
> *After we won the lottery, we lived it up for a year.*

Live out: go through a period of time
> *They lived out their days in peace.*

Live with: resign oneself to
> *He learned to live with his limitations.*

Live up to: achieve
> *How can you live up to your parents' expectations?*

Look after: take care of
> *She will look after you while I'm gone.*

Look down on: despise
> *They always looked down on the new students.*

Look for: expect
> *What can we look for in the new year?*

Look for: search
> *Look for tea in the coffee aisle of the supermarket.*

Look forward to: await with great anticipation
> *I am looking forward to our meeting.*

Look like: appear as
> *It looks like rain.*

Look on/upon: regard
> *They looked upon him with skepticism.*

Look out: be careful
> *Look out. It's a dangerous crossing.*

Look to: expect from
> *We looked to you for guidance.*

Look up: search and find
> *What words do you have to look up in a dictionary?*

Look up to: admire
> *She really looks up to her daddy.*

Lose out: fail to achieve
> *Those who came late lost out on a golden opportunity.*

Make for: promote, lead to, results in
> *That approach makes for better productivity.*

Make off: depart hastily
> *The thieves made off with their jewelry.*

Make out: discern
> *Without my glasses I can't make out this note.*

Make out: understand
> *I can't make out what he means.*

Make out: compose
Have you made out a will?
Make out: get along with
How did you make out with the new eyeglasses?
Make over: redo
She was completely made over for the new part.
Make up: construct
Let's make up a new proposal.
Make up: alter appearance
They made her up to be an old woman for the play.
Make up: apply cosmetics
She always makes herself up before she goes out.
Make up: resolve a quarrel
After an hour they decided to make up and start over again.
Make up: take an exam later
The student who had been ill had a chance to make up the math exam.

Mark down: decrease the price
They marked down the toys after the Christmas holidays.
Mark out: plan something
He marked out a course of action.
Mark up: deface
They marked up the subway car with spray paint.
Mark up: increase the price
As soon as the New Year came they marked up the new car models.

Measure up: match requirements
He just didn't measure up to our qualifications.

Meet with: be received
The outline of the plan met with his approval.

Move in/into: occupy a place
We are moving into the new offices next week.
Move on: begin a passage
It's time to move on and try something new.
Move out: leave a place
When will they be moving out of their apartment?

Mow down: destroy (as in cutting grass)
Every time the enemy soldiers attacked, they were mowed down by the machine gun.

Open up: unfold
She opened up the letter with mixed emotions.
Open up: begin the business day
We open up at 7:00 AM on Sundays.
Open up: speak candidly
Only after we became good friends did she begin to open up.
Open up: start
They opened up the newsstand as soon as the dawn came.

Pass away: die

    He passed away last year.

Pass off: offer an imitation as the original

    He tried to pass it off as a Picasso painting.

Pass out: lose consciousness

    After drinking ten bottles of beer he passed out.

Pass over: omit

    They passed over the difficult items on the agenda.

Pass over: skip

    He was passed over for promotion.

Pass up: miss an opportunity

    He passed up a chance to sing with the Beatles.

Pay off: pay the full amount

    He paid off the mortgage last year.

Pay off: return a profit

    Their investment in real estate paid off handsomely.

Pay out: spend

    He paid out twenty dollars for the gift.

Pay up: give the requested amount

    He paid up his bar tab on Friday evening.

Pick apart: refute by careful analysis

    He picked apart the prosecution's argument in front of the jury.

Pick at: pluck with fingers

    He picked at the guitar strings before playing a song.

Pick on: tease

    You shouldn't pick on your baby sister.

Pick out: select

    Pick out a nice tie for me.

Pick out: distinguish in a large group

    He could always pick her out in a crowd.

Pick up: retrieve by hand

    He picked up a newspaper on the way to work.

Pick up: organize, clean

    Let's pick up this room right now.

Play at: take half-heartedly

    He only played at being the boss.

Play back: replay

    We played back the tape.

Play down: minimize

    We want to play down the weakest aspects of our proposal.

Play on: take advantage of

    He often played on her fears.

Play out: exhaust

    This type of approach played itself out long ago.

Play up: emphasize

    They played up her good looks.

Pull away: withdraw
>*They pulled away from the attack.*

Pull away: move ahead
>*He pulled away in the public opinion polls.*

Pull back: withdraw
>*Let's pull back and regroup.*

Pull in: arrive at destination
>*The train pulled in at 10:00 PM.*

Pull out: depart
>*The train pulled out on time.*

Pull over: bring a vehicle to a stop
>*The policeman asked him to pull over.*

Pull through: endure and emerge successfully
>*He finally pulled through after much extra work.*

Pull up: bring to a halt
>*The riders pulled up at the gate.*

Put across: make comprehensible
>*He was able to put across his main points.*

Put away: renounce
>*They put away their thoughts of revolution.*

Put down: write down
>*He put down his thoughts on paper.*

Put down: to end
>*We must put down the revolt.*

Put down: criticize
>*Someone was always putting her down.*

Put forth: exert
>*He put forth his best effort in the race.*

Put forward: propose
>*He put forward his ideas in his presentation.*

Put in: apply
>*He put in for the new position at his office.*

Put in: spend time
>*He put in ten extra hours last week.*

Put off: postpone
>*They put off the meeting until after the harvest.*

Put on: clothe oneself
>*Put on a hat.*

Put out: extinguish
>*He put out the fire.*

Put out: publish
>*She put out a small literary journal.*

Put over on: get across deceptively
>*He tried to put over his schemes on the people.*

Put through: bring to a successful end
>*He put the bill through in the Senate.*

Put together: construct
>*She put together the model airplane with her dad.*

Put upon: imposed
>*He was often put upon by friends.*

Read out: read aloud
> *The teacher read out the names at the beginning of class.*

Read up: learn or study by reading
> *I'll have to read up on my history for the exam.*

Read out of: be expelled from
> *He was read out of the party organization.*

Ride out: survive
> *They rode out the latest dip in the stock market.*

Ring up: record a sale
> *I can ring those items up at this register.*

Ring up: extend out a series
> *They rang up ten victories without a loss.*

Rip into: criticize
> *She certainly ripped into him for that performance.*

Rip off: steal from, defraud
> *Several customers felt they had been ripped off at the sale.*

Rise above: be superior to
> *You must rise above these petty squabbles.*

Run across: find by chance
> *They simply ran across each other at the shopping mall.*

Run after: seek attention
> *Stop running after her and maybe she'll pay you more attention.*

Run against: encounter
> *He kept running against new obstacles.*

Run against: oppose
> *He ran against the incumbent senator.*

Run along: leave
> *Run along now, children.*

Run away: flee
> *The prisoners tried to run away.*

Run down: stop because of lack of power
> *The tractor simply ran down.*

Run down: tire
> *He was very run down after the basketball season.*

Run down: collide with
> *They ran down that poor little dog.*

Run down: chase and capture
> *They ran him down in Philadelphia.*

Run down: review
> *Let's run down the list of our options.*

Run in: take into legal custody
> *He was run in by the two officers.*

Run into: meet by chance
> *I ran into my wife at the post office.*

Run into: amount to
> *This could run into millions of dollars.*

Run off: print, duplicate
> *He ran off a hundred copies.*

Run off: escape
> *He ran off with all their money.*

Run off: flow or drain away
> *The water ran off the roof.*

Run off: decide a contest
> *They are running off the tie vote today.*

Run on: continue to talk
> *How he runs on when he gets to the podium.*

Run out: deplete
> *I never want to run out of money.*

Run over: knock down
> *Who ran over the dog?*

Run over: review quickly
> *I ran over my notes before the speech.*

Run over: overflow
> *My cup runneth over.*

Run over: exceed the limit
> *I don't want any of you to run over budget this month.*

Run through: pierce
> *He ran the knife through the butter.*

Run through: use up quickly
> *We have run through all our copy paper.*

Run through: rehearse
> *Let's run through the play one more time.*

Run through: go over main points
> *Let's run through the first two points.*

Run up: make larger
> *He ran up a huge bar bill.*

Run with: adopt an idea
> *Let's run with this idea for the time being.*

See after: take care of
> *She will see after you until I return.*

See off: take leave of
> *They saw the children off at the airport.*

See out: escort to the door
> *Judy will see you out. Please come again.*

See through: understand the true nature
> *I can see through his plans.*

See through: continue
> *I will see this deal through until they sign on the bottom line.*

See through: support in difficult times
> *My dad saw us through financially the first few years.*

See to: attend to
> *See to the new patient and I'll find his chart.*

Sell off: get rid of at discount prices
>*We will be selling off any leftover items at the end of the month.*

Sell out: dispose of all
>*The tickets were all sold out by mid-morning.*

Send for: summon
>*They sent for the police.*

Send in: cause to arrive
>*They sent in dozens of e-mail messages.*

Send out: order from
>*They sent out for two pizzas and some beer.*

Send up: confined to jail
>*He was sent up for five years on a drug charge.*

Set about: begin
>*They set about their business.*

Set apart: distinguish
>*Her qualifications clearly set her apart from the other candidates.*

Set aside: reserve
>*Can you set aside two tickets for us?*

Set aside: reject
>*Their claim was set aside by the service manager.*

Set at: attack
>*The dogs set at the two little boys throwing stones.*

Set back: slow down
>*The family was severely set back by the flood.*

Set back: cost a lot
>*That new part for the car set me back one hundred dollars.*

Set down: seat someone
>*They set the baby down at the table.*

Set down: put in writing
>*He wanted to set down his thoughts before the meeting.*

Set down: land a plane
>*The pilot set down in a grassy field.*

Set forth: express
>*He set forth his principles in his campaign speech.*

Set forth: propose
>*The attorneys set forth the necessary conditions of the tentative agreement.*

Set in: insert
>*His last words are set in stone.*

Set in: begin happening
>*The storm set in overnight.*

Set off: initiate
>*His words set off a rally on Wall Street.*

Set off: explode
>*He set off the bomb.*

Set out: undertake
>*He set out to conquer the world.*

Set out: lay out graphically
>*He set out the new plans for the museum.*

Set to: begin
>*Can we set to work?*

Set up: put forward, select
>*He was set up as the group's leader.*

Set up: assemble
>*He set up the train set in the living room.*

Set up: establish business
>*What do we still need to set up production?*

Set up: arrange
>*Please set up the glasses on the rear shelf of the cabinet.*

Set upon: attack violently
>*The dogs set upon the cat.*

Sew up: complete successfully
>*We finally sewed up the deal.*

Shake down: subject to search
>*I want you to shake down his apartment for evidence in the case.*

Shake hands: greet by clasping one another's hands
>*Americans often shake hands when they meet one another.*

Shake off: dismiss
>*He shook off the injury and continued to play.*

Shake off: get rid of
>*How can I shake off this cold?*

Shake up: upset
>*The death of his father really shook him up.*

Shake up: rearrange drastically.
>*He will really shake up the industry.*

Shape up: develop
>*This is shaping up to be a close contest.*

Shape up: improve to the standard.
>*He will have to shape up or he'll be fired.*

Shoot down: bring down
>*They shot down the enemy aircraft.*

Shoot for: aspire
>*You ought to shoot for the top job.*

Shoot up: increase dramatically
>*The stock prices shot up toward the end of the day.*

Shoot up: damage or terrorize a town
>*The guerrillas shot up the entire village.*

Shoot straight: be truthful
>*I love someone who shoots straight in negotiations.*

Shop around: look for bargains
>*The girls love to shop around at the discount stores.*

Shop around: look for something better, like a job.
>*We decided to shop around for a while, before we make a career decision.*

Show around: act as a guide
> *My daughter can show you around the city if you have time.*

Show off: display
> *The goods were shown off to their best advantage.*

Show off: behave ostentatiously
> *He always likes to show off in front of his friends.*

Show up: be visible
> *The cancer showed up clearly on the x-ray.*

Show up: arrive
> *Will they ever show up?*

Shut down: stop something from operating
> *They shut the plant down.*

Shut off: stop the flow
> *Shut off the electricity before you work on the outlet.*

Shut off: isolate
> *He was shut off from all news for two months.*

Shut out: prevent from scoring
> *We were able to shut them out in the last inning of the game.*

Shut up: silence, be silent
> *You should shut up before you get in more trouble.*

Sing out: cry out
> *He sang out from the rear of the crowd.*

Sit down: take a seat
> *Please sit down until you are called.*

Sit in: participate
> *They sat in on the discussions.*

Sit in: participate in a sit-in demonstration
> *The demonstrators intend to sit in at the plant gates tomorrow.*

Sit on: consider
> *Can we sit on this for a day or two and then give you our response?*

Sit on: suppress
> *The defense attorneys sat on the new evidence.*

Sit out: stay to the end
> *We will sit this out until it is over.*

Sit out: not participate
> *I sat out the second match and let my brother play.*

Sit up: rise from lying to sitting position
> *After his nap he sat up in bed.*

Sit up: sit with spine erect
> *Mothers always want you to sit up straight.*

Sit up: stay up late
> *They sat up until past midnight waiting for their daughter to come home.*

Sit up: become suddenly alert
> *He sat up at the sound of shots.*

Sleep in: sleep late

I like to sleep in on Sundays.

Sleep out: sleep away from one's home

The parents are sleeping out this weekend.

Sleep over: spend the night at another home

The girls slept over at their friend's house.

Sleep with: have sexual relations

He slept with her for the first time on their vacation.

Slip away: depart without taking one's leave

They just slipped away from the party.

Slip out: depart unnoticed

He slipped out for a cigarette break.

Smell out: discover through investigation

They smelled out the criminal after years of investigation.

Sound off: express an opinion

He sounded off about taxes at the town meeting.

Sound out: elicit an opinion

Sound out the board on this matter before Monday.

Speak out: talk freely

He spoke out at our weekly meeting.

Speak up: talk loud enough to be heard

We can't hear you. Would you please speak up?

Speak up: talk without fear

You must learn to speak up for your rights.

Spell out: read slowly

Try to spell it out if you can't understand the meaning.

Spell out: make clear

Would you please spell out your specific objections?

Spell out: decipher

Let's see if we can spell out the new proposal and write a response.

Spin off: develop from an existing project

They spun off two shows from the original.

Spin out: rotate out of control

The car spun out on the ice when he hit the brakes.

Split up: part company

After ten years of marriage they decided to split up.

Stand by: be ready

Stand by for the commercial.

Stand by: remain uninvolved

He just stood by and watched.

Stand by: remain loyal

She stood by me in my time of trouble.

Stand down: withdraw, cease work
> *The soldiers on duty stood down at midnight.*

Stand for: represent
> *What do you stand for?*

Stand for: put up with
> *I don't know why I stand for this nonsense.*

Stand in: replace
> *She stood in for the sick actress.*

Stand off: stay at a distance
> *They stood off and observed from afar.*

Stand on: be based on
> *These findings stand on my previous calculations.*

Stand on: insist on
> *There are times when you must stand on ceremony.*

Stand out: be conspicuous
> *She really stood out in the green dress.*

Stand out: refuse compliance
> *He is going to stand out against the tax people.*

Stand over: supervise
> *She stood over him the entire test.*

Stand to: prepare to act
> *The police were ordered to stand to.*

Stand up: remain valid
> *His conclusions stood up to various attacks.*

Stand up: miss an appointment
> *She stood him up again last evening.*

Stand up for: defend
> *I stood up for you in my meeting with the school board.*

Start out: begin a trip
> *They started out for Miami at dawn.*

Stave off: prevent
> *They staved off the attackers countless times.*

Stay put: remain in place
> *Now you kids stay put until I get the ice cream.*

Stay up: remain awake
> *They stayed up all night talking about old times.*

Stick around: remain
> *He stuck around for an hour after the press conference to sign autographs.*

Stick out: be prominent
> *He really sticks out in a crowd.*

Stick up: to rob at gunpoint
> *They were stuck up twice in six months.*

Stick up for: defend
> *He always sticks up for his kid brother.*

Stop by: visit
> *They stopped by for coffee after the theater.*

Stop off: interrupt a trip
> *They stopped off in Rome for two days.*

Strike down: fell with a blow
> *He was struck down by a lightning bolt.*

Strike out for: begin a course of action
> *He struck out for California on his own.*

Strike out: fail in one's attempts
> *He struck out in his attempts to get approval for the highway.*

Strike up: start
> *Strike up the band!*

String along: entice by giving false hope
> *They strung him along for a few weeks before telling him they had hired someone else.*

String out: prolong
> *How long can we string out these talks?*

String up: hang someone
> *They strung him up without a trial.*

Swear at: verbally abuse
> *She swore at them like a sailor.*

Swear by: rely on
> *I swear by these calculations.*

Swear by: take an oath
> *Do you swear by the Bible?*

Swear in: administer a legal oath
> *He was sworn in as Governor.*

Swear off: renounce
> *I have sworn off cigarettes.*

Swear out: process
> *The detectives swore out a warrant for his arrest.*

Sweat out: await anxiously
> *Some students sweated out the two weeks before grades were mailed home.*

Take after: follow the example of, resemble
> *She takes after her father.*

Take apart: separate
> *He took the motor apart in an afternoon.*

Take back: retract
> *I take back my original comments.*

Take down: lower
> *He was taken down a notch or two by the negative fitness report.*

Take down: record in writing
> *He took down the minutes of the meeting.*

Take for: regard
> *What do you take me for?*

Take in: grant admittance
She was taken in as a member of the law firm.
Take in: reduce
She took in his new slacks at the waist.
Take in: include
This article takes in all of the existing information.
Take in: deceive
He was taken in by her flashy business card.
Take in: observe thoroughly
He took in the entire scene with a single glance.
Take off: remove
Take off your hat indoors.
Take off: depart by aircraft
Our flight to Madrid took off on schedule.
Take off: deduct
He took off ten percent from the marked price.
Take on: hire
We took him on temporarily for the job.
Take on: accept
We took on the new responsibilities cheerfully.
Take on: oppose
He took on the taller man in a fistfight.
Take out: secure a license
I took out a hunting license.
Take out: escort
I took out our guests for a look at the city.
Take out: vent
He took out his anger on the punching bag.
Take out: kill
He took out the enemy sniper with his first shot.
Take over: assume control
I am taking over here as of today.
Take to: develop habit or ability
He took to swimming at an early age.
Take to: escape
The escapees took to the hills.
Take up: assume
He took up the burden of his family's debts.
Take up: reduce
She took up the dress a full inch.
Take up: use time
It took up all morning.

Talk around: persuade
He tried to talk me around to his point of view.
Talk around: avoid
He tried talking his way around the parking ticket.
Talk at: address
He talked at the rotary club.

Talk back: reply rudely
>*Don't talk back to your parents.*

Talk down: deprecate
>*He loves to talk down to his secretary.*

Talk down: silence
>*By the end of the meeting he had successfully talked down all the dissenting voices.*

Talk out: resolve
>*Can we not talk this out in a friendly fashion?*

Talk over: consider
>*We talked it over before deciding.*

Talk over: persuade
>*They talked her over by the end of the day.*

Talk up: promote, exaggerate
>*Let's talk up our accomplishments.*

Tear at: attack like an animal
>*They tore at the package like wild animals.*

Tear at: distress oneself
>*Stop tearing at yourself.*

Tear down: vilify
>*They love to tear other people down.*

Tear down: demolish
>*They love to tear down the walls that separate the people in our community.*

Tear into: attack vigorously
>*They tore into their opponents.*

Tear up: destroy
>*We tore up the lease.*

Tell off: reprimand
>*They certainly told him off.*

Throw away: get rid of
>*We throw the boxes away.*

Throw away: waste
>*She threw away her life's savings in Las Vegas.*

Throw away: fail to take advantage
>*They threw away their chance.*

Throw back: hinder the progress
>*They were completely thrown back by his critical comments.*

Throw back: revert
>*They were thrown back to the beginning by the new discovery.*

Throw in: insert
>*Throw in your opinions whenever ready.*

Throw off: rid oneself
>*They threw the dogs off their scent by crossing a stream.*

Throw off: emit
>*The new plant throws off a foul odor.*

Throw off: divert
>*They were thrown off course by a faulty computer.*

Throw open: make accessible
>*We must throw open our doors to every deserving student.*

Throw out: emit
>*It throws out a powerful signal to other countries.*

Throw out: reject
>*The new design was thrown out by the board of directors.*

Throw out: force to leave
>*Throw the bum out.*

Throw over: overturn
>*They threw over the leftist government in the sixties.*

Throw over: reject
>*The new tax laws were thrown over by the voters in a special vote.*

Throw up: vomit
>*I was so sick I threw up twice.*

Throw up: abandon
>*She threw up her attempts to gain the money.*

Throw up: refer to something repeatedly
>*He kept throwing up her name.*

Throw up: construct hastily
>*Those buildings were thrown up in a matter of months.*

Throw up: project
>*Please throw that image up on the screen.*

Tie in: connect
>*Can we tie in these findings with our previous data?*

Tie into: attack
>*He tied into her.*

Tie up: block
>*They tied up traffic for hours.*

Tie up: occupy
>*I was tied up in the office all last week.*

Try on: check out clothes for size
>*Try on the shoes before you buy them.*

Try out: undergo a competitive qualifying exam
>*He must try out for the soccer team.*

Try out: test or examine
>*Can I try out these new glasses before I purchase a pair?*

Turn away: dismiss
>*They were turned away at the hotel because it was full.*

Turn away: reject
>*They were turned away at the last moment by a violent counterattack.*

Turn back: reverse direction
>*Can you turn back time?*

Turn back: halt advance
>*The invaders were turned back by the courageous citizens of the village.*

Turn down: reject
>*She was turned down by the police department.*

Turn down: fold down
>The bed was turned down by the chambermaid before they returned last evening.

Turn in: give over
>Turn in your papers at the end of class.

Turn in: inform on
>They turned in their own brother to the authorities.

Turn off: stop operation
>Turn off the electricity.

Turn off: offend
>He was turned off by their use of profanity.

Turn off: cease paying attention
>He turned them off and played all by himself.

Turn on: begin operation
>Turn on the television.

Turn on: alter the mind with drugs
>In the sixties people were eager to turn on.

Turn on: interest
>That course turned him on.

Turn out: produce
>They turn out dozens of autos an hour.

Turn out: gather
>Hundreds turned out for his speech.

Turn out: develop
>The cake turned out wonderfully.

Turn over: shift position
>Turn over on your side if you snore.

Turn over: reflect upon
>He turned the request over and over in his mind for a long time.

Turn over: transfer to another
>The papers were turned over to the judge.

Turn over: sell
>How many of these cars can we turn over by the end of the month?

Turn to: seek assistance
>Whom can I turn to?

Turn to: begin
>He turned his attention to the new project.

Turn up: increase volume
>Turn up the radio. I want to hear the weather report.

Turn up: find
>Where did you turn up the missing wallet?

Turn up: appear, be found
>The ring turned up among her dirty socks.

Turn up: just happen
>In every translation, some new difficulty turns up.

Use up: exhaust the supply
>He used up all the sugar for the cake.

Wait on/upon: attend to
>She waited on him day and night.

Wait out: endure

We will have to wait out the storm in a hotel.

Wait up: postpone sleep

Daddy still waits up for his daughters even though they are grown up.

Walk out: go on strike

The workers walked out at midnight without a contract.

Walk out: leave suddenly

He just got up and walked out.

Walk over: gain easy victory

They walked all over their opponents.

Walk over: treat poorly

They walk all over the staff.

Walk through: perform

They walked through their lines for the last time.

Watch out: be careful

Watch out, it's very slippery.

Watch over: be in charge of

I was told to watch over him until the doctor came.

Watch it: be careful

I'm telling you, you'd better watch it, or they'll be trouble.

Wear down: exhaust by continuous pressure

They finally wore him down by constant interrogation.

Wear off: diminish gradually

The paint has worn off the siding.

Wear out: become unusable

These jeans will never wear out.

Win out: prevail

He finally won out over his competitors.

Win over: persuade

He won them over with his charm.

Wind down: relax

After work they wound down for an hour in the hot tub.

Wind up: end

They wound up the party at midnight.

Work in: insert

They worked in an hour of relaxation.

Work off: rid by effort

She worked off ten pounds at the gym.

Work out: accomplish

That worked out well.

Work out: develop

They worked out a satisfactory arrangement for them both.

Work out: engage in strenuous activity

She works out every afternoon for two hours.

Work over: repeat, revise
> *They are working over their papers for submission on Monday.*

Work up: get excited
> *She got all worked up over her grade.*

Work up: increase ability or capacity
> *She worked her way up to ten pages an hour.*

Wrap up: complete
> *Let's wrap up the meeting and go home.*

Wrap up: summarize
> *Can you wrap up the presentation with your main points?*

Wrap up: intensely involved
> *She's all wrapped up in her schoolwork.*

Write down: record
> *She wrote down the assignment.*

Write in: insert
> *She wrote in a new opening scene for the main actress.*

Write in: submit name of candidate not on the ballot
> *They wrote her in for the post of treasurer.*

Write in: write to organization
> *They wrote in to the maker of the toy with their complaint.*

Write off: dismiss
> *They wrote her off even before the tryouts.*

Write out: write in full
> *She had to write out the complete sentence.*

Write up: report
> *She wrote up the minutes of the meeting.*

Zero in: concentrate on
> *They zeroed in on their long-term goals during the afternoon session.*

Zip up: close, enclose
> *Please zip up your files before sending them to me.*

Another 550 Problem Verbs

Listed below are an additional 550 English Verbs whose principal parts may cause confusion or difficulty in spelling. The principal parts are listed here to correspond to the order of the full **501 English Verbs.** *Note the different spellings in the Past Tense and Participle forms, a single l, m, t for American English, a double consonant for British English.*

Basic Form	3rd Person Singular	Present Participle	Past Tense	Past Participle
abet	abets	abetting	abetted	abetted
abhor	abhors	abhorring	abhorred	abhorred
accompany	accompanies	accompanying	accompanied	accompanied
accede	accedes	acceding	acceded	acceded
access	accesses	accessing	accessed	accessed
acquit	acquits	acquitting	acquitted	acquitted
ad-lib	ad-libs	ad-libbing	ad-libbed	ad-libbed
allay	allays	allaying	allayed	allayed
allot	allots	allotting	allotted	allotted
annul	annuls	annulling	annulled	annulled
answer	answers	answering	answered	answered
antique	antiques	antiquing	antiqued	antiqued
bat	bats	batting	batted	batted
bed	beds	bedding	bedded	bedded
befit	befits	befitting	befitted	befitted
beget	begets	begetting	begot/begat	begotten/begot
behold	beholds	beholding	beheld	beheld
belie	belies	belying	belied	belied
benefit	benefits	benefit/benefitting	benefited/ benefitted	benefited/ benefitted
bereave	bereaves	bereaving	bereaved/bereft	bereaved/bereft
beseech	beseeches	beseeching	besought/ beseeched	besought/ beseeched
beset	besets	besetting	beset	beset
bestride	bestrides	bestriding	bestrode	bestridden
betake	betakes	betaking	betook	betaken
bid	bids	bidding	bade	biddne
binge	binges	binging/bingeing	binged	binged
blab	blabs	blabbing	blabbed	blabbed
blot	blots	blotting	blotted	blotted
blur	blurs	blurring	blurred	blurred
bob	bobs	bobbing	bobbed	bobbed
bobsled	bobsleds	bobsledding	bobsledded	bobsledded
boo	boos	booing	booed	booed
bop	bops	bopping	bopped	bopped
brim	brims	brimming	brimmed	brimmed
bug	bugs	bugging	bugged	bugged
bum	bums	bumming	bummed	bummed

Basic Form	3rd Person Singular	Present Participle	Past Tense	Past Participle
bus	buses/busses	busing/bussing	bused/bussed	bused/bussed
can	can		could	
cancel	cancels	canceling/ cancelling	canceled/ cancelled	canceled/ cancelled
cane	canes	caning	caned	caned
cap	caps	capping	capped	capped
catalog	catalogs	cataloging	cataloged	cataloged
catalogue	catalogues	cataloguing	catalogued	catalogued
channel	channels	channeling/ channelling	channeled/ channelled	channeled/ channelled
chap	chaps	chapping	chapped	chapped
chide	chides	chiding	chided/chid	chidden
chin	chins	chinning	chinned	chinned
chip	chips	chipping	chipped	chipped
chug	chugs	chugging	chugged	chugged
chum	chums	chumming	chummed	chummed
clad	clads	cladding	clad	clad
clap	claps	clapping	clapped	clapped
cleave	cleaves	cleaving	cleft/cleaved/ clove	cleft/cleaved/ cloven
clip	clips	clipping	clipped	clipped
clog	clogs	clogging	clogged	clogged
clot	clots	clotting	clotted	clotted
club	clubs	clubbing	clubbed	clubbed
combat	combats	combating/ combatting	combated/ combatted	combated/ combatted
commit	commits	committing	committed	committed
confer	confers	conferring	conferred	conferred
control	controls	controlling	controlled	controlled
coo	coos	cooing	cooed	cooed
cop	cops	copping	copped	copped
cope	copes	coping	coped	coped
counsel	counsels	counseling/ counselling	counseled/ counselled	counseled/ counselled
crab	crabs	crabbing	crabbed	crabbed
crop	crops	cropping	cropped	cropped
dab	dabs	dabbing	dabbed	dabbed
debug	debugs	debugging	debugged	debugged
debut	debuts	debuting	debuted	debuted
deep-freeze	deep-freezes	deep-freezing	deep-froze	deep-frozen
defat	defats	defatting	defatted	defatted
deter	deters	deterring	deterred	deterred
dip	dips	dipping	dipped	dipped
disagree	disagrees	disagreeing	disagreed	disagreed
disbar	disbars	disbarring	disbarred	disbarred

Basic Form	3rd Person Singular	Present Participle	Past Tense	Past Participle
disbud	disbuds	disbudding	disbudded	disbudded
dog	dogs	dogging	dogged	dogged
don	dons	donning	donned	donned
dot	dots	dotting	dotted	dotted
drip	drips	dripping	dripped	dripped
drivel	drivels	driveling/drivelling	driveled/drivelled	driveled/drivelled
drug	drugs	drugging	drugged	drugged
drum	drums	drumming	drummed	drummed
dry	dries	drying	dried	dried
dub	dubs	dubbing	dubbed	dubbed
duel	duels	dueling/duelling	dueled/duelled	dueled/duelled
dun	duns	dunning	dunned	dunned
emit	emits	emitting	emitted	emitted
empty	empties	emptying	emptied	emptied
entrap	entraps	entrapping	entrapped	entrapped
envy	envies	envying	envied	envied
enwrap	enwraps	enwrapping	enwrapped	enwrapped
equal	equals	equaling/equalling	equaled/equalled	equaled/equalled
equip	equips	equipping	equipped	equipped
exhibit	exhibits	exhibiting	exhibited	exhibited
expel	expels	expelling	expelled	expelled
eye	eyes	eyeing	eyed	eyed
fan	fans	fanning	fanned	fanned
fat	fats	fatting	fatted	fatted
fatten	fattens	fattening	fattened	fattened
fell	fells	felling	felled	felled
fib	fibs	fibbing	fibbed	fibbed
fine	fines	fining	fined	fined
flag	flags	flagging	flagged	flagged
flap	flaps	flapping	flapped	flapped
flip	flips	flipping	flipped	flipped
flog	flogs	flogging	flogged	flogged
flop	flops	flopping	flopped	flopped
flub	flubs	flubbing	flubbed	flubbed
fog	fogs	fogging	fogged	fogged
forbear	forbears	forbearing	forbore	forborne
forswear	forswears	forswearing	forswore	forsworn
frag	frags	fragging	fragged	fragged
fret	frets	fretting	fretted	fretted
frit	frits	fritting	fritted	fritted
fry	fries	frying	fried	fried
fuel	fuels	fueling/fuelling	fueled/fuelled	fueled/fuelled
fur	furs	furring	furred	furred
gainsay	gainsays	gainsaying	gainsaid	gainsaid

Basic Form	3rd Person Singular	Present Participle	Past Tense	Past Participle
gap	gaps	gapping	gapped	gapped
gape	gapes	gaping	gaped	gaped
gas	gases/gasses	gassing	gassed	gassed
gel	gels	gelling	gelled	gelled
geld	gelds	gelding	gelded/gelt	gelded/gelt
gem	gems	gemming	gemmed	gemmed
gib	gibs	gibbing	gibbed	gibbed
gibe	gibes	gibing	gibed	gibed
gig	gigs	gigging	gigged	gigged
gild	gilds	gilding	gilded/gilt	gilded/gilt
gin	gins	ginning	ginned	ginned
gird	girds	girding	girded/girt	girded/girt
glut	gluts	glutting	glutted	glutted
grab	grabs	grabbing	grabbed	grabbed
gravel	gravels	graveling/ gravelling	graveled/ gravelled	graveled/ gravelled
grin	grins	grinning	grinned	grinned
grip	grips	gripping	gripped	gripped
gripe	gripes	griping	griped	griped
grit	grits	gritting	gritted	gritted
grub	grubs	grubbing	grubbed	grubbed
gum	gums	gumming	gummed	gummed
gun	guns	gunning	gunned	gunned
gut	guts	gutting	gutted	gutted
gyp	gyps	gypping	gypped	gypped
ham	hams	hamming	hammed	hammed
hamstring	hamstrings	hamstringing	hamstrung	hamstrung
hat	hats	hatting	hatted	hatted
hem	hems	hemming	hemmed	hemmed
hew	hews	hewing	hewed	hewn/hewed
hide	hides	hiding	hided	hided
hoe	hoes	hoeing	hoed	hoed
hog	hogs	hogging	hogged	hogged
hug	hugs	hugging	hugged	hugged
impel	impels	impelling	impelled	impelled
imperil	imperils	imperiling/ imperilling	imperiled/ imperilled	imperiled/ imperilled
inbreed	inbreeds	inbreeding	inbred	inbred
incur	incurs	incurring	incurred	incurred
infer	infers	inferring	inferred	inferred
inherit	inherits	inheriting	inherited	inherited
input	inputs	inputting	inputted/input	inputted/input
inter	inters	interring	interred	interred
interbreed	interbreeds	interbreeding	interbred	interbred
intercrop	intercrops	intercropping	intercropped	intercropped

Basic Form	3rd Person Singular	Present Participle	Past Tense	Past Participle
intercut	intercuts	intercutting	intercut	intercut
intermit	intermits	intermitting	intermitted	intermitted
intrigue	intrigues	intriguing	intrigued	intrigued
intromit	intromits	intromitting	intromitted	intromitted
intuit	intuits	intuiting	intuited	intuited
issue	issues	issuing	issued	issued
jab	jabs	jabbing	jabbed	jabbed
jag	jags	jagging	jagged	jagged
jam	jams	jamming	jammed	jammed
jar	jars	jarring	jarred	jarred
jet	jets	jetting	jetted	jetted
jib	jibs	jibbing	jibbed	jibbed
jig	jigs	jigging	jigged	jigged
job	jobs	jobbing	jobbed	jobbed
jog	jogs	jogging	jogged	jogged
jot	jots	jotting	jotted	jotted
jug	jugs	jugging	jugged	jugged
junket	junkets	junketing	junketed	junketed
jut	juts	jutting	jutted	jutted
ken	kens	kenning	kenned/kent	kenned/kent
kid	kids	kidding	kidded	kidded
kidnap	kidnaps	kidnapping/ kidnaping	kidnapped/ kidnaped	kidnapped/ kidnaped
knap	knaps	knapping	knapped	knapped
knee	knees	kneeing	kneed	kneed
knot	knots	knotting	knotted	knotted
label	labels	labeling/labelling	labeled/labelled	labeled/labelled
lade	lades	lading	laded	laden/laded
lag	lags	lagging	lagged	lagged
lap	laps	lapping	lapped	lapped
lasso	lassos/lassoes	lassoing	lassoed	lassoed
laurel	laurels	laureling/laurelling	laureled/laurelled	laureled/laurelled
level	levels	leveling/levelling	leveled/levelled	leveled/levelled
libel	libels	libeling/libelling	libeled/libelled	libeled/libelled
lid	lids	lidding	lidded	lidded
lip	lips	lipping	lipped	lipped
lob	lobs	lobbing	lobbed	lobbed
log	logs	logging	logged	logged
loop	loops	looping	looped	looped
lop	lops	lopping	lopped	lopped
lope	lopes	loping	loped	loped
lug	lugs	lugging	lugged	lugged
mad	mads	madding	madded	madded

Basic Form	3rd Person Singular	Present Participle	Past Tense	Past Participle
madden	maddens	maddening	maddened	maddened
magic	magics	magicking	magicked	magicked
man	mans	manning	manned	manned
manumit	manumits	manumitting	manumitted	manumitted
map	maps	mapping	mapped	mapped
mar	mars	marring	marred	marred
marvel	marvels	marveling/ marvelling	marveled/ marvelled	marveled/ marvelled
mat	mats	matting	matted	matted
mate	mates	mating	mated	mated
maul	mauls	mauling/maulling	mauled/maulled	mauled/maulled
may	may		might	
medal	medals	medaling/medalling	medaled/medalled	medaled/medalled
merchandise	merchandises	merchandising	merchandised	merchandised
metal	metals	metaling/metalling	metaled/metalled	metaled/metalled
mete	metes	meting	meted	meted
midwife	midwifes/ midwives	midwifing/ midwiving	midwifed/ midwived	midwifed/ midwived
misdeal	misdeals	misdealing	misdealt	misdealt
misdo	midoes	misdoing	misdid	misdone
misfuel	misfuels	misfueling/ misfuelling	misfueled/ misfuelled	misfueled/ misfuelled
mislabel	mislabels	mislabeling/ mislabelling	mislabeled/ mislabelled	mislabeled/ mislabelled
misspeak	misspeaks	misspeaking	misspoke	misspoken
misspend	misspends	misspending	misspent	misspent
misunderstand	misunderstands	misunderstanding	misunderstood	misunderstood
miswrite	miswrites	miswriting	miswrote	miswritten
model	models	modeling/ modelling	modeled/ modelled	modeled/ modelled
monogram	monograms	monogramming/ monograming	monogrammed/ monogramed	monogrammed/ monogramed
monolog	monologs	monologging	monologed	monologed
monologue	monologues	monologuing	monologued	monologued
mope	mopes	moping	moped	moped
mortgage	mortgages	mortgaging	mortgaged	mortgaged
mosaic	mosaics	mosaicking	mosaicked	mosaicked
mud	muds	mudding	mudded	mudded
mug	mugs	mugging	mugged	mugged
mum	mums	mumming	mummed	mummed
must	must		had to	
nap	naps	napping	napped	napped
nag	nags	nagging	nagged	nagged
nap	naps	napping	napped	napped
net	nets	netting	netted	netted
nip	nips	nipping	nipped	nipped

Basic Form	3rd Person Singular	Present Participle	Past Tense	Past Participle
nod	nods	nodding	nodded	nodded
omit	omits	omitting	omitted	omitted
one-step	one-steps	one-stepping	one-stepped	one-stepped
one-up	one-ups	one-upping	one-upped	one-upped
ought	ought		ought	
outbreed	outbreeds	outbreeding	outbred	outbred
outfight	outfights	outfighting	outfought	outfought
outfit	outfits	outfitting	outfitted	outfitted
outgo	outgoes	outgoing	outwent	outgone
outgrow	outgrows	outgrowing	outgrew	outgrown
outlay	outlays	outlaying	outlaid	outlaid
outshine	outshines	outshining	outshone	outshone
outstrip	outstrips	outstripping	outstripped	outstripped
outwear	outwears	outwearing	outwore	outworn
outwork	outworks	outworking	outworked/ outwrought	outworked/ outwrought
overbear	overbears	overbearing	overbore	overborne
overbid	overbids	overbidding	overbidded	overbidded
overblow	overblows	overblowing	overblew	overblown
overcast	overcasts	overrcasting	overcast	overcast
overcommit	overcommits	overcommitting	overcommitted	overcommitted
overdo	overdoes	overdoing	overdid	overdone
overfeed	overfeeds	overfeeding	overfed	overfed
overshoot	overshoots	overshooting	overshot	overshot
pad	pads	padding	padded	padded
pal	pals	palling	palled	palled
pale	pales	paling	paled	paled
pall	palls	palling	palled	palled
pan	pans	panning	panned	panned
panel	panels	paneling/panelling	paneled/panelled	paneled/panelled
panic	panics	panicking	panicked	panicked
par	pars	parring	parred	parred
parallel	parallels	paralleling/ parallelling	paralleled/ parallelled	paralleled/ parallelled
parcel	parcels	parceling/parcelling	parceled/parcelled	parceled/parcelled
partake	partakes	partaking	partook	partaken
pat	pats	patting	patted	patted
patrol	patrols	patrolling	patrolled	patrolled
pedal	pedals	pedaling/pedalling	pedaled/pedalled	pedaled/pedalled
peg	pegs	pegging	pegged	pegged
pencil	pencils	penciling/pencilling	penciled/ pencilled	penciled/ pencilled
pep	peps	pepping	pepped	pepped
pet	pets	petting	petted	petted
photo	photos	photoing	photoed	photoed

Basic Form	3rd Person Singular	Present Participle	Past Tense	Past Participle
picnic	picnics	picnicking	picnicked	picnicked
pig	pigs	pigging	pigged	pigged
pin	pins	pinning	pinned	pinned
pine	pines	pining	pined	pined
pip	pips	pipping	pipped	pipped
pipe	pipes	piping	piped	piped
pique	piques	piquing	piqued	piqued
pit	pits	pitting	pitted	pitted
plague	plagues	plaguing	plagued	plagued
plane	planes	planing	planed	planed
plod	plods	plodding	plodded	plodded
plop	plops	plopping	plopped	plopped
plot	plots	plotting	plotted	plotted
plug	plugs	plugging	plugged	plugged
ply	plies	plying	plied	plied
pod	pods	podding	podded	podded
pop	pops	popping	popped	popped
pot	pots	potting	potted	potted
pray	prays	praying	prayed	prayed
prep	preps	prepping	prepped	prepped
prig	prigs	prigging	prigged	prigged
prim	prims	primming	primmed	primmed
prime	primes	priming	primed	primed
prod	prods	prodding	prodded	prodded
prop	props	propping	propped	propped
pry	pries	prying	pried	pried
pug	pugs	pugging	pugged	pugged
pun	puns	punning	punned	punned
putt	putts	putting	putted	putted
quip	quips	quipping	quipped	quipped
quiver	quivers	quivering	quivered	quivered
rag	rags	ragging	ragged	ragged
rage	rages	raging	raged	raged
rally	rallies	rallying	rallied	rallied
ram	rams	ramming	rammed	rammed
ramble	rambles	rambling	rambled	rambled
rattle	rattles	rattling	rattled	rattled
rebind	rebinds	rebinding	rebound	rebound
rebut	rebuts	rebutting	rebutted	rebutted
recap	recaps	recapping	recapped	recapped
recede	recedes	receding	receded	receded
recur	recurs	recurring	recurred	recurred
reflag	reflags	reflagging	reflagged	reflagged
rely	relies	relying	relied	relied
remake	remakes	remaking	remade	remade

Basic Form	3rd Person Singular	Present Participle	Past Tense	Past Participle
remit	remits	remitting	remitted	remitted
remodel	remodels	remodeling/ remodelling	remodeled/ remodelled	remodeled/ remodelled
repel	repels	repelling	repelled	repelled
reread	rereads	rereading	reread	reread
rerun	reruns	rerunning	reran	rerun
rescue	rescues	rescuing	rescued	rescued
reset	resets	resetting	reset	reset
rethink	rethinks	rethinking	rethought	rethought
retread	retreads	retreading	retreaded/retrod	retreaded/ retrodden
rev	revs	revving	revved	revved
reveal	reveals	revealing	revealed	revealed
revel	revels	reveling/revelling	reveled/revelled	reveled/revelled
rewind	rewinds	rewinding	rewound	rewound
rib	ribs	ribbing	ribbed	ribbed
rim	rims	rimming	rimmed	rimmed
rip	rips	ripping	ripped	ripped
rival	rivals	rivaling/rivalling	rivaled/rivalled	rivaled/rivalled
rive	rives	riving	rived	riven/rived
rivet	rivets	riveting	riveted	riveted
robe	robes	robing	robed	robed
rot	rots	rotting	rotted	rotted
rub	rubs	rubbing	rubbed	rubbed
rue	rues	ruing	rued	rued
sag	sags	sagging	sagged	sagged
sap	saps	sapping	sapped	sapped
scab	scabs	scabbing	scabbed	scabbed
scan	scans	scanning	scanned	scanned
scar	scars	scarring	scarred	scarred
scare	scares	scaring	scared	scared
scram	scrams	scramming	scrammed	scrammed
scrap	scraps	scrapping	scrapped	scrapped
scrape	scrapes	scraping	scraped	scraped
scrub	scrubs	scrubbing	scrubbed	scrubbed
scrunch	scrunches	scrunching	scrunched	scrunched
scud	scuds	scudding	scudded	scudded
scum	scums	scumming	scummed	scummed
shag	shags	shagging	shagged	shagged
shall	shall		should	
sham	shams	shamming	shammed	shammed
shear	shears	shearing	sheared	sheared/shorn
sheer	sheers	sheering	sheered	sheered
shellac	shellacs	shellacking	shellacked	shellacked
shin	shins	shinning	shinned	shinned
ship	ships	shipping	shipped	shipped

Basic Form	3rd Person Singular	Present Participle	Past Tense	Past Participle
shoe	shoes	shoing	shod	shod/shodden
shot	shots	shotting	shotted	shotted
shrive	shrives	shriving	shrove/shrived	shriven/shrived
shrivel	shrivels	shriveling/ shrivelling	shriveled/ shrivelled	shriveled/ shrivelled
shrug	shrugs	shrugging	shrugged	shrugged
shy	shies	shying	shied	shied
sin	sins	sinning	sinned	sinned
skid	skids	skidding	skidded	skidded
skim	skims	skimming	skimmed	skimmed
skin	skins	skinning	skinned	skinned
skip	skips	skipping	skipped	skipped
sky	skies	skying	skied	skied
slab	slabs	slabbing	slabbed	slabbed
slam	slams	slamming	slammed	slammed
slap	slaps	slapping	slapped	slapped
sled	sleds	sledding	sledded	sledded
slew	slews	slewing	slewed	slewed
slim	slims	slimming	slimmed	slimmed
slink	slinks	slinking	slunk/slinked	slunk/slinked
slog	slogs	slogging	slogged	slogged
slop	slops	slopping	slopped	slopped
slope	slopes	sloping	sloped	sloped
slot	slots	slotting	slotted	slotted
slub	slubs	slubbing	slubbed	slubbed
slue	slues	sluing	slued	slued
slug	slugs	slugging	slugged	slugged
slum	slums	slumming	slummed	slummed
slur	slurs	slurring	slurred	slurred
smite	smites	smiting	smote	smitten/smote
smut	smuts	smutting	smutted	smutted
snag	snags	snagging	snagged	snagged
snap	snaps	snapping	snapped	snapped
snip	snips	snipping	snipped	snipped
snipe	snipes	sniping	sniped	sniped
snub	snubs	snubbing	snubbed	snubbed
snug	snugs	snugging	snugged	snugged
sob	sobs	sobbing	sobbed	sobbed
sod	sods	sodding	sodded	sodded
sop	sops	sopping	sopped	sopped
spat	spats	spatting	spatted	spatted
spec	specs	spec'ing/speccing	spec'd/specced	spec'd/specced
spiral	spirals	spiraling/spiralling	spiraled/spiralled	spiraled/spiralled
spot	spots	spotting	spotted	spotted
sprig	sprigs	sprigging	sprigged	sprigged
spur	spurs	spurring	spurred	spurred
spy	spies	spying	spied	spied

Basic Form	3rd Person Singular	Present Participle	Past Tense	Past Participle
squat	squats	squatting	squatted	squatted
squelch	squelches	squelching	squelched	squelched
squib	squibs	squibbing	squibbed	squibbed
squirrel	squirrels	squirreling/ squirrelling	squirreled/ squirrelled	squirreled/ squirrelled
stab	stabs	stabbing	stabbed	stabbed
stag	stags	stagging	stagged	stagged
stage	stages	staging	staged	staged
star	stars	starring	starred	starred
stare	stares	staring	stared	stared
stave	staves	staving	staved/stove	staved/stove
steer	steers	steering	steered	steered
stem	stems	stemming	stemmed	stemmed
step	steps	stepping	stepped	stepped
stir	stirs	stirring	stirred	stirred
stitch	stitches	stitching	stitched	stitched
stoop	stoops	stooping	stooped	stooped
stope	stopes	stoping	stoped	stoped
strap	straps	strapping	strapped	strapped
strip	strips	stripping	stripped	stripped
stripe	stripes	striping	striped	striped
strop	strops	stropping	stropped	stropped
strum	strums	strumming	strummed	strummed
strut	struts	strutting	strutted	strutted
stub	stubs	stubbing	stubbed	stubbed
stud	studs	studding	studded	studded
stun	stuns	stunning	stunned	stunned
sub	subs	subbing	subbed	subbed
subdue	subdues	subduing	subdued	subdued
submit	submits	submitting	submitting	submitting
sum	sums	summing	summed	summed
summon	summons	summoning	summoned	summoned
summons	summonses	summonsing	summonsed	summonsed
sun	suns	sunning	sunned	sunned
sunburn	sunburns	sunburning	sunburned/ sunburnt	sunburned/ sunburnt
sup	sups	supping	supped	supped
swab	swabs	swabbing	swabbed	swabbed
swag	swags	swagging	swagged	swagged
swap	swaps	swapping	swapped	swapped
swivel	swivels	swiveling/ swivelling	swiveled/ swivelled	swiveled/ swivelled
tab	tabs	tabbing	tabbed	tabbed
taboo	taboos	tabooing	tabooed	tabooed
tabu	tabus	tabuing	tabued	tabued
tag	tags	tagging	tagged	tagged

Basic Form	3rd Person Singular	Present Participle	Past Tense	Past Participle
talc	talcs	talcking/talcing	talcked/talced	talcked/talced
tan	tans	tanning	tanned	tanned
tap	taps	tapping	tapped	tapped
tar	tars	tarring	tarred	tarred
tax	taxes	taxing	taxed	taxed
teasel	teasels	teaseling/teaselling	teaseled/teaselled	teaseled/teaselled
tech	techs	teching	teched	teched
tee	tees	teeing	teed	teed
telecast	telecasts	telecasting	telecast/telecasted	telecast/telecasted
thin	thins	thinning	thinned	thinned
throb	throbs	throbbing	throbbed	throbbed
thrum	thrums	thrumming	thrummed	thrummed
thud	thuds	thudding	thudded	thudded
tic	tics	ticcing	ticced	ticced
tick	ticks	ticking	ticked	ticked
ticket	tickets	ticketing	ticketed	ticketed
tin	tins	tinning	tinned	tinned
tip	tips	tipping	tipped	tipped
toe	toes	toeing	toed	toed
tog	togs	togging	togged	togged
top	tops	topping	topped	topped
total	totals	totaling/totalling	totaled/totalled	totaled/totalled
trammel	trammels	trammeling/ trammelling	trammeled/ trammelled	trammeled/ trammelled
trap	traps	trapping	trapped	trapped
travel	travels	traveling/travelling	traveled/travelled	traveled/travelled
tree	trees	treeing	treed	treed
trek	treks	trekking	trekked	trekked
trifle	trifles	trifling	trifled	trifled
trim	trims	trimming	trimmed	trimmed
trip	trips	tripping	tripped	tripped
trolley	trolleys	trolleying	trolleyed	trolleyed
trot	trots	trotting	trotted	trotted
tub	tubs	tubbing	tubbed	tubbed
tug	tugs	tugging	tugged	tugged
tumble	tumbles	tumbling	tumbled	tumbled
unbend	unbends	unbending	unbent	unbent
unbind	unbinds	unbinding	unbound	unbound
unbuckle	unbuckles	unbuckling	unbuckled	unbuckled
underbid	underbids	underbidding	underbid	underbid
underwrite	underwrites	underwriting	underwrote	underwritten
unfreeze	unfreezes	unfreezing	unfroze	unfrozen
unify	unifies	unifying	unified	unified
unmake	unmakes	unmaking	unmade	unmade
unravel	unravels	unraveling/ unravelling	unraveled/ unravelled	unraveled/ unravelled

Basic Form	3rd Person Singular	Present Participle	Past Tense	Past Participle
untie	unties	untying	untied	untied
unwind	unwinds	unwinding	unwound	unwound
up	ups	upping	upped	upped
uphold	upholds	upholding	upheld	upheld
value	values	valuing	valued	valued
van	vans	vanning	vanned	vanned
vat	vats	vatting	vatted	vatted
vet	vets	vetting	vetted	vetted
veto	vetoes	vetoing	vetoed	vetoed
vial	vials	vialing/vialling	vialed/vialled	vialed/vialled
vie	vies	vying	vied	vied
volley	volleys	volleying	volleyed	volleyed
wad	wads	wadding	wadded	wadded
wade	wades	wading	waded	waded
wag	wags	wagging	wagged	wagged
wage	wages	waging	waged	waged
wainscot	wainscots	wainscoting/ wainscotting	wainscoted/ wainscotted	wainscoted/ wainscotted
waltz	waltzes	waltzing	waltzed	waltzed
wan	wans	wanning	wanned	wanned
wane	wanes	waning	waned	waned
war	wars	warring	warred	warred
weasel	weasels	weaseling/ weaselling	weaseled/ weaselled	weaseled/ weaselled
web	webs	webbing	webbed	webbed
whet	whets	whetting	whetted	whetted
whir	whirs	whirring	whirred	whirred
whiz	whizzes	whizzing	whizzed	whizzed
whop	whops	whopping	whopped	whopped
whoop	whoops	whooping	whooped	whoopped
wig	wigs	wigging	wigged	wigged
wigwag	wigwags	wigwagging	wigwagged	wigwagged
will	will		would	
wind	winds	winding	winded	winded
woo	woos	wooing	wooed	wooed
wow	wows	wowing	wowed	wowed
wreak	wreaks	wreaking	wreaked	wreaked
yak	yaks	yakking	yakked	yakked
yap	yaps	yapping	yapped	yapped
yip	yips	yipping	yipped	yipped
yodel	yodels	yodeling/yodelling	yodeled/yodelled	yodeled/yodelled
yo-yo	yo-yos	yo-yoing	yo-yoed	yo-yoed
zag	zags	zagging	zagged	zagged

Basic Form	3rd Person Singular	Present Participle	Past Tense	Past Participle
zap	zaps	zapping	zapped	zapped
zig	zigs	zigging	zigged	zigged
zigzag	zigzags	zigzagging	zigzagged	zigzagged
zinc	zincs/zincks	zincing/zincking	zinced/zincked	zinced/zincked
zing	zings	zinging	zinged	zinged

501 Verb Drills and Exercises

The following drills and exercises will help you review and practice the material presented in the book. You will have an opportunity to work with the forms required to speak and write English correctly. The answers to all of the exercises are found beginning on page 624. As you work your way through each of these exercises, be sure to reread the material contained in the introductory pages (vi–xix) If you have any doubts you can always look up the verb form in the alphabetical listing of the 501 Verbs. Some verbs can be found in the section "Another 550 Problem Verbs."

Tip: English, like other languages, is a system. There is a reason for everything. Before you can use the correct form, you must have a reason for selecting that tense, voice, and mood. Only then can you apply the rules for the proper endings. Verbs are key words in an English sentence, but their form and function normally depend on the grammatical subject of the sentence. So first identify that subject, then examine the context, and then select the correct form. Keep in mind that irregular verbs require special handling. Good luck, and enjoy yourself on your way to mastery of the English verb forms!

Exercise 1

The Present Tense

Convert the verb in *italics* into the correct form for the blank space.

1. I promise to *try* if he _____.
2. She *asks* a lot of questions. Why don't you _____ one?
3. I promise to *begin* as soon as Mom _____.
4. Do you *believe* what your father _____?
5. To win, you must *bid* more than the other person _____.
6. If one side decides to *sue*, the other side automatically _____.
7. Who *dares* to enter where even angels _____ not go?
8. I never seem to *dream*, but my daughter _____ all the time.
9. I never *drink* alcohol when my dinner companion _____?
10. Do you *see* what I _____?
11. I rarely *guess* at the answers, but my brother often _____ correctly.
12. He *catches* fish for a living; I never _____ anything.
13. If no one *establishes* the rules of the game, who _____ the winner?
14. I don't *cry* often, but there are times when a man _____.
15. They told us to *radio* for help, but the captain never _____ without good reason.
16. I want to *go* to the movies tonight, but my sister never _____.
17. Since everyone is *pushing* back and forth, it's hard to know who _____ whom.
18. I would like to learn how to *Google* a word definition. Steve _____ all the time.
19. My computer *crashes* about once a week. They say that the new computers no longer _____ so frequently.
20. You can always *fax* me the proposal. No one _____ such an important document!
21. I *ski* every day, but my sister _____ only on weekends.

22. When you *do* the laundry, Mom _____ the dishes.
23. I *miss* my family; my family _____ me.
24. We *play* for fun; the professional golfer _____ for money.
25. When I *lie* in my bed, the dog _____ on the floor.

Exercise 2

The Present Participle and the Progressive

Insert the verb in parentheses into the correct Present Progressive form. Be sure to include the proper form of the verb "be."

Example: (go) They ____ _____ to the movies.
              They *are going* to the movies.

1. (arrive)   They _____ _____ after midnight.
2. (argue)   He ____ _____ over nothing.
3. (browse)   The young children ____ _____ the Internet.
4. (consult)   The authors _____ _____ with the editors.
5. (crash)   All of our computers ____ _____ at the same time.
6. (dine)   We _____ _____ with friends this evening.
7. (free)   They ____ _____ the captive birds tomorrow morning.
8. (sew)   The mothers _____ _____ the costumes.
9. (drive)   They ____ _____ home after the game.
10. (go)   I ___ _____ to the concert next week.
11. (sell)   _____ you _____ your house?
12. (wear)   What ___ she _____?
13. (mop)   Who ___ _____ the floor before the guests arrive?
14. (host)   We ___ _____ a major conference on that issue.
15. (lie)   She must find out which one ___ _____.
16. (transmit) I ____ _____ the e-mails at this moment.
17. (e-mail) You ___ always ____ your friends during the workday.
18. (quit)   I ___ not _____ until the job is done correctly.
19. (put)   He ___ _____ his coat on.
20. (take)   She ___ _____ her coat off.
21. (join)   We ___ _____ a dancing class this Saturday.
22. (bring)   _____ someone _____ the butter?
23. (ski)   The champion ___ _____ down the mountain.
24. (rent)   The owner ___ _____ her garage.
25. (bid)   We ___ _____ for a new computer.

Exercise 3

The Past Tense

The Past Active form of regular verbs is formed by adding "d" after a vowel and "ed" after a consonant, but there are some exceptions that you should check on page xii.

Insert the verb in parentheses into the correct Past Tense form.

1. (mention)   She _____ his name only once.
2. (realize)   I just _____ how expensive that was.
3. (move)   They _____ again last month.
4. (guess)   He never _____ the winning numbers.
5. (smile)   He always _____ at us on the way to work.
6. (order)   She _____ soup and a salad.
7. (listen)   The boss _____ for only a few minutes.
8. (bake)   Mama _____ the cookies last evening.
9. (love)   She never _____ anyone as much as her first husband.
10. (annoy)   He _____ his neighbors all evening long.
11. (agree)   We all _____ to meet next year.
12. (cry)   The baby _____ half the night.
13. (carry)   He _____ the groceries out to the car.
14. (rip)   He _____ the ad out of the newspaper.
15. (blog)   They _____ with one another for more than a year.
16. (chat)   They _____ online before they met.
17. (program)   The technician _____ the computer to shut off automatically.
18. (jog)   They _____ all around Central Park.
19. (dance)   The old couple _____ the whole night through.
20. (die)   The old woman _____ with a smile on her face.
21. (echo)   The senator _____ the words of his colleagues.
22. (wrap)   The medic _____ his injury with bandages.
23. (x-ray)   The nurse _____ his leg to search for broken bones.
24. (spill)   The baby _____ the milk all over the kitchen table.
25. (drop)   The player _____ the ball and the whistle blew.

Exercise 4

The Past Tense of Irregular Verbs

Irregular verbs (some languages call them "strong" verbs) have different ways of forming that past tense, (i.e., they do not have the normal "d" or "ed" ending). Be sure to check the correct forms provided in the alphabetical listing of verbs.

Convert the verb in *italics* into the Past Tense for the blank space.

1. I don't want to *eat* fish again today. I _____ fish yesterday.
2. Did you *see* the new film? I _____ it last week.
3. I have no money to *spend*. I _____ my allowance on my boots.

4. Did you *bring* the books back to the library? I _____ them back this morning.

5. Are you *going* home after work? The boss _____ an hour ago.

6. I can't *sing* anymore today. I _____ for three hours last night.

7. Can you *drive* me to the doctor's office? You _____ me last time.

8. I can *run* ten miles a day. Yesterday I actually _____ twelve miles.

9. Did you *find* your ring? Mom said that she _____ it in the kitchen?

10. Do we need to *wind* the clock? No, Jenny _____ it yesterday.

11. Didn't I *tell* you not to sleep so long? You _____ me no such thing.

12. What was he *thinking*? I _____ he knew where he was going.

13. How long did you *sleep* last night? Sarah _____ ten hours.

14. We have nothing to *drink*. Who _____ all the milk?

15. How did you *ring* in the New Year? We _____ it in with champagne.

16. Can I *hold* the trophy now? You _____ it yesterday.

17. Who is *choosing* the restaurant for this evening? They _____ last time.

18. You are always *forgetting* something. This morning you almost _____ to call a taxi.

19. I love to *read*. Last evening I _____ this book from cover to cover.

20. Who is *writing* the reply? I _____ the last one.

21. Do you *dream* often? I _____ the strangest thing last night.

22. Tonight the flowers might *freeze*. Last night they almost _____.

23. I wanted to *blow* out the candles! But someone already _____ them out.

24. I know what I can *do*. Do you know who _____ it?

25. Since you *can* get your homework done today, you _____ have done it yesterday.

Exercise 5

The Verb "be"

Perhaps the most frequently used and the most irregular verb in the English language is the verb "be" in all of its forms. See if you can fill in the blanks using just this verb.

"To _____, or not to _____, that is the question." Some say it _____ foolish to ____ an actor. When I _____ in high school, many students _____ actors. But since they _____ now adults, they ____ not willing to appear foolish in front of other adults. Children can _____ more natural. They do not seem to care if anyone _____ in the audience. They will ____ ready at a moment's notice to put on costumes and makeup and then _____ someone else on stage.

I sometimes wish that I _____ a child again. "____ yourself," my father used to say. He _____ a great singer, and I ____ sure that he ____ being sincere when he told me: "If you try you ____ _____ a great actor or singer too." If he _____ _____ there to see my acting debut, I _____ sure that he would ____ _____ proud of me. Mom ____ happy to see me, and we ____ never ____ sure that Dad ____ not right by her side.

Exercise 6

A Word Maze of Irregular Verbs

Find the Past Tense forms of these twenty-five irregular verbs in the maze.

1. go	6. read	11. do	16. can	21. lead
2. hit	7. rid	12. wear	17. write	22. deal
3. ride	8. spin	13. unwind	18. say	23. bite
4. bend	9. spend	14. drink	19. string	24. dig
5. wear	10. undo	15. get	20. see	25. fall

D	U	G	O	C	O	U	L	D	A
E	F	E	D	R	I	D	F	M	K
L	B	I	T	O	B	H	E	G	O
I	S	A	I	D	E	I	L	N	W
S	A	W	W	E	N	T	L	T	R
T	O	G	O	T	T	M	K	L	O
R	E	S	R	E	A	D	N	A	T
U	S	P	E	N	T	O	A	E	E
N	Z	U	N	D	I	D	R	D	P
G	U	N	W	O	U	N	D	L	A

Exercise 7

The Present Tense of Irregular Verbs

Irregular verbs do not have the normal "d" or "ed" past tense ending. The past tense form might not give all the clues necessary to find the basic dictionary form. Some of these you will simply have to memorize. Try your best. Be sure to check the correct forms provided in the alphabetical listing of verbs.

Insert the basic form of the Past Tense verb in the blank space.

1. I spoke with him last night, but we need to _____ again.
2. I forbade you to smoke. Now I must _____ you to buy any tobacco products.
3. Where did you lose your hat? Your father never _____ anything.
4. Who sat next to you last week? This week you _____ right here.
5. Who got the joker? I never seem to _____ it.
6. Your aunt caught a cold at the skating rink. She _____ the flu every winter.
7. He sped past the police officer? That car _____ past here every day.
8. Someone stole my car keys? Why would anyone _____ them?
9. We met at the party. I almost never _____ new people.

10. The first plane left an hour ago. The next one _____ in ten minutes.

11. The skater spun around on the ice. I wish I could _____ like that.

12. He stood in line for over ten hours. I _____ that long in my job.

13. They all sought freedom in America. Even today immigrants _____ a better life.

14. They fought long and hard, but you can only _____ for so long.

15. Who already took a shower? I never _____ my shower first.

16. They dug into the mine deep into the night. Sometimes they _____ all day and night.

17. The bird dove down to the surface of the water. Where did she learn how to _____ like that?

18. Yesterday we drew real faces. Usually we _____ inanimate objects.

19. She hid her money from her husband. I wonder what he _____ from her.

20. Last year the hunter shot only one deer. This year he didn't _____ a thing.

21. The child shook the tree with all her might. When she _____ it, lots of acorns fall down.

22. I was struck by your comments. It isn't often that we _____ people with our words.

23. The *Titanic* sank in a matter of hours. Do you think a cruise ship can _____ today?

24. They hung wallpaper all afternoon. Now that I have seen it, I can _____ some too.

25. Was that the first time you rode on our subway? Most New Yorkers _____ the subway to work everyday.

Exercise 8

The Passive Voice

The Passive Participle form is used for all of the Passive Voice tenses.
Convert the following verbs into the Passive Voice to complete the sentences correctly.

1. (add)   Her name was _____ to the list.

2. (attend)   The meeting was not very well _____.

3. (believe)   Those outrageous statements simply cannot be _____

4. (change)   Before we have improvements, some things have to be _____.

5. (contain)   The flu outbreak could not be _____.

6. (drop)   The charges against my defendant were _____.

7. (excuse)   You may be _____.

8. (form)   These mountain ranges were _____ millions of years ago.

9. (give)   Your word should not be _____ lightly.

10. (help)   It could not be _____.

11. (improve)   I hope that next semester your grades can be _____.

12. (knit)   These socks were _____ by his grandmother.

13. (limit)   The losses were _____ by the quick response of the emergency crew.

14. (move)   These toys on the floor will have to be _____.

15. (obtain)   Do you know whose permission has to be _____?

16. (quiz)   The boys were _____ on the accident.

17. (reduce)   The deficits should be _____ in the next five years.

18. (remember) How do you wish to be _____?

19. (shampoo)   The carpets can be _____ for better results.
20. (serve)   The country was well _____ by the general.
21. (treat)   We were _____ to homemade ice cream cones.
22. (turn)   The patient was _____ over onto her side.
23. (use)   How many gallons of fuel were _____ for the trip?
24. (watch)   Do you think the Olympics will be _____ in many nations?
25. (xerox)   Can those documents be _____ before the meeting?

Exercise 9

The Past Passive Participle of Irregular Verbs

For some irregular verbs the Past Participle form is identical to the Past Tense. But in others there are two distinct forms, one for the Past and one for the Participle. When in doubt be sure to consult the corresponding verb in the alphabetical list.

Convert the verbs in parentheses first into the Past Tense and then into the Past Participle form.

1. (begin)   The first group _____ playing at eight. By nine o'clock, all of the groups had _____.

2. (break)   She _____ the record on her first run, but even her record had been _____ by the end of the competition.

3. (drink)   The couple _____ a small bottle of wine. By evening's end, the bottle had been completely _____.

4. (catch)   Father _____ a cold. By the end of the week, all of the children had also _____ it.

5. (drive)   They _____ for hours. By nightfall, they had _____ 500 miles.

6. (forbid)   I _____ you to leave this house. For the next month, all phone calls are _____.

7. (forget)   He _____ my birthday. Such things are not to be _____.

8. (hide)   Who _____ the children's presents? Yes, they are all well _____.

9. (grow)   Last year the corn _____ slowly. This year it has already _____ over my head.

10. (hear)   I _____ his last speech. Few people before that time had _____ his name.

11. (know)   What he _____ is not everything that was _____ about the case.

12. (meet)   When we _____, we were certain that we had _____ before.

13. (lie)   He simply _____. I am not accustomed to be being _____ to.

14. (mistake)   I think we _____ the date. Yes, unfortunately you are _____.

15. (outbid)   I think we _____ the others. No, you were _____.

16. (overfeed) I'm sure I _____ the fish. They certainly appear to be _____.

17. (redo)   Last month we _____ our bathroom. Now the entire house has been _____.

18. (rent)   Last year she _____ her garage. It has been _____ before.

19. (shake)   We _____ the host's hand. How many hands have been _____ today?

20. (send)   They _____ the package last week to Martha. Why hasn't ours been _____?

21. (speak)   The critic _____ out on the movie. Nothing more need be _____.

22. (teach)   She _____ her children their manners. Her children certainly have been well
                 _____.

23. (unfreeze) The plumber _____ the pipes. Yes, the pipes are now _____.

24. (uphold)   He consistently _____ the laws of the land. His decisions were always
                 _____.

25. (write)   I wrote you last week. Why have you not _____ me?

Exercise 10

The Imperative

The Imperative Mood is used to give an order, command, demand, or request, and it sometimes is simply used in giving directions. The Active Imperative form is the same as the basic form of the verb.

For extra practice we have included here the Past Tense or Passive Participle forms of several irregular verbs. Be sure to find their correct basic form.

Convert the Past Tense verb in *italics* into the Imperative in the blank space.

1. Since Sally *began* yesterday, today it is your turn. Please _____.
2. I don't think you *bit* hard enough. _____ again.
3. You *chose* the wrong answer. _____ another one.
4. You have *cried* enough. _____ no more.
5. You *did* it perfectly the first time. ____ it again.
6. You haven't *dug* deep enough. _____ some more.
7. If you already *drank* all the orange juice, _____ some water.
8. You *ate* your potatoes; now _____ your vegetables.
9. If you already *fed* the cat, then please _____ the dog.
10. If you didn't *get* a winning number, _____ another one.
11. Joe *went* just a minute ago; _____ after him.
12. Last year the students *kept* their rooms very neat. _____ your own room just as clean and neat.
13. Who *lit* the first candle? _____ the others now.
14. Your sister *mowed* the lawn last week. _____ it before you go to town.
15. You have *overslept* once too often. Do not _____ one more time.
16. I noticed that your accomplice *pled* guilty. _____ "not guilty."
17. Since I *paid* last time, you _____ this time.
18. I *told* them not to make so much noise. _____ them again.
19. If you haven't *taken* your shower yet, then _____ one now.
20. If you *rode* the subway here, then _____ it back home.
21. Since the others *ran* this morning, you _____ this afternoon.
22. I wasn't here when you *sang* that song. Please _____ it for me.
23. I *swam* a mile this morning. Now you _____.
24. This room hasn't been *swept*. Please _____ before the guests arrive.
25. The team *won* the game yesterday. _____ this one today.

The Subjunctive

The Present Subjunctive is used with a "that" clause after verbs, adjectives, or nouns; for a condition; and in some set expressions of desire.

The Past Subjunctive describes something hypothetical or unreal. It often occurs after words like "if, as if, though, wish, suppose."

Insert the correct forms of the Subjunctive for the verbs in parentheses.

1. (frighten)   If he _____ you, he will be punished.
2. (train)   It was as if they had _____ for months, not days.
3. (serve)   He had always dreamt that he _____ his country well.
4. (recognize)   It was as if she _____ him at first sight.
5. (shave)   If you had _____, you would not have scratched me.
6. (do)   I wish that things _____ better in your office.
7. (be)   We wish that you _____ here.
8. (link)   The two networks should be _____ together.
9. (interface)   He suggested that the company _____ with its suppliers.
10. (save)   He thought that he _____ the day.
11. (market)   He insisted that they _____ their goods overseas.
12. (network)   I think you _____ with friends and former colleagues.
13. (break)   If the bone were _____, we might apply a cast to the leg.
14. (auction)   If the painting were _____, it could sell for over a million dollars.
15. (diet)   If only they had _____, they would have been able to compete.
16. (plead)   Had he only _____ "not guilty."
17. (order)   If you should _____ a dessert, I will try some.
18. (close)   If the store _____, we would have saved lots of money.
19. (love)   If you _____ her, let her go.
20. (learn)   If good manners were _____ in school, they would be apparent to us all.
21. (leave)   If you _____ before I return, please lock the door.
22. (give)   I requested that he _____ the money back to us.
23. (hit)   Had only the hurricane _____ after the city was evacuated.
24. (quit)   I wish I had _____ while I was ahead.
25. (seek)   If only peace were _____, it might be found.

More Practice on the Present Tense

Convert the verb form in *italics* into the correct form for the blank space.

1. In a compromise, I *benefit* if he _____.
2. I *can* do it, and my sister _____ too.
3. We all *envy* Joe, but he _____ no one.
4. The boys *dry* the dishes, but Mom always _____ the glasses.

5. We never *gripe*, but our teacher _____ all the time.
6. *Hide* your money where no one _____ it.
7. If you cannot *issue* a pass, please tell me who _____ them.
8. I *may* not come. Mother also _____ not come.
9. While I *fry* the bacon, Dad _____ the eggs.
10. I rarely *mop* the floor, but my brother _____ it every Saturday.
11. You can *overdo* a good thing. The wise man never _____ anything.
12. If we all want to *partake* in the glory, he too _____.
13. You will not be *fined* unless the police officer _____ you.
14. They tell us not to *panic*, but the boss _____ whenever there is a crisis.
15. I want to *rely* on the weather report, but one never _____ on just one report.
16. We *pray* for the soldier; he _____ for peace.
17. I *must* learn to download music. My student _____ learn how to play the guitar.
18. Firefighters *rescue* people every day. Who _____ a firefighter?
19. We need to *squelch* those rumors. No one _____ a rumor better than the press spokesperson!
20. All governments *tax* individuals. Who _____ businesses?
21. I *value* your loyalty. The company _____ your hard work.
22. Who can *veto* such a decision? Only the president _____ bills.
23. I love to *waltz*, and my wife _____ beautifully.
24. Some dogs *wag* their tails for joy. My dog _____ her tail when she wants to go outside.
25. I *shy* away from conflict. My husband never _____ away from it.

Exercise 13

The Present Participle and the Progressive

Convert the verb in parentheses into the correct Present Progressive form. Be sure to include the proper form of the verb "be."

Example: (go) They ____ _____ to the movies.
They *are going* to the movies.

1. (abet)   They _____ _____ the criminal.
2. (access)   He ____ _____ the Internet through his provider.
3. (bid)   My wife ____ _____ on the vacation.
4. (drip)   The melting snow _____ _____ from the trees.
5. (dry)   The clothes ____ _____ on the line outside.
6. (exhibit) We _____ _____ our paintings at the gallery next month.
7. (expel)   The school ____ _____ the disruptive students.
8. (flap)   The flag _____ _____ in the wind.
9. (fry)   They ____ _____ the fish in a pan.
10. (gape)   What ____ you _____ at?
11. (grab)   The little boy _____ _____ his mother's dress.
12. (hug)   Everyone ____ _____ one another.

13. (input)   We ___ _____ the data right now.

14. (jam)   They ___ _____ our radio signal.

15. (jog)   ___ anyone _____ with me this morning?

16. (kid)   I know that he ___ only _____.

17. (lag)   You ___ always ____ behind the others.

18. (mope)   Once again you ____ _____ around and doing nothing.

19. (nap)   The baby ___ _____ in her crib.

20. (omit)   For the next round we ___ _____ the personal interview.

21. (panic)   They ___ _____ without any reason.

22. (plot)   We do not know who ____ ____ against us.

23. (put)   Dad ___ _____ out the garbage.

24. (rally)   We ___ all _____ to her side.

25. (recede)   The floodwaters ____ _____ for the moment.

Exercise 14

More Work on the Past Tense

The Past Active form of regular verbs is formed by adding "d" after a vowel and "ed" after a consonant, but there are some exceptions that you should check on page xii.

Convert the verb in parentheses into the correct Past Tense form.

1. (answer)   She _____ correctly.

2. (allot)   I _____ him plenty of time to complete the assignment.

3. (bop)   The little boy _____ the doll on its head.

4. (cancel)   He never _____ his reservation.

5. (cap)   We _____ the increase at 3 percent.

6. (commit)   She _____ a crime in leaving the scene of the accident.

7. (control)   The boss _____ the flow of the meeting.

8. (debug)   The technician _____ my computer in a few minutes.

9. (don)   She never _____ that hat again.

10. (dot)   Small cottages _____ the landscape.

11. (empty)   We _____ all the trash cans.

12. (flip)   The monkey _____ over in his cage.

13. (grin)   He _____ at the passersby.

14. (inherit)   She _____ the entire estate.

15. (jot)   They _____ down their thoughts before they left.

16. (knot)   We _____ all the lines.

17. (lug)   He _____ the suitcase up the stairs.

18. (marr)   Rain _____ the parade.

19. (mete)   The judge _____ out a harsh sentence.

20. (nod)   The old woman _____ to the nurse.

21. (patrol)   The company _____ the woods.

22. (pin)   The kids "_____ the tail on the donkey."

23. (pry)   The carpenter _____ the nail out of the board.
24. (rub)   The mother _____ the oil over the baby's soft skin.
25. (scrape)   The little girl _____ her knee playing in the school yard.

Exercise 15

More Past Tense Irregular Verbs

Be sure to check the correct forms provided both in the main alphabetical listings and in the section "Another 550 Problem Verbs."
Insert the correct form of the Past Tense in the blank space.

1. Issues like that arise all the time. Yesterday another one _____.
2. Did you tear your new stockings? Yes, I _____ them on a nail.
3. She always loses her money at gambling. Yesterday she _____ a month's salary.
4. Did you buy the tickets? I _____ two on the Internet.
5. How far can you throw a football? I once _____ one fifty yards.
6. The boss strides about authoritatively. She just _____ off to her next meeting.
7. I can't sing anymore today. I _____ for three hours last night.
8. Did you grind the coffee beans? Yes, dear, I _____ them this morning.
9. Be careful they do not creep up on us like they _____ up yesterday.
10. Can you ever outwear a good pair of jeans? I definitely _____ this pair.
11. Be careful the watch doesn't sink. Oh, it already _____.
12. I would like to fly a plane. I never _____ one.
13. No one intentionally overeats. But I certainly _____ at their wedding reception.
14. All the children must leave before it gets dark. Sally already _____.
15. We need someone to sing the national anthem. Who _____ it at the last game?
16. The compost pile should not stink. Well, it certainly _____ this morning.
17. Why is the baby constantly falling? He _____ on his face just a minute ago.
18. The sun shines brightly in the summer. Yesterday it _____ all day long.
19. Who can send her a reminder? I _____ one last week.
20. Who stands guard this evening? I _____ my post last night.
21. I do not understand this problem. I _____ all the problems yesterday.
22. Can you undo the damage? We already _____ it.
23. We would like to underwrite your costs. We _____ your project the last time.
24. The court can uphold that decision. That judge _____ our last appeal.
25. We can withhold payment if the goods are not delivered. We _____ it once in the past month.

Exercise 16

A Word Maze of Irregular Verbs

Find the Present Tense of the twenty-five Past Tense irregular verbs in the maze.

1. told	6. bore	11. knew	16. lit	21. began
2. sat	7. kept	12. awoke	17. came	22. spoke
3. flew	8. froze	13. paid	18. wrote	23. sang
4. did	9. bought	14. slid	19. fed	24. found
5. made	10. lay	15. won	20. spent	25. left

Z	C	O	M	E	B	O	D	P	L
L	I	E	S	P	E	N	D	A	A
O	F	U	W	L	A	F	L	Y	W
S	I	N	G	E	R	R	I	T	A
P	N	T	M	A	K	E	G	E	K
E	D	I	S	V	I	E	H	L	E
A	K	S	L	E	S	Z	T	L	T
K	E	Y	I	S	F	E	E	D	I
L	E	U	D	D	K	N	O	W	R
Q	P	B	E	G	I	N	M	I	W

Exercise 17

Present or Past?

Some irregular verbs have a Past Tense that is spelled just like the Present Tense. Sometimes the pronunciation is different, however, and you should consult a good dictionary for those usages. In the third person Singular Present, these verbs have "s" or "es." In the Past Tense, there is no "s" form. In most cases you will have to determine from the context whether a verb is in the Present or Past Tense.

Read the following sentences paying close attention to words indicating present or past time; then indicate which tense the verb is in: Present or Past.

1. Yesterday he beat the odds and won the lottery.
2. Everyone bids at an auction.
3. We bet when we are on vacation.
4. The car burst into flames.
5. Our oak tree casts a long shadow.
6. The ring cost ten dollars.
7. Dad always cuts the firewood.

8. This shirt fit him well.

9. Who hit the jackpot?

10. My head hurts this morning.

11. Mama never knit him a sweater.

12. Who lets the dog out in the evening?

13. His expenses offset his earnings last year.

14. He consistently outbids his competitors.

15. A true winner never quits.

16. She read the newspaper before breakfast.

17. He rid himself of all temptations.

18. On Sundays Dad sets the table.

19. We all shed tears for their loss last week.

20. He always shreds documents with my name and address on them.

21. David shut the door.

22. She accidentally slit her finger on the knife.

23. I didn't swallow the chewing gum. I spit it out.

24. He always sweats when he jogs.

25. The rain barely wet the newly planted garden.

Exercise 18

The Past and Past Passive Participle

The Past Passive Participle is used to form the Present Perfect Tense often used in questions, such as, "Have you ever contributed to a political campaign?" The answer is frequently in the Simple Past Tense. "Yes, I contributed last year." The Past Participle for regular verbs is the same as the Past Tense form. For irregular verbs, you will have to consult the alphabetical listing.

Convert the verbs in parentheses first into the Past Participle form and then into the Past Tense.

1. (connect) Have they _____ your phone yet? They _____ my phone yesterday.

2. (base) Have they _____ their conclusion on the data? They _____ it on the latest findings.

3. (ask) Have you _____ for a glass of water? Yes, I _____ the waiter a minute ago.

4. (discover) Have they _____ the cause of the illness? Yes, they _____ it in the last set of tests.

5. (earn) Have you ever _____ any money? Yes, I _____ my allowance.

6. (form) Have you _____ a union? We _____ one last month.

7. (increase) Have they _____ your work? They _____ mine last week.

8. (listen) Have they _____ to the complaint? They _____ but took no action.

9. (handle) Have they _____ the new responsibilities well? Yes, they _____ them very well.

10. (move) Have they _____ the meeting date? Yes, they _____ it to Tuesday evening.

11. (look) Have you _____ under the bed? Yes, I _____ there first.

12. (gamble) Have you ever _____? I _____ last fall on a cruise ship.

13. (remember) Have you _____ where you put your keys? Yes, I _____ they were on my dresser.

14. (smile)   Has she ever _____? She _____ on her wedding day.

15. (shop)   Have you _____ in this mall before? Yes, we _____ here on our last visit.

16. (speak)   Have you _____of this matter with her? Yes, I _____ to her this morning.

17. (do)   Have you _____ your homework? I _____ it in school.

18. (swim)   Have you ever _____ a mile? I _____ a mile just this week.

19. (quit)   Has he _____ smoking? He _____ many years ago.

20. (send)   Have you _____ the package? We _____ it last Monday.

21. (get)   Have you _____ a flu shot? Yes, I _____ mine in October.

22. (forget)   Have you _____ his birthday again? You _____ it last year.

23. (sing)   Have you _____ in a choir before? I _____ in my school choir.

24. (see)   Have you _____ the new movie? We _____ it on Saturday evening.

25. (throw)   Have you _____ out the trash? I _____ it out after dinner.

Exercise 19

Irregular Verbs You Need to Know

The next exercise gives additional practice on the principal parts of some of the most frequently used irregular verbs.

Convert the basic form or Present Tense of the verb in *italics* into the correct forms for the blank spaces.

Example: I always *freeze* in the winter. I am _____ today. Last week I _____ at the hockey game. We were all _____ there.
I always freeze in the winter. I am *freezing* today. Last week I *froze* at the hockey game. We were all *frozen* there.

1. I *begin* each day with song. I am _____ today with a love song. Yesterday I _____ with a pop song. I have _____ each day this month with a new song.

2. I *fly* to Boston on Fridays. Today I am _____ in the evening. Last week I _____ in the morning. I have _____there for over a year.

3. He *makes* great cookies. He is _____some today. His mother _____ some for us. He has _____ cookies each day this week.

4. She *knows* all the verbs in this book. She _____ them last week. She has _____ most of them since her course.

5. My wife *runs* every day. She is _____ right now. She _____ in the marathon last year. She has _____ since she was a little girl.

6. They *stand* in the rear of the choir. They are _____ there right now. The men _____ in front only once. They have _____ in the rear ever since I can remember.

7. We all *take* showers before we swim. Who is _____ his shower now? John already _____ his. We have all _____ our showers today.

8. She *grows* tomatoes. This year she is _____ carrots. The tomatoes _____well last year. Tomatoes have been _____ here for years.

9. I always *buy* my groceries at the market. I am _____ some fresh cabbage this morning. I _____ lettuce last week. I have _____ vegetables here for a long time.

10. Who can *break* an egg? I am always _____ something. Last week I _____a light bulb. At least you can eat an egg that has been _____.

11. Can you *spin* the wheel? The wheel is already _____. Who _____ it last time? It has been _____already a dozen times.

12. I will *pay* the bill. Dad is already _____ it. You _____ last time. The important thing is that the bill has been _____.

13. He *sleeps* soundly at night. He is still _____. He _____ eight hours yesterday. He has _____ well in our new bed.

14. Can you *drive*? Mom is _____ the children to school. I _____ last week. Must you be _____ to work?

15. Can he *come*? He is _____. He _____ last time. He has _____every week.

16. I *meet* all our guests. I am _____ a new group this evening. I _____a new guest just last night. I have _____ over one hundred just this month.

17. He *swims* every morning. He is _____ right now. Last week he _____10 miles. He has _____ over 200 miles this year.

18. Babies *fall* often. That one is _____ and standing up again and again. We all _____ once. I have _____ while on skis and ice skates several times.

19. Is it time to *eat*? Who is _____ with us? They already _____. Most students have _____ before they come to visit.

20. Do you *drink* milk? The children are _____ their milk now. I already _____ a glass. Look, it's all been _____.

21. Can you *do* my hair? I am _____ your sister's first. But you _____ her hair first yesterday. Be patient. Your hair will get _____before you have to leave.

22. May I *go*? All my friends are _____? Billy _____when he was my age. I have never _____ before.

23. I always *hide* my money. Where are you _____ it? I already _____ it. Now I can't remember where it is _____.

24. What did she *say*? Can you hear what she is _____? She _____ that she was coming tonight. She has _____ that often, but she has never come.

25. You *spend* lots of money. I am _____ only what I earn. I _____ half of my salary this morning. Are your earnings all _____?

26. Do you *burn* wood for heat? Yes, we are _____oak logs. We _____ a cord of wood last winter. Has all your wood been _____ this year?

27. Who can *bring* the snacks? I am _____ the fruit. Mary _____ some vegetables. Has it all been _____ to the school?

28. I *forbid* you to go. I am also _____ your sister to go. My father _____ me. Why is it _____?

29. *Lie* down for a while. I am _____ down. I _____ down over an hour ago. I have _____ here for some time, but it has not helped.

30. *Lay* the baby in the crib. Mother is already _____ her there. She _____ her down this morning too. She will have _____ her to sleep before too long.

31. Who *keeps* the score? I am _____ it today. The other team _____ it last game. The time has always been _____ by a member of one of the teams.

32. Who *hits* our Internet site? People have been _____ it for weeks. The search engines finally _____ it last month. It was _____ over ten thousand times last week.

33. Who can *learn* this poem? We are _____ it in our class. I remember that I _____ it years ago. That poem has been _____ by thousands of schoolchildren.

34. *Lead* the way. I am _____. Who _____ last time? We were never _____ before.

35. I *read* a book a week. This week I am _____ a detective novel. Last week I _____ a romance. I have been _____ since I was a child.

36. He *bleeds* easily. His finger is _____ now. I _____ easily as a boy. My nose has _____ since last week.

37. Try not to *catch* a cold. I think I already am _____ a cold. My sister _____ one last week. Have you _____ the flu this year?

38. That dealer *sells* cars. We are _____ ours too. Last year he _____ many. This year he has already _____ a dozen cars.

39. Can you *prove* he is wrong? I am _____ it in court. I _____ our case to the judge. He ruled that our position was _____ by the evidence.

40. Did you *see* the new film? We are _____ it this afternoon. Our friends _____ it last week. The film has been _____ by millions.

41. *Choose* one color. We are _____. They _____ red. Our color was _____ for us.

42. He *builds* houses. We are _____ our own house. Our friends _____ one last year. Many houses have been recently _____ in this neighborhood.

43. She *deals* in stocks and bonds. We are _____ with just our savings. Our parents _____ only with a banker. We have _____ with the same bank for generations.

44. *Blow* out the candle. Who is _____ out the one in the living room? I already _____ that one out. All the candles have been _____ out.

45. It is not proper to *steal* a kiss. I am not _____ a kiss. You _____ one from me. That kiss was given; it was not _____.

46. *Swing* back and forth. That little boy is _____ too fast. I _____ on a trapeze once. We haven't _____ since we were children.

47. He *hangs* paintings for the museum. Today they are _____ a new exhibition. He _____ their last major show. It was _____ in just two days.

48. I *seek* an answer. I am always _____ answers. I _____ it in books. The answer to that question has been _____ since ancient times.

49. He *tears* interesting stories out of the newspaper. He is _____ one out just now. Last week I _____ out a story on London. I suspect it was _____ out by many others.

50. Who *shuts* the windows? I am _____ this one. Who _____ the other windows? They were _____ when we arrived.

51. I *am* glad I have finished. We were _____ very efficient. Yes, you _____. You have almost always _____ done on time.

501 Answers to Verb Drills and Exercises

The Present Tense

The Present Active for the first person singular and plural, second person singular and plural, and the third person plural is the basic form.

The Present Active for the third person singular (he, she, it) is normally formed by adding "s" after most consonants and all silent vowels.

After the combinations of "ss," "zz," "ch," "sh," "x," or after a vowel that is pronounced, we add "es." When a verb ends in "y" after a consonant, the "y" changes to an "i" and is followed by "es."

1. I promise to try if he *tries*. The third person singular form requires an "s." When a verb ends in "y" after a consonant, the "y" changes to an "i" and is followed by "es."

2. She asks a lot of questions. Why don't you *ask* one? The second person singular and plural use the basic form.

3. I promise to begin as soon as Mom *begins*. The third person singular (he, she, it) is normally formed by adding "s" after most consonants.

4. Do you believe what your father *believes*? The third person singular is normally formed by adding "s" after silent vowels.

5. To win, you must bid more than the other person *bids*. Add "s" after most consonants.

6. If one side decides to sue, the other side automatically *sues*. Add "s" after silent vowels.

7. Who dares to enter where even angels *dare* not go? The third person plural is the basic form.

8. I never seem to dream, but my daughter *dreams* all the time. Add "s" after most consonants.

9. I never drink alcohol when my dinner companion *drinks*. Add "s" after most consonants.

10. Do you see what I *see*? The first person singular is the basic form.

11. I rarely guess at the answers, but my brother often *guesses* correctly. After the combination of "ss," add "es."

12. He catches fish for a living; I never *catch* anything. The first person singular is the basic form.

13. If no one establishes the rules of the game, who *establishes* the winner? After the combination "sh," add "es."

14. I don't cry often, but there are times when a man *cries*. When a verb ends in "y" after a consonant, the "y" changes to an "i" and is followed by "es."

15. They told us to radio for help, but the captain never *radios* without good reason. This is an exception to the rule. Here the ending "s" is applied after two vowels that are pronounced.

16. I want to go to the movies tonight, but my sister never *goes*. After a vowel that is pronounced normally, add "es."

17. Since everyone is pushing back and forth, it's hard to know who *pushes* whom. After the combinations "sh," add "es."

18. I would like to learn how to *Google* a word definition. Steve *Googles* all the time. Add "s" after silent vowels.

19. My computer crashes about once a week. They say that the new computers no longer *crash* so frequently. The third person plural is the basic form.

20. You can always fax me the proposal. No one *faxes* such an important document! After "x," add "es."

21. I ski every day, but my sister *skis* only on weekends. This is an exception to the rule. Here the ending "s" is applied after a single vowel that is pronounced.

22. When you do the laundry, Mom *does* the dishes. After a vowel that is pronounced normally, add "es."

23. I miss my family; my family *misses* me. After the combination of "ss," add "es."

24. We play for fun; the professional golfer *plays* for money. Add "s" after consonants. Remember that "y" is a consonant.

25. When I lie in my bed, the dog *lies* on the floor. Here the ending "s" is applied after a silent vowel.

Exercise 2

The Present Participle and the Progressive

The Present Participle is used to form the Present and Future Progressive tenses. Most books simply say you form the present participle by adding "ing" to the basic form of the verb. Actually the rules for adding "ing" are similar to those for forming the past tense.

After a consonant, including "y," the letters "ing" are added:

She is working, opening, trying, marrying.

Verbs that end in a silent vowel drop the vowel and add "ing."

He is coming, deciding, hiding.

When a final vowel is pronounced, it remains before the "ing."

She will be radioing for help.

For verbs that end in "ie," that combination changes to "y" followed by "ing."

The thief is lying, and the victim is dying.

Words that end in "c" sometimes have an added "k" before the "ed" ending.

She is panicking because he is trafficking in drugs.

Sometimes the preceding consonant is doubled—when it is spelled with a single letter and the vowel before it is stressed. (In words of a single syllable, this is always the case.)

He was begging, stopping, blogging.

1. (arrive)   They *are arriving* after midnight. Verbs that end in a silent vowel drop the vowel and add "ing."

2. (argue)   He *is arguing* over nothing. Verbs that end in a silent vowel drop the vowel and add "ing."

3. (browse)   The young children *are browsing* the Internet. Verbs that end in a silent vowel drop the vowel and add "ing."

4. (consult)   The authors *are consulting* with the editors. Verbs that end in a consonant, including "y," add the letters "ing."

5. (crash)   All of our computers *are crashing* at the same time. Verbs that end in a consonant add the letters "ing."

6. (dine)   We *are dining* with friends this evening. Verbs that end in a silent vowel drop the vowel and add "ing."

7. (free)   They *are freeing* the captive birds tomorrow morning. When a final vowel or vowels are pronounced, it or they remain before the "ing."

8. (sew)   The mothers *are sewing* the costumes. Verbs that end in a consonant add the letters "ing."

9. (drive)   They *are driving* home after the game. Verbs that end in a silent vowel drop the vowel and add "ing."

10. (go)   I *am going* to the concert next week. When a final vowel is pronounced, it remains before the "ing."

11. (sell)   *Are* you *selling* your house? Verbs that end in a consonant add the letters "ing."

12. (wear)   What *is* she *wearing*? Verbs that end in a consonant add the letters "ing."

13. (mop)   Who *is mopping* the floor before the guests arrive? In words of a single syllable ending in a single consonant, the final consonant is doubled before the "ing."

14. (host)   We *are hosting* a major conference on that issue. Verbs that end in a consonant add the letters "ing."

15. (lie)   She must find out which one *is lying*. For verbs that end in "ie," that combination changes to "y" followed by "ing."

16. (transmit)   I *am transmitting* the e-mails at this moment. Sometimes the preceding consonant is doubled—when it is spelled with a single letter and the vowel before it is stressed.

17. (e-mail)   You *are* always *e-mailing* your friends during the workday. Verbs that end in a consonant add the letters "ing."

18. (quit)   I *am* not *quitting* until the job is done correctly. In words of a single syllable ending in a single consonant, the final consonant is doubled before the "ing."

19. (put)   He *is putting* his coat on. In words of a single syllable ending in a single consonant, the final consonant is doubled before the "ing."

20. (take)   She *is taking* her coat off. Verbs that end in a silent vowel drop the vowel and add "ing."

21. (join)   We *are joining* a dancing class this Saturday. Verbs that end in a consonant add the letters "ing."

22. (bring)   *Is* someone *bringing* the butter? Verbs that end in a consonant add the letters "ing."

23. (ski)   The champion *is skiing* down the mountain. When a final vowel is pronounced, it remains before the "ing."

24. (rent)   The owner *is renting* her garage. Verbs that end in a consonant add the letters "ing."

25. (bid)   We *are bidding* for a new computer. In words of a single syllable ending in a single consonant, the final consonant is doubled before the "ing."

Exercise 3

The Past Tense

The Past Active form of regular verbs is formed for all three persons, singular and plural, by adding "ed" after consonant letters and by adding "d" after a silent vowel or "e." When a "y" comes after a consonant, it changes to "i" before the ending "ed."

1. She *mentioned* his name only once. After a consonant, add "ed."

2. I just *realized* how expensive that was. Add "d" after a vowel.

3. They *moved* again last month. Add "d" after a vowel.

4. He never *guessed* the winning numbers. Add "ed" after consonant letters.

5. He always *smiled* at us on the way to work. Add "d" after a vowel.

6. She *ordered* soup and a salad. Add "ed" after consonant letters.

7. The boss *listened* for only a few minutes. Add "ed" after consonant letters.

8. Mama *baked* the cookies last evening. Add "d" after a vowel.

9. She never *loved* anyone as much as her first husband. Add "d" after a vowel.

10. He *annoyed* his neighbors all evening long. Add "ed" after consonant letters. Remember that "y" is a consonant.

11. We all *agreed* to meet again next year. Add "d" after a vowel.

12. The baby *cried* half the night. A "y" after a consonant changes to "i" before "ed."

13. He *carried* the groceries out to the car. A "y" after a consonant changes to "i" before "ed."

14. He *ripped* the ad out of the newspaper. Here the preceding consonant is doubled for a word of one syllable.

15. They *blogged* with one another for more than a year. The preceding consonant is doubled.

16. They *chatted* online before they met. The preceding consonant is doubled.

17. The technician *programmed/programed* the computer to shut off automatically. The consonant can be doubled when it is spelled with a single letter and the vowel before it is stressed. The single consonant "m" is possible in American English.

18. They *jogged* all around Central Park. The preceding consonant is doubled for a word of one syllable.

19. The old couple *danced* the whole night through. Add "d" after a vowel.

20. The old woman *died* with a smile on her face. Add "d" after a vowel.

21. The senator *echoed* the words of his colleagues. A final vowel such as "a" or "o" that is stressed is followed by "ed" as in henna—hennaed, radio—radioed.

22. The medic *wrapped* his injury with bandages. The preceding consonant is doubled.

23. The nurse *x-rayed* his leg to search for broken bones. Add "ed" after consonant letters.

24. The baby *spilled* the milk all over the kitchen table. Add "ed" after consonant letters.

25. The player *dropped* the ball and the whistle blew. The preceding consonant is doubled.

Exercise 4

The Past Tense of Irregular Verbs

There are no rules for the formation of the past tense of irregular verbs. You need to find the correct forms provided in the alphabetical listing or in the section "Another 550 Problem Verbs."

1. I don't want to eat fish again today. I *ate* fish yesterday. See page 126.

2. Did you see the new film? I *saw* it last week. See page 395.

3. I have no money to spend. I *spent* my allowance on my boots. See page 443.

4. Did you bring the books back to the library? I *brought* them back this morning. See page 53.

5. Are you going home after work? The boss *went* an hour ago. See page 185.

6. I can't sing anymore today. I *sang* for three hours last night. See page 422.

7. Can you drive me to the doctor's office? You *drove* me last time. See page 121.

8. I can run ten miles a day. Yesterday I actually *ran* twelve miles. See page 388.

9. Did you find your ring? Mom said that she *found* it in the kitchen? See page 153.

10. Do we need to wind the clock? No, Jenny *wound* it yesterday. See page 537.

11. Didn't I tell you not to sleep so long? You *told* me no such thing. See page 490.

12. What was he thinking? I *thought* he knew where he was going. See page 493.

13. How long did you sleep last night? Sarah *slept* ten hours. See page 428.

14. We have nothing to drink. Who *drank* all the milk? See page 120.

15. How did you ring in the New Year? We *rang* it in with champagne. See page 380.

16. Can I hold the trophy now? You *held* it yesterday. See page 207.

17. Who is choosing the restaurant for this evening? They *chose* last time. See page 72.

18. You are always forgetting something. This morning you almost *forgot* to call a taxi. See page 168.

19. I love to read. Last evening I *read* this book from cover to cover. See page 348.

20. Who is writing the reply? I *wrote* the last one. See page 550.

21. Do you dream often? I *dreamed/dreamt* the strangest thing last night. See page 119.

22. Tonight the flowers might freeze. Last night they almost *froze*. See page 176.

23. I wanted to blow out the candles! But someone already *blew* them out. See page 48.

24. I know what I can do. Do you know who *did* it? See page 114.

25. Since you can get your homework done today, you *could* have done it yesterday. See page 594.

Exercise 5

The Verb "be"

The forms of the verb "be" simply must be memorized. You can't get very far in English without them. See the entire set of forms on page 27.

"To *be*, or not to *be*, that is the question." The basic form is used for the infinitive.

Some say it *is* foolish to *be* an actor. The third person singular Present Tense form is "is."

When I *was* in high school, many students *were* actors. The Past Tense first person singular form is "was." The Past Tense for we, you, and they is "were."

But since they *are* now adults, they *are* not willing to appear foolish in front of other adults. The Present Tense plural for we, you, and they is "are."

Children can *be* more natural. The auxiliary verb "can" combines with the basic form of the verb.

They do not seem to care if anyone *is* in the audience. The third person singular for the Present Tense is "is."

They will *be* ready at a moment's notice to put on costumes and makeup and then *be* someone else on stage. The Simple Future combines the verb "will" with the basic form of the verb.

I sometimes wish that I *were* a child again. The Past Subjunctive for the verb "be" is "were." You will frequently encounter the form using the Past Tense: "I wish I was there."

"*Be* yourself," my father used to say. The Imperative form is the same as the basic form.

He *was* a great singer, and I *am* sure that he *was* being sincere when he told me: Third person singular Past Tense; first person singular Present; third person singular Past Tense.

"If you try, you *will be* a great actor or singer too." The Simple Future is formed from the verb "will" plus the basic form.

If he *had been* there to see my acting debut, I *am* sure that he would *have been* proud of me. Here are examples of both the Past Perfect Subjunctive and the Present Perfect Subjunctive.

Mom *was* happy to see me. The Simple Past form for the third person singular is "was."

and we *will* never *be* sure that Dad *was* not right by her side. Simple Future using "will" and the basic form. Simple Past third person singular is "was."

Exercise 6

Irregular Verb Maze

D	U	G	O	C	O	U	L	D	A
E	F	E	D	R	I	D	F	M	K
L	B	I	T	O	B	H	E	G	O
I	S	A	I	D	E	I	L	N	W
S	A	W	W	E	N	T	L	T	R
T	O	G	O	T	T	M	K	L	O
R	E	S	R	E	A	D	N	A	T
U	S	P	E	N	T	O	A	E	E
N	Z	U	N	D	I	D	R	D	P
G	U	N	W	O	U	N	D	L	A

Exercise 7

The Present Tense of Irregular Verbs

It may be difficult to find the Present Tense or basic form for irregular verbs when you only have the past tense. In general, look at the first set of consonants for a guide. Irregular verbs have different ways of forming that Past Tense, (i.e., they do not have the normal "d" or "ed" ending). Some of these you will simply have to memorize. The answers indicate the correct verbs in the alphabetical listings.

1. I spoke with him last night, but we need to *speak* again. See page 440.
2. I forbade you to smoke. Now I must *forbid* you to buy any tobacco products. See page 163.
3. Where did you lose your hat? Your father never *loses* anything. See page 262.
4. Who sat next to you last week? This week you *sit* right here. See page 425.
5. Who got the joker? I never seem to *get* it. See page 180.
6. Your aunt caught a cold at the skating rink. She *catches* the flu every winter. See page 68.
7. He sped past the police officer? That car *speeds* past here every day. See page 441.
8. Someone stole my car keys? Why would anyone *steal* them? See page 458.

9. We met at the party. I almost never *meet* new people. See page 274.

10. The first plane left an hour ago. The next one *leaves* in ten minutes. See page 242.

11. The skater spun around on the ice. I wish I could *spin* like that. See page 445.

12. He stood in line for over ten hours. I *stand* that long in my job. See page 452.

13. They all sought freedom in America. Even today immigrants *seek* a better life. See page 397.

14. They fought long and hard, but you can only *fight* for so long. See page 148.

15. Who already took a shower? I never *take* my shower first. See page 484.

16. They dug into the mine deep into the night. Sometimes they *dig* all day and night. See page 108.

17. The bird dove down to the surface of the water. Where did she learn how to *dive* like that? See page 113.

18. Yesterday we drew real faces. Usually we *draw* inanimate objects. See page 118.

19. She hid her money from her husband. I wonder what he *hides* from her. See page 205.

20. Last year the hunter shot only one deer. This year he didn't *shoot* a thing. See page 412.

21. The child shook the tree with all her might. When she *shakes* it, lots of acorns fall down. See page 406.

22. I was struck by your comments. It isn't often that we *strike* people with our words. See page 466.

23. The *Titanic* sank in a matter of hours. Do you think a cruise ship can *sink* today? See page 424.

24. They hung wallpaper all afternoon. Now that I have seen it, I can *hang* some too. See page 194.

25. Was that the first time you rode on our subway? Most New Yorkers *ride* the subway to work everyday. See page 378.

Exercise 8

The Passive Voice

The Passive Participle form is used for all of the Passive Voice tenses. The Passive Participle form for most regular verbs is identical to the Past Tense form.

1. (add)   Her name was *added* to the list. After a consonant, add "ed."

2. (attend)   The meeting was not very well *attended*. After a consonant, add "ed."

3. (believe) Those outrageous statements simply cannot be *believed*. After a vowel, add "d."

4. (change)   Before we have improvements, some things have to be *changed*. After a vowel, add "d."

5. (contain) The flu outbreak could not be *contained*. After a consonant, add "ed."

6. (drop)   The charges against my defendant were *dropped*. In this single-syllable word ending in a single consonant letter, the final consonant is doubled before adding "ed" for the Past Tense form.

7. (excuse)   You may be *excused*. After a vowel, add "d."

8. (form)   These mountain ranges were *formed* millions of years ago. After a consonant, add "ed."

9. (give)   Your word should not be *given* lightly. This is an irregular verb. See page 182.

10. (help)   It could not be *helped*. After a consonant, add "ed."

11. (improve) I hope that next semester your grades can be *improved*. After a vowel, add "d."

12. (knit)   These socks were *knit/knitted* by his grandmother. This verb has two acceptable Past Tense forms and Participles. In the second instance, the final consonant of a one-syllable word is doubled before adding "ed."

13. (limit)   The losses were *limited* by the quick response of the emergency crew. After a consonant, add "ed."

14. (move)   These toys on the floor will have to be *moved*. After a vowel, add "d."

15. (obtain)   Do you know whose permission has to be *obtained*? After a consonant, add "ed."

16. (quiz)   The boys were *quizzed* on the accident. Sometimes the preceding consonant is doubled in words of a single syllable.

17. (reduce)   The deficits should be *reduced* in the next five years. After a vowel, add "d."

18. (remember) How do you wish to be *remembered*? After a consonant, add "ed."

19. (shampoo)   The carpets can be *shampooed* for better results. After a stressed vowel or vowels, add "ed."

20. (serve)   The country was well *served* by the general. After a vowel, add "d."

21. (treat)   We were *treated* to homemade ice cream cones. After a consonant, add "ed."

22. (turn)   The patient was *turned* over onto her side. After a consonant, add "ed."

23. (use)   How many gallons of fuel were *used* for the trip? After a vowel, add "d."

24. (watch)   Do you think the Olympics will be *watched* in many nations? After a consonant, add "ed."

25. (xerox)   Can those documents be *xeroxed* before the meeting? After a consonant, add "ed."

Exercise 9

The Past Passive Participle of Irregular Verbs

For some irregular verbs the Past Participle form is identical to the Past Tense. But in others there are two distinct forms, one for the Past and one for the Participle. When in doubt be sure to consult the corresponding verb in the alphabetical list.

1. (begin)   The first group *began* playing at eight. By nine o'clock, all of the groups had *begun*. See page 34.

2. (break)   She *broke* the record on her first run, but even her record had been *broken* by the end of the competition. See page 51.

3. (drink)   The couple *drank* a small bottle of wine. By evening's end, the bottle had been completely *drunk*. See page 120.

4. (catch)   Father *caught* a cold. By the end of the week, all of the children had also *caught* it. See page 68.

5. (drive)   They *drove* for hours. By nightfall, they had *driven* 500 miles. See page 121.

6. (forbid)   I *forbade/forbad* you to leave this house. For the next month, all phone calls are *forbidden/forbid*. See page 163.

7. (forget)   He *forgot* my birthday. Such things are not to be *forgotten*. See page 168.

8. (hide)   Who *hid* the children's presents? Yes, they are all well *hidden*. See page 205.

9. (grow)   Last year the corn *grew* slowly. This year it has already *grown* over my head. See page 189.

10. (hear)   I *heard* his last speech. Few people before that time had *heard* his name. See page 200.

11. (know)   What he *knew* is not everything that was *known* about the case. See page 233.

12. (meet)   When we *met*, we were certain that we had *met* before. See page 274.

13. (lie)   He simply *lied*. I am not accustomed to be being *lied* to. See page 246.

14. (mistake) I think we *mistook* the date. Yes, unfortunately you are *mistaken*. See page 281.

15. (outbid) I think we *outbid* the others. No, you were *outbidden/outbid*. See page 300.

16. (overfeed) I'm sure I *overfed* the fish. They certainly appear to be *overfed*. See page 599.

17. (redo)   Last month we *redid* our bathroom. Now the entire house has been *redone*. See page 354.

18. (rent)   Last year she *rented* her garage. It has been *rented* before. See page 365.

19. (shake)   We *shook* the host's hand. How many hands have been *shaken* today? See page 406.

20. (send)   They *sent* the package last week to Martha. Why hasn't ours been *sent*? See page 401.

21. (speak)   The critic *spoke* out on the movie. Nothing more need be *spoken*. See page 440.

22. (teach)   She *taught* her children their manners. Her children certainly have been well *taught*. See page 488.

23. (unfreeze) The plumber *unfroze* the pipes. Yes, the pipes are now *unfrozen*. See page 604.

24. (uphold) He consistently *upheld* the laws of the land. His decisions were always *upheld*. See page 515.

25. (write)   I *wrote* you last week. Why have you not *written* me? See page 550.

Exercise 10

The Imperative

The Active Imperative form is the same as the basic form of the verb.

1. Since Sally began yesterday, today it is your turn. Please *begin*. See page 34.
2. I don't think you bit hard enough. *Bite* again. See page 43.
3. You chose the wrong answer. *Choose* another one. See page 72.
4. You have cried enough. *Cry* no more. See page 94.
5. You did it perfectly the first time. *Do* it again. See page 114.
6. You haven't dug deep enough. *Dig* some more. See page 108.
7. If you already drank all the orange juice, *drink* some water. See page 120.
8. You ate your potatoes; now *eat* your vegetables. See page 126.
9. If you already fed the cat, then please *feed* the dog. See page 145.
10. If you didn't get a winning number, *get* another one. See page 180.
11. Joe went just a minute ago; *go* after him. See page 185.
12. Last year the students kept their rooms very neat. *Keep* your own room just as clean and neat. See page 227.
13. Who lit the first candle? *Light* the others now. See page 249.
14. Your sister mowed the lawn last week. *Mow* it before you go to town. See page 285.
15. You have overslept once too often. Do not *oversleep* one more time. See page 308.

16. I noticed that your accomplice pled guilty. *Plead* "not guilty." See page 323.

17. Since I paid last time, you *pay* this time. See page 314.

18. I told them not to make so much noise. *Tell* them again. See page 490.

19. If you haven't taken your shower yet, then *take* one now. See page 484.

20. If you rode the subway here, then *ride* it back home. See page 378.

21. Since the others ran this morning, you *run* this afternoon. See page 388.

22. I wasn't here when you sang that song. Please *sing* it for me. See page 422.

23. I swam a mile this morning. Now you *swim*. See page 481.

24. This room hasn't been swept. Please *sweep* before the guests arrive. See page 479.

25. The team won the game yesterday. *Win* this one today. See page 536.

Exercise 11

The Subjunctive

The Present Subjunctive uses the basic form except for the verb "be." The third person singular form has no "s."

The Present Subjunctive Passive is made by combining "be" and the past participle.

The Past Subjunctive describes something hypothetical or unreal. It often occurs after words like "if, as if, though, wish, suppose."

The Past Subjunctive Active* (sometimes called the "were form") is identical to the forms of the past except for the verb "be" where the "were form" is used for all persons.

The Past Subjunctive Passive combines "were" with the past participle.

1. (frighten) If he *frightened* you, he will be punished. The Past Subjunctive Active is identical to the Past Tense.

2. (train) It was as if they had *trained* for months, not days. The Past Subjunctive Active is identical to the Past Tense.

3. (serve) He had always dreamt that he *served* his country well. The Past Subjunctive Active is identical to the Past Tense.

4. (recognize) It was as if she *recognized* him at first sight. The Past Subjunctive Active is identical to the Past Tense.

5. (shave) If you had *shaved*, you would not have scratched me. A Past Perfect Subjunctive can be formed with "had" and the Past Participle.

6. (do) I wish that things *were done* better in your office. The Past Subjunctive Passive combines "were" with the Past Participle.

7. (be) We wish that you *were* here. The Past Subjunctive Active for the verb "be" uses "were" for all persons.

8. (link) The two networks should *be linked* together. The Present Subjunctive Passive is made by combining "be" and the Past Participle.

9. (interface) He suggested that the company *interface* with its suppliers. The Present Subjunctive uses the basic form of the verb. The third person singular form has no "s."

---

* In modern American English the Indicative Past Tense is often substituted: "I wish I was there." A Past Perfect Subjunctive is also possible using "had" or "had been" plus the Past Participle: "If I had written, they would have come." "If we had been driven, we would not have arrived too late for the show."

10. (save)   He thought that he *saved* the day. The Past Subjunctive Active is identical to the Past.

11. (market)   He insisted that they *marketed* their goods overseas. The Past Subjunctive Active is identical to the Past.

12. (network)   I think you *networked* with friends and former colleagues. The Past Subjunctive Active is identical to the Past.

13. (break)   If the bone were *broken*, we might apply a cast to the leg. The Past Subjunctive Passive combines "were" with the Past Participle.

14. (auction)   If the painting were *auctioned*, it could sell for over a million dollars. The Past Subjunctive Passive combines "were" with the Past Participle.

15. (diet)   If only they had *dieted*, they would have been able to compete. A Past Perfect Subjunctive can be formed with "had" and the Past Participle.

16. (plead)   Had he only *pled* "not guilty." A Past Perfect Subjunctive can be formed with "had" and the Past Participle.

17. (order)   If you should *order* a dessert, I will try some. The Present Subjunctive uses the basic form.

18. (close)   If the store were *closed*, we would have saved lots of money. The Past Subjunctive Passive combines "were" with the Past Participle.

19. (love)   If you *love* her, let her go. The Present Subjunctive uses the basic form.

20. (learn)   If good manners were *learned* in school, they would be apparent to us all. The Past Subjunctive Passive combines "were" with the Past Participle.

21. (leave)   If you *leave* before I return, please lock the door. The Present Subjunctive uses the basic form.

22. (give)   I requested that he *give* the money back to us. The Present Subjunctive uses the basic form.

23. (hit)   Had only the hurricane *hit* after the city was evacuated. A Past Perfect Subjunctive can be formed with "had" and the Past Participle.

24. (quit)   I wish I had *quit* while I was ahead. A Past Perfect Subjunctive can be formed with "had" and the Past Participle.

25. (seek)   If only peace were *sought*, it might be found. The Past Subjunctive Passive combines "were" with the Past Participle.

Exercise 12

More Practice on the Present Tense

1. In a compromise, I benefit if he *benefits*. The third person singular is normally formed by adding "s."

2. I can do it, and my sister *can* too. This modal verb has no "s" in the third person singular form. See page 64.

3. We all envy Joe, but he *envies* no one. When a verb ends in "y" after a consonant, the "y" changes to an "i" and is followed by "es."

4. The boys dry the dishes, but Mom always *dries* the glasses. When a verb ends in "y" after a consonant, the "y" changes to an "i" and is followed by "es."

5. We never gripe, but our teacher *gripes* all the time. The third person singular is normally formed by adding "s" after silent vowels.

6. Hide your money where no one *hides* it. Add "s" after silent vowels.

7. If you cannot issue a pass, please tell me who *issues* them. Add "s" after silent vowels.

8. I may not come. Mother also *may* not come. This modal verb has no "s" in the third person singular form. See page 598.

9. While I fry the bacon, Dad *fries* the eggs. When a verb ends in "y" after a consonant, the "y" changes to an "i" and is followed by "es."

10. I rarely mop the floor, but my brother *mops* it every Saturday. Add "s" after most consonants.

11. You can overdo a good thing. The wise man never *overdoes* anything. After a vowel that is pronounced normally, add "es."

12. If we all want to partake in the glory, he too *partakes*. Add "s" after silent vowels.

13. You will not be fined unless the police officer *fines* you. Add "s" after silent vowels.

14. They tell us not to panic, but the boss *panics* whenever there is a crisis. Add "s" after most consonants.

15. I want to rely on the weather report, but one never *relies* on just one report. When a verb ends in "y" after a consonant, the "y" changes to an "i" and is followed by "es."

16. We pray for the soldier; he *prays* for peace. Add "s" after most consonants. Remember that "y" is a consonant.

17. I must learn to download music. My student *must* learn how to play the guitar. The modal verb "must" has no "s" for the third person singular form. See page 598.

18. Firefighters rescue people every day. Who *rescues* a firefighter? Add "s" after silent vowels.

19. We need to squelch those rumors. No one *squelches* a rumor better than the press spokesperson! After the combinations "ch," add "es."

20. All governments tax individuals. Who *taxes* businesses? After the consonant "x," add "es."

21. I value your loyalty. The company *values* your hard work. Add "s" after silent vowels.

22. Who can veto such a decision? Only the president *vetoes* bills. After a vowel that is pronounced normally, add "es."

23. I love to waltz, and my wife *waltzes* beautifully. This rare three-letter combination at the end of the verb requires the ending "es."

24. Some dogs wag their tails for joy. My dog *wags* her tail when she wants to go outside. Add "s" after most consonants.

25. I shy away from conflict. My husband never *shies* away from it. When a verb ends in "y" after a consonant, the "y" changes to an "i" and is followed by "es."

The Present Participle and the Progressive

The Present Participle ("ing" form) is used to form the Present and Future Progressive tenses. Remember that the rules for the formation of the "ing" form are similar to those for forming the Past Tense.

1. (abet)   They *are abetting* the criminal. Sometimes the preceding consonant is doubled when it is spelled with a single letter and the vowel before it is stressed.

2. (access)   He *is accessing* the Internet through his provider. Verbs that end in a consonant add the letters "ing."

3. (bid)   My wife *is bidding* on the vacation. In words of a single syllable ending in a single consonant, the final consonant is doubled before the "ing."

4. (drip)   The melting snow *is dripping* from the trees. The final consonant is doubled.

5. (dry)   The clothes *are drying* on the line outside. Verbs that end in a consonant add the letters "ing."

6. (exhibit)   We *are exhibiting* our paintings at the gallery next month. Verbs that end in a consonant add the letters "ing."

7. (expel)   The school *is expelling* the disruptive students. The final consonant is doubled.

8. (flap)   The flag *is flapping* in the wind. The final consonant is doubled before the "ing."

9. (fry)   They *are frying* the fish in a pan. Verbs that end in a consonant add the letters "ing."

10. (gape)   What *are* you *gaping* at? Verbs that end in a silent vowel drop the vowel and add "ing."

11. (grab)   The little boy *is grabbing* his mother's dress. The final consonant is doubled.

12. (hug)   Everyone *is hugging* one another. The final consonant is doubled.

13. (input)   We *are inputting* the data right now. Even thought the stress is not on the final syllable, this verb doubles the "t" based on the analogy with the verb "put."

14. (jam)   They *are jamming* our radio signal. The final consonant is doubled.

15. (jog)   *Is* anyone *jogging* with me this morning? The final consonant is doubled.

16. (kid)   I know that he *is* only *kidding*. The final consonant is doubled.

17. (lag)   You *are* always *lagging* behind the others. The final consonant is doubled.

18. (mope)   Once again you *are moping* around and doing nothing. Verbs that end in a silent vowel drop the vowel and add "ing."

19. (nap)   The baby *is napping* in her crib. The final consonant is doubled.

20. (omit)   For the next round we *are omitting* the personal interview. The final consonant is doubled.

21. (panic)   They *are panicking* without any reason. This is a special instance where "k" is inserted after the final "c" before adding "ing."

22. (plot)   We do not know who *is plotting* against us. The final consonant is doubled.

23. (put)   Dad *is putting* out the garbage. The final consonant is doubled.

24. (rally)   We *are* all *rallying* to her side. Verbs that end in a consonant add the letters "ing."

25. (recede)   The floodwaters *are receding* for the moment. Verbs that end in a silent vowel drop the vowel and add "ing."

More Work on the Past Tense

1. (answer)   She *answered* correctly. The Past Active form of regular verbs is formed by adding "ed" after consonant letters.

2. (allot)   I *allotted* him plenty of time to complete the assignment. Sometimes the consonant can be doubled when it is spelled with a single letter and the vowel before it is stressed.

3. (bop)   The little boy *bopped* the doll on its head. The preceding consonant is doubled for a word of one syllable.

4. (cancel)   He never *canceled/cancelled* his reservation. Sometimes the consonant can be doubled when it is spelled with a single letter and the vowel before it is stressed. The single consonant is sometimes found in American English even when the final syllable is not stressed.

5. (cap)   We *capped* the increase at 3 percent. The preceding consonant is doubled for a word of one syllable.

6. (commit)   She *committed* a crime in leaving the scene of the accident. Sometimes the consonant can be doubled when it is spelled with a single letter and the vowel before it is stressed.

7. (control)   The boss *controlled* the flow of the meeting. Sometimes the consonant can be doubled when it is spelled with a single letter and the vowel before it is stressed.

8. (debug)   The technician *debugged* my computer in a few minutes. Sometimes the consonant can be doubled when it is spelled with a single letter and the vowel before it is stressed.

9. (don)   She never *donned* that hat again. The final consonant is doubled for a word of one syllable.

10. (dot)   Small cottages *dotted* the landscape. The final consonant is doubled for a word of one syllable.

11. (empty)   We *emptied* all the trash cans. When a "y" comes after a consonant, it changes to "i" before the ending "ed."

12. (flip)   The monkey *flipped* over in his cage. The final consonant is doubled for a word of one syllable.

13. (grin)   He *grinned* at the passersby. The final consonant is doubled for a word of one syllable.

14. (inherit)   She *inherited* the entire estate. Add "ed" after consonant letters.

15. (jot)   They *jotted* down their thoughts before they left. The final consonant is doubled.

16. (knot)   We *knotted* all the lines. The final consonant is doubled.

17. (lug)   He *lugged* the suitcase up the stairs. The final consonant is doubled.

18. (marr)   Rain *marred* the parade. Add "ed" after consonant letters.

19. (mete)   The judge *meted* out a harsh sentence. Add "d" after a vowel letter.

20. (nod)   The old woman *nodded* to the nurse. The final consonant is doubled.

21. (patrol)   The company *patrolled* the woods. The consonant can be doubled.

22. (pin)   The kids "*pinned* the tail on the donkey." The final consonant is doubled.

23. (pry)   The carpenter *pried* the nail out of the board. When a "y" comes after a consonant, it changes to "i" before the ending "ed."

24. (rub)   The mother *rubbed* the oil over the baby's soft skin. The final consonant is doubled.

25. (scrape) The little girl *scraped* her knee playing in the school yard. Add "d" after a vowel.

Exercise 15

More Past Tense Irregular Verbs

There are no rules for the formation of the Past Tense of irregular verbs.

1. Issues like that arise all the time. Yesterday another one *arose*. See page 15.
2. Did you tear your new stockings? Yes, I *tore* them on a nail. See page 489.
3. She always loses her money at gambling. Yesterday she *lost* a month's salary. See page 262.
4. Did you buy the tickets? I *bought* two on the Internet. See page 61.
5. How far can you throw a football? I once *threw* one fifty yards. See page 497.
6. The boss strides about authoritatively. She just *strode* off to her next meeting. See page 465.
7. I can't sing anymore today. I *sang* for three hours last night. See page 422.
8. Did you grind the coffee beans? Yes, dear, I *ground* them this morning. See page 188.
9. Be careful they do not creep up on us like they *crept* up yesterday. See page 93.
10. Can you ever outwear a good pair of jeans? I definitely *outwore* this pair. See page 599.
11. Be careful the watch doesn't sink. Oh, it already *sank*. See page 424.
12. I would like to fly a plane. I never *flew* one. See page 159.
13. No one intentionally overeats. But I certainly *overate* at their wedding reception. See page 305.
14. All the children must leave before it gets dark. Sally already *left*. See page 242.
15. We need someone to sing the national anthem. Who *sang* it at the last game? See page 422.
16. The compost pile should not stink. Well, it certainly *stank* this morning. See page 461.
17. Why is the baby constantly falling? He *fell* on his face just a minute ago. See page 143.
18. The sun shines brightly in the summer. Yesterday it *shone* all day long. See page 411.
19. Who can send her a reminder? I *sent* one last week. See page 401.
20. Who stands guard this evening? I *stood* my post last night. See page 452.
21. I do not understand this problem. I *understood* all the problems yesterday. See page 511.
22. Can you undo the damage? We already *undid* it. See page 513.
23. We would like to underwrite your costs. We *underwrote* your project the last time. See page 604.
24. The court can uphold that decision. That judge *upheld* our last appeal. See page 515.
25. We can withhold payment if the goods are not delivered. We *withheld* it once in the past month. See page 539.

Present Tense of Irregular Verbs Maze

Z	C	O	M	E	B	O	D	P	L
L	I	E	S	P	E	N	D	A	A
O	F	U	W	L	A	F	L	Y	W
S	I	N	G	E	R	R	I	T	A
P	N	T	M	A	K	E	G	E	K
E	D	I	S	V	I	E	H	L	E
A	K	S	L	E	S	Z	T	L	T
K	E	Y	I	S	F	E	E	D	I
L	E	U	D	D	K	N	O	W	R
Q	P	B	E	G	I	N	M	I	W

Exercise 17

Present or Past?

1. Yesterday he beat the odds and won the lottery. Past. The word "yesterday" provides the context.

2. Everyone bids at an auction. Present. Only in the Present do you have the "s" form for the third person singular.

3. We bet when we are on vacation. Present. The second clause indicates Present tense.

4. The car burst into flames. Past. In the Past the third person singular does not have the "s" ending.

5. Our oak tree casts a long shadow. Present. Only in the Present do you have the "s" form for the third person singular.

6. The ring cost ten dollars. Past. In the Past the third person singular does not have the "s" ending.

7. Dad always cuts the firewood. Present. Only in the Present do you have the "s" form for the third person singular.

8. This shirt fit him well. Past. In the Past the third person singular does not have the "s" ending.

9. Who hit the jackpot? Past. In the Past the third person singular does not have the "s" ending.

10. My head hurts this morning. Present. Only in the Present do you have the "s" form for the third person singular.

11. Mama never knit him a sweater. Past. In the Past the third person singular does not have the "s" ending.

12. Who lets the dog out in the evening? Present. Only in the Present do you have the "s" form for the third person singular.

13. His expenses offset his earnings last year. Past. In the Past the third person singular does not have the "s" ending.

14. He consistently outbids his competitors. Present. Only in the Present do you have the "s" form for the third person singular.

15. A true winner never quits. Present. Only in the Present do you have the "s" form for the third person singular.

16. She read the newspaper before breakfast. Past. In the Past the third person singular does not have the "s" ending.

17. He rid himself of all temptations. Past. In the Past the third person singular does not have the "s" ending.

18. On Sundays Dad sets the table. Present. Only in the Present do you have the "s" form for the third person singular.

19. We all shed tears for their loss last week. Past. "Last week" indicates the Past tense.

20. He always shred documents with my name and address on them. Present. Only in the Present do you have the "s" form for the third person singular.

21. David shut the door. Past. In the Past the third person singular does not have the "s" ending.

22. She accidentally slit her finger on the knife. Past. In the Past the third person singular does not have the "s" ending.

23. I didn't swallow the chewing gum. I spit it out. Past. The context indicates the action has been completed.

24. He always sweats when he jogs. Present. Only in the Present do you have the "s" form for the third person singular.

25. The rain barely wet the newly planted garden. Past. In the Past the third person singular does not have the "s" ending.

Exercise 18

The Past and Past Passive Participle

The Past Participle for regular verbs is the same as the Past Tense form. For irregular verbs you will have to consult the alphabetical listing.

1. (connect) Have they *connected* your phone yet? They *connected* my phone yesterday. After a consonant, the Past Tense and Past Participle are formed by adding "ed."

2. (base) Have they *based* their conclusion on the data? They *based* it on the latest findings. After a silent vowel, the Past Tense and Past Participle are formed by adding "d."

3. (ask) Have you *asked* for a glass of water? Yes, I *asked* the waiter a minute ago. Add "ed."

4. (discover) Have they *discovered* the cause of the illness? Yes, they *discovered* it in the last set of tests. Add "ed."

5. (earn) Have you ever *earned* any money? Yes, I *earned* my allowance. Add "ed."

6. (form) Have you *formed* a union? We *formed* one last month. Add "ed."

7. (increase) Have they *increased* your work? They *increased* mine last week. Add "d."

8. (listen)   Have they *listened* to the complaint? They *listened* but took no action. Add "ed."

9. (handle)   Have they *handled* the new responsibilities well? Yes, they *handled* them very well. Add "d."

10. (move)   Have they *moved* the meeting date? Yes, they *moved* it to Tuesday evening. Add "d."

11. (look)   Have you *looked* under the bed? Yes, I *looked* there first. Add "ed."

12. (gamble)   Have you ever *gambled*? I *gambled* last fall on a cruise ship. Add "d."

13. (remember) Have you *remembered* where you put your keys? Yes, I *remembered* they were on my dresser. Add "ed."

14. (smile)   Has she ever *smiled*? She *smiled* on her wedding day. Add "d."

15. (shop)   Have you *shopped* in this mall before? Yes, we *shopped* here on our last visit. The final consonant of a one-syllable word is doubled before adding "ed."

16. (speak)   Have you *spoken* of this matter with her? Yes, I *spoke* to her this morning. This and the following sentences contain irregular verbs. The endings are not predictable and must be learned. See page 440.

17. (do)   Have you *done* your homework? I *did* it in school. See page 114.

18. (swim)   Have you ever *swum* a mile? I *swam* a mile just this week. See page 481.

19. (quit)   Has he *quit* smoking? He *quit* many years ago. See page 341.

20. (send)   Have you *sent* the package? We *sent* it last Monday. See page 401.

21. (get)   Have you *gotten* a flu shot? Yes, I *got* mine in October. See page 180.

22. (forget)   Have you *forgotten* his birthday again? You *forgot* it last year. See page 168.

23. (sing)   Have you *sung* in a choir before? I *sang* in my school choir. See page 422.

24. (see)   Have you *seen* the new movie? We *saw* it on Saturday evening. See page 396.

25. (throw)   Have you *thrown* out the trash? I *threw* it out after dinner. See page 497.

Exercise 19

Irregular Verbs You Need to Know

These are verbs you simply must learn to speak and write English correctly. Check your answers in the alphabetical listing.

1. I begin each day with song. I am *beginning* today with a love song. Yesterday I *began* with a pop song. I have *begun* each day this month with a new song. See page 34.

2. I fly to Boston on Fridays. Today I am *flying* in the evening. Last week I *flew* in the morning. I have *flown* there for over a year. See page 159.

3. He makes great cookies. He is *making* some today. His mother *made* some for us. He has *made* cookies each day this week. See page 265.

4. She knows all the verbs in this book. She *knew* them last week. She has *known* most of them since her course. See page 233.

5. My wife runs every day. She is *running* right now. She *ran* in the marathon last year. She has *run* since she was a little girl. See page 388.

6. They stand in the rear of the choir. They are *standing* there right now. The men *stood* in front only once. They have *stood* in the rear ever since I can remember. See page 452.

7. We all take showers before we swim. Who is *taking* his shower now? John already *took* his. We have all *taken* our showers today. See page 484.

8. She grows tomatoes. This year she is *growing* carrots. The tomatoes *grew* well last year. Tomatoes have been *grown* here for years. See page 189.

9. I always buy my groceries at the market. I am *buying* some fresh cabbage this morning. I *bought* lettuce last week. I have *bought* vegetables here for a long time. See page 61.

10. Who can break an egg? I am always *breaking* something. Last week I *broke* a light bulb. At least you can eat an egg that has been *broken*. See page 51.

11. Can you spin the wheel? The wheel is already *spinning*. Who *spun* it last time? It has been *spun* already a dozen times. See page 445.

12. I will pay the bill. Dad is already *paying* it. You *paid* last time. The important thing is that the bill has been *paid*. See page 314.

13. He sleeps soundly at night. He is still *sleeping*. He *slept* eight hours yesterday. He has *slept* well in our new bed. See page 428.

14. Can you drive? Mom is *driving* the children to school. I *drove* last week. Must you be *driven* to work? See page 121.

15. Can he come? He is *coming*. He *came* last time. He has *come* every week. See page 78.

16. I meet all our guests. I am *meeting* a new group this evening. I *met* a new guest just last night. I have *met* over one hundred just this month. See page 279.

17. He swims every morning. He is *swimming* right now. Last week he *swam* 10 miles. He has *swum* over 200 miles this year. See page 481.

18. Babies fall often. That one is *falling* and standing up again and again. We all *fell* once. I have *fallen* while on skis and ice skates several times. See page 143.

19. Is it time to eat? Who is *eating* with us? They already *ate*. Most students have *eaten* before they come to visit. See page 126.

20. Do you drink milk? The children are *drinking* their milk now. I already *drank* a glass. Look, it's all been *drunk*. See page 120.

21. Can you do my hair? I am *doing* your sister's first. But you *did* her hair first yesterday. Be patient. Your hair will get *done* before you have to leave. See page 114.

22. May I go? All my friends are *going*? Billy *went* when he was my age. I have never *gone* before. See page 186.

23. I always hide my money. Where are you *hiding* it? I already *hid* it. Now I can't remember where it is *hidden*. See page 205.

24. What did she say? Can you hear what she is *saying*? She *said* that she was coming tonight. She has *said* that often, but she has never come. See page 392.

25. You spend lots of money. I am *spending* only what I earn. I *spent* half of my salary this morning. Are your earnings all *spent*? See page 443.

26. Do you burn wood for heat? Yes, we are *burning* oak logs. We *burned/burnt* a cord of wood last winter. Has all your wood been *burned/burnt* this year? See page 58.

27. Who can bring the snacks? I am *bringing* the fruit. Mary *brought* some vegetables. Has it all been *brought* to the school? See page 53.

28. I forbid you to go. I am also *forbidding* your sister to go. My father *forbade/forbad* me. Why is it *forbidden/forbid*? See page 163.

29. Lie down for a while. I am *lying* down. I *lay* down over an hour ago. I have *lain* here for some time, but it has not helped. See page 246.

30. Lay the baby in the crib. Mother is already *laying* her there. She *laid* her down this morning too. She will have *laid* her to sleep before too long. See page 236.

31. Who keeps the score? I am *keeping* it today. The other team *kept* it last game. The time has always been *kept* by a member of one of the teams. See page 227.

32. Who hits our Internet site? People have been *hitting* it for weeks. The search engines finally *hit* it last month. It was *hit* over ten thousand times last week. See page 206.

33. Who can learn this poem? We are *learning* it in our class. I remember that I *learned /learnt* it years ago. That poem has been *learned/learnt* by thousands of schoolchildren. See page 241.

34. Lead the way. I am *leading*. Who *led* last time? We were never *led* before. See page 237.

35. I read a book a week. This week I am *reading* a detective novel. Last week I *read* a romance. I have been *reading* since I was a child. See page 348.

36. He bleeds easily. His finger is *bleeding* now. I *bled* easily as a boy. My nose has *bled* since last week. See page 44.

37. Try not to catch a cold. I think I already am *catching* a cold. My sister *caught* one last week. Have you *caught* the flu this year? See page 68.

38. That dealer sells cars. We are *selling* ours too. Last year he *sold* many. This year he has already *sold* a dozen cars. See page 400.

39. Can you prove he is wrong? I am *proving* it in court. I *proved* our case to the judge. He ruled that our position was *proven* by the evidence. See page 334.

40. Did you see the new film? We are *seeing* it this afternoon. Our friends *saw* it last week. The film has been *seen* by millions. See page 395.

41. Choose one color. We are *choosing*. They *chose* red. Our color was *chosen* for us. See page 72.

42. He builds houses. We are *building* our own house. Our friends *built* one last year. Many houses have been recently *built* in this neighborhood. See page 57.

43. She deals in stocks and bonds. We are *dealing* with just our savings. Our parents *dealt* only with a banker. We have *dealt* with the same bank for generations. See page 98.

44. Blow out the candle. Who is *blowing* out the one in the living room? I already *blew* that one out. All the candles have been *blown* out. See page 48.

45. It is not proper to steal a kiss. I am not *stealing* a kiss. You *stole* one from me. That kiss was given; it was not *stolen*. See page 458.

46. Swing back and forth. That little boy is *swinging* too fast. I *swung* on a trapeze once. We haven't *swung* since we were children. See page 482.

47. He hangs paintings for the museum. Today they are *hanging* a new exhibition. He *hung* their last major show. It was *hung* in just two days. See page 194.

48. I seek an answer. I am always *seeking* answers. I *sought* it in books. The answer to that question has been *sought* since ancient times. See page 397.

49. He tears interesting stories out of the newspaper. He is *tearing* one out just now. Last week I *tore* out a story on London. I suspect it was *torn* out by many others. See page 489.

50. Who shuts the windows? I am *shutting* this one. Who *shut* the other windows? They were *shut* when we arrived. See page 421.

51. I am glad I have finished. We were *being* very efficient. Yes, you *were*. You have almost always *been* done on time. See page 198.

Index of the 501 English Verbs

All of the verbs conjugated in *501 English Verbs* are listed below in alphabetical order. Irregular (or possibly confusing) principal parts are listed in *italics* underneath each verb to assist you in finding the basic form of the verb you need.

rebound
rebounding,
rebounded
rebuild
rebuilt
receive
recognize
redo
redid, redone
reduce
refer
regret
relate
re-lay
re-laid,
re-laying
relay
relayed,
relaying
remain
remember
remove
rend
rent
rent
rented
repay
repaid
reply
report
represent
require
rescue
rest
result
retell
retold
return
rewrite
rewrote,
rewritten
rid
ridding,
ridded
ride
riding, rode,
ridden
rig
ring
rang, rung

ring
ringed
rip
rise
rose, risen
rob
robbing,
robbed
rout
routing,
routed
route
routing,
routed
ruin
run
ran

save
saw
sawn
say
said
seat
see
saw, seen
seek
sought
seem
sell
sold
send
sent
serve
set
sew
sewn
shake
shook, shaken
shampoo
shape
shave
shaven
shed
shine
shone
shoot
shot
shop
short

shorten
shovel
show
shown
shred
shrink
shrank,
shrunk,
shrunken
shut
sing
sang, sung
singe
sink
sank, sunk
sit
sat
ski
slay
slew, slain
sleep
slept
slide
slid
sling
slung
slip
slit
smell
smelt
smile
sneak
snuck
snowboard
sound
sow
sown
spam
speak
spoke, spoken
speed
sped
spell
spelt
spend
spent
spill
spilt
spin
span, spun

spit
spat
split
spoil
spoilt
spread
spring
sprang,
sprung
stalk
stand
stood
start
state
stay
steal
stole, stolen
stick
stuck
sting
stung
stink
stank, stunk
stop
strategize
strew
strewn
stride
strode,
stridden
strike
struck,
stricken
string
strung
strive
strove, striven
stroke
study
sue
suggest
support
suppose
surf
surprise
swear
swore, sworn
sweat
sweep
swept

swell
swim
swam, swum
swing
swung
sync
synch

take
took, taken
talk
taxi
taxies, taxying
teach
taught
tear
tore, torn
tell
told
text
think
thought
thread
thrive
throve,
thriven
throw
threw,
thrown
thrust
tie
tying
train
transfer
transmit
tread
trod,
trodden
treat
try
turn

uncover
undergo
underwent,
undergone
understand
understood

undertake
undertook,
undertaken
undo
undid, undone
unite
uphold
upheld
upset
use

vary
visit

wait
wake
woke,
woken
waken
walk
want
watch
waylay
waylaid
wear
wore,
worn

weave
wove, woven
wed
weep
wept
wet
whip
whipt
will
win
won
wind
wound

wish
withhold
withheld
withstand
withstood
wonder
work
wrought
worry
worship
wound
wrap
wrapt
wreck

wring
wrung
write
wrote,
written

x-ray
xerox

yes

zero
zip

Minimum Systems Requirement for the CD-ROM

Windows

- Pentium II or higher recommeded
- Windows 98, ME, NT4, 2000, XP
- 64 MB of installed RAM, 128 MB recommended
- CD-ROM drive
- 1024 X 768 color display

Apple

- Power Macintosh Power PC processor (G3 or higher recommended)
- Mac OS® X 10.2 – 10.4 64 MB of installed RAM,
- 128 MB recommended
- CD-ROM drive
- 1024 x 768 color display

Launching Instructions for the PC	Launching Instructions for the MAC
Windows Users:	Macintosh Users:
Insert the CD-ROM into your CD-ROM drive. The application should start in a few moments. If it doesn't follow the steps below. 1. Click on the Start button on the Desktop and select Run. 2. Type "D:/501Verbs" (where D is the letter of your CD-ROM drive). 3. Click OK.	The CD will open to the desktop automatically when inserted into the CD drive. Double click the 501Verbs Flash icon to launch the program.